BUSINESS
ESSENTIALS

NINTH EDITION

BUSINESS
ESSENTIALS

Ronald J. Ebert

Ricky W. Griffin

Boston   Columbus   Indianapolis   New York   San Francisco   Upper Saddle River
Amsterdam   Cape Town   Dubai   London   Madrid   Milan   Munich   Paris   Montréal   Toronto
Delhi   Mexico City   São Paulo   Sydney   Hong Kong   Seoul   Singapore   Taipei   Tokyo

Editorial Director: Sally Yagan
Acquisitions Editor: James Heine
Editorial Project Manager: Karin Williams
Editorial Assistant: Ashlee Bradbury
Director of Marketing: Patrice Lumumba Jones
Senior Marketing Manager: Maggie Moylan
Senior Managing Editor: Judy Leale
Production Project Manager: Jacqueline A. Martin
Senior Operations Supervisor: Arnold Vila
Operations Specialist: Cathleen Petersen
Senior Art Director: Kenny Beck
Text and Cover Designer: Tamara Newnam

Manager, Visual Research: Karen Sanatar
Photo Researcher: Sarah Peavey
Manager, Rights and Permissions: Estelle Simpson
Cover Art: © Viktor1/Shutterstock.com
Media Director: Lisa Rinaldi
Lead Media Project Manager: Allison Longley
**Full-Service Project Management and
  Composition:** Integra
Printer/Binder: Courier/Kendallville
Cover Printer: Courier/Kendallville
Text Font: 10/12 Palatino

Credits and acknowledgments borrowed from other sources and reproduced, with permission, in this textbook appear on the appropriate page within the text.

Many of the designations by manufacturers and sellers to distinguish their products are claimed as trademarks. Where those designations appear in this book, and the publisher was aware of a trademark claim, the designations have been printed in initial caps or all caps.

Library of Congress Cataloging-in-Publication Data
Ebert, Ronald J.
  Business essentials / Ronald J. Ebert, Ricky W. Griffin. — 9th ed.
    p. cm.
  Includes bibliographical references and index.
  ISBN-13: 978-0-13-266402-8
  ISBN-10: 0-13-266402-X
  1. Industrial management—United States.   2. Business enterprises—United States.
    I. Griffin,
Ricky W. II. Title.
HD70.U5E2 2013
658—dc22
                                          2011049403

10 9 8 7 6 5 4 3 2 1

ISBN 10: 0-13-266402-X
ISBN 13: 978-0-13-266402-8

To Fran, for bringing a lifetime of friendship, fun, and love into our family. —R. J. E.

For Paul and Sherry—Friends for life. —R. W. G.

Brief Contents

Contents

Part 3: People in Organizations

From the Authors

RON EBERT and RICKY GRIFFIN

Businesses today face constant change—change in their competitive landscape, change in their workforce, change in governmental regulation, change in economic conditions, change in technology, change in … well, you get the idea. As we began to plan this revision, we too recognized the need for change. Changing demands from instructors, changing needs and preferences by students, and changing views on what material to cover in this course and how to cover it have all affected how we planned and revised the book.

A new editorial team was assembled to guide and shape the creation and development of the book. Along with suggestions from many loyal users, the business world itself provided us with dozens of new examples, new challenges, new successes and failures, and new perspectives on what they must do to remain competitive. And a new dedication to relevance guided our work from beginning to end. For example, we know that some business students will go to work for big companies. Others will work for small firms. Some will start their own business. Still others may join a family business. Nonbusiness students, too, as interested citizens, are curious about its "whys" and "hows." So, we accepted the challenge of striving to make the book as relevant as possible to all students, regardless of their personal and career goals and objectives.

We also carefully reviewed the existing book line by line. Extraneous material was removed, and new material was added. Examples were updated or replaced with newer ones. We worked extra hard to make our writing as clear and as crisp as possible. More recent business practices and issues are included throughout the text. We've also engaged the student by opening each chapter with the question "What's in It for Me?" We then answer that question by identifying the key elements in the chapter that are most central to the student's future relationships to business—be it as employee, manager, consumer, investor, or interested citizen. And because so much work in modern organizations is performed by teams, we added a special team ethics exercise at the end of each chapter and reinstated the companion individual ethics exercises that have been so popular in previous editions.

These are just some of the many changes, additions, and improvements we've made to the book.

We are proud of what we have accomplished and believe that we have taken this book to a higher level of excellence. Its content is stronger, its learning framework is better, its design is more accessible, and its support materials are the best in the market. We hope that you enjoy reading and learning from this book as much as we enjoyed creating it. And who knows? Perhaps one day we can tell your story of business success to other students.

Preface

About the Authors

Ronald J. Ebert is Emeritus Professor at the University of Missouri-Columbia where he lectures in the Management Department and serves as advisor to students and student organizations. Dr. Ebert draws upon more than 30 years of teaching experience at such schools as Sinclair College, University of Washington, University of Missouri, Lucian Blaga University of Sibiu (Romania), and Consortium International University (Italy). His consulting alliances have included such firms as Mobay Corporation, Kraft Foods, Oscar Mayer, Atlas Powder, and John Deere. He has designed and conducted management development programs for such diverse clients as the American Public Power Association, the United States Savings and Loan League, and the Central Missouri Manufacturing Training Consortium.

His experience as a practitioner has fostered an advocacy for integrating concepts with best business practices in business education. The five business books he has coauthored have been translated into Spanish, Chinese, Malaysian, and Romanian languages.

Dr. Ebert has served as the Editor of the *Journal of Operations Management*. He is a Past-President and Fellow of the Decision Sciences Institute. He has served as consultant and external evaluator for *Quantitative Reasoning for Business Studies*, an introduction-to-business project sponsored by the National Science Foundation.

Ricky Griffin received his Ph.D. in management from the University of Houston. After spending three years on the faculty at the University of Missouri-Columbia, he moved to Texas A&M University. During his career at Texas A&M he has taught undergraduate and graduate courses in management, organizational behavior, human resource management, and international business.

Dr. Griffin's research interests include workplace aggression and violence, organizational security, workplace culture, and leadership. His work has been published in such journals as *Academy of Management Review*, *Academy of Management Journal*, *Administrative Science Quarterly*, and *Journal of Management*. He served as Associate Editor and then as Editor of *Journal of Management*.

In addition, Dr. Griffin has also authored or coauthored several leading textbooks and coedited three scholarly books. His books are used in more than 500 colleges and universities in the United States and abroad, and have been translated into Spanish, Russian, Polish, and Chinese.

He has served the Academy of Management as Chair of the Organizational Behavior Division and as Program Chair of the Research Methods Division. He has served as President of the Southwest Division of the Academy of Management and on the Board of Directors of the Southern Management Association. Dr. Griffin is a Fellow of both the Academy of Management and the Southern Management Association. He has also won several awards for research and been supported by over $400,000 in federal research funding.

Dr. Griffin has served as Director of the Center for Human Resource Management and Head of the Department of Management at Texas A&M University. He has also served as Executive Associate Dean and Interim Dean at the Mays Business School. He currently serves as Head of the Department of Management.

What's New to This Edition

- Six kinds of chapter-ending involvement activities—to reinforce and practice the use of chapter concepts—are back by popular demand (see below for detailed descriptions)
- Hundreds of new real-life business examples added throughout the text, as requested by reviewers and users.
- Five brand new chapter-opening cases cover key concepts in Chapter 4 (The Global Context of Business), Chapter 6 (Organizing the Business), Chapter 7 (Operations Management and Quality), Chapter 10 (Human Resource Management and Labor Relations), and Chapter 15 (Money and Banking).
- Substantially updated Marketing Processes and Consumer Behavior (Chapter 11), with all-new sections covering the new product development process, customer relationship management, geo-demographic segmentation, and behavior segmentation.
- Five new sections added to illustrate the modernization of Pricing, Distributing, and Promoting Products (Chapter 12), including the role of e-intermediaries, non-physical storage (warehousing for digital data), direct interactive marketing, combining just-in-time and supply chains for a competitive advantage, as well as marketing strategies of distribution via supply chains.
- Four new sections cover the latest changes in Information Technology for Business (Chapter 13), including computer-aided manufacturing (CAM), applications software ("apps"), computer-based voice technology, and recent ethical issues arising from IT.

Features

"What's in It for Me?"

Each chapter opens with a section called "What's in It for Me?" In this section, we answer that question by identifying the key elements in the chapter that are most central to your future careers in business, be it as an employee, manager, investor, or as an outside consumer or interested citizen—making it clear why each chapter really matters.

Two-Part Chapter Case Vignettes

We've updated or completely replaced the chapter-opening cases, keeping them fresh, relevant, and up-to-date. Covering companies from British Petroleum to iTunes and Starbucks to Google, these chapter case vignettes pique your interest at the beginning of the chapter and reinforce concepts you've learned throughout the chapter by adding a new case wrap-up with discussion questions at the end.

"Entrepreneurship and New Ventures"

If your plan is to work for a large corporation, start your own business, or anything in between, you need to be both entrepreneurial and *intrapreneurial*. These updated, popular boxed features touch upon entrepreneurs who have really made a difference.

"Managing in Turbulent Times"

Whatever your role with any business, as employee, customer, or investor, you need to see the challenges and consequences firms encounter during economic downturns. Experiences from real companies reveal both disappointments and unexpected new opportunities arising from the 2008–2010 recession and the uncertainties of economic recovery.

We've also brought back several End-of-Chapter features that are designed to help you review and apply chapter concepts and build skills.

- **Summary of Learning Objectives** offers a quick guide for you to review the major topics covered in each chapter.
- **Key Terms** with page references to help reinforce chapter concepts.
- **Building Your Business Skills** activities allow you to apply your knowledge and critical thinking skills to an extended problem drawn from a wide range of realistic business experiences.
- **Exercising Your Ethics: Individual Exercises & Team Exercises** ask you to examine an ethical dilemma and think critically about how you would approach and resolve it.
- **Video Exercises** help you see how real-life businesses and the people who run them apply fundamental business principles on a daily basis.

What's in It for You?

If you're like many other students, you may be starting this semester with some questions about why you're here. Whether you're taking this course at a two-year college, at a four-year university, or at a technical school, in a traditional classroom setting or online, you may be wondering just what you're supposed to get from this course and how it will benefit you. In short, you may be wondering, "What's in it for me?"

Regardless of what it may be called at your school, this is a survey course designed to introduce you to the many exciting and challenging facets of business, both in the United States and elsewhere. The course fits the needs of a wide variety of students. You may be taking this course as the first step toward earning a degree in business, you may be thinking about business and want to know more about it, or you may know you want to study business but are unsure of the area you want to pursue. Maybe you plan to major in another field but want some basic business background and are taking this course as an elective. Or you may be here because, frankly, this course is required or is a prerequisite to another course.

For those of you with little work experience, you may be uncertain as to what the business world is all about. If you have a lot of work experience, you may even be a bit skeptical about what you can actually learn about business from an introductory course. One of our biggest challenges as authors is to write a book that meets the needs of such a diverse student population, especially when we acknowledge the legitimacy of your right to ask "What's in it for me?" We also want to do our best to ensure that you find the course challenging, interesting, and useful.

The world today is populated with a breathtaking array of businesses and business opportunities. Big and small businesses, established and new businesses, broad-based and niche businesses, successful and unsuccessful businesses, global and domestic businesses—throughout this book we'll discuss how they get started and how they work, why they grow and why some fail, and how they affect you. Regardless of where your future takes you, we hope that you look back on this course as one of your first steps.

Going forward, we also urge you to consider that what you get out of this course—what's in it for you—is shaped by at least three factors. One factor is this book and the various learning aids that accompany it. Another factor is your instructor. He or she is a dedicated professional who wants to help you grow and develop intellectually and academically.

The third factor? You. Learning is an active process that requires you to be a major participant. Simply memorizing the key terms and concepts in this book may help you achieve an acceptable course grade. But true learning requires that you read, study, discuss, question, review, experience, and evaluate as you go along. While tests and homework may be a "necessary evil," we believe we will have done our part if you finish this course with new knowledge and increased enthusiasm for the world of business. We know your instructor will do his or her best to facilitate your learning. The rest, then, is up to you. We wish you success.

To help lay the foundation for meeting these challenges, let's look at the various "hats" that you may wear, both now and in the future.

Wearing the Hats

There's an old adage that refers to people wearing different "hats." In general, this is based on the idea that any given person usually has different roles to play in different settings. For example, your roles may include student, child, spouse, employee, friend, and/or parent. You could think of each of these roles as needing a different hat—when you play the role of a student, for example, you wear one hat, but when you leave campus and go to your part-time job, you put on a different hat. From the perspective of studying and interfacing with the world of *business*, there are at least four distinct "hats" that you might wear:

- *The Employee Hat.* One business hat is as an employee working for a business. Many people wear this hat during the early stages of their career. To wear the hat successfully, you will need to understand your "place" in the organization—your job duties and responsibilities, how to get along with others, how to work with your boss, what your organization is all about, and so on. You'll begin to see how to best wear this hat as you learn more about organizing business enterprises in Chapter 6 and how organizations manage their human resources in Chapter 10, as well as in several other places in this book.

- *The Employer or Boss Hat.* Another business hat that many people wear is as an employer or boss. Whether you start your own business or get promoted within someone else's business, one day people will be working for you. You'll still need to know your job duties and responsibilities. But you'll now also need to understand how to manage other people—how to motivate and reward them, how to lead them, how to deal with conflict among them, and the legal parameters that may affect how you treat them. Chapters 3, 5, 8, and 9 provide a lot of information about how you can best wear this hat, although the role of employer runs throughout the entire book.

- *The Consumer Hat.* Even if you don't work for a business, you will still wear the hat of a consumer. Whenever you fill your car with Shell gasoline, bid for something on eBay, buy clothes at Urban Outfitters, or download a song from iTunes, you're consuming products or services created by business. To wear this hat effectively, you need to understand how to assess the value of what you're buying, your rights as a consumer, and so on. We discuss how you can best wear this hat in Chapters 4, 11, and 12.

- *The Investor Hat.* The final business hat many people wear is that of an investor. You may buy your own business or work for a company that allows you to buy its own stock. You may also invest in other companies through the purchase of stocks or shares of a mutual fund. In order for you to invest wisely, you must understand some basics, such as financial markets, business earnings, and the basic costs of investment. Chapters 4, 14, 15, 16, and an appendix will help you learn how to best wear this hat.

Many people wear more than one of these hats at the same time. Regardless of how many hats you wear or when you may be putting them on, it should be clear that you have in the past, do now, and will in the future interface with many businesses in different ways. Knowing how to best wear all these hats is what this book is all about.

BUSINESS ESSENTIALS

1

The U.S. Business Environment

What Goes Up...Can Go Even Higher!

The sign in front of a Texas Mobil gasoline station summed it up nicely: The "prices" for the three grades of gasoline sold at the station were listed as "an arm," "a leg," and "your first born." While the sign no doubt led to a few smiles from motorists, its sentiments were far from a laughing matter. The stark reality is that gas prices have fluctuated dramatically in recent years, reaching an all-time high of over $4.00 per gallon in early 2008 before dropping back to less than $2.00 per gallon in 2009. By 2011, though, prices were surging again, and some experts suggested that they could hit $5.00 per gallon in the near future. Indeed, the dramatic price fluctuations that began in mid-2004 have left consumers, government officials, and business leaders struggling to cope with uncertainty about future prices.

What makes this gas crisis unusual is that it began with an unusual mix of supply, demand, and global forces. In the past, gas prices generally increased only when the supply was reduced. But the circumstances underlying the increases that started in 2004 and continued through 2011 were much more complex. First, global supplies of gasoline have been increasing at a rate that has more than offset the steady decline in U.S. domestic production of gasoline since 1972. As a result, the United States has been relying more on foreign producers and is, therefore, subject to whatever prices those producers want to charge. Second, demand for gasoline in the United States has continued to rise as a result of a

After reading this chapter, you should be able to:

1 Define the nature of U.S. business and identify its main goals and functions.
2 Describe the external environments of business and discuss how these environments affect the success or failure of any organization.
3 Describe the different types of global economic systems according to the means by which they control the factors of production.
4 Show how markets, demand, and supply affect resource distribution in the United States, identify the elements of private enterprise, and explain the various degrees of competition in the U.S. economic system.
5 Explain the importance of the economic environment to business and identify the factors used to evaluate the performance of an economic system.

growing population, the continued popularity of large gas-guzzling vehicles, and a strong demand for other petroleum-based products.

Another major piece of the puzzle has been a surging global economy that until recently caused a higher demand for oil and gasoline. China, in particular, has become a major consumer of petroleum, passing Japan in 2005 to trail only the United States in total consumption. The global recession that started in 2008, however, reduced demand in most industrialized countries. The recession, in fact, probably played a role in the dip in prices in 2009 just as the gradual recovery that started in 2010 has helped spur higher prices once again. Political turmoil in the Middle East in 2011 also played a major role.

The price fluctuations have also led to a wide array of related consequences. Automobile manufacturers stepped up their commitment to making more fuel-efficient cars even as automobile sales

WHAT'S IN IT FOR ME?

The forces that have caused jumps in gas prices reflect both the opportunities and challenges you'll find in today's business world. All businesses are subject to the influences of economic forces. But these same economic forces also provide astute managers and entrepreneurs with opportunities for profits and growth. By understanding these economic forces and how they interact, you'll be better able to (1) appreciate how managers must contend with the challenges and opportunities resulting from economic forces from the standpoint of an employee and a manager or business owner, and (2) understand why prices fluctuate from the perspective of a consumer.

In this chapter, we'll look at some basic elements of economic systems and describe the economics of market systems. We'll also introduce and discuss several indicators that are used to gauge the vitality of our domestic economic system. But first, let's start with some business basics.

MyBizLab Where you see MyBizLab in this chapter, go to **www.mybizlab.com** for additional activities on the topic being discussed.

Heather A. Craig/Shutterstock

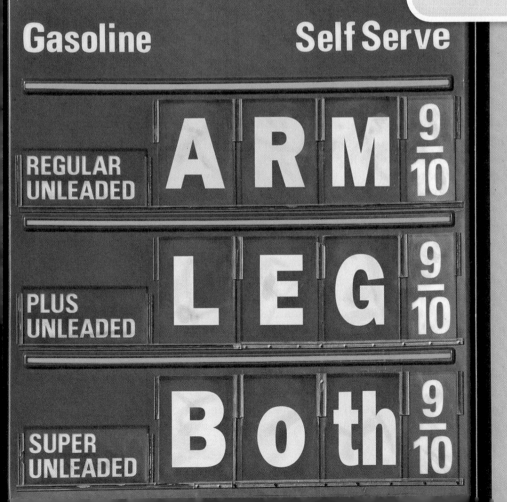

Gasoline   Self Serve

REGULAR UNLEADED   ARM 9/10

PLUS UNLEADED   LEG 9/10

SUPER UNLEADED   Both 9/10

plummeted during the recent recession. Refiners posted record profits (indeed, some critics charged that the energy companies were guilty of price gouging). And even local police officers were kept busy combating a surge in gasoline theft, yet another indication that gas was becoming an increasingly valuable commodity![1]

Our opening story continues on page 24.

1 Define the nature of U.S. business and identify its main goals and functions.

The Concept of Business and the Concept of Profit

What do you think of when you hear the word *business*? Does it conjure up images of successful corporations, such as Apple and Google? Or of less successful companies, such as Borders Books and Kmart? Are you reminded of smaller firms, such as your local supermarket or favorite restaurant? Or do you think of even smaller family-owned operations, such as your neighborhood pizzeria or the florist down the street?

All these organizations are **businesses**—organizations that provide goods or services that are then sold to earn profits. Indeed, the prospect of earning **profits**—the difference between a business's revenues and its expenses—is what encourages people to open and expand businesses. After all, profits are the rewards owners get for risking their money and time. The right to pursue profits distinguishes a business from those organizations—such as most universities, hospitals, and government agencies—that run in much the same way but that generally don't seek profits.[2]

Consumer Choice and Demand In a capitalistic system, such as that in the United States, businesses exist to earn profits for owners; within certain broad constraints an owner is free to set up a new business, grow that business, sell it, or even shut it down. But consumers also have freedom of choice. In choosing how to pursue profits, businesses must take into account what consumers want and/or need. No matter how efficient a business is, it won't survive if there is no demand for its goods or services. Neither a snowblower shop in Florida nor a beach-umbrella store in Alaska is likely to do well.

Opportunity and Enterprise If enterprising businesspeople can spot a promising opportunity and then develop a good plan for capitalizing on it, they can succeed. For example, as large retailers like Circuit City and Linens-N-Things closed their doors in 2009, other firms profited by handling the inventory liquidations of those failed retailers. The opportunity always involves goods or services that consumers need and/or want—especially if no one else is supplying them or if existing businesses are doing so inefficiently or incompletely.

The Benefits of Business So what are the benefits of businesses? Businesses produce most of the goods and services we consume, and they employ most working people. They create most new innovations and provide a vast range of opportunities for new businesses, which serve as their suppliers. A healthy business climate also contributes to the quality of life and standard of living of people in a society. Business profits enhance the personal incomes of millions of owners and stockholders, and business taxes help to support governments at all levels. Many businesses support charities and provide community leadership. However, some businesses also harm the environment, and their decision makers sometimes resort to unacceptable practices for their own personal benefit.

In this chapter, we begin our introduction to business by examining the environment in which businesses operate. This provides a foundation for our subsequent discussions dealing with economic forces that play a major role in the success and failure of businesses everywhere.

MyBizLab

Gain hands-on experience through an interactive, real-world scenario. This chapter's simulation entitled Supply and Demand is located at **www.mybizlab.com.**

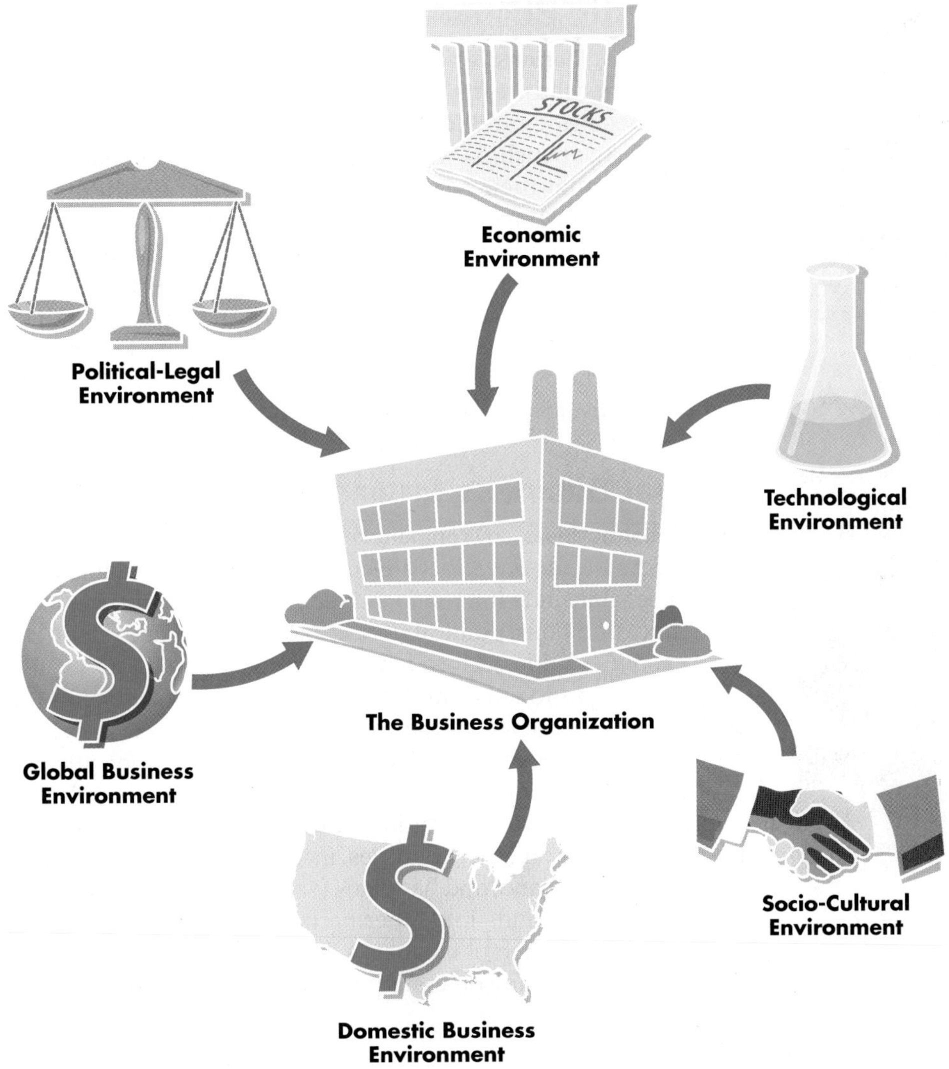

Figure 1.1 **Dimensions of the External Environment**

Economic Environment

Political-Legal Environment

Technological Environment

Global Business Environment

The Business Organization

Socio-Cultural Environment

Domestic Business Environment

The External Environments of Business

2 Describe the external environments of business and discuss how these environments affect the success or failure of any organization.

All businesses, regardless of their size, location, or mission, operate within a larger external environment. This **external environment** consists of everything outside an organization's boundaries that might affect it. (Businesses also have an *internal environment*, more commonly called *corporate culture*; we discuss this in Chapter 5.) Not surprisingly, the external environment plays a major role in determining the success or failure of any organization. Managers must, therefore, have a complete and accurate understanding of their environment and then strive to operate and compete within it. Businesses can also influence their environments.

Figure 1.1 shows the major dimensions and elements of the external environment as it affects businesses today. As you can see, these include the *domestic business environment*, the *global business environment*, the *technological environment*, the *political-legal environment*, the *sociocultural environment*, and the *economic environment*.

Business organization that provides goods or services to earn profits

Profits difference between a business's revenues and its expenses

External Environment everything outside an organization's boundaries that might affect it

LE Robshaw/Alamy

Urban Outfitters is affected by the external environment in many different ways.

Domestic Business Environment

The **domestic business environment** refers to the environment in which a firm conducts its operations and derives its revenues. In general, businesses seek to be close to their customers, to establish strong relationships with their suppliers, and to distinguish themselves from their competitors. Take Urban Outfitters, for example. The firm initially located its stores near urban college campuses; it now also locates stores in other, often more upscale, areas as well. The company also has a strong network of suppliers and is itself a wholesale supplier to other retailers through its Free People division. And it has established a clear identity for itself within the domestic business environment that enables it to compete alongside such competitors as Aeropostale and dELiA*s.

Global Business Environment

The **global business environment** refers to the international forces that affect a business. Factors affecting the global environment at a general level include international trade agreements, international economic conditions, political unrest, and so forth. For example, as political protests spread through much of the Middle East in 2011 oil prices began to surge and companies with operations in the region took emergency measures to protect their employees. At a more immediate level, any given business is likely to be affected by international market opportunities, suppliers, cultures, competitors, and currency values. For instance, Urban Outfitters currently has stores in several other countries, including Canada, the United Kingdom, and Ireland, and has plans for other international expansion. But as it expands into other parts of the world, it will have to contend with different languages, more diverse cultures, and so forth. Even now, many of its suppliers are foreign companies.

Technological Environment

The **technological environment** generally includes all the ways by which firms create value for their constituents. Technology includes human knowledge, work methods, physical equipment, electronics and telecommunications, and various processing systems that are used to perform business activities. For instance, Urban Outfitters relies on a sophisticated information system that tracks sales and inventory levels in order to be highly responsive to its customers. The firm also enjoys considerable success with its e-commerce websites. Urban Outfitters has developed a strong market presence in Japan, for example, even though it has no retail outlets in that country.

Political-Legal Environment

The **political-legal environment** reflects the relationship between business and government, usually in the form of government regulation of business. It is important for several reasons. First, the legal system defines in part what an organization can and can't do. For instance, Urban Outfitters is subject to a variety of political and legal forces, including product identification laws and local zoning requirements. Likewise, various government agencies regulate important areas, such as advertising practices, safety and health considerations, and acceptable standards of business conduct. Pro- or anti-business sentiment in government and political stability are also important considerations, especially for international firms. For instance, shortly after President Obama took office in 2009, a number of new regulations were imposed on businesses. And the president himself forced the resignation of General Motors' CEO in exchange for infusing new capital into the struggling automaker.

Sociocultural Environment

The **sociocultural environment** includes the customs, mores, values, and demographic characteristics of the society in which an organization functions. Sociocultural processes also determine the goods and services, as well as the standards of business conduct, that a society is likely to value and accept. For example, a few years ago, Urban Outfitters introduced a Monopoly-like game called Ghettopoly. The company received a lot of unfavorable publicity about the game, based on critics' charges that it made light of poverty and other social problems. In response, Urban Outfitters pulled it from shelves and discontinued its sale.

Economic Environment

The **economic environment** refers to relevant conditions that exist in the economic system in which a company operates. For example, if an economy is doing well enough that most people have jobs, a growing company may find it necessary to pay higher wages and offer more benefits in order to attract workers from other companies. But if many people in an economy are looking for jobs, as was the case during the 2009–2010 recession, a firm may be able to pay less and offer fewer benefits.

The rest of this chapter is devoted to the economic environment; the other environments of business are covered throughout the rest of the book.

Economic Systems

A U.S. business operates differently from a business in France or the People's Republic of China, and businesses in these countries differ from those in Japan or Brazil. A key factor in these differences is the economic system of a firm's *home country*—the nation in which it does most of its business. An **economic system** is a nation's system for allocating its resources among its citizens, both individuals and organizations.

3 Describe the different types of global economic systems according to the means by which they control the factors of production.

Factors of Production

A basic difference between economic systems is the way in which a system manages its **factors of production**—the resources that a country's businesses use to produce goods and services. Economists have long focused on four factors of production: *labor, capital, entrepreneurs,* and *physical resources.* In addition to these traditional four factors, *information resources* are now included as well. Note that the concept of factors of production can also be applied to the resources that an individual organization *manages* to produce goods and services.

Labor   People who work for businesses provide labor. **Labor**, sometimes called **human resources**, includes the physical and intellectual contributions people make while engaged in economic production. Starbucks, for example, employs over 176,000 people.[3] The firm's workforce includes the baristas who prepare coffees for customers, store managers, regional managers, coffee tasters, quality control experts, coffee buyers, marketing experts, financial specialists, and other specialized workers and managers.

Capital   Obtaining and using labor and other resources requires **capital**—the financial resources needed to operate a business. You need capital to start a new business and

---

Domestic Business Environment the environment in which a firm conducts its operations and derives its revenues

Global Business Environment the international forces that affect a business

Technological Environment all the ways by which firms create value for their constituents

Political-Legal Environment the relationship between business and government

Sociocultural Environment the customs, mores, values, and demographic characteristics of the society in which an organization functions

Economic Environment relevant conditions that exist in the economic system in which a company operates

Economic System a nation's system for allocating its resources among its citizens

Factors of Production resources used in the production of goods and services—labor, capital, entrepreneurs, physical resources, and information resources

Labor (Human Resources) physical and mental capabilities of people as they contribute to economic production

Capital funds needed to create and operate a business enterprise

Starbucks uses various factors of production, including (a) labor, such as this Starbucks barrista; (b) entrepreneurs, such as CEO Howard Schultz; and (c) physical resources, including coffee beans.

(a)

Xinhua/Photoshot

(b)

UPPA/Photoshot

(c)

foodfolio/Alamy

then to keep it running and growing. For example, when Howard Schultz decided to buy the fledgling Starbucks coffee outfit back in 1987, he used personal savings and a loan to finance his acquisition. As Starbucks grew, he came to rely more on Starbucks' profits. Eventually, the firm sold stock to other investors to raise even more money. Starbucks continues to rely on a blend of current earnings and both short- and long-term debt to finance its operations and fuel its growth. Moreover, even when the firm decided to close several hundred coffee shops in 2008 and early 2009, it employed capital to pay off leases and provide severance pay to employees who lost their jobs.

Entrepreneurs An **entrepreneur** is a person who accepts the risks and opportunities entailed in creating and operating a new business. Three individuals founded Starbucks back in 1971 and planned to emphasize wholesale distribution of fresh coffee beans. However, they lacked either the interest or the vision to see the retail potential for coffee. But Howard Schultz was willing to accept the risks associated with retail growth and, after buying the company, he capitalized on the market opportunities for rapid growth. Had his original venture failed, Schultz would have lost most of his savings. Most economic systems encourage entrepreneurs, both to start new businesses and to make the decisions that allow them to create new jobs and make more profits for their owners.

— *LAND* —
Physical Resources **Physical resources** are the tangible things that organizations use to conduct their business. They include natural resources and raw materials, offices, storage and production facilities, parts and supplies, computers and peripherals, and a variety of other equipment. For example, Starbucks relies on coffee beans and other food products, the equipment it uses to make its coffee drinks, paper products for packaging, and other retail equipment, as well as office equipment and storage facilities for running its business at the corporate level.

MANAGING IN TURBULENT TIMES

What Goes Around...

It seems like just yesterday. In 2005 the global economy was booming. In the United States, for example, business profits were soaring, jobs were plentiful, and home ownership was at any all-time high. The stock market reached unprecedented highs, pension plans were burgeoning, and new business opportunities were plentiful.

Fast-forward just five short years to 2010, and things looked a lot different. Business profits were down, hundreds of thousands of jobs were lost and unemployment claims soared, and mortgage foreclosures were the order of the day. The stock market plummeted, pension plans went broke, and it seemed like no one wanted to start a new business (and even those who did had a hard time getting financing).

What happened in this short period of time? Economists call it the business cycle. Historically, our economy has followed long periods of growth and prosperity, with periods of cutbacks and retreats. And that's where we were in 2010. During extended periods of prosperity, people sometimes start to act as though good times will last forever. They continue to bid up stock prices, for instance, far beyond rational value. They also take on too much debt, save too little money, and spend beyond their means. But things have a way of correcting themselves, and that's what happened when our economy went into recession beginning in 2008.

So what does the future hold? Well, while no one has a real crystal ball, most experts agree that the bad times will run their course, and then things will start looking up again. Indeed, by mid-2011

Lilli Day/iStockphoto.com

the stock market was inching back up and many businesses were cautiously hiring again. It may take awhile longer for growth to really take off again, but one day soon profits will again start to surge, businesses will embark on ambitious hiring plans, the stock market will surpass all previous highs, and business opportunities will again be plentiful. Until then, though, managers have to focus on following core business principles and do their best to steer their organizations through today's turbulence.

MyBizLab

Information Resources   The production of tangible goods once dominated most economic systems. Today, **information resources**—data and other information used by businesses—play a major role. Information resources that businesses rely on include market forecasts, the specialized knowledge of people, and economic data. In turn, much of what they do results either in the creation of new information or the repackaging of existing information for new users. For example, Starbucks uses various economic statistics to decide where to open new outlets. It also uses sophisticated forecasting models to predict the future prices of coffee beans. And consumer taste tests help the firm decide when to introduce new products.

Types of Economic Systems

Different types of economic systems manage these factors of production differently. In some systems, all ownership is private; in others, all factors of production are owned or controlled by the government. Most systems, however, fall between these extremes.

Economic systems also differ in the ways decisions are made about production and allocation. A **planned economy** relies on a centralized government to control all

---

Entrepreneur individual who accepts the risks and opportunities involved in creating and operating a new business venture

Physical Resources tangible items organizations use in the conduct of their businesses

Information Resources data and other information used by businesses

Planned Economy economy that relies on a centralized government to control all or most factors of production and to make all or most production and allocation decisions

or most factors of production and to make all or most production and allocation decisions. In a **market economy**, individual producers and consumers control production and allocation by creating combinations of supply and demand. Let's look at each of these types of economic systems as well as mixed market economies in more detail.

Planned Economies   There are two basic forms of planned economies: *communism* (discussed here) and *socialism* (discussed as a mixed market economy). As envisioned by nineteenth-century German economist Karl Marx, **communism** is a system in which the government owns and operates all factors of production. Under such a system, the government would assign people to jobs; it would also own all business and control business decisions—what to make, how much to charge, and so forth. Marx proposed that individuals would contribute according to their abilities and receive benefits according to their needs. He also expected government ownership of production factors to be temporary: Once society had matured, government would wither away, and workers would take direct ownership of the factors of production.

The former Soviet Union and many Eastern European countries embraced communism until the end of the twentieth century. In the early 1990s, however, one country after another renounced communism as both an economic and a political system. Today, North Korea, Vietnam, and the People's Republic of China are among the few nations with openly communist systems. Even in these countries, however, planned economic systems are making room for features of the free enterprise system.

Market Economies   A **market** is a mechanism for exchange between the buyers and sellers of a particular good or service. (Like *capital*, the term *market* can have multiple meanings.) Market economies rely on capitalism and free enterprise to create an environment in which producers and consumers are free to sell and buy what they choose (within certain limits). As a result, items produced and prices paid are largely determined by supply and demand. The underlying premise of a market economy is to create shared value—in theory, at least, effective businesses benefit because they earn profits on what they sell while customers also benefit by getting what they want for the best price available.[4]

To understand how a market economy works, consider what happens when you go to a fruit market to buy apples. While one vendor is selling apples for $1 per pound, another is charging $1.50. Both vendors are free to charge what they want, and you are free to buy what you choose. If both vendors' apples are of the same quality, you will buy the cheaper ones. If the $1.50 apples are fresher, you may buy them instead. In short, both buyers and sellers enjoy freedom of choice.

Taken to a more general level of discussion, individuals in a market system are free to not only buy what they want but also to work where they want and to invest, save, or spend their money in whatever manner they choose. Likewise, businesses are free to decide what products to make, where to sell them, and what prices to charge. This process contrasts markedly with that of a planned economy, in which individuals may be told where they can and cannot work, companies may be told what they can and cannot make, and consumers may have little or no choice in what they purchase or how much they pay. The political basis of market processes is called **capitalism**, which allows the private ownership of the factors of production and encourages entrepreneurship by offering profits as an incentive. The economic basis of market processes is the operation of demand and supply, which we discuss in the next section.

Mixed Market Economies   In reality, there are really no "pure" planned or "pure" market economies. Most countries rely on some form of **mixed market economy** that features characteristics of both planned and market economies. Even a market economy that strives to be as free and open as possible, such as the U.S. economy, restricts certain activities. Some products can't be sold legally, others can be sold only to people of a certain age, advertising must be truthful, and so forth. And the People's Republic of China, the world's most important planned economy, is increasingly allowing certain forms of private ownership and entrepreneurship (although with government oversight).

When a government is making a change from a planned economy to a market economy, it usually begins to adopt market mechanisms through **privatization**—the process of converting government enterprises into privately owned companies. In Poland, for example, the national airline was sold to a group of private investors. In recent years, this practice has spread to many other countries as well. For example, the postal system in many countries is government-owned and government-managed. The Netherlands, however, recently privatized its TNT Post Group N.V., already among the world's most efficient post-office operations. Canada has also privatized its air traffic control system. In each case, the new enterprise reduced its payroll, boosted efficiency and productivity, and quickly became profitable.

In the partially planned system called **socialism**, the government owns and operates selected major industries. In such mixed market economies, the government may control banking, transportation, or industries producing such basic goods as oil and steel. Smaller businesses, such as clothing stores and restaurants, are privately owned. Many Western European countries, including England and France, allow free market operations in most economic areas but keep government control of others, such as health care. And when the U.S. government took an ownership stake in General Motors and Chrysler as part of the recession-driven bail out in 2009 many critics of President Obama called the decision an act of socialism.

Many formerly planned economies have moved toward a more mixed economic model.

Geoff A Howard/Alamy

The Economics of Market Systems

Understanding the complex nature of the U.S. economic system is essential to understanding the environment in which U.S. businesses operate. In this section, we describe the workings of the U.S. market economy. Specifically, we examine the nature of *demand and supply*, *private enterprise*, and *degrees of competition*. We will then discuss private enterprise and forms of competition.

4 Show how markets, demand, and supply affect resource distribution in the United States, identify the elements of private enterprise, and explain the various degrees of competition in the U.S. economic system.

Demand and Supply in a Market Economy

A market economy consists of many different markets that function within that economy. As a consumer, for instance, the choices you have and the prices you pay for gas, food, clothing, and entertainment are all governed by different sets of market forces. Businesses also have many different choices about buying and selling their products. Dell Computer, for instance, can purchase keyboards from literally hundreds of different manufacturers. Its managers also have to decide what inventory levels should be, at what prices they should sell their goods, and how they will distribute these goods. Literally billions of exchanges take place every day between businesses and individuals; between businesses; and among individuals, businesses, and governments. Moreover, exchanges conducted in one area often affect exchanges elsewhere. For instance, the high cost of gas may also lead to prices going up for other products, ranging from food to clothing to delivery services. Why? Because each of these businesses relies heavily on gas to transport products.

Market Economy economy in which individuals control production and allocation decisions through supply and demand

Communism political system in which the government owns and operates all factors of production

Market mechanism for exchange between buyers and sellers of a particular good or service

Capitalism system that sanctions the private ownership of the factors of production and encourages entrepreneurship by offering profits as an incentive

Mixed Market Economy economic system featuring characteristics of both planned and market economies

Privatization process of converting government enterprises into privately owned companies

Socialism planned economic system in which the government owns and operates only selected major sources of production

The Laws of Demand and Supply On all economic levels, decisions about what to buy and what to sell are determined primarily by the forces of demand and supply.[5] **Demand** is the willingness and ability of buyers to purchase a product (a good or a service). **Supply** is the willingness and ability of producers to offer a good or service for sale. Generally speaking, demand and supply follow basic laws:

- The **law of demand**: Buyers will purchase (demand) *more* of a product as its price *drops* and *less* of a product as its price *increases*.
- The **law of supply**: Producers will offer (supply) *more* of a product for sale as its price *rises* and *less* of a product as its price *drops*.

The Demand and Supply Schedule To appreciate these laws in action, consider the market for pizza in your town (or neighborhood). If everyone is willing to pay $25 for a pizza (a relatively high price), the town's only pizzeria will produce a large supply. But if everyone is willing to pay only $5 (a relatively low price), it will make fewer pizzas. Through careful analysis, we can determine how many pizzas will be sold at different prices. These results, called a **demand and supply schedule**, are obtained from marketing research, historical data, and other studies of the market. Properly applied, they reveal the relationships among different levels of demand and supply at different price levels.

Demand and Supply Curves The demand and supply schedule can be used to construct demand and supply curves for pizza in your town. A **demand curve** shows how many products—in this case, pizzas—will be demanded (bought) at different prices. A **supply curve** shows how many pizzas will be supplied (baked or offered for sale) at different prices.

Figure 1.2 shows demand and supply curves for pizzas. As you can see, demand increases as price decreases; supply increases as price increases. When demand and supply curves are plotted on the same graph, the point at which they intersect is the **market price** (also called the **equilibrium price**)—the price at which the quantity of goods demanded and the quantity of goods supplied are equal. In Figure 1.2, the equilibrium price for pizzas in our example is $10. At this point, the quantity of pizzas demanded and the quantity of pizzas supplied are the same: 1,000 pizzas per week.

Surpluses and Shortages What if the pizzeria decides to make some other number of pizzas? For example, what would happen if the owner tried to increase profits by making *more* pizzas to sell? Or what if the owner wanted to lower overhead, cut back on store hours, and *reduce* the number of pizzas offered for sale? In either case, the result would be an inefficient use of resources and lower profits. For instance, if the pizzeria supplies 1,200 pizzas and tries to sell them for $10 each, 200 pizzas will not be bought. Our demand schedule shows that only 1,000 pizzas will be demanded at this price. The pizzeria will therefore have a **surplus**—a situation in which the quantity supplied exceeds the quantity demanded. It will lose the money that it spent making those extra 200 pizzas.

Conversely, if the pizzeria supplies only 800 pizzas, a **shortage** will result. The quantity demanded will be greater than the quantity supplied. The pizzeria will "lose" the extra profit that it could have made by producing 200 more pizzas. Even though consumers may pay more for pizzas because of the shortage, the pizzeria will still earn lower total profits than if it had made 1,000 pizzas. It will also risk angering customers who cannot buy pizzas and encourage other entrepreneurs to set up competing pizzerias to satisfy unmet demand. Businesses should seek the ideal combination of price charged and quantity supplied so as to maximize profits, maintain goodwill among customers, and discourage competition. This ideal combination is found at the equilibrium point.

Our example involves only one company, one product, and a few buyers. The U.S. economy—indeed, any market economy—is far more complex. Thousands of companies sell hundreds of thousands of products to millions of buyers every day. In the end, however, the result is much the same: Companies try to supply the quantity and selection of goods that will earn them the largest profits.

Figure 1.2 **Demand and Supply**
Source: Adapted from Karl E. Case and Ray C. Fair, *Principles of Economics*, 8th ed., updated (Upper Saddle River, NJ: Prentice Hall, 2007).

DEMAND AND SUPPLY SCHEDULES

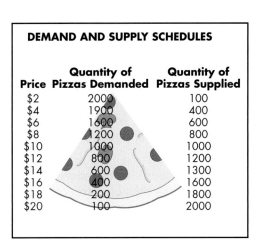

Price	Quantity of Pizzas Demanded	Quantity of Pizzas Supplied
$2	2000	100
$4	1900	400
$6	1600	600
$8	1200	800
$10	1000	1000
$12	800	1200
$14	600	1300
$16	400	1600
$18	200	1800
$20	100	2000

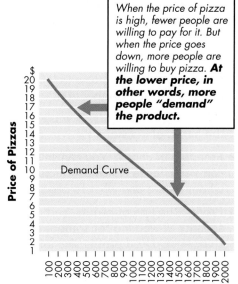

When the price of pizza is high, fewer people are willing to pay for it. But when the price goes down, more people are willing to buy pizza. **At the lower price, in other words, more people "demand" the product.**

When the price of pizza is low, more people are willing to buy pizza. Pizza makers, however, do not have the money to invest in making pizzas and so they make fewer. Supply, therefore, is limited, and **only when the price goes up will pizza makers be willing and able to increase supply**.

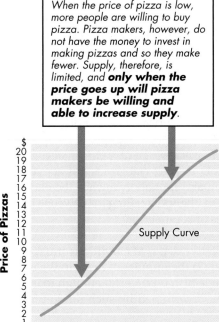

When the pizza makers increase supply in order to satisfy demand, there will be **a point at which the price that suppliers can charge is the same as the price that a maximum number of customers is willing to pay**. That point is the market price, or **equilibrium** price.

EQUILIBRIUM PRICE (DEMAND AND SUPPLY)

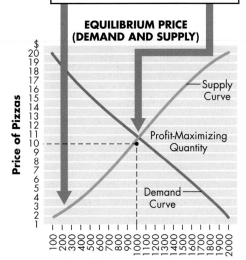

Demand the willingness and ability of buyers to purchase a good or service

Supply the willingness and ability of producers to offer a good or service for sale

Law of Demand principle that buyers will purchase (demand) more of a product as its price drops and less as its price increases

Law of Supply principle that producers will offer (supply) more of a product for sale as its price rises and less as its price drops

Demand and Supply Schedule assessment of the relationships among different levels of demand and supply at different price levels

Demand Curve graph showing how many units of a product will be demanded (bought) at different prices

Supply Curve graph showing how many units of a product will be supplied (offered for sale) at different prices

Market Price (Equilibrium Price) profit-maximizing price at which the quantity of goods demanded and the quantity of goods supplied are equal

Surplus situation in which quantity supplied exceeds quantity demanded

Shortage situation in which quantity demanded exceeds quantity supplied

Private Enterprise and Competition in a Market Economy

Market economies rely on a **private enterprise** system—one that allows individuals to pursue their own interests with minimal government restriction. In turn, private enterprise requires the presence of four elements: private property rights, freedom of choice, profits, and competition.

1 *Private property rights.* Ownership of the resources used to create wealth is in the hands of individuals.

2 *Freedom of choice.* You can sell your labor to any employer you choose. You can also choose which products to buy, and producers can usually choose whom to hire and what to produce.

3 *Profits.* The lure of profits (and freedom) leads some people to abandon the security of working for someone else and to assume the risks of entrepreneurship. Anticipated profits also influence individuals' choices of which goods or services to produce.

4 *Competition.* If profits motivate individuals to start businesses, competition motivates them to operate those businesses efficiently. **Competition** occurs when two or more businesses vie for the same resources or customers. To gain an advantage over competitors, a business must produce its goods or services efficiently and be able to sell at a reasonable profit. To achieve these goals, it must convince customers that its products are either better or less expensive than those of its competitors. Competition, therefore, forces all businesses to make products better or cheaper. A company that produces inferior, expensive products is likely to fail.

Degrees of Competition Even in a free enterprise system, not all industries are equally competitive. Economists have identified four degrees of competition in a private enterprise system: *perfect competition, monopolistic competition, oligopoly,* and *monopoly.* Note that these are not always truly distinct categories but actually tend to fall along a continuum; perfect competition and monopoly anchor the ends of the continuum, with monopolistic competition and oligopoly falling in between. Table 1.1 summarizes the features of these four degrees of competition.

Perfect Competition For **perfect competition** to exist, two conditions must prevail: (1) all firms in an industry must be small, and (2) the number of firms in the industry must be large. Under these conditions, no single firm is powerful enough to influence the price of its product. Prices are, therefore, determined by such market forces as supply and demand.

TABLE 1.1 Degrees of Competition				
Characteristic	**Perfect Competition**	**Monopolistic Competition**	**Oligopoly**	**Monopoly**
Example	Local farmer	Stationery store	Steel industry	Public utility
Number of competitors	Many	Many, but fewer than in perfect competition	Few	None
Ease of entry into industry	Relatively easy	Fairly easy	Difficult	Regulated by government
Similarity of goods or services offered by competing firms	Identical	Similar	Can be similar or different	No directly competing goods or services
Level of control over price by individual firms	None	Some	Some	Considerable

In addition, these two conditions also reflect four principles:

1 The products of each firm are so similar that buyers view them as identical to those of other firms.

2 Both buyers and sellers know the prices that others are paying and receiving in the marketplace.

3 Because each firm is small, it is easy for firms to enter or leave the market.

4 Going prices are set exclusively by supply and demand and accepted by both sellers and buyers.

U.S. agriculture is a good example of perfect competition. The wheat produced on one farm is the same as that from another. Both producers and buyers are aware of prevailing market prices. It is relatively easy to start producing wheat and relatively easy to stop when it's no longer profitable.

Monopolistic Competition In **monopolistic competition**, there are numerous sellers trying to make their products at least seem to be different from those of competitors. While there are many sellers involved in monopolistic competition, there tend to be fewer than in pure competition. Differentiating strategies include brand names (Tide versus Cheer), design or styling (Diesel versus Lucky jeans), and advertising (Coke versus Pepsi). For example, in an effort to attract health-conscious consumers, Kraft Foods promotes such differentiated products as low-fat Cool Whip, low-calorie Jell-O, and sugar-free Kool-Aid.

Monopolistically competitive businesses may be large or small, but they can still enter or leave the market easily. For example, many small clothing stores compete successfully with large apparel retailers, such as Abercrombie & Fitch, Banana Republic, and J. Crew. A good case in point is bebe stores. The small clothing chain controls its own manufacturing facilities and can respond just as quickly as firms like the Gap to changes in fashion tastes. Likewise, many single-store clothing businesses in college towns compete by developing their own T-shirt and cap designs with copyrighted slogans and logos.

Product differentiation also gives sellers some control over prices. For instance, even though Target shirts may have similar styling and other features, Ralph Lauren Polo shirts can be priced with little regard for lower Target prices. But the large number of buyers relative to sellers applies potential limits to prices: Although Polo might be able to sell shirts for $20 more than a comparable Target shirt, it could not sell as many shirts if they were priced at $200 more.

Oligopoly When an industry has only a handful of sellers, an **oligopoly** exists. As a general rule, these sellers are quite large. The entry of new competitors is hard because large capital investment is needed. Thus, oligopolistic industries (the automobile, airline, and steel industries) tend to stay that way. Only two companies make large commercial aircraft: Boeing (a U.S. company) and Airbus (a European consortium). Furthermore, as the trend toward globalization continues, most experts believe that oligopolies will become increasingly prevalent.

Oligopolists have more control over their strategies than do monopolistically competitive firms, but the actions of one firm can significantly affect the sales of every other firm in the industry. For example, when one firm cuts prices or offers incentives to increase sales, the others usually protect sales by doing the same.

Private Enterprise economic system that allows individuals to pursue their own interests without undue governmental restriction

Competition vying among businesses for the same resources or customers

Perfect Competition market or industry characterized by numerous small firms producing an identical product

Monopolistic Competition market or industry characterized by numerous buyers and relatively numerous sellers trying to differentiate their products from those of competitors

Oligopoly market or industry characterized by a handful of (generally large) sellers with the power to influence the prices of their products

ENTREPRENEURSHIP AND NEW VENTURES

Business...and Pleasure

Americans are multitaskers. We sip lattes while driving, we walk the dog while checking stock quotes, and we pay our bills online while watching TV; it is no surprise that this trend has taken on bigger dimensions. In many sectors business and entertainment are no longer considered two separate entities. Entertainment used to be defined as amusement parks, miniature golf, baseball games, and movies. Business was business: work, dine, shop, etc. But now, in a recessionary market economy, industries feel even more pressure to mix business with entertainment. The brightly colored play structures in McDonald's and the first mall roller coaster paved the way for this upsurge of integration that is now almost impossible to avoid.

Apple and Starbucks recently announced a partnership that allows customers to preview Apple iTunes songs while waiting in line for their coffee. The customers also have the option to buy or download music onto their iPod touch, iPhone, PC, or Mac. JetBlue is partnering with XM Radio to offer passengers a sample of the new wave of satellite radio, and United offers DirecTV satellite television viewing on some of its flights. Select Wal-Mart stores host live broadcasts of concerts enticing shoppers to linger just a little longer. This growing trend is not likely to change anytime soon. But businesses should be wary of new business cycles created in the entertainment realm. Entertainment-driven corporations are always at a high risk of deflation when the economy falters. Those businesses that rely on partnerships with these high-risk firms may not be as grounded as they seem.

MyBizLab

Ian Shaw/Alamy

Likewise, when one firm raises prices, others generally follow suit. Therefore, the prices of comparable products are usually similar. When an airline announces new fare discounts, others adopt the same strategy almost immediately. Just as quickly, when discounts end for one airline, they usually end for everyone else.

Monopoly A **monopoly** exists when an industry or market has only one producer (or else is so dominated by one producer that other firms cannot compete with it). A sole supplier enjoys complete control over the prices of its products. Its only constraint is a decrease in consumer demand due to increased prices. In the United States, laws, such as the Sherman Antitrust Act (1890) and the Clayton Act (1914), forbid many monopolies and regulate prices charged by **natural monopolies**—industries in which one company can most efficiently supply all needed goods or services.[3] Many electric companies are natural monopolies because they can supply all the power needed in a local area. Duplicate facilities—such as two power plants and two sets of power lines—would be wasteful.

5 Explain the importance of the economic environment to business and identify the factors used to evaluate the performance of an economic system.

Economic Indicators

Because economic forces are so volatile and can be affected by so many things, the performance of a country's economic system varies over time. Sometimes it gains strength and brings new prosperity to its members (this describes the U.S. economy during the early years of the 21st century); other times it weakens and damages their fortunes (as was the case during 2009–2010). Clearly, then, knowing how an economy is performing is useful for both business owners and investors alike.

Most experts look to various **economic indicators**—statistics that show whether an economic system is strengthening, weakening, or remaining stable—to help assess the performance of an economy.

Economic Growth, Aggregate Output, and Standard of Living

At one time, about half the U.S. population was involved in producing the food that we needed. Today, less than 2.5 percent of the U.S. population works in agriculture, and this number is expected to decrease slightly over the next decade.[6] But agricultural efficiency has improved because better ways of producing products have been devised, and better technology has been invented for getting the job done. We can say that agricultural productivity has increased because we have been able to increase total output in the agricultural sector.

We can apply the same concepts to a nation's economic system, although the computations are more complex. Fundamentally, how do we know whether an economic system is growing or not? Experts call the pattern of short-term ups and downs (or, better, expansions and contractions) in an economy the **business cycle**. The primary measure of growth in the business cycle is **aggregate output**—the total quantity of goods and services produced by an economic system during a given period.[7]

To put it simply, an increase in aggregate output is growth (or economic growth). When output grows more quickly than the population, two things usually follow:

- Output per capita—the quantity of goods and services per person—goes up.
- The system provides more of the goods and services that people want.

When these two things occur, people living in an economic system benefit from a higher **standard of living**, which refers to the total quantity and quality of goods and services that they can purchase with the currency used in their economic system. To know how much your standard of living is improving, you need to know how much your nation's economic system is growing (see Table 1.2). For instance, while the U.S. economy reflects overall growth in most years, in 2009 the economy actually shrank by 2.6 percent due to the recession.

Gross Domestic Product   **Gross domestic product (GDP)** refers to the total value of all goods and services produced within a given period by a national economy through domestic factors of production. GDP is a measure of aggregate output. Generally speaking, if GDP is going up, aggregate output is going up; if aggregate output is going up, the nation is experiencing *economic growth*.

TABLE 1.2 U.S. GDP and GDP per Capita		
2009 Gross Domestic Product (GDP) ($ Trillion)	**2009 GDP: Real Growth Rate (%)**	**2009 GDP per Capita: Purchasing Power Parity**
$14.14	−2.6%	$46,000

Monopoly market or industry in which there is only one producer that can therefore set the prices of its products

Natural Monopoly industry in which one company can most efficiently supply all needed goods or services

Economic Indicator a statistic that helps assess the performance of an economy

Business Cycle short-term pattern of economic expansions and contractions

Aggregate Output the total quantity of goods and services produced by an economic system during a given period

Standard of Living the total quantity and quality of goods and services people can

purchase with the currency used in their economic system

Gross Domestic Product (GDP) total value of all goods and services produced within a given period by a national economy through domestic factors of production

Sometimes, economists also use the term **gross national product (GNP)**, which refers to the total value of all goods and services produced by a national economy within a given period regardless of where the factors of production are located. What, precisely, is the difference between GDP and GNP? Consider a General Motors automobile plant in Brazil. The profits earned by the factory are included in U.S. GNP—but not in GDP—because its output is not produced domestically (that is, in the United States). Conversely, those profits are included in Brazil's GDP—but not GNP—because they are produced domestically (that is, in Brazil). Calculations quickly become complex because of different factors of production. The labor, for example, will be mostly Brazilian but the capital mostly American. Thus, wages paid to Brazilian workers are part of Brazil's GNP even though profits are not.

Real Growth Rate GDP and GNP usually differ by less than 1 percent, but economists argue that GDP is a more accurate indicator of domestic economic performance because it focuses only on domestic factors of production. With that in mind, let's look at the middle column in Table 1.2. Here we find that the real growth rate of U.S. GDP—the growth rate of GDP *adjusted for inflation and changes in the value of the country's currency*—was –2.6 percent in 2009. This is in contrast to growth of 2.20 percent in 2007 and 1.4 percent in 2008 (as the recession was taking hold). But what do these numbers actually mean? Remember that *growth depends on output increasing at a faster rate than population*. The U.S. population is growing at a rate of 0.97 percent per year.[8] The *real growth rate* of the U.S. economic system, therefore, has for the past few years been only modest.

GDP per Capita The number in the third column of Table 1.2 is a reflection of the standard of living: *GDP per capita* means GDP per person. We get this figure by dividing total GDP ($14.14 trillion) by total population, which happens to be a bit over about 301 million.[9] In a given period (usually calculated on an annual basis), the United States produces goods and services equal in value to $46,000 for every person in the country. Figure 1.3 shows both GDP and GDP per capita in the United States between 1950 and 2009. GDP per capita is a better measure than GDP itself of the economic well-being of the average person.

Real GDP **Real GDP** means that GDP has been adjusted to account for changes in currency values and price changes. To understand why adjustments are necessary, assume that pizza is the only product in a hypothetical economy. In 2010, a pizza cost $10; in 2011, a pizza cost $11. In both years, exactly 1,000 pizzas were produced. In 2010, the local GDP was $10,000 ($10 × 1,000); in 2011, the local GDP was $11,000 ($11 × 1,000). Has the economy grown? No. Because 1,000 pizzas were produced in both years, *aggregate output* remained the same. The point is to not be misled into believing that an economy is doing better than it is. If it is not adjusted, local GDP for 2011 is **nominal GDP**—GDP measured in current dollars or with all components valued at current prices.[10]

Purchasing Power Parity In the example, *current prices* would be 2011 prices. On the other hand, we calculate real GDP when we adjust GDP to account for changes in *currency values and price changes*. When we make this adjustment, we account for both GDP and **purchasing power parity**—the principle that exchange rates are set so that the prices of similar products in different countries are about the same. Purchasing power parity gives us a much better idea of *what people can actually buy with the financial resources allocated to them by their respective economic systems*. In other words, it gives us a better sense of standards of living across the globe. Figure 1.4 illustrates a popular approach to see how purchasing power parity works in relation to a Big Mac. For instance, the figure pegs the price of a Big Mac in the United States at $3.73. Based on currency exchange rates, a Big Mac would cost $7.20 in Norway and $4.91 in Brazil. But the same burger would cost only $1.90 in Hong Kong and $1.78 in Argentina.

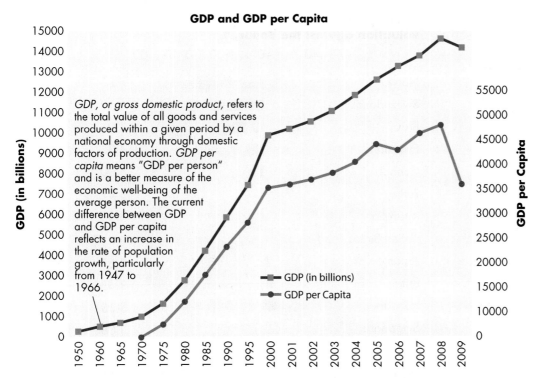

GDP and GDP per Capita

GDP, or gross domestic product, refers to the total value of all goods and services produced within a given period by a national economy through domestic factors of production. GDP per capita means "GDP per person" and is a better measure of the economic well-being of the average person. The current difference between GDP and GDP per capita reflects an increase in the rate of population growth, particularly from 1947 to 1966.

Note: This graph is shown in five-year increments until the year 2000, after which it is shown in one-year increments so as to provide more detail for recent periods. Hence, the curve artificially "flattens" after 2000.

Figure 1.3 GDP and GDP per Capita
Source: Data obtained from U.S. Department of Commerce Bureau of Economic Analysis, **www.bea.gov/bea/dn/gdplev.xls**; U.S. Census Bureau, **www.census.gov/popest/states/tables/NST-EST2005–01.xls**; www.census.gov/popest/archives/1990s; National Economic Accounts, at **http://www.bea.gov/national/nipaweb/TableView.asp#Mid**; From World Bank Development Indicators 2007–Feb 2008: International Comparison Program (May 29, 2008), at http://www.finfacts.com/biz10/globalworldincomepercapita.htm.

Productivity   A major factor in the growth of an economic system is **productivity**, which is a measure of economic growth that compares how much a system produces with the resources needed to produce it. Let's say that it takes 1 U.S. worker and 1 U.S. dollar to make 10 soccer balls in an 8-hour workday. Let's also say that it takes 1.2 Saudi workers and the equivalent of 1.2 riyals, the currency of Saudi Arabia, to make 10 soccer balls in the same 8-hour workday. We can say that the U.S. soccer-ball industry is more productive than the Saudi soccer-ball industry. The two factors of production in this extremely simple case are labor and capital.

If more products are being produced with fewer factors of production, the prices of these products will likely go down. As a consumer, therefore, you would need less of your currency to purchase the same quantity of these products. In short, your standard of living—at least with regard to these products—has improved. If your entire economic system increases its productivity, then your overall standard of living improves. In fact, *standard of living improves only through increases in productivity.*[11] Real growth in GDP reflects growth in productivity.

Gross National Product (GNP) total value of all goods and services produced by a national economy within a given period regardless of where the factors of production are located

Real GDP gross domestic product (GDP) adjusted to account for changes in currency values and price changes

Nominal GDP gross domestic product (GDP) measured in current dollars or with all components valued at current prices

Purchasing Power Parity the principle that exchange rates are set so that the prices of similar products in different countries are about the same

Productivity a measure of economic growth that compares how much a system produces with the resources needed to produce it

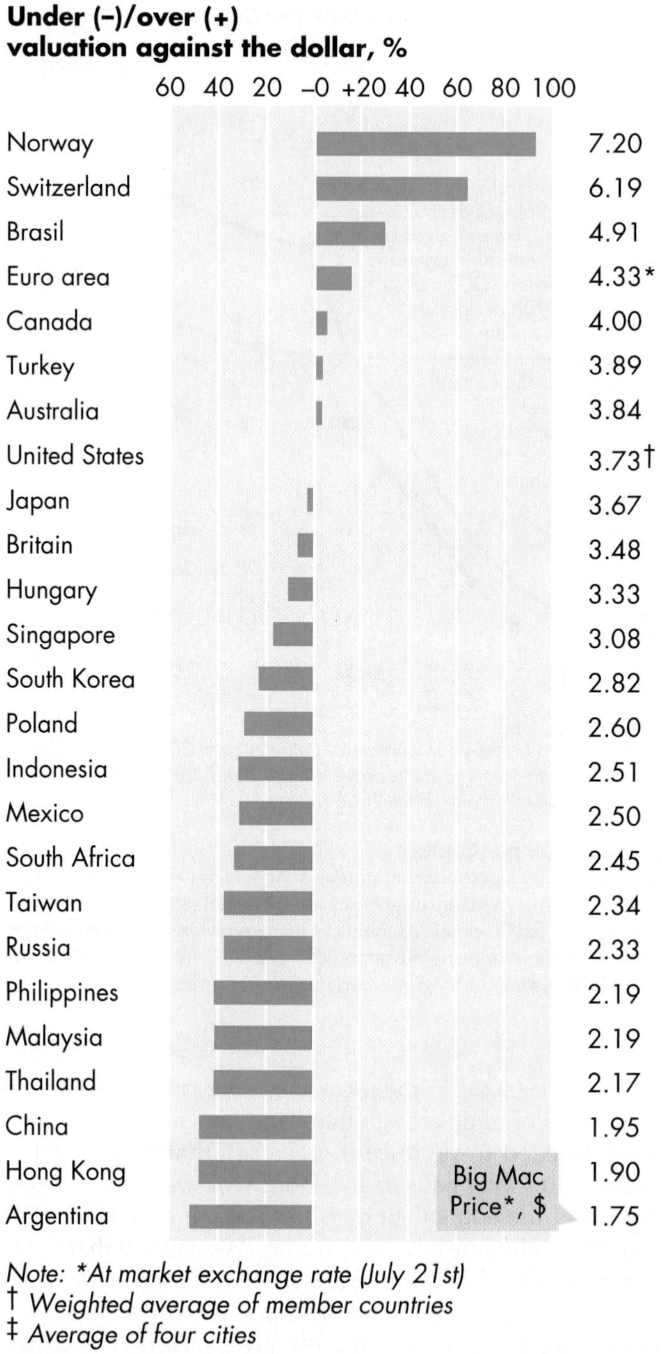

Figure 1.4 The Big Mac Index
Source: Data obtained from Big Mac
Index Review 2007 (May 29, 2008), at
**http://www.woopidoo.com/reviews/
news/big-mac-index.htm**

**Under (−)/over (+)
valuation against the dollar, %**

	Big Mac Price*, $
60 40 20 −0 +20 40 60 80 100	
Norway	7.20
Switzerland	6.19
Brasil	4.91
Euro area	4.33*
Canada	4.00
Turkey	3.89
Australia	3.84
United States	3.73†
Japan	3.67
Britain	3.48
Hungary	3.33
Singapore	3.08
South Korea	2.82
Poland	2.60
Indonesia	2.51
Mexico	2.50
South Africa	2.45
Taiwan	2.34
Russia	2.33
Philippines	2.19
Malaysia	2.19
Thailand	2.17
China	1.95
Hong Kong	1.90
Argentina	1.75

*Note: *At market exchange rate (July 21st)*
† Weighted average of member countries
‡ Average of four cities

   Productivity in the United States is generally increasing, and as a result, so are GDP and GDP per capita in most years (excluding the 2009–2010 recession). Ultimately, increases in these measures of growth mean an improvement in the standard of living. However, things don't always proceed so smoothly. Several factors can inhibit the growth of an economic system, including *balance of trade* and the *national debt*.

Balance of Trade A country's **balance of trade** is the economic value of all the products that it exports minus the economic value of its imported products. The principle here is quite simple:

- A *positive* balance of trade results when a country exports (sells to other countries) more than it imports (buys from other countries).
- A *negative* balance of trade results when a country imports more than it exports.

   A negative balance of trade is commonly called a *trade deficit*. In 2008, the U.S. trade deficit was almost $400 billion. The United States is a *debtor nation* rather

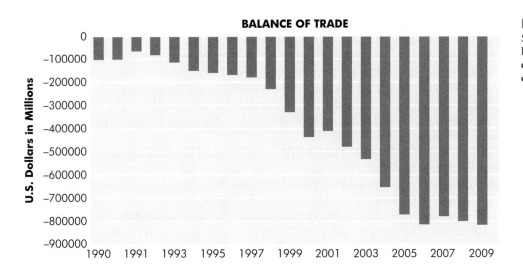

Figure 1.5 **Balance of Trade**
Source: Data obtained from U.S. Census Bureau (June 19, 2008), at **http://www.census.gov/foreign-trade/balance/c0004.html#2005.**

than a *creditor nation*. Recent trends in the U.S. balance of trade are shown in Figure 1.5.

Trade deficit affects economic growth because the amount of money spent on foreign products has not been paid in full. Therefore, it is, in effect, borrowed money, and borrowed money costs more in the form of interest. The money that flows out of the country to pay off the deficit can't be used to invest in productive enterprises, either at home or overseas.

National Debt Its **national debt** is the amount of money that the government owes its creditors. As of this writing, the U.S. national debt is over $13.6 trillion. You can find out the national debt on any given day by going to any one of several Internet sources, including the U.S. National Debt Clock at www.brillig.com/debt_clock.

How does the national debt affect economic growth? While taxes are the most obvious way the government raises money, it also sells *bonds*—securities through which it promises to pay buyers certain amounts of money by specified future dates. (In a sense, a bond is an IOU with interest.)[12] These bonds are attractive investments because they are extremely safe: The U.S. government is not going to default on them (that is, fail to make payments when due). Even so, they must also offer a decent return on the buyer's investment, and they do this by paying interest at a competitive rate. By selling bonds, therefore, the U.S. government competes with every other potential borrower for the available supply of loanable money. The more money the government borrows, the less money is available for the private borrowing and investment that increase productivity.

Economic Stability

Stability is a condition in which the amount of money available in an economic system and the quantity of goods and services produced in it are growing at about the same rate. A chief goal of an economic system, stability can be threatened by certain factors.

Inflation   **Inflation** occurs when an economic system experiences widespread price increases. Instability results when the amount of money injected into an

---

Balance of Trade the economic value of all the products that a country exports minus the economic value of all the products it imports

National Debt the amount of money the government owes its creditors

Stability condition in which the amount of money available in an economic system and the quantity of goods and services produced in it are growing at about the same rate

Inflation occurs when widespread price increases occur throughout an economic system

economy exceeds the increase in actual output, so people have more money to spend but the same quantity of products available to buy. As supply and demand principles tell us, as people compete with one another to buy available products, prices go up. These high prices will eventually bring the amount of money in the economy back down. However, these processes are imperfect—the additional money will not be distributed proportionately to all people, and price increases often continue beyond what is really necessary. As a result, purchasing power for many people declines.

Keeping in mind that our definition of inflation is the occurrence of widespread price increases throughout an economic system, it stands to reason that we can measure inflation by measuring price increases. Price indexes such as the **consumer price index (CPI)** measure the prices of typical products purchased by consumers living in urban areas.[13] The CPI is expressed as a percentage of prices as compared to a base period. The current base period used to measure inflation is 1982–1984, which is set at 100 (indicating a percentage). For comparison purposes, the CPI index was 172.2 in 2000, 195.3 in 2005, and 214.2 in 2010. So, prices in 2010 were slightly more than double the level in the 1982–1984 base period.

While we tend to view inflation as bad, however, in most ways it is better than *deflation*, which happens when there are widespread price cuts. While inflation creates instability, it also generally indicates the overall economy is growing (just in an erratic manner). But deflation generally means the overall economy is shrinking, a more serious problem by most measures.

Unemployment   Finally, we need to consider the effect of unemployment on economic stability. **Unemployment** is the level of joblessness among people actively seeking work in an economic system. When unemployment is low, there is a shortage of labor available for businesses to hire. As businesses compete with one another for the available supply of labor, they raise the wages they are willing to pay. Then, because higher labor costs eat into profit margins, they raise the prices of their products. Although consumers have more money to inject into the economy, this increase is soon undone by higher prices, so purchasing power declines.

There are at least two related problems:

- If wage rates get too high, businesses will respond by hiring fewer workers and unemployment will go up.
- Businesses could raise prices to counter increased labor costs, but they won't be able to sell as many of their products at higher prices. Because of reduced sales, they will cut back on hiring and, once again, unemployment will go up.

What if the government tries to correct this situation by injecting more money into the economic system—say by cutting taxes or spending more money? Prices in general may go up because of increased consumer demand. Again, purchasing power declines and inflation may set in.[14] During the recession of 2008–2009 millions of workers lost their jobs as businesses like Circuit City closed their doors and others, such as General Motors and Kodak, cut thousands of jobs in an effort to stem losses. Indeed, in early 2010 unemployment in the United States reached a 25-year high of 10.2 percent. By January 2011, as the economy was gradually pulling out of recession unemployment had dropped to around 9.5 percent.

Recessions and Depressions   Unemployment is sometimes a symptom of a system-wide disorder in the economy. During a downturn in the business cycle, people in different sectors may lose their jobs at the same time. As a result, overall income and spending may drop. Feeling the pinch of reduced revenues, businesses may cut spending on the factors of production—including labor. Yet more people will be put out of work, and unemployment will only increase further. Unemployment that results from this vicious cycle is called *cyclical unemployment*.

If we look at the relationship between unemployment and economic stability, we are reminded that when prices get high enough, consumer demand for goods and services goes down. We are also reminded that when demand for products goes down, producers cut back on hiring and, not surprisingly, eventually start producing less. Consequently, aggregate output decreases. When we go through a period during which aggregate output declines, we have a recession. During a *recession*, producers need fewer employees—less labor—to produce products. Unemployment, therefore, goes up.

To determine whether an economy is going through a recession, we start by measuring aggregate output. Recall that this is the function of real GDP, which we find by making necessary adjustments to the total value of all goods and services produced within a given period by a national economy through domestic factors of production. A **recession** is more precisely defined as a period during which aggregate output, as measured by real GDP, declines. As noted earlier, most economists agree that the U.S. economy went into recession in 2008; most also predicted that we were gradually emerging from recession in early 2011. A prolonged and deep recession is a **depression**. The last major depression in the United States started in 1929 and lasted over 10 years. Most economists believe that the 2008–2010 recession, while the worst in decades, was not really a depression.

Managing the U.S. Economy

The government acts to manage the U.S. economic system through two sets of policies: fiscal and monetary. It manages the collection and spending of its revenues through **fiscal policies**. Tax rates, for example, can play an important role in fiscal policies helping to manage the economy. One key element of President Barack Obama's presidential platform was an overhaul of the U.S. tax system. Among other things, he proposed cutting taxes for the middle class while simultaneously raising taxes for both higher-income people and businesses.

Monetary policies focus on controlling the size of the nation's money supply. Working primarily through the Federal Reserve System (the nation's central bank, often referred to simply as "the Fed"), the government can influence the ability and willingness of banks throughout the country to lend money.[15] For example, to help offset the 2008–2009 recession, the government injected more money into the economy through various stimulus packages. On the one hand, officials hoped that these funds would stimulate business growth and the creation of new jobs. On the other hand, though, some experts feared that increasing the money supply might also lead to inflation.

Taken together, fiscal policy and monetary policy make up **stabilization policy**—government economic policy whose goal is to smooth out fluctuations in output and unemployment and to stabilize prices. In effect, the economic recession that started in 2008 was a significant departure from stabilization as business valuations dropped and jobs were eliminated. The various government interventions, such as financial bailouts, represented strategies to restore economic stability.

Consumer Price Index (CPI) a measure of the prices of typical products purchased by consumers living in urban areas

Unemployment the level of joblessness among people actively seeking work in an economic system

Recession a period during which aggregate output, as measured by GDP, declines

Depression a prolonged and deep recession

Fiscal Policies policies used by a government regarding how it collects and spends revenue

Monetary Policies policies used by a government to control the size of its money supply

Stabilization Policy government economic policy intended to smooth out fluctuations in output and unemployment and to stabilize prices

Heather A. Craig/Shutterstock

Continued from page 4

Hitting the Peak?

While surging oil and gas prices occupied the thoughts of consumers in 2011, government officials began to worry about the bigger picture. The surging global demand for gasoline has been forcing experts to face a stark reality—the global supply of petroleum will soon peak and then slowly begin to decline. While no one can pinpoint when this will happen, virtually all the experts agree that it will happen well before the middle of this century.

So then what? The laws of supply and demand will continue to work, but in perhaps different ways. First, just because the supply of oil will decline doesn't mean that it will disappear immediately. While there may be gradual reductions in supply, oil and gas will remain available for at least another century—but at prices that may make those of today seem like a bargain. New technology may also allow businesses to extract petroleum from locations that are not currently accessible, such as from the deepest areas under the oceans.

Second, and more significantly, there will be market incentives for businesses everywhere to figure out how to replace today's dependence on oil and gas with alternatives. For instance, automobile manufacturers are already seeing increased demand for their hybrid products—cars and trucks that use a combination of gasoline and electrical power. Hence, firms that can produce alternative sources of energy will spring up, and those who find viable answers will prosper. And companies that can figure out how to replace today's plastic products with new products that don't rely on petroleum will also find willing buyers.

QUESTIONS FOR DISCUSSION

1 What were the basic factors of production in the petroleum industry? What do you think the factors of production might be in the future?
2 Explain how the concepts of the demand and supply of petroleum combine to determine market prices.
3 What are the economic indicators most directly affected by energy prices?
4 Does the global energy situation increase or decrease your confidence in a capitalistic system based on private enterprise?
5 Should there be more government intervention in the exploration for and pricing of petroleum products? Why or why not?

SUMMARY OF LEARNING OBJECTIVES MyBizLab

1. **Define the nature of U.S. business and identify its main goals and functions. (p. 4)**
A *business* is an organization that provides goods or services to earn profits. The prospect of earning *profits*—the difference between a business's revenues and expenses—encourages people to open and expand businesses. Businesses produce most of the goods and services that Americans consume and employ most working people. New forms of technology, service businesses, and international opportunities promise to keep production, consumption, and employment growing indefinitely.

2. **Describe the external environments of business and discuss how these environments affect the success or failure of any organization. (pp. 5–7)**
The *external environment* of business refers to everything outside its boundaries that might affect it. Both the *domestic* and the *global business environment* affect virtually all businesses. The *technological, political-legal, sociocultural,* and *economic environments* are also important.

3. **Describe the different types of global economic systems according to the means by which they control the factors of production. (pp. 7–11)**
Economic systems differ in the ways in which they manage the five *factors of production* (1) *labor*, or *human resources*, (2) *capital*, (3) *entrepreneurship*, (4) *physical resources*, and (5) *information resources*. A *planned economy* relies on a centralized government to control factors of production and make decisions. Under *communism*, the government owns and operates all sources of production. In a *market economy*, individuals—producers and consumers—control production and allocation decisions through supply and demand. A *market* is a mechanism for exchange between the buyers and sellers of a particular product or service. Sellers can charge what they want, and customers can buy what they choose. The political basis of market processes is *capitalism*, which fosters private ownership of the factors of production and encourages entrepreneurship by offering profits as an incentive. Most countries rely on some form of *mixed market economy*—a system featuring characteristics of both planned and market economies.

4. **Show how markets, demand, and supply affect resource distribution in the United States, identify the elements of private enterprise, and explain the various degrees of competition in the U.S. economic system. (pp. 11–16)**
Decisions about what to buy and what to sell are determined by the forces of demand and supply. *Demand* is the willingness and ability of buyers to purchase a product or service. *Supply* is the willingness and ability of producers to offer a product or service for sale. A *demand and supply schedule* reveals the relationships among different levels of demand and supply at different price levels.

Market economies reflect the operation of a *private enterprise system*—a system that allows individuals to pursue their own interests without government restriction. Private enterprise works according to four principles: (1) private property rights, (2) freedom of choice, (3) profits, and (4) competition. Economists have identified four degrees of competition in a private enterprise system: (1) *perfect competition*, (2) *monopolistic competition*, (3) *oligopoly*, and (4) *monopoly*.

5. **Explain the importance of the economic environment to business and identify the factors used to evaluate the performance of an economic system. (pp. 16–23)**
Economic indicators are statistics that show whether an economic system is strengthening, weakening, or remaining stable. The overall health of the economic environment—the economic system in which they operate—affects organizations. The two key goals of the U.S. system are *economic growth* and *economic stability*. Growth is assessed by *aggregate output*. Among the factors that can inhibit growth, two of the most important are *balance of trade* and the *national debt*. *Economic stability* means that the amount of money available in an economic system and the quantity of goods and services produced in it are growing at about the same rate. There are two key threats to stability: *inflation* and *unemployment*. The government manages the economy through two sets of policies: *fiscal policies* (such as tax increases) and *monetary policies* that focus on controlling the size of the nation's money supply.

KEY TERMS MyBizLab

aggregate output (p. 17)
balance of trade (p. 20)
business (p. 4)
business cycle (p. 17)
capital (p. 7)
capitalism (p. 10)
communism (p. 10)
competition (p. 14)
consumer price index (CPI) (p. 22)
demand (p. 12)

demand and supply schedule (p. 12)
demand curve (p. 12)
depression (p. 23)
domestic business environment (p. 6)
economic environment (p. 7)
economic indicators (p. 17)
economic system (p. 7)
entrepreneur (p. 8)
external environment (p. 5)
factors of production (p. 7)

fiscal policies (p. 23)
global business environment (p. 6)
gross domestic product (GDP) (p. 17)
gross national product (GNP) (p. 18)
inflation (p. 21)
information resources (p. 9)
labor (human resources) (p. 7)
law of demand (p. 12)
law of supply (p. 12)
market (p. 10)

QUESTIONS AND EXERCISES

QUESTIONS FOR REVIEW

1. What are the factors of production? Is one factor more important than the others? If so, which one? Why?
2. What is a demand curve? A supply curve? What is the term for the point at which they intersect?
3. What is GDP? Real GDP? What does each measure?
4. Why is inflation both good and bad? How does the government try to control it?

QUESTIONS FOR ANALYSIS

5. In recent years, many countries that previously used planned economies have moved to market economies. Why do you think this has occurred? Can you envision a situation that would cause a resurgence of planned economies?
6. Cite an instance in which a surplus of a product led to decreased prices. Cite an instance in which a shortage led to increased prices. What eventually happened in each case? Why?
7. Explain how current economic indicators, such as inflation and unemployment, affect you personally. Explain how they may affect you as a manager.

8. At first glance, it might seem as though the goals of economic growth and stability are inconsistent with one another. How can you reconcile this apparent inconsistency?

APPLICATION EXERCISES

9. Visit a local shopping mall or shopping area. List each store that you see and determine what degree of competition it faces in its immediate environment. For example, if there is only one store in the mall that sells shoes, that store represents a monopoly. Note those businesses with direct competitors (two jewelry stores) and show how they compete with one another.
10. Interview a business owner or senior manager. Ask this individual to describe for you the following things: (1) how demand and supply affect the business, (2) what essential factors of production are most central to the firm's operations, and (3) how fluctuations in economic indicators affect his or her business.

BUILDING YOUR BUSINESS SKILLS

Paying the Price of Doing E-Business

Goal
To help you understand how the economic environment affects a product's price.

Background Information
Assume that you own a local business that provides Internet access to individuals and businesses. Yours is one of four such businesses in the local market. Each one charges the same price: $12 per month for standard DSL service. You also provide e-mail service, as do two of your competitors. Two competitors give users free personal web pages. One competitor just dropped its price to $10 per month, and the other two have announced that they'll follow suit. Your break-even price is $7 per customer—that is, you must charge $7 for your service package in order to cover your costs. You are concerned about getting into a price war that may destroy your business.

Method

Step 1
Divide into groups of four or five people. Each group should develop a general strategy for responding to competitors' price changes. Be sure to consider the following factors:
- How demand for your product is affected by price changes
- The number of competitors selling the same or a similar product
- The methods you can use—other than price—to attract new customers and retain current customers

Step 2
Develop specific pricing strategies based on each of the following situations:
- A month after dropping the price to $10, one of your competitors raises it back to $12.

- Two of your competitors drop their prices even further—to $8 a month. As a result, your business falls off by 25 percent.
- One of the competitors who offers free web pages announces that the service will become optional for an extra $2 a month.
- Two competitors announce that they will charge individual users $8 a month but will charge a higher price (not yet announced) for businesses.
- All four providers (including you) are charging $8 a month. One goes out of business, and you know that another is in poor financial health.

1. Discuss the role that various inducements other than price might play in affecting demand and supply in this market.
2. Is it always in a company's best interest to feature the lowest prices?
3. Eventually, what form of competition is likely to characterize this market?

EXERCISING YOUR ETHICS: INDIVIDUAL EXERCISE

Prescribing a Dose of Competitive Medicine

The Situation
You are a businessperson in a small town, where you run one of two local pharmacies. The population and economic base are fairly stable. Each pharmacy controls about 50 percent of the market. Each is reasonably profitable, generating solid if unspectacular revenues.

The Dilemma
You have just been approached by the owner of the other pharmacy. He has indicated an interest either in buying your pharmacy or in selling his to you. He argues that neither of you can substantially increase your profits and complains that if one pharmacy raises its prices, customers will simply go to the other one. He tells you outright that if you sell to him, he plans to raise prices by 10 percent. He believes that the local market will have to accept the increase for two reasons: (1) The town is too small to attract national competitors, such as Walgreens or CVS, and (2) local customers can't go elsewhere to shop because the nearest town with a pharmacy is 40 miles away.

QUESTIONS TO ADDRESS
1 What are the roles of supply and demand in this scenario?
2 What are the underlying ethical issues?
3 What would you do if you were actually faced with this situation?

EXERCISING YOUR ETHICS: TEAM EXERCISE

Making the Right Decision

The Situation
Hotel S is a large hotel in the heart of a southern city. The hotel is a franchise operation run by an international hotel chain. The primary source of revenue for the hotel is convention business. A major tropical storm is about to hit the city, which in the past has been prone to heavy flooding.

The Dilemma
Because Hotel S is a licensed operation, it must maintain numerous quality standards in order to keep its license. This license is important because the international management company handles advertising, reservations, and so on. If it were to lose its license, it is almost certain that the hotel would have to reduce its staff.

For the past few years, members of the Hotel S team have been lobbying the investors who own the hotel to undertake a major renovation. They fear that without such a renovation, the hotel will lose its license when it comes up for renewal in a few months. The owners, however, have balked at investing more of their funds in the hotel itself but have indicated that hotel management can use revenues earned above a specified level for upgrades.

The tropical storm approaching the city has cut off most major transportation avenues, and telephone service is also down. The Hotel S staff is unable to reach the general manager, who has been traveling on business. Because the city is full of conventioneers, hotel rooms are in high demand. Unfortunately, because of the disrepair at the hotel, it only has about 50 percent occupancy. Hotel S staff have been discussing what to do and have identified three basic options:

1 The hotel can reduce room rates in order to help both local citizens as well as out-of-town visitors. The hotel can also provide meals at reduced rates. A few other hotels are also doing this.
2 The hotel can maintain its present pricing policies. Most of the city's hotels are adopting this course of action.
3 The hotel can raise its rates by approximately 15 percent without attracting too much attention. It can also start charging for certain things it has been providing for free, such as local telephone calls, parking, and morning coffee. None of the staff members favors this option out of greed, but instead see it as a way to generate extra profits for renovation and to protect jobs.

Team Activity
Assemble a group of four students and assign each group member to one of the following roles:
- A member of the hotel staff
- The Hotel S manager
- A customer at the hotel
- A Hotel S investor

ACTION STEPS

1 Before hearing any of your group's comments on this situation, and from the perspective of your assigned role, which of the three options do you think is the best choice? Write down the reasons for your position.

2 Before hearing any of your group's comments on this situation, and from the perspective of your assigned role, what are the underlying ethical issues, if any, in this situation? Write down the issues.

3 Gather your group together and reveal, in turn, each member's comments on the best choice of the three options. Next, reveal the ethical issues listed by each member.

4 Appoint someone to record main points of agreement and disagreement within the group. How do you explain the results? What accounts for any disagreement?

5 From an ethical standpoint, what does your group conclude is the most appropriate action that should have been taken by the hotel in this situation?

6 Develop a group response to the following question: Can your team identify other solutions that might help satisfy both extreme views?

VIDEO EXERCISE   MyBizLab

Bancfirst

Learning Objectives

The purpose of this video is to help you:

1 Describe the impact of the external environment on a business.

2 Identify factors that influence demand and supply curves and the equilibrium price.

3 Understand the impact of the business cycle.

Synopsis

BancFirst is a multi-branch bank located in Oklahoma. While many banks faced serious crises during the past few years, BancFirst has remained strong. A relaxed regulatory environment allowed banks to make mortgage loans to buyers who were unlikely to be able to repay the loans. When these buyers began to default on their loans, banks foreclosed on the loans and became the owners of these homes. In the past, banks were typically able to resell foreclosed homes and recover the amount of the loan. However, with a large number of homes for sale and a shrinking pool of buyers, banks found themselves unable to sell the foreclosed homes and began to face serious challenges. While the number of bank failures was less than ten for most of the last decade, rates began to skyrocket in 2009. BancFirst avoided much of this crisis by sticking to well-established lending guidelines.

DISCUSSION QUESTIONS

1 What are the major elements of the external environment? Of these, which is most important to BancFirst?

2 What are the factors that caused the demand curve for houses to shift to the right? How did this affect the equilibrium price?

3 Which factors created a shift in the supply curve? How did this affect the equilibrium price for houses?

4 There are four stages in the business cycle: prosperity, recession, depression, and recovery. Where was the U.S. economy when the housing crisis began? Where are we today?

5 The U.S. government "bailed out" a number of banks during this crisis. Do you think that this prevented a depression? Do you think that this is the proper role of government?

Online Exploration

Visit the BancFirst website (www.bancfirst.com) and click on Investor Relations. From this page, you will be able to access the bank's latest annual report (Latest 10-K). Although the report is very long, you can read through the first few pages to learn more about the bank. Beginning on page 13, BancFirst identifies a number of risk factors. What are the primary concerns that BancFirst has identified? What plans have they made to address each concern?

END NOTES

1 "If Unrest Spreads, Gas May Hit $5," *USA Today*, February 22, 2011, p. 1A; "Why the World Is One Storm Away from Energy Crisis," *Wall Street Journal*, September 24, 2005, A1, A2; "Higher and Higher—Again: Gasoline Prices Set a Record," *USA Today*, May 25, 2004, p. B1; "Who Wins and Loses When Gas Prices Skyrocket?" *Time*, May 8, 2006, p. 28; "Gas Prices Climbing Despite Hefty Supply," *USA Today*, February 2, 2011, pp. B1, B2; "Fear and Loathing in the Oil Markets," *Time*, March 14, 2011, p. 22.

2 See Paul Heyne, Peter J. Boetke, and David L. Prychitko, *The Economic Way of Thinking*, 11th ed. (Upper Saddle River, NJ: Prentice Hall, 2005), 171–176.

3 *Hoover's Handbook of American Business* 2011 (Austin: Hoover's, 2011), pp. 793–794.

4 Michael Porter and Mark Kramer, "Creating Shared Value," *Harvard Business Review*, January–February 2011, pp. 62–77.

5 See Karl E. Case and Ray C. Fair, *Principles of Economics*, 10th ed., updated (Upper Saddle River, NJ: Prentice Hall, 2011), 103–105.

6 http://quickfacts.census.gov/qfd/states/00000.html (February 15, 2010).

7 Case and Fair, *Principles of Economics*, 432–433.

8 The World Factbook: United States. (February 15, 2011), at https://www.cia.gov/library/publications/the-world-factbook/geos/us.html

9 Ibid.

[10] See Olivier Blanchard, *Macroeconomics*, 4th ed. (Upper Saddle River, NJ: Prentice Hall, 2005), 24–26.

[11] See Jay Heizer and Barry Render, *Operations Management*, 8th ed. (Upper Saddle River, NJ: Prentice Hall, 2006), 14.

[12] This section is based on Paul Heyne, Peter J. Boetke, and David L. Prychitko, *The Economic Way of Thinking*, 11th ed. (Upper Saddle River, NJ: Prentice Hall, 2005), 491–493.

[13] This section follows Ronald M. Ayers and Robert A. Collinge, *Economics: Explore and Apply*, (Upper Saddle River, NJ: Prentice Hall, 2004), 163–167.

[14] See Heyne, Boetke, and Prychitko, *The Economic Way of Thinking*, 403–409, 503–504.

[15] See "The New Fed," *BusinessWeek*, November 7, 2005, pp. 30–34.

Business Ethics and Social Responsibility

Under the Guise of Green

Oil companies aren't necessarily known for their environmentally responsible reputations. Exxon Mobil, for example, is remembered for the damage inflicted off the coast of Alaska when one of its tankers ran aground, and Royal Dutch Shell has been widely criticized for environmental damage resulting from its explorations in the Amazon basin. Another global energy giant, BP, however, has been making a concerted effort to create and market an environmentally friendly image. For the most part, this strategy has worked—ironically leading many to overlook the facts suggesting that BP is not entirely the environmentally responsible exception it claims to be.

For the past several years, BP has been charged with major environmental offenses almost annually. In 2000 the company was convicted of an environmental felony for failing to report that its subcontractor was dumping hazardous waste in Alaska. In 2005, BP allegedly ignored knowledge that its Texas City refinery was unsafe in a cost-cutting effort that led to an explosion, 15 deaths, and dozens more injuries. The following year, BP's negligence at its Prudhoe Bay oil field caused a 200,000-gallon oil spill and misdemeanor violation of the Clean Water Act. Then, in 2007, BP lobbied Indiana regulators for an exemption allowing it to increase its daily release of ammonia and sludge into Lake Michigan. Finally, the BP oil spill in the Gulf of Mexico in 2010, when the firm's *Deepwater Horizon* rig collapsed, led to a significant backlash against the firm and ultimately resulted in the ouster of CEO Tony Hayward.

After reading this chapter, you should be able to:

1 **Explain how individuals develop their personal codes of ethics and why ethics are important in the workplace.**

2 **Distinguish social responsibility from ethics, identify organizational stakeholders, and characterize social consciousness today.**

3 **Show how the concept of social responsibility applies both to environmental issues and to a firm's relationships with customers, employees, and investors.**

4 **Identify four general approaches to social responsibility and describe the four steps that a firm must take to implement a social responsibility program.**

5 **Explain how issues of social responsibility and ethics affect small business.**

Despite these misdeeds, however, BP still tries to maintain its image as a "green" company. The Natural Resource Defense Council has even praised it for being a leader in the industry's move toward renewable energy. Indeed, true to the tag line, "Beyond Petroleum," that accompanies its green logo, BP's 2010 Sustainability Report projects spending $8 billion over the next ten years on renewable energy products. Its website even offers a carbon footprint calculator that lets visitors see how their own choices affect the environment.

Indeed, even a cursory look at the BP website conveys an image of environmental awareness and social responsibility. The BP logo, an image that combines elements of a classic solar rendering and a flower, is clearly intended to convey an image of "nature friendliness," for example, and the color green is used prominently across the site. There are also links to descriptions of

David Robertson/Alamy

WHAT'S IN IT FOR ME?

Business practices in the energy industry exemplify a growing issue in the business world today: the economic imperatives (real or imagined) facing managers versus pressures to function as good world citizens. Oil companies have to balance the pressure to earn profits for owners and help meet the growing demand for energy against the need to help protect and preserve the fragile natural environment. By understanding the material in this chapter, you'll be better able to assess ethical and socially responsible issues facing you as an employee and as a boss or business owner and understand the ethical and socially responsible actions of businesses you deal with as a consumer and as an investor.

In this chapter, we'll look at ethics and social responsibility—what they mean and how they apply to environmental issues and to a firm's relationships with customers, employees, and investors. Along the way, we look at general approaches to social responsibility, the steps businesses must take to implement social responsibility programs, and how issues of social responsibility and ethics affect small businesses. But first, we begin this chapter by discussing ethics in the workplace—individual, business, and managerial.

MyBizLab Where you see MyBizLab in this chapter, go to **www.mybizlab.com** for additional activities on the topic being discussed.

the firm's environment initiatives and policies and practices regarding "green" business practices.[1]

Our opening story continues on page 52.

Ethics in the Workplace

Just what is ethical behavior? **Ethics** are beliefs about what's right and wrong or good and bad. An individual's values and morals, plus the social context in which his or her behavior occurs, determine whether behavior is regarded as ethical or unethical. In other words, **ethical behavior** is behavior that conforms to individual beliefs and social norms about what's right and good. **Unethical behavior** is behavior that conforms to individual beliefs and social norms about what is defined as wrong and bad. **Business ethics** is a term often used to refer to ethical or unethical behaviors by employees in the context of their jobs.

Individual Ethics

Because ethics are based on both individual beliefs and social concepts, they vary from person to person, from situation to situation, and from culture to culture. Social standards are broad enough to support differences in beliefs. Without violating general standards, people may develop personal codes of ethics reflecting a wide range of attitudes and beliefs.

Thus, ethical and unethical behaviors are determined partly by the individual and partly by the culture. For instance, virtually everyone would agree that if you see someone drop $20, it would be ethical to return it to the owner. But there'll be less agreement if you find $20 and don't know who dropped it. Should you turn it in to the lost-and-found department? Or, since the rightful owner isn't likely to claim it, can you just keep it?

Ambiguity, the Law, and the Real World Societies generally adopt formal laws that reflect prevailing ethical standards or social norms. For example, because most people regard theft as unethical, we have laws against such behavior and ways of punishing those who steal. We try to make unambiguous laws, but interpreting and applying them can still lead to ethical ambiguities. Real-world situations can often be interpreted in different ways, and it isn't always easy to apply statutory standards to real-life behavior. For instance, during the aftermath of Hurricane Katrina, desperate survivors in New Orleans looted grocery stores for food. While few people criticized this behavior, such actions were technically against the law.

Unfortunately, the epidemic of scandals that dominated business news over the past decade shows how willing people can be to take advantage of potentially ambiguous situations—indeed, to create them. For example, Tyco sold itself to the smaller ADT Ltd. Because its new parent company was based in the tax haven of Bermuda, Tyco no longer had to pay U.S. taxes on its non-U.S. income. Tyco's subsidiaries in such tax-friendly nations soon doubled, and the company slashed its annual U.S. tax bill by $600 million. "Tyco," complained a U.S. congressman, "has raised tax avoidance to an art," but one tax expert replies that Tyco's schemes "are very consistent with the [U.S.] tax code."[2] Even in the face of blistering criticism and the indictment of its former CEO, Tyco retains its offshore ownership structure.[3]

Individual Values and Codes How should we deal with business behavior that we regard as unethical, especially when it's legally ambiguous? No doubt we have to start with the individuals in a business—its managers, employees, and other legal representatives. Each person's personal code of ethics is determined by a combination of factors. We start to form ethical standards as children in response to our perceptions of the behavior of parents and other adults. Soon, we enter school, where we're influenced by peers, and as we grow into adulthood, experience shapes our lives and contributes to our ethical beliefs and our behavior. We also develop values

MANAGING IN TURBULENT TIMES

Just When They Need It Most

In many ways, it's a pretty bitter irony. Volunteer organizations and charitable enterprises like the American Red Cross, the Salvation Army, and the United Way do much good in our society. When emergency strikes, the Red Cross is usually first on the scene. The Salvation Army provides much-needed relief for people without means. And the United Way supports a wide array of charities and social programs.

All three of these organizations depend on contributions from people and businesses to provide the services people often need. Salvation Army volunteers, for example, ring holiday bells outside retailers and collect spare change in red kettles. The United Way helps organize giving campaigns within business and government organizations. And the Red Cross calls on the assistance of more than a million volunteers each year.

But when the economy takes a downturn, as it did from 2008 through 2010, charitable giving almost always goes down. Most individuals and businesses, for example, find that they have less discretionary income and so have to reduce their spending. And giving to help others is one area that gets cut back. Indeed, the Red Cross, Salvation Army, and United Way all reported a drop in income in all three years of the recession. While a small increase is forecast for 2011, it will still be well below the pre-recession levels of 2006 and 2007.

Ironically, it's in these very times that more people than ever need just the kind of assistance these organizations provide. When people lose their jobs, when their savings disappear, when they can't make their mortgage payment or when

Dorothy Alexander/Alamy

second jobs during holiday periods are reduced, people need to be able to turn to the Salvation Army, for example, to help feed their children.

Fortunately, the leadership at these organizations anticipates difficult times and has plans in place that allow them to dip into reserves and cut back on their own expenses as necessary. As a result, at least for the time being, they have been able to provide the same basic levels of support as in past years. Hopefully, economic conditions will begin to improve soon, and they can begin to once again think about expanding services and providing more support to those who need it most.

MyBizLab

and morals that contribute to ethical standards. If you put financial gain at the top of your priority list, you may develop a code of ethics that supports the pursuit of material comfort. If you set family and friends as a priority, you'll no doubt adopt different standards.

Business and Managerial Ethics

Managerial ethics are the standards of behavior that guide individual managers in their work.[4] Although your ethics can affect your work in any number of ways, it's helpful to classify them in terms of three broad categories.

Behavior toward Employees This category covers such matters as hiring and firing, wages and working conditions, and privacy and respect. Ethical and legal guidelines suggest that hiring and firing decisions should be based solely on the

---

Ethics beliefs about what is right and wrong or good and bad in actions that affect others

Ethical Behavior behavior conforming to generally accepted social norms concerning beneficial and harmful actions

Unethical Behavior behavior that does not conform to generally accepted social norms concerning beneficial and harmful actions

Business Ethics ethical or unethical behaviors by employees in the context of their jobs

Managerial Ethics standards of behavior that guide individual managers in their work

ability to perform a job. A manager who discriminates against African Americans or women in hiring exhibits both unethical and illegal behavior. But what about the manager who hires a friend or relative when someone else might be more qualified? Although such decisions may not be illegal, they may be objectionable on ethical grounds.

Wages and working conditions, while regulated by law, are also areas for controversy. Consider a manager who pays a worker less than he deserves because the manager knows that the employee can't afford to quit or risk his job by complaining. While some people will see the behavior as unethical, others will see it as smart business. Cases such as these are hard enough to judge, but consider the behavior of Enron management toward company employees. It encouraged employees to invest retirement funds in company stock and then, when financial problems began to surface, refused to permit them to sell the stock (even though top officials were allowed to sell). Ultimately, the firm's demise cost thousands of these very employees to lose their jobs and much of their pensions.

Behavior toward the Organization Ethical issues also arise from employee behavior toward employers, especially in such areas as conflict of interest, confidentiality, and honesty. A *conflict of interest* occurs when an activity may benefit the individual to the detriment of his or her employer. Most companies have policies that forbid buyers from accepting gifts from suppliers since such gifts might be construed as a bribe or an attempt to induce favoritism. Businesses in highly competitive industries—software and fashion apparel, for example—have safeguards against designers selling company secrets to competitors.

Relatively common problems in the general area of honesty include such behavior as stealing supplies, padding expense accounts, and using a business phone to make personal long-distance calls. Most employees are honest, but many organizations are nevertheless vigilant. Again, Enron is a good example of employees' unethical behavior toward an organization: Top managers not only misused corporate assets, but they often committed the company to risky ventures in order to further their own personal interests.

Behavior toward Other Economic Agents Ethics also comes into play in the relationship of a business and its employees with so-called *primary agents of interest*—mainly customers, competitors, stockholders, suppliers, dealers, and unions. In dealing with such agents, there is room for ethical ambiguity in just about every activity—advertising, financial disclosure, ordering and purchasing, bargaining and negotiation, and other business relationships. Bernard Madoff's investment scams cost hundreds of his clients their life savings. He led them to believe their money was safe and that they were earning large returns when in fact their money was being hidden and used to support his own extravagant lifestyle. He used funds from new clients to pay returns to older clients. Madoff's scheme showed a blatant disregard for his investors.

From a more controversial perspective, businesses in the pharmaceutical industry are often criticized because of the rising prices of drugs. Critics argue that pharmaceutical companies reap huge profits at the expense of the average consumer. In its defense, the pharmaceutical industry argues that prices must be set high in order to cover the costs of research and development programs to develop new drugs. The solution to such problems seems obvious: Find the right balance between reasonable pricing and price gouging (responding to increased demand with overly steep price increases). But like so many questions involving ethics, there are significant differences of opinion about the proper balance.

Another problem is global variations in business practices. In many countries, bribes are a normal part of doing business. U.S. law, however, forbids bribes, even if rivals from other countries are paying them. A U.S. power-generating company recently lost a $320 million contract in the Middle East because it refused to pay bribes that a Japanese firm used to get the job. We'll discuss some of the ways in which social, cultural, and legal differences among nations affect international business in Chapter 4.

Assessing Ethical Behavior

What distinguishes ethical from unethical behavior is often subjective and subject to differences of opinion. So how can we decide whether a particular action or decision is ethical? The following three steps set a simplified course for applying ethical judgments to situations that may arise during the course of business activities:

1 Gather the relevant factual information. *(just facts)*

2 Analyze the facts to determine the most appropriate moral values.

3 Make an ethical judgment based on the rightness or wrongness of the proposed activity or policy.

Unfortunately, the process doesn't always work as smoothly as these three steps suggest. What if the facts aren't clear-cut? What if there are no agreed-upon moral values? Nevertheless, a judgment and a decision must be made. Experts point out that, otherwise, trust is impossible. And trust is indispensable in any business transaction.

The Ethical Soft Shoe To bribe or not to bribe? That is the question. Well, actually, it's not really a question at all because the textbook answer is a non-negotiable no. No matter what business environment you're in, whatever culture or country you're in, the answer is always no.

In reality, it's a little more complicated than that. Business dealings that ignore the strict letter of the law happen all the time—more so in some countries than in others. Not just bribes, but offering or accepting incentives to get things done or extracting a personal favor or two. We do it all the time in the United States—using the power and influence of people we know to get things done the way we want. Granted, American business practices overseas are subject to certain constraints, such as those embodied in the Foreign Corrupt Practices Act.

Elsewhere, however, the answer to the question is not necessarily no. A hallmark of Brazilian business culture, for example, is a creative approach to problem solving known as *jeitinho*. *Jeitinho* means "to find a way." For Brazilians, there's always another way to get something done. If you need some kind of official document, for instance, you might set out on the straight and narrow path, determined to take all the proper bureaucratic steps to get it. Unfortunately, you may soon find yourself in a maze of rules and regulations from which it's impossible to extricate yourself. That's when you're most likely to resort to *jeitinho*—using personal connections, bending the rules, making a "contribution," or simply approaching the problem from a different angle.

The focus of *jeitinho* appears to be on the goal—in this case, obtaining a document. For Brazilians, however, it's really on *the process of accomplishing it*—on being willing and able to find another way, no matter what the obstacle. After all, every obstacle forces you in another direction, and during the process of negotiating the maze, you may be forced to change your original destination. *Jeitinho* almost never involves butting heads with authority. Rather, it's a complex dance that enables individuals to go around problems instead of having to go through them. It's a philosophy in which ends sometimes justify a complicated web of means.

Even if you're operating in a country (like Brazil) in which sidestepping the rules is business as usual, you don't *have* to do an ethical soft shoe. Many global companies have strict ethical guidelines for doing business, and the steps generally don't change just because you're dancing with a foreign partner. The key is understanding the culture of the host country—observing the way business is conducted and preparing yourself for any challenges—before you get out on the dance floor.

To assess more fully the ethics of specific behavior, we need a more complex perspective. Consider a common dilemma faced by managers with expense accounts. Companies routinely provide managers with accounts to cover work-related expenses—hotel bills, meals, rental cars, or taxis—when they're traveling on company business or entertaining clients for business purposes. They expect employees to claim only work-related expenses.

If a manager takes a client to dinner and spends $100, submitting a $100 reimbursement receipt for that dinner is accurate and appropriate. But suppose that this manager has a $100 dinner the next night with a good friend for purely social purposes. Submitting that receipt for reimbursement would be unethical, but some managers rationalize that it's okay to submit a receipt for dinner with a friend. Perhaps they'll tell themselves that they're underpaid and just "recovering" income due to them.

Ethical *norms* also come into play in a case like this. Consider four such norms and the issues they entail:[5]

1 *Utility.* Does a particular act optimize the benefits to those who are affected by it? (That is, do all relevant parties receive "fair" benefits?)

2 *Rights.* Does it respect the rights of all individuals involved?

3 *Justice.* Is it consistent with what's fair?

4 *Caring.* Is it consistent with people's responsibilities to each other?

Figure 2.1 incorporates the consideration of these ethical norms into a model of ethical judgment making.

Now let's return to our case of the inflated expense account. While the utility norm acknowledges that the manager benefits from a padded account, others, such as coworkers and owners, don't. Most experts would also agree that the act doesn't respect the rights of others (such as investors, who have to foot the bill). Moreover, it's clearly unfair and compromises the manager's responsibilities to others. This particular act, then, appears to be clearly unethical.

Figure 2.1, however, also provides mechanisms for dealing with unique circumstances—those that apply only in limited situations. Suppose, for example, that our manager loses the receipt for the legitimate dinner but retains the receipt for the social dinner. Some people will now argue that it's okay to submit the illegitimate receipt because the manager is only doing so to get proper reimbursement. Others, however, will reply that submitting the alternative receipt is wrong under any circumstances. We won't pretend to arbitrate the case, and we will simply make the following point: Changes in most situations can make ethical issues either more or less clear-cut.

Company Practices and Business Ethics

As unethical and even illegal activities by both managers and employees plague more companies, many firms have taken additional steps to encourage ethical behavior in the workplace. Many set up codes of conduct and develop clear ethical positions on how the firm and its employees will conduct business. An increasingly controversial area regarding business ethics and company practices involves the privacy of e-mail and other communications that take place inside an organization. For instance, some companies monitor the web searches conducted by their employees; the appearance of certain key words may trigger a closer review of how an employee is using the company's computer network. While some companies argue they do this for business reasons, some employees claim that it violates their privacy.[5]

Perhaps the single most effective step that a company can take is to demonstrate top management support of ethical standards. This policy contributes to a corporate culture that values ethical standards and announces that the firm is as concerned with good citizenship as with profits. For example, when United Technologies (UT), a Connecticut-based industrial conglomerate, published its 21-page code of ethics, it also named a vice president for business practices to see that UT conducted business ethically and responsibly. With a detailed code of ethics and a senior official to enforce it, the firm sends a signal that it expects ethical conduct from its employees.

Two of the most common approaches to formalizing top management commitment to ethical business practices are *adopting written codes* and *instituting ethics programs.*

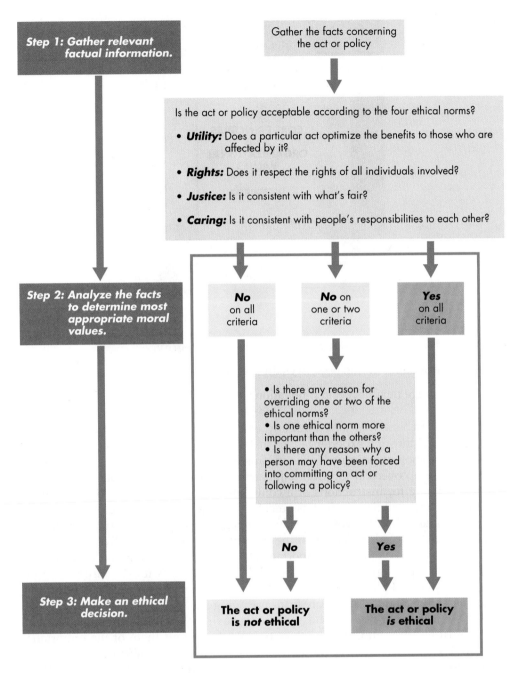

Figure 2.1 Model of Ethical Judgment Making
Source: Cavanagh, Gerald F. American Business Values: With International Perspectives, 4th edition, © 1998. Reprinted by permission of Pearson Education, Inc., Upper Saddle River, NJ.

Step 1: Gather relevant factual information.

Gather the facts concerning the act or policy

Is the act or policy acceptable according to the four ethical norms?

- **Utility:** Does a particular act optimize the benefits to those who are affected by it?
- **Rights:** Does it respect the rights of all individuals involved?
- **Justice:** Is it consistent with what's fair?
- **Caring:** Is it consistent with people's responsibilities to each other?

Step 2: Analyze the facts to determine most appropriate moral values.

No on all criteria

No on one or two criteria

Yes on all criteria

- Is there any reason for overriding one or two of the ethical norms?
- Is one ethical norm more important than the others?
- Is there any reason why a person may have been forced into committing an act or following a policy?

No

Yes

Step 3: Make an ethical decision.

The act or policy is *not* ethical

The act or policy *is* ethical

Adopting Written Codes   Many companies, like UT, have written codes that formally announce their intent to do business in an ethical manner. The number of such companies has risen dramatically in the last three decades, and today almost all major corporations have written codes of ethics. Even Enron had a code of ethics, but managers must follow the code if it's going to work. On one occasion, Enron's board of directors voted to set aside the code in order to complete a deal that would violate it; after the deal was completed, they then voted to reinstate it!

Figure 2.2 illustrates the role that corporate ethics and values should play in corporate policy. You can use it to see how a good ethics statement might be structured. Basically, the figure suggests that although strategies and practices can change frequently and objectives can change occasionally, an organization's core principles and values should remain steadfast. Hewlett-Packard, for example, has had the same written code of ethics, called *The HP Way*, since 1957. Its essential elements are these:

- We have trust and respect for individuals.

- We focus on a high level of achievement and contribution.

Figure 2.2 Core Principles and Organizational Values
Source: Baron, David P. *Business and Its Environment,* 4th edition, © 2003. Reprinted by permission of Pearson Education, Inc., Upper Saddle River, NJ.

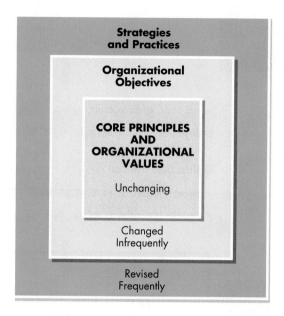

- We conduct our business with uncompromising integrity.
- We achieve our common objectives through teamwork.
- We encourage flexibility and innovation.

Instituting Ethics Programs   Many examples suggest that ethical responses can be learned through experience. For instance, in a classic case several years ago, a corporate saboteur poisoned Tylenol capsules, resulting in the deaths of several consumers. Employees at Johnson & Johnson, the maker of Tylenol, all knew that, without waiting for instructions or a company directive, they should get to retailers' shelves and pull the product as quickly as possible. In retrospect, they reported simply knowing that this was what the company would want them to do. But can business ethics be taught, either in the workplace or in schools? Not surprisingly, business schools have become important players in the debate about ethics education. Most analysts agree that even though business schools must address the issue of ethics in the workplace, companies must take the chief responsibility for educating employees. In fact, more and more firms are doing so.

For example, both ExxonMobil and Boeing have major ethics programs. All managers must go through periodic ethics training to remind them of the importance of ethical decision making and to update them on the most current laws and regulations that might be particularly relevant to their firms. Interestingly, some of the more popular ethics training programs today are taught by former executives who have spent time in prison for their own ethical transgressions.[6] Others, such as Texas Instruments, have ethical hotlines—numbers that an employee can call, either to discuss the ethics of a particular problem or situation or to report unethical behavior or activities by others.

Social Responsibility

Ethics affect individual behavior in the workplace. **Social responsibility** is a related concept, but it refers to the overall way in which a business attempts to balance its commitments to relevant groups and individuals in its social environment. These groups and individuals are often called **organizational stakeholders**—those groups, individuals, and organizations that are directly affected by the practices of an organization and, therefore, have a stake in its performance.[6] Major corporate stakeholders are identified in Figure 2.3.

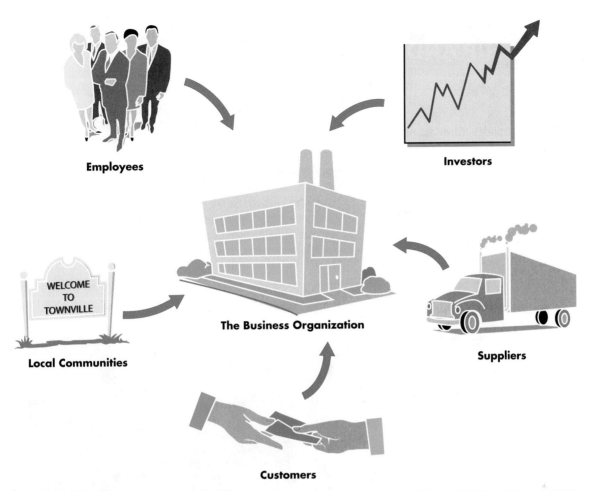

Figure 2.3 Major Corporate Stakeholders

The Stakeholder Model of Responsibility

Most companies that strive to be responsible to their stakeholders concentrate first and foremost on five main groups: *customers, employees, investors, suppliers,* and the *local communities* where they do business. They may then select other stakeholders that are particularly relevant or important to the organization and try to address their needs and expectations as well.

Customers   Businesses that are responsible to their customers strive to treat them fairly and honestly. They also seek to charge fair prices, honor warranties, meet delivery commitments, and stand behind the quality of the products they sell. L.L.Bean, Lands' End, Dell Computer, and Johnson & Johnson are among those companies with excellent reputations in this area. In recent years, many small banks have increased their profits by offering much stronger customer service than the large national banks (such as Wells Fargo and Bank of America). For instance, some offer their customers free coffee and childcare while they're in the bank conducting business. According to Gordon Goetzmann, a leading financial services executive, "Big banks just don't get it" when it comes to understanding what customers want. As a result, for the past few years, small bank profits have been growing at a faster rate than profits at larger chain banks.

Social Responsibility the attempt of a business to balance its commitments to groups and individuals in its environment, including customers, other businesses, employees, investors, and local communities

Organizational Stakeholders those groups, individuals, and organizations that are directly affected by the practices of an organization and who therefore have a stake in its performance

ENTREPRENEURSHIP AND NEW VENTURES

The Electronic Equivalent of Paper Shredding

In virtually every major corporate scandal of the last few years, the best-laid plans of managerial miscreants have come unraveled, at least in part, when supposedly private e-mail surfaced as a key piece of evidence. At Citigroup, for example, analyst Jack Grubman changed stock recommendations in exchange for favors from CEO Sandy Weill and then sent an e-mail to confirm the arrangement. Investigators found that David Duncan, Arthur Andersen's head Enron auditor, had deleted incriminating e-mails shortly after the start of the Justice Department's investigation. After Tim Newington, an analyst for Credit Suisse First Boston, refused to give in to pressure to change a client's credit rating, an e-mail circulated on the problem of Newington's troublesome integrity: "Bigger issue," warned an upper manager, "is what to do about Newington in general. I'm not sure he's salvageable at this point."

Many corporations are nervous about the potential liability that employee e-mail may incur, but some entrepreneurs detect an opportunity in this same concern. A few software-development houses are busily designing programs to meet the needs of cautious corporate customers.

One such software house is Omniva Policy Systems. E-mail senders using Omniva's e-mail software can send encrypted messages and specify an expiration date after which encrypted e-mail messages can no longer be decrypted—the electronic equivalent of paper shredding. In addition, Omniva software can also prevent resending or printing, and users cannot unilaterally delete their own e-mail on their own initiative. In the event of a lawsuit or investigation, administrators can hit a "red button" that prevents all deletions.

"Our goal," says Omniva CEO Kumar Sreekanti, "is to keep the honest people honest.... We help organizations comply with regulations automatically so they don't have to rely on people to do it." Removing responsibility (and temptation) has become an increasingly popular strategy among executives who, like those at Metropolitan Life, the CIA, Eli Lilly, and many other organizations, are looking to e-mail-security systems to help them avoid the kind of exposure encountered by Citigroup, Arthur Andersen, and Credit Suisse.

MyBizLab

John Harrington/Black Star/Newscom

Employees Businesses that are socially responsible in their dealings with employees treat workers fairly, make them a part of the team, and respect their dignity and basic human needs. Organizations, such as The Container Store, Starbucks, Microsoft, FedEx, and American Express, have established strong reputations in this area. In addition, many of the same firms also go to great lengths to find, hire, train, and promote qualified minorities. Each year, *Fortune* magazine publishes lists of the "Best Companies to Work for in America" and the "Best Companies for Minorities." These lists attract more individuals who are eager to work for such highly regarded employers.

Investors To maintain a socially responsible stance toward investors, managers should follow proper accounting procedures, provide appropriate information to shareholders about financial performance, and manage the organization to protect shareholder rights and investments. These managers should be accurate and candid in assessing future growth and profitability, and they should avoid even the appearance of impropriety in such sensitive areas as insider trading, stock-price manipulation, and the withholding of financial data.

In 2002, for example, WorldCom, a giant telecommunications business and owner of MCI, announced that it had overstated previous years' earnings by as much as $6 billion. The SEC also announced that it was investigating the firm's accounting practices, and investors learned that the firm had lent CEO Bernard Ebbers $366 million that he might not be able to repay. On the heels of these problems, WorldCom's stock price dropped by more than 43 percent, and the company eventually had to seek bankruptcy protection as it attempted to dig out of the hole it had created for itself. As for Ebbers, he was subsequently indicted on several charges related to the accounting scandal. In 2005, he was found guilty and sentenced to 25 years in prison.

Suppliers   Relations with suppliers should also be managed with care. For example, it might be easy for a large corporation to take advantage of suppliers by imposing unrealistic delivery schedules and reducing profit margins by constantly pushing for lower prices. Many firms now recognize the importance of mutually beneficial partnership arrangements with suppliers. Thus, they keep them informed about future plans, negotiate delivery schedules and prices that are acceptable to both firms, and so forth. Toyota and Amazon.com are among the firms acknowledged to have excellent relationships with their suppliers.

Local and International Communities   Most businesses try to be socially responsible to their local communities. They may contribute to local programs, such as Little League baseball, get actively involved in charitable programs, such as the United Way, and strive to simply be good corporate citizens by minimizing their negative impact on communities. Target, for example, donates a percentage of sales to the local communities where it does business. The company says it gives over $3 million each week to neighborhoods, programs, and schools across the country.[7]

The stakeholder model can also provide some helpful insights into the conduct of managers in international business. In particular, to the extent that an organization acknowledges its commitments to its stakeholders, it should also recognize that it has multiple sets of stakeholders in each country where it does business. Daimler, for example, has investors not only in Germany but also in the United States, Japan, and other countries where its shares are publicly traded. It also has suppliers, employees, and customers in multiple countries, and its actions affect many different communities in dozens of different countries. Similarly, international businesses must also address their responsibilities in areas, such as wages, working conditions, and environmental protection, across different countries that have varying laws and norms regulating such responsibilities. ExxonMobil, for instance, has helped build hospitals and expand schools in the west African nation of Angola, where it has established a growing oil business. The firm also supports a local anti-malaria program in the area.

Contemporary Social Consciousness

Social consciousness and views toward social responsibility continue to evolve. The business practices of such entrepreneurs as John D. Rockefeller, J. P. Morgan, and Cornelius Vanderbilt raised concerns about abuses of power and led to the nation's first laws regulating basic business practices. In the 1930s, many people blamed the Great Depression on a climate of business greed and lack of restraint. Out of this economic turmoil emerged new laws that dictated an expanded role for business in protecting and enhancing the general welfare of society. Hence, the concept of *accountability* was formalized.

In the 1960s and 1970s, business was again characterized as a negative social force. Some critics even charged that defense contractors had helped to promote the Vietnam War to spur their own profits. Eventually, increased social activism prompted increased government regulation in a variety of areas. Health warnings were placed on cigarettes, for instance, and stricter environmental protection laws were enacted.

During the 1980s and 1990s, the general economic prosperity enjoyed in most sectors of the economy led to another period of laissez-faire attitudes toward business. While the occasional scandal or major business failure occurred, people for the most part seemed to view business as a positive force in society and one that was generally able to police itself through self-control and free-market forces. Many businesses continue to operate in enlightened and socially responsible ways. For example, retailers such as Sears and Target have policies against selling handguns and other weapons.

GameStop refuses to sell Mature-rated games to minors and Anheuser-Busch promotes the concept of responsible drinking in some of its advertising.

Firms in numerous other industries have also integrated socially conscious thinking into their production plans and marketing efforts. The production of environmentally safe products has become a potential boom area as many companies introduce products designed to be environmentally friendly. Electrolux, a Swedish appliance maker, has developed a line of water-efficient washing machines, a solar-powered lawn mower, and ozone-free refrigerators. Ford and General Motors are both aggressively studying and testing ways to develop and market low-pollution vehicles fueled by electricity, hydrogen, and other alternative energy sources.

Unfortunately, the spate of corporate scandals and incredible revelations in the last few years may revive negative attitudes and skepticism toward business. As just a single illustration, widespread moral outrage erupted when some of the perquisites provided to former Tyco International CEO Dennis Kozlowski were made public. These perks included such extravagances as a $50 million mansion in Florida and an $18 million apartment in New York, along with $11 million for antiques and furnishings (including a $6,000 shower curtain). The firm even paid for a $2.1 million birthday party in Italy for Kozlowski's wife. It's not as though Kozlowski was a pauper—he earned almost $300 million between 1998 and 2001 in salary, bonuses, and stock proceeds. In late 2005, Kozlowski was sentenced to 8-to-25 years in prison.

3 Show how the concept of social responsibility applies both to environmental issues and to a firm's relationships with customers, employees, and investors.

Areas of Social Responsibility

When defining its sense of social responsibility, a firm typically confronts four areas of concern: responsibilities toward the *environment*, its *customers*, its *employees*, and its *investors*.

Responsibility toward the Environment

The topic of global warming has become a major issue for business and government alike. However, while most experts agree that the earth is, in fact, warming, the causes, magnitude, and possible solutions are all subject to widespread debate. At present it appears that climate change is occurring at a relatively mild pace and we are experiencing few day-to-day changes in the weather. We are, however, increasing the likelihood of having troublesome weather around the globe—droughts, hurricanes, winter sieges, and so forth.[8] The charges leveled against greenhouse emissions are disputed, but as one researcher puts it, "The only way to prove them for sure is to hang around 10, 20, or 30 more years, when the evidence would be overwhelming. But in the meantime, we're conducting a global experiment. And we're all in the test tube." The movie *The Day After Tomorrow* portrayed one possible scenario of rapid climate changes wrought by environmental damage and 2011's *Contagion* illustrated the possible effects of a global pandemic.

Controlling *pollution*—the injection of harmful substances into the environment—is a significant challenge for contemporary business. Although noise pollution is now attracting increased concern, air, water, and land pollution remain the greatest problems in need of solutions from governments and businesses alike. In the following sections, we focus on the nature of the problems in these areas and on some of the current efforts to address them.

Air Pollution   Air pollution results when several factors combine to lower air quality. Carbon monoxide emitted by cars contributes to air pollution, as do smoke and other chemicals produced by manufacturing plants. Air quality is usually worst in certain geographic locations, such as the Denver area and the Los Angeles basin, where pollutants tend to get trapped in the atmosphere. For this very reason, the air around Mexico City is generally considered to be the most polluted in the entire world.

Legislation has gone a long way toward controlling air pollution. Under new laws, many companies must now install special devices to limit the pollutants they expel into the air, and such efforts are costly. Air pollution is compounded by such problems as acid rain, which occurs when sulfur is pumped into the atmosphere, mixes with natural moisture, and falls to the ground as rain. Much of the damage to forests and streams in the eastern United States and Canada has been attributed to acid rain originating in sulfur from manufacturing and power plants in the midwestern United States. The North American Free Trade Agreement (NAFTA) also includes provisions that call for increased controls on air pollution, especially targeting areas that affect more than one member nation.

Water Pollution   Water becomes polluted primarily from chemical and waste dumping. For years, businesses and cities dumped waste into rivers, streams, and lakes with little regard for the consequences. Cleveland's Cuyahoga River was once so polluted that it literally burst into flames one hot summer day. After an oil spill, a Houston ship channel burned for days.

Thanks to new legislation and increased awareness, water quality in many areas of the United States is improving. The Cuyahoga River now boasts fish and is even used for recreation. Laws in New York and Florida forbidding dumping of phosphates (an ingredient found in many detergents) have helped to make Lake Erie and other major waters safe again for fishing and swimming. Both the Passaic River in New Jersey and the Hudson River in New York are much cleaner now than they were just a few years ago.

Land Pollution   Two key issues characterize land pollution. The first is how to restore the quality of land that has already been damaged. Land and water damaged by toxic waste, for example, must be cleaned up for the simple reason that people still need to use them. The second problem is the prevention of future contamination. New forms of solid-waste disposal constitute one response to these problems. Combustible wastes can be separated and used as fuels in industrial boilers, and decomposition can be accelerated by exposing waste matter to certain microorganisms.

Toxic Waste Disposal   An especially controversial problem in land pollution is toxic waste disposal. Toxic wastes are dangerous chemical or radioactive by-products of manufacturing processes. U.S. manufacturers produce between 40 and 60 million tons of such material each year. As a rule, toxic waste must be stored; it cannot be destroyed or processed into harmless material. Few people, however, want toxic waste storage sites in their backyards. A few years ago, American Airlines pled guilty—and became the first major airline to gain a criminal record—to a felony charge that it had mishandled some hazardous materials packed as cargo in passenger airplanes. While fully acknowledging the firm's guilt, Anne McNamara, American's general counsel, argued that "this is an incredibly complicated area with many layers of regulation. It's very easy to inadvertently step over the line."

Recycling   Recycling is another controversial area in land pollution. Recycling—the reconversion of waste materials into useful products—has become an issue not only for municipal and state governments but also for many companies engaged in high-waste activities. Certain products, such as aluminum cans and glass, can be very efficiently recycled. Others, such as plastics, are more troublesome. For example, brightly colored plastics, such as some detergent and juice bottles, must be recycled separately from clear plastics, such as milk jugs. Most plastic bottle caps, meanwhile, contain a vinyl lining that can spoil a normal recycling batch. Nevertheless, many local communities actively support various recycling programs, including curbside pickup of aluminum, plastics, glass, and pulp paper. Unfortunately, consumer awareness and interest in this area—and the policy priorities of businesses—are more acute at some times than at others.

Responsibility toward Customers

A company that does not act responsibly toward its customers will ultimately lose their trust and their business. To encourage responsibility, the FTC regulates advertising and pricing practices, and the FDA enforces labeling guidelines for food products. These government regulating bodies can impose penalties against violators, who may also face civil litigation. For example, in 2006, the FTC fined the social networking site Xanga $1 million for allowing children under the age of 13 to create accounts in clear violation of the Children's Online Privacy Protection Act.[9] Table 2.1 summarizes the central elements of so-called "green marketing"—the marketing of environmentally friendly goods.

Consumer Rights   Current interest in business responsibility toward customers can be traced to the rise of **consumerism**—social activism dedicated to protecting the rights of consumers in their dealings with businesses. The first formal declaration of consumer rights protection came in the early 1960s, when President John F. Kennedy identified four basic consumer rights. Since then, general agreement on two additional rights has emerged; these rights are described in Figure 2.4. The Consumer Bill of Rights is backed by numerous federal and state laws.

Merck provides an instructive example of what can happen to a firm that violates one or more of these consumer rights. For several years the firm aggressively marketed the painkiller Vioxx, which it was forced to recall in 2004 after clinical trials linked it to an increased risk of heart attacks and strokes. After the recall was announced, it was revealed that Merck had known about these risks as early as 2000 and downplayed them so that they could continue selling it. In 2007, Merck agreed to pay $4.85 billion to individuals or families of those who were injured or died as a result of taking the drug.[13]

Unfair Pricing   Interfering with competition can take the form of illegal pricing practices. **Collusion** occurs when two or more firms collaborate on such wrongful acts as price fixing. In 2007, the European airlines Virgin and Lufthansa admitted to colluding with rivals to raise the prices of fuel surcharges on passenger flights as much as 12 times the regular price between August 2004 and January 2006. British Airways and Korean Air Lines were heavily fined, but in exchange for turning them in, Virgin and Lufthansa were not penalized.[14]

Firms can also come under attack for *price gouging*—responding to increased demand with overly steep (and often unwarranted) price increases. For example, during threats of severe weather, people often stock up on bottled water and batteries. Unfortunately, some retailers take advantage of this pattern by marking up

---

TABLE 2.1   The Elements of Green Marketing

- **Production Processes** Businesses, like Ford Motors and General Electric, modify their production processes to limit the consumption of valuable resources like fossil fuels by increasing energy efficiency and reduce their output of waste and pollution by cutting greenhouse gas emissions.
- **Product Modification** Products can be modified to use more environmentally friendly materials, a practice S.C. Johnson encourages with its Greenlist of raw materials classified according to their impact on health and the environment. Committed to only using the safest materials on this list, S.C. Johnson eliminated 1.8 million pounds of volatile organic compounds from its glass cleaner Windex.[10]
- **Carbon Offsets** Many companies are committed to offsetting the CO2 produced by their products and manufacturing processes. In 2007, Volkswagen began a program of planting trees (which consume CO2 during photosynthesis) in the so-called VW Forest in the lower Mississippi alluvial valley to offset the CO2 emissions of every car they sell.[11]
- **Packaging Reduction** Reducing and reusing materials used in packaging products is another important strategy of green marketing, which Starbucks has pioneered. In 2004 the U.S. Food and Drug Administration gave the coffee retailer the first-ever approval to use recycled materials in its food and beverage packaging. Starbucks estimates that using cups composed of 10 percent recycled fibers reduces its packaging waste by more than 5 million pounds per year.[12]
- **Sustainability** Using renewable resources and managing limited resources responsibly and efficiently are important goals for any business pursuing a green policy. For example, Whole Foods Market is committed to buying food from farmers who use sustainable agriculture practices that protect the environment and agricultural resources, like land and water.

Figure 2.4 **Consumer Bill of Rights**

Consumer Bill of Rights

1   Consumers have a right to safe products.

2   Consumers have a right to be informed about all relevant aspects of a product.

3   Consumers have a right to be heard.

4   Consumers have a right to choose what they buy.

5   Consumers have a right to be educated about purchases.

6   Consumers have a right to courteous service.

prices. Reports were widespread of gasoline retailers doubling or even tripling prices immediately after the events of September 11, 2001, and following the U.S. invasion of Iraq in 2003. Similar problems arose after hurricanes Katrina and Rita damaged oil refineries along the Gulf Coast in late 2005.

Ethics in Advertising   In recent years, increased attention has been given to ethics in advertising and product information. Controversy arose when *Newsweek* magazine reported that Sony had literally created a movie critic who happened to be particularly fond of movies released by Sony's Columbia Pictures. When advertising its newest theatrical releases, the studio had been routinely using glowing quotes from a fictitious critic. After the story broke, Sony hastily stopped the practice and apologized.

Another issue concerns advertising that some consumers consider morally objectionable—for products such as underwear, condoms, alcohol, tobacco products, and firearms. Laws regulate some of this advertising (for instance, tobacco cannot be promoted in television commercials but can be featured in print ads in magazines), and many advertisers use common sense and discretion in their promotions. But some companies, such as Calvin Klein and Victoria's Secret, have come under fire for being overly explicit in their advertising.

This magazine ad for cigarettes is legal in India but not in the United States.

Consumerism form of social activism dedicated to protecting the rights of consumers in their dealings with businesses

Collusion illegal agreement between two or more companies to commit a wrongful act

Responsibility toward Employees

In Chapter 10, we show how a number of human resource management activities are essential to a smoothly functioning business. These activities—recruiting, hiring, training, promoting, and compensating—are also the basis for social responsibility toward employees.

Legal and Social Commitments

By law, businesses cannot practice a wide variety of forms of discrimination against people in any facet of the employment relationship. For example, a company cannot refuse to hire someone because of ethnicity or pay someone a lower salary than someone else on the basis of gender. A company that provides its employees with equal opportunities without regard to race, sex, or other irrelevant factors is meeting both its legal and its social responsibilities. Firms that ignore these responsibilities risk losing good employees and leave themselves open to lawsuits.

Most would also agree that an organization should strive to ensure that the workplace is physically and socially safe. Companies with a heightened awareness of social responsibility also recognize an obligation to provide opportunities to balance work and life pressures and preferences, help employees maintain job skills, and, when terminations or layoffs are necessary, treat them with respect and compassion.

Ethical Commitments: The Special Case of Whistle-Blowers Respecting employees as people also means respecting their behavior as ethical individuals. Ideally, an employee who discovers that a business has been engaging in illegal, unethical, or socially irresponsible practices should be able to report the problem to higher-level management and feel confident that managers will stop the questionable practices. However, if no one in the organization will take action, the employee might elect to drop the matter, or he or she may inform a regulatory agency or the media and become what is known as a **whistle-blower**—an employee who discovers and tries to put an end to a company's unethical, illegal, or socially irresponsible actions by publicizing them.[15]

Unfortunately, whistle-blowers may be demoted, fired, or, if they remain in their jobs, treated with mistrust, resentment, or hostility by coworkers. One recent study suggests that about half of all whistle-blowers eventually get fired, and about half of those who get fired subsequently lose their homes and/or families.[16] The law offers some recourse to employees who take action. The current whistle-blower law stems from the False Claims Act of 1863, which was designed to prevent contractors from selling defective supplies to the Union Army during the Civil War. With 1986 revisions to the law, the government can recover triple damages from fraudulent contractors. If the Justice Department does not intervene, a whistle-blower can proceed with a civil suit. In that case, the whistle-blower receives 25 to 30 percent of any money recovered.[17] Unfortunately, however, the prospect of large cash awards has generated a spate of false or questionable accusations.[18] In the wake of the Bernard Madoff investment scams, news broke that a Boston fraud investigator had for years been trying to convince the Securities and Exchange Commission (SEC) that Madoff was engaging in illegal and unethical practices. His warnings, though, had been ignored. This embarrassing revelation led to the SEC's recent announcement that it was reviewing all of its procedures regarding whistle-blowing and a pledge from the SEC chairman that new procedures would be put into place to safeguard against future problems.

Responsibility toward Investors

Managers can abuse their responsibilities to investors in several ways. As a rule, irresponsible behavior toward shareholders means abuse of a firm's financial resources so that shareholder-owners do not receive their due earnings or dividends. Companies can also act irresponsibly toward shareholder-owners by misrepresenting company resources.

Improper Financial Management   Blatant financial mismanagement—such as paying excessive salaries to senior managers, sending them on extravagant "retreats" to exotic resorts, and providing frivolous perks—may be unethical but not necessarily illegal. In such situations, creditors and stockholders have few options for recourse. Forcing a management changeover is a difficult process that can drive down stock prices—a penalty that shareholders are usually unwilling to impose on themselves.

Insider Trading   **Insider trading** is using confidential information to gain from the purchase or sale of stocks. Suppose, for example, that a small firm's stock is currently trading at $50 a share. If a larger firm is going to buy the smaller one, it might have to pay as much as $75 a share for a controlling interest. Individuals aware of the impending acquisition before it is publicly announced, such as managers of the two firms or the financial institution making the arrangements, could gain by buying the stock at $50 in anticipation of selling it for $75 after the proposed acquisition is announced.

Informed executives can also avoid financial loss by selling stock that's about to drop in value. Legally, stock can only be sold on the basis of public information available to all investors. Potential violations of this regulation were at the heart of the recent Martha Stewart scandal. Sam Waksal, president of ImClone, learned that the company's stock was going to drop in value and hastily tried to sell his own stock. He also allegedly tipped off close friend Martha Stewart, who subsequently sold her stock as well. Stewart, who argued that she never received Waksal's call and sold her stock only because she wanted to use the funds elsewhere, eventually pled guilty to other charges (lying to investigators) and served time in prison. Waksal, meanwhile, received a much stiffer sentence because his own attempts to dump his stock were well documented.

Misrepresentation of Finances   In maintaining and reporting its financial status, every corporation must conform to generally accepted accounting principles (GAAP; see Chapter 14). Unethical managers might project profits in excess of what they actually expect to earn, hide losses and/or expenses in order to boost paper profits, or slant financial reports to make the firm seem stronger than is really the case. In 2002, the U.S. Congress passed the *Sarbanes-Oxley Act*, which requires an organization's chief financial officer to personally guarantee the accuracy of all financial reporting (see Chapter 14).

Implementing Social Responsibility Programs

4   Identify four general approaches to social responsibility and describe the four steps that a firm must take to implement a social responsibility program.

Opinions differ dramatically concerning social responsibility as a business goal. While some oppose any business activity that threatens profits, others argue that social responsibility must take precedence. Some skeptics fear that businesses will gain too much control over the ways social projects are addressed by society as a whole, or that they lack the expertise needed to address social issues. Still, many believe that corporations should help improve the lives of citizens because they are citizens themselves, often control vast resources, and may contribute to the very problems that social programs address.

Whistle-blower employee who detects and tries to put an end to a company's unethical, illegal, or socially irresponsible actions by publicizing them

Insider Trading illegal practice of using special knowledge about a firm for profit or gain

Figure 2.5 Spectrum of Approaches to Corporate Social Responsibility

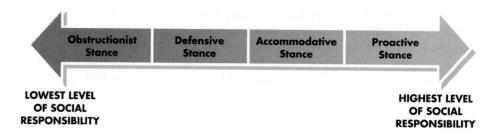

LOWEST LEVEL OF SOCIAL RESPONSIBILITY

HIGHEST LEVEL OF SOCIAL RESPONSIBILITY

Approaches to Social Responsibility

Given these differences of opinion, it is little wonder that corporations have adopted a variety of approaches to social responsibility. As Figure 2.5 illustrates, the four stances that an organization can take concerning its obligations to society fall along a continuum ranging from the lowest to the highest degree of socially responsible practices.

Obstructionist Stance   The few organizations that take an **obstructionist stance** to social responsibility usually do as little as possible to solve social or environmental problems, have little regard for ethical conduct, and will go to great lengths to deny or cover up wrongdoing. For example, IBP, a leading meat-processing firm, has a long record of breaking environmental protection, labor, and food processing laws and then trying to cover up its offenses. Similarly, in 2009 a Georgia peanut processing plant owned by Peanut Corporation of America shipped products contaminated with salmonella. The firm's top manager allegedly knew that the products had failed safety tests but shipped them anyway in order to avoid losing money.

Defensive Stance   Organizations that take a **defensive stance** will do everything that is legally required, including admitting to mistakes and taking corrective actions, but nothing more. Defensive stance managers insist that their job is to generate profits and might, for example, install pollution-control equipment dictated by law but not higher-quality equipment to further limit pollution.

Tobacco companies generally take this position in their marketing efforts. In the United States, they are legally required to include product warnings and to limit advertising to prescribed media. Domestically, they follow these rules to the letter of the law, but in many Asian and African countries, which don't have these rules, cigarettes are heavily promoted, contain higher levels of tar and nicotine, and carry few or no health warning labels.

Accommodative Stance   A firm that adopts an **accommodative stance** meets and, in certain cases exceeds, its legal and ethical requirements. Such firms will agree to participate in social programs if solicitors convince them that given programs are worthy of their support. Both Shell and IBM, for example, will match contributions made by their employees to selected charitable causes.

Proactive Stance   Firms with the highest degree of social responsibility exhibit the **proactive stance;** they take to heart the arguments in favor of social responsibility, view themselves as citizens in a society, indicate sincere commitment to improve the general social welfare, and surpass the accommodative stance by proactively seeking opportunities to contribute. The most common—and direct—way to implement this stance is to set up a foundation for providing direct financial support for various social programs. Table 2.2 lists the top 50 corporate foundations using the most recent data available.

An excellent example of a proactive stance is the McDonald's Corporation's Ronald McDonald House program. These houses, located close to major medical

TABLE 2.2 Top 25 Corporate Foundations

Rank	Name/(state)	Total Giving	As of Fiscal Year End Date
1	sanofi-aventis Patient Assistance Foundation (NJ)	$321,376,881	12/31/2009
2	The Wal-Mart Foundation, Inc. (AR)	216,557,131	01/31/2009
3	The Bank of America Charitable Foundation, Inc. (NC)	186,149,230	12/31/2009
4	Novartis Patient Assistance Foundation, Inc. (NJ)	177,195,258	12/31/2009
5	GE Foundation (CT)	103,573,293	12/31/2009
6	The Wachovia Wells Fargo Foundation, Inc. (NC)	99,435,085	12/31/2009
7	The JPMorgan Chase Foundation (NY)	77,145,399	12/31/2008
8	ExxonMobil Foundation (TX)	73,544,150	12/31/2009
9	Wells Fargo Foundation (CA)	68,367,615	12/31/2009
10	Citi Foundation (NY)	66,507,524	12/31/2009
11	Verizon Foundation (NJ)	56,289,332	12/31/2009
12	Johnson & Johnson Family of Companies Contribution Fund (NJ)	49,556,298	12/31/2009
13	The Merck Company Foundation (NJ)	42,238,719	12/31/2009
14	The Coca-Cola Foundation, Inc. (GA)	40,968,382	12/31/2009
15	Intel Foundation (OR)	40,481,300	12/31/2009
16	MetLife Foundation (NY)	39,465,498	12/31/2009
17	The UPS Foundation (GA)	38,913,155	12/31/2009
18	AT&T Foundation (TX)	38,176,693	12/31/2009
19	BP Foundation, Inc. (TX)	37,210,977	12/31/2009
20	California Physicians' Service Foundation (CA)	34,725,931	12/31/2009
21	Abbott Fund (IL)	34,202,053	12/31/2009
22	Caterpillar Foundation (IL)	31,239,085	12/31/2009
23	Eli Lilly and Company Foundation (IN)	30,345,734	12/31/2009
24	The Boeing Company Charitable Trust (TX)	30,053,296	12/31/2009
25	The PNC Foundation (PA)	29,694,921	12/31/2009

Source: 50 Largest Corporate Foundations by Total Giving, 2009 © 2011 The Foundation Center. Used by permission.

centers, can be used for minimal cost by families while their sick children are receiving medical treatment nearby. However, these categories are not sharply distinct: Organizations do not always fit neatly into one category or another. The Ronald McDonald House program has been widely applauded, but McDonald's has also been accused of misleading consumers about the nutritional value of its food products.

Obstructionist Stance approach to social responsibility that involves doing as little as possible and may involve attempts to deny or cover up violations

Defensive Stance approach to social responsibility by which a company meets only minimum legal requirements in its commitments to groups and individuals in its social environment

Accommodative Stance approach to social responsibility by which a company, if specifically asked to do so, exceeds legal minimums in its commitments to groups and individuals in its social environment

Proactive Stance approach to social responsibility by which a company actively seeks opportunities to contribute to the well-being of groups and individuals in its social environment

Managing Social Responsibility Programs

A full commitment to social responsibility requires a carefully organized and managed program and managers who take steps to foster a companywide sense of social responsibility:[19]

1 *Social responsibility must start at the top and be considered a factor in strategic planning.* No program can succeed without the support of top management, who must embrace a strong stand on social responsibility and develop a policy statement outlining that commitment.

2 *A committee of top managers must develop a plan detailing the level of management support.* Companies may set aside percentages of profits for social programs or set specific priorities, such as supporting the arts.

3 *One executive must be put in charge of the firm's agenda.* Whether a separate job or part of an existing one, the selected individual must monitor the program and ensure implementation consistent with the firm's policy statement and strategic plan.

4 *The organization must conduct occasional social audits—systematic analyses of its success in using funds earmarked for its social responsibility goals.* Consider the case of a company whose strategic plan calls for spending $200,000 to train 300 unemployed people and to place 275 of them in jobs. If, at the end of a year, the firm has spent $198,000, trained 305 people, and filled 270 jobs, a **social audit** will confirm the program's success. But if the program has cost $350,000, trained only 190 people, and placed only 40 of them, the audit will reveal the program's failure. Such failure should prompt a rethinking of the program's implementation and its priorities.

So far, we have discussed social responsibility as if there were some agreement on how organizations should behave. Opinions differ dramatically concerning the role of social responsibility as a business goal. Some people oppose any business activity that threatens profits. Others argue that social responsibility must take precedence over profits.

Even businesspeople who agree on the importance of social responsibility will cite different reasons for their views. Some skeptics of business-sponsored social projects fear that if businesses become too active, they will gain too much control over the ways in which those projects are addressed by society as a whole. These critics point to the influence that many businesses have been able to exert on the government agencies that are supposed to regulate their industries. Other critics claim that business organizations lack the expertise needed to address social issues. They argue, for instance, that technical experts, not businesses, should decide how to clean up polluted rivers.

Proponents of socially responsible business believe that corporations are citizens and should, therefore, help to improve the lives of fellow citizens. Still others point to the vast resources controlled by businesses and note that they help to create many of the problems social programs are designed to alleviate.

5 Explain how issues of social responsibility and ethics affect small business.

Social Responsibility and the Small Business

As the owner of a garden supply store, how would you respond to a building inspector's suggestion that a cash payment will speed your application for a building permit? As the manager of a liquor store, would you call the police, refuse to sell, or sell to a customer whose identification card looks forged? As the owner of a small laboratory, would you call the state board of health to make sure that it has licensed the company with whom you want to contract to dispose of medical waste? Who will really be harmed if a small firm pads its income statement to help it get a much-needed bank loan?

Many of the examples in this chapter illustrate big-business responses to ethical and social responsibility issues. Such examples, however, show quite clearly that small businesses must answer many of the same questions. Differences are primarily differences of scale.

At the same time, these are largely questions of *individual* ethics. What about questions of social responsibility? Can a small business, for example, afford a social agenda? Should it sponsor Little League baseball teams, make donations to the United Way, and buy lightbulbs from the Lion's Club? Do joining the chamber of commerce and supporting the Better Business Bureau cost too much? Clearly, ethics and social responsibility are decisions faced by all managers in all organizations, regardless of rank or size. One key to business success is to decide in advance how to respond to the issues that underlie all questions of ethical and social responsibility.

Social Audit systematic analysis of a firm's success in using funds earmarked for meeting its social responsibility goals

David Robertson/Alamy

Continued from page 32

Green ... But Not Too Green

The *Deepwater Horizon* disaster clearly dealt a blow to BP's efforts to portray itself as the leading environmentally friendly oil company. Not only were 11 workers killed in the explosion, but millions of gallons of crude oil gushed into the Gulf of Mexico for months as the firm seemed hapless in its efforts to stop the leak. Businesses across the entire Gulf Coast were affected, and thousands of people lost their jobs—permanently or temporarily. BP also faced a major crisis as it attempted to stop the leak, minimize the environmental damage, and assure people it would provide adequate compensation once everything was settled.

But BP is nothing if not bold. For example, the oil giant continues to risk compromising its green image by engaging in what Greenpeace calls the "greatest climate crime" in history—extracting oil from the tar sands of Alberta, Canada. The project is energy- and water-intensive, produces excessive amounts of greenhouse gases, destroys acres of forest, and harms indigenous communities, but it comes at a time when oil prices are high and western consumers are dependent on Middle Eastern oil. It remains to be seen whether BP's seemingly socially responsible ends can justify their environmentally damaging means.

QUESTIONS FOR DISCUSSION

1 What are the major ethical issues in this case?
2 Aside from personal greed, what factors might lead an oil company to compile a long list of environmental damages?
3 Which approach to social responsibility does BP appear to be taking?
4 Distinguish between ethical issues and social responsibility issues as they apply to this problem.

SUMMARY OF LEARNING OBJECTIVES   MyBizLab

1. **Explain how individuals develop their personal codes of ethics and why ethics are important in the workplace. (pp. 32–38)**
   Ethics are beliefs about what's right and wrong or good and bad. *Ethical behavior* conforms to individual beliefs and social norms about what's right and good. *Unethical behavior* is behavior that individual beliefs and social norms define as wrong and bad. *Managerial ethics* are standards of behavior that guide managers. There are three broad categories of ways in which managerial ethics can affect people's work: (1) *behavior toward employees*, (2) *behavior toward the organization*, and (3) *behavior toward other economic agents*.

   One model for applying ethical judgments to business situations recommends the following three steps: (1) Gather relevant factual information, (2) analyze the facts to determine the most appropriate moral values, and (3) make an ethical judgment based on the rightness or wrongness of the proposed activity or policy. Perhaps the single most effective step that a company can take is to *demonstrate top management support*. In addition to promoting attitudes of honesty and openness, firms can also take specific steps to formalize their commitment: (1) *adopting written codes* and (2) *instituting ethics programs*.

2. **Distinguish social responsibility from ethics, identify organizational stakeholders, and characterize social consciousness today. (pp. 38–42)**
   Ethics affect individuals. *Social responsibility* refers to the way a firm attempts to balance its commitments to organizational stakeholders—those groups, individuals, and organizations that are directly affected by the practices of an organization and, therefore, have a stake in its performance. Many companies concentrate on five main groups: (1) *customers*, (2) *employees*, (3) *investors*, (4) *suppliers*, and (5) *local communities*.

   Attitudes toward social responsibility have changed. The late nineteenth century, though characterized by the entrepreneurial spirit and the laissez-faire philosophy, also featured labor strife and predatory business practices. Concern about unbridled business activity was soon translated into laws regulating business practices. Out of the economic turmoil of the 1930s, when greed was blamed for business failures and the loss of jobs, came new laws protecting and enhancing social well-being. During the 1960s and 1970s, activism prompted increased government regulation in many areas of business. Today's attitudes stress a greater social role for business. This view, combined with the economic prosperity of the 1980s and 1990s, marked a return to the laissez-faire philosophy, but the recent epidemic of corporate scandals threatens to revive the 1930s call for more regulation and oversight.

3. **Show how the concept of social responsibility applies both to environmental issues and to a firm's relationships with customers, employees, and investors. (pp. 42–47)**
   A firm confronts four areas of concern: (1) *responsibility toward the environment*, (2) *responsibility toward customers*, (3) *responsibility toward employees*, and (4) *responsibility toward investors*. Organizations and managers may be guilty of *financial mismanagement*—offenses that are unethical but not necessarily illegal. Certain unethical practices are illegal. Using confidential information to gain from a stock transaction is *insider trading*. Certain behavior regarding financial representation is also unlawful.

4. **Identify four general approaches to social responsibility and describe the four steps that a firm must take to implement a social responsibility program. (pp. 47–50)**
   A business can take one of four stances concerning its social obligations to society: (1) *obstructionist stance*, (2) *defensive stance*, (3) *accommodative stance*, or (4) *proactive stance*. One model suggests a four-step approach to fostering a companywide sense of social responsibility: (1) Social responsibility must start at the top and be included in strategic planning. (2) Top managers must develop a plan detailing the level of management support. (3) One executive must be put in charge of the agenda. (4) The organization must conduct occasional social audits—analyses of its success in using funds earmarked for social responsibility goals.

5. **Explain how issues of social responsibility and ethics affect small business. (pp. 50–51)**
   For small businesspeople, ethical issues are questions of individual ethics. But in questions of social responsibility, they must ask themselves if they can afford a social agenda, such as sponsoring Little League baseball teams or making donations to the United Way. They should also realize that managers in *all* organizations face issues of ethics and social responsibility.

KEY TERMS   MyBizLab

accommodative stance (p. 48)
business ethics (p. 32)
collusion (p. 44)
consumerism (p. 44)
defensive stance (p. 48)
ethical behavior (p. 32)

ethics (p. 32)
insider trading (p. 47)
managerial ethics (p. 33)
obstructionist stance (p. 48)
organizational
   stakeholders (p. 38)

proactive stance (p. 48)
social audit (p. 50)
social responsibility (p. 38)
unethical behavior (p. 32)
whistle-blower (p. 46)

QUESTIONS AND EXERCISES

QUESTIONS FOR REVIEW

1. What basic factors should be considered in any ethical decision?
2. Who are an organization's stakeholders? Who are the major stakeholders with which most businesses must be concerned?
3. What are the major areas of social responsibility with which businesses should be concerned?
4. What are the four basic approaches to social responsibility?
5. In what ways do you think your personal code of ethics might clash with the operations of some companies? How might you try to resolve these differences?

QUESTIONS FOR ANALYSIS

6. What kind of wrongdoing would most likely prompt you to be a whistle-blower? What kind of wrongdoing would be least likely? Why?

7. In your opinion, which area of social responsibility is most important? Why? Are there areas other than those noted in the chapter that you consider important?
8. Identify some specific ethical or social responsibility issues that might be faced by small-business managers and employees in each of the following areas: environment, customers, employees, and investors.

APPLICATION EXERCISES

9. Develop a list of the major stakeholders of your college or university. How do you think the school prioritizes these stakeholders? Do you agree or disagree with this prioritization?
10. Using newspapers, magazines, and other business references, identify and describe at least three companies that take a defensive stance to social responsibility, three that take an accommodative stance, and three that take a proactive stance.

BUILDING YOUR BUSINESS SKILLS

To Lie or Not to Lie: That Is the Question

Goal
To encourage you to apply general concepts of business ethics to specific situations.

Background Information
It seems workplace lying has become business as usual. According to one survey, one-quarter of working adults in the United States said that they had been asked to do something illegal or unethical on the job. Four in 10 did what they were told. Another survey of more than 2,000 secretaries showed that many employees face ethical dilemmas in their day-to-day work.

Method

Step 1
Working with a small group of other students, discuss ways in which you would respond to the following ethical dilemmas. When there is a difference of opinion among group members, try to determine the specific factors that influence different responses.

- Would you lie about your supervisor's whereabouts to someone on the phone? Would it depend on what the supervisor was doing?
- Would you lie about who was responsible for a business decision that cost your company thousands of dollars to protect your own or your supervisor's job?
- Would you inflate sales and revenue data on official company accounting statements to increase stock value? Would you do so if your boss ordered it?
- Would you say that you witnessed a signature when you did not if you were acting in the role of a notary?

- Would you keep silent if you knew that the official minutes of a corporate meeting had been changed? Would the nature of the change matter?
- Would you destroy or remove information that could hurt your company if it fell into the wrong hands?

Step 2
Research the commitment to business ethics at Johnson & Johnson (www.jnj.com) and Texas Instruments (www.ti.com/corp/docs/ethics/home.htm) by checking out their respective websites. As a group, discuss ways in which these statements are likely to affect the specific behaviors mentioned in Step 1.

Step 3
Working with group members, draft a corporate code of ethics that would discourage the specific behaviors mentioned in Step 1. Limit your code to a single printed page, but make it sufficiently broad to cover different ethical dilemmas.

FOLLOW-UP QUESTIONS

1. What personal, social, and cultural factors do you think contribute to lying in the workplace?
2. Do you agree or disagree with the statement "The term business ethics is an oxymoron." Support your answer with examples from your own work experience or that of someone you know.
3. If you were your company's director of human resources, how would you make your code of ethics a "living document"?
4. If you were faced with any of the ethical dilemmas described in Step 1, how would you handle them? How far would you go to maintain your personal ethical standards?

EXERCISING YOUR ETHICS: INDIVIDUAL EXERCISE

Taking a Stance

The Situation

A perpetual debate revolves around the roles and activities of business owners in contributing to the greater social good. Promoting the so-called proactive stance, some people argue that businesses should be socially responsible by seeking opportunities to benefit the society in which they are permitted to conduct their affairs. Others promoting the defensive stance maintain that because businesses exist to make profits for owners, they have no further obligation to society.

The Dilemma

Assume that you are the manager of a restaurant near a major manufacturing plant. Many of your customers are employees at the plant. Due to inflation, you are about to raise your prices 10 to 15 percent. You have had new menus created and updated your posters. You have been planning to implement the higher prices in about three weeks.

You have just heard that another plant owned by the same company has been shut down for two weeks due to an explosion.

The plant near you will be expected to ____ ing workers to put in longer hours, a ____ forth. You anticipate a substantial jur ____ diately. You are now trying to make a quick ____ pricing. One option is to go ahead and roll out your higher prices now. Combined with the big jump in traffic, your profits would skyrocket. The other option is to follow your original timetable and wait three weeks to increase your prices. You will have then passed up the opportunity to capitalize on the temporary jump in business.

QUESTIONS TO ADDRESS

1 Which course of action is easier to defend? Why?
2 What is your personal opinion about the appropriate stance that a business should take regarding social responsibility?
3 To what extent is the concept of social responsibility relevant to nonbusiness organizations such as universities, government units, health care organizations, and so forth?

EXERCISING YOUR ETHICS: TEAM EXERCISE

Finding the Balance

The Situation

Managers often find it necessary to find the right balance among the interests of different stakeholders. For instance, paying employees the lowest possible wages can enhance profits, but paying a living wage might better serve the interests of workers. As more businesses outsource production to other countries, these trade-offs become even more complicated.

The Dilemma

The Delta Company currently uses three different suppliers in Southeast Asia for most of its outsourced production. Due to increased demand for its products, it needs to double the amount of business it currently subcontracts to one of these suppliers. (For purposes of this exercise, assume that the company must award the new supplier contract to a single firm, and that it must be one of these three. You can also assume that the quality provided is about the same for all three companies.)

Subcontractor A provides a spartan but clean work environment for its workers; even though the local weather conditions are hot and humid much of the year, the plant is not air conditioned. Delta Company safety experts have verified, though, that the conditions are not dangerous, simply a bit uncomfortable at times. The firm pays its workers the same prevailing wage rate that is paid by its local competitors. While it has never had a legal issue with its workforce, it does push its employees to meet production

quotas and it has a very tough policy regarding discipline for tardiness. For instance, an employee who is late gets put on probation; a second infraction within three months results in termination. This supplier provides production to Delta Company at a level such that Delta can attach a 25 percent markup.

Subcontractor B also provides a spartan work environment. It pays its workers about 5 percent above local wage levels and hence is an attractive employer. Because of its higher pay, this firm is actually quite ruthless with some of its policies, however. For instance, any employee who reports to work more than 15 minutes late without a medical excuse is automatically terminated. This supplier's costs are such that Delta Company can achieve a 20 percent markup.

Subcontractor C runs a much nicer factory; the plant is air conditioned, for instance. It also pays its workers about 10 percent above local wage levels. The company also operates an on-site school for the children of its employees, and provides additional training for its workers so they can improve their skills. Due to its higher costs, Delta Company's markup on this firm's products is only around 15 percent.

Team Activity

Assemble a group of four students and assign each group member to one of the following roles:
• Delta Company executive
• Delta Company employee
• Delta Company customer
• Delta Company investor

STEPS

before hearing any of your group's comments on this situation, and from the perspective of your assigned role, which firm do you think should get the additional business? Which firm is your second choice? Write down the reasons for your position.

2 Before hearing any of your group's comments on this situation, and from the perspective of your assigned role, what are the underlying ethical issues in this situation? Write down the issues.

3 Gather your group together and reveal, in turn, each member's comments on their choices. Next, reveal the ethical issues listed by each member.

4 Appoint someone to record main points of agreement and disagreement within the group. How do you explain the results? What accounts for any disagreement?

5 From an ethical standpoint, what does your group conclude is the most appropriate choice for the company in this situation?

6 Develop a group response to the following question: Would your decision have been any different if you were able to break up the new contract across different suppliers? Why?

VIDEO EXERCISE   MyBizLab

Jones Soda

Learning Objectives

The purpose of this video is to help you:
1 Define social responsibility.
2 Describe the stakeholder model of social responsibility.
3 Identify areas of social responsibility.

Synopsis

Jones Soda is a Seattle-based company founded in 1987 by Peter van Stolk. Although the company first began as a beverage distributor, it quickly evolved into a manufacturer of alternatives to highly popular bottled sodas. Their quirky natural products feature customer pictures on the labels and include unique flavors such as bug juice, blue bubble gum, and turkey and gravy. Jones Soda differs from its larger competitors in many ways, including their use of cane sugar as a sweetener. More recently, in response to changes in customer demand, Jones has introduced a line of zero-calorie products, Zilch. Jones products are available today all over the United States and Canada in a variety of retailers, including Starbucks and Panera Bread. Jones is highly committed to the Seattle area and hands out free sodas every Friday from its headquarters, a tradition that they maintained, even through difficult economic times.

DISCUSSION QUESTIONS

1 Who are Jones Soda's stakeholders?
2 What are the six areas of social responsibility? Which of these areas are highlighted in the video?
3 How did Jones Soda get involved in the 2008 presidential election? Do you think that this was appropriate?
4 Jones Soda shares the core values of its loyal customer base. While this costs them money, do you think that this is a wise business decision? Why or why not?
5 Although this video focuses on social responsibility, do you think that Jones Soda's strategy influences the ethics of its employees? If so, how?

Online Exploration

Visit the Jones Soda website (www.jonessoda.com) and do a little exploration. Find out more about their products and marketing strategy. After you've done a little looking around, click on "Jones Soda Co" on the top right side of the page and select "Keeping it Real." What is Jones Soda doing to "keep it real"? How is Jones Soda making an impact on its customers as well as the Seattle area?

END NOTES

[1] *Hoover's Handbook of World Business 2011* (Austin: Hoover's Business Press, 2011), pp. 79–80; "Oil Company BP Pleads Guilty to Environmental Crime," *International Herald Tribune* (November 29, 2007), p. 5; Michael Hawthorne, "BP Gets Break on Dumping in Lake," *Chicago Tribune* (July 15, 2007), p. B7; Terry Macalister "Greenpeace Calls BP's Oil Sands Plan an Environmental Crime," *guardian. co.uk* (December 7, 2007), pp. 15–16; Sharon Epperson, "BP's Fundamental But Obscured Energy Contradiction," cnbc.com (May 21, 2008), at **http://www.cnbc.com/ id/24758394**; Brad Hem, "10 plaintiffs in BP Case Will Seek $950 Million," *Houston Chronicle* (May 23, 2008), pp. C1, C4.

[2] William G. Symonds, Geri Smith, "The Tax Games Tyco Played," *BusinessWeek* (July 1, 2002), 40–41.

[3] "Tyco Votes to Stay Offshore," *BBC News* (March 6, 2003), p. 18.

[4] This section follows the logic of Gerald F. Cavanaugh, *American Business Values: A Global Perspective*, 5th ed. (Upper Saddle River, NJ: Prentice Hall, 2006), Chapter 3.

[5] Manuel G. Velasquez, *Business Ethics: Concepts and Cases*, 6th ed. (Upper Saddle River, NJ: Prentice Hall, 2006), Chapter 2. See also John R. Boatright, *Ethics and the Conduct of Business*, 4th ed. (Upper Saddle River, NJ: Prentice Hall, 2003), 34–35, 57–59.

[6] Jeffrey S. Harrison, R. Edward Freeman, "Stakeholders, Social Responsibility, and Performance: Empirical Evidence and

Theoretical Perspectives," *Academy of Management Journal*, 1999, vol. 42, no. 5, 479–485. See also David P. Baron, *Business and Its Environment*, 5th ed. (Upper Saddle River, NJ: Prentice Hall, 2006), Chapter 18.

[7] http://target.com/target_group/community_giving/index.jhtml, accessed February 20, 2011.

[8] For a recent summary of these questions see "Can Geoengineering Put the Freeze on Global Warming? *USA Today*, February 25, 2011, pp. 1B, 2B.

[9] Bob Sullivan, "FTC Fines Xanga for Violating Kids' Privacy," (September 7, 2006), at http://www.msnbc.msn.com/id/14718350.

[10] http://money.cnn.com/galleries/2007/fortune/0703/gallery.green_giants.fortune/7.html, accessed May 30, 2008; http://www.scjohnson.com/environment/growing_1.asp, accessed May 30, 2008.

[11] http://www.nytimes.com/2008/01/09/business/09offsets.html?_r=1&ex=1357707600&en=05dc8be5247f9737&ei=5088&partner=rssnyt&emc=rss&oref=slogin, accessed May 30, 2008.

[12] http://www.starbucks.com/csrnewsletter/winter06/csrEnvironment.asp, accessed May 30, 2008.

[13] Alex Berenson, "Merck Agrees to Pay $4.85 Billion in Vioxx Claims," *New York Times*, (November 9, 2007), at http://www.nytimes.com/2007/11/09/business/09cnd-merck.html?ref=business; Rita Rubin, "How Did Vioxx Debacle Happen?" *USA Today*, (October 12, 2004), at http://www.usatoday.com/news/health/2004-10-12-vioxx-cover_x.htm.

[14] "British Airways and Korean Air Lines Fined in Fuel Collusion," *New York Times* (August 2, 2007), at http://www.nytimes.com/2007/08/02/business/worldbusiness/02air.html?scp=2&sq=british+airways+price+fixing&st=nyt.

[15] Jerald Greenberg and Robert A. Baron, *Behavior in Organizations: Understanding and Managing the Human Side of Work*, 8th ed. (Upper Saddle River, NJ: Prentice Hall, 2003), 410–413.

[16] Cora Daniels, "It's a Living Hell," *Fortune* (April 15, 2002), 367–368.

[17] Henry R. Cheeseman, *Business Law: Legal, E-Commerce, Ethical, and International Environments*, 5th ed. (Upper Saddle River, NJ: Prentice Hall, 2004), 128–129.

[18] http://www.usdoj.gov/usao/iln/pr/chicago/2008/pr0318_01.pdf, accessed May 30, 2008; Jacob Goldstein, "CVS to Pay $37.5 Million to Settle Pill Switching Case," *Wall Street Journal* (March 18, 2008), at http://blogs.wsj.com/health/2008/03/18/cvs-to-pay-375-million-to-settle-pill-switching-case.

[19] Michael E. Porter and Mark R. Kramer, "Philanthropy's New Agenda: Doing Well by Doing Good," *Sloan Management Review* (Winter 2000), 75–85.

3 Entrepreneurship, New Ventures, and Business Ownership

Harvard Dropout Turned Billionaire

D o you Facebook? An estimated 175 million people in the United States do, and almost half are college students. The immensely popular social-networking website was started by Harvard sophomore Mark Zuckerberg in February 2004 as a way for his classmates to network. The site proved to be so popular that he quickly opened it up to other schools. By November 2004, the site boasted 1 million users. A mere 18 months later, membership had ballooned to 7 million members at 2,100 colleges and 22,000 high schools. When it began accepting nonstudents in October 2006, membership doubled from 12 million to 24 million in just 8 months. Today, Facebook.com is one of the most visited sites on the Internet, running neck-and-neck with Google among U.S. college students. The total number of worldwide Facebook users was approaching 700 million in 2011.

Although Facebook began as a noncommercial enterprise, it wasn't long before Zuckerberg realized that if he had more cash he could convert it into a business. PayPal cofounder Peter Thiel invested $500,000 in 2004, and substantial investments of additional venture capital followed. The new company lost $3.6 million in fiscal 2005, but with projected revenues of $150 million in 2007, Microsoft paid $240 million for a 1.6 percent stake in the company, pushing its valuation to $15 billion. Bear in mind that Facebook is not a publicly

After reading this chapter, you should be able to:

1 Define *small business*, discuss its importance to the U.S. economy, and explain popular areas of small business.

2 Explain entrepreneurship and describe some key characteristics of entrepreneurial personalities and activities.

3 Describe the business plan and the start-up decisions made by small businesses and identify sources of financial aid available to such enterprises.

4 Discuss the trends in small business start-ups and identify the main reasons for success and failure among small businesses.

5 Explain sole proprietorships, partnerships, and cooperatives and discuss the advantages and disadvantages of each.

6 Describe corporations, discuss their advantages and disadvantages, and identify different kinds of corporations; explain the basic issues involved in managing a corporation and discuss special issues related to corporate ownership.

traded company—its stock can't be purchased on the open market. It's all privately held, and that $15 billion figure reflects the prices being paid at the time for the company's preferred stock by Microsoft and other major investors.

But as a business, Facebook has a problem that is not widely known—it's actually finding it hard to make a profit. Approximately 85 percent of the company's total revenue comes from advertising (about $210 million in 2009), with another $35 million to $50 million coming from sales of virtual gifts—those little icons that pop up in certain Facebook programs and that users can exchange for about $1. In 2009, Facebook sold about $3 million worth of virtual gifts every month, but revenues for the year—about $260 million—fell short of the company's $300 million projection. It was time to get serious about profit.

If we look even more closely at these numbers, we notice an interesting phenomenon: User

WHAT'S IN IT FOR ME?

Mark Zuckerberg displayed many of the characteristics key to entrepreneurial success. Facebook also highlights some of the problems inherent in converting a great business idea into profits for owners. This chapter will discuss these and additional issues important for starting and owning a business, including the business plan, reasons for success and failure, and the advantages and disadvantages of different kinds of ownership. First, we'll start by defining a small business and identifying its importance in the U.S. economy.

MyBizLab Where you see MyBizLab in this chapter, go to **www.mybizlab.com** for additional activities on the topic being discussed.

TomBham/Alamy

rates and revenues aren't going in the same direction. Since its inception, Facebook has had a problem with monetization—how to make a profit. It's a problem that Facebook shares with MySpace, which still commands a substantial share of the income from social networking. The solution, of course, is ad revenue—user fees are negligible, and even $3 million a month in virtual-gift sales won't begin to cover server costs. When they first appeared on the Internet scene, social networks seemed like turbocharged revenue generators, but both Facebook and MySpace have found that selling spots on web pages dedicated to personal profiles and group interchanges isn't as easy as it seemed.[1]

Our opening story continues on page 80.

What Is a "Small" Business?

1 Define *small business*, discuss its importance to the U.S. economy, and explain popular areas of small business.

The term *small business* defies easy definition. Locally owned and operated restaurants, dry cleaners, and hair salons are obviously small businesses, and giant corporations, such as Dell, Starbucks, Apple, and Best Buy, are clearly big businesses. Between these two extremes, though, fall thousands of companies that cannot be easily categorized.

The U.S. Department of Commerce considers a business "small" if it has fewer than 500 employees. The U.S. **Small Business Administration (SBA),** a government agency that assists small businesses, regards some companies with as many as 1,500 employees as small, but only if the business has relatively low annual revenues. Because strict numerical terms sometimes lead to contradictory classifications, we will consider a **small business** to be one that is independent (that is, not part of a larger business) and that has relatively little influence in its market. A small neighborhood grocer would be small, assuming it is not part of a chain and that the prices it pays to wholesalers and that it can charge its customers are largely set by market forces. Dell Computer was a small business when founded by Michael Dell in 1984, but today it's number one in the personal computer market and is not small in any sense of the term. Hence, it can negotiate from a position of strength with its suppliers and can set its prices with less consideration for what other computer firms are charging.

The Importance of Small Business in the U.S. Economy

As Figure 3.1 shows, most U.S. businesses employ fewer than 100 people, and most U.S. workers are employed by small business. Moreover, this same pattern exists across most free market economies.

Figure 3.1(a) shows that 85.95 percent of all businesses employ 20 or fewer people. Another 11.65 percent employ between 20 and 99 people, and 2.15 percent employ between 100 and 499. Only about one-tenth of 1 percent employ 1,000 or more people. Figure 3.1(b) also shows that 24.55 percent of all workers are employed by firms with fewer than 20 people, and 29.61 percent are employed by firms with between 20 and 99 people. Another 25.52 percent are employed by firms with between 100 and 499 people. Only 13.44 percent of all workers are employed by firms with 500 or more employees.

We can measure the contribution of small business in terms of its impact on key aspects of the U.S. economic system, including *job creation*, *innovation*, and their *contributions to big business*.

Job Creation   Small businesses—especially in certain industries—are an important source of new (and often well-paid) jobs. In recent years, small businesses have

MyBizLab

Gain hands-on experience through an interactive, real-world scenario. This chapter's simulation entitled Are You an Entrepreneur? Getting Your Business Off the Ground is located at www.mybizlab.com.

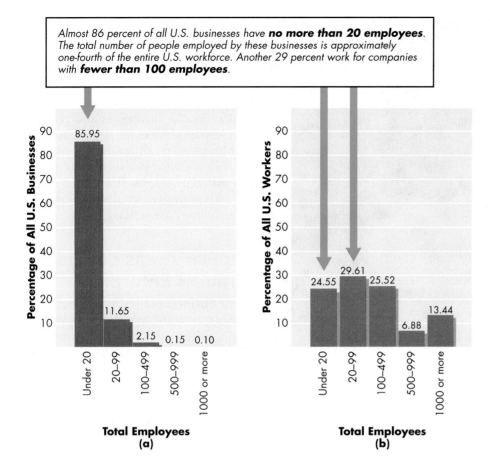

Almost 86 percent of all U.S. businesses have **no more than 20 employees**. The total number of people employed by these businesses is approximately one-fourth of the entire U.S. workforce. Another 29 percent work for companies with **fewer than 100 employees**.

Figure 3.1 **The Importance Small Business in the United States**
Source: Data from **www.sba.gov**, accessed 3/6/2010, and U.S. Census Bureau, "Statistics About Business Size (including Small Business) from the U.S. Census Bureau," at **www.census .gov/epcd/www/smallbus.html**, accessed 4/25/2011.

accounted for around 40 percent of all new jobs in high-technology sectors of the economy.[2] Jobs are created by companies of all sizes, all of which hire and lay off workers. Although small firms often hire at a faster rate, they also tend to cut jobs at a higher rate. They are generally the first to hire in times of economic recovery, while big firms are generally the last to lay off workers during downswings.

However, relative job growth among businesses of different sizes is not easy to determine. For one thing, when a successful small business starts adding employees at a rapid clip, it may quickly cease being small. For example, Dell Computer had 1 employee in 1984 (Michael Dell himself). But the payroll grew to 100 employees in 1986, 2,000 in 1992, more than 39,000 in 2004, and 94,300 in 2010. While there was no precise point at which Dell turned from "small" into "large," some of the jobs it created could be counted in the small business sector and some in the large.

Innovation   History reminds us that major innovations are as likely to come from small businesses (or individuals) as from big ones. Small firms and individuals invented the personal computer, the stainless-steel razor blade, the photocopier, the jet engine, and the self-developing photograph. Innovations are not always new products. Michael Dell didn't invent the PC; he developed an innovative way to build it (buy finished components and then assemble them) and an innovative way to sell it (directly to consumers, first by telephone and now via the Internet). Today, small businesses produce 13 times as many patents per employee as large patenting firms.[3]

Contributions to Big Business   Most of the products made by big businesses are sold to consumers by small ones. For example, most dealerships that sell Fords, Toyotas, and Volvos are independently operated. Even as more shoppers turn to the

Small Business Administration (SBA) government agency charged with assisting small businesses

Small Business independently owned business that has relatively little influence in its market

Thomas Nord/Shutterstock

New businesses often emerge in response to emerging opportunities. For instance, an increase in the number of working families with pets has created an opportunity for professional dog-walkers. Most dog-walkers, in turn, are individual entrepreneurs.

Internet, smaller businesses still play critical roles. For instance, most larger online retailers actually outsource the creation of their websites and the distribution of their products to other firms, many of them small or regional companies. Smaller businesses also provide data storage services for larger businesses. Moreover, small businesses provide big ones with many of their services and raw materials. Microsoft, for instance, relies on hundreds of small firms for most of its routine code-writing functions.

Popular Areas of Small-Business Enterprise

Small businesses play a major role in services, retailing, construction, wholesaling, finance and insurance, manufacturing, and transportation. Generally, the more resources that are required, the harder a business is to start and the less likely an industry is dominated by small firms. Remember, too, that small is a relative term. The criteria (number of employees and total annual sales) differ among industries and are often meaningful only when compared with truly large businesses. Figure 3.2 shows the distribution of all U.S. businesses employing fewer than 20 people across industry groups.

Services   About 50.74 percent of businesses with fewer than 20 employees are involved in the service industry, which ranges from marriage counseling to computer software, from management consulting to professional dog walking. Partly because they require few resources, service providers are the fastest-growing segment of small business.

Retailing   Retailers, which sell products made by other firms directly to consumers, account for about 13 percent of these firms. Usually, people who start small retail businesses favor specialty shops—big men's clothing or gourmet coffees, for example—that let them focus limited resources on narrow or small market segments.

Figure 3.2 Small Business by Industry
Source: U.S. Census Bureau, "Statistical Abstract of the United States," at *http://www.census.gov/prod/www/statistical-abstract.html.*

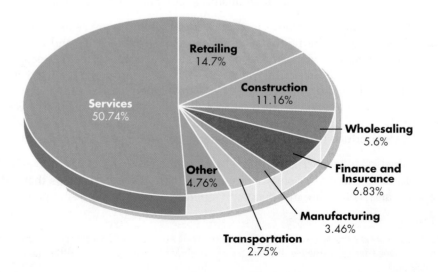

Retailing
14.7%

Construction
11.16%

Wholesaling
5.6%

Services
50.74%

Finance and Insurance
6.83%

Other
4.76%

Manufacturing
3.46%

Transportation
2.75%

MANAGING IN TURBULENT TIMES

The Wide World of Risk

One reason why globalization has become such a factor in everyday business life is the expanded reach and power of multinational companies. Many large corporations have actually become engines for innovation as well as growth, adapting to new markets and new economic circumstances. In a highly interconnected world, however, it's often hard to figure out the complex ownership and organizational structures of many global corporations. Sometimes, for example, their branding strategies and management structures lead people to think that they're local companies when, in fact, the real source of corporate power may lie thousands of miles away on another continent. One thing's for sure: If you're going to be dealing with a company overseas, you'd better have a good idea of where and how decisions are made, and who has the real power to make them.

Remember, too, that different cultures have different attitudes when it comes to entrepreneurship. In some countries and cultures, like that of the United States, there's a lively entrepreneurial spirit. Businesspeople are open to taking risks, and if they fail, they tend to pick themselves up and move on to something else. In some Asian countries, the entrepreneurial spirit is often tempered by the need for consensus and getting everyone on board. This approach requires a lot of patience and the ability to compromise.

Baris Simsek/iStockphoto.com

Knowing the cultural forces that shape both a business organization and people's attitudes toward risk, success, and failure is an elementary but important component of international business.

MyBizLab

Construction   About 14.7 percent of all U.S. businesses are involved in construction. Because many construction jobs are small local projects, like a homeowner adding a garage or remodeling a room, local contractors are often best suited to handle them.

Wholesaling   Small-business owners often do well in wholesaling, which accounts for about 5.6 percent of businesses with fewer than 20 employees. Wholesalers buy products in bulk from manufacturers or other producers and store them in quantities and locations convenient for selling them to retailers.

Finance and Insurance   Financial and insurance firms account for about 6.83 percent. Most of these businesses, such as local State Farm Insurance offices, are affiliates of or agents for larger national firms. Small locally owned banks are also common in smaller communities and rural areas.

Manufacturing   More than any other industry, manufacturing lends itself to big business, but it still accounts for about 3.46 percent of firms with fewer than 20 employees. Indeed, small manufacturers sometimes outperform big ones in such innovation-driven industries as electronics, equipment and machine parts, and computer software.

Transportation   About 2.75 percent of these small companies are in transportation and related businesses, including many taxi and limousine companies, charter airplane services, and tour operators.

Other The remaining 4.76 percent or so are in other industries, such as small research-and-development laboratories and independent media companies, like start-up web channels, small-town newspapers, and radio broadcasters.

Entrepreneurship

2 Explain entrepreneurship and describe some key characteristics of entrepreneurial personalities and activities.

We noted earlier that Dell Computer started as a one-person operation and grew into a giant corporation. Dell's growth was spurred by the imagination and skill of Michael Dell, the entrepreneur who founded the company. **Entrepreneurs** are people, like Michael Dell, who assume the risk of business ownership. **Entrepreneurship** is the process of seeking business opportunities under conditions of risk. However, not all entrepreneurs have the same goals.

For instance, many entrepreneurs seek to launch a new business with the goal of independence—independence from working for someone else coupled with some reasonable degree of financial security. Such entrepreneurs want to achieve a safe and secure financial future for themselves and their families but do not aspire to grow their business beyond their capacity to run it. Consider Jack Matz, a former corporate executive in Houston who lost his job when his firm merged with another. Rather than look for another management position, Matz opened a photocopying business near a local university. His goal is to earn enough money to lead a comfortable life until he retires in 10 years. The term *small business* is most closely associated with these kinds of enterprises.

Other entrepreneurs, however, launch new businesses with the goal of growth and expansion—that is, to transform their venture into a large business. This was Michael Dell's vision when he started his business; likewise, when Howard Schultz took over Starbucks, he too had plans to grow and develop the fledgling coffee company into a much larger enterprise. Terms such as *new ventures* and *start-ups* are often used to refer to these kinds of businesses.

In still other cases, the goals of an entrepreneur may not always be clear in the early stages of business development. For instance, one entrepreneur might launch a business with little or no expectation that it will have huge growth potential but then find that it can grow dramatically. Mark Zuckerberg, for example, had no idea that his Facebook firm would grow to its present size. Another entrepreneur might start out with ambitious growth plans but find that expected opportunities cannot be realized—perhaps there really is no large market or another firm establishes dominance over that market first.

Entrepreneurial Characteristics

Regardless of their goals, many successful entrepreneurs share certain characteristics—for example, resourcefulness and a concern for good, often personal, customer relations. Most of them also have a strong desire to be their own bosses. Many express a need to "gain control over my life" or "build for the family" and believe that building successful businesses will help them do it. They can also deal with uncertainty and risk.

Yesterday's entrepreneur was often stereotyped as "the boss"—self-reliant, male, and able to make quick, firm decisions. Today's entrepreneur is seen more often as an open-minded leader who relies on networks, business plans, and consensus. Although today's entrepreneur may be male, she is just as likely to be female. Past and present entrepreneurs also have different views on such topics as how to succeed, how to automate business, and when to rely on experience in the trade or on basic business acumen.[4]

Consider Yoshiko Shinohara, who had lost her father by the age of 8, was divorced by the age of 28, and never received a college education. At the age of 70, she is president of Tempstaff, a Japanese temp agency that she started out of her one-room apartment more than 30 years ago. Fueled by Japan's need for temps during a period of stagnation in the 1990s and Shinohara's ambition, Tempstaff is now a $1.5 billion company with a high-rise headquarters in Tokyo.[5]

Among other things, Shinohara's story illustrates what is almost always a key element in entrepreneurship: risk. Interestingly, most successful entrepreneurs seldom see what they do as risky. Whereas others may focus on possibilities for failure and balk at gambling everything on a new venture, most entrepreneurs are so passionate about their ideas and plans that they see little or no likelihood of failure. For example, when Shinohara started Tempstaff, few Japanese businesses understood or had even heard of the temporary-worker concept. But Shinohara felt that she "had nothing to lose anyway" and preferred taking that risk to ending up "serving tea or just being a clerical assistant."[6]

Starting and Operating a New Business

3 Describe the business plan and the start-up decisions made by small businesses and identify sources of financial aid available to such enterprises.

The Internet has changed the rules for starting and operating a small business. Setting up is easier and faster than ever, there are more potential opportunities than at any other time, and the ability to gather and assess information is at an all-time high. Today, for example, many one-person retailers do most of their business—both buying and selling—on Internet auction sites, such as eBay.

Even so, would-be entrepreneurs must make the right start-up decisions. They must decide how to get into business—should they buy an existing business or build from the ground up? They must know when to seek expert advice and where to find sources of financing. If, for example, a new firm needs financial backing from investors or a line of credit from vendors or distributors, the entrepreneur must have in place a comprehensive, well-crafted business plan.

Crafting a Business Plan

The starting point for virtually every new business is a **business plan** in which the entrepreneur describes her or his business strategy for the new venture and demonstrates how it will be implemented.[7] A real benefit of a business plan is the fact that in the act of preparing it, the would-be entrepreneur must develop the business idea on paper and firm up his or her thinking about how to launch it before investing time and money in it. The idea of the business plan isn't new. What is new is the use of specialized business plans, mostly because creditors and investors demand them as tools for deciding whether to finance or invest.

Setting Goals and Objectives   A business plan describes the match between the entrepreneur's abilities and experiences and the requirements for producing and/or marketing a particular product. It also defines strategies for production and marketing, legal elements and organization, and accounting and finance. In particular, a business plan should answer three questions: (1) What are the entrepreneur's goals and objectives? (2) What strategies will be used to obtain them? (3) How will these strategies be implemented?

Sales Forecasting   While a key element of any business plan is sales forecasts, plans must carefully build an argument for likely business success based on sound logic and research. Entrepreneurs, for example, can't forecast sales revenues without

---

Entrepreneur businessperson who accepts both the risks and the opportunities involved in creating and operating a new business venture

Entrepreneurship the process of seeking businesses opportunities under conditions of risk

Business Plan document in which the entrepreneur summarizes her or his business strategy for the proposed new venture and how that strategy will be implemented

first researching markets. Simply asserting that the new venture will sell 100,000 units per month is not credible. Instead, the entrepreneur must demonstrate an understanding of the current market, of the strengths and weaknesses of existing firms, and of the means by which the new venture will compete. Without the sales forecast, no one can estimate the required size of a plant, store, or office or decide how much inventory to carry and how many employees to hire.

Financial Planning   Financial planning refers to the entrepreneur's plan for turning all other activities into dollars. It generally includes a cash budget, an income statement, balance sheets, and a breakeven chart. The cash budget shows how much money you need before you open for business and how much you need to keep the business going before it starts earning a profit.[7]

Starting the Small Business

An old Chinese proverb says that a journey of a thousand miles begins with a single step. This is also true of a new business. The first step is the individual's commitment to becoming a business owner. In preparing a business plan, the entrepreneur must choose the industry and market in which he or she plans to compete. This choice means assessing not only industry conditions and trends but also one's own abilities and interests. Like big-business managers, small-business owners must understand the nature of the enterprises in which they are engaged.

Buying an Existing Business   Next, the entrepreneur must decide whether to buy an existing business or start from scratch. Many experts recommend the first approach because, quite simply, the odds are better: If it's successful, an existing business has already proven its ability to attract customers and generate profit. It has also established relationships with lenders, suppliers, and other stakeholders. Moreover, an existing track record gives potential buyers a much clearer picture of what to expect than any estimate of a start-up's prospects.

Ray Kroc bought McDonald's as an existing business, added entrepreneurial vision and business insight, and produced a multinational giant. Both Southwest Airlines and Starbucks were small but struggling operations when entrepreneurs took over and grew them into large businesses. About 35 percent of all new businesses that were started in the past decade were bought from someone else.

Franchising   Most McDonald's, Subway, 7-Eleven, RE/Max, Ramada, and Blockbuster outlets are franchises operating under licenses issued by parent companies to local owners. A **franchise** agreement involves two parties, a *franchisee* (the local owner) and a *franchiser* (the parent company).[8]

Franchisees benefit from the parent corporation's experience and expertise, and the franchiser may even supply financing. It may pick the store location, negotiate the lease, design the store, and purchase equipment. It may train the first set of employees and managers and issue standard policies and procedures. Once the business is open, the franchiser may offer savings by allowing the franchisee to purchase from a central location. Marketing strategy (especially advertising) may also be handled by the franchiser. In short, franchisees receive—that is, invest in—not only their own ready-made businesses but also expert help in running them.

Franchises have advantages for both sellers and buyers. Franchises can grow rapidly by using the investment money provided by franchisees. The franchisee gets to own a business and has access to big-business management skills. The franchisee does not have to build a business step by step, and because each franchise outlet is probably a carbon copy of every other outlet, failure is less likely. Recent statistics show that franchising is on the upswing, having increased by over 20 percent during the past decade.

Perhaps the most significant disadvantage in owning a franchise is start-up cost. Franchise prices vary widely. The fee for a Fantastic Sam's hair salon is $30,000; however, the franchisee must also invest additional funds in building and outfitting the salon. A McDonald's franchise has an initial fee of $45,000 but again requires the additional funds to construct and outfit a restaurant; the costs generally run the total outlay to around $1 million. And professional sports teams (which are also franchises) can cost several hundred million dollars. Franchisees may also be obligated to contribute a percentage of sales to parent corporations. From the perspective of the parent company, some firms choose not to franchise in order to retain more control over quality and earn more profits for themselves. Starbucks, for instance, does not franchise its coffee shops. (Starbucks does have licensing agreements where other firms operate Starbucks kiosks and other niche outlets; it does not, though, franchise individual free-standing coffee shops to individuals.)

Starting from Scratch   Despite the odds, some people seek the satisfaction that comes from planting an idea and growing it into a healthy business. There are also practical reasons to start from scratch. A new business doesn't suffer the ill effects of a prior owner's errors, and the start-up owner is free to choose lenders, equipment, inventories, locations, suppliers, and workers. Of all new businesses begun in the past decade, about 64 percent were started from scratch. Dell Computer, Wal-Mart, Microsoft, and Facebook are among today's most successful businesses that were started from scratch by an entrepreneur.

But as we have already noted, the risks of starting a business from scratch are greater than those of buying an existing firm. New-business founders can only make projections about their prospects. Success or failure depends on identifying a genuine opportunity, such as a product for which many customers will pay well but which is currently unavailable. To find openings, entrepreneurs must study markets and answer the following questions:

- Who and where are my customers?
- How much will those customers pay for my product?
- How much of my product can I expect to sell?
- Who are my competitors?
- Why will customers buy my product rather than the product of my competitors?

Financing the Small Business

Although the choice of how to start a business is obviously important, it's meaningless unless you can get the money. Among the more common sources for funding are family and friends, personal savings, lending institutions, investors, and governmental agencies. Lending institutions are more likely to help finance the purchase of an existing business because the risks are better understood. Individuals starting new businesses will probably have to rely on personal resources. One of the many causes of the 2008–2010 recession was a sharp reduction in the availability of credit, including funds to help start new businesses. This credit crunch, in turn, limited both new start-up funding and funding for existing businesses wanting to make new investments.

According to the National Federation of Independent Business, personal resources, not loans, are the most important sources of money. Including money borrowed from friends and relatives, personal resources account for over two-thirds of all money invested in new small businesses, and one-half of that is used to purchase existing businesses. Getting money from banks, independent investors, and government loans requires extra effort. At a minimum, banks and private investors will want to review business plans, and government loans have strict eligibility guidelines.

Franchise arrangement in which a buyer (franchisee) purchases the right to sell the good or service of the seller (franchiser)

Other Sources of Investment **Venture capital companies** are groups of small investors seeking to make profits on companies with rapid growth potential. Most of these firms do not lend money. They invest it, supplying capital in return for partial ownership (like stocks, discussed later in this chapter). They may also demand representation on boards of directors. In some cases, managers need approval from the venture capital company before making major decisions. In most cases, venture capitalists do not provide money to start a new business; instead, once a business has been successfully launched and its growth potential established, they provide the funds to fuel expansion. Of all venture capital currently committed in the United States, about 30 percent comes from true venture capital firms.

Small-business investment companies (SBICs) also invest in companies with potential for rapid growth. They are federally licensed to borrow money from the SBA and to invest it in or lend it to small businesses, and they are themselves investments for their shareholders. Past beneficiaries of SBIC capital include Apple Computer, Intel, and FedEx. The government also sponsors *minority enterprise small-business investment companies (MESBICs).* As the name suggests, MESBICs target minority-owned businesses.

SBA Financial Programs Since its founding in 1953, the SBA has sponsored financing programs for small businesses that meet standards in size and independence. Eligible firms must be unable to get private financing at reasonable terms. The most common form of SBA financing, its *7(a) loans programs,* allows small businesses to borrow from commercial lenders and guarantees to repay a maximum of 75 percent. The SBA's *special purpose loans* target businesses with specific needs, such as meeting international demands or implementing pollution-control measures. For loans under $35,000, the SBA offers the *micro-loan program*. The *Certified Development Company (504) program* offers fixed interest rates on loans from nonprofit community-based lenders to boost local economies.[9]

Other SBA Programs The SBA also helps entrepreneurs improve their management skills. The Service Corps of Retired Executives (SCORE) is made up of retired executives who volunteer to help entrepreneurs start new businesses. The **Small Business Development Center (SBDC)** program consolidates information from various disciplines and institutions for use by new and existing small businesses.

4 Discuss the trends in small business start-ups and identify the main reasons for success and failure among small businesses.

Trends, Successes, and Failures in New Ventures

For every Sam Walton, Mark Zuckerberg, Mary Kay Ash, or Bill Gates—entrepreneurs who transformed small businesses into big ones—there are many entrepreneurs who fail. Each year there are generally between 600,000 and 650,000 new businesses launched in the United States. On the other hand, there are also between 500,000 and 600,000 failures each year as well.[10] In 2009, for instance, 627,200 new firms started operations and another 595,600 closed down. In this section, we look first at a few key trends in small-business start-ups. Then we examine some of the reasons for success and failure in small-business undertakings.

Trends in Small-Business Start-Ups

As noted previously, thousands of new businesses are started in the United States every year. Several factors account for this trend, and in this section, we focus on five of them.

Emergence of E-Commerce The most significant recent trend is the rapid emergence of electronic commerce. Because the Internet provides fundamentally new ways of doing business, savvy entrepreneurs have created and expanded new businesses faster and easier than ever before. Such leading-edge firms as Google, Amazon.com, and eBay owe their very existence to the Internet. Figure 3.3 underscores this point by summarizing the growth in online commerce from 2003 through 2010.

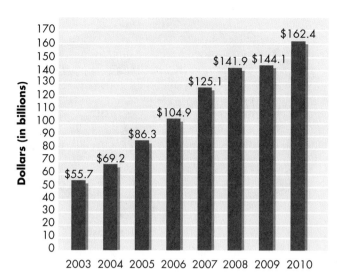

Figure 3.3 **Growth of Online Retail Spending**

Crossovers from Big Business   More businesses are being started by people who have opted to leave big corporations and put their experience to work for themselves.[9] In some cases, they see great new ideas that they want to develop. Others get burned out in the corporate world. Some have lost their jobs, only to discover that working for themselves was a better idea anyway. John Chambers spent several years working at IBM and Wang Laboratories/GLOBAL before he decided to try his hand at entrepreneurship. After resigning from Wang, he signed on to help Cisco, then a small and struggling firm. Under his leadership and entrepreneurial guidance, Cisco has become one of the largest and most important technology companies in the world.

Opportunities for Minorities and Women   More small businesses are also being started by minorities and women.[11] The number of businesses owned by African Americans increased by 48 percent during the most recent five-year period for which data are available and now totals about 2 million. The number of Hispanic-owned businesses has grown 31 percent and now totals about 2.25 million. Ownership among Asians has increased 24 percent and among Pacific Islanders 64 percent.[12]

Almost 8 million businesses are now owned by women. Together, they generate a combined $200 trillion in revenue a year and employ about 10 million workers.[13] Figure 3.4 shows some of the reasons women cite for starting their own businesses.

Global Opportunities   Many entrepreneurs are also finding new opportunities in foreign markets. Doug Mellinger is founder and CEO of PRT Group, a software development company. One of Mellinger's biggest problems was finding trained programmers. There aren't enough U.S.-based programmers to go around, and foreign-born programmers face strict immigration quotas. So Mellinger set up shop on Barbados, a Caribbean island where the government helps him attract foreign programmers and does everything it can to make things easier. Today, PRT has customers and suppliers from dozens of nations.

Better Survival Rates   More people are encouraged to test their skills as entrepreneurs because the small-business failure rate has declined. During the 1960s and 1970s, less than half of all new start-ups survived more than 18 months; only one in five lasted 10 years. Now, however, 44 percent can expect to survive for at least four years.[14]

Venture Capital Company group of small investors who invest money in companies with rapid growth potential

Small-Business Investment Company (SBIC) government-regulated investment company that borrows money from the SBA to invest in or lend to a small business

Small Business Development Center (SBDC) SBA program designed to consolidate information from various disciplines and make it available to small businesses

Figure 3.4 **Reasons Women Give for Starting Businesses**

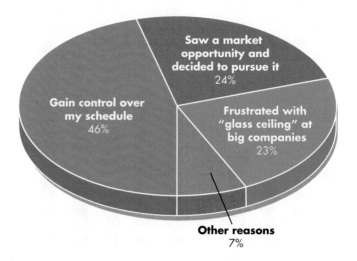

Saw a market opportunity and decided to pursue it
24%

Gain control over my schedule
46%

Frustrated with "glass ceiling" at big companies
23%

Other reasons
7%

Reasons for Failure

Unfortunately, over half of all new businesses will not enjoy long-term success. Why do some succeed and others fail? Although no set pattern has been established, four general factors contribute to failure:

1 *Managerial incompetence or inexperience.* Some entrepreneurs put too much faith in common sense, overestimate their own managerial skills, or believe that hard work alone ensures success. If managers don't know how to make basic business decisions or don't understand basic management principles, they aren't likely to succeed in the long run.

2 *Neglect.* Some entrepreneurs try to launch ventures in their spare time, and others devote only limited time to new businesses. But starting a small business demands an overwhelming time commitment. If you aren't willing to put in the time and effort that a business requires, you aren't likely to survive.

3 *Weak control systems.* Effective control systems keep a business on track and alert managers to potential trouble. If your control systems don't signal impending problems, you may be in serious trouble before you spot more obvious difficulties. For instance, some businesses fail because they do a poor job of managing their credit collection policies—anxious to grow, they may be too liberal in extending credit to their customers and then end up not being able to collect all the money that is owed to them.

4 *Insufficient capital.* Some entrepreneurs are overly optimistic about how soon they'll start earning profits. In most cases, it takes months or even years. Amazon.com didn't earn a profit for 10 years but obviously still required capital to pay employees and to cover other expenses. Experts say you need enough capital to operate at least six months without earning a profit; some recommend enough to last a year.[15]

Reasons for Success

Four basic factors are also typically cited to explain small-business success:

1 *Hard work, drive, and dedication.* Small-business owners must be committed to succeeding and willing to spend the time and effort to make it happen. Gladys Edmunds, a single mother in Pittsburgh, wanted to open a travel agency but did not have enough money to get started. So, she washed laundry, made chicken dinners to sell to cab drivers, and sold fire extinguishers door to door to earn

ENTREPRENEURSHIP AND NEW VENTURES

Being Savvy and Lucky Make a Great Combination

One day a few years ago an ex-Marine named Reed Hastings rented a movie from his neighborhood video rental store. After watching the movie, he discovered that he had misplaced the plastic case for the videocassette. It took him several days to locate it but by then he had racked up some hefty late fees. Hastings dropped off the movie on his way to the gym for a workout, and left fuming over the fees. A bit later, as he was walking on the gym's treadmill he had an inspiration: maybe a video rental business could be run just like a gym, where members play a flat monthly fee but then get to use the gym as much as they wanted. From this basic idea came one of today's hottest businesses—Netflix.

Hastings launched Netflix in 1997, offering members unlimited video rentals through the mail with no late fees. Customers pay a monthly service charge and register online to receive movies of their choice. Whenever they receive a movie, they can keep it as long as they like with no additional fees. Whenever they send a movie back to Netflix—whether its two days or two months later—they get their next movie. Over 17 million subscribers belong to Netflix, and the company has successfully fended off threats from Blockbuster, Amazon, and Google.

But new threats are on the horizon. More and more home viewers are shifting away from renting movies through the mail and instead are buying streaming video. Netflix was actually one of the first businesses to move into this emerging market and currently has the largest market share. At the same time, though, streaming video requires entirely new licensing agreements with content providers like Disney, CBS, and Sony. While these and other firms have remained partners with Netflix, they are also keeping their options open. Meanwhile, other streaming video competitors emerge almost daily and who knows when one of these companies might develop a new business model that can offset Netflix's current advantages.

For his part, though, Reed Hastings continues to enjoy the fruits of his brilliant idea. In 2010, for example, he received a base salary as Netflix's CEO of over $2.5 million. In addition, he is also the company's largest individual shareholder. In this case, then, a mix of entrepreneurial savvy and some old-fashioned good luck have combined to provide another great success story in the history of American entrepreneurship.[16]

MyBizLab

w51/ZUMA Press/Newscom

start-up money. Today, Edmunds Travel Consultants employs eight people and earns about $6 million a year.[17]

2 *Market demand for the products or services being provided.* Careful analysis of market conditions can help small-business owners assess the probable reception of their products. Attempts to expand restaurants specializing in baked potatoes, muffins, and gelato often struggle, but hamburger and pizza chains continue to expand.

3 *Managerial competence.* Successful owners may acquire competence through training or experience or by drawing on the expertise of others. Few, however, succeed alone or straight out of college. Most spend time in successful companies or partner with others to bring expertise to a new business.[13]

4 *Luck.* After Alan McKim started Clean Harbors, an environmental cleanup firm in New England, he struggled to keep his business afloat. Then the U.S. government committed $1.6 billion to toxic waste cleanup—McKim's specialty. He landed several large government contracts and put his business on solid financial footing. Had the government fund not been created at just the right time, McKim might well have failed.

5 Explain sole proprietorships, partnerships, and
cooperatives and discuss the
advantages and disadvantages
of each.

Noncorporate Business Ownership

Whether they intend to launch a small local business or a new venture projected to grow rapidly, all entrepreneurs must decide which form of legal ownership best suits their goals: *sole proprietorship, partnership,* or *corporation.* Because this choice affects a host of managerial and financial issues, few decisions are more critical. Entrepreneurs must consider their own preferences, their immediate and long-range needs, and the advantages and disadvantages of each form. Table 3.1 compares the most important differences among the three major ownership forms.

Sole Proprietorships

The **sole proprietorship** is owned and usually operated by one person. About 72 percent of all U.S. businesses are sole proprietorships; however, they account for only about 5 percent of total business revenues. Though usually small, they may be as large as steel mills or department stores.

Advantages of Sole Proprietorships   Freedom may be the most important benefit of sole proprietorships. Because they own their businesses, sole proprietors answer to no one but themselves. Sole proprietorships are also easy to form. Sometimes, you can go into business simply by putting a sign on the door. The simplicity of legal setup procedures makes this form appealing to self-starters and independent spirits, as do low start-up costs.

Another attractive feature is the tax benefits extended to businesses that are likely to suffer losses in their early stages. Tax laws permit owners to treat sales revenues and operating expenses as part of their personal finances, paying taxes based on their personal tax rate. They can cut taxes by deducting business losses from income earned from personal sources other than the business.

Disadvantages of Sole Proprietorships   A major drawback is **unlimited liability:** A sole proprietor is personally liable for all debts incurred by the business. If it fails to generate enough cash, bills must be paid out of the owner's pocket. Another disadvantage is lack of continuity: A sole proprietorship legally dissolves when the owner dies. Although the business can be reorganized by a successor, executors or heirs must otherwise sell its assets.

Finally, a sole proprietorship depends on the resources of one person whose managerial and financial limitations may constrain the business. Sole proprietors often find it hard to borrow money to start up or expand. Many bankers fear that they won't be able to recover loans if owners become disabled or insolvent.

TABLE 3.1   Comparative Summary: Three Forms of Business

Business Form	Liability	Continuity	Management	Sources of Investment
Proprietorship	Personal, unlimited	Ends with death or decision of owner	Personal, unrestricted	Personal
General Partnership	Personal, unlimited	Ends with death or decision of any partner	Unrestricted or depends on partnership agreement	Personal by partner(s)
Corporation	Capital invested	As stated in charter, perpetual or for specified period of years	Under control of board of directors, which is selected by stockholders	Purchase of stock

Partnerships

The most common type of partnership, the **general partnership,** is similar to a sole proprietorship but is owned by more than one person. Partners may invest equal or unequal sums of money. In most cases, partners share the profits equally or in proportion to their investment. In certain cases, though, the distribution of profits may be based on other things. A locally prominent athlete, for instance, may lend her or his name to the partnership and earn profits without actually investing funds. And sometimes one partner invests all of the funds needed for the business but plays no role in its management; this person is usually called a *silent partner.* Another partner might invest nothing but provide all the labor. In this case, the financial investor likely owns the entire business, and the labor partner owns nothing. But over time, and as specified in a contract, the labor partner gradually gains an ownership stake in the business (usually called *sweat equity*).

Advantages of Partnerships
The most striking advantage of general partnerships is the ability to grow by adding new talent and money. Because banks prefer to make loans to enterprises that are not dependent on single individuals, partnerships find it easier to borrow than sole proprietorships. They can also invite new partners to join by investing money.

Like a sole proprietorship, a partnership can be organized by meeting only a few legal requirements. Even so, all partnerships must begin with an agreement of some kind. In all but two states, the Revised Uniform Limited Partnership Act requires the filing of specific information about the business and its partners. Partners may also agree to bind themselves in ways not specified by law. In any case, an agreement should answer questions such as the following:

- Who invested what sums?

- Who will receive what share of the profits?

- Who does what, and who reports to whom?

- How may the partnership be dissolved? In the event of dissolution, how will assets be distributed?

- How will surviving partners be protected from claims made by a deceased partner's heirs?

The partnership agreement is strictly a private document. No laws require partners to file agreements with any government agency. Nor are partnerships regarded as legal entities. In the eyes of the law, a partnership is just two or more people working together. Because partnerships have no independent legal standing, the Internal Revenue Service (IRS) taxes partners as individuals.

Disadvantages of Partnerships
For general partnerships as for sole proprietorships, unlimited liability is the greatest drawback. Each partner may be liable for all debts incurred by the partnership. If any partner incurs a business debt, all partners may be liable, even if some of them did not know about or agree to the new debt.

Partnerships also share with sole proprietorships the potential lack of continuity. When one partner dies or leaves, the original partnership dissolves, even if one or more of the other partners want it to continue. But dissolution need not mean a loss of sales revenues. Survivors may form a new partnership to retain the old firm's business.

A related disadvantage is difficulty in transferring ownership. No partner may sell out without the consent of the others. A partner who wants to retire or to transfer interest to a son or daughter must have the other partners' consent.

Sole Proprietorship business owned and usually operated by one person who is responsible for all of its debts

Unlimited Liability legal principle holding owners responsible for paying off all debts of a business

General Partnership business with two or more owners who share in both the operation of the firm and the financial responsibility for its debts

Alternatives to General Partnerships   Because of these disadvantages, general partnerships are among the least popular forms of business. Roughly 1.79 million U.S. partnerships generate only 5.8 percent of total sales revenues.[15] To resolve some of the problems inherent in general partnerships, especially unlimited liability, some partners have tried alternative agreements. The **limited partnership** allows for **limited partners** who invest money but are liable for debts only to the extent of their investments. They cannot, however, take active roles in business operations. A limited partnership must have at least one **general (or active) partner,** mostly for liability purposes. This is usually the person who runs the business and is responsible for its survival and growth.

Under a **master limited partnership,** an organization sells shares (partnership interests) to investors on public markets such as the New York Stock Exchange. Investors are paid back from profits. The master partner retains at least 50 percent ownership and runs the business, while minority partners have no management voice. (The master partner differs from a general partner, who has no such ownership restriction.) The master partner must regularly provide minority partners with detailed operating and financial reports.

Cooperatives

Sometimes, groups of sole proprietorships or partnerships agree to work together for their common benefit by forming cooperatives. **Cooperatives** combine the freedom of sole proprietorships with the financial power of corporations. They give members greater production power, greater marketing power, or both. On the other hand, they are limited to serving the specific needs of their members. Although cooperatives make up only a minor segment of the U.S. economy, their role is still important in agriculture. Ocean Spray, the Florida Citrus Growers, Riceland, and Cabot Cheese are among the best-known cooperatives.

Corporations

6 Describe corporations, discuss their advantages and disadvantages, and identify different kinds of corporations; explain the basic issues involved in managing a corporation and discuss special issues related to corporate ownership.

There are about 4.93 million corporations in the United States. As you can see from Figure 3.5, they account for about 20 percent of all U.S. businesses but generate about 85 percent of all sales revenues.[18] Almost all large businesses use this form, and corporations dominate global business. As we will see, corporations need not be large—indeed, many small businesses also elect to operate as corporations.

According to the most recent data, Wal-Mart, the world's largest corporation, posted annual revenue of over $408 billion, with total profits of over $100 billion. Even "smaller" large corporations post huge sales figures. The New York Times Company, though five-hundredth in size among U.S. corporations, posted a profit of $1.4 billion on annual sales of $2.4 billion. Given the size and influence of this form of ownership, we devote a great deal of attention to various aspects of corporations.

The Corporate Entity

When you think of corporations, you probably think of giant operations such as General Motors and IBM. The very word *corporation* inspires images of size and power. In reality, however, your corner newsstand has as much right to incorporate as a giant automaker. Moreover, the newsstand and GM would share the characteristics of all **corporations:** legal status as separate entities, property rights and obligations, and indefinite life spans.

In 1819, the U.S. Supreme Court defined a corporation as "an artificial being, invisible, intangible, and existing only in contemplation of the law." The court defined the corporation as a legal person. Corporations may, therefore, perform the following activities:

- Sue and be sued

- Buy, hold, and sell property

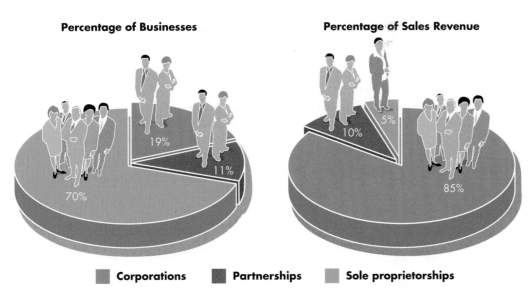

Percentage of Businesses

19%

11%

70%

Percentage of Sales Revenue

5%

10%

85%

■ **Corporations**   ■ **Partnerships**   ■ **Sole proprietorships**

Figure 3.5 **Proportions of U.S. Firms in Terms of Organization Type and Sales Revenue**

- Make and sell products
- Commit crimes and be tried and punished for them

Advantages of Incorporation   The biggest advantage of corporations is **limited liability:** Investor liability is limited to personal investment (through stock ownership, covered later) in the corporation. In the event of failure, the courts may seize and sell a corporation's assets but cannot touch the investors' personal possessions. If, for example, you invest $1,000 in stock in a corporation that ends up failing, you may lose your $1,000, but no more. In other words, your liability is limited to the $1,000 you invested.

Another advantage is continuity. Because it has a legal life independent of founders and owners, a corporation can, at least in theory, continue forever. Shares of stock may be sold or passed on to heirs, and most corporations also benefit from the continuity provided by professional management. Finally, corporations have advantages in raising money. By selling stock, they expand the number of investors and the amount of available funds. Continuity and legal status tend to make lenders more willing to grant loans.

Disadvantages of Incorporation   Although a chief attraction is ease of transferring ownership, this same feature can create complications. For example, using a legal process called a **tender offer**—an offer to buy shares made by a prospective buyer directly to a corporation's shareholders—a corporation can be taken over against the will of its managers. Another disadvantage is start-up cost. Corporations are heavily regulated, and incorporation entails meeting the complex legal requirements of the state in which the firm is chartered.

Limited Partnership type of partnership consisting of limited partners and a general (or managing) partner

Limited Partner partner who does not share in a firm's management and is liable for its debts only to the limits of said partner's investment

General (or Active) Partner partner who actively manages a firm and who has unlimited liability for its debts

Master Limited Partnership form of ownership that sells shares to investors who receive profits and that pays taxes on income from profits

Cooperative form of ownership in which a group of sole proprietorships and/or partnerships agree to work together for common benefits

Corporation business that is legally considered an entity separate from its owners and is liable for its own debts; owners' liability extends to the limits of their investments

Limited Liability legal principle holding investors liable for a firm's debts only to the limits of their personal investments in it

Tender Offer offer to buy shares made by a prospective buyer directly to a target corporation's shareholders, who then make individual decisions about whether to sell

The biggest disadvantage of incorporation, however, is **double taxation.** First, a corporation pays income taxes on company profits. In addition, stockholders then pay taxes on income returned by their investments in the corporation. Thus, the profits earned by corporations are taxed twice—once at the corporate level and then again at the ownership level. Because profits are treated as owners' personal income, sole proprietorships and partnerships are taxed only once.

The advantages and disadvantages of corporate ownership have inspired laws establishing different kinds of corporations. Most are intended to help businesses take advantage of the benefits of the corporate model without assuming all the disadvantages. We discuss these corporate forms next.

Types of Corporations

We can classify corporations as either *public* or *private*. But within these broad categories, we can identify several specific types of corporations, some of which are summarized in Table 3.2.

- The most common form of U.S. corporation is the **closely held (or private) corporation.** Stock is held by only a few people and is not available for sale to the public. The controlling group of stockholders may be a family, a management group, or even the firm's employees. Most smaller corporations fit this profile.

- When shares are publicly issued, the firm becomes a **publicly held (or public) corporation.** Stock is widely held and available for sale to the public. Many large businesses are of this type.

TABLE 3.2	Types of Corporations	
Type	**Distinguishing Features**	**Examples**
Closely Held	Stock held by only a few people	Blue Cross/Blue Shield
	Subject to corporate taxation	MasterCard
		Primestar
Publicly Held	Stock widely held among many investors	Dell Computer
	Subject to corporate taxation	Starbucks
		Texas Instruments
Subchapter S	Organized much like a closely held corporation	Minglewood Associates
	Subject to additional regulation	Entech Pest Systems
	Subject to partnership taxation	Frontier Bank
Limited Liability	Organized much like a publicly held corporation	Pacific Northwest Associates
	Subject to additional regulation	Global Ground Support
	Subject to partnership taxation	Ritz Carlton
Professional	Subject to partnership taxation	Norman Hui, DDS &
	Limited business liability	Associates
	Unlimited professional liability	B & H Engineering
		Anderson, McCoy & Oria
Multinational	Spans national boundaries	Toyota
	Subject to regulation in multiple countries	Nestlé
		General Electric

- The **S corporation** (more fully called the *Subchapter S corporation*) is a hybrid of a closely held corporation and a partnership. It is organized and operates like a corporation, but it is treated like a partnership for tax purposes. To qualify, firms must meet stringent legal conditions. For instance, stockholders must be individual U.S. citizens.

- Another hybrid is the **limited liability corporation (LLC).** Owners are taxed like partners, each paying personal taxes only. However, they also enjoy the benefits of limited liability accorded to publicly held corporations. LLCs have grown in popularity in recent years, partially because of IRS rulings that allow corporations, partnerships, and foreign investors to be partial owners.

- **Professional corporations** are most likely composed of doctors, lawyers, accountants, or other professionals. While the corporate structure protects from unlimited financial liability, members are not immune from unlimited liability. Professional negligence by a member can entail personal liability on the individual's part.

- As the term implies, the **multinational** (or **transnational**) **corporation** spans national boundaries. Stock may be traded on the exchanges of several countries, and managers are likely to be of different nationalities.

Managing a Corporation

Creating any type of corporation can be complicated, due to the various legal conditions that must be met. In addition, once the corporate entity comes into existence, it must be managed by people who understand the principles of **corporate governance**—the roles of shareholders, directors, and other managers in corporate decision making and accountability. In this section, we discuss the principles of *stock ownership* and *stockholders' rights* and describe the role of *boards of directors*. We then examine some special issues related to corporate ownership.

Corporate Governance   Corporate governance is established by the firm's bylaws and usually involves three distinct bodies. **Stockholders** (or **shareholders**) are the owners of a corporation—investors who buy ownership shares in the form of stock. The *board of directors* is a group elected by stockholders to oversee corporate management. Corporate *officers* are top managers hired by the board to run the corporation on a day-to-day basis.

Stock Ownership and Stockholders' Rights   Corporations sell shares, called *stock*, to investors who then become stockholders, or shareholders. Profits are distributed among stockholders in the form of *dividends*, and corporate managers serve at stockholders' discretion. In a closely held corporation, only a few people own stock. Shares of publicly held corporations are widely held.

Double Taxation situation in which taxes may be payable both by a corporation on its profits and by shareholders on dividend incomes

Closely Held (or Private) Corporation corporation whose stock is held by only a few people and is not available for sale to the general public

Publicly Held (or Public) Corporation corporation whose stock is widely held and available for sale to the general public

S Corporation hybrid of a closely held corporation and a partnership, organized and operated like a corporation but treated as a partnership for tax purposes

Limited Liability Corporation (LLC) hybrid of a publicly held corporation and a partnership in which owners are taxed as partners but enjoy the benefits of limited liability

Professional Corporation form of ownership allowing professionals to take advantage of corporate benefits while granting them limited business liability and unlimited professional liability

Multinational (or Transnational) Corporation form of corporation spanning national boundaries

Corporate Governance roles of shareholders, directors, and other managers in corporate decision making and accountability

Stockholder (or Shareholder) owner of shares of stock in a corporation

Boards of Directors The governing body of a corporation is its **board of directors.** Boards communicate with stockholders and other stakeholders through such channels as an annual report—a summary of a firm's financial health. They also set policy on dividends, major spending, and executive compensation. They are legally responsible and accountable for corporate actions and are increasingly being held personally liable for them.

Officers Although board members oversee operations, most do not participate in day-to-day management. Rather, they hire a team of managers to run the firm. This team, called **officers,** is usually headed by the firm's **chief executive officer (CEO),** who is responsible for overall performance. Other officers typically include a *president*, who is responsible for internal management, and *vice presidents*, who oversee various functional areas such as marketing and operations.

Special Issues in Corporate Ownership

In recent years, several issues have grown in importance in the area of corporate ownership, including *joint ventures and strategic alliances, employee stock ownership plans*, and *institutional ownership*. Other important issues in contemporary corporate ownership involve *mergers, acquisitions, divestitures*, and *spin-offs*.

Joint Ventures and Strategic Alliances

In a **strategic alliance,** two or more organizations collaborate on a project for mutual gain. When partners share ownership of what is essentially a new enterprise, it is called a **joint venture.** The number of strategic alliances has increased rapidly in recent years on both domestic and international fronts.

Employee Stock Ownership Plans

An **employee stock ownership plan (ESOP)** allows employees to own a significant share of the corporation through trusts established on their behalf. Current estimates count about 11,500 ESOPs in the United States. The growth rate in new ESOPs has slowed a bit in recent years, but they still are an important part of corporate ownership patterns in the United States.

Institutional Ownership

Most individual investors don't own enough stock to exert influence on corporate managers. In recent years, however, more stock has been purchased by **institutional investors.** Because they control enormous resources, these investors—especially mutual and pension funds—can buy huge blocks of stock. The national teachers' retirement system (TIAA-CREF) has assets of over $400 billion, much of it invested in stocks. Institutional investors own almost 55 percent of all the stock issued in the United States.

Mergers, Acquisitions, Divestitures, and Spin-Offs

Another important set of issues includes mergers, acquisitions, divestitures, and spin-offs. Mergers and acquisitions involve the legal joining of two or more corporations. A divestiture occurs when a corporation sells a business operation to another corporation; with a spin-off, it creates a new operation.

Mergers and Acquisitions (M&As) A **merger** occurs when two firms combine to create a new company. For example, United Airlines and Continental recently merged to create the world's largest airline. The new airline bears the United name but retains the equipment design of Continental. Continental's CEO assumed control of the new company. The firm took two years to integrate their respective operations into a unified new firm.

In an **acquisition,** one firm buys another outright. Many deals that are loosely called mergers are really acquisitions. Why? Because one of the two firms will usually control the newly combined ownership. In general, when the two firms are roughly the same size, the combination is usually called a merger even if one firm is taking control of the other. When the acquiring firm is substantially larger than the acquired firm, the deal is really an acquisition. So-called M&As are an important form of corporate strategy. They let firms increase product lines, expand operations, go international, and create new enterprises.

Divestitures and Spin-Offs Sometimes, a corporation decides to sell a part of its existing business operations or set it up as a new and independent corporation. There may be several reasons for such a step. A firm might decide, for example, that it should focus more specifically on its core businesses, and thus it will sell off unrelated and/or underperforming businesses. Such a sale is called a **divestiture.** When a firm sells part of itself to raise capital, the strategy is known as a **spin-off.** A spin-off may also mean that a firm deems a business unit more valuable as a separate company. The Limited, for example, spun off three of its subsidiaries—Victoria's Secret, Bath & Body Works, and White Barn Candle Co.—to create a new firm, Intimate Brands, which it then offered through an Initial Public Offering (IPO). The Limited retained 84 percent ownership of Intimate Brands while getting an infusion of new capital.

Board of Directors governing body of a corporation that reports to its shareholders and delegates power to run its day-to-day operations while remaining responsible for sustaining its assets

Officers top management team of a corporation

Chief Executive Officer (CEO) top manager who is responsible for the overall performance of a corporation

Strategic Alliance strategy in which two or more organizations collaborate on a project for mutual gain

Joint Venture strategic alliance in which the collaboration involves joint ownership of the new venture

Employee Stock Ownership Plan (ESOP) arrangement in which a corporation holds its own stock in trust for its employees, who gradually receive ownership of the stock and control its voting rights

Institutional Investor large investor, such as a mutual fund or a pension fund, that purchases large blocks of corporate stock

Merger the union of two corporations to form a new corporation

Acquisition the purchase of one company by another

Divestiture strategy whereby a firm sells one or more of its business units

Spin-Off strategy of setting up one or more corporate units as new, independent corporations

TomBham/Alamy

Continued from page 60

Conjuring Up Profits?

Facebook has been trying to figure how to best link members and advertisers since 2007. Its first effort, called Facebook Platform, involved allowing developers to build their own businesses on a platform supported by Facebook. By October, the Facebook site had been flooded with more than 4,000 social apps, and the wave of attention—coupled with an upsurge in the number of Facebook users—sealed the investment deal with Microsoft. The next phase, called Beacon, consisted of linking ads with a user's photo when that user bought a product or expressed an opinion about it. Ads and photos were then sent automatically to all the user's Facebook "friends"—the accumulated network of people with whom a user shares comments, photos, and profiles. Advertisers responded quite favorably to the Beacon initiative, and marketers from several companies—including Blockbuster, Condé Nast, and Coke—announced that they intended to make spending on social-networking sites a priority.

The Beacon process called for getting the user's permission to broadcast a commercial message to all his or her friends—but not for consulting those friends, who were unable to avoid any commercial messages. Not surprisingly, critics of the initiative quickly expressed concern about privacy issues, and within a month, the company was presented with a petition containing the names of 50,000 users who objected to its tactics in rolling out the advertising plan. For one thing, it seems that Facebook didn't actually *ask* users' permission to piggyback ads on their personal messages. Rather, it posted less-than-conspicuous notices of its intent to do so and then proceeded to assume that everyone who ignored them was giving tacit permission. In addition, Facebook neglected to inform advertisers that users had to take overt action to opt out of Beacon.

Facebook's "social-advertising" strategy has since evolved into a process called *hypertargeting*, which allows advertisers to select an audience—say, Florida college students who watch the cable TV sports network ESPN—and target simple ads at its members. In February 2009, Facebook announced an initiative called Engagement Ads, which is designed to attract advertisers to the site's potential for market research rather than sales.

Critics point out, however, that Facebook users aren't very good candidates for survey responses. In particular, they tend to use the site strictly for the activities that attracted them to it in the first place—commenting on friends' photos, leaving wall posts, and adding the applications that they want. "Social networks are some of the stickiest sites out there," says advertising consultant Andrew Chen. "They have very low click-through rates." In other words, users stick to the site and don't click on the ads. In fact, while 79 percent of all Internet users click through, only 57 percent of users on sites such as Facebook and MySpace leave the lively interactive environments of the host sites. It's a proclivity that doesn't bode well for monetization in the online social-networking business. The business model, adds Chen, "has to mature significantly before any sort of real revenue or value can be created."

QUESTIONS FOR DISCUSSION

1 Why do you think Facebook has been so successful?
2 Facebook is a corporation. Why do you think the firm uses this form of ownership?
3 What threats might derail Facebook's success? What steps might the firm take today in order to thwart those threats?
4 Suppose Mark Zuckerberg asked you for advice on how to generate more profits from Facebook. What would you tell him?

SUMMARY OF LEARNING OBJECTIVES   MyBizLab

1. **Define *small business*, discuss its importance to the U.S. economy, and explain popular areas of small business. (pp. 60–64)**

A *small business* is independently owned and managed and has relatively little influence in its market. The importance of small business includes (1) *job creation*, (2) *innovation*, and (3) *contributions to big business*. The major small-business industry groups are (1) *services*, (2) *retailing*, (3) *construction*, (4) *wholesaling*, (5) *finance and insurance*, (6) *transportation*, and (7) *manufacturing*.

2. **Explain entrepreneurship and describe some key characteristics of entrepreneurial personalities and activities. (pp. 64–65)**

Entrepreneurs are people who assume the risk of business ownership. *Entrepreneurship* is the process of seeking business opportunities under conditions of risk. Some entrepreneurs have a goal of independence and financial security, while others want to launch a new venture that can be grown into a large business. Most successful entrepreneurs are resourceful and concerned for customer relations. They have a strong desire to be their own bosses and can handle ambiguity and surprises. Today's entrepreneur is often an open-minded leader who relies on networks, business plans, and consensus and is just as likely to be female as male. Finally, although successful entrepreneurs understand the role of risk, they do not necessarily regard what they do as being risky.

3. **Describe the business plan and the start-up decisions made by small businesses and identify sources of financial aid available to such enterprises. (pp. 65–68)**

The starting point for virtually every new business is a *business plan*, in which the entrepreneur summarizes business strategy for the new venture and shows how it will be implemented. Business plans are increasingly important because creditors and investors demand them as tools for deciding whether to finance or invest. Entrepreneurs must also decide whether to buy an existing business, operate a franchise, or start from scratch.

Common funding sources include personal funds, family and friends, savings, lenders, investors, and governmental agencies. *Venture capital companies* are groups of small investors seeking to make profits on companies with rapid growth potential. Most of these firms do not lend money but rather invest it, supplying capital in return for partial ownership. Lending institutions are more likely to finance an existing business than a new business because the risks are better understood.

4. **Discuss the trends in small business start-ups and identify the main reasons for success and failure among small businesses. (pp. 68–71)**

Five factors account for the fact that thousands of new businesses are started in the United States every year: (1) *the emergence of e-commerce*; (2) *entrepreneurs who cross over from big business*; (3) *increased opportunities for minorities and women*; (4) *new opportunities in global enterprise*; and (5) *improved rates of survival among small businesses*.

Four factors contribute to most small-business failure: (1) *managerial incompetence or inexperience*; (2) *neglect*; (3) *weak control systems*; and (4) *insufficient capital*. Likewise, four basic factors explain most small-business success: (1) *hard work, drive, and dedication*; (2) *market demand for the products or services being provided*; (3) *managerial competence*; and (4) *luck*.

5. **Explain sole proprietorships, partnerships, and cooperatives and discuss the advantages and disadvantages of each. (pp. 72–74)**

The *sole proprietorship* is owned and usually operated by one person. There are tax benefits for new businesses that are likely to suffer losses in early stages. A major drawback is *unlimited liability*. Another disadvantage is lack of continuity. Finally, a sole proprietorship depends on the resources of a single individual. The *general partnership* is a sole proprietorship multiplied by the number of partner-owners. The biggest advantage is its ability to grow by adding new talent and money. A partnership is not a legal entity. It is just two or more people working together. Partners are taxed as individuals, and *unlimited liability* is a drawback. Partnerships may lack continuity, and transferring ownership may be hard. No partner may sell out without the consent of the others. *Cooperatives* combine the freedom of sole proprietorships with the financial power of corporations.

6. **Describe corporations, discuss their advantages and disadvantages, and identify different kinds of corporations; explain the basic issues involved in managing a corporation and discuss special issues related to corporate ownership. (pp. 74–79)**

All *corporations* share certain characteristics: legal status as separate entities, property rights and obligations, and indefinite life spans. They may sue and be sued; buy, hold, and sell property; make and sell products; and commit crimes and be tried and punished for them. The biggest advantage of incorporation is *limited liability*: Investor liability is limited to one's personal investments in the corporation. Another advantage is continuity. Finally, corporations have advantages in raising money. By selling stock, they expand the number of investors and the amount of available funds. Legal protections tend to make lenders more willing to grant loans.

One disadvantage is that a corporation can be taken over against the will of its managers. Another disadvantage is start-up cost. Corporations are heavily regulated and must meet complex legal requirements in the states in which they're chartered. The greatest potential drawback to incorporation is *double taxation*. Different kinds of corporations help businesses take advantage of incorporation without assuming all of the disadvantages.

Corporations sell shares, called *stock*, to investors who then become *stockholders* (or shareholders) and the real owners. Profits are distributed among stockholders in the form of *dividends*, and managers serve at their discretion.

The governing body of a corporation is its *board of directors*. Most board members do not participate in day-to-day management but rather hire a team of managers. This team, called *officers*, is usually headed by a *chief executive officer (CEO)* who is responsible for overall performance. Several issues have grown in importance in the area of corporate ownership. In a *strategic alliance*, two or more organizations collaborate on a project for mutual gain. When partners share ownership of a new enterprise, the arrangement is called a *joint venture*. The *employee stock ownership plan (ESOP)* allows employees to own a significant share of the corporation through trusts established on their behalf. More stock is now being purchased by institutional investors. A *merger* occurs when two firms combine to create a new company. In an *acquisition*, one firm buys another outright. A *divestiture* occurs when a corporation sells a part of its existing business operations or sets it up as a new and independent corporation. When a firm sells part of itself to raise capital, the strategy is known as a *spin-off*.

KEY TERMS   MyBizLab

acquisition (p. 78)
board of directors (p. 78)
business plan (p. 65)
chief executive
    officer (CEO) (p. 78)
closely held (or private)
    corporation (p. 76)
cooperative (p. 74)
corporate governance (p. 77)
corporation (p. 74)
divestiture (p. 79)
double taxation (p. 76)
employee stock ownership
    plan (ESOP) (p. 78)
entrepreneur (p. 64)
entrepreneurship (p. 64)
franchise (p. 66)

general (or active) partner (p. 74)
general partnership (p. 73)
institutional investor (p. 78)
joint venture (p. 78)
limited liability (p. 75)
limited liability corporation
    (LLC) (p. 77)
limited partner (p. 74)
limited partnership (p. 74)
master limited partnership (p. 74)
merger (p. 78)
multinational (or transnational)
    corporation (p. 77)
officers (p. 78)
professional corporation (p. 77)
publicly held (or public)
    corporation (p. 76)

S corporation (p. 77)
small business (p. 60)
Small Business Administration
    (SBA) (p. 60)
Small Business Development
    Center (SBDC) (p. 68)
small-business investment
    company (SBIC) (p. 68)
sole proprietorship (p. 72)
spin-off (p. 79)
stockholder
    (or shareholder) (p. 77)
strategic alliance (p. 78)
tender offer (p. 75)
unlimited liability (p. 72)
venture capital
    company (p. 68)

QUESTIONS AND EXERCISES

QUESTIONS FOR REVIEW

1. Why are small businesses important to the U.S. economy?
2. Which industries are easiest for start-ups to enter? Which are hardest? Why?
3. What are the primary reasons for new business failure and success?
4. What are the basic forms of noncorporate business ownership? What are the key advantages and disadvantages of each?

QUESTIONS FOR ANALYSIS

5. Why might a closely held corporation choose to remain private? Why might it choose to be publicly traded?
6. If you were going to open a new business, what type would it be? Why?

7. Would you prefer to buy an existing business or start from scratch? Why?
8. Under what circumstances might it be wise for an entrepreneur to reject venture capital? Under what circumstances might it be advisable to take more venture capital than he or she actually needs?

APPLICATION EXERCISES

9. Interview the owner/manager of a sole proprietorship or a general partnership. What characteristics of that business form led the owner to choose it? Does he or she ever contemplate changing the form of the business?
10. Identify two or three of the fastest growing businesses in the United States during the last year. What role has entrepreneurship played in the growth of these firms?

BUILDING YOUR BUSINESS SKILLS

Working the Internet

Goal
To encourage you to define the opportunities and problems for new companies doing business on the Internet.

Background Information
Let's say that you and two partners plan to launch a new business. Using a virtual storefront on the Internet, you intend to offer local delivery services for books and magazines. Customers can select books and magazines after perusing any online retailer's listings. But rather than placing an order with that retailer, which then entails paying postage and waiting several days for delivery, customers can place their order with your local company. You will purchase the desired item from a local discounter, deliver it within two hours, and collect a full retail price from the customer. Your profit margin will be the difference between the discount price you pay and the full retail price you collect from your customers.

Method

Step 1
Join with two other students and assume the role of business partners. Start by discussing this idea among yourselves. Identify as many strengths and weaknesses as possible for your potential new venture.

Step 2
Based on your assessment, now determine the importance of the following new business issues:
- Analyzing your competitive marketplace and how you should go about promoting your service
- Identifying sources of management advice as expansion proceeds
- The role of technology consultants in launching and maintaining a website
- Customer-service policies and costs in a virtual environment
- The primary pitfalls that could derail your business

FOLLOW-UP QUESTIONS
1. Do you think this business would be successful? Why or why not?
2. Based on your analysis, what future developments could most affect your business? How might you best prepare yourself for these developments?
3. Do you think that operating a virtual storefront will be harder or easier than doing business from a traditional brick-and-mortar operation? Explain your answer.

EXERCISING YOUR ETHICS: INDIVIDUAL EXERCISE

Breaking Up Is Hard to Do

The Situation
Connie and Mark began a 25-year friendship after finishing college and discovering their mutual interest in owning a business. Established as a general partnership, their home-furnishings center is a successful business sustained for 20 years by a share-and-share-alike relationship. Start-up cash, daily responsibilities, and profits have all been shared equally. The partners both work four days each week except when busy seasons require both of them to be in the store. Shared goals and compatible personalities have led to a solid give-and-take relationship that helps them overcome business problems while maintaining a happy interpersonal relationship.

The division of work is a natural match and successful combination because of the partners' different but complementary interests. Mark buys the merchandise and maintains up-to-date contacts with suppliers; he also handles personnel matters (hiring and training employees). Connie manages the inventory, buys shipping supplies, keeps the books, and manages the finances. Mark does more selling, with Connie helping out only during busy seasons. Both partners share in decisions about advertising and promotions.

The Dilemma
Things began changing two years ago, when Connie became less interested in the business and got more involved in other activities. Whereas Mark's enthusiasm remained high, Connie's time was increasingly consumed by travel, recreation, and community-service activities. At first, she reduced her work commitment from four to three days a week. Then she indicated that she wanted to cut back further, to just two days. "In that case," Mark replied, "we'll have to make some changes."

Mark insisted that profit sharing be adjusted to reflect his larger role in running the business. He proposed that Connie's monthly salary be cut in half (from $4,000 to $2,000). Connie agreed. He recommended that the $2,000 savings be shifted to his salary because of his increased workload, but this time Connie balked, arguing that Mark's current $4,000 salary already compensated him for his contributions. She proposed to split the difference, with Mark getting a $1,000 increase and the other $1,000 going into the firm's cash account. Mark said no and insisted on a full $2,000 raise. To avoid a complete falling out, Connie finally gave in, even though she thought it unfair for Mark's salary to jump from $4,000 per month to $6,000. At that point, she made a promise to herself: "To even things out, I'll find a way to get $2,000 worth of inventory for personal use each month."

QUESTIONS TO ADDRESS
1 Identify the ethical issues, if any, regarding Mark's and Connie's respective positions on Mark's proposed $2,000 salary increase.
2 What kind of salary adjustments do you think would be fair in this situation? Explain why.
3 There is another way for Mark and Connie to solve their differences: Because the terms of participation have changed, it might make sense to dissolve the existing partnership. What do you recommend in this regard?

EXERCISING YOUR ETHICS: TEAM EXERCISE

Public or Private? That Is the Question

The Situation

The Thomas Corporation is a very well-financed, private corporation with a solid and growing product line, little debt, and a stable workforce. However, in the past few months, there has been a growing rift among the board of directors that has created considerable differences of opinion as to the future directions of the firm.

The Dilemma

Some board members believe the firm should "go public" with a stock offering. Since each board member owns a large block of corporate stock, each would make a considerable amount of money if the company went public.

Other board members want to maintain the status quo as a private corporation. The biggest advantage of this approach is that the firm maintains its current ability to remain autonomous in its operations.

The third faction of the board also wants to remain private, but clearly has a different agenda. Those board members have identified a small public corporation that is currently one of the company's key suppliers. Their idea is to buy the supplying company, shift its assets to the parent firm, sell all of its remaining operations, terminate employees, and then outsource the production of the parts it currently buys from the firm. Their logic is that the firm would gain significant assets and lower its costs.

Team Activity

Assemble a group of four students and assign each group member to one of the following roles:

- An employee at the Thomas Corporation
- A customer of the Thomas Corporation
- An investor in the Thomas Corporation
- A board member who has not yet decided which option is best

ACTION STEPS

1 Before hearing any of your group's comments on this situation, and from the perspective of your assigned role, which option do you think is best? Write down the reasons for your position.

2 Before hearing any of your group's comments on this situation, and from the perspective of your assigned role, what are the underlying ethical issues, if any, in this situation? Write down the issues.

3 Gather your group together and reveal, in turn, each member's comments on the situation. Next, reveal the ethical issues listed by each member.

4 Appoint someone to record main points of agreement and disagreement within the group. How do you explain the results? What accounts for any disagreement?

5 From an ethical standpoint, what does your group conclude is the most appropriate action that should have been taken by the Thomas Corporation in this situation?

6 Develop a group response to the following question: What do you think most people would do in this situation?

VIDEO EXERCISE   MyBizLab

WILD PLANET

Learning Objectives

The purpose of this video is to help you:

1 Define entrepreneurship and describe the entrepreneurial personality.
2 Identify the sources of financing for small businesses.
3 List the advantages and disadvantages of the primary forms of business ownership.

Synopsis

Wild Planet is a strong player in the toy industry, focusing on toys that are fun, imaginative, and unique. Wild Planet offers toys for children of all ages, even adults. Some of their most popular toys include Aquapets, Crayon Town activity sets, and Squatz Fizz-and-Find collectible toys. The Spy Gear TRAKR is a remote controlled vehicle that transmits color video as well as audio, perfect for every aspiring spy. Daniel Grossman began the company in 1993, already having experience in the toy industry. Starting out as a small business, he was unable to produce toys in-house. He focused on design and contracted out production operations overseas, where the cost of production was much lower. Wild Planet's success is largely due to the creativity of the design team, who work collaboratively to develop fun and distinctive products. Today, Wild Planet's toys can be found in over 50 countries, in small specialty stores as well as mast-market retailers.

DISCUSSION QUESTIONS

1 What is an entrepreneur? Do you think that Daniel Grossman possesses the characteristics commonly associated with entrepreneurs? Why or why not?

2 How did Wild Planet get its initial financing? Is this typical of small business?

3 What are the primary advantages and disadvantages of organizing as a sole proprietorship or partnership? Why do you think that Wild Planet decided not to chose either of these forms?

4 What are the advantages and disadvantages of organizing as a corporation? How do these relate to Wild Planet and their decision on a form of ownership?

5 DBA ultimately decided to organize as a private corporation. What factors led to this decision?

Online Exploration

Wild Planet's success is built on creativity and innovation, as well as the ability to adapt and change over time. After visiting the company's website, www.wildplanet.com, you will be able to find out more about their latest products, as well as management team. As the company grows, the company could choose to go public and sell stock. What are the advantages and disadvantages of going public to the owners and employees of Wild Planet? Do you think that this is a viable option? Why or why not?

END NOTES

[1] David Kushner, "The Web's Hottest Site: Facebook.com," *Rolling Stone*, April 7, 2006, pp. 5–7; Brad Stone, "Microsoft Buys Stake in Facebook," *New York Times*, October 25, 2007, p. B1; Michael Arrington, "Social Networking: Will Facebook Overtake MySpace in the U.S. in 2009?" *Tech Crunch*, January 13, 2009, p. 4; "MySpace Might Have Friends, but It Wants Ad Money," *New York Times*, June 16, 2008, p. 9; C. T. Moore, "The Future of Facebook Revenues," *ReveNews*, February 15, 2009, pp. 4–6.

[2] See http://www.sba.gov.

[3] See http://www.sba.gov/aboutsba.

[4] "A New Generation Re-Writes the Rules," *Wall Street Journal* (May 22, 2002), R4; See also Mark Henricks, "Up to the Challenge," *Entrepreneur* (February 2006), 64–67.

[5] "Special Report—Stars of Asia," *BusinessWeek* (July 12, 2004), p. 18.

[6] "Special Report—Stars of Asia," *BusinessWeek* (July 12, 2004), at 18.

[7] See Thomas Zimmerer and Norman Scarborough, *Essentials of Entrepreneurship and Small Business Management*, 5th ed. (Upper Saddle River, NJ: Prentice Hall, 2008).

[8] James Combs, David Ketchen, Christopher Shook, and Jeremy Short, "Antecedents and Consequences of Franchising: Past Accomplishments and Future Challenges, *Journal of Management*, January 2011, pp. 99–126.

[9] U.S. Small Business Administration, "Finance Primer: A Guide to SBA's Loan Guaranty Programs," http://app1.sba.gov/training/sbafp/, accessed February 20, 2011.

[10] Ibid.

[11] U.S. Census Bureau, "1997 Economic Census Surveys of Minority- and Women-Owned Business Enterprises," at http://www.census.gov/csd/mwb.

[12] Peter Hoy, "Minority- and Women-Owned Businesses Skyrocket," *Inc.* (May 1, 2006), pp. 20–24.

[13] Zimmerer and Scarborough, 20.

[14] See U.S. Small Business Administration, "Frequently Asked Questions," at http://app1.sba.gov/faqs/faqIndexAll.cfm?areaid=24, accessed February 20, 2011.

[15] Zimmerer and Scarborough.

[16] *Hoover's Handbook of Emerging Companies 2011* (Austin: Hoover's Business Press, 2011), p. 299; "A Pioneer in One-Stop Home Entertainment," *Time*, April 26, 2011, p. 49; "Is Netflix Looking Over its Shoulder?" *Business Week*, February 19, 2011, pp. 84-85; "Hire the Best, Keep the Best—Neflix's Recipe for Success," *HR Magazine*, January 2011, pp. 51-53.

[17] See "Gladys Edmunds Biography," at http://biography.jrank.org/pages/2404/Edmunds-Gladys.html, accessed February 20, 2011.

[18] Ibid.

4 The Global Context of Business

Delicious Chocolate...But at What Price?

Did you ever wonder where the chocolate in your favorite candy bar comes from? It might surprise you to know that virtually all of the chocolate you consume starts out halfway around the world. Chocolate comes from small beans that grow on cocoa trees. It takes about 400 beans to make a pound of chocolate. To harvest the beans, laborers have to chop them from the trees, slice them open, scoop out the beans, spread them on mats, and cover them to ferment. Once the beans are fermented, they're dried, packed in heavy bags, and carried to waiting trucks by the same laborers. At that point, they've entered the supply chain that will take them to the United States or Europe, where they'll be turned into Snickers candy bars or Dreyer's Double Fudge Brownie ice cream.

Over 40 percent of the world's cocoa bean supply comes from small farms scattered throughout the West African nation of Ivory Coast, which may ship as much as 47,000 tons per month to the United States. Unfortunately, though, according to reports issued about ten years ago by the United Nations Children's Fund and the U.S. State Department, much of the labor involved in Ivory Coast cocoa production is performed by children, mostly boys ranging in age from 12 to 16. The children—perhaps as many as 15,000 of them—work 12 hours a day, 7 days a week. They are often beaten to maintain productivity quotas and they sleep on bare wooden planks in cramped rooms. Most of them were tricked or sold into forced labor, many by destitute parents

After reading this chapter, you should be able to:

1 **Discuss the rise of international business and describe the major world marketplaces, trade agreements, and alliances.**
2 **Explain how differences in import-export balances, exchange rates, and foreign competition determine the ways in which countries and businesses respond to the international environment.**
3 **Discuss the factors involved in deciding to do business internationally and in selecting the appropriate levels of international involvement and international organizational structure.**
4 **Describe some of the ways in which social, cultural, economic, legal, and political differences among nations affect international business.**

who couldn't feed them. In the decade following the initial reports of abusive conditions, efforts to alleviate the problem have met with relatively little success.

How did enslaving children become business as usual in the Ivory Coast cocoa industry? Because a full one-third of the country's economy is based on cocoa exports, Ivory Coast is heavily dependent on world market prices for cocoa. Unfortunately, cocoa is an extremely unstable commodity—global prices fluctuate significantly. Profitability in the cocoa industry, therefore, depends on prices over which farmers have no control. This problem is compounded by unpredictable natural conditions, such as drought, over which they also have no control. To improve their chances of making a profit, they look for ways to cut costs, and the use of slave labor—in their mind—is the most effective money-saving measure.

Photo Researchers

WHAT'S IN IT FOR ME?

Regardless of whether you see yourself living abroad, working for a big company, or starting your own business, the global economy will affect you in some way. Exchange rates for different currencies and global markets for buying and selling are all of major importance to everyone, regardless of their role or perspective. As a result, this chapter will better enable you to (1) understand how global forces affect you as a customer, (2) understand how globalization affects you as an employee, and (3) assess how global opportunities and challenges can affect you as a business owner and as an investor. You will also gain insights into how wages and working conditions in different regions are linked to what we buy and the prices we pay.

This chapter explores the global context of business. We begin with an exploration of the major world marketplaces and trade agreements that affect international business. Next, we examine several factors that help determine how countries and businesses respond to international opportunities and challenges. We then direct our attention to some of the decisions managers must make if they intend to compete in international markets. Finally, we conclude with a discussion of some of the social, cultural, economic, legal, and political factors that affect international business.

MyBizLab Where you see MyBizLab in this chapter, go to **www.mybizlab.com** for additional activities on the topic being discussed.

This is where the idea of "fair trade" comes in. *Fair trade* refers to programs designed to ensure that export-dependent farmers in developing countries receive fair prices for their crops. Several such programs are sponsored by Fairtrade Labelling Organizations International (FLO), a global nonprofit network of fair-trade groups headquartered in Germany. Here's how it works. FLO partners with cooperatives representing cocoa producers in Africa and Latin America to establish certain standards, not only for the producers' products but also for their operations and socially relevant policies (such as enforcing anti–child labor laws and providing education and health care services). In return, FLO guarantees producers a "Fairtrade Minimum Price" for their products. In early 2011, FLO guaranteed cocoa farmers a price of $1,750 per ton. If the market price falls below that level, FLO covers the difference. If the market price tops $1,750, FLO pays producers a premium of $150 per ton.

Where does the money come from? The cost is borne by the importers, manufacturers, and distributors who buy and sell cocoa from FLO-certified producers. These companies are in turn monitored by a network of FLO-owned organizations called TransFair, which ensures that FLO criteria are met and that FLO-certified producers receive the fair prices guaranteed by FLO. Products that meet the appropriate FLO-TransFair criteria are entitled to bear labels attesting that they're "Fair Trade Certified™." At present, semifinished and branded chocolate products certified by TransFair USA can be found in more than 1,600 U.S. retail locations, including Safeway and Whole Foods stores.

What incentive encourages importers, manufacturers, and distributors not only to adopt FLO-TransFair standards but also to bear the costs of subsidizing overseas producers? They get the right to promote their chocolate products not only as "fair-trade" but, often, as "organic" products as well—categories that typically command premium retail prices. In fact, FLO pays an even higher premium on organically certified cocoa—$200 instead of $150 per ton—and the extra cost, of course, shows up in retail prices. Organic chocolate products are priced in the same range as luxury chocolates, but consumers appear to be willing to pay the relatively high asking prices—not only for organic products but also for all kinds of chocolate products bearing the Fair Trade Certified label. TransFair USA chief executive Paul Rice explains that when consumers know they're supporting programs to empower farmers in developing countries, sellers and resellers can charge "dramatically higher prices, often two to three times higher." Consumers, he says, "put their money where their mouth is and pay a little more."

A 3.5-ounce candy bar labeled "organic fair trade" may sell for $3.49, compared to about $1.50 for one that's not. Why so much? Because the fair-trade candy bar, says TransFair USA spokesperson Nicole Chettero, still occupies a niche market. "As the demand and volume of Fair Trade-certified products increase," she predicts, "the market will work itself out….[R]etailers will naturally start to drop prices to remain competitive." Ultimately, she concludes, "there is no reason why fair-trade [products] should cost astronomically more than traditional products."[1]

Our opening story continues on page 106.

The Contemporary Global Economy

1 Discuss the rise of international business and describe the major world marketplaces, trade agreements, and alliances.

The total volume of world trade is immense—over $12 trillion in merchandise trade each year. Foreign investment in the United States is over $150 billion, and U.S. investment abroad exceeds $300 billion. As more firms engage in international business, the world economy is fast becoming an interdependent system—a process called **globalization.**

We often take for granted the diversity of products we can buy as a result of international trade. Your television, your shoes, and even your morning coffee or juice are probably **imports**—products made or grown abroad and sold domestically in the United States. At the same time, the success of many U.S. firms depends on **exports**—products made or grown here, such as machinery, electronic equipment, and grains, and shipped for sale abroad.

Firms like McDonald's, Microsoft, Apple, and Starbucks have found international markets to be a fruitful area for growth. But firms sometime stumble when they try to expand abroad. Home Depot has closed most of the stores it opened in China, for example, because labor costs are so low there few homeowners are interested in "do-it-yourself" projects. Similarly, Best Buy also closed its stores in China because consumers there tend to buy their electronics goods at lower prices from local merchants or from online merchants.[2]

And the impact of globalization doesn't stop with firms looking to open locations abroad or having to close locations that fail. Small firms with no international operations (such as an independent coffee shop) may still buy from international suppliers, and even individual contractors or self-employed people can be affected by fluctuations in exchange rates.

Indeed, international trade is becoming increasingly important to most nations and their businesses. Many countries that once followed strict policies to protect domestic business now encourage trade just as aggressively. They are opening borders to foreign business, offering incentives for domestic businesses to expand internationally, and making it easier for foreign firms to partner with local firms. Likewise, as more industries and markets become global, so, too, are the firms that compete in them.

Several forces have combined to spark and sustain globalization. For one thing, governments and businesses are more aware of the benefits of globalization to businesses and shareholders. These benefits include the potential for higher standards of living and improved business profitability. New technologies have made international travel, communication, and commerce faster and cheaper than ever before. Finally, there are competitive pressures: Sometimes a firm must expand into foreign markets simply to keep up with competitors.

Gain hands-on experience through an interactive, real-world scenario. This chapter's simulation entitled Going Global is located at www.mybizlab.com.

Globalization process by which the world economy is becoming a single interdependent system

Import product made or grown abroad but sold domestically

Export product made or grown domestically but shipped and sold abroad

Islemount Images/Alamy

Some globalization protestors like this man fear that multinational companies will wipe out small domestic businesses like family farms.

Globalization is not without its detractors. Some critics charge that globalization allows businesses to exploit workers in less developed countries and bypass domestic environmental and tax regulations. They also charge that globalization leads to the loss of cultural heritages and often benefits the rich more than the poor. As a result, many international gatherings of global economic leaders are marked by protests and demonstrations.

The Major World Marketplaces

Managers involved with international businesses need to have a solid understanding of the global economy, including the major world marketplaces. This section examines some fundamental economic distinctions between countries based on wealth and then looks at some of the world's major international marketplaces.

Distinctions Based on Wealth   The World Bank, an agency of the United Nations, uses per-capita income—average income per person—to make distinctions among countries. Its current classification method consists of four different categories of countries:[3]

1 *High-income countries.* Those with annual per-capita income greater than $11,115

2 *Upper-middle-income countries.* Those with annual per-capita income of $11,115 or less but more than $3,595

3 *Lower-middle-income countries.* Those with annual per-capita income of $3,595 or lower but more than $905

4 *Low-income countries (often called developing countries).* Those with annual per-capita income of $905 or less

Geographic Clusters   The world economy revolves around three major marketplaces: North America, Europe, and Pacific Asia. In general, these clusters include relatively more of the upper-middle and high-income nations but relatively few low- and lower-middle-income countries.

North America   As the world's largest marketplace and most stable economy, the United States dominates the North American market. Canada also plays a major role in the international economy, and the United States and Canada are each other's largest trading partners.

Mexico has become a major manufacturing center, especially along the U.S. border, where cheap labor and low transportation costs have encouraged many firms from the United States and other countries to build factories. However, Mexico's role as a low-cost manufacturing center may have peaked. The emergence of China as a low-cost manufacturing center may lead companies to begin to shift their production from Mexico to China.[4] (The escalating drug-related violence along the northern Mexican border is also contributing to this shift.)

Europe   Europe is often regarded as two regions—Western and Eastern. Western Europe, dominated by Germany, the United Kingdom, and France, has long been a mature but fragmented marketplace. The transformation of this region via the European Union (discussed later) into an integrated economic system has further increased its importance. E-commerce and technology have also become increasingly important in this region. There has been a surge in Internet start-ups in southeastern England, the Netherlands, and the Scandinavian countries; Ireland is now one of the world's largest exporters of software; Strasbourg, France, is a major center for biotech start-ups; Barcelona, Spain, has many flourishing software and Internet companies; and the Frankfurt region of Germany is dotted with software and biotech start-ups.

Eastern Europe, once primarily communist, has also gained in importance, both as a marketplace and as a producer. Such multinational corporations as Daewoo, Nestlé, General Motors, and ABB Asea Brown Boveri have all set up operations in Poland. Ford, General Motors, Suzuki, and Volkswagen have all built new factories in Hungary. On the other hand, governmental instability has hampered development in parts of Russia, Bulgaria, Albania, Romania, and other countries.

Pacific Asia Pacific Asia is generally agreed to consist of Japan, China, Thailand, Malaysia, Singapore, Indonesia, South Korea, Taiwan, the Philippines, and Australia. Fueled by strong entries in the automobile, electronics, and banking industries, the economies of these countries grew rapidly in the 1970s and 1980s. After a currency crisis in the late 1990s that slowed growth in virtually every country of the region, Pacific Asia was showing clear signs of revitalization until the global recession in 2009. As the global economy begins to regain its momentum, Pacific Asia is expected to again be on the forefront. This is especially true of Japan, which—led by firms such as Toyota, Toshiba, and Nippon Steel—dominates the region. South Korea (home to firms Samsung and Hyundai, among others), Taiwan (owner of Chinese Petroleum and the manufacturing home of many foreign firms), and Hong Kong (a major financial center) are also successful players in the international economy.

China, the world's most densely populated country, has emerged as an important market and now boasts the world's third-largest economy, behind only the European Union and the United States.[5] Although its per-capita income remains low, the sheer number of potential consumers makes it an important market. India, though not part of Pacific Asia, is also rapidly emerging as one of the globe's most important economies.

As in North America and Europe, technology promises to play an increasingly important role in the future of this region. In some parts of Asia, however, poorly developed electronic infrastructures, slower adoption of computers and information technology, and a higher percentage of lower-income consumers hamper the emergence of technology firms.

Trade Agreements and Alliances

Various legal agreements have sparked international trade and shaped the global business environment. Indeed, virtually every nation has formal trade treaties with other nations. A *treaty* is a legal agreement that specifies areas in which nations will cooperate with one another. Among the most significant treaties is the *North American Free Trade Agreement*. The *European Union*, the *Association of Southeast Asian Nations*, and the *World Trade Organization*, all governed by treaties, are also instrumental in promoting international business activity.

North American Free Trade Agreement   The **North American Free Trade Agreement (NAFTA)** removes most tariffs and other trade barriers among the United States, Canada, and Mexico and includes agreements on environmental issues and labor abuses.

Most observers agree that NAFTA is achieving its basic purpose—to create a more active North American market. It has created several hundred thousand new jobs, although this number is smaller than NAFTA proponents had hoped. One thing is clear, though—the flood of U.S. jobs lost to Mexico predicted by NAFTA critics, especially labor unions, has not occurred.

North American Free Trade Agreement (NAFTA) agreement to gradually eliminate tariffs and other trade barriers among the United States, Canada, and Mexico

The European Union   The **European Union (EU)** includes most European nations, as shown in Figure 4.1. These nations have eliminated most quotas and set uniform tariff levels on products imported and exported within their group. In 1992, virtually all internal trade barriers went down, making the EU the largest free marketplace in the world. The adoption of a common currency—the euro—by most member nations further solidified the EU's position in the world economy.

The Association of Southeast Asian Nations (ASEAN)   The **Association of Southeast Asian Nations (ASEAN)** was founded in 1967 as an organization for economic, political, social, and cultural cooperation. In 1995, Vietnam became the group's first Communist member. Figure 4.2 shows a map of the ASEAN countries. Because of its relative size, ASEAN does not have the same global economic significance as NAFTA and the EU.

The World Trade Organization   The **General Agreement on Tariffs and Trade (GATT)** was signed in 1947. Its purpose was to reduce or eliminate trade barriers, such as tariffs and quotas. It did so by encouraging nations to protect domestic industries within agreed-upon limits and to engage in multilateral negotiations. The GATT proved to be relatively successful. So, to further promote globalization, most of the world's countries joined to create the **World Trade Organization (WTO)**, which began on January 1, 1995. (The GATT is the actual treaty that governs the WTO.) The 152 member countries are required to open markets to international trade, and the WTO is empowered to pursue three goals:[6]

1 Promote trade by encouraging members to adopt fair trade practices.

2 Reduce trade barriers by promoting multilateral negotiations.

3 Establish fair procedures for resolving disputes among members.

Figure 4.1 The Nations of the European Union
Source: Europe, at *http://europa.eu/abc/maps/index_en.htm*, accessed October 22, 2011.

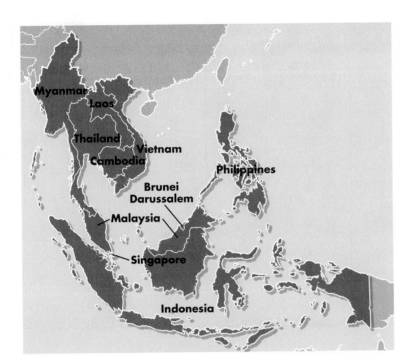

Figure 4.2 **The Nations of the Association of Southeast Asian Nations (ASEAN)**
Source: Association of Southeast Asian Nations, at *http://www.aseansec.org/ 74.htm*, accessed October 22, 2011.

International Trade

The global economy is essentially defined by international trade. International trade occurs when an exchange takes place across national boundaries. Although international trade has many advantages, it can also pose problems if a country's imports and exports don't maintain an acceptable balance. Table 4.1 lists the major trading partners of the United States. The left of the table shows the 10 largest markets for exports from the United States, while the right of the table shows the 10 largest markets that import to the United States.

Note that many countries are on both lists (China and Canada, for instance). However, the United States also does business with many more countries. For instance, in 2010, the United States exported $3.8 billion to Egypt, $1.96 billion to Kuwait, $645 million to Poland, and $29 million to Zambia; imports from those same countries were $1.14 billion, $1.55 billion, $1.27 billion, and $8.8 million, respectively. In deciding whether an overall balance exists between imports and exports, economists use two measures: *balance of trade* and *balance of payments*.

Balance of Trade   A country's **balance of trade** is the total economic value of all the products that it exports minus the economic value of all the products that it imports. A *positive balance of trade* results when a country exports (sells to other countries) more than it imports (buys from other countries). A *negative balance of trade* results when a country imports more than it exports.

Relatively small trade imbalances are common and are unimportant. Large imbalances, however, are another matter. The biggest concern about trade balances involves the flow of currency. When U.S. consumers and businesses buy foreign

2 Explain how differences in import-export balances, exchange rates, and foreign competition determine the ways in which countries and businesses respond to the international environment.

European Union (EU) agreement among major European nations to eliminate or make uniform most trade barriers affecting group members

Association of Southeast Asian Nations (ASEAN) organization for economic, political, social, and cultural cooperation among Southeast Asian nations

General Agreement on Tariffs and Trade (GATT) international trade agreement to encourage the multilateral reduction or elimination of trade barriers

World Trade Organization (WTO) organization through which member nations negotiate trading agreements and resolve disputes about trade policies and practices

Balance of Trade economic value of all products a country exports minus the economic value of all products it imports

TABLE 4.1   Major Trading Partners of the U.S.

Country	Imports ($ billions)	Rank	Country	Exports ($ billions)	Rank
China	345	1	Canada	235	1
Canada	258	2	Mexico	153	2
Mexico	215	3	China	90	3
Japan	112	4	Japan	61	4
Federal Republic of Germany	77	5	United Kingdom	49	5
United Kingdom	49	6	Federal Republic of Germany	48	6
South Korea	47	7	South Korea	39	7
France	38	8	Brazil	35	8
Taiwan	35	9	Netherlands	34	9
Ireland	32	10	Singapore	30	10

products, dollars flow from the United States to other countries; when U.S. businesses are selling to foreign consumers and businesses, dollars flow back into the United States. A large negative balance of trade means that many dollars are controlled by interests outside the United States.

Trade Deficits and Surpluses   When a country's imports exceed its exports—that is, when it has a negative balance of trade—it suffers a **trade deficit.** When exports exceed imports, the nation enjoys a **trade surplus.** Several factors, such as general economic conditions and the effect of trade agreements, influence trade deficits and surpluses. For example, higher domestic costs, greater international competition, and continuing economic problems among some of its regional trading partners have slowed the tremendous growth in exports that Japan once enjoyed. But rising prosperity in China and India has led to strong increases in both exports from and imports to those countries.

Figures 4.3 and 4.4 highlight two series of events: (1) recent trends in U.S. exports and imports and (2) the resulting trade deficit. As Figure 4.3 shows, both U.S. imports and U.S. exports have, with minor variations, increased over the past eight years—a trend that's projected to continue.

Trade deficits between 2000 and 2010 are shown in Figure 4.4. There was a deficit in each of these years because more money flowed out to pay for foreign imports than flowed in to pay for U.S. exports. For example, in 2008, the United States exported $1,300.50 billion in goods and services and imported $2,100.4 billion in goods and services. Because imports exceeded exports, the United States had a *trade deficit* of $800 billion (the difference between exports and imports). Note also that both experts and imports declined in 2008 and 2009 from the previous year. This was due to the global economic slowdown.

Balance of Payments   The **balance of payments** refers to the flow of *money* into or out of a country. The money that a country pays for imports and receives for exports—its balance of trade—accounts for much of its balance of payments. Other financial exchanges are also factors. Money spent by tourists in a country, money spent by a country on foreign-aid programs, and money exchanged by buying and selling currency on international money markets affect the balance of payments.

For instance, suppose that the United States has a negative balance of trade of $1 million. Now, suppose that this year, U.S. citizens travel abroad as tourists and spend a total of $200,000 in other countries. This amount gets added to the balance of trade to form the balance of payments, which is now a negative $1.2 million dollars. Now, further suppose that tourists from other countries come to the United States and spend the equivalent of $300,000 while they are here. This has the effect of

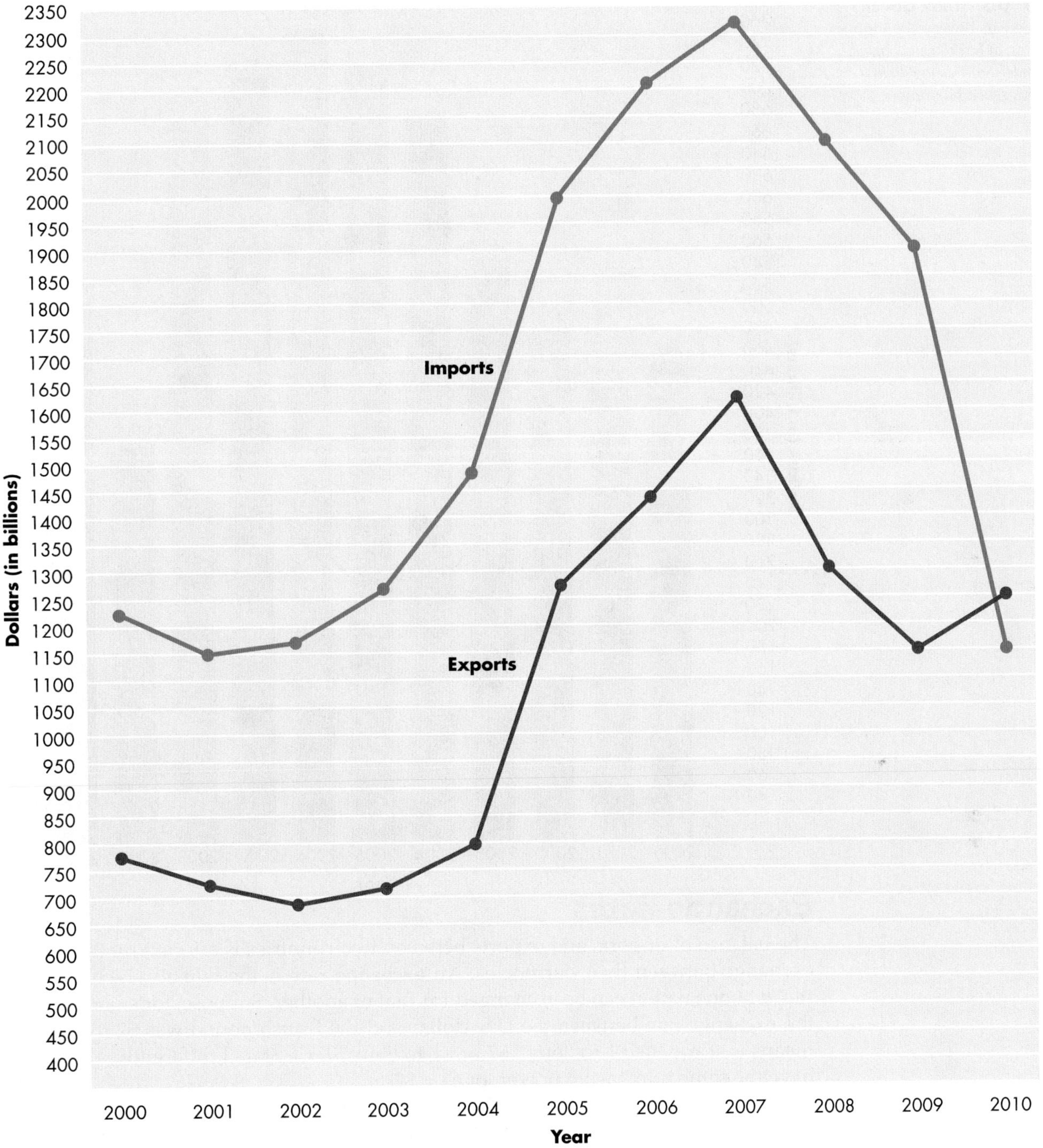

Figure 4.3 **U.S. Imports and Exports**
Source: U.S. Census Bureau: Foreign Trade Statistics, at *http://www.census.gov/foreign-trade/statistics/highlights/annual.html*, accessed November 11, 2011.

reducing the negative balance of payments to $900,000. Then, further suppose that the United States then sends $600,000 in aid to help the victims of a tsunami-ravaged country in Asia. Because this represents additional dollars leaving the United States, the balance of payments is now a negative $1.5 million. For many years, the United States enjoyed a positive balance of payments. Recently, however, the overall balance has become negative.

Trade Deficit situation in which a country's imports exceed its exports, creating a negative balance of trade	**Trade Surplus** situation in which a country's exports exceed its imports, creating a positive balance of trade	**Balance of Payments** flow of all money into or out of a country

Figure 4.4 U.S. Trade Deficit
Source: U.S. Census Bureau: Foreign Trade Statistics, at *http://www.census.gov/foreign-trade/statistics/highlights/annual.html*, accessed November 11, 2011.

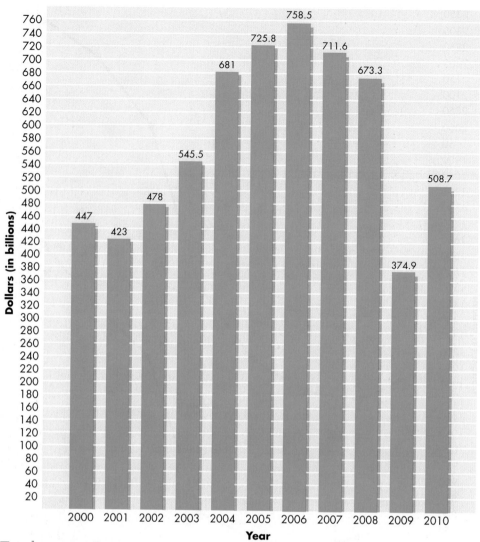

Exchange Rates

The balance of imports and exports between two countries is affected by the rate of exchange between their currencies. An **exchange rate** is the rate at which the currency of one nation can be exchanged for that of another. Suppose, for example, that the exchange rate between the U.S. dollar and the British pound was $2 to £1. This means that it costs £1 to "buy" $2 or $1 to "buy" £0.5. Stated differently, £1 and $2 have the same purchasing power, or £1 = $2.

At the end of World War II, the major nations of the world agreed to set *fixed exchange rates*. The value of any country's currency relative to that of another would remain constant. The goal was to allow the global economy to stabilize. Today, however, *floating exchange rates* are the norm, and the value of one country's currency relative to that of another varies with market conditions. For example, when many British citizens want to spend pounds to buy U.S. dollars (or goods), the value of the dollar relative to the pound increases. Demand for the dollar is high, and a currency is strong when demand for it is high. It's also strong when there's high demand for the goods manufactured with that currency. On a daily basis, exchange rates fluctuate very little. Significant variations usually occur over longer time spans. Highly regulated economic systems like China are among the few that still use fixed exchange rates. The Chinese government regulates the flow of currency—its own as well as all others—into and out of China and determines the precise rate of exchange within its borders.

Exchange-rate fluctuation can have an important impact on balance of trade. Suppose you want to buy some English tea for £10 per box. At an exchange rate of $2 to £1, a box will cost you $20 (£10 × 2 = 20). But what if the pound is weaker? At an exchange rate of, say, $1.25 to £1, the same box would cost you only $12.50 (£10 ×

1.25 = 12.50). If the dollar is strong in relation to the pound, the prices of all United States–made products will rise in England, and the prices of all English-made products will fall in the United States. The English would buy fewer U.S. products, and Americans would be prompted to spend more on English-made products. The result would probably be a U.S. trade deficit with England.

One of the most significant developments in foreign exchange has been the introduction of the **euro**—the common currency of the European Union. The euro was officially introduced in 2002 and has replaced other currencies, such as the German Deutsche Mark and the French franc. The EU anticipates that the euro will become as important as the dollar and the yen in international commerce. When the euro was first introduced, its value was pegged as being equivalent to the dollar: €1 = $1. But because the dollar has been relatively weak in recent years, its value has eroded relative to that of the euro. In January 2011, for example, $1 was worth only about €0.75.

Companies with international operations must watch exchange-rate fluctuations closely because changes affect overseas demand for their products and can be a major factor in competition. In general, when the value of a country's currency rises—becomes stronger—companies based there find it harder to export products to foreign markets and easier for foreign companies to enter local markets. It also makes it more cost-efficient for domestic companies to move operations to lower-cost foreign sites. When the value of a currency declines—becomes weaker—the opposite occurs. As the value of a country's currency falls, its balance of trade usually improves because domestic companies should experience a boost in exports. There should also be less reason for foreign companies to ship products into the domestic market and less reason to establish operations in other countries.

Forms of Competitive Advantage

Before we discuss the fundamental issues involved in international business management, we must consider one last factor: forms of *competitive advantage*. Because no country can produce everything that it needs, countries tend to export what they can produce better or less expensively than other countries and use the proceeds to import what they can't produce as effectively. This principle doesn't fully explain why nations export and import what they do. Such decisions hinge partly on the advantages that a particular country enjoys regarding its abilities to create and/or sell certain products and resources.[7] Economists traditionally focused on absolute and comparative advantage to explain international trade. But because this approach focuses narrowly on such factors as natural resources and labor costs, a more contemporary view of national competitive advantage has emerged.

Absolute Advantage   An **absolute advantage** exists when a country can produce something that is cheaper and/or of higher quality than any other country. Saudi oil, Brazilian coffee beans, and Canadian timber come close (because these countries have such abundant supplies of these resources), but examples of true absolute advantage are rare. For example, many experts say that the vineyards of France produce the world's finest wines. But the burgeoning wine business in California demonstrates that producers there can also make very good wine—wines that rival those from France but come in more varieties and at lower prices.

Comparative Advantage   A country has a **comparative advantage** in goods that it can produce more efficiently or better than other nations. If businesses in a given country can make computers more efficiently than they can make automobiles, then that nation has a comparative advantage in computer manufacturing.

Exchange Rate rate at which the currency of one nation can be exchanged for the currency of another nation

Euro a common currency shared among most of the members of the European Union (excluding Denmark, Sweden, and the United Kingdom)

Absolute Advantage the ability to produce something more efficiently than any other country can

Comparative Advantage the ability to produce some products more efficiently than others

ENTREPRENEURSHIP AND NEW VENTURES

Rolling in the Worldwide Dough

Is any business more confined to a local market than a bakery? Breads and pastries get stale quickly, and even the largest operations, such as those that make buns for McDonald's, only move products over short distances. But a bakery in Paris has refused to accept geographic limitations and is now selling its famous bread in global markets.

When Lionel Poilâne took over the family business more than 30 years ago, he was determined to return breadmaking to its roots. Poilâne built clay ovens based on sixteenth-century plans and technology, trained his breadmakers in ancient techniques, and began selling old-style dark bread with a thick, chewy, fire-tinged flavor. It quickly became a favorite in Parisian bistros, and demand soared.

To help meet demand, Poilâne built two more bakeries in Paris; today they sell over 15,000 loaves of bread a day. Poilâne also opened a bakery in London, but his efforts to expand to Japan were stymied: Local ordinances prohibited wood-burning ovens, and Poilâne refused to compromise. During the negotiation process, however, he came to realize that he didn't really even *want* to build new bakeries all over the world.

Instead, he turned to modern technology to expand his old-fashioned business. The key was the big FedEx hub at Paris Roissy Charles de Gaulle Airport near Poilâne's largest Paris bakery. After launching a website, Poilâne started taking international orders. New orders are packaged as the bread cools and then picked up by FedEx. A quick warm-up in the customer's oven gives it the same taste as it had when it came out of Poilâne's oven. Today, a loaf of bread baked in Paris in the morning can easily be reheated for tomorrow night's dinner in more than 25 countries.[8]

MyBizLab

Brenda A. Carson/iStockphoto

In general, both absolute and comparative advantages translate into competitive advantage. Brazil, for instance, can produce and market coffee beans knowing full well that there are few other countries with the right mix of climate, terrain, and altitude to enter the coffee bean market. The United States has comparative advantages in the computer industry (because of technological sophistication) and in farming (because of large amounts of fertile land and a temperate climate). South Korea has a comparative advantage in electronics manufacturing because of efficient operations and cheap labor. As a result, U.S. firms export computers and grain to South Korea and import DVD players from South Korea. South Korea can produce food, and the United States can build DVD players, but each nation imports certain products because the other holds a comparative advantage in the relevant industry.

National Competitive Advantage   In recent years, a theory of national competitive advantage has become a widely accepted model of why nations engage in international trade.[9] **National competitive advantage** derives from four conditions:

1 *Factor conditions* are the factors of production we discussed in Chapter 1—*labor, capital, entrepreneurs, physical resources,* and *information resources.*

2 *Demand conditions* reflect a large domestic consumer base that promotes strong demand for innovative products.

3 *Related and supporting industries* include strong local or regional suppliers and/or industrial customers.

4 *Strategies, structures, and rivalries* refer to firms and industries that stress cost reduction, product quality, higher productivity, and innovative products.

When all attributes of national competitive advantage exist, a nation is likely to be heavily involved in international business. Japan, for instance, has an abundance of natural resources and strong domestic demand for automobiles. Its carmakers have well-oiled supplier networks, and domestic firms have competed intensely with one another for decades. These circumstances explain why Japanese car companies like Toyota and Honda are successful in foreign markets.

International Business Management

Regardless of where a firm is located, its success depends largely on how well it's managed. International business is so challenging because basic management tasks—planning, organizing, directing, and controlling—are much more difficult when a firm operates in markets scattered around the globe.

Managing means making decisions. In this section, we examine the three basic decisions that a company must make when considering globalization. The first decision is whether to go international at all. Once that decision has been made, managers must decide on the level of international involvement and on the organizational structure that will best meet the firm's global needs.

3 Discuss the factors involved in deciding to do business internationally and in selecting the appropriate levels of international involvement and international organizational structure.

Going International

As the world economy becomes globalized, more firms are conducting international operations. U.S. firms are aggressively expanding abroad, while foreign companies such as BP and Nestlé continue to expand into foreign markets as well, including the U.S. market. This route, however, isn't appropriate for every company. If you buy and sell fresh fish, you'll find it more profitable to confine your activities to limited geographic areas because storage and transport costs may be too high to make international operations worthwhile. As Figure 4.5 shows, several factors affect the decision to go international.

Gauging International Demand   In considering international expansion, a company must consider whether there is a demand for its products abroad. Products that are successful in one country may be useless in another. Even when there is demand, advertising may still need to be adjusted. For example, bicycles are largely used for recreation in the United States but are seen as basic transportation in China. Hence, a bicycle maker would need to have different advertising strategies in each of these two countries. Market research and/or the prior market entry of competitors may indicate whether there's an international demand for a firm's products.

Adapting to Customer Needs   If its product is in demand, a firm must decide whether and how to adapt it to meet the special demands of foreign customers. For example, to satisfy local tastes, McDonald's sells wine in France, beer in Germany, and provides some vegetarian sandwiches in India. Likewise, consumer electronics companies have to be aware that different countries use different kinds of electric sockets and different levels of electric power. Therefore, regardless of demand, customer needs must still be considered.

Outsourcing and Offshoring   **Outsourcing**—the practice of paying suppliers and distributors to perform certain business processes or to provide needed materials or services—has become a very popular option for going international. It has become so popular because (1) it helps firms focus on their core activities and avoid getting

National Competitive Advantage international competitive advantage stemming from a combination of factor conditions, demand conditions, related and supporting industries, and firm strategies, structures, and rivalries

Outsourcing the practice of paying suppliers and distributors to perform certain business processes or to provide needed materials or services

Figure 4.5 Going International

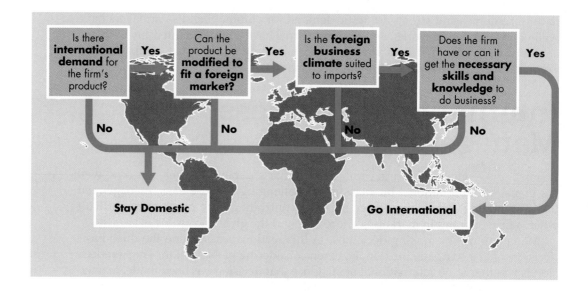

sidetracked on secondary activities, and (2) it reduces costs by locating certain business functions in areas where relevant costs are low.[10]

The practice of outsourcing to foreign countries is more specifically referred to as **offshoring.** Many companies today contract their manufacturing to low-cost factories in Asia. Similarly, many service call centers today are outsourced to businesses located in India. The 2008 Oscar winner *Slumdog Millionaire* featured a young Indian man who worked for an international call center in Mumbai.

Levels of International Involvement

After deciding to go international, a firm must determine the level of its involvement. Several levels are possible: A firm may act as an exporter or importer, organize as an international firm, or (like most of the world's largest industrial firms) operate as a multinational firm.

Exporters and Importers   An **exporter** makes products in one country to distribute and sell in others. An **importer** buys products in foreign markets and brings them home for resale. Both conduct most of their business in their home nations. Both entail the lowest level of involvement in international operations, and both are good ways to learn the fine points of global business. Many large firms entered international business as exporters. IBM and Coke, among others, exported to Europe for several years before setting up production sites there.

International Firms   As exporters and importers gain experience and grow, many move to the next level of involvement. **International firms** conduct a good deal of their business abroad and may even maintain overseas manufacturing facilities. An international firm may be large, but it's still basically a domestic company with international operations. Hershey, for instance, buys ingredients for its chocolates from several foreign suppliers, but makes all of its products in the United States. Moreover, while it sells its products in approximately 50 other countries, it generates most of its revenues from its domestic market.[11]

Multinational Firms   Most **multinational firms**—firms that design, produce, and market products in many nations—such as ExxonMobil, Nestlé, IBM, and Ford, don't think of themselves as having domestic and international divisions. Headquarters locations are almost irrelevant, and planning and decision making are geared to international markets. The world's largest multinationals in 2010 based on sales, profits, and employees are shown in Table 4.2.

TABLE 4.2 The World's Largest Non-U.S. Companies By Sales, Profits, and Number of Employees (2010)			
Company	**Sales ($ million)**	**Profits ($ million)**	**Employees**
BP p.l.c.	246,138		
China Petroleum & Chemical	196,781		
Royal Dutch Shell	285,129		
Saudi Arabian Oil	233,300		
Toyota	204,443		
Barclays PLC		16,385	
BP p.l.c.		16,578	
China Mobile		16,849	
OAO Gazprom		25,722	
PETROBRAS		15,448	
Carrefour SA			475,976
Deutsche Post			436,651
OAO Gazprom			393,600
Siemens			405,000
Tesco PLC			472,094

We can't underestimate the economic impact of multinational firms. Consider just the impact of the 500 largest multinationals: In 2010, these 500 firms generated $12.3 trillion in revenues and $819.3 billion in owner profits. They employed tens of millions of people, bought materials and equipment from literally thousands of other firms, and paid billions in taxes. Moreover, their products affected the lives of hundreds of millions of consumers, competitors, investors, and even protestors.

International Organization Structures

Different levels of international involvement entail different kinds of organizational structure. A structure that would help coordinate an exporter's activities would be inadequate for those of a multinational. In this section, we consider the spectrum of organizational strategies, including *independent agents*, *licensing arrangements*, *branch offices*, *strategic alliances*, and *foreign direct investment*.

Independent Agents   An **independent agent** is a foreign individual or organization that represents an exporter in foreign markets. Independent agents often act as sales representatives: They sell the exporter's products, collect payment, and make sure that customers are satisfied. They often represent several firms at once and usually don't specialize in a particular product or market. Peter So operates an import-export office in Hong Kong. He and his staff of three handle imports from about 15 foreign companies into Hong Kong and about 10 Hong Kong firms that export products abroad.

Offshoring the practice of outsourcing to foreign countries

Exporter firm that distributes and sells products to one or more foreign countries

Importer firm that buys products in foreign markets and then imports them for resale in its home country

International Firm firm that conducts a significant portion of its business in foreign countries

Multinational Firm firm that designs, produces, and markets products in many nations

Independent Agent foreign individual or organization that agrees to represent an exporter's interests

MANAGING IN TURBULENT TIMES

The Ups and Downs of Globalization

International business has been around for thousands of years. For example, as far back as 2000 B.C., tribes in northern Africa took dates and clothing to Babylonia and Assyria in the Middle East and traded them for spices and olive oil. By 500 B.C., Chinese merchants were actively exporting silk and jade to India and Europe, and trade routes were being established between many countries in Europe, Asia, and Africa.

But even as recently as 100 years ago, international trade was only a small part of the global economy. The effects of any given country's economy had a minimal effect on the rest of the world. Indeed, it wasn't until the Great Depression that swept the world in 1929 that experts realized how interdependent the global economy had become.

Globalization—the process through which the world's economy is becoming one interdependent system—brings with it both advantages and disadvantages. On the plus side, globalization has increased the standard of living of billions of people and has helped to create enormous wealth in many different parts of the globe. On the other hand, there are many people who have not shared in the benefits of globalization, and some critics believe that globalization has both hurt less developed countries and destroyed or damaged the unique cultures that exist in different parts of the world.

Globalization has also led to such a high degree of interdependence that no major country's economy is immune from what happens in the rest of the world. The recession of 2008–2009 demonstrated this fact once again: As the economy of the United States ground to a halt, so did the economies of virtually all major European and Asian countries as well. Global stock trading, real-time information available on

Alexander Tovstenko/iStockphoto

the Internet, and worldwide financial networks combined to bring to a grinding halt just about every major business in the world.

Managers seeking to reverse the tide and get their businesses going again had to juggle more factors than ever before. Domestic forces such as consumer demand, interest rates, and production costs all had to be considered. But so too did international business conditions. And many businesses—Circuit City and Chrysler, for example—struggled mightily, and some failed. But those with managers and leaders who really understood the global economy did in fact regain their footing. And as global economic conditions improve, so too does the outlook for these businesses.

MyBizLab

Licensing Arrangements Companies seeking more involvement may opt for **licensing arrangements.** Firms give foreign individuals or companies exclusive rights (called *licensing agreements*) to manufacture or market their products in that market. In return, the exporter receives a fee plus ongoing payments (royalties) that are calculated as a percentage of the license holder's sales. Franchising is an increasingly popular form of licensing. For example, McDonald's and Pizza Hut franchise around the world.

Branch Offices Instead of developing relationships with foreign agents or licensing companies, a firm may send its own managers to overseas **branch offices,** where the firm has more direct control than it does over agents or license holders. Branch offices also furnish a more visible public presence in foreign countries, and foreign customers tend to feel more secure when there's a local branch office. Halliburton, a Houston-based oil field supply and services company, recently opened a branch office in Dubai in order to more effectively establish relationships with customers in the Middle East.

Strategic Alliances In a **strategic alliance,** a company finds a partner in the country in which it wants to do business. Each party agrees to invest resources and capital into a new business or to cooperate in some mutually beneficial way. This new business—the alliance—is owned by the partners, who divide its profits. Such alliances are sometimes called *joint ventures,* but the term *strategic alliance* has arisen because such partnerships are playing increasingly important roles in the strategies of major companies. Ford and Russian automaker Sollers recently launched a new joint venture; Sollers will manufacture Ford products in Russia and the two partners will then work together on marketing them.[12] In many countries, such as Mexico, India, and China, laws make alliances virtually the only way to do international business. Mexico, for example, requires that all foreign firms investing there have local partners.

In addition to easing the way into new markets, alliances give firms greater control over foreign activities than agents and licensees. Alliances also allow firms to benefit from the knowledge and expertise of foreign partners. Microsoft, for example, relies heavily on alliances as it expands into international markets. This approach has helped the firm learn the intricacies of doing business in China and India, two of the hardest emerging markets to crack.

Foreign Direct Investment **Foreign direct investment (FDI)** involves buying or establishing tangible assets in another country. Dell Computer, for example, has built assembly plants in Europe and China. Volkswagen has built a factory in Brazil, and Disney has built theme parks in France and Hong Kong. Each of these activities represents FDI by a firm in another country.

Barriers to International Trade

4 Describe some of the ways in which social, cultural, economic, legal, and political differences among nations affect international business.

Whether a business is truly multinational or sells to only a few foreign markets, several factors will affect its international operations. Success in foreign markets will largely depend on the ways it responds to *social*, *economic*, *legal*, and *political barriers* to international trade.

Social and Cultural Differences

Any firm planning to conduct business abroad must understand the social and cultural differences between host country and home country. Some differences are obvious. You must, for example, consider language factors when adjusting packaging, signs, and logos. Pepsi is the same product in Seattle and Moscow—except for the lettering on the bottle. Less universal products, however, face several conditions that force them to make adjustments. When Bob's Big Boy launched new restaurants in Thailand, it had to add deep-fried shrimp to the menu. KFC has altered menus, ingredients, and hours of operation to suit Thai culture.

A wide range of subtle value differences can also affect operations. For example, many Europeans shop daily for groceries. To U.S. consumers accustomed to weekly supermarket trips, the European pattern may seem like a waste of time. For many Europeans, however, shopping is not just a matter of buying food; it's also an outlet for meeting friends and exchanging political views. Consider the implications of this difference for U.S. firms selling food and food-related products in Europe where large American supermarkets are not the norm in many parts of Europe.

Economic Differences

Although cultural differences are often subtle, economic differences can be fairly pronounced. As we discussed in Chapter 1, in dealing with mixed market economies like those of France and Sweden, firms must know when—and to what extent—the government is involved in a given industry. The French government, for instance, is heavily involved in all aspects of airplane design and manufacturing. The impact of

Licensing Arrangement arrangement in which firms choose foreign individuals or organizations to manufacture or market their products in another country

Branch Office foreign office set up by an international or multinational firm

Strategic Alliance arrangement (also called joint venture) in which a company finds a foreign partner to contribute approximately half of the resources needed to establish and operate a new business in the partner's country

Foreign Direct Investment (FDI) arrangement in which a firm buys or establishes tangible assets in another country

economic differences can be even greater in planned economies like those of China and Vietnam, where the government owns and operates many factors of production.

Legal and Political Differences

Governments can affect international business in many ways. They can set conditions for doing business within their borders and even prohibit doing business altogether. They can control the flow of capital and use tax legislation to discourage or encourage activity in a given industry. They can even confiscate the property of foreign-owned companies. In this section, we discuss some of the more common legal and political issues in international business: *quotas, tariffs,* and *subsidies; local content laws;* and *business practice laws.*

Quotas, Tariffs, and Subsidies

Even free market economies, such as the United States, have some quotas and/or tariffs, both of which affect prices and quantities of foreign-made products. A **quota** restricts the number of products of a certain type that can be imported and, by reducing supply, raises the prices of those imports. That's why Belgian ice-cream makers can't ship more than 922,315 kilograms to the United States each year, and Canada can ship no more than 14.7 billion board feet of softwood timber per year. Quotas are often determined by treaties. Better terms are often given to friendly trading partners, and quotas are typically adjusted to protect domestic producers.

The ultimate quota is an **embargo:** a government order forbidding exportation and/or importation of a particular product—or even all products—from a specific country. Many nations control bacteria and disease by banning certain agricultural products. Because the United States has embargoes against Cuba and Libya, American firms can't invest in these countries, and their products can't legally be sold on American markets.

Tariffs are taxes on imported products. They raise the prices of imports by making consumers pay not only for the products but also for tariff fees. Tariffs take two forms. Revenue tariffs are imposed to raise money for governments, but most tariffs, called protectionist tariffs, are meant to discourage particular imports. Did you know that firms that import ironing-board covers into the United States pay a 7-percent tariff on the price of the product? Firms that import women's athletic shoes pay a flat rate of $0.90 per pair plus 20 percent of the product price. Such figures are determined through a complicated process designed to put foreign and domestic firms on competitive footing (that is, to make the foreign goods about the same cost as the domestic goods).

Quotas and tariffs are imposed for numerous reasons. The U.S. government aids domestic automakers by restricting the number of Japanese cars imported into this country. Because of national security concerns, we limit the export of technology (for example, computer and nuclear technology to China). The United States isn't the only country that uses tariffs and quotas. To protect domestic firms, Italy imposes high tariffs on electronic goods. As a result, CD players are prohibitively expensive.

A **subsidy** is a government payment to help a domestic business compete with foreign firms. They're actually indirect tariffs that lower the prices of domestic goods rather than raise the prices of foreign goods. For example, many European governments subsidize farmers to help them compete against U.S. grain imports.

The Protectionism Debate In the United States, **protectionism**—the practice of protecting domestic business at the expense of free market competition—is controversial. Supporters argue that tariffs and quotas protect domestic firms and jobs as well as shelter new industries until they're able to compete internationally. They contend that we need such measures to counter steps taken by other nations. Other advocates justify protectionism in the name of national security. A nation, they argue, must be able to produce efficiently the goods needed for survival in case of war. Thus, the U.S. government requires the Air Force to buy planes only from U.S. manufacturers.

Critics cite protectionism as a source of friction between nations. They also charge that it drives up prices by reducing competition. They maintain that although jobs in some industries would be lost as a result of free trade, jobs in other industries (for example, electronics and automobiles) would be created if all nations abandoned protectionist tactics.

Protectionism sometimes takes on almost comic proportions. Neither Europe nor the United States grows bananas, but both European and U.S. firms buy and sell bananas in foreign markets. Problems arose when the EU put a quota on bananas imported from Latin America—a market dominated by two U.S. firms, Chiquita and Dole—in order to help firms based in current and former European colonies in the Caribbean. To retaliate, the United States imposed a 100-percent tariff on certain luxury products imported from Europe, including Louis Vuitton handbags, Scottish cashmere sweaters, and Parma ham.

Local Content Laws   Many countries, including the United States, have **local content laws**—requirements that products sold in a country be at least partly made there. Firms seeking to do business in a country must either invest there directly or take on a domestic partner. In this way, some of the profits from doing business in a foreign country stay there rather than flow out to another nation. In some cases, the partnership arrangement is optional but wise. In Mexico, for instance, Radio Shack de México is a joint venture owned by Tandy Corp. (49 percent) and Mexico's Grupo Gigante (51 percent). This allows the retailer to promote a strong Mexican identity; it also makes it easier to address certain import regulations that are easier for Mexican than for U.S. firms. Both China and India currently require that when a foreign firm enters into a joint venture with a local firm, the local partner must have the controlling ownership stake.

Business Practice Laws   Many businesses entering new markets encounter problems in complying with stringent regulations and bureaucratic obstacles. Such practices are affected by the **business practice laws** by which host countries govern business practices within their jurisdictions. As part of its entry strategy in Germany several years ago, Wal-Mart had to buy existing retailers rather than open brand-new stores because, at the time, the German government was not issuing new licenses to sell food products. Wal-Mart also was not allowed to follow its normal practice of refunding price differences on items sold for less by other stores because the practice is illegal in Germany. In addition, Wal-Mart had to comply with business-hour restrictions: Stores can't open before 7:00 A.M., must close by 8:00 P.M. on weeknights and 4:00 P.M. on Saturday, and must remain closed on Sunday. After a few years, Wal-Mart eventually decided its meager profits in Germany didn't warrant the effort it required to generate them and closed all of its stores there.

Cartels and Dumping   Sometimes, a legal—even an accepted—practice in one country is illegal in another. In some South American countries, for example, it is sometimes legal to bribe business and government officials. The existence of **cartels**—associations of producers that control supply and prices—gives tremendous power to some nations, such as those belonging to the Organization of Petroleum Exporting Countries (OPEC). U.S. law forbids both bribery and cartels.

Finally, many (but not all) countries forbid **dumping**—selling a product abroad for less than the cost of production at home. U.S. antidumping legislation sets two conditions for determining whether dumping is being practiced:

1 Products are being priced at "less than fair value."

2 The result unfairly harms domestic industry.

Just a few years ago, the United States charged Japan and Brazil with dumping steel at prices 70 percent below normal value. To protect local manufacturers, the U.S. government imposed a significant tariff on steel imported from those countries.

Quota restriction on the number of products of a certain type that can be imported into a country

Embargo government order banning exportation and/or importation of a particular product or all products from a particular country

Tariff tax levied on imported products

Subsidy government payment to help a domestic business compete with foreign firms

Protectionism practice of protecting domestic business against foreign competition

Local Content Law law requiring that products sold in a particular country be at least partly made there

Business Practice Law law or regulation governing business practices in given countries

Cartel association of producers whose purpose is to control supply and prices

Dumping practice of selling a product abroad for less than the cost of production

Photo Researchers

Continued from page 89

Fair Trade—Worth the Price?

Some critics of fair-trade practices and prices agree in principle with those who advocate its use but contend that consumers don't need to be paying such excessive prices even under *current* market conditions. They point out that, according to TransFair's own data, cocoa farmers get only 3 cents of the $3.49 that a socially conscious consumer pays for a Fair Trade–certified candy bar. "Farmers often receive very little," reports consumer researcher Lawrence Solomon. "Often fair trade is sold at a premium," he charges, "but the entire premium goes to the middlemen." Critics like Solomon suggest that sellers of fair-trade products are taking advantage of consumers who are socially but not particularly price conscious. They point out that if sellers priced that $3.49 candy bar at $2.49, farmers would still be entitled to 3 cents. The price, they charge, is inflated to $3.49 only because there's a small segment of the market willing to pay it (while farmers still get only 3 cents). Fair-trade programs, advises English economist Tim Harford, "make a promise that the producers will get a good deal. They do not promise that the consumer will get a good deal. That's up to you as a savvy shopper."

QUESTIONS FOR DISCUSSION

1 Do you think fair-trade is a viable solution to child-labor and related problems?
2 Are you willing to pay more for fair-trade products? Why or why not?
3 What other options can you identify that might help deal with child labor and other problems in the global cocoa market?

SUMMARY OF LEARNING OBJECTIVES   MyBizLab

1. **Discuss the rise of international business and describe the major world marketplaces, trade agreements, and alliances. (pp. 89–92)**
Several forces combine to sustain *globalization*: (1) Governments and businesses are more aware of the benefits of globalization; (2) new technologies make international travel, communication, and commerce faster and cheaper; (3) competitive pressures sometimes force firms to expand into foreign markets just to keep up with competitors; (4) treaties and trade agreements also play a major role. The most important influences are (1) the *North American Free Trade Agreement (NAFTA)*; (2) the *European Union (EU)*; and (3) the *General Agreement on Tariffs and Trade (GATT)* and the *World Trade Organization (WTO)*. The contemporary world economy revolves around three major marketplaces: North America, Europe, and Asia.

2. **Explain how differences in import-export balances, exchange rates, and foreign competition determine the ways in which countries and businesses respond to the international environment. (pp. 93–99)**
A nation's *balance of trade* is the total economic value of all products that it exports minus the total economic value of all products that it imports. When a country's imports exceed its exports—when it has a *negative balance of trade*—it suffers a *trade deficit*; a *positive balance of trade* occurs when exports exceed imports, resulting in a *trade surplus*. The *balance of payments* refers to the flow of money into or out of a country.

An *exchange rate* is the rate at which one nation's currency can be exchanged for that of another. Under *floating exchange rates*, the value of one currency relative to that of another varies with market conditions.

Countries *export* what they can produce better or less expensively than other countries and use the proceeds to *import* what they can't produce as effectively. Economists once focused on two forms of advantage to explain international trade: *absolute advantage* and *comparative advantage*. Today, the theory of *national competitive advantage* is a widely accepted model of why nations engage in international trade.

3. **Discuss the factors involved in deciding to do business internationally and in selecting the appropriate levels of international involvement and international organizational structure. (pp. 99–103)**
Several factors enter into the decision to go international. One overriding factor is the *business climate* in other nations. A company should also consider at least two other issues: (1) Is there a *demand* for its products abroad? (2) If so, must it *adapt* those products for international consumption?

After deciding to go international, a firm must decide on its level of involvement. Several levels are possible: (1) *exporters and importers*; (2) *international firms*; and (3) *multinational firms*. Different levels of involvement require different kinds of organizational structure. The spectrum of international organizational strategies includes the following: (1) *independent agents*; (2) *licensing arrangements*; (3) *branch offices*; (4) *strategic alliances* (or *joint ventures*); and (5) *foreign direct investment (FDI)*.

4. **Describe some of the ways in which social, cultural, economic, legal, and political differences among nations affect international business. (pp. 103–106)**
Some social and cultural differences, like language, are obvious, but a wide range of subtle value differences can also affect operations. Economic differences can be fairly pronounced. Common legal and political issues in international business include *quotas, tariffs, subsidies, local content laws*, and *business practice laws*.

KEY TERMS   MyBizLab

absolute advantage (p. 97)
Association of Southeast Asian Nations (ASEAN) (p. 92)
balance of payments (p. 94)
balance of trade (p. 93)
branch office (p. 102)
business practice law (p. 105)
cartel (p. 105)
comparative advantage (p. 97)
dumping (p. 105)
embargo (p. 104)
euro (p. 97)
European Union (EU) (p. 92)
exchange rate (p. 96)

export (p. 89)
exporter (p. 100)
foreign direct investment (FDI) (p. 103)
General Agreement on Tariffs and Trade (GATT) (p. 92)
globalization (p. 89)
import (p. 89)
importer (p. 100)
independent agent (p. 101)
international firm (p. 100)
licensing arrangement (p. 102)
local content law (p. 105)
multinational firm (p. 100)

national competitive advantage (p. 98)
North American Free Trade Agreement (NAFTA) (p. 91)
offshoring (p. 100)
outsourcing (p. 99)
protectionism (p. 104)
quota (p. 104)
strategic alliances (p. 102)
subsidy (p. 104)
tariff (p. 104)
trade deficit (p. 94)
trade surplus (p. 94)
World Trade Organization (WTO) (p. 92)

QUESTIONS AND EXERCISES

QUESTIONS FOR REVIEW

1. How does the balance of trade differ from the balance of payments?
2. What are the three possible levels of involvement in international business? Give examples of each.
3. How does a country's economic system affect the decisions of foreign firms interested in doing business there?
4. What aspects of the culture in your state or region would be of particular interest to a foreign firm thinking about locating there?

QUESTIONS FOR ANALYSIS

5. List all the major items in your bedroom, including furnishings. Try to identify the country in which each item was made. Offer possible reasons why a given nation might have a comparative advantage in producing a given good.
6. Suppose that you're the manager of a small firm seeking to enter the international arena. What basic information would you need about the market that you're thinking of entering?

7. Do you support protectionist tariffs for the United States? If so, in what instances and for what reasons? If not, why not?
8. Do you think that a firm operating internationally is better advised to adopt a single standard of ethical conduct or to adapt to local conditions? Under what kinds of conditions might each approach be preferable?

APPLICATION EXERCISES

9. Interview the manager of a local firm that does at least some business internationally. Why did the company decide to go international? Describe the level of the firm's international involvement and the organizational structure(s) it uses for international operations.
10. Select a product familiar to you. Using library reference works to gain some insight into the culture of India, identify the problems that might arise in trying to market this product to Indian consumers.

BUILDING YOUR BUSINESS SKILLS

Finding Your Place

Goal

To encourage you to apply global business strategies to a small-business situation.

Background Information

Some people might say that Yolanda Lang is a bit too confident. Others might say that she needs confidence—and more—to succeed in the business she's chosen. But one thing is certain: Lang is determined to grow INDE, her handbag design company, into a global enterprise. At only 28 years of age, she has time on her side—if she makes the right business moves now.

These days, Lang spends most of her time in Milan, Italy. Backed by $50,000 of her parents' personal savings, she is trying to compete with Gucci, Fendi, and other high-end handbag makers. Her target market is American women willing to spend $200 on a purse. Ironically, Lang was forced to set up shop in Italy because of the snobbishness of these customers, who buy high-end bags only if they're European-made. "Strangely enough," she muses, "I need to be in Europe to sell in America."

To succeed, she must first find ways to keep production costs down—a tough task for a woman in a male-dominated business culture. Her fluent Italian is an advantage, but she's often forced to turn down inappropriate dinner invitations. She also has to figure out how to get her 22-bag collection into stores worldwide. Retailers are showing her bags in Italy and Japan, but she's had little luck in the United States. "I intend to be a global company," says Lang. The question is how to succeed first as a small business.

Method

Step 1

Join together with three or four other students to discuss the steps that Lang has taken so far to break into the U.S. retail market. These steps include:

- Buying a mailing list of 5,000 shoppers from high-end department store Neiman Marcus and selling directly to these customers.
- Linking with a manufacturer's representative to sell her line in major U.S. cities while she herself concentrates on Europe.

Step 2

Based on what you learned in this chapter, suggest other strategies that might help Lang grow her business. Working with group members, consider whether the following options would help or hurt Lang's business. Explain why a strategy is likely to work or likely to fail.

- Lang could relocate to the United States and sell abroad through an independent agent.
- Lang could relocate to the United States and set up a branch office in Italy.
- Lang could find a partner in Italy and form a strategic alliance that would allow her to build her business on both continents.

FOLLOW-UP QUESTIONS

1. What are the most promising steps that Lang can take to grow her business? What are the least promising?
2. Lang thinks that her trouble breaking into the U.S. retail market stems from the fact that her company is unknown. How would this circumstance affect the strategies suggested in Steps 1 and 2?

3. When Lang deals with Italian manufacturers, she is a young woman in a man's world. Often she must convince men that her purpose is business and nothing else. How should Lang handle personal invitations that get in the way of business? How can she say no while still maintaining business relationships? Why is it often difficult for American women to do business in male-dominated cultures?

4. The American consulate has given Lang little business help because her products are made in Italy. Do you think the consulate's treatment of an American businessperson is fair or unfair? Explain your answer.
5. Do you think Lang's relocation to Italy will pay off? Why or why not?
6. With Lang's goals of creating a global company, can INDE continue to be a one-person operation?

EXERCISING YOUR ETHICS: INDIVIDUAL EXERCISE

Paying Heed to Foreign Practices

The Situation

Assume that you're an up-and-coming manager in a regional U.S. distribution company. Firms in your industry are just beginning to enter foreign markets, and you've been assigned to head up your company's new operations in a Latin American country. Because at least two of your competitors are also trying to enter this same market, your boss wants you to move as quickly as possible. You also sense that your success in this assignment will likely determine your future with the company.

You have just completed meetings with local government officials, and you're pessimistic about your ability to get things moving quickly. You've learned, for example, that it will take 10 months to get a building permit for a needed facility. Moreover, once the building's up, it will take another 6 months to get utilities. Finally, the phone company says that it may take up to two years to install the phone lines that you need for high-speed Internet access.

The Dilemma

Various officials have indicated that time frames could be considerably shortened if you were willing to pay special "fees." You realize that these "fees" are bribes, and you're well aware that the practice of paying such "fees" is both unethical and illegal in the United States. In this foreign country, however, it's not illegal and not even considered unethical. Moreover, if you don't pay and one of your competitors does, you'll be at a major competitive disadvantage. In any case, your boss isn't likely to understand the long lead times necessary to get the operation running. Fortunately, you have access to a source of funds that you could spend without the knowledge of anyone in the home office.

QUESTIONS TO ADDRESS

1 What are the key ethical issues in this situation?
2 What do you think most managers would do in this situation?
3 What would you do?

EXERCISING YOUR ETHICS: TEAM EXERCISE

Weighing the Trade-offs

The Situation

A medium-size regional banking corporation has its headquarters in a small city in the Midwestern United States. The firm is privately owned; all managers own stock in the bank corporation. The company's senior managers (and majority owners) have decided to sell the bank to a major international banking company within the next two to three years. First, though, the bank corporation needs to trim its expenses in order to make it more attractive to a potential buyer.

The Dilemma

Because the bank corporation has been a locally owned and operated enterprise, it has maintained a full slate of operations within the local market. For instance, its corporate offices, many banking outlets, and all of its support activities are housed locally. The latter category includes a large call center—a staff of 300 people who handle most customer calls with questions about their accounts.

There has been a growing trend in banking, though, to outsource call centers to foreign countries, most notably India. Such markets have an abundance of potential English-speaking employees, excellent technology, and low wages. One senior manager has argued that the bank corporation should outsource its call center immediately. This would enable the firm to lower its costs, thus making it even more attractive to a potential buyer. When confronted with the prospect of cutting 300 jobs, the manager acknowledges that that will be tough but is certain that any buyer will eventually do the same anyway.

Another vocal senior manager, though, is opposed to this idea. This person argues that because the bank corporation was started locally and has longstanding ties throughout the local community, it should maintain its current operations until the bank is sold. Then, this manager argues, if a new owner decides to cut jobs, "it will be on their conscience, not ours."

Team Activity

Assemble a group of four students and assign each group member to one of the following roles:
- Senior manager (majority owner) of the bank
- Call center employee
- Bank customer
- Bank corporation investor

ACTION STEPS

1 Before hearing any of your group's comments on this situation, and from the perspective of your assigned role, do you think that the call center should be outsourced immediately? Write down the reasons for your position.

2 Before hearing any of your group's comments on this situation, and from the perspective of your assigned role, what are the underlying ethical issues, if any, in this situation? Write down the issues.

3 Gather your group together and reveal, in turn, each member's comments on whether the call center should be outsourced immediately. Next, reveal the ethical issues listed by each member.

4 Appoint someone to record main points of agreement and disagreement within the group. How do you explain the results? What accounts for any disagreement?

5 From an ethical standpoint, what does your group conclude is the most appropriate action for the bank to take in this situation?

6 Develop a group response to the following question: Can your team identify other solutions that might help satisfy both senior managers' views?

CRAFTING A BUSINESS PLAN

Part 1: The Contemporary Business Environment

Goal of the Exercise

In Chapter 3 we discussed how the starting point for virtually every new business is a *business plan*. Business plans describe the business strategy for any new business and demonstrate how that strategy will be implemented. One benefit of a business plan is that in preparing it, would-be entrepreneurs must develop their idea on paper and firm up their thinking about how to launch their business before investing time and money in it. In this exercise, you'll get started on creating your own business plan.

Exercise Background: Part 1 of the Business Plan

The starting point for any business plan is coming up with a "great idea." This might be a business that you've already considered setting up. If you don't have ideas for a business already, look around. What are some businesses that you come into contact with on a regular basis? Restaurants, childcare services, and specialty stores are a few examples you might consider. You may also wish to create a business that is connected with a talent or interest you have, such as crafts, cooking, or car repair. It's important that you create a company from "scratch" rather than use a company that already exists. You'll learn more if you use your own ideas.

Once you have your business idea, your next step is to create an "identity" for your business. This includes determining a name for your business and an idea of what your business will do. It also includes identifying the type of ownership your business will take, topics we discussed in Chapter 3. The first part of the plan also briefly looks at who your ideal customers are as well as how your business will stand out from the crowd. Part 1 of the plan also looks at how the business will interact with the community and demonstrate social responsibility, topics we discussed in Chapter 2. Finally, almost all business plans today include a perspective on the impact of global business.

Your Assignment

Step 1

To complete this assignment, you first need to download the *Business Plan Student Template* file from the book's Companion website at www.prenhall.com/ebert. This is a Microsoft Word file

you can use to complete your business plan. For this assignment, you will fill in "Part 1" of the plan.

Step 2

Once you have the *Business Plan Student Template* file, you can begin to answer the following questions in "Part 1: The Contemporary Business Environment."

1 What is the name of your business?
Hint: When you think of the name of your business, make sure that it captures the spirit of the business you're creating.

2 What will your business do?
Hint: Imagine that you are explaining your idea to a family member or a friend. Keep your description to 30 words or less.

3 What form of business ownership (sole proprietorship, partnership, or corporation) will your business take? Why did you choose this form?
Hint: For more information on types of business ownership, refer to the discussion in Chapter 3.

4 Briefly describe your ideal customer. What are they like in terms of age, income level, and so on?
Hint: You don't have to give too much detail in this part of the plan; you'll provide more details about customers and marketing in later parts of the plan.

5 Why will customers choose to buy from your business instead of your competition?
Hint: In this section, describe what will be unique about your business. For example, is the product special or will you offer the product at a lower price?

6 All businesses have to deal with ethical issues. One way to address these issues is to create a code of ethics. List three core principles your business will follow.
Hint: To help you consider the ethical issues that your business might face, refer to the discussion in Chapter 2.

7 A business shows social responsibility by respecting all of its stakeholders. What steps will you take to create a socially responsible business?
Hint: Refer to the discussion of social responsibility in Chapter 2. What steps can you take to be a "good citizen" in the community? Consider also how you may need to be socially responsible toward your customers and, if applicable, investors, employees, and suppliers.

8 Will you sell your product in another country? If so, what countries and why? What challenges will you face?
Hint: To help you consider issues of global business, refer to Chapter 4. Consider how you will expand internationally (i.e., independent agent, licensing, etc.). Do you expect global competition for your product? What advantages will foreign competitors have?

Note: **Once you have answered the questions, save your Word document. You'll be answering additional questions in later chapters.**

VIDEO EXERCISE   MyBizLab

Mini

Learning Objectives

The purpose of this video is to help you:
1 Identify three levels of international involvement and describe how a firm selects the most appropriate level.
2 Discuss the ways in which social, cultural, and economic differences affect businesses with international operations.
3 Explain how legal and political differences influence international businesses.

Synopsis

The Mini was first introduced in 1959 by British Motor Corporation. It was sold briefly in the United States in the 1960s, but received a lukewarm reception from the American market who was interested in much larger vehicles. While the brand continued to be successful in Great Britain and Europe, it was not reintroduced into the American market until 2002. Mini, now owned by the German BMW auto group, has positioned itself as the premium small car brand, incorporating all the equipment, technology, and driving fun of larger and often more expensive competitors. With the exception of the Countryman, all Minis are produced in Oxford, England. Minis are now sold all over the world, including Argentina, Chile, Luxemburg, Malaysia, South Africa, and Turkey.

DISCUSSION QUESTIONS

1 A company wishing to enter the international market can consider several levels of involvement, including operating as an importer or exporter, international firm, or multinational firm. Which of these best describes Mini? Support your conclusion.
2 How do social and cultural factors influence the sales of Minis in the United States and around the world?
3 How does the buying process in the United States differ from other international markets?
4 Legal and political factors can influence a firm operating in the global economy. How would import tariffs influence the sales of Minis in the United States? What would be the potential impact of a quota on imported vehicles?
5 The most recent addition to the Mini product line is the Countryman. Do you think that this vehicle is well suited to the American market?

Online Exploration

Mini has sales operations around the globe. Start by taking a look at Mini's U.S. website at www.miniusa.com. After you have checked out the links on this site, take a look at a site from a few other countries, including Ireland (www.mini.ie), South Africa (www.mini.co.za), and Germany (www.mini.de). What similarities and differences do you notice between these sites? How do these reflect social, cultural, economic, political, and legal differences between the countries?

END NOTES

[1] "Slaves Feed World's Taste for Chocolate," Knight Ridder News Service, January 9, 2011; "Chocolate and Slavery: Child Labor in Côte d'Ivoire," TED Case Studies, No. 664 (2009), "Abolishing Child Labor on West African Cocoa Farms," SocialFunds.com, April 4, 2009; "Stop Child Labor: Cocoa Campaign," International Labor Rights Forum, 2008, April 3, 2010; and Jennifer Alsever, "Fair Prices for Farmers: Simple Idea, Complex Reality," *New York Times*, March 19, 2006.

[2] "Best Buy, Home Depot Find China Market a Tough Sell," *USA Today*, February 23, 2011, p. 5B.

[3] Ricky W. Griffin and Michael W. Pustay, *International Business: A Managerial Perspective*, 7th ed. (Upper Saddle River, NJ: Prentice Hall, 2012).

[4] Thomas Friedman, *The World Is Flat* (New York: Farrar, Straus, and Giroux, 2005).

[5] "World," *Time*, February 28, 2011, p. 15.

[6] World Trade Organization, at http://www.wto.org/English/thewto_e/whatis_e/tif_e/org6_e.htm, accessed February 27, 2011.

[7] Griffin and Pustay, *International Business: A Managerial Perspective*, 125–127. See also Steven Husted and Michael

Melvin, *International Economics*, 5th ed. (Boston: Addison Wesley Longman, 2001), 54–61; and Karl E. Case and Ray C. Fair, *Principles of Economics*, 8th ed. (Upper Saddle River, NJ: Prentice Hall, 2007), 700–708.

[8] Ron Lieber, "Give Us This Day Our Global Bread," *Fast Company*, March 2001, 164–167; Poilâne: "Our History," at http://www.poilane.fr/pages/en/company_univers_histoire.php, accessed May 14, 2008; "Les Boulangeries-Pâtisseries de Paris: Poilâne," (June 14, 2006), at http://louisrecettes.blogspot.com/2006/06/les-boulangeries-ptisseries-de-paris.html.

[9] This section is based on Michael Porter, *The Competitive Advantage of Nations* (Boston: Addison-Wesley Longman, 2001), 54–61; and Case and Fair, *Principles of Economics*, 669–677.

[10] Lee J. Krajewski, Manoj Malhotra, and Larry P. Ritzman, *Operations Management: Processes and Value Chains*, 8th ed. (Upper Saddle River, NJ: Prentice Hall, 2007), 401–403.

[11] *Hoover's Handbook of American Business 2011* (Austin, Texas: Hoover's Business Press, 20116), 432–433.

[12] "Ford, Russian Automaker Make Deal," *USA Today*, February 21, 2011, p. 1B.

5 Business Management

Google Keeps Growing

Sergey Brin and Larry Page met at Stanford University in 1995, when both were graduate students in computer science. At the time, Page was working on a software-development project designed to create an index of websites by scouring sites for key words and other linkages. Brin joined him on the project, and when they were satisfied that they'd developed something with commercial value, they tried to license the technology to other search companies. As luck would have it, they couldn't find a buyer and settled instead for procuring enough investment capital to keep refining and testing their product.

In 2000, Brin and Page ran across the description of a business model based on the concept of selling advertising in the form of sponsored links and search-specific ads. They adapted it to their own concept and went into business for themselves, eventually building Google into the world's largest search engine, with an index of more than 10 billion web pages and a user base of 380 million people per month in 112 different countries. Following an IPO in 2004, the company's market capitalization rose steadily; it stood at more than $157 billion by 2008, when Google controlled 61.5 percent of the U.S. search market (compared to Yahoo!'s 29.9 percent and Microsoft's 9.2 percent). Google, however, is much more than a mere search engine. Services include searches for news, shopping, local businesses, interactive maps, and discussion groups, as well as blogs, web-based e-mail and voice mail, and a digital photo-management system. You can access the results of any Google search from the Google website, from your own user's toolbar, from your

> *After reading this chapter, you should be able to:*
>
> 1 **Describe the nature of management and identify the four basic functions that constitute the management process.**
> 2 **Identify different types of managers likely to be found in an organization by level and area.**
> 3 **Describe the basic skills required of managers.**
> 4 **Explain the importance of strategic management and effective goal setting in organizational success.**
> 5 **Discuss contingency planning and crisis management in today's business world.**
> 6 **Describe the development and explain the importance of corporate culture.**

Windows taskbar, and from wireless devices such as phones and PDAs.

How did two young computer scientists build this astoundingly successful company, and where will they take it in the future? For one thing, Brin and Page remain in the forefront of Google's search for technological innovations. They believe in the power of mathematics and have developed unique algorithms for just about every form of activity in the firm. One of the most successful is an algorithm for auctioning advertising placements that ensures the highest possible prices.

Brin and Page have also been remarkably successful in attracting talented and creative employees and providing them with a work environment and culture that foster the kind of productivity and innovation for which they were hired. Finally, although the founders avoid formal strategic planning, they've managed to diversify

UPPA/Photoshot

WHAT'S IN IT FOR ME?

Sergey Brin and Larry Page are clearly effective managers, and they understand what it takes to build a business and then keep it at the forefront of its industry. After reading this chapter, you'll be better positioned to carry out various management responsibilities yourself. And from the perspective of a consumer or investor, you'll be able to more effectively assess and appreciate the quality of management in various companies.

In this chapter, we explore the importance of strategic management and effective goal setting to organizational success. We also examine the functions that constitute the management process and identify different types of managers likely to be found in an organization by level and area. Along the way, we look at basic management skills and explain the importance of corporate culture.

MyBizLab Where you see MyBizLab in this chapter, go to **www.mybizlab.com** for additional activities on the topic being discussed.

extensively through acquisitions and key alliances. Typically, Google absorbs an acquired firm and then improves on its technology, thereby adding variety to its own online offerings. Recent acquisitions include YouTube, a leader in online video sharing (2006), Postini, a leader in communications-security products (2007), and Double Click, a leader in online advertising services (2008). Strategic alliances include those with foreign online service providers that offer Google searches on their sites.[1]

Our opening story continues on page 132.

1 Describe the nature of management and identify the four basic functions that constitute the management process.

The Management Process

All corporations depend on effective management. Whether they run a multibillion-dollar business like Google or a small local fashion boutique, managers perform many of the same functions and have many of the same responsibilities. These include analyzing their competitive environments and planning, organizing, directing, and controlling day-to-day operations of their business. Ultimately, they are also responsible for the performance and effectiveness of the teams, divisions, or companies that they head.

Although our focus is on managers in business settings, remember that the principles of management apply to all kinds of organizations. Managers work in charities, churches, social organizations, educational institutions, and government agencies. The prime minister of Canada, curators at the Museum of Modern Art, the dean of your college, and the chief administrator of your local hospital are all managers. Remember, too, that managers bring to small organizations much the same kinds of skills—the ability to make decisions and respond to a variety of challenges—that they bring to large ones. Regardless of the nature and size of an organization, managers are among its most important resources.

Management itself is the process of planning, organizing, leading, and controlling an organization's financial, physical, human, and information resources to achieve its goals. Managers oversee the use of all these resources in their respective firms. All aspects of a manager's job are interrelated. Any given manager is likely to be engaged in each of these activities during the course of any given day.

Planning

Determining what the organization needs to do and how best to get it done requires planning. **Planning** has three main components. It begins when managers determine the firm's goals. Next, they develop a comprehensive *strategy* for achieving those goals. After a strategy is developed, they design *tactical and operational plans* for implementing the strategy. We discuss these three components in more detail later in this chapter.

When Yahoo! was created, for example, the firm's top managers set a strategic goal of becoming a top firm in the then-emerging market for Internet search engines. But then came the hard part—figuring out how to do it. The company started by assessing the ways in which people actually use the web and concluded that users wanted to be able to satisfy a wide array of needs, preferences, and priorities by going to as few sites as possible to find what they were looking for. One key component of Yahoo!'s strategy was to foster partnerships and relationships with other companies so that potential web surfers could draw upon several sources through a single site, or portal—which would be Yahoo!. The goal of partnering emerged as one set of *tactical plans* for moving forward.

Yahoo! managers then began fashioning alliances with such diverse partners as Reuters, Standard & Poor's, and the Associated Press (for news coverage), RE/Max

MyBizLab

Gain hands-on experience through an interactive, real-world scenario. This chapter's simulation entitled Plan for Success is located at **www.mybizlab.com.**

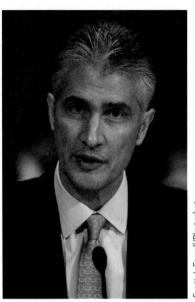

Kenneth Chenault, CEO of American Express; Indra Nooyi, Chairman and CEO of PepsiCo; and Jeffrey Smisek, President and CEO of United Airlines, are all senior managers responsible for overseeing the planning, organizing, leading, and control functions in their businesses.

(for real estate information), and a wide array of information providers specializing in sports, weather, entertainment, shopping, and travel. The creation of individual partnership agreements with each of these partners represents a form of *operational planning*.

Organizing

Managers must also organize people and resources. For example, some businesses prepare charts that diagram the various jobs within the company and how those jobs relate to one another. These so-called *organization charts* help everyone understand roles and reporting relationships, key parts of the organizing function. Some businesses go so far as to post their organization chart on an office wall. But in most larger businesses, roles and reporting relationships, while important, may be too complex to draw as a simple box-and-line diagram. To better appreciate the complexities and importance of organizing in a big business, let's consider the following example.

Once one of the leading-edge, high-tech firms in the world, Hewlett-Packard (HP) began to lose some of its luster a few years ago. Ironically, one of the major reasons for its slide could be traced back to what had once been a major strength. Specifically, HP had long prided itself on being little more than a corporate confederation of individual businesses. Sometimes, these businesses even ended up competing among themselves. This approach had been beneficial for much of the firm's history: It was easier for each business to make its own decisions quickly and efficiently, and the competition kept each unit on its toes. By the late 1990s, however, problems had become apparent, and no one could quite figure out what was going on.

Enter Ann Livermore, then head of the firm's software and services business. Livermore realized that the structure that had served so well in the past was now holding the firm back. To regain its competitive edge, HP needed an integrated, organization-wide strategy. Unfortunately, the company's highly decentralized

Management process of planning, organizing, leading, and controlling an organization's resources to achieve its goals

Planning management process of determining what an organization needs to do and how best to get it done

organization made that impossible. Livermore led the charge to create one organization united behind one strategic plan. "I felt we could be the most powerful company in the industry," she said, "if we could get our hardware, software, and services aligned." Eventually, a new team of top managers was handed control of the company, and every major component of the firm's structure was reorganized. As a result, while the firm still has a long way to go, it appears to be back on solid footing and set to regain its place as one of the world's preeminent technology businesses.[2] The process that was used to revive HP—determining the best way to arrange a business's resources and activities into a coherent structure—is called **organizing.** We explore organizing in more detail in Chapter 6.

Leading

Managers have the power to give orders and demand results. Leading, however, involves more complex activities. When **leading,** a manager works to guide and motivate employees to meet the firm's objectives. Legendary management figures like Walt Disney, Sam Walton (of Wal-Mart), and Herb Kelleher (of Southwest Airlines) had the capacity to unite their employees in a clear and targeted manner and motivate them to work in the best interests of their employer. Their employees respected them, trusted them, and believed that by working together, both the firm and themselves as individuals would benefit.

Until his recent death, Steve Jobs was one of the most widely recognized business leaders today. As head of both Pixar Animation Studios and Apple Computer, Jobs was responsible for some astonishing developments. Jobs helped produce the first mass-market personal computer, mouse, and graphical user interface (which uses icons rather than commands to send instructions to the computer). More recently, of course, Jobs led the introduction of the iPod, iPhone, and iPad. Pixar also holds numerous awards for its revolutionary animation technology, including several Oscars for Best Animated Feature. Apple has won eighteen International Design Excellence Awards (IDEA), more than any other company except Sony.

Jobs's leadership was more about vision than about technical proficiency. "On the technical side, there are people here with skills I can't possibly match," claimed Jobs. How then did Jobs create an environment in which engineers, computer scientists, and designers can produce cutting-edge products over and over again? According to Jobs, a leader must establish a strategic vision, hire a great group of people, provide a supportive atmosphere, and then get out of their way. We discuss leadership and decision making more fully in Chapter 9.

Controlling

Controlling is the process of monitoring a firm's performance to make sure that it is meeting its goals. All CEOs must pay close attention to costs and performance. Managers at United Airlines, for example, focus almost relentlessly on numerous indicators of performance that they can constantly measure and adjust. Everything from on-time arrivals to baggage-handling errors to the number of empty seats on an airplane to surveys of employee and customer satisfaction are regularly and routinely monitored. If on-time arrivals start to slip, managers focus on the problem and get it fixed. If customers complain too much about the food, catering managers figure out how to improve. As a result, no single element of the firm's performance can slip too far before it's noticed and fixed.

Figure 5.1 illustrates the control process that begins when management establishes standards, often for financial performance. If, for example, a company sets a goal of increasing its sales by 20 percent over the next 10 years, an appropriate standard to assess progress toward the 20-percent goal might be an increase of about 2 percent a year.

Managers then measure actual performance each year against standards. If the two amounts agree, the organization continues along its present course. If they vary significantly, however, one or the other needs adjustment. If sales have increased 2.1 percent by the end of the first year, things are probably fine. If sales have dropped 1

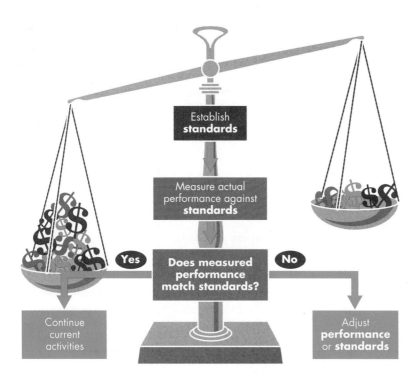

Figure 5.1 **The Control Process**

percent, some revision in plans may be needed. Perhaps the original goal should be lowered or more money should be spent on advertising.

Control can also show where performance is running better than expected and can serve as a basis for providing rewards or reducing costs. For example, when Chevrolet introduced the Super Sport Roadster (a classic, late-1940s pickup-style vehicle with a two-seat roadster design), the firm thought it had a major hit on its hands. But poor sales led to Chevrolet's decision to suspend production of the vehicle. On the other hand, Apple's iPad has been so successful that the firm has not been forced to discount or offer incentives for people to buy the device.

Types of Managers

Although all managers plan, organize, lead, and control, not all managers have the same degree of responsibility for these activities. It is helpful to classify managers according to levels and areas of responsibility.

Levels of Management

The three basic levels of management are *top*, *middle*, and *first-line* management. As summarized in Table 5.1, most firms have more middle managers than top managers and more first-line managers than middle managers. Both the power of managers and the complexity of their duties increase as they move up the ladder.

2 Identify different types of managers likely to be found in an organization by level and area.

Organizing management process of determining how best to arrange an organization's resources and activities into a coherent structure

Leading management process of guiding and motivating employees to meet an organization's objectives

Controlling management process of monitoring an organization's performance to ensure that it is meeting its goals

TABLE 5.1   The Three Levels of Management

Level	Examples	Responsibilities
Top managers	President, vice president, treasurer, chief executive officer (CEO), chief financial officer (CFO)	• Responsible for the overall performance and effectiveness of the firm • Set general policies, formulate strategies, and approve all significant decisions • Represent the company in dealings with other firms and with government bodies
Middle managers	Plant manager, operations manager, division manager, regional sales manager	• Responsible for implementing the strategies and working toward the goals set by top managers
First-line managers	Supervisor, office manager, project manager, group leader, sales manager	• Responsible for supervising the work of employees who report to them • Ensure employees understand and are properly trained in company policies and procedures

Top Managers   Like Sergey Brin, Larry Page, and the late Steve Jobs, the fairly small number of executives who get the chance to guide the fortunes of most companies are top managers. Common titles for top managers include *president*, *vice president*, *treasurer*, *chief executive officer (CEO)*, and *chief financial officer (CFO)*. **Top managers** are responsible for the overall performance and effectiveness of the firm. They set general policies, formulate strategies, approve all significant decisions, and represent the company in dealings with other firms and with government bodies.

Middle Managers   Just below the ranks of top managers is another group of managers who also occupy positions of considerable autonomy and importance and who are called middle managers. Titles such as *plant manager*, *operations manager*, and *division manager* designate middle-management slots. In general, **middle managers** are responsible for implementing the strategies and working toward the goals set by top managers.[3] For example, if top management decides to introduce a new product in 12 months or to cut costs by 5 percent in the next quarter, middle management are primarily responsible for determining how to meet these goals. The manager of an American Express service center or a regional sales manager of Frito-Lay snack products will likely be a middle manager.

First-Line Managers   Those who hold such titles as *supervisor*, *office manager*, *project manager*, and *group leader* are **first-line managers.** Although they spend most of their time working with and supervising the employees who report to them, first-line managers' activities are not limited to that arena. At a building site, for example, the project manager not only ensures that workers are carrying out construction as specified by the architect, but also interacts extensively with materials suppliers, community officials, and middle- and upper-level managers at the home office. The supervisor of delivery drivers for Frito-Lay products in a city would be considered to be a first-line manager.

Areas of Management

In any large company, top, middle, and first-line managers work in a variety of areas, including human resources, operations, marketing, information, and finance. For the most part, these areas correspond to the types of basic management skills described later in this chapter and to the wide range of business principles and activities discussed in the rest of this book.

Human Resource Managers   Most companies have *human resource managers* who hire and train employees, evaluate performance, and determine compensation. At large firms, separate departments deal with recruiting and hiring, wage and salary levels, and labor relations. A smaller firm may have a single department—or a single person—responsible for all human resource activities. (We discuss some key issues in human resource management in Chapter 10.)

Operations Managers   As we will see in Chapter 7, the term *operations* refers to the systems by which a firm produces goods and services. Among other duties, *operations managers* are responsible for production, inventory, and quality control. Manufacturing companies such as Texas Instruments, Ford, and Caterpillar have a strong need for operations managers at many levels. Such firms typically have a *vice president for operations* (top manager), *plant managers* (middle managers), and *production supervisors* (first-line managers). In recent years, sound operations management practices have become increasingly important to a variety of service organizations.

Marketing Managers   As we will see in Chapter 11, marketing encompasses the development, pricing, promotion, and distribution of goods and services. *Marketing managers* are responsible for getting products from producers to consumers. Marketing is especially important for firms that manufacture consumer products, such as Nike, Coca-Cola, and Apple. Such firms often have large numbers of marketing managers at several levels. For example, a large consumer products firm is likely to have a *vice president for marketing* (top manager), several *regional marketing managers* (middle managers), and several *district sales managers* (first-line managers).

Information Managers   Occupying a fairly new managerial position in many firms, *information managers* design and implement systems to gather, organize, and distribute information. Huge increases in both the sheer volume of information and the ability to manage it have led to the emergence of this important function. Although still relatively few in number, the ranks of information managers are growing at all levels. Some firms have a top-management position for a *chief information officer* (*CIO*). Middle managers help design information systems for divisions or plants. Computer systems managers within smaller businesses are usually first-line managers. We'll discuss information management in more detail in Chapter 13.

Financial Managers   Nearly every company has *financial managers* to plan and oversee its accounting functions and financial resources. Levels of financial management may include *CFO* or *vice president for finance* (top), a *division controller* (middle), and an *accounting supervisor* (first-line manager). Some financial institutions— NationsBank and Prudential, for example—have even made effective financial management the company's reason for being. We'll discuss financial management in more detail in Chapters 14 and 15.

Other Managers   Some firms also employ other specialized managers. Many companies, for example, have public relations managers. Chemical and pharmaceutical companies such as Monsanto and Merck have research and development managers. The range of possibilities is wide, and the areas of management are limited only by the needs and imagination of the firm.

Top Manager manager responsible for a firm's overall performance and effectiveness

Middle Manager manager responsible for implementing the strategies and working toward the goals set by top managers

First-Line Manager manager responsible for supervising the work of employees

3   Describe the basic skills required of managers.

Basic Management Skills

Although the range of managerial positions is almost limitless, the success that people enjoy in those positions is often limited by their skills and abilities. Effective managers must develop *technical, human relations, conceptual, decision-making*, and *time management skills*. Unfortunately, these skills are quite complex, and it is the rare manager who excels in every area.

Technical Skills

The skills needed to perform specialized tasks are called **technical skills.** A programmer's ability to write code, an animator's ability to draw, and an accountant's ability to audit a company's records are all examples of technical skills. People develop technical skills through a combination of education and experience. Technical skills are especially important for first-line managers. Many of these managers spend considerable time helping employees solve work-related problems, training them in more efficient procedures, and monitoring performance.

Human Relations Skills

Effective managers also generally have good **human relations skills**—skills that enable them to understand and get along with other people. A manager with poor human relations skills may have trouble getting along with subordinates, cause valuable employees to quit or transfer, and contribute to poor morale. Although human relations skills are important at all levels, they are probably most important for middle managers, who must often act as bridges between top managers, first-line managers, and managers from other areas of the organization. Managers should possess good communication skills. Many managers have found that being able both to understand others and to get others to understand them can go a long way toward maintaining good relations in an organization.

Conceptual Skills

Conceptual skills refer to a person's ability to think in the abstract, to diagnose and analyze different situations, and to see beyond the present situation. Conceptual skills help managers recognize new market opportunities and threats. They can also help managers analyze the probable outcomes of their decisions. The need for conceptual skills differs at various management levels. Top managers depend most on conceptual skills, first-line managers least. Although the purposes and everyday needs of various jobs differ, conceptual skills are needed in almost any job-related activity. In many ways, conceptual skills may be the most important ingredient in the success of executives in e-commerce businesses. For example, the ability to foresee how a particular business application will be affected by or can be translated to the Internet is clearly conceptual in nature.

Decision-Making Skills

Decision-making skills include the ability to define problems and to select the best course of action. These skills involve gathering facts, identifying solutions, evaluating alternatives, and implementing the chosen alternative. Periodically following up and evaluating the effectiveness of the choice are also part of the decision-making process. These skills allow some managers to identify effective strategies for their firm, such as Michael Dell's commitment to direct marketing as the firm's distribution model. But poor decision-making skills can also lead to failure and ruin. Indeed, poor decision making played a major role in the downfall of such U.S. business stalwarts as Montgomery Ward, Studebaker, and Enron. We'll discuss decision making more fully in Chapter 9.

Time Management Skills

Time management skills refer to the productive use that managers make of their time. Suppose, for example, that a CEO is paid $2 million in base salary (this is not an especially large CEO salary, by the way!). Assuming that she works 50 hours a week and takes two weeks' vacation, our CEO earns $800 an hour—a little more than $13 per minute. Any amount of time that she wastes clearly represents a large cost to the firm and its stockholders. Most middle and lower-level managers receive much smaller salaries than this, of course, but their time is still very valuable, and poor use of it still translates into costs and wasted productivity.

To manage time effectively, managers must address four leading causes of wasted time:

1 *Paperwork.* Some managers spend too much time deciding what to do with letters and reports. Most documents of this sort are routine and can be handled quickly. Managers must learn to recognize those documents that require more attention.

2 *Telephone calls.* Experts estimate that managers get interrupted by the telephone every five minutes. To manage this time more effectively, they suggest having an assistant screen all calls and setting aside a certain block of time each day to return the important ones. Unfortunately, the explosive use of cell phones seems to be making this problem even worse for many managers.

3 *Meetings.* Many managers spend as much as four hours a day in meetings. To help keep this time productive, the person handling the meeting should specify a clear agenda, start on time, keep everyone focused on the agenda, and end on time.

4 *E-mail.* Increasingly, managers are relying heavily on e-mail and other forms of electronic communication. Time is wasted when managers have to sort through spam and a variety of electronic folders, in-boxes, and archives.

Management Skills for the Twenty-First Century

Although the skills discussed in this chapter have long been important parts of every successful manager's career, new skill requirements continue to emerge. Today, most experts point to the growing importance of skills involving *global management* and *technology*.

Global Management Skills   Tomorrow's managers must equip themselves with the special tools, techniques, and skills needed to compete in a global environment. They will need to understand foreign markets, cultural differences, and the motives and practices of foreign rivals. They also need to understand how to collaborate with others around the world on a real-time basis.

On a more practical level, businesses will need more managers who are capable of understanding international operations. In the past, most U.S. businesses hired local managers to run their operations in the various countries in which they operated. More recently, however, the trend has been to transfer U.S. managers to foreign locations. This practice helps firms transfer their corporate cultures to foreign operations. In addition, foreign assignments help managers become better prepared for

---

Technical Skills skills needed to perform specialized tasks

Human Relations Skills skills in understanding and getting along with people

Conceptual Skills abilities to think in the abstract, diagnose and analyze different situations, and see beyond the present situation

Decision-Making Skills skills in defining problems and selecting the best courses of action

Time Management Skills skills associated with the productive use of time

international competition as they advance within the organization. The top management teams of large corporations today are also likely to include directors from other countries.

Management and Technology Skills   Another significant issue facing tomorrow's managers is technology, especially as it relates to communication. Managers have always had to deal with information. In today's world, however, the amount of information has reached staggering proportions. In the United States alone, people exchange hundreds of millions of e-mail messages every day. New forms of technology have added to a manager's ability to process information while simultaneously making it even more important to organize and interpret an ever-increasing wealth of input.

Technology has also begun to change the way the interaction of managers shapes corporate structures. Elaborate computer networks control the flow of a firm's life-blood—information. This information no longer flows strictly up and down through hierarchies. It now flows to everyone simultaneously. As a result, decisions are made quicker, and more people are directly involved. With e-mail, videoconferencing, and other forms of communication, neither time nor distance—nor such corporate boundaries as departments and divisions—can prevent people from working more closely together. More than ever, bureaucracies are breaking down, while planning, decision making, and other activities are beginning to benefit from group building and teamwork. We discuss the effects technology has on business in more detail in Chapter 13.

Strategic Management: Setting Goals and Formulating Strategy

4   Explain the importance of strategic management and effective goal setting in organizational success.

As we noted earlier, planning is a critical part of the manager's job. Managers today are increasingly being called on to think and act strategically. **Strategic management** is the process of helping an organization maintain an effective alignment with its environment. For instance, if a firm's business environment is heading toward fiercer competition, the business may need to start cutting its costs and developing more products and services before the competition really starts to heat up. Likewise, if an industry is globalizing, a firm's managers may need to start entering new markets, developing international partnerships, and so forth during the early stages of globalization rather than waiting for its full effects.

The starting point in effective strategic management is setting **goals**—objectives that a business hopes and plans to achieve. Every business needs goals. Remember, however, that deciding what it intends to do is only the first step for an organization. Managers must also make decisions about what actions will and will not achieve company goals. Decisions cannot be made on a problem-by-problem basis or merely to meet needs as they arise. In most companies, a broad program underlies those decisions. That program is called a **strategy,** which is a broad set of organizational plans for implementing the decisions made for achieving organizational goals. Let's begin by examining business goals more closely.

Setting Business Goals

Goals are performance targets—the means by which organizations and their managers measure success or failure at every level. For example, Marjorie Scardino's goals at Pearson are currently tied to cost reductions and improved profitability; in the future, she will likely focus more on growth. At AmEx, however, Kenneth Chenault is focusing more on revenue growth and the firm's stock price. Indra Nooyi's goals at Pepsi include keeping abreast of changing consumer tastes and leveraging the firm's current products

ENTREPRENEURSHIP AND NEW VENTURES

Samuel Adams Makes Headway

In 1984 James Koch was a high-flying management consultant earning over $250,000 a year. To the surprise of his family and friends, however, he quit this job and invested his life's savings to start a business from scratch and go head-to-head with international competitors in a market that had not had a truly successful specialty product in decades. To everyone's even greater surprise, he succeeded.

Koch's company is Boston Beer, and its flagship product is a premium beer called Samuel Adams. James set up shop in an old warehouse in Boston, bought some surplus equipment from a large brewery, and started operations. Because he used only the highest-quality ingredients, Koch had to price his product at about $1 more per case than such premium imports as Heineken. Most distributors, doubting consumers would pay $6 per six-pack for an American beer, refused to carry it. So Koch began selling directly to retailers and bars.

His big break came when Samuel Adams Lager won the consumer preference poll at the Great American Beer Festival. Koch quickly turned this victory into an advertising mantra, proclaiming Samuel Adams "The Best Beer in America." As sales took off, national distributors came calling; to meet surging demand, Koch contracted parts of his brewing operations to facilities in Pittsburgh and Cincinnati.

During the early 1990s, annual sales of Samuel Adams products grew at a rate of over 50 percent and today exceed $340 million. The 2008 purchase of a brewery outside Philadelphia increased the firm's brewing capacity by over 1.6 million barrels per year. Boston Beer even exports Samuel Adams to Germany, where it's become popular among finicky beer drinkers. Koch, who retains controlling interest in the business, still oversees day-to-day brewing operations. Indeed, he claims to have sampled at least one of the firm's products every day.[4]

MyBizLab

Samuel Adams handout/MCT/Newscom

into new markets. And Jeffrey Smisek's goals at United are to continue the smooth integration of Continental and United into the world's largest airline.

Purposes of Goal Setting   An organization functions systematically because it sets goals and plans accordingly. An organization commits its resources on all levels to achieve its goals. Specifically, we can identify four main purposes in organizational goal setting:

1   *Goal setting provides direction and guidance for managers at all levels.* If managers know precisely where the company is headed, there is less potential for error in the different units of the company. Starbucks, for example, has a goal of increasing capital spending by 10 percent, with all additional expenditures devoted to opening new stores. This goal clearly informs everyone in the firm that expansion into new territories is a high priority for the firm.

Strategic Management process of helping an organization maintain an effective alignment with its environment

Goal objective that a business hopes and plans to achieve

Strategy broad set of organizational plans for implementing the decisions made for achieving organizational goals

2 *Goal setting helps firms allocate resources.* Areas that are expected to grow will get first priority. The company allocates more resources to new projects with large sales potential than it allocates to mature products with established but stagnant sales potential. Thus, Starbucks is primarily emphasizing new store expansion, while its e-commerce initiatives are currently given a lower priority. "Our management team," says CEO Howard Schultz, "is 100 percent focused on growing our core business without distraction ... from any other initiative."

3 *Goal setting helps to define corporate culture.* For years, the goal at General Electric has been to push each of its divisions to first or second in its industry. The result is a competitive (and often stressful) environment and a corporate culture that rewards success and has little tolerance for failure. At the same time, however, GE's appliance business, television network (NBC), aircraft engine unit, and financial services business are each among the very best in their respective industries. Eventually, the firm's CEO set an even higher companywide standard—to make the firm the most valuable in the world.

4 *Goal setting helps managers assess performance.* If a unit sets a goal of increasing sales by 10 percent in a given year, managers in that unit who attain or exceed the goal can be rewarded. Units failing to reach the goal will also be compensated accordingly. GE has a long-standing reputation for evaluating managerial performance, richly rewarding those who excel—and getting rid of those who do not. Each year, the lower 10 percent of GE's managerial force are informed that either they make dramatic improvements in performance or consider alternative directions for their careers.

Kinds of Goals   Goals differ from company to company, depending on the firm's purpose and mission. Every enterprise has a purpose, or a reason for being. Businesses seek profits, universities seek to discover and transmit new knowledge, and government agencies seek to set and enforce public policy. Many enterprises also have missions and **mission statements**—statements of how they will achieve their purposes in the environments in which they conduct their businesses.

A company's mission is usually easy to identify, at least at a basic level. Starbucks sums up its mission very succinctly: the firm intends to "establish Starbucks as the premier purveyor of the finest coffee in the world while maintaining our uncompromising principles while we grow." But businesses sometimes have to rethink their strategies and mission as the competitive environment changes. A few years ago, for example, Starbucks announced that Internet marketing and sales were going to become core business initiatives. Managers subsequently realized, however, that this initiative did not fit the firm as well as they first thought. As a result, they scaled back this effort and made a clear recommitment to their existing retail business. The demands of change force many companies to rethink their missions and revise their statements of what they are and what they do.

In addition to its mission, every firm also has long-term, intermediate, and short-term goals:

- **Long-term goals** relate to extended periods of time, typically five years or more. For example, AmEx might set a long-term goal of doubling the number of participating merchants during the next 10 years. Kodak might adopt a long-term goal of increasing its share of the digital picture processing market by 10 percent during the next eight years.

- **Intermediate goals** are set for a period of one to five years. Companies usually set intermediate goals in several areas. For example, the marketing department's goal might be to increase sales by 3 percent in two years. The production department might want to reduce expenses by 6 percent in four years. Human resources might seek to cut turnover by 10 percent in two years. Finance might aim for a 3-percent increase in return on investment in three years.

- **Short-term goals** are set for perhaps one year and are developed for several different areas. Increasing sales by 2 percent this year, cutting costs by 1 percent next quarter, and reducing turnover by 4 percent over the next six months are examples of short-term goals.

After a firm has set its goals, it then focuses attention on strategies to accomplish them.

Types of Strategy

As shown in Figure 5.2, the three types of strategy that are usually considered by a company are *corporate strategy*, *business* (or *competitive*) *strategy*, and *functional strategy*.

Corporate Strategy   The purpose of **corporate strategy** is to determine what business or businesses a company will own and operate. Some corporations own and operate only a single business. The makers of WD-40, for example, concentrate solely on that brand. Other corporations own and operate many businesses. A company may decide to *grow* by increasing its activities or investment or to *retrench* by reducing them.

Sometimes a corporation buys and operates multiple businesses in compatible industries as part of its corporate strategy. For example, the restaurant chains operated by YUM! (KFC, Pizza Hut, and Taco Bell) are clearly related to one another. This strategy is called *related diversification*. However, if the businesses are not similar, the strategy is called *unrelated diversification*. Samsung, which owns electronics, construction, chemicals, catering, and hotel businesses is following this approach. Under Kenneth Chenault, AmEx corporate strategy calls for strengthening operations through a principle of growth called *e-partnering*—buying shares of small companies that can provide technology that AmEx itself does not have.

Business (or Competitive) Strategy   When a corporation owns and operates multiple businesses, it must develop strategies for each one. **Business (or competitive) strategy,** then, takes place at the level of the business unit or product line and focuses on improving the company's competitive position. For example, at this level, AmEx makes decisions about how best to compete in an industry that includes Visa,

Figure 5.2 **Hierarchy of Strategy**
Source: Based on Thomas L. Wheelen and J. David Hunger, *Strategic Management and Business Policy*, 8th ed. (Upper Saddle River, NJ: Prentice Hall, 2002), 14.

Mission Statement organization's statement of how it will achieve its purpose in the environment in which it conducts its business

Long-Term Goal goal set for an extended time, typically five years or more into the future

Intermediate Goal goal set for a period of one to five years into the future

Short-Term Goal goal set for the very near future

Corporate Strategy strategy for determining the firm's overall attitude toward growth and the way it will manage its businesses or product lines

Business (or Competitive) Strategy strategy, at the business-unit or product-line level, focusing on improving a firm's competitive position

MasterCard, and other credit card companies. In this respect, the company has committed heavily to expanding its product offerings and serving customers through new technology. Pepsi, meanwhile, has one strategy for its soft drink business as it competes with Coca-Cola and a different strategy for its sports drink business and yet another strategy for its New Age beverage company. It has still other strategies for its snack foods businesses.

Functional Strategy   At the level of **functional strategy,** managers in specific areas such as marketing, finance, and operations decide how best to achieve corporate goals by performing their functional activities most effectively. At AmEx, for example, each business unit has considerable autonomy in deciding how to use the single website at which the company has located its entire range of services. Pepsi, meanwhile, develops functional strategies for marketing its beverage and snack foods products and operations strategies for distributing them. The real challenges—and opportunities—lie in successfully creating these strategies. Therefore, we now turn our attention to the basic steps in strategy formulation.

Formulating Strategy

Planning is often concerned with the nuts and bolts of setting goals, choosing tactics, and establishing schedules. In contrast, *strategy* tends to have a wider scope. By definition, it is a broad concept that describes an organization's intentions. Further, a strategy outlines how the business intends to meet its goals and includes the organization's responsiveness to new challenges and new needs. Because a well-formulated strategy is so vital to a business's success, most top managers devote substantial attention and creativity to this process. **Strategy formulation** involves the three basic steps summarized in Figure 5.3 and discussed next.

Step 1:   *Setting Strategic Goals* **Strategic goals** are derived directly from a firm's mission statement. For example, Martin Winterkorn, CEO of Volkswagen, has clear strategic goals for the European carmaker. When he took over, Volkswagen was only marginally profitable, was regarded as an also-ran in the industry, and was thinking about pulling out of the U.S. market altogether because its sales were so poor. Over the next few years, however, Winterkorn totally revamped the firm, acquired Audi, Skoda, Scania, and Porsche, and is now making big profits. Volkswagen is also now a much more formidable force in the global automobile industry.

Step 2:   *Analyzing the Organization and the Environment: SWOT Analysis* After strategic goals have been established, managers usually attempt to assess

Figure 5.3 Strategy Formulation
Source: Adapted from Stephen P. Robbins and Mary Coulter, *Management,* 9th ed. (Upper Saddle River, NJ: Prentice Hall, 2007), 199.

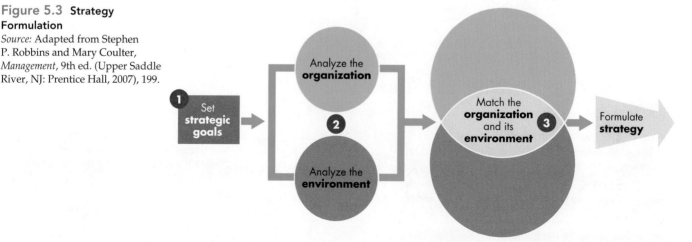

both their organization and its environment. A common framework for this assessment is called a **SWOT analysis.** This process involves assessing organizational strengths and weaknesses (the **S** and **W**) and environmental opportunities and threats (the **O** and **T**). In formulating strategy, managers attempt to capitalize on organizational strengths and take advantage of environmental opportunities. During this same process, they may seek ways to overcome or offset organizational weaknesses and avoid or counter environmental threats.

Scanning the business environment for threats and opportunities is often called **environmental analysis.** Changing consumer tastes and hostile takeover offers are threats, as are new government regulations that will limit a firm's opportunities. Even more important threats come from new products and new competitors. For example, online music services like iTunes are a major threat to manufacturers of CDs and CD players. Likewise, the emergence of digital photography has dramatically weakened companies tied to print photography. Opportunities, meanwhile, are areas in which the firm can potentially expand, grow, or take advantage of existing strengths. For example, when Pepsi managers recognized the growing market potential for bottled water, they moved quickly to launch their Aquafina brand and to position it for rapid growth.

In addition to analyzing external factors by performing an environmental analysis, managers must also examine internal factors. The purpose of such an **organizational analysis** is to better understand a company's strengths and weaknesses. Strengths might include surplus cash, a dedicated workforce, an ample supply of managerial talent, technical expertise, or little competition. For example, Pepsi's strength in beverage distribution through its network of soft drink distributors was successfully extended to distribution of bottled water. A cash shortage, aging factories, a heavily unionized workforce, and a poor public image can all be important weaknesses.

Step 3: *Matching the Organization and Its Environment* The final step in strategy formulation is matching environmental threats and opportunities against corporate strengths and weaknesses. This matching process is at the heart of strategy formulation. That is, a firm should attempt to leverage its strengths so as to capitalize on opportunities and counteract threats; it should also attempt to shield its weaknesses, or at least not allow them to derail other activities. For instance, knowing how to distribute consumer products (a strength) allows Pepsi to add new businesses and extend existing ones that use the same distribution models. But a firm that lacked a strong understanding of consumer product distribution would be foolish to add new products whose success relied heavily on efficient distribution.

Understanding strengths and weaknesses may also determine whether a firm typically takes risks or behaves more conservatively. Either approach can be successful. Blue Bell, for example, is one of the most profitable ice-cream makers in the world, even though it sells its products

---

Functional Strategy strategy by which managers in specific areas decide how best to achieve corporate goals through productivity

Strategy Formulation creation of a broad program for defining and meeting an organization's goals

Strategic Goal goal derived directly from a firm's mission statement

SWOT Analysis identification and analysis of organizational strengths and weaknesses and environmental opportunities and threats as part of strategy formulation

Environmental Analysis process of scanning the business environment for threats and opportunities

Organizational Analysis process of analyzing a firm's strengths and weaknesses

MANAGING IN TURBULENT TIMES

Best Buy—Built to Last

Recent times have seen the demise of retailing giants like Circuit City and Linens-N-Things, as well as the weakening of others like Ann Taylor and Sears. But one industry stalwart, Best Buy, continues to thrive. Down the hall from the CEO's office at the Best Buy headquarters in Minneapolis, there's a row of hospital beds, each containing the effigy of an ailing or deceased U.S. retailer. Bedside charts reveal dire financial results. A nearby sign reads: "This is where companies go when their strategies get sick."

What are the keys to success at Best Buy? Former CEO Brad Anderson saw his job as keeping the company in strategic good health. So, for one thing, he went to great lengths to stay in tune with customer tastes and preferences. He also decided that the company would stop paying commissions to its sales staff and put these employees on salary instead. The move didn't go over well with the big suppliers who expected a retailer's salespeople to push their premium products, but customers appreciated the break from high-pressure sales tactics, and revenues at Best Buy jumped by 25 percent a year in the early 1990s.

Anderson also made the decision to buy a Minneapolis start-up that specialized in installing and fixing PCs. And by 2005, there was a Geek Squad presence in every store in the chain. Whether working at the customer's home, in a Best Buy outlet, over the phone, or online, the Geeks constitute a first line of defense against the technological frustrations that can sap the value out of an electronics purchase and the goodwill out of a customer experience. Anderson was confident from the first that the technical-services market would continue to grow, but perhaps more importantly, he realized that competitors like Wal-Mart and Costco would never offer the kind of customer service that Best Buy could offer through the Geek Squad. On sales of $1 billion, the Geek Squad now generates about $280 million in profits annually.

By far, however, Anderson's most ambitious strategic gambit has been the "customer-centricity"—or just plain "centricity"—initiative. The keys to centricity are demographics and segmentation. From store to store, the most valuable customers—the ones whose patronage is most lucrative—don't necessarily belong to the same group of people. At one outlet, for example, the most profitable customers might be affluent tech enthusiasts; elsewhere, they may be suburban mothers, price-conscious family guys, or youthful gadget fiends. Beginning in 2003, Anderson started "centrizing" Best

Kristoffer Tripplaar/Alamy

Buy stores—realigning them to cater to their most profitable segments (or combination of segments). A given location, for instance, may be geared toward young gadget fiends, another toward suburban mothers. The first will have a broader range of video games and special stations for trying out accessories; the second will have a staff of personal shopping assistants to help a homemaker find the right digital camera for recording family activities. If a store caters to affluent tech enthusiasts (as about 40 percent of them do), there will be a home theater expert on hand.

In a sign of the volatile times, Best Buy announced in November 2008 that it expected revenues for fiscal 2009 to fall short of projections. When the smoke had cleared, however, sales had gone up 4 percent, thanks in part to another Brad Anderson gamble that had paid off: Although comparable-store sales (sales in stores that have been open for at least a year) had declined 6.8 percent, the losses were offset by revenues from 138 new stores that had been opened in the preceding 12 months. "While the environment continues to be as challenging as we expected," said Anderson, "consumers are being drawn to brands that they trust, and they are responding to our customer-centric model. In this light, we believe that the market-share gains we've been making will be sustained."[5]

MyBizLab

in only about a dozen states. Based in Brenham, Texas, Blue Bell controls more than 50 percent of the market in each state where it does business. The firm, however, has resisted the temptation to expand too quickly. Its success is based on product freshness and frequent deliveries—strengths that may suffer if the company grows too large.

A Hierarchy of Plans

The final step in formulating strategy is translating the strategy into more operational language. This process generally involves the creation of actual plans. Plans can be viewed on three levels: strategic, tactical, and operational. Managerial responsibilities are defined at each level. The levels constitute a hierarchy because implementing plans is practical only when there is a logical flow from one level to the next.

- **Strategic plans** reflect decisions about resource allocations, company priorities, and the steps needed to meet strategic goals. They are usually created by the firm's top management team but, as noted earlier, often rely on input from others in the organization. So, the fundamental outcome of the strategic planning process is the creation of a strategic plan. General Electric's decision that viable businesses must rank first or second within their respective markets is a matter of strategic planning.

- **Tactical plans** are shorter-term plans for implementing specific aspects of the company's strategic plans. That is, after a strategic plan has been created, managers then develop shorter-term plans to guide decisions so they are consistent with the strategic plan. They typically involve upper and middle management. Dell's efforts to extend its distribution expertise into the markets for televisions and other home electronics is an example of tactical planning.

- **Operational plans,** which are developed by mid-level and lower-level managers, set short-term targets for daily, weekly, or monthly performance. Starbucks, for instance, has operational plans dealing with how its stores must buy, store, and brew coffee.

Contingency Planning and Crisis Management

5 Discuss contingency planning and crisis management in today's business world.

Because business environments are often difficult to predict and because the unexpected can create major problems, most managers recognize that even the best-laid plans sometimes simply do not work out. For instance, when Walt Disney announced plans to launch a cruise line replete with familiar Disney characters and themes, managers also began aggressively developing and marketing packages linking three- and four-day cruises with visits to Disney World in Florida. The inaugural sailing was sold out more than a year in advance, and the first year was booked solid six months before the ship was launched. Three months before the first sailing, however, the shipyard constructing Disney's first ship (the *Disney Magic*) notified the company that it was behind schedule and that delivery would be several weeks late. When similar problems befall other cruise lines, they can offer to rebook passengers on alternative itineraries. But because Disney had no other ship, it had no choice but to refund the money it had collected as prebooking deposits for its first 15 cruises.

The 20,000 displaced customers were offered big discounts if they rebooked on a later cruise. Many of them, however, could not rearrange their schedules and

---

Strategic Plan plan reflecting decisions about resource allocations, company priorities, and steps needed to meet strategic goals

Tactical Plan generally short-term plan concerned with implementing specific aspects of a company's strategic plans

Operational Plan plan setting short-term targets for daily, weekly, or monthly performance

requested full refunds. Moreover, quite a few blamed Disney for the problem, and a few expressed outrage at what they saw as poor planning by the entertainment giant. Fortunately for Disney, however, the *Disney Magic* was eventually launched and has now become very popular and very profitable. Because managers know such things can happen, they often develop alternative plans in case things go awry. Two common methods of dealing with the unknown and unforeseen are *contingency planning* and *crisis management*.

Contingency Planning

Contingency planning seeks to identify in advance important aspects of a business or its market that might change. It also identifies the ways in which a company will respond to changes. Suppose, for example, that a company develops a plan to create a new division. It expects sales to increase at an annual rate of 10 percent for the next five years, and it develops a marketing strategy for maintaining that level. But suppose that sales have increased by only 5 percent by the end of the first year. Does the firm (1) abandon the venture, (2) invest more in advertising, or (3) wait to see what happens in the second year? Whichever choice the firm makes, its efforts will be more efficient if managers decide in advance what to do in case sales fall below planned levels.

Contingency planning helps them do exactly that. Disney learned from its mistake with its first ship—when the second ship was launched a year later, managers allowed for an extra two weeks between when the ship was supposed to be ready for sailing and its first scheduled cruise.

Crisis Management

A crisis is an unexpected emergency requiring immediate response. **Crisis management** involves an organization's methods for dealing with emergencies. Seeing the consequences of poor crisis management after the terrorist attacks of September 11, 2001, and the hurricanes that hit the Gulf Coast in 2005, many firms today are working to create new and better crisis management plans and procedures.

For example, both Reliant Energy and Duke Energy rely on computer trading centers where trading managers actively buy and sell energy-related commodities. If a terrorist attack or natural disaster were to strike their trading centers, they would essentially be out of business. Consequently, Reliant and Duke have created secondary trading centers at other locations. In the event of a shutdown at their main trading centers, these firms can quickly transfer virtually all their core trading activities to their secondary centers within 30 minutes or less.[6] Still, however many firms do not have comprehensive crisis management strategies. For example, as concerns grew about the outbreak of H1N1 (swine) flu in 2009 and some officials warned of a possible pandemic, a survey found that only about 57 percent of U.S. businesses had plans in place to deal with a flu pandemic.

6 Describe the development and explain the importance of corporate culture.

Management and the Corporate Culture

Every organization—big or small, more successful or less successful—has an unmistakable "feel" to it. Just as every individual has a unique personality, every company has a unique identity, a **corporate culture:** the shared experiences, stories, beliefs, and norms that characterize an organization. This culture helps define the work and business climate that exists in an organization.

A strong corporate culture serves several purposes. For one thing, it directs employees' efforts and helps everyone work toward the same goals. Some cultures, for example, stress financial success to the extreme, whereas others focus more on quality of life. In addition, corporate culture helps newcomers learn accepted behaviors. If financial success is the key to a culture, newcomers quickly learn that they are expected to work long, hard hours and that the "winner" is the one who brings in the most revenue. But if quality of life is more fundamental, newcomers learn that it's more acceptable to spend less time at work and that balancing work and nonwork is encouraged.

Where does a business's culture come from? In some cases, it emanates from the days of an organization's founder. Firms such as Walt Disney, Hewlett-Packard, Wal-Mart, and J. C. Penney, for example, still bear the imprint of their founders. In other cases, an organization's culture is forged over a long period of time by a constant and focused business strategy. Pepsi, for example, has an achievement-oriented culture tied to its long-standing goal of catching its biggest competitor, Coca-Cola. Similarly, Google has a sort of "work hard, play hard" culture stemming from its constant emphasis on innovation and growth coupled with lavish benefits and high pay.

Sam Walton honed his craft as a retailer at Walton's five and dime. He then used his experience to create a unique corporate culture when he founded Wal-Mart.

Communicating the Culture and Managing Change

Corporate culture influences management philosophy, style, and behavior. Managers, therefore, must carefully consider the kind of culture they want for their organizations and then work to nourish that culture by communicating with everyone who works there.

Communicating the Culture   To use a firm's culture to its advantage, managers must accomplish several tasks, all of which hinge on effective communication. First, managers themselves must have a clear understanding of the culture. Second, they must transmit the culture to others in the organization. Thus, training and orientation for newcomers in an organization often includes information about the firm's culture. A clear and meaningful statement of the organization's mission is also a valuable communication tool. Finally, managers can maintain the culture by rewarding and promoting those who understand it and work toward maintaining it.

Managing Change   Organizations must sometimes change their cultures. In such cases, they must also communicate the nature of the change to both employees and customers. According to the CEOs of several companies that have undergone radical change in the last decade or so, the process usually goes through three stages:

1 *At the highest level, analysis of the company's environment highlights extensive change as the most effective response to its problems.* This period is typically characterized by conflict and resistance.

2 *Top management begins to formulate a vision of a new company.* Whatever that vision, it must include renewed focus on the activities of competitors and the needs of customers.

3 *The firm sets up new systems for appraising and compensating employees who enforce the firm's new values.* The purpose is to give the new culture solid shape from within the firm.

Contingency Planning identifying aspects of a business or its environment that might entail changes in strategy

Crisis Management organization's methods for dealing with emergencies

Corporate Culture the shared experiences, stories, beliefs, and norms that characterize an organization

UPPA/Photoshot

Continued from page 114

Want to Know the Future? Just Google It...

For the immediate future, at least, Google plans on following its basic proven recipe for success, competing head to head with financial-service providers for stock information and with iTunes for music and videos. Also committed to the in-house development of new features and services, Google spent $2.4 billion on R&D in 2010 (up from $1.2 billion in 2006) and another $1 billion to acquire new IT assets. Innovations in the works include an automated universal language translator for translating documents in any language into any other language and personalized home pages that will allow users to design automatic searches and display the results in personal "newspapers."

Nobody knows for sure what else is on the drawing board. In fact, outsiders—notably potential investors—often criticize Google for being a "black box" when they want a few more details about such topics of investor interest as long-range strategy. "We don't talk about our strategy," explains Page, "… because it's strategic. I would rather have people think we're confused than let our competitors know what we're going to do."

QUESTIONS FOR DISCUSSION

1 Describe examples of each of the management functions illustrated in this case.
2 Which management skills seem to be most exemplified in Sergey Brin and Larry Page?
3 What role have goals and strategy played in the success of Google?
4 How would you describe the corporate culture at Google?

SUMMARY OF LEARNING OBJECTIVES   MyBizLab

1. **Describe the nature of management and identify the four basic functions that constitute the management process. (pp. 114–117)**
Management is the process of planning, organizing, leading, and controlling all of a firm's resources to achieve its goals. *Planning* is determining what the organization needs to do and how best to get it done. The process of arranging resources and activities into a coherent structure is called *organizing*. When *leading*, a manager guides and motivates employees to meet the firm's objectives. *Controlling* is the process of monitoring performance to make sure that a firm is meeting its goals.

2. **Identify different types of managers likely to be found in an organization by level and area. (pp. 117–119)**
There are three levels of management. The few executives who are responsible for the overall performance of large companies are *top managers*. Just below top managers are *middle managers*, including plant, operations, and division managers, who implement strategies, policies, and decisions made by top managers. Supervisors and office managers are the *first-line managers* who work with and supervise the employees who report to them.
  In any large company, most managers work in one of five areas. *Human resource managers* hire and train employees, assess performance, and fix compensation. *Operations managers* are responsible for production, inventory, and quality control. *Marketing managers* are responsible for getting products from producers to consumers. *Information managers* design and implement systems to gather, organize, and distribute information. Some firms have a top manager called a *chief information officer (CIO)*. *Financial managers*, including the chief financial officer (top), division controllers (middle), and accounting supervisors (first-line), oversee accounting functions and financial resources.

3. **Describe the basic skills required of managers. (pp. 120–122)**
Effective managers must develop a number of important skills. *Technical skills* are skills needed to perform specialized tasks. *Human relations skills* are skills in understanding and getting along with other people. *Conceptual skills* refer to the ability to think abstractly as well as diagnose and analyze different situations. *Decision-making skills* include the ability to define problems and select the best courses of action. *Time management skills* refer to the productive use of time. *Global management skills* include understanding foreign markets, cultural differences, and the motives and practices of foreign rivals. *Technology management skills* include the ability to process, organize, and interpret an ever-increasing amount of information.

4. **Explain the importance of strategic management and effective goal setting in organizational success. (pp. 122–129)**
Strategic management is the process of helping an organization maintain an effective alignment with its environment. It starts with setting *goals*—objectives that a business hopes (and plans) to achieve. Determined by the board and top management, *strategies* reflect decisions about resource allocations, company priorities, and plans. The three types of strategy that are usually considered by a company are *corporate strategy*, *business* (or *competitive*) *strategy*, and *functional strategy*.

5. **Discuss contingency planning and crisis management in today's business world. (pp. 129–130)**
Companies often develop alternative plans in case things go awry. There are two common methods of dealing with the unforeseen, *contingency planning* and *crisis management*. Contingency planning is planning for change: It seeks to identify in advance important aspects of a business or its market that might change. It also identifies the ways in which a company will respond to changes. Crisis management involves an organization's methods for dealing with emergencies.

6. **Describe the development and explain the importance of corporate culture. (pp. 130–131)**
Every company has a unique identity called *corporate culture*: its shared experiences, stories, beliefs, and norms. It helps define the work and business climate of an organization. A strong corporate culture directs efforts and helps everyone work toward the same goals. If an organization must change its culture, it must communicate the nature of the change to both employees and customers.

KEY TERMS   MyBizLab

business (or competitive) strategy (p. 125)
conceptual skills (p. 120)
contingency planning (p. 130)
controlling (p. 116)
corporate culture (p. 130)
corporate strategy (p. 125)
crisis management (p. 130)
decision-making skills (p. 120)
environmental analysis (p. 127)
first-line manager (p. 118)
functional strategy (p. 126)

goal (p. 122)
human relations skills (p. 120)
intermediate goal (p. 124)
leading (p. 116)
long-term goal (p. 124)
management (p. 114)
middle manager (p. 118)
mission statement (p. 124)
operational plan (p. 129)
organizational analysis (p. 127)
organizing (p. 116)
planning (p. 114)

short-term goal (p. 125)
strategic goal (p. 126)
strategic management (p. 122)
strategic plan (p. 129)
strategy (p. 122)
strategy formulation (p. 126)
SWOT analysis (p. 127)
tactical plan (p. 129)
technical skills (p. 120)
time management skills (p. 121)
top manager (p. 118)

QUESTIONS AND EXERCISES

QUESTIONS FOR REVIEW

1. Relate the five basic management skills (technical, human relations, conceptual, decision-making, and time management) to the four activities in the management process (planning, organizing, leading, and controlling). For example, which skills are most important in leading?
2. What are the four main purposes of setting goals in an organization?
3. Identify and explain the three basic steps in strategy formulation.
4. What is corporate culture? How is it formed? How is it sustained?

QUESTIONS FOR ANALYSIS

5. Select any group of which you are a member (your company, your family, or a club or organization, for example). Explain how planning, organizing, leading, and controlling are practiced in that group.
6. Identify managers by level and area at your school, college, or university.

7. In what kind of company would the technical skills of top managers be more important than human relations or conceptual skills? Are there organizations in which conceptual skills are not important?
8. What differences might you expect to find in the corporate cultures of a 100-year-old manufacturing firm based in the Northeast and a 1-year-old e-commerce firm based in Silicon Valley?

APPLICATION EXERCISES

9. Interview the manager at any level of a local company. Identify that manager's job according to level and area. Show how planning, organizing, leading, and controlling are part of this person's job. Inquire about the manager's education and work experience. Which management skills are most important for this manager's job?
10. Compare and contrast the corporate cultures of two companies that do business in your community. Be sure to choose two companies in the same industry—for example, a Sears department store and a Wal-Mart discount store.

BUILDING YOUR BUSINESS SKILLS

Speaking with Power

Goal
To encourage you to appreciate effective speaking as a critical human relations skill.

Background Information
A manager's ability to understand and get along with supervisors, peers, and subordinates is a critical human relations skill. At the heart of this skill, says Harvard University Professor of Education Sarah McGinty, is the ability to speak with power and control. McGinty defines "powerful speech" in terms of the following characteristics:
- The ability to speak at length and in complete sentences
- The ability to set a conversational agenda
- The ability to deter interruptions
- The ability to argue openly and to express strong opinions about ideas, not people
- The ability to make statements that offer solutions rather than pose questions
- The ability to express humor
    Taken together, says McGinty, "all this creates a sense of confidence in listeners."

Method

Step 1
Working alone, compare your own personal speaking style with McGinty's description of powerful speech by taping yourself as you speak during a meeting with classmates or during a phone conversation. (Tape both sides of the conversation only if the person to whom you are speaking gives permission.) Listen for the following problems:
- Unfinished sentences
- An absence of solutions
- Too many disclaimers ("I'm not sure I have enough information to say this, but ...")
- The habit of seeking support from others instead of making definitive statements of personal conviction (saying, "I recommend consolidating the medical and fitness functions," instead of, "As Emily stated in her report, I recommend consolidating the medical and fitness functions")
- Language fillers (saying, "you know," "like," and "um" when you are unsure of your facts or uneasy about expressing your opinion)

Step 2
Join with three or four other classmates to evaluate each other's speaking styles. Finally,
- Have a 10-minute group discussion on the importance of human relations skills in business.
- Listen to other group members, and take notes on the "power" content of what you hear.
- Offer constructive criticism by focusing on what speakers say rather than on personal characteristics (say, "Bob, you sympathized with Paul's position, but I still don't know what you think," instead of, "Bob, you sounded like a weakling").

FOLLOW-UP QUESTIONS

1. How do you think the power content of speech affects a manager's ability to communicate? Evaluate some of the ways in which effects may differ among supervisors, peers, and subordinates.
2. How do you evaluate yourself and group members in terms of powerful and powerless speech? List the strengths and weaknesses of the group.
3. Do you agree or disagree with McGinty that business success depends on gaining insight into your own language habits? Explain your answer.
4. In our age of computers and e-mail, why do you think personal presentation continues to be important in management?
5. McGinty believes that power language differs from company to company and that it is linked to the corporate culture. Do you agree, or do you believe that people express themselves in similar ways no matter where they are?

EXERCISING YOUR ETHICS: INDIVIDUAL EXERCISE

Making Room for Alternative Actions

The Situation

Assume that you are the manager of a large hotel adjacent to a medical center in a major city. The medical center itself consists of 10 major hospitals and research institutes. Two of the hospitals are affiliated with large universities and two with churches. Three are public and three are private. The center has an international reputation and attracts patients from around the world.

Because so many patients and their families travel great distances to visit the medical center and often stay for days or weeks, there are also eight large hotels in the area, including three new ones. The hotel that you manage is one of the older ones and, frankly, is looking a bit shabby. Corporate headquarters has told you that the hotel will either be closed or undergo a major remodeling in about two years. In the meantime, you are expected to wring every last cent of profit out of the hotel.

The Dilemma

A tropical storm has just struck the area and brought with it major flooding and power outages. Three of the medical center hospitals have been shut down indefinitely, as have six of the nearby hotels. Fortunately, your hotel sustained only minor damage and is fully functional. You have just called a meeting with your two assistant managers to discuss what actions, if any, you should take.

One assistant manager has urged you to cut room rates immediately for humanitarian reasons. This manager also wants you to open the hotel kitchens 24 hours a day to prepare free food for rescue workers and meals to donate to the hospitals, whose own food-service operations have been disrupted. The other assistant manager, meanwhile, has urged just the opposite approach: raise room rates by at least 20 percent and sell food to rescue workers and hospitals at a premium price. You can also choose to follow the advice of neither and continue doing business as usual.

QUESTIONS TO ADDRESS

1. What are the ethical issues in this situation?
2. What do you think most managers would do in this situation?
3. What would you do?

EXERCISING YOUR ETHICS: TEAM EXERCISE

Clean Up Now, or Clean Up Later?

The Situation

The top management team of a medium-sized manufacturing company is on a strategic planning "retreat" where it is formulating ideas and plans for spurring new growth in the company. As one part of this activity, the team, working with the assistance of a consultant, has conducted a SWOT analysis. During this activity, an interesting and complex situation has been identified. Next year, the Environmental Protection Agency (EPA) will be issuing new—and much more stringent—pollution standards for the company's industry. The management team sees this as a potential "threat" in that the company will have to buy new equipment and change some of its manufacturing methods in order to comply with the new standards.

The Dilemma

One member of the team, James Smith, has posed an interesting option—not complying. His logic can be summarized as follows:

1. The firm has already developed its capital budgets for the next two years. Any additional capital expenditures will cause major problems with the company's cash flow and budget allocations.
2. The company has a large uncommitted capital budget entry available in three years; those funds could be used to upgrade pollution control systems at that time.
3. Because the company has a spotless environmental record, James Smith argues that if the company does not buy the equipment for three years, the most likely outcomes will be (a) a warning in year 1; (b) a small fine in year 2; and (c) a substantial

fine in year 3. However, the total amounts of the years 2 and 3 fines will be much lower than the cost of redoing the company budgets and complying with the new law next year.

Team Activity

Assemble a group of four students and assign each group member to one of the following roles:
- Management team member
- Lower-level employee at the company
- Company customer
- Company investor

ACTION STEPS

1 Before hearing any of your group's comments on this situation, and from the perspective of your assigned role, do you think that James Smith's suggestion regarding ignoring pollution standards is a good one? Write down the reasons for your position.

2 Before hearing any of your group's comments on this situation, and from the perspective of your assigned role, what are the underlying ethical issues in this situation? Write down the issues.

3 Gather your group together and reveal, in turn, each member's comments on James Smith's suggestion. Next, reveal the ethical issues listed by each member.

4 Appoint someone to record main points of agreement and disagreement within the group. How do you explain the results? What accounts for any disagreement?

5 From an ethical standpoint, what does your group conclude is the most appropriate action that should be taken by the company in this situation?

6 Develop a group response to the following question: What are the respective roles of profits, obligations to customers, and obligations to the community for the firm in this situation?

VIDEO EXERCISE   MyBizLab

Pizza Hut

Learning Objectives

The purpose of this video is to help you:
1 Describe the four functions of management and differentiate between the three levels of management.
2 Discuss the five key skill areas for managers.
3 Explain how managers analyze the environment and create plans.

Synopsis

Pizza Hut began over 50 years ago as the first national pizza chain in the United States. Pizza Hut is part of a larger parent company, Yum! Brands, which also includes Taco Bell and KFC. Most individual Pizza Hut restaurants are franchises owned by a local businessperson who licenses the rights to operate from the parent company. Effective management at the corporate, brand, and franchise level has kept the company profitable. Although long established in the pizza industry, Pizza Hut has needed to continually evaluate their strategy in order to maintain their competitive position. On April 1, 2008, Pizza Hut launched an intensive promotional campaign, announcing that they were changing their name to Pasta Hut. While this was a clever April Fool's joke, it coincided with the launch of their Tuscani pasta line, targeted at the carry out and home delivery markets. While the campaign developed a lot of visibility in the media, the company hedged their position by creating contingency plans in the event of consumer backlash against the marketing ploy.

DISCUSSION QUESTIONS

1 Describe the three levels of management for Pizza Hut, as described in the video. Briefly discuss the types of decisions made by each level of manager.

2 What are the four functions of management? Give an example of each for a Pizza Hut restaurant manager.

3 The text and video identify five management skills. Give an example of each for a first-line manager at a Pizza Hut restaurant.

4 Pizza Hut conducted organizational or SWOT analysis, as described in the video. What did this analysis reveal and how did the company respond?

5 In order to launch the new Tuscani pasta line, Pizza Hut brand managers had to develop tactical and operational plans. Define and give an example of each.

Online Exploration

An organization's culture is its unique personality; it helps to define the work and business climate. Corporate culture can be reflected in the shared experiences, stories, beliefs, and norms that characterize an organization. Go the Pizza Hut's website (www.pizzahut.com) and look for signs of the company's culture. In particular, you may wish to look at the Careers and Diversity links. How would you characterize Pizza Hut's corporate culture?

END NOTES

1 Google, "Corporate Information," March 10, 2011, at http://www.google.com; "The Secret to Google's Success," *BusinessWeek*, March 6, 2008, http://www.businessweek.com; "In Search of the Real Google," *Time*, February 20, 2007, http://www.time.com.

2 *Hoover's Handbook of American Business 2011* (Austin, Texas: Hoover's Business Press, 2011), pp. 230–231.

3 Anneloes Raes, Mrielle Heijltjes, Ursula Glunk, and Robert Row, "The Interface of the Top Management Team and Middle Managers: A Process Model," *Academy of Management Review*, January 2011, pp. 102–126.

4 "Sam Adams Beer to Expand Cincinnati Brewery," *USA Today* (January 6, 2005); Christopher Edmunds, "Bottom of the Barrel: Boston Beer's Winning Formula," RealMoney.com

(March 5, 2003); "Boston Beer Company - Company Profile, Information, Business Description, History, Background Information on Boston Beer Company," at http://www.referenceforbusiness.com/history2/74/Boston-Beer-Company.html, accessed March 5, 2011.

[5] Matthew Boyle, "Best Buy's Giant Gamble," Fortune, April 3, 2006; Kristina Bell, "Q&A with Best Buy CEO Brad Anderson," *Time*, June 12, 20; "How to Break Out of Commodity Hell," *BusinessWeek*, March 27, 2006; "Best Buy Reports December Revenue of $8.2 Billion, Continues Market Share Gains," Best Buy Inc., news release, January 9, 2011,.

[6] Del Jones, "Next Time," *USA Today* (October 4, 2005), 1B, 2B.

6 Organizing the Business

A New Chinese-American Recipe For Success

Lenovo was started by Chinese entrepreneur Liu Chuanzhi in 1984. The firm dabbled in a variety of high-tech industries before it began to focus on the personal computer market. Initially Lenovo made computers for other firms, most notably AST Research. In 1990, though, the firm launched its own brand of PC and by 1997 Lenovo was the top selling PC company in its home country. Unfortunately, the company was not very successful in getting its computers accepted outside of China. One reason for this was the lack of brand recognition. Another was that Lenovo simply did not have very many top managers with global experience. Hence, they did not really understand foreign markets or how to penetrate them.

But that began to change in 2005. During the early 2000s IBM, one of the world's most recognized computer companies, was developing a new strategy emphasizing informational technology and business services and concentrating on business clients. IBM also felt that PCs were dropping in price so quickly that reasonable profit margins would be difficult to maintain. When the company finally decided to sell its PC operation in 2005, Lenovo was quick to jump on the opportunity and bought IBM's PC business for $1.75 billion. Lenovo was allowed to continue using the IBM name through 2007 but then began to brand all of its PCs with the Lenovo name.

After reading this chapter, you should be able to:

1 Discuss the factors that influence a firm's organizational structure.
2 Explain specialization and departmentalization as two of the building blocks of organizational structure.
3 Describe centralization and decentralization, delegation, and authority as the key ingredients in establishing the decision-making hierarchy.
4 Explain the differences among functional, divisional, matrix, and international organizational structures and describe the most popular new forms of organizational design.
5 Describe the informal organization and discuss intrapreneuring.

Along with the PC business itself, Lenovo also got another extremely important asset—a team of skilled top managers well-versed in global PC markets. Senior IBM executives were integrated into the top management structure and one of them, Stephen Ward, was appointed CEO of Lenovo. Chuanzhi, meanwhile, moved into the background but remained a director. But almost from the start problems began to surface. Ward, for example, was extremely autocratic in how he made decisions and this alienated his new Chinese colleagues. And at a more general level, the U.S. managers tried to impose a rigid, centralized, and bureaucratic structure on the new Lenovo. The Chinese, meanwhile, were highly resistant to these efforts, strongly preferring the more traditional consensus-style structure that they had used previously.

Within a matter of months things came to a head. Among other changes, Ward was pushed

QILAI SHEN/EPA/Newscom

WHAT'S IN IT FOR ME?

Lenovo has been undergoing changes over the past several years, most of them aimed at improving the organization's structure. As a result, people who work for Lenovo have had to continually work to understand their "place" in the organization. By understanding the material in this chapter, you'll also be prepared to understand your "place" in the organization that employs you. Similarly, as a boss or owner, you'll be better equipped to create the optimal structure for your own organization.

This chapter examines factors that influence a firm's organizational structure. We discuss the building blocks of organizational structure as well as the differences between decision making in different types of organizations. Along the way, we look at a variety of organizational structures and describe the most popular new forms of organizational design.

MyBizLab Where you see MyBizLab in this chapter, go to **www.mybizlab.com** for additional activities on the topic being discussed.

out and replaced with William Amelio, a senior executive recruited from Dell Computer Asia/Pacific operations. Amelio expressed an interest in trying to move Lenovo back toward the traditional Chinese structure. He also thought that the firm could benefit from an infusion of additional perspectives, so he began to aggressively recruit new executives from other international high-tech firms. His Chinese colleagues, meanwhile, took a wait-and-see attitude.[1]

Our opening story continues on page 158.

1 Discuss the factors that influence a firm's organizational structure.

What Is Organizational Structure?

One key decision that business owners and managers must address is how best to structure their organization. Stated differently, they must decide on an appropriate organizational structure. We can define **organizational structure** as the specification of the jobs to be done within an organization and the ways in which those jobs relate to one another.[2] Perhaps the easiest way to understand structure is in terms of an *organization chart.*

Organization Charts

Most businesses prepare **organization charts** to clarify structure and to show employees where they fit into a firm's operations. Figure 6.1 is an organization chart for Contemporary Landscape Services, a small but thriving business in Bryan, Texas. Each box in the chart represents a job. The solid lines define the **chain of command**, or *reporting relationships,* within the company. For example, the retail shop, nursery, and landscape operations managers all report to the owner and president, Mark Ferguson. Within the landscape operation is one manager for residential accounts and another for commercial accounts. Similarly, there are other managers in the retail shop and the nursery.

The organization charts of large firms are far more complex and include individuals at many more levels than those shown in Figure 6.1. Size prevents many large firms from even having charts that include all their managers. Typically, they create one organization chart showing overall corporate structure, separate charts for each division, and even more charts for individual departments or units.

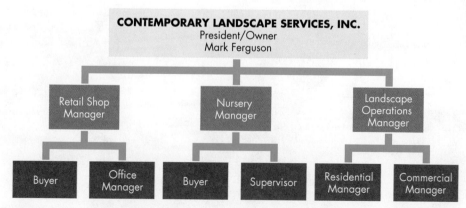

Figure 6.1 The Organization Chart

Recall our definition of organizational structure: the specification of the jobs to be done within an organization and the ways in which those jobs relate to one another. The boxes in the organization chart represent the jobs, and the lines connecting the boxes show how the jobs are related. As we will see, however, even though organizational structure can be broken down into a series of boxes and lines, virtually no two organizations will have the same structure. What works for Texas Instruments will not work for Google, Shell Oil, Amazon.com, or the U.S. Department of Justice. Likewise, the structure of the American Red Cross will probably not work for Urban Outfitters, Union Carbide, Starbucks, or the University of Minnesota.

Determinants of Organizational Structure

How is an organization's structure determined? Ideally, managers carefully assess a variety of important factors as they plan for and then create an organizational structure that will allow their organization to function efficiently.

Many factors play a part in determining an organization's optimal structure. Chief among them are the organization's *mission* and *strategy*. A dynamic and rapidly growing business, for example, needs an organizational structure that allows it to be flexible, to respond to changes in its environment and strategy, and to grow. A stable organization with only modest growth goals and a more conservative strategy will most likely function best with a different organizational structure.

Size of the company and aspects of the organization's environment also affect organizational structure. As we saw in Chapter 5, organizing is a key part of the management process. As such, it must be conducted with an equal awareness of both a firm's external and internal environments. A large manufacturer operating in a strongly competitive environment—for example, American Airlines or Hewlett-Packard—requires a different organizational structure than a local barbershop or video store. Even after an organizational structure has been created, it is rarely free from tinkering—or even outright re-creation. Most organizations change their structures on an almost continuing basis.

Since it was first incorporated in 1903, Ford Motor Company has undergone literally dozens of major structural changes, hundreds of moderate changes, and thousands of minor changes. In the last twenty years alone, Ford has initiated several major structural changes. In 1994, for instance, the firm announced a major restructuring plan called Ford 2000, which was intended to integrate all of Ford's vast international operations into a single, unified structure by the year 2000.

By 1998, however, midway through implementation of the grand plan, top Ford executives announced major modifications, indicating that (1) additional changes would be made, (2) some previously planned changes would not be made, and (3) some recently realigned operations would be changed again. In early 1999, managers announced another set of changes intended to eliminate corporate bureaucracy, speed decision making, and improve communication and working relationships among people at different levels of the organization. Early in 2001, Ford announced yet more sweeping changes intended to boost the firm's flagging bottom line and stem a decline in product quality. More significant changes followed in both 2003 and 2004, and in 2006, the firm announced several plant closings, resulting in even more changes. Not surprisingly, yet another major reorganization was announced in 2010 as the firm sought to deal with a global recession and a major slump in automobile sales.[3] And in 2011 the firm announced even more restructuring in order to gain more international market share.[4]

Organizational Structure specification of the jobs to be done within an organization and the ways in which they relate to one another

Organization Chart diagram depicting a company's structure and showing employees where they fit into its operations

Chain of Command reporting relationships within a company

2 Explain specialization and departmentalization as two of the building blocks of organizational structure.

The Building Blocks of Organizational Structure

The first step in developing the structure of any business, large or small, involves three activities:

1 *Specialization.* Determining who will do what

2 *Departmentalization.* Determining how people performing certain tasks can best be grouped together

3 *Establishment of a Decision-Making Hierarchy.* Deciding who will be empowered to make which decisions and who will have authority over others

These three activities are the building blocks of all business organizations. In this section, we discuss specialization and departmentalization. Because the decision-making hierarchy actually includes several elements, we cover it in more detail in the next section.

Specialization

The process of identifying the specific jobs that need to be done and designating the people who will perform them leads to **job specialization**. In a sense, all organizations have only one major job, such as making cars (Ford), selling finished goods to consumers (Lenova), or providing telecommunications services (Verizon). Usually, that job is more complex in nature. For example, the job of Chaparral Steel is converting scrap steel (such as wrecked automobiles) into finished steel products (such as beams and reinforcement bars).

To perform this one overall job, managers actually break it down, or specialize it, into several smaller jobs. Thus, some workers transport the scrap steel to the company's mill in Midlothian, Texas. Others operate shredding equipment before turning raw materials over to the workers who then melt them into liquid form. Other specialists oversee the flow of the liquid into molding equipment, where it is transformed into new products. Finally, other workers are responsible for moving finished products to a holding area before they are shipped out to customers. When the overall job of the organization is broken down like this, workers can develop real expertise in their jobs, and employees can better coordinate their work with that done by others.

Specialization and Growth In a very small organization, the owner may perform every job. As the firm grows, however, so does the need to specialize jobs so that others can perform them. To see how specialization can evolve in an organization, consider the case of the Walt Disney Company. When Walt Disney first opened his animation studio, he and his brother Roy did everything. For example, when they created their very first animated feature, *Steamboat Willy*, they wrote the story, drew the pictures, transferred the pictures to film, provided the voices, and went out and sold the cartoon to theater operators.

Today, however, a Disney animated feature is made possible only through the efforts of hundreds of people. The job of one animator may be to create the face of a single character throughout an entire feature. Another artist may be charged with coloring background images in certain scenes. People other than artists are responsible for the subsequent operations that turn individual computer-generated images into a moving picture or for the marketing of the finished product.

Job specialization is a natural part of organizational growth. It also has certain advantages. For example, specialized jobs are learned more easily and can be performed more efficiently than nonspecialized jobs, and it is also easier to replace people who leave an organization if they have highly specialized jobs. However, jobs at lower levels of the organization are especially susceptible to overspecialization. If such jobs become too narrowly defined, employees may become bored and careless, derive less satisfaction from their jobs, and lose sight of their roles in the organization.

Pictorial Press Ltd/Alamy

AF archive/Alamy

When Walt Disney was just starting out, he did most of the work on his animated features all by himself. But today's features like Disney's 2011 hit *Cars II* require the work of hundreds of people.

Departmentalization

After jobs are specialized, they must be grouped into logical units, which is the process of **departmentalization**. Departmentalized companies benefit from this division of activities: Control and coordination are narrowed and made easier, and top managers can see more easily how various units are performing.

Departmentalization allows the firm to treat each department as a **profit center**—a separate company unit responsible for its own costs and profits. Thus, Sears can calculate the profits it generates from men's clothing, appliances, home furnishings, and every other department within a given store separately. Managers can then use this information in making decisions about advertising and promotional events, space allocation, budgeting, and so forth.

Managers do not departmentalize jobs randomly. They group them logically, according to some common thread or purpose. In general, departmentalization may occur along *product*, *process*, *functional*, *customer*, or *geographic* lines (or any combination of these).

Product Departmentalization
Manufacturers and service providers often opt for **product departmentalization**—dividing an organization according to the specific product or service being created. Kraft Foods uses this approach to divide departments: for example, the Oscar Mayer division focuses on hot dogs and lunch meats, the Kraft Cheese division focuses on cheese products, the Maxwell House and Post division focus on coffee and breakfast cereal, respectively, and so on.[5] Because each division represents a defined group of products or services, managers at Kraft Foods are able—in theory—to focus on *specific* product lines in a clear and defined way.

Process Departmentalization
Other manufacturers favor **process departmentalization**, in which the organization is divided according to production processes used to create a good or service. This principle is logical for Vlasic, which has three separate departments to transform cucumbers into either fresh-packed pickles, pickles cured in brine, or relishes. Cucumbers destined to become fresh-packed pickles

---

Job Specialization the process of identifying the specific jobs that need to be done and designating the people who will perform them

Departmentalization process of grouping jobs into logical units

Profit Center separate company unit responsible for its own costs and profits

Product Departmentalization dividing an organization according to specific products or services being created

Process Departmentalization dividing an organization according to production processes used to create a good or service

must be packed into jars immediately, covered with a solution of water and vinegar, and prepared for sale. Those slated to be brined pickles must be aged in brine solution before packing. Relish cucumbers must be minced and combined with a host of other ingredients. Each process requires different equipment and worker skills, and different departments were created for each.

Functional Departmentalization Many service and manufacturing companies, especially smaller ones, use **functional departmentalization** to develop departments according to a group's functions or activities. Such firms typically have production, marketing and sales, human resources, and accounting and finance departments. Departments may be further subdivided. For example, the marketing department might be divided into separate staffs for market research and advertising.

Customer Departmentalization Retail stores actually derive their generic name—department stores—from the manner in which they are structured—a men's department, a women's department, a luggage department, a lawn and garden department, and so on. Each department targets a specific customer category (men, women, people who want to buy luggage, people who want to buy a lawn mower) by using **customer departmentalization** to create departments that offer products, and meet the needs of, identifiable customer groups. Thus, a customer shopping for a baby's playpen at Sears can bypass lawn and garden supplies and head straight for children's furniture. In general, the store is more efficient, and customers get better service because salespeople tend to specialize and gain expertise in their departments. Another illustration of customer departmentalization is reflected in most banks. A customer wanting a consumer loan goes to the retail banking office, whereas a small business owner goes to the commercial banking office.

Geographic Departmentalization **Geographic departmentalization** divides firms according to the areas of the country or the world that they serve. Levi Strauss, for instance, has one division for North and South America; one for Europe, the Middle East, and North Africa; and one for the Asia Pacific region.[6] Within the United States, geographic departmentalization is common among utilities. For example, Southern Company organizes its power subsidiaries into four geographic departments—Alabama, Georgia, Gulf, and Mississippi Power.[7]

Multiple Forms of Departmentalization Because different forms of departmentalization have different advantages, as firms grow in size they tend to adopt different types of departmentalization for various levels. The company illustrated in Figure 6.2 uses functional departmentalization at the top level. At the middle level,

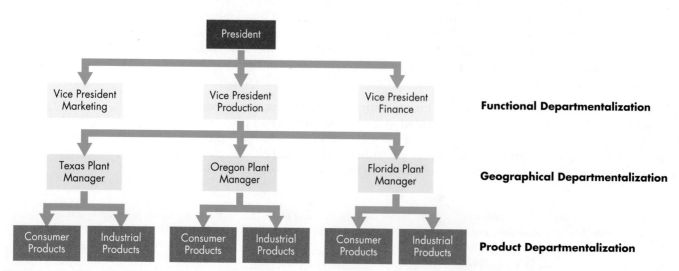

Figure 6.2 Multiple Forms of Departmentalization

MANAGING IN TURBULENT TIMES

Force-feeding the Market

Some business crises hit quickly, like the 2008–2010 recession. Others come more slowly. PepsiCo is facing one of the slow kind but is taking rapid action to turn things around. For years, consumption of soft drinks has been slowly declining. Driven primarily by health concerns, consumers in most countries are simply drinking fewer cans and bottles of the stuff. While there are no-sugar versions available, of course, Pepsi and Coke just don't taste quite the same when preceded by the word "Diet." Pepsi, for instance, shipped about 1 billion cases of soft drinks in 2007, down 20 percent from 2000.

To compensate, PepsiCo has been heavily promoting its juice, bottled water, and fruity soda brands. But the 2008–2010 recession took its toll on those products as well. PepsiCo CEO Indra Nooyi knew action was needed, so she promoted Massimo F. d'Amore to the position of CEO of PepsiCo Americas Beverages and gave him a mandate: Get the beverage business back on track.

d'Amore, in turn, decided to use organization structure as the primary driver to fix things. When he took over, the three major brands at PepsiCo Americas Beverages were Pepsi, Gatorade, and Tropicana—each operating as an independent division. d'Amore concluded that this independence was actually a problem in that the three brands were competing for the same resources, that there was too little coordination between the divisions, and that all too often, market information that should have been communicated across the divisions was instead treated as proprietary and not shared with others.

To help offset these problems, d'Amore created one large operating division for all three of the major brands, as well

Richard Levine/Alamy

as four others. This move rankled some key executives, who saw it as a reduction in their own power, and a few left the company. But d'Amore stuck to his guns and has maintained this new structure. He believes that a unified and coordinated approach to brand management will be the key that revives growth at PepsiCo Americas Beverages and will help the firm establish increased market share across all product lines and in all markets the unit serves. And if he is right, he will also have staked a major claim as Indra Nooyi's successor when she decides it's time to step down.[8]

MyBizLab

production is divided along geographic lines. At a lower level, marketing is departmentalized by product group. Larger firms are certain to use all of these different forms of departmentalization in various areas.

Establishing the Decision-Making Hierarchy

3 Describe centralization and decentralization, delegation, and authority as the key ingredients in establishing the decision-making hierarchy.

The third major building block of organizational structure is the establishment of a decision-making hierarchy. This is usually done by formalizing reporting relationships. When the focus is on the reporting relationships among individual managers

Functional Departmentalization dividing an organization according to groups' functions or activities

Customer Departmentalization dividing an organization to offer products and meet needs for identifiable customer groups

Geographic Departmentalization dividing an organization according to the areas of the country or the world served by a business

and the people who report to them, it is most commonly referred to as *delegation*. However, when the focus is on the overall organization, it becomes a question of *decentralization* versus *centralization*.

Distributing Authority: Centralization and Decentralization

Some managers make the conscious decision to retain as much decision-making authority as possible at the higher levels of the organizational structure; others decide to push authority as far down the hierarchy as possible. While we can think of these two extremes as anchoring a continuum, most companies fall somewhere between the middle of such a continuum and one end point or the other.

Centralized Organizations In a **centralized organization**, most decision-making authority is held by upper-level managers.[9] McDonald's practices centralization as a way to maintain standardization. All restaurants must follow precise steps in buying products and making and packaging menu items. Most advertising is handled at the corporate level, and any local advertising must be approved by a regional manager. Restaurants even have to follow prescribed schedules for facilities' maintenance and upgrades like floor polishing and parking lot cleaning. Centralized authority is most commonly found in companies that face relatively stable and predictable environments and is also typical of small businesses.

Decentralized Organizations As a company gets larger, more decisions must be made; thus, the company tends to adopt **decentralized organization**, in which much decision-making authority is delegated to levels of management at various points below the top. Decentralization is typical in firms that have complex and dynamic environmental conditions. It makes a company more responsive by allowing managers more discretion to make quick decisions in their areas of responsibility. For example, Urban Outfitters practices relative decentralization in that it allows individual store managers considerable discretion over merchandising and product displays. Whole Foods Market takes things even further in its decentralization. Stores are broken up into small teams, which are responsible for making decisions on issues such as voting on which new staff members to hire and which products to carry based on local preferences. This practice taps into the idea that the people who will be most affected by decisions should be the ones making them.[10]

Tall and Flat Organizations Decentralized firms tend to have relatively fewer layers of management, resulting in a **flat organizational structure** like that of the hypothetical law firm shown in Figure 6.3(a). Centralized firms typically require multiple layers of management and thus **tall organizational structures**, as in the U.S. Army example in Figure 6.3(b). Because information, whether upward or downward bound, must pass through so many organizational layers, tall structures are prone to delays in information flow.

As organizations grow in size, it is both normal and necessary that they become at least somewhat taller. For instance, a small firm with only an owner-manager and a few employees is likely to have two layers—the owner-manager and the employees who report to that person. As the firm grows, more layers will be needed. A manager must ensure that he or she has only the number of layers his or her firm needs. Too few layers can create chaos and inefficiency, whereas too many layers can create rigidity and bureaucracy.

Span of Control As you can see in Figure 6.3, the distribution of authority in an organization also affects the number of people who work for any individual manager. In a flat organizational structure, the number of people directly managed by one supervisor—the manager's **span of control**—is usually wide. In tall organizations, span of control tends to be narrower. Employees' abilities and the

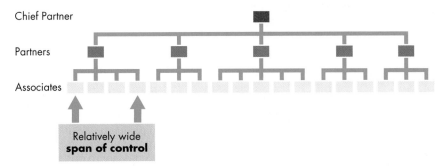

(a) FLAT ORGANIZATION: Typical Law Firm

Chief Partner

Partners

Associates

Relatively wide **span of control**

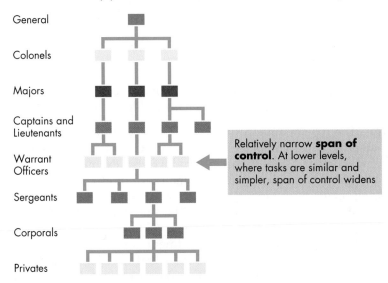

(b) TALL ORGANIZATION: United States Army

General

Colonels

Majors

Captains and Lieutenants

Warrant Officers

Sergeants

Corporals

Privates

Relatively narrow **span of control**. At lower levels, where tasks are similar and simpler, span of control widens

Figure 6.3   **Organizational Structures and Span of Control**

supervisor's managerial skills influence how wide or narrow the span of control should be, as do the similarity and simplicity of tasks and the extent to which they are interrelated.

If lower-level managers are given more decision-making authority, their supervisors will have less work to do and may then be able to take on a widened span of control. Similarly, when several employees perform either the same simple task or a group of interrelated tasks, a wide span of control is possible and often desirable. For instance, because of the routine and interdependent nature of jobs on an assembly line, one supervisor may well control the entire line.

In contrast, when jobs are more diversified or prone to change, a narrow span of control is preferable. Consider how Electronic Arts develops video games. Design,

Centralized Organization organization in which most decision-making authority is held by upper-level management

Decentralized Organization organization in which a great deal of decision-making authority is delegated to levels of management at points below the top

Flat Organizational Structure characteristic of decentralized companies with relatively few layers of management

Tall Organizational Structure characteristic of centralized companies with multiple layers of management

Span of Control number of people supervised by one manager

art, audio, and software development teams have specialized jobs whose products must come together in the end to create a coherent game. Although related, the complexities involved with and the advanced skills required by each job mean that one supervisor can oversee only a small number of employees.

The Delegation Process

Delegation is the process through which a manager allocates work to subordinates. In general, the delegation process involves:

1 Assigning **responsibility**, the duty to perform an assigned task

2 Granting **authority**, or the power to make the decisions necessary to complete the task

3 Creating **accountability**, the obligation employees have for the successful completion of the task

For the delegation process to work smoothly, responsibility and authority must be equivalent. Table 6.1 lists some common obstacles that hinder the delegation process, along with strategies for overcoming them.

Three Forms of Authority

As individuals are delegated responsibility and authority, a complex web of interactions develops in the form of *line*, *staff*, and *committee and team* authorities.

Line Authority   The type of authority that flows up and down the chain of command is **line authority**. Most companies rely heavily on **line departments** linked directly to the production and sales of specific products. For example, in the division of Clark Equipment that produces forklifts and small earthmovers, line departments include purchasing, materials handling, fabrication, painting, and assembly (all of which are directly linked to production) along with sales and distribution (both of which are directly linked to sales).

As the doers and producers, each line department is essential to an organization's ability to sell and deliver finished goods. A bad decision by the manager in one department can hold up production for an entire plant. For example, the painting department manager at Clark Equipment changes a paint application on a batch of forklifts, which then show signs of peeling paint. The batch will have to be repainted (and perhaps partially reassembled) before the machines can be shipped.

TABLE 6.1   Learning to Delegate Effectively

I'm afraid to delegate because...	Solution
My team doesn't know how to get the job done.	If members of your team are exhibiting opportunities for improved performance, offer them the training necessary for them to become more effective at their jobs.
I like controlling as many things as possible.	Recognize that trying to accomplish everything yourself while your team does nothing only sets you up for burnout and failure. As you begin to relinquish control, you will come to trust your team more as you watch your team members succeed.
I don't want anyone on my team outperforming me.	High-performing team members are a reflection of your success as a manager. Encourage them to excel, praise them for it, and share the success of *your* team with the rest of the organization.
I don't know how to delegate tasks effectively.	Consider taking a management training course or reading some books on the topic of delegating effectively.

Staff Authority   Some companies also rely on **staff authority**, which is based on special expertise and usually involves advising line managers in areas such as law, accounting, and human resources. A corporate attorney, for example, may advise the marketing department as it prepares a new contract with the firm's advertising agency, but will not typically make decisions that affect how the marketing department does its job. **Staff members** help line departments make decisions, but do not usually have the authority to make final decisions.

Typically, the separation between line authority and staff responsibility is clearly delineated and is usually indicated in organization charts by solid lines (line authority) and dotted lines (staff responsibility), as shown in Figure 6.4. It may help to understand this separation by remembering that whereas *staff members* generally provide services to management, *line managers* are directly involved in producing the firm's products.

Committee and Team Authority   Recently, more organizations have started to grant **committee and team authority** to groups that play central roles in daily operations. A committee, for example, may consist of top managers from several major areas. If the work of the committee is especially important and if the committee members will be working together for an extended time, the organization may even grant it special authority as a decision-making body beyond the individual authority possessed by each of its members.

At the operating level, many firms today use **work teams** that are empowered to plan, organize, and perform their work with minimal supervision and often

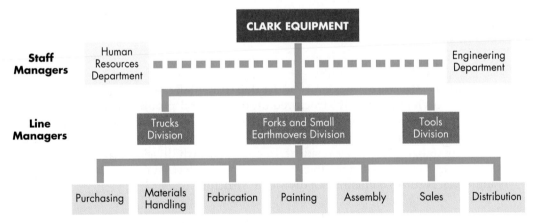

Figure 6.4 **Line and Staff Organization**

Delegation process through which a manager allocates work to subordinates

Responsibility duty to perform an assigned task

Authority power to make the decisions necessary to complete a task

Accountability obligation employees have to their manager for the successful completion of an assigned task

Line Authority organizational structure in which authority flows in a direct chain of command from the top of the company to the bottom

Line Department department directly linked to the production and sales of a specific product

Staff Authority authority based on expertise that usually involves counseling and advising line managers

Staff Members advisers and counselors who help line departments in making decisions but who do not have the authority to make final decisions

Committee and Team Authority authority granted to committees or teams involved in a firm's daily operations

Work Team groups of operating employees who are empowered to plan and organize their own work and to perform that work with a minimum of supervision with special authority as well. Most U.S. companies today use teams in at least some areas; some make widespread use of teams throughout every area of their operations.

Basic Forms of Organizational Structure

4   Explain the differences among functional, divisional, matrix, and international organizational structures and describe the most popular new forms of organizational design.

Organizations can structure themselves in an almost infinite number of ways—according to specialization, for example, or departmentalization, or the decision-making hierarchy. Nevertheless, it is possible to identify four basic forms of organizational structure that reflect the general trends followed by most firms: *functional*, *divisional*, *matrix*, and *international*.

Functional Structure

Under a **functional structure**, relationships between group functions and activities determine authority. Functional structure is used by most small to medium-sized firms, which are usually structured around basic business functions: a marketing department, an operations department, and a finance department. The benefits of this approach include specialization within functional areas and smoother coordination among them.

In large firms, coordination across functional departments becomes more complicated. Functional structure also fosters centralization (which can be desirable, but is usually counter to the goals of larger businesses) and makes accountability more difficult. As organizations grow, they tend to shed this form and move toward one of the other three structures. Figure 6.5 illustrates a functional structure.

Divisional Structure

A **divisional structure** relies on product departmentalization. Organizations using this approach are typically structured around several product-based **divisions** that resemble separate businesses in that they produce and market their own products. The head of each division may be a corporate vice president or, if the organization is large enough, a divisional president. In addition, each division usually has its own identity and operates as a relatively autonomous business under the larger corporate umbrella. Figure 6.6 illustrates a divisional structure.

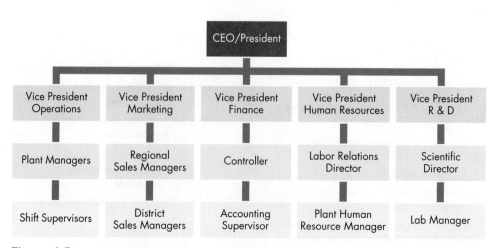

Figure 6.5 Functional Structure

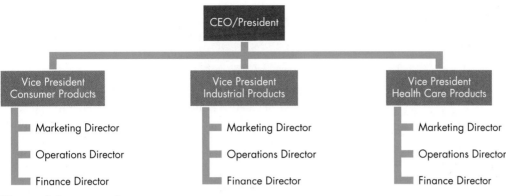

Figure 6.6 **Divisional Structure**

Johnson & Johnson, one of the most recognizable names in health care products, organizes its company into three major divisions: consumer health care products, medical devices and diagnostics, and pharmaceuticals. Each major division is then broken down further. The consumer health care products division relies on product departmentalization to separate baby care, skin and hair care, topical health care, oral health care, women's health, over-the-counter medicines, and nutritionals. These divisions reflect the diversity of the company, which can protect it during downturns, such as the one in 2008–2010, which showed the slowest pharmaceutical growth in four decades. Because they are divided, the other divisions are protected from this blight and can carry the company through it.

Consider that Johnson & Johnson's over-the-counter pain management medicines are competition for their pain management pharmaceuticals. Divisions can maintain healthy competition among themselves by sponsoring separate advertising campaigns, fostering different corporate identities, and so forth. They can also share certain corporate-level resources (such as market research data). However, if too much control is delegated to divisional managers, corporate managers may lose touch with daily operations. Also, competition between divisions can become disruptive, and efforts in one division may duplicate those of another.[11]

Matrix Structure

Sometimes a **matrix structure**—a combination of two separate structures—works better than either simpler structure alone. This structure gets its matrix-like appearance, when shown in a diagram, by using one underlying "permanent" organizational structure (say, the divisional structure flowing up-and-down in the diagram), and then superimposing a different organizing framework on top of it (e.g., the functional form flowing side-to-side in the diagram). This highly flexible and readily adaptable structure was pioneered by NASA for use in developing specific space programs.

Suppose a company using a functional structure wants to develop a new product as a one-time special project. A team might be created and given responsibility for that product. The project team may draw members from existing

Functional Structure organization structure in which authority is determined by the relationships between group functions and activities

Divisional Structure organizational structure in which corporate divisions operate as autonomous businesses under the larger corporate umbrella

Division department that resembles a separate business in that it produces and markets its own products

Matrix Structure organizational structure created by superimposing one form of structure onto another

ENTREPRENEURSHIP AND NEW VENTURES

Making the Grade

In 1965, undistinguished Yale undergrad Fred Smith wrote a paper describing how automated technology necessitated quicker, more reliable transportation. According to legend, the paper received a poor grade. But Smith himself debunks this myth. "It's become a well-known story because everybody likes to flout authority. But to be honest, I don't really remember what grade I got."

Whatever the grade, the idea was a winner. After serving in Vietnam, Smith invested his own money to start the air transport business Federal Express. FedEx, as the firm is now named, was revolutionary in pioneering the hub-and-spoke system and using bar codes, handheld PDAs, and package tracking to compete with the monopolistic U.S. Postal Service.

When rival UPS entered the airfreight segment in 2000, FedEx acquired several key players in the ground transportation industry. "The economics of airplanes are such that we couldn't just keep taking prices down," Smith says. "We finally realized that if we wanted to grow, we had to get into surface transportation." FedEx's new fleet capitalized on the brand's reputation for speed and reliability: "People say 'FedEx this' when they mean 'Get it someplace fast,'" says investor Timothy M. Ghriskey. "No one says 'UPS this.'"

Although standardization is important, FedEx's commitment to decentralization breeds innovation. Managers are encouraged and rewarded for questioning, challenging, and developing new ideas, which are always given serious consideration. Developments have included teaming up with Motorola and Microsoft to create a proprietary pocket-size PC, sending package information to cell phones, and creating software products for small business logistics. "Engage in constant change," is a mantra for CEO Smith, and he adds, "Companies that don't take risks—some of which are going to work and some of which aren't—are going to end up getting punched up by the marketplace."[12]

MyBizLab

Caro/Alamy

functional departments, such as finance and marketing, so that all viewpoints are represented as the new product is being developed; the marketing member may provide ongoing information about product packaging and pricing issues, for instance, and the finance member may have useful information about when funds will be available.

In some companies, the matrix organization is a temporary measure installed to complete a specific project and affecting only one part of the firm. In these firms, the end of the project usually means the end of the matrix—either a breakup of the team or a restructuring to fit it into the company's existing line-and-staff structure. Ford, for example, uses a matrix organization to design new models, such as the newest Mustang. A design team composed of people with engineering, marketing, operations, and finance expertise was created to design the new car. After its work was done, the team members moved back to their permanent functional jobs.

In other settings, the matrix organization is a semipermanent fixture. Figure 6.7 shows how Martha Stewart Living Omnimedia has created a permanent matrix organization for its lifestyle business. As you can see, the company is organized broadly into media and merchandising groups, each of which has specific product and product groups. For instance, there is an Internet group housed within the media group. Layered on top of this structure are teams of

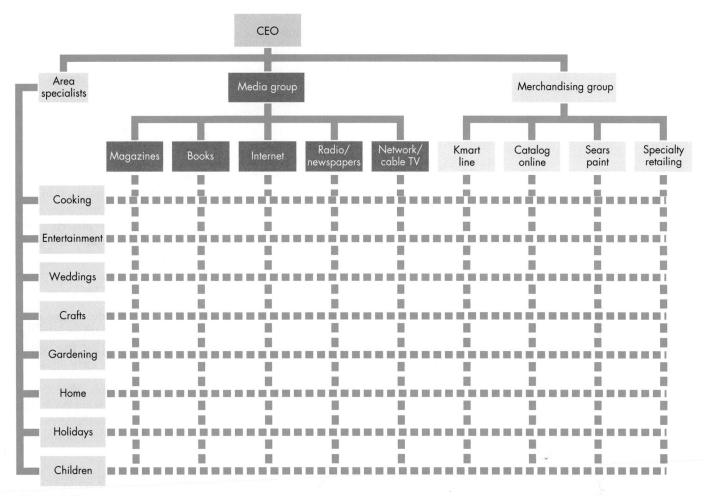

Figure 6.7   Matrix Organization of Martha Stewart Living Omnimedia

lifestyle experts led by area specialists organized into groups, such as cooking, entertainment, weddings, crafts, and so forth. Although each group targets specific customer needs, they all work, as necessary, across all product groups. An area specialist in weddings, for example, might contribute to an article on wedding planning for an Omnimedia magazine, contribute a story idea for an Omnimedia cable television program, and supply content for an Omnimedia site. This same individual might also help select fabrics suitable for wedding gowns that are to be retailed.

International Structure

Several different **international organizational structures** have emerged in response to the need to manufacture, purchase, and sell in global markets.

For example, when Wal-Mart opened its first store outside the United States in 1992, it set up a special projects team. In the mid-1990s, the firm created a small international department to handle overseas expansion. By 1999 international sales

International Organizational Structures
approaches to organizational structure developed in response to the need to manufacture, purchase, and sell in global markets

and expansion had become such a major part of operations that a separate international division headed up by a senior vice president was created. By 2002, international operations had become so important that the international division was further divided into geographic areas, such as Mexico and Europe. And as the firm expands into more foreign markets, such as Russia and India, new units are created to oversee those operations.[13]

Some companies adopt a truly global structure in which they acquire resources (including capital), produce goods and services, engage in research and development, and sell products in whatever local market is appropriate, without consideration of national boundaries. Until a few years ago, General Electric (GE) kept its international business operations as separate divisions, as illustrated in Figure 6.8. Now, however, the company functions as one integrated global organization. GE businesses around the world connect and interact with each other constantly, and managers freely move back and forth among them. This integration is also reflected in GE's executive team, which includes executives from Spain, Japan, Scotland, Ireland, and Italy.[14]

Organizational Design for the Twenty-first Century

As the world grows increasingly complex and fast-paced, organizations also continue to seek new forms of organization that permit them to compete effectively. Among the most popular of these new forms are the *team organization*, the *virtual organization*, and the *learning organization*.

Team Organization   *Team organization* relies almost exclusively on project-type teams, with little or no underlying functional hierarchy. People float from project to project as dictated by their skills and the demands of those projects. As the term suggests, team authority is the underlying foundation of organizations that adopt this organizational structure.

Virtual Organization   Closely related to the team organization is the *virtual organization*. A virtual organization has little or no formal structure. Typically, it has only a handful of permanent employees, a very small staff, and a modest administrative facility. As the needs of the organization change, its managers bring in temporary workers, lease facilities, and outsource basic support services to meet the demands of each unique situation. As the situation changes, the temporary workforce changes in parallel, with some people leaving the organization and others entering. Facilities and the subcontracted services also change. In other words, the virtual organization exists only in response to its own needs.[15] This structure would be applicable to research or consulting firms that hire consultants based on the specific content knowledge required by each unique project. As the projects change, so too does the composition of the organization. Figure 6.9 illustrates a hypothetical virtual organization.

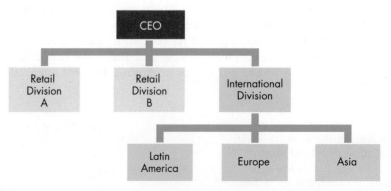

Figure 6.8 International Division Structure

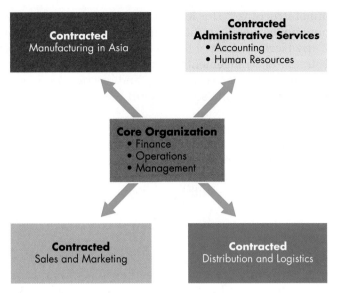

Figure 6.9 **The Virtual Organization**

Learning Organization The so-called *learning organization* works to integrate continuous improvement with continuous employee learning and development. Specifically, a learning organization works to facilitate the lifelong learning and personal development of all of its employees while continually transforming itself to respond to changing demands and needs.

While managers might approach the concept of a learning organization from a variety of perspectives, the most frequent goals are superior quality, continuous improvement, and performance measurement. The idea is that the most consistent and logical strategy for achieving continuous improvement is to constantly upgrade employee talent, skill, and knowledge. For example, if each employee in an organization learns one new thing each day and can translate that knowledge into work-related practice, continuous improvement will logically follow. Indeed, organizations that wholeheartedly embrace this approach believe that only through constant employee learning can continuous improvement really occur. Shell Oil's Shell Learning Center boasts state-of-the-art classrooms and instructional technology, lodging facilities, a restaurant, and recreational amenities. Line managers rotate through the center to fulfill teaching assignments, and Shell employees routinely attend training programs, seminars, and related activities.

Informal Organization

5 Describe the informal organization and discuss intrapreneuring.

The structure of a company, however, is by no means limited to the *formal organization* as represented by the organization chart and the formal assignment of authority. Frequently, the **informal organization**—everyday social interactions among employees that transcend formal jobs and job interrelationships—effectively alters

Informal Organization network, unrelated to the firm's formal authority structure, of everyday social interactions among company employees

a company's formal structure.[16] This level of organization is sometimes just as powerful—if not more powerful—than the formal structure. In 2005, Hewlett-Packard fired its CEO, Carly Fiorina. Much of the discussion that led to her firing took place outside formal structural arrangements in the organization—members of the board of directors, for example, held secret meetings and reached confidential agreements among themselves before Fiorina's future with the company was addressed in a formal manner.[17]

On the negative side, the informal organization can reinforce office politics that put the interests of individuals ahead of those of the firm and can disseminate distorted or inaccurate information. For example, if the informal organization is highlighting false information about impending layoffs, valuable employees may act quickly (and unnecessarily) to seek other employment.

Informal Groups

Informal groups are simply groups of people who decide to interact among themselves. They may be people who work together in a formal sense or who just get together for lunch, during breaks, or after work. They may talk about business, the boss, or nonwork-related topics like families, movies, or sports. Their impact on the organization may be positive (if they work together to support the organization), negative (if they work together in ways that run counter to the organization's interests), or irrelevant (if what they do is unrelated to the organization).

Organizational Grapevine

The **grapevine** is an informal communication network that can run through an entire organization. Grapevines are found in all organizations except the very smallest, but they do not always follow the same patterns as formal channels of authority and communication, nor do they necessarily coincide with them. Because the grapevine typically passes information orally, such information often becomes distorted in the process.

Attempts to eliminate the grapevine are fruitless, but, fortunately, managers do have some control over it. By maintaining open channels of communication and responding vigorously to inaccurate information, they can minimize the damage the grapevine can cause. The grapevine can actually be an asset. By getting to know the key people in the grapevine, for example, the manager can partially control the information they receive and use the grapevine to sound out employee reactions to new ideas (for example, a change in human resource policies or benefit packages). The manager can also get valuable information from the grapevine and use it to improve decision making.

Intrapreneuring

Good managers recognize that the informal organization exists whether they want it or not and can use it not only to reinforce the formal organization, but also to harness its energy to improve productivity.

Many firms, including Rubbermaid, 3M, and Xerox, support **intrapreneuring**—creating and maintaining the innovation and flexibility of a small-business environment within a large, bureaucratic structure. Historically, most innovations have come from individuals in small businesses. As businesses increase in size, however, innovation and creativity tend to become casualties in the battle for more sales and profits. In some large companies, new ideas are even discouraged, and champions of innovation have been stalled in midcareer. At Lockheed Martin, the Advanced Development Programs (ADP) encourages intrapreneurship in the tradition of Skunk Works, a legendary team developed in 1943 as engineer Kelly Johnson's response to Lockheed's need for a powerful jet fighter. Johnson's innovative organization approach broke all the rules, and not only did it work, but it also taught Lockheed the value of encouraging that kind of thinking.[18]

Grapevine informal communication network that runs through an organization

Intrapreneuring process of creating and maintaining the innovation and flexibility of a small-business environment within the confines of a large organization

QILAI SHEN/EPA/Newscom

Continued from page 140

Tweaking the Recipe

William Amelio's efforts at Lenovo yielded mixed results. He led the development of a sophisticated and long-term international strategy that is still being followed today. He also successfully integrated numerous divisions and functions between the old IBM unit and Lenovo. But there were also major problems. For one thing, Lenovo began to lose market share. Its new products were not well received in the marketplace, and profits began to drop. Internal conflict also became more significant, with the old-guard IBM executives in one camp, the Chinese executives who grew up in Lenovo in a different camp, and the newly recruited executives from other firms in still a third camp.

Finally, in 2010 Liu Chuanzhi decided that he had to take action. He pushed Amelio to resign and took control of the firm himself. He then quickly restructured the upper ranks of Lenovo to fall more in line with the traditional Chinese approach. Under Amelio's U.S.-style approach, the CEO had made most of the major decisions and then worked with business unit heads to execute them. Chuanzhi, though, formed the eight top managers at Lenovo into a close-knit team and then they all worked together to make decisions and formulate plans.

Right now it's too soon to know if the changes at Lenovo will improve its fortunes or not. But Chuanzhi believes that his new approach, which he calls a blend of old Chinese thinking and modern global thinking, will soon carry the day.

QUESTIONS FOR DISCUSSION

1 Identify as many examples related to organization structure as possible in this case.
2 The case illustrates how culture might affect structure in different countries. If Lenovo established a major division in the United States, do you think its structure should be closer to the Chinese model or the U.S. model? Why?
3 Research Lenovo's current performance relative to the performance of HP and Dell and comment on how well Chuanzhi's plans seem to be working.
4 Ask ten of your friends not enrolled in this course if they are familiar with the Lenovo brand. What are the implications of your findings?

SUMMARY OF LEARNING OBJECTIVES   MyBizLab

1. **Discuss the factors that influence a firm's organizational structure. (pp. 140–141)**
Each organization must develop an appropriate *organizational structure*—the specification of the jobs to be done and the ways in which those jobs relate to one another. Most organizations change structures almost continuously. Firms prepare *organization charts* to clarify structure and to show employees where they fit into a firm's operations. Each box represents a job, and solid lines define the *chain of command*, or *reporting relationships*. The charts of large firms are complex and include individuals at many levels. Because size prevents them from charting every manager, they may create single organization charts for overall corporate structure and separate charts for divisions.

2. **Explain specialization and departmentalization as two of the building blocks of organizational structure. (pp. 142–145)**
The process of identifying specific jobs and designating people to perform them leads to *job specialization*. After they're specialized, jobs are grouped into logical units—the process of *departmentalization*. Departmentalization follows one (or any combination) of five forms: (1) *product departmentalization*, (2) *process departmentalization*, (3) *functional departmentalization*, (4) *customer departmentalization*, or (5) *geographic departmentalization*. Larger companies take advantage of different types of departmentalization for various levels.

3. **Describe centralization and decentralization, delegation, and authority as the key ingredients in establishing the decision-making hierarchy. (pp. 145–150)**
After jobs have been specialized and departmentalized, firms establish decision-making hierarchies. One major issue addressed through the creation of the decision-making hierarchy involves whether the firm will be relatively *centralized* or relatively *decentralized*. Centralized authority systems typically require multiple layers of management and thus *tall organizational structures*. Decentralized firms tend to have relatively fewer layers of management, resulting in a *flat organizational structure*. *Delegation* is the process through which a manager allocates work to subordinates. In general, the delegation process involves three steps: (1) the assignment of *responsibility*, (2) the granting of *authority*, and (3) the creation of *accountability*. As individuals are delegated responsibility and authority in a firm, a complex web of interactions develops. These interactions may take one of three forms of authority: *line, staff*, or *committee and team*.

4. **Explain the differences among functional, divisional, matrix, and international organizational structures and describe the most popular new forms of organizational design. (pp. 150–155)**
Most firms rely on one of four basic forms of organizational structure: (1) *functional*, (2) *divisional*, (3) *matrix*, or (4) *international*. As global competition becomes more complex, companies may experiment with ways to respond. Some adopt truly global structures, acquiring resources and producing and selling products in local markets without consideration of national boundaries. Organizations also continue to seek new forms of organization that permit them to compete effectively. The most popular new forms include (1) *team organization*, (2) *virtual organization*, and (3) *learning organization*.

5. **Describe the informal organization and discuss intrapreneuring. (pp. 155–157)**
The *formal organization* is the part that can be represented in chart form. The *informal organization*—everyday social interactions among employees that transcend formal jobs and job interrelationships—may alter formal structure. There are two important elements in most informal organizations. *Informal groups* consist of people who decide to interact among themselves. Their impact on a firm may be positive, negative, or irrelevant. The *grapevine* is an informal communication network that can run through an entire organization. Because it can be harnessed to improve productivity, some organizations encourage the informal organization. Many firms also support *intrapreneuring*—creating and maintaining the innovation and flexibility of a small business within the confines of a large, bureaucratic structure.

KEY TERMS   MyBizLab

accountability (p. 148)
authority (p. 148)
centralized organization (p. 146)
chain of command (p. 140)
committee and team authority (p. 149)
customer departmentalization (p. 144)
decentralized organization (p. 146)
delegation (p. 148)
departmentalization (p. 143)
division (p. 150)
divisional structure (p. 150)
flat organizational structure (p. 146)

functional departmentalization (p. 144)
functional structure (p. 150)
geographic departmentalization (p. 144)
grapevine (p. 156)
informal organization (p. 155)
international organizational
   structures (p. 153)
intrapreneuring (p. 156)
job specialization (p. 142)
line authority (p. 148)
line department (p. 148)
matrix structure (p. 151)

organization chart (p. 140)
organizational structure (p. 140)
process departmentalization (p. 143)
product departmentalization (p. 143)
profit center (p. 143)
responsibility (p. 148)
span of control (p. 146)
staff authority (p. 149)
staff members (p. 149)
tall organizational structure (p. 146)
work team (p. 149)

QUESTIONS AND EXERCISES

QUESTIONS FOR REVIEW

1. What is an organization chart? What purpose does it serve?
2. Explain the significance of size as it relates to organizational structure. Describe the changes that are likely to occur as an organization grows.
3. What is the difference between responsibility and authority?
4. Why do some managers have difficulties in delegating authority?
5. Why is a company's informal organization important?

QUESTIONS FOR ANALYSIS

6. Draw up an organization chart for your college or university.
7. Describe a hypothetical organizational structure for a small printing firm. Describe changes that might be necessary as the business grows.

8. Compare and contrast the matrix and divisional approaches to organizational structure. How would you feel personally about working in a matrix organization in which you were assigned simultaneously to multiple units or groups?

APPLICATION EXERCISES

9. Interview the manager of a local service business, such as a fast-food restaurant. What types of tasks does this manager typically delegate? Is the appropriate authority also delegated in each case?
10. Using books, magazines, or personal interviews, identify a person who has succeeded as an intrapreneur. In what ways did the structure of the intrapreneur's company help this individual succeed? In what ways did the structure pose problems?

BUILDING YOUR BUSINESS SKILLS

Getting with the Program

Goal
To encourage you to understand the relationship between organizational structure and a company's ability to attract and keep valued employees.

Background Information
You are the founder of a small but growing high-tech company that develops new computer software. With your current workload and new contracts in the pipeline, your business is thriving, except for one problem: You cannot find computer programmers for product development. Worse yet, current staff members are being lured away by other high-tech firms. After suffering a particularly discouraging personnel raid in which competitors captured three of your most valued employees, you schedule a meeting with your director of human resources to plan organizational changes designed to encourage worker loyalty. You already pay top dollar, but the continuing exodus tells you that programmers are looking for something more.

Method
Working with three or four classmates, identify some ways in which specific organizational changes might improve the working environment and encourage employee loyalty. As you analyze the following factors, ask yourself the obvious question: If I were a programmer, what organizational changes would encourage me to stay?

- *Level of job specialization.* With many programmers describing their jobs as tedious because of the focus on detail in a narrow work area, what changes, if any, would you make in job specialization? Right now, for instance, few of your programmers have any say in product design.
- *Decision-making hierarchy.* What decision-making authority would encourage people to stay? Is expanding employee authority likely to work better in a centralized or decentralized organization?
- *Team authority.* Can team empowerment make a difference? Taking the point of view of the worker, describe the ideal team.
- *Intrapreneuring.* What can your company do to encourage and reward innovation?

FOLLOW-UP QUESTIONS

1. With the average computer programmer earning nearly $70,000, and with all competitive firms paying top dollar, why might organizational issues be critical in determining employee loyalty?
2. If you were a programmer, what organizational factors would make a difference to you? Why?
3. As the company founder, how willing would you be to make major organizational changes in light of the shortage of qualified programmers?

EXERCISING YOUR ETHICS: INDIVIDUAL EXERCISE

Minding Your Own Business

The Situation
Assume that you have recently gone to work for a large high-tech company. You have discovered an interesting arrangement in which one of your coworkers is engaging. Specifically, he blocks his schedule for the hour between 11:00 A.M. and 12:00 noon each day and does not take a lunch break. During this one-hour interval, he is actually running his own real estate business.

The Dilemma
You recently asked this employee how he manages to pull this off. "Well," he responded, "the boss and I never talked about it, but she knows what's going on. They know they can't replace me, and I always get my work done. I don't use any company resources. So, what's the harm?" Interestingly, you also have a business opportunity that could be pursued in the same way.

QUESTION TO ADDRESS
1 What are the ethical issues in this situation?
2 What do you think most people would do in this situation?
3 What would you do in this situation?

EXERCISING YOUR ETHICS: TEAM EXERCISE

To Poach, or Not to Poach ...

The Situation
The Hails Corporation, a manufacturing plant, has recently moved toward an all-team-based organization structure. That is, all workers are divided into teams. Each team has the autonomy to divide up the work assigned to it among its individual members. In addition, each team handles its own scheduling for members to take vacations and other time off. The teams also handle the interviews and hiring of new team members when the need arises. Team A has just lost one of its members who moved to another city to be closer to his ailing parents.

The Dilemma
Since moving to the team structure, every time a team has needed new members, it has advertised in the local newspaper and hired someone from outside the company. However, Team A is considering a different approach to fill its opening. Specifically, a key member of another team (Team B) has made it known that she would like to join Team A. She likes the team members, sees the team's work as being enjoyable, and is somewhat bored with her team's current assignment.

The concern is that if Team A chooses this individual to join the team, several problems may occur. For one thing, her current team will clearly be angry with the members of Team A. Further, "poaching" new team members from other teams inside the plant is likely to become a common occurrence. On the other hand, though, it seems reasonable that she should have the same opportunity to join Team A as an outsider would. Team A needs to decide how to proceed.

Team Activity
Assemble a group of four students and assign each group member to one of the following roles:

- Member of Team A
- Member of Team B
- Manager of both teams
- Hails investor

ACTION STEPS
1 Before hearing any of your group's comments on this situation, and from the perspective of your assigned role, do you think that the member of Team B should be allowed to join Team A? Write down the reasons for your position.
2 Before hearing any of your group's comments on this situation, and from the perspective of your assigned role, what are the underlying ethical issues, if any, in this situation? Write down the issues.
3 Gather your group together and reveal, in turn, each member's comments on the situation. Next, reveal the ethical issues listed by each member.
4 Appoint someone to record main points of agreement and disagreement within the group. How do you explain the results? What accounts for any disagreement?
5 From an ethical standpoint, what does your group conclude is the most appropriate action that should be taken by Hails in this situation? Should Team B's member be allowed to join Team A?
6 Develop a group response to the following questions: Assuming Team A asks the Team B member to join its team, how might it go about minimizing repercussions? Assuming Team A does not ask the Team B member to join its team, how might it go about minimizing repercussions?

VIDEO EXERCISE   MyBizLab

My Gym

Learning Objectives

The purpose of this video is to help you:

1 Explain how specialization and departmentalization create organizational structure.
2 Describe the role of centralization and decentralization in the management of an organization.
3 Identify the characteristics, advantages, and disadvantages of a functional structure.

Synopsis

My Gym is an international enterprise that has developed fitness programs for children from infancy to age 13 that focus on their psychological, as well as physiological needs. Through their programming, My Gym hopes to make fitness fun and help to reverse a trend of increased rates of childhood obesity. My Gym began operations in 1983 when the three cofounders, William Caplin and Yacov and Susi Sherman, opened the first two locations in Santa Monica and Van Nuys, California. The company added new partners over the next 12 years and refined their business model and developed custom-made equipment. In 1995, My Gym began selling franchises. In 2011, there are more than 200 My Gyms in the United States and over 25 countries around the world. The company has ambitious goals, hoping to expand to more than 300 facilities in more than 50 countries by the end of 2012. The company also hopes to expand through their mobile program, bringing My Gym programming to schools, community centers, camps, or any other location with children in need of fun and exercise.

DISCUSSION QUESTIONS

1. As My Gym grew as an organization, jobs became more specialized. What are the advantages to more specialized jobs at My Gym?
2. Envisioning the My Gym organization as a headquarters operation, with more than 200 locations, each directed by a branch manager/franchise owner, what form of departmentalization is being used? Be sure to support your conclusion.
3. What is centralization? What types of decisions do you think would be centralized at the headquarters for My Gym? What are the advantages of this type of centralization to My Gym?
4. What is decentralization? What types of decisions do you think would be decentralized to individual locations? What are the advantages of this type of decentralization to My Gym and franchise owners?
5. My Gym's headquarters has a functional structure, with managers heading divisions for accounting and finance, marketing, training, and franchise development. What are the advantages and disadvantages of a functional structure?

Online Exploration

Although there over 200 My Gym locations around the world, many of us have never had the opportunity to step inside. Visit the company's website at www.my-gym.com to learn more about their programming and organizational structure. As the company continues to expand, both domestically and internationally, and opens more locations, how do you think that the organizational structure may change?

END NOTES

[1] "Lenovo's Legend Returns," *Time*, May 10, 2010, pp. 65–68; "Lenovo: A Company Without a Country," *Business Week*, January 23, 2010, pp. 49–50; "Lenovo's Turnaround Man," *Forbes*, May 4, 2010, p. 88.

[2] See Royston Greenwood and Danny Miller, "Tackling Design Anew: Getting Back to the Heart of Organizational theory," *Academy of Management Perspectives*, November 2010, pp. 78–88.

[3] Joann S. Lublin, "Place vs. Product: It's Tough to Choose a Management Model," *Wall Street Journal*, June 27, 2001, A1, A4; Joann Muller, "Ford: Why It's Worse Than You Think," *BusinessWeek*, June 25, 2001, pp. 58–59; *Hoover's Handbook of American Business 2011*, (Austin, Texas: Hoover's Business Press, 2011), pp. 145–146.

[4] "How Mulally Helped Turn Ford Around," *USA Today*, July 18, 2011, p. 2B.

[5] AllBusiness.com, "Kraft Foods North America Announces New Management Structure," September 28, 2000 (March 5, 2011), at http://www.allbusiness.com/food-beverage/food-beverage-overview/6505848-1.html.

[6] See Levi Strauss & Co., at http://www.levistrauss.com/Company/WorldwideRegions.aspx.

[7] "Blowing Up Pepsi," *BusinessWeek*, April 27, 2009, pp. 32–36; *Hoover's Handbook of American Business 2011* (Austin, Texas: Hoover's Business Press, 2011), pp. 643–644.

[8] See Southern Company, http://investor.southerncompany.com/governance.cfm.

[9] Michael E. Raynor and Joseph L. Bower, "Lead From the Center," *Harvard Business Review*, May 2001, 93–102.

[10] Gary Hamel, "What Google, Whole Foods Do Best," *Fortune*, September 27, 2007, p. 59.

[11] *Hoover's Handbook of American Business 2011* (Austin, Texas: Hoover's Business Press, 2011); Brian Dumaine, "How I Delivered the Goods," *Fortune Small Business*, October 2002 (*quote); Charles Haddad, "FedEx: Gaining on the Ground," *BusinessWeek*, December 16, 2002, 126–128; Claudia H. Deutsch, "FedEx Has Hit the Ground Running, but Will Its Legs Tire?" *New York Times*, October 13, 2002, BU7; http://www.Forbes.com/finance (February 16, 2006); PBS.org, "Who Made America" (June 19, 2008), at

http://www.pbs.org/wgbh/theymadeamerica/whomade/fsmith_hi.html.

12 John Simons, "Prognosis Looks Good for J&J," *Fortune*, November 16, 2007, pp. 70–71; Johnson & Johnson, "Company Structure" (June 19, 2008), at http://www.jnj.com/connect/about-jnj/company-structure/.

13 "Wal-Mart Acquires Interspar," Management Ventures (July 20, 2001), at http://www.mvi-insights.com/Index.aspx; Kerry Capell et al., "Wal-Mart's Not-So-Secret British Weapon," *BusinessWeek Online* (July 20, 2001), at http://www.businessweek.com/2000/00_04/b3665095.htm; Brent Schlender, "Wal-Mart's $288 Billion Meeting," *Fortune*, April 18, 2005, 90–106; see http://walmartstores.com.

14 Thomas A. Stewart, "See Jack. See Jack Run," *Fortune*, September 27, 1999, 124–271; Jerry Useem, "America's Most Admired Companies," *Fortune*, March 7, 2005, 67–82; See GE.com, "Executive Leaders," at http://www.ge.com/company/leadership/executives.html.

15 Leslie P. Willcocks and Robert Plant, "Getting from Bricks to Clicks," *Sloan Management Review*, Spring 2001, 50–60.

16 "The Office Chart That Really Counts," *BusinessWeek*, February 27, 2006, 48–49.

17 Carol Loomis, "How the HP Board KO'd Carly," *Fortune*, March 7, 2005, 99–102.

18 Lockheed Martin, "Skunk Works" (June 19, 2008), at http://www.lockheedmartin.com/aeronautics/skunkworks/index.html.

7 Operations Management and Quality

Passengers and Airlines: Friends, or Foes? [1]

Poor treatment by airlines has customers in an uproar, as the many services that go into their flight experiences continue to deteriorate. Disturbances include everything from higher fares, inconvenient scheduling activities and discourteous airline personnel before getting to the airport, then to unpleasant surprises at the airport such as overbooked flights, rude gate agents, additional baggage fees, long waits, and inaccurate information. While airlines continue to eliminate onboard services, those that remain are available, increasingly, only with add-on fees. Because planes land late, departing passengers miss their connecting flights and are left stranded, often with little or no assistance from airline personnel. As to the customers' problems—the airlines don't seem to care.

How would you feel after landing, to discover your bag isn't there? Airlines lose 26 million passengers' bags annually due to theft, mishandling, and labeling errors. Even worse, imagine being stranded for eight hours awaiting takeoff on a crowded runway without food, water, and air conditioning. While the overtaxed bathrooms are unfit for further use, passengers are not allowed off the plane. Little wonder that passengers are increasingly vocal, irritated, and sometimes even violent.

Airline scheduling, too, has become increasingly abusive to customers. Consider, for example, four friends who scheduled a trip together from Chicago to New York, booking airline reservations four months in

> *After reading this chapter, you should be able to:*
>
> 1 Explain the meaning of the term *production* or *operations*.
> 2 Describe the three kinds of utility that operations processes provide for adding customer value.
> 3 Explain how companies with different business strategies are best served by having different operations capabilities.
> 4 Identify the major factors that are considered in operations planning.
> 5 Discuss the information contained in four kinds of operations schedules—the master production schedule, detailed schedule, staff schedule, and project schedule.
> 6 Discuss the two key activities required for operations control.
> 7 Identify the activities and underlying objectives involved in total quality management.
> 8 Explain how a supply chain strategy differs from traditional strategies for coordinating operations among firms.

advance. Before departure, the airline rescheduled their flights three times, including one assignment that separated the group onto different planes, and placed a child and mother on different flights. After each involuntary rescheduling, passengers faced the hassle of revising their personal non-airline arrangements (hotels, land travel, personal appointments, job absences, etc.), then re-revising them, then again re-re-revising them at considerable inconvenience and even added costs. In contrast, if the travelers had requested those same changes, the airline would have imposed a $50 service fee on each passenger for each rescheduling, for a total charge of $600.

As the list of service complaints grows, so too are the feelings of helplessness and frustration among customers. Little wonder, then, the number of passengers on U.S. airlines in

WHAT'S IN IT FOR ME?

If, like the thousands of airline customers disrupted by inconvenience and mistreatment, you've ever been disappointed in a good or service that you bought, you'll find it easy to relate to the topics in this chapter. We'll explore the numerous ways companies align their operations processes with their business plans, and discuss how these decisions contribute to a firm's ability to create a high-quality product. Gaining an appreciation for the many steps it takes to bring high-quality goods and services to market will help make you a smarter consumer and more effective employee. And if you're a manager, understanding that production activities are pliable and should be reoriented to better support new business strategies will help you redefine your company and its marketplace over time.

MyBizLab Where you see MyBizLab in this chapter, go to **www.mybizlab.com** for additional activities on the topic being discussed.

Ben Stansall/AFP/Getty Images/Newscom

2009 dropped, with fewer flyers than any time since 2004, as poor economic conditions were aided by equally poor service quality in the airlines industry. With so many complaints, it is hardly a surprise that one 2010 poll shows that more U.S. passengers hold a negative, rather than positive view of airlines.

Why is all this happening? The airlines say they have to cut services and start charging for "extras" to stay profitable, or else go out of business.

Our opening story continues on page 188.

1 Explain the meaning of the term *production* or *operations*.

What Does *Operations* Mean Today?

Although you're not always aware of it, as a customer you are constantly involved in business activities that provide goods and services to customers. You wake up to the sound of your favorite radio station, and on your bus ride to work or school you are texting on a cell phone. Your instructors, the bus driver, the messaging provider, and the morning radio announcer all work in **service operations** (or **service production**). They provide intangible and tangible service products, such as entertainment, transportation, education, and communications services. Firms that make only tangible products—radios, cell phones, buses, textbooks—are engaged in activities for **goods operations** (or **goods production**).

The term **operations** (or **production**) refers to all the activities involved in making products—goods and services—for customers. In modern societies, much of what we need or want, from health care to fast food, is produced by service operations. As a rule, managers in the service sector give more consideration to the human element in operations (as opposed to the equipment or technology involved) because success or failure depends often on provider-customer contact. As we saw with airlines in the opening story, employees who deal directly with customers affect customer feelings about the service. As we will see, a key difference between goods and services operations is the customer's involvement in the latter.

Although companies are typically classified as either goods producers or service providers, the distinction is often blurred. Consider General Electric. When you think of GE, you most likely think of appliances and jet engines. However, GE is not just a goods producer. According to its annual report, GE's "growth engines"—its most vibrant business activities—are service operations, including media and entertainment (NBC Universal), consumer and commercial finance, investment, transportation services, and health care information, which account for over 80 percent of the company's revenues.[2]

MyBizLab

Gain hands-on experience through an interactive, real-world scenario. This chapter's simulation entitled Improving a Business is located at www.**mybizlab**.com.

2 Describe the three kinds of utility that operations processes provide for adding customer value.

Creating Value Through Operations

To understand a firm's production processes, we need to know what kinds of benefits its production provides, both for itself and for its customers. Production provides businesses with economic results: profits, wages, and goods purchased from other companies. At the same time, it adds customer value by providing **utility**—the ability of a product to satisfy a want or need—in terms of form, time, and place:

- Production makes products available: By converting raw materials and human skills into finished goods and services, production creates *form utility*, as when

Len Wilcox/Alamy

AF archive/Alamy

General Electric (GE) can be classified as both a goods producer (for example, of the GE Wind Turbine, shown here) and a service provider (for example, of media and entertainment shows such as *Saturday Night Live*).

Regal Cinemas combines building materials, theater seats, and projection equipment to create entertainment.

- When a theater offers midday, afternoon, and evening shows seven days a week, it creates *time utility*; that is, it adds customer value by making products available when consumers want them.

- When a theater offers a choice of 15 movies, all under one roof at a popular location, it creates *place utility*: It makes products available where they are convenient for consumers.

Creating a product that customers value, then, is no accident, but instead results from organized effort. **Operations (production) management** is the systematic direction and control of the activities that transform resources into finished services and goods that create value for and provide benefits to customers. In overseeing production, **operations (production) managers** are responsible for ensuring that operations activities create what customers want and need.

As Figure 7.1 shows, operations managers draw up plans to transform resources into products. First, they bring together basic resources: knowledge, physical materials, information, equipment, the customer, and human skills. Then they put them to effective use in a production facility. As demand for a product increases, they schedule and control work to produce the required amount. Finally, they control

Service Operations (Service Production) activities producing intangible and tangible products, such as entertainment, transportation, and education

Goods Operations (Goods Production) activities producing tangible products, such as radios, newspapers, buses, and textbooks

Operations (Production) activities involved in making products—goods and services—for customers

Utility product's ability to satisfy a human want or need

Operations (Production) Management systematic direction and control of the activities that transform resources into finished products that create value for and provide benefits to customers

Operations (Production) Managers managers responsible for ensuring that operations activities create value and provide benefits to customers

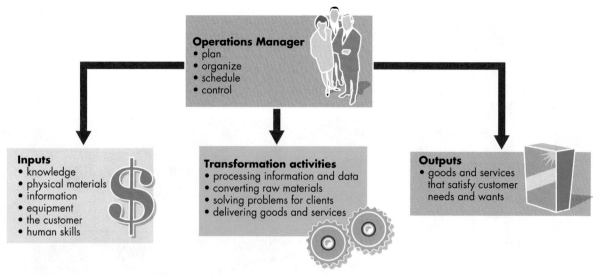

Figure 7.1 **The Resource Transformation Process**

costs, quality levels, inventory, and facilities and equipment. In some businesses, the operations manager is one person. Typically, different employees work together to complete these different responsibilities.

Some operations managers work in factories; others work in offices, restaurants, hospitals, and stores. Farmers are operations managers who create utility by transforming soil, seeds, fuel, and other inputs into soybeans, milk, and other outputs. They may hire crews of workers to plant and harvest, opt instead for automated machinery, or prefer some combination of workers and machinery. These decisions affect costs and determine the kinds of buildings and equipment in operations and the quality and quantity of goods produced.

Differences between Service and Goods Manufacturing Operations

Both service and manufacturing operations transform raw materials into finished products. In service operations, however, the raw materials, or inputs, are not things like glass or steel. Rather, they are people who have either unsatisfied needs or possessions needing care or alteration. In service operations, finished products or outputs are people with needs met and possessions serviced.

Thus, there are several obvious differences between service and manufacturing operations. Four aspects of service operations can make them more complicated than simple goods production. These include (1) interacting with customers, (2) the intangible and unstorable nature of some services, (3) the customer's presence in the process, and (4) service quality considerations.

Interacting with Customers   Manufacturing operations emphasize outcomes in terms of physical goods—for example, a new jacket. But the products of most *service* operations are really combinations of goods and services—both making a pizza *and* delivering (serving) it. Service workers need different skills. For example, gas company employees may need interpersonal skills to calm frightened customers who have reported gas leaks. Thus, the job includes more than just repairing pipes. In contrast, factory workers who install gas pipes in manufactured homes without any customer contact don't need such skills.

Services Can Be Intangible and Unstorable   Two prominent characteristics—*intangibility* and *unstorability*—set services apart from physical goods:

- **Intangibility.** Often, services can't be touched, tasted, smelled, or seen, but they're still there. An important satisfier for customers, therefore, is the *intangible* value they receive in the form of pleasure, gratification, or a feeling of safety. For example, when you hire an attorney, you purchase not only the intangible quality of legal expertise but also the equally intangible reassurance that help is at hand.

- **Unstorability.** Many services—such as trash collection, transportation, child care, and house cleaning—can't be produced ahead of time and then stored for high-demand periods. If a service isn't used when available, it's usually wasted. Services, then, are typically characterized by a high degree of *unstorability*.

Customers' Presence in the Operations Process   Because service operations transform customers or their possessions, the customer is often present in the operations process. To get a haircut, for example, most of us have to go to the barbershop or hair salon. As physical participants in the operations process, customers can affect it. As a customer, you expect the salon to be conveniently located (place utility), to be open for business at convenient times (time utility), to provide safe and comfortable facilities, and to offer high-quality grooming (form utility) at reasonable prices (value for money spent). Accordingly, the manager sets hours of operation, available services, and an appropriate number of employees to meet customer requirements. But what happens if a customer, scheduled to receive a haircut, also asks for additional services, such as highlights or a shave when he or she arrives? In this case, the service provider must quickly adjust the service activities to provide customer satisfaction. High customer contact has the potential to affect the process significantly.

Intangibles Count for Service Quality   Consumers use different measures to judge services and goods because services include intangibles, not just physical objects. Most service managers know that quality of work and quality of service are not necessarily the same thing. Your car, for example, may have been flawlessly repaired (quality of work), but you'll probably be unhappy with the service if you're forced to pick it up a day later than promised (quality of service).

Operations Processes

To better understand the diverse kinds of production in various firms and industries, it is helpful to classify production according to differences in operations processes. An **operations process** is a set of methods and technologies used to produce a good or a service. Banks, for example, use two processes—document shredding and data encryption—to protect confidential information. Automakers use precision painting methods (equipment and materials) to produce a glittering paint finish.

We can classify goods production into broad groupings, by asking whether its operations process has a "make-to-order" or a "make-to-stock" emphasis. We can classify services according to the extent of customer contact required.

Goods Production Processes: Make-to-Order versus Make-to-Stock Processes   Clothing, such as evening gowns, is available either off-the-shelf in department stores or custom-made at a designer/tailor shop. The designer/tailor's **make-to-order operations** respond to one-of-a-kind gown requirements, including unique patterns, materials, sizes, and shapes, depending on customers' unique characteristics. **Make-to-stock operations**, in contrast, produce standard gowns in large quantities to be stocked on store shelves or in displays for mass consumption. The production processes are quite different for the two settings, including procedures for designing gowns; planning for materials purchases; equipment and work methods for cutting, sewing, and assembling gowns; and employee skills for production.

Operations Process set of methods and technologies used to produce a good or a service

Make-to-Order Operations activities for one-of-a-kind or custom-made production

Make-to-Stock Operations activities for producing standardized products for mass consumption

Because service operations transform customers or their possessions, the customer is often present in the operations process.

Service Production Processes: Extent of Customer Contact

In classifying services, we may ask whether a service can be provided without customers being present in the production system. In answering this question, we classify services according to *extent of customer contact.*

Low-Contact Systems Consider the postal delivery operations at your local U.S. post office. Postal employees gather mail, sort it, and send it on its journey to addressees. This operation is a **low-contact system**: Customers are not in contact with the post office while the service is performed. They receive the service—mail sent and mail received—without setting foot in the processing center. Gas and electric companies, auto repair shops, and lawn-care services are other examples of low-contact systems.

High-Contact Systems Think about your local public transit system. The service is transportation, and when you purchase transportation, you board a bus or train. For example, the Bay Area Rapid Transit (BART) system, which connects San Francisco with outlying suburbs is, like all public transit systems, a **high-contact system**: To receive the service, the customer must be part of the system. Thus, managers must worry about the cleanliness of trains and the appearance of stations. By contrast, a firm that ships coal is not concerned with the appearance of its trains since no paying passengers are riding on them. It's a low-contact system.

3 Explain how companies with different business strategies are best served by having different operations capabilities.

Business Strategy as the Driver of Operations

There is no one standard way for doing production. Rather, it is a flexible activity that can be molded into many shapes to give quite different operations capabilities for different purposes. How, then, do companies go about selecting the kind of production that is best for them? They adopt the kind of production that best achieves the firm's larger business strategy.

The Many Faces of Production Operations

Consider the four firms listed in Table 7.1. Two are in goods production (Toyota and 3M), and two are in services. These companies have contrasting business strategies and, as we shall see, they have chosen different operations capabilities. All four firms have been successful, but they've taken quite different operations paths to get there. Each company has identified a business strategy that it uses for attracting customers in its industry. For Toyota, *quality* was chosen, more than 35 years ago, as the strategy for competing in selling autos. Save-A-Lot grocery stores, in contrast to others in the grocery industry, offer customers *lower prices.* The *flexibility* strategy at 3M emphasizes new product development in an ever-changing line of products for home and office. FedEx captures the overnight delivery market by emphasizing delivery *dependability*, first and foremost.

Business Strategy Determines Operations Capabilities Successful firms design their operations to support the company's business strategy.[3] In other words, production operations are adjusted to support the firms' target markets. Since our four firms use different business strategies, we should expect to see differences in their operations, too. The top-priority **operations capability (production capability)**—the special ability that

TABLE 7.1 Business Strategies That Win Customers for Four Companies

Company	Strategy for Attracting Customers	What the Company Does to Implement Its Strategy
Toyota	Quality	Cars perform reliably, have an appealing fit and finish, and consistently meet or exceed customer expectations at a competitive price
Save-A-Lot	Low price	Foods and everyday items offered at savings up to 40 percent less than conventional food chains
3M	Flexibility	Innovation, with more than 55,000 products in a constantly changing line of convenience items for home and office
FedEx	Dependability	Every delivery is fast and on time, as promised

TABLE 7.2 Operations Capabilities and Characteristics for Four Companies

Operations Capability	Key Operations Characteristics
Quality (Toyota)	• High-quality standards for materials suppliers • Just-in-time materials flow for lean manufacturing • Specialized, automated equipment for consistent product buildup • Operations personnel are experts on continuous improvement of product, work methods, and materials
Low Cost (Save-A-Lot)	• Avoids excessive overhead and costly inventory (no floral departments, sushi bars, or banks that drive up costs) • Limited assortment of products, staples, in one size only for low-cost restocking, lower inventories, and less paperwork • Many locations; small stores—less than half the size of conventional grocery stores—for low construction and maintenance costs • Reduces labor and shelving costs by receiving and selling merchandise out of custom shipping cartons
Flexibility (3M)	• Maintains some excess (expensive) production capacity available for fast startup on new products • Adaptable equipment/facilities for production changeovers from old to new products • Hires operations personnel who thrive on change • Many medium- to small-sized manufacturing facilities in diverse locations, which enhances creativity
Dependability (FedEx)	• Customer automation: uses electronic and online communications tools with customers to shorten shipping time • Wireless information system for package scanning by courier, updating of package movement, and package tracking by customer • Maintains a company air force, global weather forecasting center, and ground transportation for pickup and delivery, with backup vehicles for emergencies • Each of 30 automated regional distribution hubs processes up to 45,000 packages per hour for next-day deliveries

production does especially well to outperform the competition—is listed for each firm in Table 7.2, along with key operations characteristics for implementing that capability. Each company's operations capability matches up with its business strategy so that the firm's activities—from top to bottom—are focused in a particular direction.

Low-Contact System level of customer contact in which the customer need not be part of the system to receive the service

High-Contact System level of customer contact in which the customer is part of the system during service delivery

Operations Capability (Production Capability) special ability that production does especially well to outperform the competition

For example, because Toyota's top priority focuses on quality, its operations—the resource inputs for production, the transformation activities, and the outputs from production—are devoted first and foremost to that characteristic. Its car designs and production processes emphasize appearance, reliable performance, and desirable features at a reasonable price. All production processes, equipment, and training are designed to build better cars. The entire culture supports a quality emphasis among employees, suppliers, and dealerships. Had Toyota instead chosen to compete as the low-price car in the industry, as some successful car companies do, then a cost-minimization focus would have been appropriate, giving Toyota's operations an altogether different form. Toyota's operations support its chosen business strategy, and did it successfully until problems arose in 2008. Before that downfall the company had more than 35 consecutive years of increasing sales for which quality was the foundation for greatness.

Expanding into Additional Capabilities Finally, it should be noted that excellent firms learn, over time, how to achieve more than just one competence. Our four example firms eventually became excellent in several capabilities. FedEx, for example, in addition to dependability, is noted for world-class service quality and cost containment, too. But in the earlier start-up years, its primary and distinguishing capability, which set it apart from the competition, was dependability, the foundation upon which future success was built.

Operations Planning

4 Identify the major factors that are considered in operations planning.

Let's turn now to a discussion of production activities and resources that are considered in every business organization. Like all good managers, we start with planning. Managers from many departments contribute to decisions about operations. As Figure 7.2 shows, however, no matter how many decision makers are involved, the process is a logical sequence of decisions.

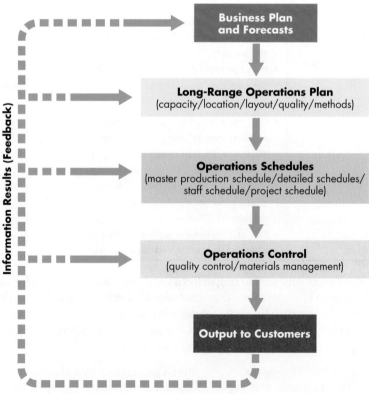

Figure 7.2 **Operations Planning and Control**

ENTREPRENEURSHIP AND NEW VENTURES

A Better Path to Planning Meals (and Better Eating, Too)

Want to eat better at home, while saving time and money, too? Folks at Bradenton, FL, are doing exactly that, using Erika Vitiene's newly launched online meal-planning venture, *Grocery Dash*. Vitiene has used her personal shopping experience, together with carefully developed meal-planning steps, to design the *grocerydash.com* website where subscribers get help for their at-home dinner planning.

Vitiene's motivation is to save over-burdened moms the time and money ordinarily spent on planning meals—deciding on menus, exploring grocery aisles to compare prices and staying within budget—and meal preparation. Every family's meal planner, eventually, feels the challenge of finding new and different dishes, instead of serving "the same old thing, week after week." Although new meal ideas provide greater variety, they also require more time searching for and using different recipes, and buying new ingredients at the right price.[4]

While the website doesn't use formal terms such as "methods improvement" and "process flowchart," its contents nevertheless reflect Erika's intuitive understanding of the sequence of steps for improving the "meal planning" process: It identifies the meal planner (the user who will gain better meal planning), the planner's objectives (good meals at lower cost and time savings), and provides information resources such as ready-made menus, lists of ingredients, and local stores currently offering the ingredients at reduced prices. Menus for seven dinners are displayed weekly, along with their recipes, lists of ingredients, and an aisle-by-aisle shopping list, all arranged around the price specials at local grocery stores. The menus are based on the USDA food pyramid for better nutrition, and recipes minimize the use of processed ingredients.

Subscribers can download additional free resources—printable grocery lists, a freezer guide showing how long food will keep (and a list of foods that do not freeze well), and a pantry checklist for an up-to-date inventory of foods on hand at home.[5]

Erika used her system a long time, and proved its effectiveness to herself—saving 25 to 50 percent on her grocery bill—before presenting it online. Although originally intended for moms, and with a subscription price at $4.95 per month, *grocerydash.com* can also become a valued resource to singles, students, and others whose busy schedules and tight budgets can benefit from nutritious ready-planned meals at lower cost, instead of just fast foods.[6]

MyBizLab

Grant Jefferies/MCT/Newscom

The business plan and forecasts developed by top managers provide guidance for long-term operations plans. Covering a two- to five-year period, the operations plan anticipates the number of plants or service facilities and the amount of labor, equipment, transportation, and storage needed to meet future demand for new and existing products. The planning activities fall into five categories: *capacity, location, layout, quality,* and *methods planning*.

Capacity Planning

The amount of a product that a company can produce under normal conditions is its **capacity**. A firm's capacity depends on how many people it employs and the number and size of its facilities. A supermarket's capacity for customer checkouts, for instance, depends on its number of checkout stations. A typical store has excess capacity—more cash registers than it needs—on an average day, but on Saturday morning or during the three days before Thanksgiving, they'll all be running at full capacity.

Capacity amount of a product that a company can produce under normal conditions

Long-range capacity planning considers both current and future requirements. If capacity is too small for demand, the company must turn away customers—a situation that cuts into profits and alienates both customers and salespeople. If capacity greatly exceeds demand, the firm is wasting money by maintaining facilities that are too large, keeping excess machinery online, or employing too many workers.

The stakes are high in capacity decisions: While expanding fast enough to meet future demand and to protect market share from competitors, the costs of expanding must also be considered. When markets are growing, greater capacity is desirable. In troubled times, however, existing capacity may be too large and too expensive to maintain, requiring a reduction in size. To open her start-up "green laundry," for example, Deborah Dower found plenty of empty commercial space was available in the sagging 2010 economy. Business slowdowns forced other Sacramento, CA, area firms to abandon excess capacity, making space available at below-market prices for Dower's Paradise Laundry, with its motto, "Wash Green. Save Green." Encouraged by a favorable public response, and a willingness to take a financial risk, Dower has expanded capacity by opening a second Paradise Laundry.[7]

Location Planning

Because location affects production costs and flexibility, sound location planning is crucial for factories, offices, and stores. Depending on its site, a company may be able to produce low-cost products, or it may find itself at a cost disadvantage relative to its competitors.

Consider the reasons why Slovakia has become known as "Detroit East." With the worldwide slowdown in car sales, Slovakia's auto production is suffering. Still, as recently as 2008 it produced more cars per capita—including Volkswagen SUVs, Peugeot Citroens, and Kias—than any other country. Its auto factories are well-positioned to resume high-volume production as the worldwide economy improves. The central European country is an ideal place to produce cars. It has a good railroad system and nearby access to the Danube River, meaning economical transportation for incoming materials and outgoing cars once auto factories are in operation. The area also has skilled, hard-working laborers, and wages lower than those of surrounding countries.[8]

In contrast to manufacturing, consumer services concentrate on being located near customers. Thus, fast-food restaurants, such as Taco Bell and McDonald's, are located in areas with high traffic, such as dormitories, hospital cafeterias, and shopping malls. At retail giant Wal-Mart, managers of the company's huge distribution centers regard Wal-Mart outlets as their customers. To ensure that truckloads of merchandise flow quickly to stores, distribution centers are located near the hundreds of Wal-Mart stores that they supply, not near the companies that supply them.

Layout Planning

Layout is the physical location or floor plan for machinery, equipment, customers, service stations, and supplies. It determines whether a company can respond efficiently to demand for more and different products or whether it finds itself unable to match competitors' speed and convenience. Among the many layout possibilities, two well-known alternatives—*custom-products layouts and same-steps layouts*—are presented here to illustrate how different layouts serve different purposes for operations.

Custom-Products Layouts
In a **custom-products layout**, which is well suited to *make-to-order shops* (or *job shops*) specializing in custom work, equipment and people are grouped according to function. Kinko's Copy Centers, for example, use custom-products layouts to accommodate a variety of custom jobs. Specific activities, such as photocopying, computing, binding, photography, and laminating, are performed in separate, specialized areas of the store.

The main advantage of custom-products layouts is flexibility—at any time, the shop can process individual customer orders, each requiring different kinds of work. Depending on its work requirements, a job may flow through three activity areas, another through just one area, and still others through four or more work zones. Machining, woodworking, and dry cleaning shops, as well as health clinics and physical fitness studios, are among the many facilities using custom-products layouts.

Same-Steps Layouts   A **same-steps layout** is set up to make one type of product in a fixed sequence of production steps. All units go through the same set of steps. It is efficient for large-volume make-to-stock operations that mass-produce many units of a product quickly, often using an **assembly line**: A partially finished product moves step by step through the plant on conveyor belts or other equipment, often in a straight line, as it passes through each stage until the product is completed. Automobile, food-processing, and television-assembly plants use same-steps layouts, as do mail-processing facilities, such as UPS or FedEx.

Same-steps layouts are efficient because the work skill is built into the equipment, allowing unskilled labor to perform simple tasks. But they are often inflexible, especially where they use specialized equipment that's hard to rearrange for new applications.

Quality Planning

Every operations plan includes activities for ensuring that products meet the firm's and customers' quality standards. The American Society for Quality defines **quality** as the combination of "characteristics of a product or service that bear on its ability to satisfy stated or implied needs."[9] Such characteristics may include a reasonable price and dependability in delivering the benefits it promises.

Planning for quality begins when products are being designed. Early in the process, goals are established for both performance and consistency. **Performance** refers to how well the product does what it is supposed to do. For loyal buyers of Godiva premium chocolates, performance includes such sensory delights as aroma, flavor, color, and texture. "Truly fine chocolates," observes master chocolatier Thiery Muret, "are always fresh, contain high-quality ingredients like cocoa beans and butter … and feature unusual textures and natural flavors." The recipe was designed to provide these features. Superior performance helps Godiva remain one of the world's top brands.[10]

In addition to performance, quality also includes **consistency**—the sameness of product quality from unit to unit. Business travelers using Courtyard by Marriott, for example, enjoy high consistency with each overnight stay, which is one reason Courtyard by Marriott is among the best-selling brands in the lodging industry. This is achieved by maintaining the same features at all of Marriott's nearly 700 U.S. locations. Designed for business travelers, most guest rooms include a Courtyard Suite with high-speed Internet access, meeting space, and access to an exercise room, restaurant and lounge, swimming pool, and 24-hour access to food. The layout of the suites is identical at many locations, the rooms are always clean, and check-in/checkout procedures are identical so that lodgers know what to expect with each overnight stay. This consistency is achieved by monitoring for uniformity of materials and supplies, encouraging conscientious work, training employees, and maintaining equipment.

Custom-Products Layout physical arrangement of production activities that groups equipment and people according to function

Same-Steps Layout physical arrangement of production steps designed to make one type of product in a fixed sequence of activities according to its production requirements

Assembly Line a same-steps layout in which a product moves step by step through a plant on conveyor belts or other equipment until it is completed

Quality combination of "characteristics of a product or service that bear on its ability to satisfy stated or implied needs"

Performance dimension of quality that refers to how well a product does what it is supposed to do

Consistency dimension of quality that refers to sameness of product quality from unit to unit

In addition to product design, quality planning includes employees deciding what constitutes a high-quality product—for both goods and services—and determining how to measure these quality characteristics.

Methods Planning

In designing operations systems, managers must identify each production step and the specific methods for performing it. They can then reduce waste and inefficiency by examining procedures on a step-by-step basis—an approach called *methods improvement*.

Improving Process Flows   Improvements for operations begin by documenting current production practices. A detailed description, often using a diagram called a *process flowchart*, is helpful in organizing and recording information. The flowchart identifies the sequence of production activities, movements of materials, and work performed at each stage of the process. It can then be analyzed to isolate wasteful activities, sources of delay, and other inefficiencies in both goods and services operations. The final step is implementing improvements.

Improving Customer Service   Consider, for example, the traditional checkout method at hotels. The process flowchart in Figure 7.3 shows five stages of customer activities. As is widely known among guests and employees, hotel checkout can be time consuming for customers standing in line to pay. They become impatient and annoyed, especially during popular checkout times when lines are long. Other hotel tasks are disrupted, too, as employees, called to assist with surging checkout lines, are reassigned from their normal jobs that are left until later. An improved checkout method was developed that avoids wasting time in line for customers and reduces interruptions of other staff duties as well. It saves time by eliminating steps 1, 2, 3A, and 5. Customers now scan their bills on television in the privacy of their rooms any time before departure. If the bill is correct, no further checkout is required, and the hotel submits the charges against the credit card that the customer submitted during check-in.

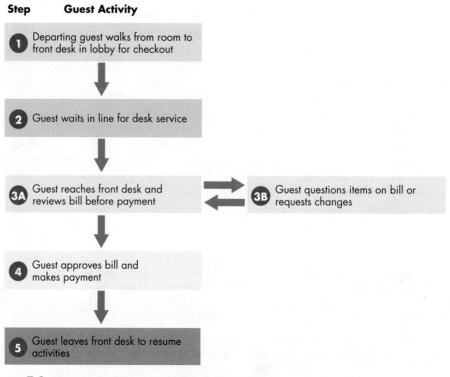

Figure 7.3 Flowchart of Traditional Guest Checkout

Operations Scheduling

5 Discuss the information contained in four kinds of operations schedules—the master production schedule, detailed schedule, staff schedule, and project schedule.

Continuing with the flow of activities in Figure 7.2, once operations plans have been determined, managers then develop timetables for implementing them. This aspect of operations, called *operations scheduling*, identifies times when specific production activities will occur.

In this section we consider four general kinds of schedules. (1) The *master schedule* is "the game plan" for upcoming production. (2) *Detailed schedules* show day-to-day activities that will occur in production. (3) *Staff schedules* identify who and how many employees will be working, and when. (4) Finally, *project schedules* provide coordination for completing large-scale projects.

The Master Production Schedule

Scheduling of production occurs at different levels. First, a top-level **master production schedule** shows which products will be produced, and when, in upcoming time periods. Logan Aluminum, for example, makes coils of aluminum that it supplies to customer companies that use it to make beverage cans. Logan's master schedule, with a format like the partial schedule shown in Figure 7.4, covers production for 60 weeks in which more than 300,000 tons will be produced. For various types of coils (products), it specifies how many tons will be produced each week, helping managers determine the kinds of materials, equipment, and other resources that will be needed for each week's production.

Detailed Schedules

While the master production schedule is the backbone for overall scheduling, additional information comes from **detailed schedules**—schedules showing daily work assignments with start and stop times for assigned jobs at each work station. Logan's production personnel need to know the locations of all coils in the plant and their various stages of completion. Start and stop times must be assigned, and employees need scheduled work assignments daily, not just weekly. Detailed short-term schedules allow managers to use customer orders and information about equipment status to update sizes and the variety of coils to be made each day.

Staff Schedules and Computer-Based Scheduling

Scheduling is useful for employee staffing in service companies, too, including restaurants, hotels, transportation, and landscaping. **Staff schedules**, in general, specify assigned working times in upcoming days—perhaps for as many as 30 days or more—for each employee on each work shift. They consider employees' needs and the company's efficiency and costs, including the ebbs and flows of demand for production.

Coil # (Product)	8/6/07	8/13/07	8/20/07	...	11/5/07	11/12/07
TC016	1,500	2,500			2,100	600
TC032	900		2,700		3,000	
TR020	300		2,600			1,600

Figure 7.4 **Example of Partial Master Production Schedule**

Master Production Schedule schedule showing which products will be produced, and when, in upcoming time periods

Detailed Schedule schedule showing daily work assignments with start and stop times for assigned jobs

Staff Schedule assigned working times in upcoming days for each employee on each work shift

Computer-based scheduling, using tools such as the *ABS Visual Staff Scheduler® PRO* (VSS Pro) software, can easily handle multi-shift activities for many employees—both part-time and full-time. It accommodates vacation times, holiday adjustments, and daily adjustments in staffing for unplanned absences and changes in production schedules.

Project Scheduling

Special projects, such as new business construction or redesigning a product, require close coordination and precise timing among many activities. In these cases, project management is facilitated by project scheduling tools, including Gantt charts and PERT.

The Gantt Graphical Method   Named after its developer, Henry Gantt, a **Gantt chart** breaks down large projects into steps to be performed and specifies the time required to perform each one. The project manager lists all activities needed to complete the work, estimates the time required for each step, records the progress on the chart, and checks the progress against the time scale on the chart to keep the project moving on schedule. If work is ahead of schedule, some employees may be shifted to another project. If it's behind schedule, workers may be added or completion delayed.

Figure 7.5 shows a Gantt chart for the renovation of a college classroom. It shows progress to date and schedules for remaining work. It also shows that some steps can be performed at the same time (e.g., step D can be performed during the same time as steps C and E), but others cannot (e.g., step A must be completed before any of the others can begin). Step E is behind schedule; it should have been completed before the current date.

Project Scheduling with PERT Charts   The *Program Evaluation and Review Technique (PERT)* provides even more information for controlling the progress of large projects. Along with times required to perform the activities, the layout of the **PERT chart** uses arrows to show the necessary *sequence* among activities, from start to finish, for completing the project. It also identifies the *critical path*—the most time-consuming set of activities—for completing the project.

Figure 7.6 shows a PERT chart for renovating the college classroom. The project's nine activities and the times required to complete them are identified. Each activity

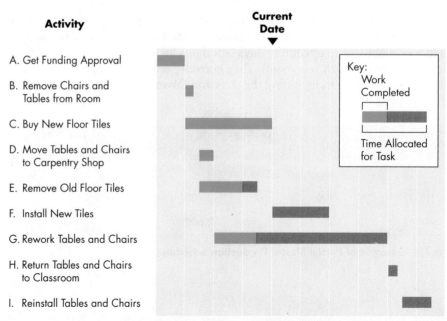

Figure 7.5 Gantt Chart

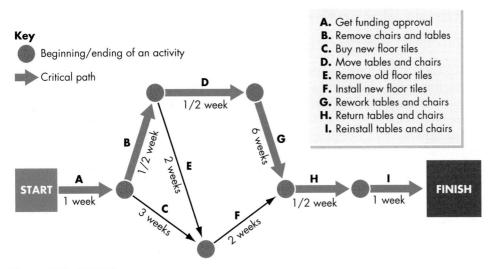

A. Get funding approval
B. Remove chairs and tables
C. Buy new floor tiles
D. Move tables and chairs
E. Remove old floor tiles
F. Install new floor tiles
G. Rework tables and chairs
H. Return tables and chairs
I. Reinstall tables and chairs

Figure 7.6 **PERT Chart**

is represented by an arrow. The arrows are positioned to show the required sequence for performing the activities. For example, chairs and tables can't be returned to the classroom (H) until after they've been reworked (G) and after new floor tiles are installed (F). Accordingly, the diagram shows arrows for G and F coming before activity H. Similarly, funding approval (A) has to occur before anything else can get started.

The critical path is informative because it reveals the most time-consuming path for project completion, and for most projects speed of completion is vital. The critical path for classroom renovation consists of activities A, B, D, G, H, and I, requiring 9.5 weeks. It's critical because a delay in completing any of those activities will cause corresponding lateness beyond the planned completion time (9.5 weeks after startup). Project managers will watch those activities and, if potential delays arise, take special action—by reassigning workers and equipment—to speed up late activities and stay on schedule.

Operations Control

6 Discuss the two key activities required for operations control.

Once long-range plans have been put into action and schedules have been drawn up, **operations control** requires managers to monitor performance by comparing results with detailed plans and schedules. If schedules or quality standards aren't met, managers can take corrective action. **Follow-up**—checking to ensure that production decisions are being implemented—is a key and ongoing facet of operations.

Operations control includes *materials management* and *quality control*. Both activities ensure that schedules are met and products delivered, both in quantity and in quality.

Gantt Chart production schedule that breaks down large projects into steps to be performed and specifies the time required to perform each step

Pert Chart production schedule specifying the sequence of activities, time requirements, and critical path for performing the steps in a project

Operations Control process of monitoring production performance by comparing results with plans and taking corrective action when needed

Follow-Up operations control activity for ensuring that production decisions are being implemented

Materials Management

Most of us have difficulty keeping track of personal items now and then—clothes, books, cell phones, and so on. Imagine keeping track of thousands or even millions of things at any one time. That's the challenge in **materials management**—the process by which managers plan, organize, and control the flow of materials from sources of supply through distribution of finished goods. For manufacturing firms, typical materials costs make up 50 to 75 percent of total product costs. For service firms, too, the materials stakes are high. UPS delivers 16 million packages every day and promises that all of them will arrive on schedule. It keeps this promise by tracking the locations, schedules, and on-time performance of 600 aircraft and 100,000 vehicles as they carry packages through the delivery system.

It's All in the Timing **Lean production systems**, pioneered by Toyota, are designed for smooth production flows that avoid inefficiencies, eliminate unnecessary inventories, and continuously improve production processes. **Just-in-time (JIT) production**, a type of lean system, brings together all needed materials at the precise moment they are required for each production stage, not before, thus creating fast and efficient responses to customer orders. All resources flow continuously—from arrival as raw materials to final assembly and shipment of finished products.

JIT production reduces to practically nothing the number of goods in process (goods not yet finished). It minimizes inventory costs, reduces storage space requirements for inventories, and saves money by replacing stop-and-go production with smooth movement. Once smooth flow is the norm, disruptions are more visible and are resolved more quickly. Finding and eliminating disruptions by the continuous improvement of production is a major objective of JIT production.

Materials Management Activities   Once a product has been designed, successful materials flows depend on five activities. From selecting suppliers on through the distribution of finished goods, materials managers engage in the following areas that compose materials management:

- **Supplier selection** means finding and choosing suppliers of services and materials to buy from. It includes evaluating potential suppliers, negotiating terms of service, and maintaining positive buyer–seller relationships.
- **Purchasing** is the acquisition of all the raw materials and services that a company needs to produce its products. Most large firms have purchasing departments to buy proper services and materials in the amounts needed.
- **Transportation** includes the means of transporting resources to the producer and finished goods to customers.
- **Warehousing** is the storage of both incoming materials for production and finished goods for distribution to customers.
- **Inventory control** includes the receiving, storing, handling, and counting of all raw materials, partly finished goods, and finished goods. It ensures that enough materials inventories are available to meet production schedules, while at the same time avoiding expensive excess inventories.

Quality Control

Quality control means taking action to ensure that operations produce goods or services that meet specific quality standards. Consider, for example, service operations where customer satisfaction depends largely on the employees who provide the service. By monitoring services, mistakes can be detected and corrections made. First, however, managers or other personnel must establish specific standards and measurements. At a bank, for example, quality control for teller services might require supervisors to observe employees periodically and evaluate their work according to a checklist. The results would then be reviewed with employees and would either confirm proper performance or indicate changes for bringing performance up to standards.

The quality of customer-employee interactions is no accident in firms that monitor customer encounters and provide training for employee skills development. Many managers realize that without employees trained in customer-relationship skills, quality suffers, and businesses, such as airlines—as we saw in our opening story—and hotels, can lose customers to better-prepared competitors.

Quality control means taking action to ensure that operations produce products that meet specific quality standards.

Quality Improvement and Total Quality Management

7 Identify the activities and underlying objectives involved in total quality management.

It is not enough to *control* quality by inspecting products and monitoring service operations as they occur, as when a supervisor listens in on a catalog sales service representative's customer calls. Businesses must also consider *building* quality into goods and services. In order to compete on a global scale, U.S. companies continue to emphasize a quality orientation. All employees, not just managers, participate in quality efforts, and firms have embraced new methods to measure progress and to identify areas for improvement. In many organizations, quality improvement has become a way of life.

Managing for Quality

Total quality management (TQM) includes all the activities necessary for getting high-quality goods and services into the marketplace. TQM begins with leadership and a desire for continuously improving both processes and products. It must consider all aspects of a business, including customers, suppliers, and employees. To marshal the interests of all these stakeholders, TQM first evaluates the costs of poor quality. It then involves assigning and accepting responsibility for quality improvement.

Materials Management process of planning, organizing, and controlling the flow of materials from sources of supply through distribution of finished goods

Lean Production System production system designed for smooth production flows that avoid inefficiencies, eliminate unnecessary inventories, and continuously improve production processes

Just-in-Time (Jit) Production type of lean production system that brings together all materials at the precise time they are required at each production stage

Supplier Selection process of finding and choosing suppliers from whom to buy

Purchasing acquisition of the materials and services that a firm needs to produce its products

Transportation activities in transporting resources to the producer and finished goods to customers

Warehousing storage of incoming materials for production and finished goods for distribution to customers

Inventory Control process of receiving, storing, handling, and counting of all raw materials, partly finished goods, and finished goods

Quality Control action of ensuring that operations produce products that meet specific quality standards

Total Quality Management (TQM) all activities involved in getting high-quality goods and services into the marketplace

MANAGING IN TURBULENT TIMES

Leaner Operations Are Restoring the U.S. Auto Industry

Recent signs of recovery for the U.S. auto industry stem from more than financial bailouts. General Motors and Chrysler, suffering grave financial losses in 2008, needed to demonstrate that they can survive and repay the bridge loans received from the U.S. Department of the Treasury. Under the guise of restructuring or reorganization, the steps automakers have taken can be summarized in just two words: *leaner operations*. GM, Chrysler, and Ford are adopting business strategies that Japanese producers have been using (and have mastered) for three decades to simplify production and capture a greater market share.

A reduction in product offerings is the foundation for leaner operations: A smaller number of makes, models, and options such as colors, engine sizes, trims, etc. simplifies product design, production, and distribution. It leads to lower costs, higher quality, and better customer service. Because it's easier to design a few rather than many different products, design and engineering requirements are vastly lowered. Designers strive for commonality of component parts so that all models use the same parts [e.g., all use the same door handles] rather than having separate designs for each model. Parts reductions simplify the supply chain, too: Fewer suppliers are needed, communications are easier and faster, and closer relationships with suppliers provide faster supplier responses on short notice.

Design simplification is a blessing for assembly operations, too, because fewer production steps are required, and when quality problems arise, they are easier to find and are quickly corrected. Because fewer components require less inventory space and equipment, smaller factories—which are less costly and easier to maintain—become possible. Production scheduling is simpler, as are materials movements during production, so there is less work stoppage and fewer mistakes, product quality improves, and on-time deliveries to customers increase.

x10/ZUMA Press/Newscom

The company's distribution network is simplified, too, when some of its auto brands are eliminated. GM has downsized to just four core brands—Buick, Cadillac, Chevrolet, and GMC—after ending the Oldsmobile, Pontiac, Saturn, Hummer, and Saab brands under the GM label. Chrysler's roster includes just three major brands: Chrysler, Jeep, and Dodge. Ford has discontinued its Mercury brand. Fewer brands means some auto dealerships are no longer needed, thus lowering distribution costs. With speedier product designs and production operations, newer products get into the marketplace more quickly than those of competitors, and customer service improves. When the benefits of lower costs, higher quality, and lower prices are added together, it becomes apparent that lean production systems offer significant competitive advantages. Causing it to happen, and quickly, at GM, Chrysler, and Ford continues to be a massive challenge for survival in turbulent times.

MyBizLab

The Cost of Poor Quality   As seen prominently in the popular press, Toyota recalled more than 10 million cars in 2009–2010, costing the world's then-number-one automaker billions of dollars and a severe blemish to its high-quality image. Problems ranging from sticking gas pedals and stalling engines, to malfunctioning fuel pumps were dangerous and costly not only to Toyota, but to many consumers, too.

As with goods producers, service providers and customers, too, suffer financial distress from poor-quality service products. The banking industry is a current example. As a backbone of the U.S. financial system, banks and their customers are still suffering because of bad financial products, most notably home mortgage loans. Lenders during "good times" began relaxing (or even ignoring altogether) traditional lending standards for determining whether borrowers are creditworthy (are they qualified to borrow and likely to repay mortgage loans?). Lenders in some cases intentionally overstated property values so customers could borrow more money than the property justified. Borrowers were sometimes encouraged to overstate (falsify) their incomes and were not required to present evidence of income or even employment. Some borrowers, unaware of the terms of their loan agreements, were surprised after an initial time lapse when a much higher interest rate (and monthly payment) suddenly kicked in. Unable to meet their payments, borrowers had to abandon their homes. Meanwhile, banks were left holding foreclosed properties, unpaid (defaulted) loans, and no cash. With shortages of bank funds threatening to shut down the entire financial system, the entire nation felt the widespread costs of poor quality.

Quality Ownership: Taking Responsibility for Quality   To ensure high-quality goods and services, many firms assign responsibility for some aspects of TQM to specific departments or positions. These specialists and experts may be called in to assist with quality-related problems in any department, and they keep everyone informed about the latest developments in quality-related equipment and methods. They also monitor quality-control activities to identify areas for improvement.

The backbone of TQM, however, and its biggest challenge, is motivating all employees throughout the company and its suppliers to achieve quality goals. Leaders of the quality movement use various methods and resources to foster a quality focus—training, verbal encouragement, teamwork, and tying compensation to work quality. When those efforts succeed, employees and suppliers will ultimately accept **quality ownership**— the idea that quality belongs to each person who creates it while performing a job.

With TQM, everyone—purchasers, engineers, janitors, marketers, machinists, suppliers, and others—must focus on quality. At Saint Luke's Hospital of Kansas City, for example, every employee receives the hospital's "balanced scorecard" showing whether the hospital is meeting its goals: fast patient recovery for specific illnesses, 94 percent or better patient-satisfaction rating, every room cleaned when a patient is gone to X-ray, and the hospital's return on investment being good enough to get a good bond rating in the financial markets. Quarterly scores show the achievement level reached for each goal. Every employee can recite where the hospital is excelling and where it needs improvement. In recognition of its employees' dedication to quality performance, Saint Luke's received the Malcolm Baldrige National Quality Award—the prestigious U.S. award for excellence in quality—and is a three-time winner of the Missouri Quality Award.[11]

Tools for Total Quality Management

Hundreds of tools have proven useful for quality improvement, ranging from statistical analysis of product data, to satisfaction surveys of customers, to **competitive product analysis**—a process by which a company analyzes a competitor's products to identify desirable improvements. Using competitive analysis, for example, Toshiba might take apart a Xerox copier and test each component. The results would help managers decide which Toshiba product features are satisfactory, which features should be upgraded, and which operations processes need improvement.

In this section, we survey five of the most commonly used tools for TQM: *value-added analysis, quality improvement teams, getting closer to the customer, the ISO series,* and *business process reengineering*.

Value-Added Analysis   **Value-added analysis** refers to the evaluation of all work activities, materials flows, and paperwork to determine the value that they add for customers. It often reveals wasteful or unnecessary activities that can be eliminated without jeopardizing customer service. The basic tenet is so important that Tootsie Roll Industries, the venerable candy company, employs it as a corporate principle: "We run a trim operation and continually strive to eliminate waste, minimize cost, and implement performance improvements." [12]

Quality Ownership principle of total quality management that holds that quality belongs to each person who creates it while performing a job

Competitive Product Analysis process by which a company analyzes a competitor's products to identify desirable improvements

Value-Added Analysis process of evaluating all work activities, materials flows, and paperwork to determine the value that they add for customers

Quality Improvement Teams   Companies throughout the world have adopted **quality improvement teams** patterned after the successful Japanese concept of *quality circles*: collaborative groups of employees from various work areas who meet regularly to define, analyze, and solve common production problems. Their goal is to improve both their own work methods and the products they make. Quality improvement teams organize their own work, select leaders, and address problems in the workplace. For years, Motorola has sponsored companywide team competitions to emphasize the value of the team approach, to recognize outstanding team performance, and to reaffirm the team's role in the company's continuous-improvement culture.

Getting Closer to the Customer   Successful businesses take steps to know what their customers want in the products they consume. On the other hand, struggling companies have often lost sight of customers as the driving force behind all business activity. Such companies waste resources by designing products that customers do not want. Sometimes, they ignore customer reactions to existing products or fail to keep up with changing tastes.

Successful firms take steps to know what their customers want in the products they consume. Caterpillar financial services, for example, received the Malcolm Baldrige National Quality Award for high ratings by its customers (that is, dealers and buyers of caterpillar equipment). Buying and financing equipment from Cat Financial became easier as Cat moved its services increasingly online. Customers now have 24/7 access to information on how much they owe on equipment costing anywhere from $30,000 to $2 million, and they can make payments around the clock, too. In the past, the 60,000 customers had to phone a Cat representative, who was often unavailable, resulting in delays and wasted time. The improved online system is testimony to Cat Financial's dedication in knowing what customers want, and then providing it.[13]

Identifying Customers—Internal and External   Improvement projects are undertaken for both external and internal customers. Internal suppliers and internal customers exist wherever one employee or activity relies on others. For example, marketing managers rely on internal accounting information—costs for materials, supplies, and wages—to plan marketing activities for coming months. The marketing manager is a customer of the firm's accountants—the information user relies on the information supplier. Accountants in a TQM environment recognize this supplier–customer connection and take steps to improve information for marketing.

The ISO Series   Perhaps you've driven past companies proudly displaying large banners announcing, "This Facility Is ISO Certified." The ISO (pronounced ICE-oh) label is a mark of quality achievement that is respected throughout the world and, in some countries, it's a requirement for doing business.

ISO 9000   **ISO 9000** is a certification program attesting that a factory, a laboratory, or an office has met the rigorous quality management requirements set by the International Organization for Standardization. Today, more than 160 countries have adopted ISO 9000 as a national standard. Nearly 1 million certificates have been issued to organizations worldwide meeting the ISO standards.

The standards of *ISO 9000* allow firms to show that they follow documented procedures for testing products, training workers, keeping records, and fixing defects. It allows international companies to determine (or be assured of) quality of product (or the business) when shipping for/from/to suppliers across borders. To become certified, companies must document the procedures followed by workers during every stage of production. The purpose is to ensure that a company's processes can create products exactly the same today as it did yesterday and as it will tomorrow.

ISO 14000   The **ISO 14000** program certifies improvements in environmental performance by requiring a firm to develop an *environmental management system*: a plan documenting how the company has acted to improve its performance in using resources (such as raw materials) and in managing pollution. A company must not only identify hazardous wastes that it expects to create, but it must also stipulate plans for treatment and disposal.

Business Process Reengineering Every business consists of processes—activities that it performs regularly and routinely in conducting business, such as receiving and storing materials from suppliers, billing patients for medical treatment, filing insurance claims for auto accidents, and filling customer orders from Internet sales. Any business process can increase customer satisfaction by performing it well. By the same token, any business process can disappoint customers when it's poorly managed.

Business process reengineering focuses on improving a business process—rethinking each of its steps by starting from scratch. *Reengineering* is the fundamental rethinking and radical redesign of business processes to achieve dramatic improvements as measured by cost, quality, service, and speed. The discussion of Caterpillar's changeover to an online system for customers is an example. Cat reengineered the whole payments and financing process by improving equipment, retraining employees, and connecting customers to Cat's databases. As the example illustrates, redesign is guided by a desire to improve operations and thereby provide higher-value services for customers.

Adding Value Through Supply Chains

8 Explain how a supply chain strategy differs from traditional strategies for coordinating operations among firms.

The term *supply chain* refers to the group of companies and stream of activities that work together to create a product. A **supply chain** (or **value chain**) for any product is the flow of information, materials, and services that starts with raw-materials suppliers and continues adding value through other stages in the network of firms until the product reaches the end customer.

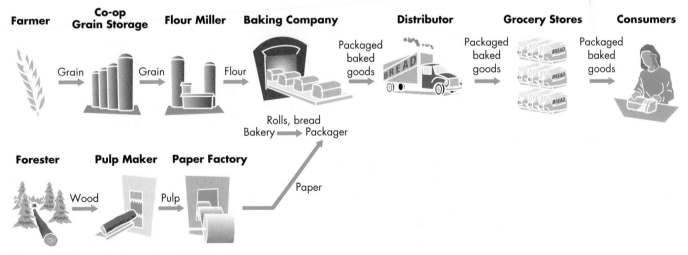

Figure 7.7 **Supply Chain for Baked Goods**

Quality Improvement Team TQM tool in which collaborative groups of employees from various work areas work together to improve quality by solving common shared production problems

ISO 9000 program certifying that a factory, laboratory, or office has met the quality management standards set by the International Organization for Standardization

ISO 14000 certification program attesting to the fact that a factory, laboratory, or office has improved its environmental performance

Business Process Reengineering rethinking and radical redesign of business processes to improve performance, quality, and productivity

Supply Chain (Value Chain) flow of information, materials, and services that starts with raw-materials suppliers and continues adding value through other stages in the network of firms until the product reaches the end customer

Figure 7.7 shows the chain of activities for supplying baked goods to consumers. Each stage adds value for the final customer. This bakery example begins with raw materials (grain harvested from the farm). It also includes storage and transportation activities, factory operations for baking and wrapping, and distribution to retailers. Each stage depends on the others for success in getting freshly baked goods to consumers. However, a failure by any link can spell disaster for the entire chain.

The Supply Chain Strategy

Traditional strategies assume that companies are managed as individual firms rather than as members of a coordinated supply system. Supply chain strategy is based on the idea that members of the chain will gain competitive advantage by working as a coordinated unit. Although each company looks out for its own interests, it works closely with suppliers and customers throughout the chain. Everyone focuses on the entire chain of relationships rather than on just the next stage in the chain.

A traditionally managed bakery, for example, would focus simply on getting production inputs from flour millers and paper suppliers, and then on supplying baked goods to distributors. Unfortunately, this approach limits the chain's performance and doesn't allow for possible improvements when activities are more carefully coordinated. Proper management and better coordination among supply chain activities can provide fresher baked goods at lower prices.

Supply Chain Management   **Supply chain management (SCM)** looks at the chain as a whole to improve the overall flow through a system composed of companies working together. Because customers ultimately get better value, supply chain management gains competitive advantage for each of the chain's members.

An innovative supply chain strategy was the heart of Michael Dell's vision when he established Dell Inc. Dell's concept improves performance by sharing information among chain members. Dell's long-term production plans and up-to-the-minute sales data are available to suppliers via the Internet. The process starts when customer orders are automatically translated into updated production schedules in the factory. These schedules are used not only by operations managers at Dell but also by such parts suppliers as Sony, which adjust their own production and shipping activities to better meet Dell's production needs. In turn, parts suppliers' updated schedules are transmitted to their materials suppliers, and so on up the chain. As Dell's requirements change, suppliers up and down the chain synchronize their schedules to produce only the right materials and parts. As a result, Dell's prices are low and turnaround time for shipping PCs to customers is reduced to a matter of hours instead of days.

Reengineering Supply Chains for Better Results   Process improvements and reengineering often are applied in supply chains to lower costs, speed up service, and coordinate flows of information and material. Because the smoother flow of accurate information along the chain reduces unwanted inventories and transportation, avoids delays, and cuts supply times, materials move faster to business customers and individual consumers. SCM offers faster deliveries and lower costs than customers could get if each member acted only according to its own operations requirements.

Outsourcing and Global Supply Chains

Outsourcing is the strategy of paying suppliers and distributors to perform certain business processes or to provide needed materials or services. The decision to outsource expands supply chains. The movement of manufacturing and service operations from the United States to countries such as China, Mexico, and India has reduced U.S. employment in traditional jobs. It has also created new operations jobs for supply chain management. Maytag, for example, had to develop its own internal global operations expertise before it could decide to open a new refrigerator factory in Mexico, import refrigerators from South Korea's Daewoo, and get laundry appliances from South Korea's Samsung Electronics. In departing from a long-standing practice of domestic production, Maytag adopted new supply chain skills for evaluating prospective outsourcing partners.

Skills for coordinating Maytag's domestic activities with those of its cross-border partners didn't end with the initial decision to get appliances from Mexico and Korea. Maytag personnel in their Newton, Iowa, headquarters have near-constant interaction with their partners on a host of continuing new operations issues. Product redesigns are transferred from the United States and used at remote manufacturing sites. Arrangements for cross-border materials flows require compliance with each country's commerce regulations. Production and global transportation scheduling are coordinated with U.S. market demand so that outsourced products arrive in the right amounts and on time without tarnishing Maytag's reputation for high quality. Although manufacturing operations are located remotely, they are closely integrated with the firm's home-base activities. That tightness of integration demands on-site operations expertise on both sides of the outsourcing equation. Global communication technologies are essential. The result for outsourcers is a greater need of operations skills for integration among dispersed facilities.

Supply Chain Management (SCM) principle of looking at the supply chain as a whole to improve the overall flow through the system

Ben Stansall/AFP/Getty Images/Newscom

Continued from page 166

Some Airlines Are "Getting It Right"

Unlike many carriers, better-performing airlines are proving that good service quality need not be sacrificed to remain profitable. JetBlue Airways, for example, continues to be profitable while also receiving fewer complaints than most other U.S. airlines. Among larger carriers, Southwest Airlines has demonstrated consistently that the two—high-quality service and profitability—go hand-in-hand. Southwest's service quality has attracted a loyal customer following. Passenger testimonials cite Southwest's refusal to charge extra for baggage, for booking flights on the phone, or for changing flights. They receive exceptionally high ratings for baggage handling (fewer lost bags), orderly boarding practices, and consistent on-time performance.[14] Southwest had the fewest number of consumer complaints for the most recent three consecutive years in the U.S. Department of Transportation's (DOT) official reports.[15] Along with quality, profitability continues to grow, while other airlines are operating at a loss: "Yearend results for 2009 marked Southwest's 37th consecutive year of profitability."[16]

Airline quality ratings are well-documented, using measurements from airport operations records and from customer complaints on numerous service activities. At the DOT, for example, the Aviation Consumer Protection Division gathers data on flight delays, mishandled baggage, oversales (number of confirmed passengers denied boarding), and customer complaints (on cancellations, misconnections, delays, baggage, fares, ticketing mistakes, and rude or unhelpful employees). Airlines are ranked each month, from top (fewest complaints) to bottom on each service activity, and Southwest Airlines is at or near the top consistently.[17] Several other well-known brands, near the bottom, seem to have little interest in improving. Many passengers are left wondering, "Why don't more airlines adopt the Southwest model?"

QUESTIONS FOR DISCUSSION

1 How would you define *quality* and how is quality measured in this industry? Are some measurements more useful than others? Explain.

2 Some *service activities*, such as delayed departures, are not under total control by airlines, but are also affected by outside factors. Among all service activities that affect quality for customers, identify three or more that are totally controlled by airlines, and three or more that airlines cannot totally control. Should both sets of activities be included in the airlines' quality ratings? Explain.

3 Describe how *process flowcharts* may be helpful for methods improvement in airline service operations. What kinds of information would you hope to gain from the flowcharts?

4 Identify a major U.S. airline that has received *poor quality ratings*. Who are its customers, and what are the basic causes that led to declining quality?

5 U.S. airplane passengers must choose between two controversial security-screening procedures: full-body image detection or probing pat-downs. How might these procedures affect customers' *perceptions of airlines' services*? What actions would you recommend be considered by airlines to overcome negative perceptions?

SUMMARY OF LEARNING OBJECTIVES   MyBizLab

1. **Explain the meaning of the term *production* or *operations*. (p. 166)**

   Operations (or *production*) refers to all the activities involved in making products—goods and services—for customers. Through their operations processes—using knowledge, physical materials, information, equipment, the customer, and human skills—firms provide benefits for themselves and for their customers. Production provides businesses with economic results: profits, wages, and goods purchased from other companies. At the same time, it adds value and benefits for customers by providing products that satisfy a want or need.

2. **Describe the three kinds of utility that operations processes provide for adding customer value. (pp. 166–170)**

   Production or operations adds customer value by providing *utility*—the ability of a product to satisfy a want or need—in terms of form, time, and place: (1) *Form utility*: By turning raw materials and human skills into finished goods and services, production adds customer value by making products available. (2) *Time utility*: Production provides customer value by making products available when customers want them. (3) *Place utility*: Production adds customer value by making products available where they are convenient for customers.

3. **Explain how companies with different business strategies are best served by having different operations capabilities. (pp. 170–172)**

   Production is a flexible activity that can be molded into many shapes to give different operations capabilities (production capabilities) for different purposes. Its design is best driven from above by the firm's larger business strategy. When firms adopt different strategies for winning customers in specific target markets, they should also adjust their *operations capabilities*—what production must do especially well—to match the chosen strategy. The operations capability that is appropriate for a low-cost strategy, for example, is different than the kind of competence that is best for a dependability strategy. Accordingly, the operations characteristics—such as number and size of production facilities, employee skills, kinds of equipment—and its operations activities will be different, resulting in different operations capabilities to better support their different purposes.

4. **Identify the major factors that are considered in operations planning. (pp. 172–176)**

   Operations planning includes five major considerations: (1) *Capacity planning* considers current and future capacity requirements for meeting anticipated customer demand. The amount of a product that a company can produce under normal conditions is its *capacity*, and it depends on how many people it employs and the number and size of its facilities. (2) *Location planning* is crucial because a firm's location affects costs of production, ease of transporting, access to skilled workers, and convenient accessibility for customers. (3) *Layout planning* determines the physical location of machinery, equipment, and facilities and affects how efficiently a company can respond to customer demand. A *custom-products layout* is effective for make-to-order production specializing in custom jobs. A *same-steps layout*, such as assembly lines, is often used for large-volume, make-to-stock production. (4) *Quality planning* begins when products are being designed and extends into production operations for ensuring that the desired performance and consistency are built into products. (5) *Methods planning* considers each production step and the specific methods for performing it. The purpose is to reduce waste and inefficiency by methods improvement procedures.

5. **Discuss the information contained in four kinds of operations schedules—the master production schedule, detailed schedule, staff schedule, and project schedule. (pp. 177–179)**

   Operations scheduling identifies times when specific production activities will occur. The *master production schedule*, the top-level schedule for upcoming production, shows how many of which products will be produced in each time period, in weeks or months ahead, to meet upcoming customer demand. *Detailed schedules* take a shorter-range perspective by specifying daily work assignments with start and stop times for assigned jobs at each workstation. *Staff schedules* identify who and how many employees will be working, and their assigned working times on each work shift for up to 30 days ahead. Finally, *project schedules* provide information for completing large-scale projects. Project scheduling tools such as *PERT* break down special large projects into the sequence of steps to be performed and when to perform them. PERT shows the necessary sequence among activities, and identifies the critical path—the most time-consuming set of activities for completing the project.

6. **Discuss the two key activities required for operations control. (pp. 179–181)**

   Once plans and schedules have been drawn up, *operations control* requires managers to monitor performance by comparing results against those plans and schedules. If schedules or quality standards are not met, managers take corrective action. *Follow-up*—checking to ensure that decisions are being implemented—is an essential facet of operations control. *Materials management*—including supplier selection, purchasing, transportation, warehousing, and inventory control—facilitates the flow of materials. It may use lean production systems, such as *just-in-time operations*, for smooth production flows that avoid inefficiencies, comply with schedules, eliminate unnecessary inventories, and continuously improve production processes. *Quality control* means taking action to ensure that operations produce goods or services that meet specific quality standards.

7. **Identify the activities and underlying objectives involved in total quality management. (pp. 181–185)**
Total quality management (TQM) is a customer-driven culture for offering products with characteristics that customers want. It includes all the activities necessary for getting customer-satisfying goods and services into the marketplace and, internally, getting every job to give better service to internal customers. TQM begins with leadership and a desire for continuously improving both processes and products. It considers all aspects of a business, including customers, suppliers, and employees. The TQM culture fosters an attitude of quality ownership among employees and suppliers—the idea that quality belongs to each person who creates it while performing a job—so that quality improvement becomes a continuous way of life. It identifies the costs of poor quality, and applies the process improvement tools of TQM to reduce those costs.

8. **Explain how a supply chain strategy differs from traditional strategies for coordinating operations among firms. (pp. 185–187)**
The supply chain strategy is based on the idea that members of the *supply chain*—the stream of all activities and companies that add value in creating a product—will gain competitive advantage by working together as a coordinated unit. In contrast, traditional strategies assume that companies are managed as individual firms, each acting in its own interest. By managing the chain as a whole—using *supply chain management*—companies can more closely coordinate activities throughout the chain. By sharing information, overall costs and inventories can be reduced, quality can be improved, overall flow through the system improves, thus providing customers higher value from faster deliveries and lower costs.

KEY TERMS   MyBizLab

assembly line (p. 175)
business process reengineering (p. 185)
capacity (p. 173)
competitive product analysis (p. 183)
consistency (p. 175)
custom-products layout (p. 174)
detailed schedule (p. 177)
follow-up (p. 179)
Gantt chart (p. 178)
goods operations (goods production) (p. 166)
high-contact system (p. 170)
inventory control (p. 180)
ISO 9000 (p. 184)
ISO 14000 (p. 184)
just-in-time (JIT) production (p. 180)
lean production system (p. 180)

low-contact system (p. 170)
make-to-order operations (p. 169)
make-to-stock operations (p. 169)
master production schedule (p. 177)
materials management (p. 180)
operations capability (production capability) (p. 170)
operations control (p. 179)
operations process (p. 169)
operations (production) (p. 166)
operations (production) management (p. 167)
operations (production) managers (p. 167)
performance (p. 175)
PERT chart (p. 178)
purchasing (p. 180)
quality (p. 175)

quality control (p. 180)
quality improvement team (p. 184)
quality ownership (p. 183)
same-steps layout (p. 175)
service operations (service production) (p. 166)
staff schedule (p. 177)
supplier selection (p. 180)
supply chain management (SCM) (p. 186)
supply chain (value chain) (p. 185)
total quality management (TQM) (p. 181)
transportation (p. 180)
utility (p. 166)
value-added analysis (p. 183)
warehousing (p. 180)

QUESTIONS AND EXERCISES

QUESTIONS FOR REVIEW

1. What are the major differences between goods-production operations and service operations?
2. What are the major differences between high-contact and low-contact service systems?
3. What are the five major categories of operations planning?
4. What are the major activities in materials management?
5. What activities are involved in total quality management?

QUESTIONS FOR ANALYSIS

6. What are the input resources and finished products in the following services: a real estate firm, a child care facility, a bank, and a hotel?

7. Choose a consumer item, such as an iPod, packaged food, or another everyday product, and trace its supply chain. Identify at least four upstream stages in the chain. Based on your familiarity with the product and the supply chain stages you identified, what recommendations would you make to improve the supply chain?
8. Develop a list of internal customers and internal suppliers for some business that you use frequently (or where you work), such as a cafeteria, a dormitory or hotel, or a movie theater. Identify areas for potential quality improvement in these internal customer–supplier activity relationships.
9. Find good examples of a make-to-order production process and a make-to-stock process in both goods operations and in service operations. Explain your choices.

APPLICATION EXERCISES

10. Think of an everyday activity, either personal or professional, that you would like to streamline for faster performance or more convenience. It could be something like gassing up your car, going to work or school, enrolling in classes at school, or any other activity that involves several stages with which you are familiar. Describe how you would use methods planning as described in the chapter to improve the activity. Draw a process flowchart that shows the stages in the activity you chose, then tell how you would use it.

11. Interview the manager of a local service business, or speak to a food service, bookstore, or other manager at your school. Identify the major decisions involved in planning that business's service operations.

BUILDING YOUR BUSINESS SKILLS

The One-On-One Entrepreneur

Goal
To encourage you to apply the concept of customization to an entrepreneurial idea.

Background Information
You are an entrepreneur who wants to start your own service business. You are intrigued with the idea of creating some kind of customized one-on-one service that would appeal to baby boomers, who often like to be pampered, and working women, who have little time to get things done.

Method

Step 1
Get together with three or four other students to brainstorm ideas for services that would appeal to harried working people. Here are just a few:

- A concierge service in office buildings that would handle such personal and business services as arranging children's birthday parties and booking guest speakers for business luncheons.
- A personal-image consultation service aimed at helping clients improve appearance, etiquette, and presentation style.
- A mobile pet-care network through which vets and groomers make house calls.

Step 2
Choose one of these ideas or one that your team thinks of. Then write a memo explaining why you think your idea will succeed. Research may be necessary as you target any of the following:

- A specific demographic group or groups (Who are your customers, and why would they buy your service?)
- Features that make your service attractive to this group
- The social factors in your local community that would contribute to success

FOLLOW-UP QUESTIONS

1 Why is the customization of and easy access to personal services so desirable?

2 As services are personalized, do you think quality will become more or less important? Why?

3 Why does the trend toward personalized, one-on-one service present unique opportunities for entrepreneurs?

4 In a personal one-on-one business, how important are the human relations skills of those delivering the service? Can you make an argument that they are more important than the service itself?

EXERCISING YOUR ETHICS: INDIVIDUAL EXERCISE

Promises, Promises

The Situation
Unfortunately, false promises are not uncommon when managers feel pressure to pump up profits. Many operations managers no doubt recall times when excited marketing managers asked for unrealistic commitments from production to get a new customer contract. This exercise will introduce you to some ethical considerations pertaining to such promises and commitments.

The Dilemma
You are an operations manager for a factory that makes replacement car mufflers and tailpipes. Your products are distributed throughout the country to muffler-repair shops that install them on used vehicles. After several years of modest but steady growth, your company recently suffered a downturn and shut down 5 percent of the factory's production capacity. Two supervisors and 70 production workers were laid off.

After returning from lunch, you get a phone call from the general manager of King Kong Mufflers, one of the nation's top three muffler-repair chains, who says the following:

I suppose you know that we're about to sign a contract for your firm to supply us with replacement parts in large volumes, *beginning two months from now. Your sales manager assures me that you can reliably meet my needs, and I just want to confirm that promise with you before I sign the contract.*

This is the first you've heard about this contract. While your potential customer is talking, you realize that meeting his needs will require a 20-percent increase in your current production capacity. Two months, however, isn't enough time to add more equipment, acquire tools, hire and train workers, and contract for supplies. An increase this large might even require a bigger building (which would take considerably more than two months to arrange). On the other hand, you also know how much your firm needs the business. Your thoughts are interrupted when the caller says, "So what's your production situation insofar as meeting our needs?" The caller waits in silence while you gather your thoughts.

QUESTIONS TO ADDRESS

1 What are the underlying ethical issues in this situation?

2 From an ethical standpoint, what is an appropriate response to the customer's question? What steps should you take in responding to it? Explain.

3 What would you say on the phone at this time to this customer?

EXERCISING YOUR ETHICS: TEAM EXERCISE

Calculating the Cost of Conscience

The Situation
Product quality and cost affect every firm's reputation and profitability, as well as the satisfaction of customers. This exercise will expose you to some ethical considerations that pertain to certain cost and service decisions that must be made by operations managers.

The Dilemma
As director of quality for a major appliance manufacturer, Ruth was reporting to the executive committee on the results of a program for correcting problems with a newly redesigned compressor (the motor that cools the refrigerator) that the company had recently begun using in its refrigerators. Following several customer complaints, the quality lab had determined that some of the new compressor units ran more loudly than expected. One corrective option was simply waiting until customers complained and responding to each complaint if and when it occurred. Ruth, however, decided that this approach was inconsistent with the company's policy of being the high-quality leader in the industry. Insisting on a proactive, "pro-quality" approach, Ruth initiated a program for contacting all customers who had purchased refrigerators containing the new compressor.

Unfortunately, her "quality-and-customers-first" policy was expensive. Service representatives nationwide had to phone every customer, make appointments for home visits, and replace original compressors with a newer model. Because replacement time was only 30 minutes, customers were hardly inconvenienced, and food stayed refrigerated without interruption. Customer response to the replacement program was overwhelmingly favorable.

Near the end of Ruth's report, an executive vice president was overheard to comment, "Ruth's program has cost this company $400 million in service expenses." Two weeks later, Ruth was fired.

Team Activity
Assemble a group of four students and assign each group member to one of the following roles:
- Ruth
- Ruth's boss
- customer
- company investor

ACTION STEPS
1 Before hearing any of your group's comments on this situation, and from the perspective of your assigned role, do you think that Ruth's firing is consistent with the company's desire for industry leadership in quality? Write down the reasons for your position.
2 Before hearing any of your group's comments on this situation, and from the perspective of your assigned role, what are the underlying ethical issues, if any, in this situation? Write down the issues.
3 Gather your group together and reveal, in turn, each member's comments on Ruth's firing. Next, reveal the ethical issues listed by each member.
4 Appoint someone to record main points of agreement and disagreement within the group. How do you explain the results? What accounts for any disagreement?
5 From an ethical standpoint, what does your group conclude is the most appropriate action that should have been taken by the company in this situation?
6 Develop a group response to the following question: What are the respective roles of profits, obligations to customers, and employee considerations for the firm in this situation?

VIDEO EXERCISE   MyBizLab

Method

Learning Objectives
The purpose of this video is to help you:
1 Explain how utility is created through the production process.
2 Describe the advantages and disadvantages of outsourcing for an organization.
3 Identify the activities and underlying objectives involved in total quality management.

Synopsis
While soap has been around for centuries, Method has taken a new approach to the production of this essential product. Method, founded by Adam Lowry and Eric Ryan, seeks to make fundamental change through the design, production, and distribution of their home cleaning and laundry products. A core value of the company is adherence to the Cradle to Cradle philosophy, which seeks to produce products that are infinitely renewable and recyclable. Cradle to Cradle certification is administered through MBDC (McDonough Braungart Design Chemistry), a global sustainability consulting and product certification firm. While being committed to environmental goals, Method must also produce their products in a cost efficient manner to keep prices close to their competition. One option for Method would be to design and build their own manufacturing facility. This would create assurance that they could address environmental concerns, but it would increase costs. To maintain their competitive position, Method has chosen to contract with outside manufacturers to produce Method products according to their exacting standards.

DISCUSSION QUESTIONS
1 Utility is the ability of a product to satisfy a want or need. What types of utility does Method create through their product line?
2 How are Method's products different from those of their competition?
3 Why did Method choose to outsource production of their products? What are the advantages and disadvantages of outsourcing?
4 How is Method's packaging different?
5 Method seeks to meet ISO 14000 standards, including ISO 14001 which seeks improved environmental performance. How do they achieve this goal?

Online Exploration

By visiting Method's website www.methodhome.com, you will gain insight into the company's mission, values, and products. Method works to reduce its impact on the environment in every decision that it makes, from the ingredients in their products to the manufacturing process to packaging decisions. Method carefully weighed the alternatives in packaging from post-consumer PET to bio-plastics and ultimately decided that traditional plastics were better for the environment. Read more about this, clicking on "sustainable packaging" under the "inside the bottle" heading on the right side of the page. What factors led Method to decide to use a more traditional plastic, post-consumer PET, for their packaging? Do you agree with their decision?

END NOTES

[1] "Number of Airline Passengers Declines 11.8 Percent," *Credit Unions Online*, May 15, 2009, at http://www.creditunionsonline.com/news/2009/Number-of-Airline-Passengers-Declines-11.8-Percent.html; Charisse Jones, "U.S. Airlines Flew Fewer Passengers in 2009," *USATODAY.com*, March 12, 2010, at http://www.usatoday.com/travel/flights/2010-03-12-airtravel12_ST_N.htm; Gary Stoller, "Extra Fees Add to Travelers' Distain for Bigger Airlines," *USATODAY.com*, April 15, 2010, at http://travel.usatoday.com/flights/2010-09-15-airlinecomplaints15_ST2_N.htm.

[2] General Electric Company, *Annual Report for Year Ended Dec. 31, 2008, FORM 10-K*, (U.S. Securities and Exchange Commission, February 19, 2009).

[3] Terry Hill, *Manufacturing Strategy*, 3rd edition (Boston: Irwin McGraw-Hill, 2000), Chapters 2–4; James A. Fitzsimmons, Mona J. Fitzsimmons, *Service Management: Operations Strategy, Information Technology*, 6th edition (Boston: Irwin McGraw-Hill, 2008), 46–48.

[4] Grace Gagliano, "Turning Meal Planning into a Business," *BRADENTON.COM*, August 19, 2010, at http://www.bradenton.com/2010/08/19/2515525/turning-meal-planning-into-a-business.html#ixzz0x3CL8WIj; http://www.grocerydash.com.

[5] Star-Ledger Wire Services, "Moms Combine Tech with Frugality to Save Money, Time at Supermarket," *NJ.com*, August 24, 2010, at http://www.nj.com/business/index.ssf/2010/08/moms_combine_tech_with_frugali.html; http://www.grocerydash.com.

[6] http://www.grocerydash.com.

[7] The Sacramento Bee, "Paradise Found," September 1, 2010, *Columbia Daily Tribune*, 6B.

[8] Jack Ewing, "The Auto Slump Hits Slovakia," *SPIEGEL ONLINE*, June 19, 2009, at http://www.spiegel.de/international/business/0,1518,druck-631388,00.html; Gail Edmondson, Willam Boston, Andrea Zammert, "Detroit East," *BusinessWeek* (July 25, 2005), at http://www.businessweek.com/print/magazine/content/05_30/b3944003.htm?chan=gl/.

[9] American Society for Quality, "ASQ Glossary of Terms," **http://www.asq.org/glossary/q.html**, accessed April 10, 2009.

[10] "Savoring Fine Chocolates," at **http://www.godiva.com/godivacollection/guideToGodiva.aspx**, accessed April 10, 2009.

[11] "Missouri Quality Award: Fifth Win for Saint Luke's, Second Time as a Health System," November 2010, at https://www.saintlukeshealthsystem.org/article/missouri-quality-award; Del Jones, "Baldrige Award Honors Record 7 Quality Winners," *USA Today*, November 26, 2003, 6B.

[12] Tootsie Roll Industries, Inc., *Annual Report 2009* (Chicago: 2010), p. 1.

[13] Del Jones, "Baldrige Award Honors Record 7 Quality Winners," *USA Today*, November 26, 2003, 6B.

[14] Gary Stoller, "Extra Fees Add to Travelers' Distain for Bigger Airlines," *USATODAY.com*, April 15, 2010, at http://travel.usatoday.com/flights/2010-09-15-airlinecomplaints15_ST2_N.htm

[15] Valaer Murray, "Most-Complained-About Airlines," *Travel And Leisure.com*, June 2010, at http://www.travelandleisure.com/articles/most-complained-about-airlines/1; "Air Travel Consumer Report," *Office of Aviation Enforcement and Proceedings: U.S. Department of Transportation*, November 9, 2010, at http://airconsumer.dot.gov/reports/index.htm.

[16] "Southwest Airlines Fact Sheet," Southwest.com, August 15, 2010.

[17] "Air Travel Consumer Report," *Office of Aviation Enforcement and Proceedings: U.S. Department of Transportation*, November 9, 2010, at http://airconsumer.dot.gov/reports/index.htm.

8 Employee Behavior and Motivation

What's the Deal About Work?

The "plight" of the American worker is common subject matter for television shows, movies, and stand-up comedians. The stereotypic image often shows people overworked, underpaid, and generally unhappy about their work life. Unfortunately, this stereotype is all too often a true reflection of what some workers face. Increased competition, longer working hours, heightened pressures to do more with less, economic uncertainty, and technology that "allows" workers to be on call 24/7 are all culprits. Some employees of video game maker Electronic Arts, for example, claim they routinely work between 65 and 85 hours a week without overtime pay; this claim has led to some unhappy workers and at least one lawsuit. Some managers at both Taco Bell and Radio Shack have made similar arguments—they are expected to run a business but must then also do a lot of other chores as well.

The consequences for businesses, in terms of increased employee turnover, lost efficiency, low morale, and so on, are high, and the consequences for workers are even worse. Although statistics are inconclusive, observers report that white-collar injuries, illnesses, and even suicides related to work have risen recently. For instance, one recent study found that 23 percent of male stockbrokers in the United States were clinically depressed, three times the national average. Other studies find that many workers feel overworked and constantly worry about both their job security and financial stability. In Japan, there is even a term for "death by overwork"—*jaroshi*, which is a legally recognized cause of death.[1]

> *After reading this chapter, you should be able to:*
>
> 1 **Identify and discuss the basic forms of behaviors that employees exhibit in organizations.**
> 2 **Describe the nature and importance of individual differences among employees.**
> 3 **Explain the meaning and importance of psychological contracts and the person-job fit in the workplace.**
> 4 **Identify and summarize the most important models and concepts of employee motivation.**
> 5 **Describe some of the strategies and techniques used by organizations to improve employee motivation.**

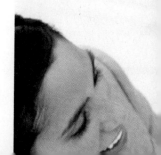

Yet there are also many individuals who find happiness and fulfillment at work. One study describes 40 percent of U.S. workers as excited about their jobs, eager to begin work on Monday mornings, and loving what they do.[2] In many cases, happy workers have jobs that are easy to love. Sandor Zombori was working as an engineer but always longed to cook. He walked away from his job, invested his savings in a restaurant, and 20 years later is the owner and chef of an award-winning restaurant. "All the time, I am soaking it up, like a sponge, trying to learn as much as I can," Zombori explains.

For others, traditional careers hold rewards. Robert Sunday, associate marketing manager of Cheerios brand at General Mills, says about his job, "I truly love it! As the parent of a toddler, it's exciting to have the coolest job at

Jacob Wackerhausen/iStockphoto.com

WHAT'S IN IT FOR ME?

The connections that people have with their jobs can go a long way toward determining how happy employees are with their work. At the extremes, some people truly love their jobs, while others just as truly hate them. Most people, however, fall somewhere in between. By understanding the basic elements of this chapter, you'll be better able to (1) understand your own feelings toward your work from the perspective of an employee and (2) understand the feelings of others toward their work from the perspective of a boss or owner.

So, what causes one employee to work hard and have a positive attitude and another worker to do just enough to get by while constantly grumbling about how awful things are? Successful managers usually have at least a fundamental understanding of what accounts for such differences. To start developing your understanding, let's begin by describing the different forms of behaviors that employees can exhibit at work. Later in the chapter, we'll look at some important models and concepts of employee motivation, as well as some strategies and techniques used by organizations to improve employee motivation.

MyBizLab Where you see MyBizLab in this chapter, go to **www.mybizlab.com** for additional activities on the topic being discussed.

preschool." For college professors, nurses, bank loan officers, and others, job happiness often comes from satisfying intellectual curiosity, helping others, giving back to the community, and feeling needed.

Sometimes jobholders can change or define their work in ways that bring them more satisfaction. Richard Karlgaard is the publisher of *Forbes* magazine. At first, his job primarily involved assessing and managing the reporting of financial data, a task he quickly decided was mundane and unexciting. So, he created a new set of responsibilities for himself, serving as an editor-at-large and writing about technology, while leaving most of the financial reporting to others.

Unfortunately, other individuals don't find their jobs rewarding but also cannot change the work they are doing. In these cases, looking elsewhere may be the best option. Mary Lou Quinlan was the CEO of a New York advertising agency, the pinnacle of her profession, but chose to quit and start a small consulting business. The pay is less, but she is happier. "Finally, I'm doing something I can picture doing for a long, long time," Quinlan says.

Our opening story continues on page 214.

Forms of Employee Behavior

Employee behavior is the pattern of actions by the members of an organization that directly or indirectly influences the organization's effectiveness. Some employee behaviors, called *performance behaviors*, directly contribute to productivity and performance. Other behaviors, referred to as *organizational citizenship*, provide positive benefits to the organization but in more indirect ways. *Counterproductive behaviors* detract from performance and actually cost the organization. Let's look at each of these types of behavior in a bit more detail.

Performance Behaviors

Performance behaviors are the total set of work-related behaviors that the organization expects employees to display. Essentially, these are the behaviors directly targeted at performing a job. For some jobs, performance behaviors can be narrowly defined and easily measured. For example, an assembly-line worker who sits by a moving conveyor and attaches parts to a product as it passes by has relatively few performance behaviors. He or she is expected to remain at the workstation for a predetermined number of hours and correctly attach the parts. Such performance can often be assessed quantitatively by counting the percentage of parts correctly attached.

For many other jobs, however, performance behaviors are more diverse and difficult to assess. For example, consider the case of a research-and-development scientist at Merck Pharmaceuticals. The scientist works in a lab trying to find new scientific breakthroughs that have commercial potential. The scientist must apply knowledge and experience gained from previous research. Intuition and creativity are also important. But even with all the scientist's abilities and effort, a desired breakthrough may take months or even years to accomplish.

Organizational Citizenship

Employees can also engage in positive behaviors that do not directly contribute to the bottom line. Such behaviors are often called **organizational citizenship.**[3] Organizational citizenship refers to the behavior of individuals who make a positive overall contribution to the organization. Consider, for example, an employee who does work that is highly acceptable in terms of both quantity and quality. However, she refuses to work overtime, won't help newcomers learn the ropes, and is generally unwilling to make any contribution beyond the strict performance requirements of her job. This person may be seen as a good performer, but she is not likely to be seen as a good organizational citizen. Another employee may exhibit a comparable level of performance. In addition, however, she always works late when the boss asks her to, she takes time to help newcomers learn their way around, and she is perceived as being helpful and committed to the organization's success. She is likely to be seen as a better organizational citizen.

A number of factors, including individual, social, and organizational variables, play roles in promoting or minimizing organizational citizenship behaviors. For example, the personality, attitudes, and needs of the individual may cause some people to be more helpful than others. Similarly, the individual's work group may encourage or discourage such behaviors. And the organization itself, especially its corporate culture, may or may not promote, recognize, and reward these types of behaviors.

Counterproductive Behaviors

Still other work-related behaviors are counterproductive. **Counterproductive behaviors** are those that detract from, rather than contribute to, organizational performance. **Absenteeism** occurs when an employee does not show up for work. Some absenteeism has a legitimate cause, such as illness, jury duty, or death or illness in the family. Other times, the employee may report a feigned legitimate cause that's actually just an excuse to stay home. When an employee is absent, legitimately or not, his or her work does not get done at all, a substitute must be hired to do it, or others in the organization must pick up the slack, In any event, though, absenteeism results in direct costs to a business.

Turnover occurs when people quit their jobs. An organization usually incurs costs in replacing workers who have quit—lost productivity while seeking a replacement, training someone new, etc. Turnover results from a number of factors, including aspects of the job, the organization, the individual, the labor market, and family influences. In general, a poor person-job fit (which we'll discuss later in the chapter) is also a likely cause of turnover. There are some employees whose turnover doesn't hurt the business; however, when productive employees leave an organization, it does reflect counterproductive behavior.

Other forms of counterproductive behavior may be even more costly for an organization. *Theft and sabotage,* for example, result in direct financial costs for an organization. *Sexual and racial harassment* also cost an organization, both indirectly (by lowering morale, producing fear, and driving off valuable employees) and directly (through financial liability if the organization responds inappropriately). *Workplace aggression and violence* are also a growing concern in some organizations.

Employee Behavior the pattern of actions by the members of an organization that directly or indirectly influences the organization's effectiveness

Performance Behaviors the total set of work-related behaviors that the organization expects employees to display

Organizational Citizenship positive behaviors that do not directly contribute to the bottom line

Counterproductive Behaviors behaviors that detract from organizational performance

Absenteeism when an employee does not show up for work

Turnover annual percentage of an organization's workforce that leaves and must be replaced

MANAGING IN TURBULENT TIMES

Tragedy in the Workplace

A few years ago, James Davis walked through the doors of the Union Butterfield tool company in Asheville, North Carolina. He had been fired by Union Butterfield just two days before, and now he wanted revenge for what he felt was a grave injustice. To extract that revenge, Davis carried a semiautomatic rifle and a pistol. Once inside the doors, he opened fire, getting off about 50 shots and killing 3 of his former coworkers. After he finished shooting, Davis lit a cigarette and calmly waited for the police to arrive; then he quietly surrendered and was led away in handcuffs.

Unfortunately, tragedies such as this one are not all that uncommon. According to recent statistics, 1 employee is killed at a U.S. workplace by a current or former coworker an average of once each week. In addition, another 25 are seriously injured by violent assaults. Overall, some 2 million U.S. workers are victims of some form of workplace violence each year.

The National Institute for Occupational Safety and Health (NIOSH) defines *workplace violence* as any physical assault, threatening behavior, or verbal abuse that occurs in a work setting. Experts also suggest that U.S. businesses lose billions of dollars each year in lost work time and productivity, litigation expenses, and security measures in the aftermath of workplace violence. Among the most common reasons often given for increasing workplace violence are economic fears regarding job security, heightened concerns for personal safety after the September 11, 2001, terrorist attacks, and generalized stress and anxiety among workers.

The recession of 2008–2010 only served to heighten these concerns. Massive layoffs, few prospects for new jobs, a spike in home foreclosures—any one of these might push a desperate person over the edge. But many people have encountered all three of these setbacks at the same time. Fortunately, most people are resilient and on a relative basis, few resort to the type of twisted revenge James Davis used.

Still, though, managers should be aware of how they treat people. Probably the most important advice is to always treat people with respect, dignity, fairness, and honesty; this

Eric Hood/iStockphoto.com

applies in all conditions, of course, not just during an economic downturn. When it becomes necessary to cut jobs or reduce pay and/or work hours, managers should provide as much advance information as possible so the cuts do not come as a surprise. They should also make sure each person who is being laid off or taking a cut in pay understands the basis for the decision—job performance, seniority, and so forth.

People should also be given a reasonable severance package. Two weeks of pay was once the standard for hourly workers, but some companies in recent times have provided no pay at all. Displaced workers should be informed about future prospects—does the company expect to hire again in the future, and if so, will they be considered for reemployment? Many larger firms also have additional security on-site when large layoffs are being announced.

MyBizLab

---

2 Describe the nature and importance of individual differences among employees.

Individual Differences Among Employees

What causes some employees to be more productive than others, to be better citizens than others, or to be more counterproductive than others? As we already noted, every individual is unique. **Individual differences** are personal attributes that vary from one person to another. Individual differences may be physical, psychological, and emotional. The individual differences that characterize a specific person make that person unique. As we see in the sections that follow, basic categories of individual differences include *personality* and *attitudes*.[4]

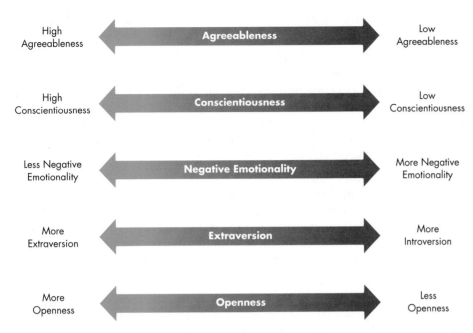

Figure 8.1 The "Big Five" Personality Traits

Personality at Work

Personality is the relatively stable set of psychological attributes that distinguish one person from another. In recent years, researchers have identified five fundamental traits that are especially relevant to organizations. These are commonly called the *"big five" personality traits. Emotional intelligence,* while not part of the "big five," also plays a large role in employee personality.

The "Big Five" Personality Traits   The **"big five" personality traits** are shown in Figure 8.1 and can be summarized as follows.

- *Agreeableness* is a person's ability to get along with others. A person with a *high* level of agreeableness is gentle, cooperative, forgiving, understanding, and good-natured in their dealings with others. A person with a *low* level of agreeableness is often irritable, short-tempered, uncooperative, and generally antagonistic toward other people. Highly agreeable people are better at developing good working relationships with coworkers, whereas less agreeable people are not likely to have particularly good working relationships.

- *Conscientiousness* in this context is a reflection of the number of things a person tries to accomplish. *Highly conscientious* people tend to focus on relatively few tasks at one time; as a result, they are likely to be organized, systematic, careful, thorough, responsible, and self-disciplined. *Less conscientious* people tend to pursue a wider array of tasks; as a result, they are often more disorganized and irresponsible, as well as less thorough and self-disciplined. Highly conscientious people tend to be relatively higher performers in a variety of different jobs.

- *Emotionality* refers to the degree to which people tend to be positive or negative in their outlook and behaviors toward others. People with *positive* emotionality are relatively poised, calm, resilient, and secure; people with negative emotionality are more excitable, insecure, reactive, and subject to mood swings. People with positive emotionality might be expected to better handle job stress, pressure, and tension. Their stability might also lead them to be seen as being more reliable than their less-stable counterparts.

- *Extraversion* refers to a person's comfort level with relationships. *Extroverts* are sociable, talkative, assertive, and open to establishing new relationships. *Introverts* are much less sociable, talkative, and assertive, and more reluctant to begin new relationships. Extroverts tend to be higher overall job performers than introverts and are more likely to be attracted to jobs based on personal relationships, such as sales and marketing positions.

- *Openness* reflects how open or rigid a person is in terms of his or her beliefs. People with *high* levels of openness are curious and willing to listen to new ideas and to change their own ideas, beliefs, and attitudes in response to new information. People with *low* levels of openness tend to be less receptive to new ideas and less willing to change their minds. People with more openness are often better performers due to their flexibility and the likelihood that they will be better accepted by others in the organization.

The "big five" framework continues to attract the attention of both researchers and managers. The potential value of this framework is that it encompasses an integrated set of traits that appear to be valid predictors of certain behaviors in certain situations. Thus, managers who can both understand the framework and assess these traits in their employees are in a good position to understand how and why they behave as they do.[2]

Emotional Intelligence The concept of emotional intelligence has also been identified in recent years and provides some interesting insights into personality. **Emotional intelligence, or emotional quotient (EQ),** refers to the extent to which people are self-aware, can manage their emotions, can motivate themselves, express empathy for others, and possess social skills.[5] These various dimensions can be described as follows:

- *Self-awareness* refers to a person's capacity for being aware of how they are feeling. In general, more self-awareness allows people to more effectively guide their own lives and behaviors.

- *Managing emotions* refers to a person's capacities to balance anxiety, fear, and anger so that they do not overly interfere with getting things accomplished.

- *Motivating oneself* refers to a person's ability to remain optimistic and to continue striving in the face of setbacks, barriers, and failure.

- *Empathy* refers to a person's ability to understand how others are feeling even without being explicitly told.

- *Social skills* refers to a person's ability to get along with others and to establish positive relationships.

Preliminary research suggests that people with high EQs may perform better than others, especially in jobs that require a high degree of interpersonal interaction and that involve influencing or directing the work of others. Moreover, EQ appears to be something that isn't biologically based but which can be developed.

Attitudes at Work

People's attitudes also affect their behavior in organizations. **Attitudes** reflect our beliefs and feelings about specific ideas, situations, or other people. Attitudes are important because they are the mechanism through which we express our feelings. An employee's comment that he feels underpaid by the organization reflects his feelings about his pay. Similarly, when a manager says that she likes the new advertising campaign, she is expressing her feelings about the organization's marketing efforts.

People in an organization form attitudes about many different things. Employees are likely to have attitudes about their salary, their promotion possibilities, their boss, employee benefits, and so on. Especially important attitudes are *job satisfaction* and *organizational commitment*.

- **Job satisfaction** reflects the extent to which people have positive attitudes toward their jobs. (Some people use the word *morale* instead of job satisfaction.) A satisfied employee tends to be absent less often, to be a good organizational citizen, and to stay with the organization. Dissatisfied employees may be absent more often, may experience stress that disrupts coworkers, and may be continually looking for another job. Contrary to what a lot of managers believe, however, high levels of job satisfaction do not necessarily lead to higher levels of productivity.

- **Organizational commitment,** sometimes called *job commitment*, reflects an individual's identification with the organization and its mission. A highly committed person will probably see herself as a true member of the firm (for example, referring to the organization in personal terms, such as "we make high-quality products"), overlook minor sources of dissatisfaction, and see herself remaining a member of the organization. A less committed person is more likely to see himself as an outsider (for example, referring to the organization in less personal terms, such as "they don't pay their employees very well"), to express more dissatisfaction about things, and to not see himself as a long-term member of the organization.

There are a few critical things managers can do to promote satisfaction and commitment. For one thing, if the organization treats its employees fairly and provides reasonable rewards and job security, its employees are more likely to be satisfied and committed. Allowing employees to have a say in how things are done can also promote these attitudes. Designing jobs so that they are stimulating can enhance both satisfaction and commitment. Another key element is understanding and respecting what experts call *psychological contracts*, which we will discuss in the next section.

Matching People and Jobs

3 Explain the meaning and importance of psychological contracts and the person-job fit in the workplace.

Given the array of individual differences that exists across people and the many different forms of employee behaviors that can occur in organizations, it stands to reason that managers would like to have a good match between people and the jobs they are performing. Two key methods for helping to understand how this match can be better understood are *psychological contracts* and the *person-job fit*.

Psychological Contracts

A **psychological contract** is the overall set of expectations held by employees and the organization regarding what employees will contribute to the organization and what the organization will provide in return. Unlike a business contract, a psychological contract is not written on paper, nor are all of its terms explicitly negotiated.[6]

Figure 8.2 illustrates the essential nature of a psychological contract. The individual makes a variety of *contributions* to the organization—such things as effort, ability, loyalty, skills, and time. These contributions satisfy their obligation under the contract. For example, Jill Henderson, a branch manager for Merrill Lynch, uses

---

Emotional Intelligence (Emotional Quotient, EQ) the extent to which people are self-aware, can manage their emotions, can motivate themselves, express empathy for others, and possess social skills

Attitudes a person's beliefs and feelings about specific ideas, situations, or people

Job Satisfaction degree of enjoyment that people derive from performing their jobs

Organizational Commitment an individual's identification with the organization and its mission

Psychological Contract set of expectations held by an employee concerning what he or she will contribute to an organization (referred to as contributions) and what the organization will in return provide the employee (referred to as inducements)

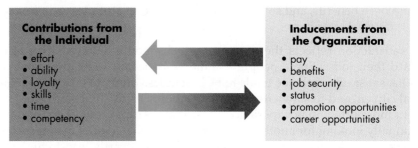

Figure 8.2 **The Psychological Contract**

her knowledge of financial markets and investment opportunities to help her clients make profitable investments. Her MBA in finance, coupled with hard work and motivation, have led her to become one of the firm's most promising young managers. The firm believed she had these attributes when it hired her and expected that she would do well.

In return for these contributions, the organization provides *inducements* to the individual. These inducements satisfy the organization's contract obligation. Some inducements, such as pay and career opportunities, are tangible rewards. Others, such as job security and status, are more intangible. Jill Henderson started at Merrill Lynch at a very competitive salary and has received a salary increase each of the six years she has been with the firm. She has also been promoted twice and expects another promotion in the near future.

In this instance, both Jill Henderson and Merrill Lynch apparently perceive that the psychological contract is fair and equitable. Both will be satisfied with the relationship and will do what they can to continue it. Henderson is likely to continue to work hard and effectively, and Merrill Lynch is likely to continue to increase her salary and give her promotions. In other situations, however, things might not work out as well. If either party sees an inequity in the contract, that party may initiate a change. The employee might ask for a pay raise or promotion, put forth less effort, or look for a better job elsewhere. The organization can also initiate change by training the worker to improve his skills, transferring him to another job, or by firing him.

All organizations face the basic challenge of managing psychological contracts. They want value from their employees, and they need to give employees the right inducements. For instance, underpaid employees may perform poorly or leave for better jobs elsewhere. Similarly, an employee may even occasionally start to steal from the company as a way to balance the psychological contract.

Recent trends in downsizing and cutbacks have complicated the process of managing psychological contracts. For example, many organizations used to offer at least reasonable assurances of job permanence as a fundamental inducement to employees. Now, however, job permanence is less likely so alternative inducements may be needed. Among the new forms of inducements, some companies are providing additional training opportunities and increased flexibility in working schedules.

The Person-Job Fit

The **person-job fit** refers to the extent to which a person's contributions and the organization's inducements match one another. A good person-job fit is one in which the employee's contributions match the inducements the organization offers. In theory, each employee has a specific set of needs that she wants fulfilled and a set of job-related behaviors and abilities to contribute. If the organization can take perfect advantage of those behaviors and abilities and exactly fulfill her needs, it will have achieved a perfect person-job fit. Good person-job fit, in turn, can result in higher performance and more positive attitudes. A poor person-job fit, though, can have just the opposite effects.

Basic Motivation Concepts and Theories

4   Identify and summarize the most important models and concepts of employee motivation.

Broadly defined, **motivation** is the set of forces that cause people to behave in certain ways.[5] One worker may be motivated to work hard to produce as much as possible, whereas another may be motivated to do just enough to survive. Managers must understand these differences in behavior and the reasons for them.

Over the years, a steady progression of theories and studies has attempted to address these issues. In this section, we survey the major studies and theories of employee motivation. In particular, we focus on three approaches to human relations in the workplace that reflect a basic chronology of thinking in the area: (1) *classical theory* and *scientific management*, (2) *early behavioral theory*, and (3) *contemporary motivational theories*.

Classical Theory

According to the so-called **classical theory of motivation,** workers are motivated solely by money. In his 1911 book, *The Principles of Scientific Management*, industrial engineer Frederick Taylor proposed a way for both companies and workers to benefit from this widely accepted view of life in the workplace. If workers are motivated by money, Taylor reasoned, paying them more should prompt them to produce more. Meanwhile, the firm that analyzed jobs and found better ways to perform them would be able to produce goods more cheaply, make higher profits, and pay and motivate workers better than its competitors.

Taylor's approach is known as *scientific management*. His ideas captured the imagination of many managers in the early twentieth century. Soon, manufacturing plants across the United States were hiring experts to perform time-and-motion studies: Industrial engineering techniques were applied to each facet of a job to determine how to perform it most efficiently. These studies were the first scientific attempts to break down jobs into easily repeated components and to devise more efficient tools and machines for performing them. [7]

Early Behavioral Theory

In 1925, a group of Harvard researchers began a study at the Hawthorne Works of Western Electric outside Chicago. With an eye to increasing productivity, they wanted to examine the relationship between changes in the physical environment and worker output.

The results of the experiment were unexpected, even confusing. For example, increased lighting levels improved productivity. For some reason, however, so did lower lighting levels. Moreover, against all expectations, increased pay failed to increase productivity. Gradually, the researchers pieced together the puzzle. The explanation lay in the workers' response to the attention they were receiving. The researchers concluded that productivity rose in response to almost any management action that workers interpreted as special attention. This finding—known today as the **Hawthorne effect**—had a major influence on human relations theory, although in many cases it amounted simply to convincing managers that they should pay more attention to employees.

Person-Job Fit the extent to which a person's contributions and the organization's inducements match one another

Motivation the set of forces that cause people to behave in certain ways

Classical Theory of Motivation theory holding that workers are motivated solely by money

Hawthorne Effect tendency for productivity to increase when workers believe they are receiving special attention from management

TABLE 8.1   Theory X and Theory Y

Theory X	Theory Y
People are lazy.	People are energetic.
People lack ambition and dislike responsibility.	People are ambitious and seek responsibility.
People are self-centered.	People can be selfless.
People resist change.	People want to contribute to business growth and change.
People are gullible and not very bright.	People are intelligent.

Following the Hawthorne studies, managers and researchers alike focused more attention on the importance of good human relations in motivating employee performance. Stressing the factors that cause, focus, and sustain workers' behavior, most motivation theorists became concerned with the ways in which management thinks about and treats employees. The major motivation theories include the *human resources model*, the *hierarchy of needs model*, and *two-factor theory*.

Human Resources Model: Theories X and Y In one important book, behavioral scientist Douglas McGregor concluded that managers had radically different beliefs about how best to use the human resources employed by a firm. He classified these beliefs into sets of assumptions that he labeled "Theory X" and "Theory Y." The basic differences between these two theories are shown in Table 8.1.

Managers who subscribe to **Theory X** tend to believe that people are naturally lazy and uncooperative and must be either punished or rewarded to be made productive. Managers who are inclined to accept **Theory Y** tend to believe that people are naturally energetic, growth-oriented, self-motivated, and interested in being productive.

McGregor argued that Theory Y managers are more likely to have satisfied and motivated employees. Theory X and Y distinctions are somewhat simplistic and offer little concrete basis for action. Their value lies primarily in their ability to highlight and classify the behavior of managers in light of their attitudes toward employees.

Maslow's Hierarchy of Needs Model Psychologist Abraham Maslow's **hierarchy of human needs model** proposed that people have several different needs that they attempt to satisfy in their work. Maslow classified these needs into five basic types and suggested that they be arranged in the hierarchy of importance, as shown in Figure 8.3. According to Maslow, needs are hierarchical because lower-level needs must be met before a person will try to satisfy higher-level needs.

Once a set of needs has been satisfied, it ceases to motivate behavior. For example, if you feel secure in your job (that is, your security needs have been met), additional opportunities to achieve even more security, such as being assigned to a long-term project, will probably be less important to you than the chance to fulfill social or esteem needs, such as working with a mentor or becoming the member of an advisory board.

If, however, a lower-level need suddenly becomes unfulfilled, most people immediately refocus on that lower level. Suppose, for example, you are seeking to meet your self-esteem needs by working as a divisional manager at a major company. If you learn that your division and, consequently, your job may be eliminated, you might very well find the promise of job security at a new firm as motivating as a promotion once would have been at your old company.

Two-Factor Theory After studying a group of accountants and engineers, psychologist Frederick Herzberg concluded that job satisfaction and dissatisfaction depend on two factors: *hygiene factors*, such as working conditions, and *motivation factors*, such as recognition for a job well done.

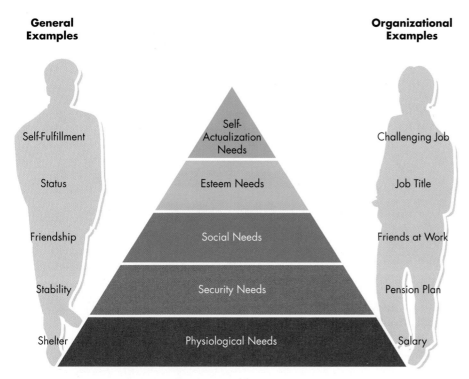

Figure 8.3 Maslow's Heirarchy of Human Needs
Source: A. H. Maslow, *Motivation and Personality*, 2nd ed. (Upper Saddle River, NJ: Prentice Hall, 1970). Reprinted by permission of Prentice Hall Inc.

According to Herzberg's **two-factor theory,** hygiene factors affect motivation and satisfaction only if they are absent or fail to meet expectations. For example, workers will be dissatisfied if they believe they have poor working conditions. If working conditions are improved, however, they will not necessarily become satisfied; they will simply not be dissatisfied. If workers receive no recognition for successful work, they may be neither dissatisfied nor satisfied. If recognition is provided, they will likely become more satisfied.

Figure 8.4 illustrates the two-factor theory. Note that motivation factors lie along a continuum from satisfaction to no satisfaction. Hygiene factors, in contrast, are likely to produce feelings that lie on a continuum from dissatisfaction to no dissatisfaction. Whereas motivation factors are directly related to the work that employees actually perform, hygiene factors refer to the environment in which they work.

This theory suggests that managers should follow a two-step approach to enhancing motivation. First, they must ensure that hygiene factors—working conditions, for example, or clearly stated policies—are acceptable. This practice will result in an absence of dissatisfaction. Then they must offer motivation factors—recognition or added responsibility—as a way to improve satisfaction and motivation.

Theory X theory of motivation holding that people are naturally lazy and uncooperative

Theory Y theory of motivation holding that people are naturally energetic, growth-oriented, self-motivated, and interested in being productive

Hierarchy of Human Needs Model theory of motivation describing five levels of human needs and arguing that basic needs must be fulfilled before people work to satisfy higher-level needs

Two-Factor Theory theory of motivation holding that job satisfaction depends on two factors, hygiene and motivation

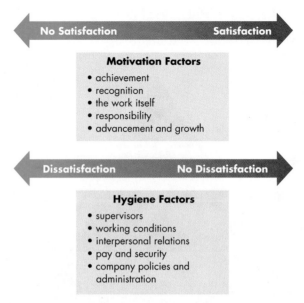

Figure 8.4 Two-Factor Theory of Motivation

Contemporary Motivation Theory

Recently, other more complex models of employee behavior and motivation have been developed.[8] Two of the more interesting and useful ones are *expectancy theory* and *equity theory*.

Expectancy Theory **Expectancy theory** suggests that people are motivated to work toward rewards that they want and that they believe they have a reasonable chance—or expectancy—of obtaining. A reward that seems out of reach is likely to be undesirable even if it is intrinsically positive. Figure 8.5 illustrates expectancy theory in terms of issues that are likely to be considered by an individual employee.

Consider the case of an assistant department manager who learns that her firm needs to replace a retiring division manager three levels above her in the organization. Even though she wants the job, she does not apply because she doubts she will be selected. In this case, she considers the performance-reward issue: She believes that her performance will not get her the position. She also learns that the firm is looking for a production manager on the night shift. She thinks she could get this job but does not apply because she does not want to work nights (the rewards–personal goals issue). Finally, she learns of an opening one level higher—department manager—in her own division. She may well apply for this job because she both wants it and thinks that she has a good chance of getting it. In this case, her consideration of all the issues has led to an expectancy that she can reach a goal.

Figure 8.5 Expectancy Theory Model

Expectancy theory helps explain why some people do not work as hard as they can when their salaries are based purely on seniority. Paying employees the same whether they work very hard or just hard enough to get by removes the financial incentive for them to work harder. In other words, they ask themselves, "If I work harder, will I get a pay raise?" (the performance–reward issue) and conclude that the answer is no. Similarly, if hard work will result in one or more undesirable outcomes—for example, a transfer to another location or a promotion to a job that requires unpleasant travel (the rewards–personal goal issue)—employees will not be motivated to work hard.

Equity Theory   **Equity theory** focuses on social comparisons—people evaluating their treatment by the organization relative to the treatment of others. This approach holds that people begin by analyzing inputs (what they contribute to their jobs in terms of time, effort, education, experience) relative to outputs (what they receive in return—salary, benefits, recognition, security). This comparison is very similar to the psychological contract. As viewed by equity theory, the result is a ratio of contribution to return. When they compare their own ratios with those of other employees, they ask whether their ratios are equal to, greater than, or less than those of the people with whom they are comparing themselves. Depending on their assessments, they experience feelings of equity or inequity. Figure 8.6 illustrates the three possible results of such an assessment.

For example, suppose a new college graduate gets a starting job at a large manufacturing firm. His starting salary is $45,000 a year, he gets an inexpensive company car, and he shares an assistant with another new employee. If he later learns that another new employee has received the same salary, car, and staff arrangement, he will feel equitably treated (result 1 in Figure 8.6). If the other newcomer, however, has received $70,000, a more expensive company car, and a personal assistant, he may feel inequitably treated (result 2 in Figure 8.6).

Note, however, that for an individual to feel equitably treated, the two ratios do not have to be identical, only equitable. Assume, for instance, that our new employee has a bachelor's degree and two years of work experience. Perhaps he learns subsequently that the other new employee has an advanced degree and 10 years of experience. After first feeling inequity, the new employee may conclude that the person with whom he compared himself is actually contributing more to the organization. That employee is equitably entitled, therefore, to receive more in return (result 3 in Figure 8.6).

When people feel they are being inequitably treated, they may do various constructive and some not so constructive things to restore fairness. For example, they may speak to their boss about the perceived inequity. Or (less constructively) they may demand a raise, reduce their efforts, work shorter hours, or just complain to their coworkers. They may also rationalize ("management succumbed to pressure to promote a woman/Asian American"), find different people with whom to compare themselves, or leave their jobs.

Strategies and Techniques for Enhancing Motivation

5 Describe some of the strategies and techniques used by organizations to improve employee motivation.

Understanding what motivates workers is only one part of the manager's job. The other part is applying that knowledge. Experts have suggested—and many companies have implemented—a range of programs designed to make jobs more

Expectancy Theory theory of motivation holding that people are motivated to work toward rewards that they want and that they believe they have a reasonable chance of obtaining

Equity Theory theory of motivation holding that people evaluate their treatment by the organization relative to the treatment of others

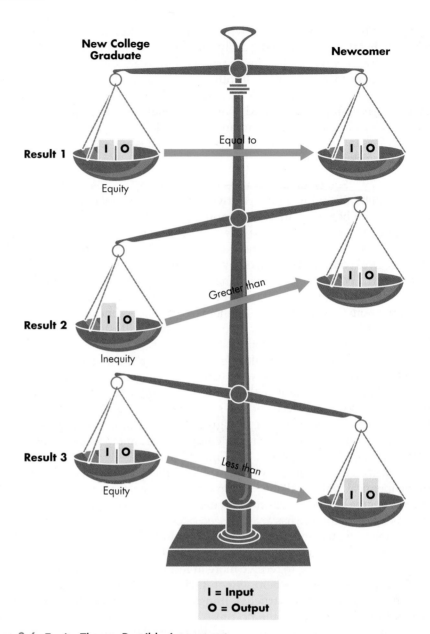

Figure 8.6 Equity Theory: Possible Assessments

interesting and rewarding, to make the work environment more pleasant, and to motivate employees to work harder.

Reinforcement/Behavior Modification

Some companies try to control—and even alter or modify—workers' behavior through systematic rewards and punishments for specific behaviors. Such companies first try to define the specific behaviors that they want their employees to exhibit (working hard, being courteous to customers, stressing quality) and the specific behaviors they want to eliminate (wasting time, being rude to customers, ignoring quality). Then they try to shape employee behavior by linking positive reinforcement with desired behaviors and punishment with undesired behaviors.

Positive reinforcement is used when a company or manager provides a reward when employees exhibit desired behaviors—working hard, helping others, and so forth. When rewards are tied directly to performance, they serve as positive reinforcement. For example, paying large cash bonuses to salespeople who exceed quotas prompts them to work even harder during the next selling period. John Deere

ENTREPRENEURSHIP AND NEW VENTURES

Extreme Employee Empowerment

In the mid-1980s, Roger Sant and Dennis Bakke decided to take advantage of the Public Utility Regulatory Policy Act and establish what would become a huge international energy company built on the values of social responsibility, integrity, fairness, and fun. To achieve these ideals, Sant and Bakke established AES Corporation under a management structure, or more accurately a lack of one, that has been called "adhocracy" and "empowerment gone mad."

Under an organizational structure AES dubs a "honeycomb," small, multifunctional teams manage themselves without the assistance of any legal, human resources, or other functional department or any written policies or procedures. AES strives to have as few supervisory layers as possible, and no one person is in charge of the teams. Employees make HR decisions, such as how much time to take for maternity leave, for themselves, and they consult outside experts on matters such as finance when necessary.

As a result of this structure, employees are empowered, flexible, multidimensional, and constantly learning. Furthermore, the company is high-functioning and can make decisions and

complete projects efficiently. AES continues to adapt to its increasing growth, though, and in 2002 added five executive officer positions and has since expanded its corporate leaders while remaining true to its honeycomb roots.

MyBizLab

w85/ZUMA Press/Newscom

has adopted a reward system based on positive reinforcement. The firm gives pay increases when its workers complete college courses and demonstrate mastery of new job skills.

Punishment is designed to change behavior by presenting people with unpleasant consequences if they exhibit undesired behaviors. Employees who are repeatedly late for work, for example, may be suspended or have their pay docked. Similarly, when the National Football League or Major League Baseball fines or suspends players found guilty of substance abuse, the organization is seeking to change players' behavior.

Using Goals to Motivate Behavior

Performance goals are also commonly used to direct and motivate behavior. The most frequent method for setting performance goals is called **management by objectives (MBO),** which is a system of collaborative goal setting that extends from the top of an organization to the bottom. MBO involves managers and subordinates in setting goals and evaluating progress. After the program is started, the organization specifies its overall goals and plans. Managers then collaborate with each of their subordinates to set individual goals that will best contribute to the organization's goals. Managers meet periodically to review progress toward individual goals, and then, usually on an annual basis, goal achievement is evaluated and used as a basis for starting the cycle over again.

Positive Reinforcement reward that follows desired behaviors

Punishment unpleasant consequences of an undesirable behavior

Management by Objectives (MBO) set of procedures involving both managers and subordinates in setting goals and evaluating progress

According to many experts, motivational impact is the biggest advantage of MBO. When employees sit down with managers to set upcoming goals, they learn more about companywide objectives, feel that they are an important part of a team, and see how they can improve companywide performance by reaching their own goals. If an MBO system is used properly, employees should leave meetings not only with an understanding of the value of their contributions but also with fair rewards for their performances. They should also accept and be committed to the moderately difficult and specific goals they have helped set for themselves.[9]

Participative Management and Empowerment

In **participative management and empowerment,** employees are given a voice in how they do their jobs and in how the company is managed—they become empowered to take greater responsibility for their own performance. Not surprisingly, participation and empowerment often makes employees feel more committed to organizational goals they have helped to shape.

Participation and empowerment can be used in large firms or small firms, both with managers and operating employees. For example, managers at General Electric who once needed higher-level approval for any expenditure over $5,000 now have the autonomy to make their own expense decisions up to as much as $50,000. At Adam Hat Company, a small firm that makes men's dress, military, and cowboy hats, workers who previously had to report all product defects to supervisors now have the freedom to correct problems themselves or even return products to the workers who are responsible for them. Sports gear company And1 also practices empowerment by allowing its designers considerable latitude in testing new ideas. For instance, a designer can make a few prototypes of a new product, distribute them to kids on a neighborhood basketball court, and then get their feedback.

Although some employees thrive in participative programs, such programs are not for everyone. People may be frustrated by responsibilities they are not equipped to handle. Moreover, participative programs may actually result in dissatisfied employees if workers see the invitation to participate as more symbolic than substantive. One key, say most experts, is to invite participation only to the extent that employees want to have input and only if participation will have real value for an organization.

Team Structures

We have already noted the increased use of teams in organizations. Yet another benefit that some companies get from using teams is increased motivation and enhanced job satisfaction among those employees working in teams. Although teams are often less effective in traditional and rigidly structured bureaucratic organizations, they often help smaller, more flexible organizations make decisions more quickly and effectively, enhance companywide communication, and encourage organizational members to feel more like a part of an organization. In turn, these attitudes usually lead to higher levels of both employee motivation and job satisfaction.[10]

But managers should remember that teams are not for everyone. Levi Strauss, for example, encountered major problems when it tried to use teams. Individual workers previously performed repetitive, highly specialized tasks, such as sewing zippers into jeans, and were paid according to the number of jobs they completed each day. In an attempt to boost productivity, company management reorganized everyone into teams of 10 to 35 workers and assigned tasks to the entire group. Each team member's pay was determined by the team's level of productivity. In practice, however, faster workers became resentful of slower workers because they reduced the group's total output. Slower workers, meanwhile, resented the pressure put on them by faster-working coworkers. As a result, motivation, satisfaction, and morale all dropped, and Levi Strauss eventually abandoned the teamwork plan altogether.

Job Enrichment and Job Redesign

Whereas goal setting and MBO programs and empowerment can work in a variety of settings, *job enrichment* and *job redesign* programs are generally used to increase satisfaction in jobs significantly lacking in motivating factors.[10]

Job Enrichment Programs   **Job enrichment** is designed to add one or more motivating factors to job activities. For example, *job rotation* programs expand growth opportunities by rotating employees through various positions in the same firm. Workers gain not only new skills but also broader overviews of their work and their organization. Other programs focus on increasing responsibility or recognition. At United Airlines, for example, flight attendants now have more control over their own scheduling. The jobs of flight service managers were enriched when they were given more responsibility and authority for assigning tasks to flight crew members.

Job Redesign Programs   **Job redesign** acknowledges that different people want different things from their jobs. By restructuring work to achieve a more satisfactory fit between workers and their jobs, job redesign can motivate individuals with strong needs for career growth or achievement. Job redesign is usually implemented in one of three ways: through *combining tasks, forming natural work groups*, or *establishing client relationships*.

Combining Tasks   The job of combining tasks involves enlarging jobs and increasing their variety to make employees feel that their work is more meaningful. In turn, employees become more motivated. For example, the job done by a programmer who maintains computer systems might be redesigned to include some system design and system development work. While developing additional skills, the programmer also gets involved in the overall system development.

Forming Natural Work Groups   People who do different jobs on the same projects are candidates for natural work groups. These groups are formed to help employees see the place and importance of their jobs in the total structure of the firm. They are valuable to management because the people working on a project are usually the most knowledgeable about it and the most capable problem solvers.

Establishing Client Relationships   Establishing client relationships means letting employees interact with customers. This approach increases job variety. It gives workers both a greater sense of control and more feedback about performance than they get when their jobs are not highly interactive. For example, software writers at Microsoft watch test users work with programs and discuss problems with them directly rather than receive feedback from third-party researchers.

Modified Work Schedules

As another way of increasing job satisfaction, many companies are experimenting with *modified work schedules*—different approaches to working hours and the workweek. The two most common forms of modified scheduling are *work-share programs* and *flextime programs*, including alternative workplace strategies.[11]

Work-Share Programs   At Steelcase, the country's largest maker of office furnishings, two very talented women in the marketing division both wanted to work only part-time. The solution: They now share a single full-time job. With each working

---

Participative Management and Empowerment method of increasing job satisfaction by giving employees a voice in the management of their jobs and the company

Job Enrichment method of increasing job satisfaction by adding one or more motivating factors to job activities

Job Redesign method of increasing job satisfaction by designing a more satisfactory fit between workers and their jobs

2.5 days a week, both got their wish and the job gets done—and done well. The practice, known as **work sharing** (or **job sharing**), has "brought sanity back to our lives," according to at least one Steelcase employee.

Job sharing usually benefits both employees and employers. Employees, for instance, tend to appreciate the organization's attention to their personal needs. At the same time, the company can reduce turnover and save on the cost of benefits. On the negative side, job-share employees generally receive fewer benefits than their full-time counterparts and may be the first to be laid off when cutbacks are necessary.

Flextime Programs and Alternative Workplace Strategies   **Flextime programs** allow people to choose their working hours by adjusting a standard work schedule on a daily or weekly basis. There are limits to flextime. The Steelcase program, for instance, requires all employees to work certain core hours. This practice allows everyone to reach coworkers at a specified time of day. Employees can then decide whether to make up the rest of the standard eight-hour day by coming in and leaving early (by working 6:00 A.M. to 2:00 P.M. or 7:00 A.M. to 3:00 P.M.) or late (9:00 A.M. to 5:00 P.M. or 10:00 A.M. to 6:00 P.M.).

In one variation, companies may also allow employees to choose four, five, or six days on which to work each week. Some, for instance, may choose Monday through Thursday, others Tuesday through Friday. Still others may work Monday and Tuesday and Thursday and Friday and take Wednesday off. By working 10 hours over four workdays, employees still complete 40-hour weeks.

Telecommuting   A rapidly growing number of U.S. workers do a significant portion of their work via **telecommuting**—performing some or all of a job away from standard office settings. Working from a home office outfitted with a PC, high-speed Internet, and a company intranet connection, telecommuters can keep abreast of everything going on at the office. In 2004, at least 14 million U.S. workers spent at least part of their working hours telecommuting. This trend is on the rise: In 2005, 44 percent of U.S. companies offered some telecommuting options, up from 32 percent in 2001.[12] And in 2010 almost 80 percent of white collar and other professional workers in the United States performed at least some of their work from a location other than their office.

Advantages and Disadvantages of Modified Schedules and Alternative Workplaces   Flextime gives employees more freedom in their professional and personal lives. It allows workers to plan around the work schedules of spouses and the school schedules of young children. Studies show that the increased sense of freedom and control reduces stress and improves individual productivity.

Companies also benefit in other ways. In urban areas, for example, such programs can reduce traffic congestion and similar problems that contribute to stress and lost work time. Furthermore, employers benefit from higher levels of commitment and job satisfaction. John Hancock Insurance, Shell Oil, and Metropolitan Life are among the major U.S. corporations that have successfully adopted some form of flextime.

Conversely, flextime sometimes complicates coordination because people are working different schedules. In addition, if workers are paid by the hour, flextime may make it difficult for employers to keep accurate records of when employees are actually working.

As for telecommuting, it may not be for everyone. For example, consultant Gil Gordon points out that telecommuters are attracted to the ideas of "not having to shave and put on makeup or go through traffic, and sitting in their blue jeans all day." However, he suggests that would-be telecommuters ask themselves several other questions: "Can I manage deadlines? What will it be like to be away from the social context of the office five days a week?" One study has shown that even though telecommuters may be producing results, those with strong advancement ambitions may miss networking and rubbing elbows with management on a day-to-day basis.

Another obstacle to establishing a telecommuting program is convincing management that it can be beneficial for all involved. Telecommuters may have to fight the perception from both bosses and coworkers that if they are not being supervised, they are not working. Managers, admits one experienced consultant, "usually have to be dragged kicking and screaming into this. They always ask 'How can I tell if someone is working when I can't see them?'" By the same token, he adds, "that's based on the erroneous assumption that if you can see them, they are working." Most experts agree that reeducation and constant communication are requirements of a successful telecommuting arrangement. Both managers and employees must determine expectations in advance.

As we have illustrated in this chapter, employee behavior and motivation are important concepts for managers to understand. They are also complex processes that require careful consideration by managers. For example, a clumsy attempt to motivate employees to work harder without fully considering all factors can actually have just the opposite effect. But managers who do take the time to understand the people with whom they work can better appreciate their efforts. Another important factor that affects employee behavior is *leadership*, the subject of our next chapter.

Work Sharing (Job Sharing) method of increasing job satisfaction by allowing two or more people to share a single full-time job

Flextime Programs method of increasing job satisfaction by allowing workers to adjust work schedules on a daily or weekly basis

Telecommuting form of flextime that allows people to perform some or all of a job away from standard office settings

Jacob Wackerhausen/iStockphoto.com

Continued from page 196

Thinking About Work and Pay

Many white-collar workers have options to enhance their motivation and job satisfaction. But what about low-skill workers? *New York Times* journalist Daniel Akst points out that workplace unhappiness "is not a new phenomenon. Work is not a picnic. It's always tough for people." Akst admonishes his readers, "If you find the modern, air-conditioned workplace stressful—all that e-mail!—just think back to the work most Americans used to do." For instance, just contrast today's modern office work with farming, the most common occupation a century ago. Farmers at that time performed hard outdoor labor seven days per week, for uncertain pay, in social isolation, and with no benefits or retirement plans.

Just as a focus on the past shows us how really fortunate most middle-class workers truly are, so too does a comparison of middle- and working-class employees. The Bureau of Labor Statistics reports that in 2009, 10.9 million U.S. managers earned an average salary of $83,400, while 13.8 million food service workers earned only $17,400. The disparity is even greater when benefits and other rewards are considered.

Organizations face a stiff challenge in designing and creating jobs for low-skill workers that are richer and more rewarding. Even if pay were greater, motivation theory would predict that repetitive, routine jobs with little autonomy will not create worker happiness or motivation. Innovative job design for barbers, grounds workers, fishing crews, and nursing aides seems very difficult, yet could affect tens of millions of individuals nationwide.

The U.S. Census reports that 8.7 million individuals in households headed by full-time year-round workers were below the federal poverty threshold. If money and an appealing job create happiness, low-skill workers must be pretty unhappy. So, what's a manager to do? Perhaps the most basic suggestion is just this: remember that workers want to be treated with respect and dignity. Even if you can't pay them a lot of money or make their jobs exciting, you can nevertheless treat them as you would want to be treated if you were in their shoes. And, come to think of it, the same could be said of any worker performing any job.

QUESTIONS FOR DISCUSSION

1 Some experts warn that we are creating more and more disparity between higher-paid workers and lower-paid workers. If this is true, what are the implications?

2 Recall a low-skill, low-wage job you have held. What could your boss have done to motivate you?

3 Have you ever had a chance to change or modify a job so as to make it more interesting? If so, how? If not, select a job you can observe (such as a Starbucks barista) and then discuss how it could be made more interesting.

4 Are there some jobs that simply cannot be improved? If so, provide examples. If not, then why aren't all jobs made more interesting and motivating?

5 Describe the "perfect" job that you can envision for yourself. What would be the parts of the job that would really motivate you?

SUMMARY OF LEARNING OBJECTIVES   MyBizLab

1. **Identify and discuss the basic forms of behaviors that employees exhibit in organizations. (pp. 196–198)**
Employee behavior is the pattern of actions by the members of an organization that directly or indirectly influences the organization's effectiveness. *Performance behaviors* are the total set of work-related behaviors that the organization expects employees to display. *Organizational citizenship* refers to the behavior of individuals who make a positive overall contribution to the organization. *Counterproductive behaviors* are those that detract from, rather than contribute to, organizational performance.

2. **Describe the nature and importance of individual differences among employees. (pp. 198–201)**
Individual differences are personal attributes that vary from one person to another. *Personality* is the relatively stable set of psychological attributes that distinguish one person from another. The *"big five" personality traits* are *agreeableness, conscientiousness, emotionality, extraversion,* and *openness. Emotional intelligence,* or *emotional quotient (EQ),* refers to the extent to which people are self-aware, can manage their emotions, can motivate themselves, express empathy for others, and possess social skills. *Attitudes* reflect our beliefs and feelings about specific ideas, situations, or other people. Especially important attitudes are *job satisfaction* and *organizational commitment*.

3. **Explain the meaning and importance of psychological contracts and the person-job fit in the workplace. (pp. 201–202)**
A *psychological contract* is the overall set of expectations held by employees and the organization regarding what employees will contribute to the organization and what the organization will provide in return. A good *person-job fit* is achieved when the employee's contributions match the inducements the organization offers. Having a good match between people and their jobs can help enhance performance, job satisfaction, and motivation.

4. **Identify and summarize the most important models and concepts of employee motivation. (pp. 203–207)**
Motivation is the set of forces that cause people to behave in certain ways. Early approaches to motivation were based first on the assumption that people work only for money and then on the assumption that social needs are the primary way to motivate people. The *hierarchy of human needs* model holds that people at work try to satisfy one or more of five different needs. The *two-factor theory* argues that satisfaction and dissatisfaction depend on *hygiene factors,* such as working conditions, and *motivation factors,* such as recognition for a job well done. *Expectancy theory* suggests that people are motivated to work toward rewards that they have a reasonable expectancy of obtaining. *Equity theory* focuses on social comparisons—people evaluating their treatment by the organization relative to the treatment of others.

5. **Describe some of the strategies and techniques used by organizations to improve employee motivation. (pp. 207–213)**
There are several major strategies and techniques often used to make jobs more interesting and rewarding. *Positive reinforcement* is used when a company or manager provides a reward when employees exhibit desired behaviors. *Punishment* is designed to change behavior by presenting employees with unpleasant consequences if they exhibit undesired behaviors. *Management by objectives (MBO)* is a system of collaborative goal setting that extends from the top of an organization to the bottom. In *participative management and empowerment,* employees are given a voice in how they do their jobs and in how the company is managed. Using *teams* can also enhance motivation. *Job enrichment* adds motivating factors to job activities. *Job redesign* is a method of increasing job satisfaction by designing a more satisfactory fit between workers and their jobs. Some companies also use *modified work schedules*—different approaches to working hours. Common options include *work sharing (job sharing), flextime programs,* and *telecommuting*.

KEY TERMS   MyBizLab

absenteeism (p. 197)
attitudes (p. 200)
"big five" personality traits (p. 199)
classical theory of
    motivation (p. 203)
counterproductive behavior (p. 197)
emotional intelligence (emotional
    quotient, EQ) (p. 200)
employee behavior (p. 196)
equity theory (p. 207)
expectancy theory (p. 206)
flextime programs (p. 212)
Hawthorne effect (p. 203)

hierarchy of human needs model
    (p. 204)
individual differences (p. 198)
job enrichment (p. 211)
job redesign (p. 211)
job satisfaction (p. 201)
management by objectives
    (MBO) (p. 209)
motivation (p. 203)
organizational citizenship (p. 197)
organizational commitment (p. 201)
participative management and
    empowerment (p. 210)

performance behaviors (p. 196)
personality (p. 199)
person-job fit (p. 202)
positive reinforcement (p. 208)
psychological contract (p. 201)
punishment (p. 209)
telecommuting (p. 212)
Theory X (p. 204)
Theory Y (p. 204)
turnover (p. 197)
two-factor theory (p. 205)
work sharing (or job sharing) (p. 212)

QUESTIONS AND EXERCISES

QUESTIONS FOR REVIEW

1. Describe the psychological contract you currently have or have had in the past with an employer. If you have never worked, describe the psychological contract that you have with the instructor in this class.
2. Do you think that most people are relatively satisfied or dissatisfied with their work? What factors do you think most contribute to satisfaction or dissatisfaction?
3. Compare and contrast the hierarchy of human needs with the two-factor theory of motivation.
4. How can participative management programs enhance employee satisfaction and motivation?

QUESTIONS FOR ANALYSIS

5. Some evidence suggests that recent college graduates show high levels of job satisfaction. Levels then drop dramatically as they reach their late twenties, only to increase gradually once they get older. What might account for this pattern?

6. As a manager, under what sort of circumstances might you apply each of the theories of motivation discussed in this chapter? Which would be easiest to use? Which would be hardest? Why?
7. Suppose you realize one day that you are dissatisfied with your job. Short of quitting, what might you do to improve your situation?
8. Describe what you would tell a low-skill worker performing a simple and routine job who wants more challenge and enjoyment from work.

APPLICATION EXERCISES

9. Assume you are about to start your own business. What might you do from the very beginning to ensure that your employees will be satisfied and motivated?
10. Interview the manager of a local manufacturing company. Identify as many different strategies for enhancing job satisfaction at that company as you can.

BUILDING YOUR BUSINESS SKILLS

Too Much of a Good Thing

Goal
To encourage you to apply different motivational theories to a workplace problem involving poor productivity.

Background Information
For years, working for George Uhe, a small chemicals broker in Paramus, New Jersey, made employees feel as if they were members of a big family. Unfortunately, this family was going broke because too few "members" were working hard enough to make money for it. Employees were happy, comfortable, complacent—and lazy.

With sales dropping in the pharmaceutical and specialty-chemicals division, Uhe brought in management consultants to analyze the situation and to make recommendations. The outsiders quickly identified a motivational problem affecting the sales force: Sales representatives were paid a handsome salary and received automatic, year-end bonuses regardless of performance. They were also treated to bagels every Friday and regular group birthday lunches that cost as much as $200. Employees felt satisfied but had little incentive to work very hard. Eager to return to profitability, Uhe's owners waited to hear the consultants' recommendations.

Method
Step 1
In groups of four, step into the role of Uhe's management consultants. Start by analyzing your client's workforce-motivation

problems from the following perspectives (our questions focus on key motivational issues):

- *Job satisfaction and morale.* As part of a 77-year-old, family-owned business, Uhe employees were happy and loyal, in part because they were treated so well. Can high morale have a downside? How can it breed stagnation, and what can managers do to prevent stagnation from taking hold?
- *Theory X versus Theory Y.* Although the behavior of these workers seems to make a case for Theory X, why is it difficult to draw this conclusion about a company that focuses more on satisfaction than on sales and profits?
- *Two-factor theory.* Analyze the various ways in which improving such motivational factors as recognition, added responsibility, advancement, and growth might reduce the importance of hygiene factors, including pay and security.
- *Expectancy theory.* Analyze the effect on productivity of redesigning the company's sales force compensation structure—namely, by paying lower base salaries while offering greater earnings potential through a sales-based incentive system. Why would linking performance with increased pay that is achievable through hard work motivate employees? Why would the threat of a job loss also motivate greater effort?

Step 2
Write a short report based on your analysis making recommendations to Uhe's owners. The goal of your report is to change the working environment in ways that will motivate greater effort and generate greater productivity.

FOLLOW-UP QUESTIONS

1. What is your group's most important recommendation? Why do you think it is likely to succeed?
2. Changing the corporate culture to make it less paternalistic may reduce employees' sense of belonging to a family. If you

were an employee, would you consider a greater focus on profits to be an improvement or a problem? How would it affect your motivation and productivity?

3. What steps would you take to improve the attitude and productivity of longtime employees who resist change?

EXERCISING YOUR ETHICS: INDIVIDUAL EXERCISE

Practicing Controlled Behavior

The Situation

Some companies try to control—or alter—workers' behavior through systematic rewards and punishments for specific behaviors. In other words, they first try to define the specific behaviors they want their employees to exhibit (such as working hard, being courteous to customers, stressing quality) and the specific behaviors they want them to eliminate (wasting time, being rude to customers, ignoring quality). They then try to shape employee behavior by linking positive reinforcement to desired behaviors and punishment to undesired behaviors.

Some critics, though, argue that these techniques rely too much on subconscious processes. That is, they equate these methods to laboratory experiments where you "give the rat some cheese when it pulls on the bar," and then it will pull on the bar again. Some people even question the ethics of this practice, since the target of the reward is not explicitly informed of how their behavior is being shaped.

The Dilemma

Assume that you are the new human resources manager in a medium-sized organization. Your boss has just ordered you to

implement a behavior-modification program by creating a network of rewards and punishments to be linked to specific desired and undesired behaviors. Specifically, you have been instructed to specify a set of rewards that will be provided when people engage in "positive" behaviors (such as an encouraging e-mail from the boss when an employee exceeds production quotas) and punishments to be provided following "negative" behaviors (such as a critical e-mail from the boss).

However, you are uncomfortable with this approach because of how it manipulates people's behaviors without their consent. Instead, you would prefer to use rewards in a way that is consistent with expectancy theory—that is, by letting employees know in advance how they can most effectively reach the rewards they most want. You have tried to change your boss's mind but to no avail. She says to proceed with behavior modification with no further discussion.

QUESTIONS TO ADDRESS

1 What are the ethical issues in this case?
2 What do you think most managers would do in this situation?
3 What would you do?

EXERCISING YOUR ETHICS: TEAM EXERCISE

Taking One for the Team

The Situation

You are a skilled technician who has worked for a major electronics firm for the past 10 years. You love your job—it is interesting, stimulating, and enjoyable, and you are well paid for what you do. The plant where you work is one of five manufacturing centers your firm operates in a major metropolitan area. The firm is currently developing a new prototype for one of its next-generation products. To ensure that all perspectives are reflected, the company has identified a set of technicians from each plant who will work together as a team for the next two months.

The Dilemma

You have just met with your new teammates and are quite confused about what you might do next. As it turns out, the technicians from two of the manufacturing centers have heard rumors that your company is planning to close at least three of the centers and move production to a lower-cost factory in another country. These individuals are very upset. Moreover, they have made it clear that they (1) do not intend to put forth much extra effort on this project and (2) they are all looking for new jobs. You and the other technicians, though, have heard none of these rumors. Moreover, these individuals seem as excited as you about their jobs.

Team Activity

First, working alone, write a brief summary of how you would handle this situation. For instance, would you seek more information or just go about your work? Would you start looking for another job, would you try to form a subgroup just with those technicians who share your views, or would you try to work with everyone?

Second, form a small group with some of your classmates. Share with each other the various ideas you each identified. Then, formulate a group description of what you think most people in your situation would do. Then, share your description with the rest of the class.

VIDEO EXERCISE   MyBizLab

Whole Foods

Learning Objectives

The purpose of this video is to help you:
1 Explain and apply the classical theory of motivation.
2 Use Maslow's hierarchy of needs theory, Theories X and Y, and expectancy theory to explain employee motivation.
3 Describe the role of teams in employee motivation.

Synopsis

Whole Foods Market opened its first store in 1980 in Austin, Texas. The store had a bumpy start—just eight months after opening, the store was severely damaged by a flood. Without insurance, the store depended on employees and members of the community to rebuild and reopen. Today, Whole Foods has more than 300 stores, each reflecting Whole Foods' unique personality. One key to Whole Foods' success has been their ability to find employees passionate about healthy foods. Once hired, employees are placed on autonomous teams who manage their own area, with separate budgets and profit and loss statements for each team. Finally, the company uses a variety of strategies to motivate employees to be engaged and focus on the mission of Whole Foods Market. The company employs extrinsic motivators such as good pay and profit sharing, as well as intrinsic factors such as commitment to the company's mission and culture.

DISCUSSION QUESTIONS

1 Summarize the classical theory of motivation. How can this theory be used to explain motivation at Whole Foods Market?
2 Maslow's hierarchy of needs theory states that human needs can be organized into five levels. On which needs does Whole Foods focus in its efforts to motivate employees?
3 Douglas McGregor concluded that managers may have differing assumptions about employee motivation and performance. Briefly describe Theory X and Theory Y managers. Which of these best describes managers at Whole Foods Market?
4 Victor Vroom's expectancy theory is a contemporary theory that can be very useful in explaining employee behavior and motivation. Use this theory to explain how managers motivate employees at Whole Foods.
5 Whole Foods Market has long used autonomous teams in the workplace. What are the advantages and disadvantages to this approach? Do you think that Whole Foods has made the right decision?

Online Exploration

Because healthy foods often come at a higher price, Whole Foods must work diligently to motivate customers to shop at their stores. One way that Whole Foods motivates customers is by hiring and rewarding excellent employees who provide excellent customer service. Visit Whole Foods' website (www.wholefoods.com) to find other ways that the company motivates customers to shop at the store. List and describe at least three of these strategies.

END NOTES

1 "Death by overwork in Japan," *The Economist*, December 19, 2007, (June 4, 2008), at http://www.economist.com/world/asia/displaystory.cfm?story_id=10329261.

2 Smith, Tom W. "Job Satisfaction in the United States," March 20, 2011 at http://www.norc.org/NR/rdonlyres/2874B40B-7C50-4F67-A6B2-26BD3B06EA04/0/JobSatisfactionintheUnitedStates.pdf.

3 Dennis W. Organ, Philip M. Podsakoff, and Nathan P. Podsakoff, "Expanding the Criterion Domain to Include Organizational Citizenship Behavior: Implications for Employee Selection," in Sheldon Zedeck, (Ed.), *Handbook of Industrial and Organizational Psychology* (American Psychological Association: Washington, D.C., 2010).

4 Oleksandr S. Chernyshenko, Stephen Stark, and Fritz Drasgow, "Individual Differences: Their Measurement and Validity," in Sheldon Zedeck, (Ed.), *Handbook of Industrial and Organizational Psychology* (American Psychological Association: Washington, D.C., 2010).

5 See Daniel Goleman, *Emotional Intelligence: Why It Can Matter More Than IQ* (New York: Bantam Books, 1995); see also Kenneth Law, Chi-Sum Wong, and Lynda Song, "The Construct and Criterion Validity of Emotional Intelligence and Its Potential Utility for Management Studies," *Journal of Applied Psychology*, 2004, vol 89, no. 3, 483–596.

6 Denise M. Rousseau, "The Individual-Organization Relationship: The Psychological Contract," in Sheldon Zedeck, (Ed.),

Handbook of Industrial and Organizational Psychology (American Psychological Association: Washington, D.C., 2010).

[7] See Daniel Wren, *The History of Management Thought*, 5th ed. (New York: John Wiley & Sons), 2004.

[8] Lyman Porter, Gregory Bigley, and Richard Steers, *Motivation and Work Behavior*, 8th ed. (New York: McGraw-Hill), 2008.

[9] Gary P. Latham, "The Importance of Understanding and Changing Employee Outcome Expectancies for Gaining Commitment to an Organizational Goal," *Personnel Psychology*, 2001, vol. 54, 707–720.

[10] Adam M. Grant, Yitzhak Fried, and Tina Juillerat, "Work Matters: Job Design in Classic and Contemporary Perspectives," in Sheldon Zedeck, (Ed.), *Handbook of Industrial and Organizational Psychology* (American Psychological Association: Washington, D.C., 2010).

[11] Stephanie Armour, "Working 9-to-5 No Longer," *USA Today*, December 6, 2004, 1B, 2B.

[12] Foss, Brad. "Telecommuters Tout Perks of Lifestyle," *Boston Globe*, March 14, 2006, (June 4, 2008), at http://www.boston.com/business/personalfinance/articles/2006/03/14/telecommuters_tout_perks_of_lifestyle/?page=2.

9 Leadership and Decision Making

Leadership Stretched to the Brink

It isn't easy leading a U.S. business these days. Leaving aside the global recession, the passion for "lean and mean" operations means that there are fewer workers to do more work. Globalization means keeping abreast of cross-cultural differences. Knowledge industries present unique leadership challenges requiring better communication skills and greater flexibility. Advances in technology have opened unprecedented channels of communication. Now more than ever, leaders must be able to do just about everything and more of it. As U.S. Senator and former presidential candidate John McCain puts it, "[Leadership is] a game of pinball, and you're the ball." Fortunately, a few of Corporate America's veteran leaders have some tips for those who still want to follow their increasingly treacherous path.

First of all, if you think you're being overworked—if your hours are too long and your schedule's too demanding—odds are, you're right: most people—including executives—*are* overworked. And in some industries, they're *particularly* overworked. U.S. airlines, for example, now serve 100 million more passengers annually than they did just four years ago—with 70,000 fewer workers. "I used to manage my time," quips one airline executive. "Now I manage my energy." In fact, many high-ranking managers have realized that energy is a key factor in their ability to complete their tasks on tough schedules. Most top corporate leaders work 80 to 100 hours a week, and a lot of

> After reading this chapter, you should be able to:
>
> 1 Define *leadership* and distinguish it from management.
> 2 Summarize early approaches to the study of leadership.
> 3 Discuss the concept of situational approaches to leadership.
> 4 Describe transformational and charismatic perspectives on leadership.
> 5 Identify and discuss leadership substitutes and neutralizers.
> 6 Discuss leaders as coaches and examine gender and cross-cultural issues in leadership.
> 7 Describe strategic leadership, ethical leadership, and virtual leadership.
> 8 Relate leadership to decision making and discuss both rational and behavioral perspectives on decision making.

them have found that regimens that allow them to rebuild and refresh make it possible for them to keep up the pace.

Carlos Ghosn, who's currently president of Renault *and* CEO of Nissan, believes in regular respites from his workweek routine. "I don't bring my work home. I play with my four children and spend time with my family on weekends," says Ghosn. "I come up with good ideas as a result of becoming stronger after being recharged." Google VP Marissa Mayer admits that "I can get by on four to six hours of sleep," but she also takes a weeklong vacation three times a year. Many leaders report that playing racquetball, running marathons, practicing yoga, or just getting regular exercise helps them to recover from overwork.

Effective leaders also take control of information flow—which means managing it, not reducing the flow until it's as close to a trickle as you can get it. Like most executives, for example, Mayer

Toru Yamanaka/AFP/Getty Images/Newscom

WHAT'S IN IT FOR ME?

In Chapter 8 we described the primary determinants of employee behavior and noted that managers can influence the behavior and enhance the motivation of employees. It is time to examine in detail how leaders—who may or may not also be managers such as Carlos Ghosn or Marissa Mayer—actually go about affecting employee behavior and motivating employee performance. We shall place these strategies and tactics in the context of various approaches to leadership throughout the years, including the situational perspective accepted today. Understanding these concepts will help you function more effectively as a leader and give you more insight into how your manager or boss strives to motivate you through his or her own leadership.

We start this chapter by taking a look at the nature of leadership. We then describe early approaches to leadership, as well as the situational perspective accepted today. Next, we examine leadership through the eyes of followers as well as alternatives to leadership. The changing nature of leadership and emerging issues in leadership are discussed next. Finally, we describe the very important related concept of decision making.

MyBizLab Where you see MyBizLab in this chapter, go to **www.mybizlab.com** for additional activities on the topic being discussed.

can't get by without multiple sources of information: "I always have my laptop with me," she reports, and "I adore my cell phone." Starbucks CEO Howard Schultz receives a morning voice mail summarizing the previous day's sales results and reads three newspapers a day. Mayer watches the news all day, and Bill Gross, a securities portfolio manager, keeps an eye on six monitors displaying real-time investment data.

On the other hand, Gross stands on his head to force himself to take a break from communicating. When he's upright again, he tries to find time to concentrate. "Eliminating the noise," he says, "is critical.…I only pick up the phone three or four times a day.…I don't want to be connected—I want to be disconnected." Ghosn, whose schedule requires weekly intercontinental travel, uses bilingual assistants to screen and translate information—one assistant for information from Europe (where Renault is), one for information from Japan (where Nissan is), and one for information from the United States (where Ghosn often has to be when he doesn't have to be in Europe or Japan). Clothing designer Vera Wang also uses an assistant to filter information. "The barrage of calls is so enormous," she says, "that if I just answered calls I'd do nothing else.…If I were to go near e-mail, there'd be even more obligations, and I'd be in [a mental hospital] with a white jacket on."[1]

Our opening story continues on page 236.

The Nature of Leadership

1 Define *leadership* and distinguish it from management.

Because *leadership* is a term that is often used in everyday conversation, you might assume that it has a common and accepted meaning. It is also, however, a word that is often misused. We define **leadership** as the processes and behaviors used by someone, such as a manager, to motivate, inspire, and influence the behaviors of others. One of the biggest errors people make is assuming that leadership and management mean the same thing when they are really different concepts. A person can be a manager, a leader, both, or neither.[2] Some of the basic distinctions between the two are summarized in Figure 9.1. As illustrated in the circle on the left, management focuses primarily on the activities of planning, organizing, leading, and controlling. Leadership, in contrast, is much more closely related to activities such as agenda

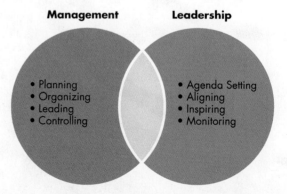

Figure 9.1 **Distinctions Between Management and Leadership**

setting, aligning, inspiring, and monitoring. As also illustrated in the figure, management and leadership may occasionally overlap but each is also a discrete and separate set of activities. Hence, a person may be a manager (but not a leader), a leader (but not a manager), or both a manager and a leader.

Consider the various roles of managers and leaders in a hospital setting. The chief of staff (chief physician) of a large hospital, though clearly a manager by virtue of his position, may not be respected or trusted by others and may have to rely solely on the authority vested in the position to get people to do things. On the other hand, an emergency-room nurse with no formal authority may be quite effective at taking charge of a chaotic situation and directing others in dealing with specific patient problems. The chief of staff is a manager but not really a leader, while the nurse is a leader but not really a manager.

Finally, the head of pediatrics, supervising a staff of 20 other doctors, nurses, and attendants, may also enjoy the staff's complete respect, confidence, and trust. They readily take her advice and follow directives without question, and often go far beyond what is necessary to help carry out the unit's mission. Thus, the head of pediatrics is both a manager (by virtue of the position she occupies) and a leader (by virtue of the respect she commands from others and their willingness to follow her direction).

Organizations need both management and leadership if they are to be effective. Management in conjunction with leadership can help achieve planned orderly change, and leadership in conjunction with management can keep the organization properly aligned with its environment.

Early Approaches to Leadership

2 Summarize early approaches to the study of leadership.

Although leaders and leadership have profoundly influenced history, careful scientific study of them began only about a century ago. Early studies focused on the *traits*, or personal characteristics, of leaders. Later research shifted to examine actual leader *behaviors*.

Trait Approaches to Leadership

Early researchers believed that notable leaders had some unique set of qualities or traits that distinguished them from their peers and endured throughout history. This **trait approach to leadership** led researchers to focus on identifying the essential leadership traits, including intelligence, dominance, self-confidence, energy, activity (versus passivity), and knowledge about the job. Unfortunately, the list of potential leadership traits quickly became so long that it lost any practical value. In addition, the results of many studies were inconsistent. For example, one argument stated that the most effective leaders were tall, like Abraham Lincoln. But critics were quick to point out that neither Napoleon Bonaparte nor Adolf Hitler was tall, but both were effective leaders in their own way.

Although the trait approach was all but abandoned several decades ago, in recent years, it has resurfaced. For example, some researchers have again started to focus on a limited set of traits. These traits include emotional intelligence, mental intelligence, drive, motivation, honesty and integrity, self-confidence, knowledge of the business, and charisma. Some people even believe that biological factors, such as appearance or height, may play a role in leadership. However, it is too early to know whether these traits really do relate to leadership.

Leadership the processes and behaviors used by someone, such as a manager, to motivate, inspire, and influence the behaviors of others

Trait Approach to Leadership focused on identifying the essential traits that distinguished leaders

Behavioral Approaches to Leadership

In the late 1940s, most researchers began to shift away from the trait approach and to look at leadership as a set of actual behaviors. The goal of the **behavioral approach to leadership** was to determine what *behaviors* were employed by effective leaders. These researchers assumed that the behaviors of effective leaders differed somehow from the behaviors of less effective leaders, and that the behaviors of effective leaders would be the same across all situations.

This research led to the identification of two basic forms of leader behavior. While different researchers applied different names, the basic leader behaviors identified during this period were

- **Task-focused leader behavior:** Task-focused leader behavior occurs when a leader focuses on how tasks should be performed in order to meet certain goals and to achieve certain performance standards.
- **Employee-focused leader behavior:** Employee-focused leader behavior occurs when a leader focuses on the satisfaction, motivation, and well-being of his or her employees.

During this period, people believed that leaders should always try to engage in a healthy dose of both behaviors, one to increase performance and the other to increase job satisfaction and motivation. Experts also began to realize that they could train managers to engage in these behaviors in a systematic manner. But they also discovered that there were other leader behaviors that needed to be considered, and that there were circumstances in which different combinations of leader behavior might be more effective than other combinations.

For instance, suppose a new manager takes over a work site that is plagued by low productivity and whose workers, while perhaps satisfied, are not motivated to work hard. The leader should most likely focus on task-focused behaviors in order to improve lagging productivity. But now suppose the situation is different—productivity is very high, but workers are stressed out about their jobs and have low levels of job satisfaction. In this instance, the manager should most likely concentrate on employee-focused behaviors to help improve job satisfaction. This line of thinking led to the creation of *situational theories*.

The Situational Approach to Leadership

3 Discuss the concept of situational approaches to leadership.

The **situational approach to leadership** assumes that appropriate leader behavior varies from one situation to another. This approach is shown in Figure 9.2. The trait and behavioral approaches to leadership were both universal in nature—they attempted to prescribe leader behaviors that would lead to a set of universal set of outcomes and consequences. For instance, proponents of these universal perspectives might argue that tall and intelligent people or people who are always employee-focused will always be good leaders. In reality, though, research has found this to simply be untrue. So, the situational approach to leadership attempt to identify various forms of leader behavior that result in contingent outcomes and consequences. By contingent, we mean that they depend on elements of the situation and characteristics of both the leader and followers.

Leadership characteristics include the manager's value system, confidence in subordinates, personal inclinations, feelings of security, and actual behaviors. Subordinate characteristics include the subordinates' need for independence, readiness to assume responsibility, tolerance for ambiguity, interest in the problem, understanding of goals, knowledge, experience, and expectations. Situational characteristics that affect decision making include the type of organization, group effectiveness, the problem itself, and time pressures.

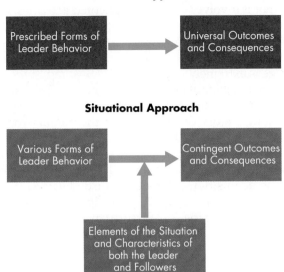

Figure 9.2 **The Situational Approach to Leadership**

Leadership Through the Eyes of Followers

4 Describe transformational and charismatic perspectives on leadership.

Another recent perspective that has been adopted by some leadership experts focuses on how leaders are seen through the eyes of their followers. The two primary approaches to leadership through the eyes of followers are *transformational leadership* and *charismatic leadership*. Barrack Obama's successful bid for the U.S. presidency in 2008 was fueled in part by many people's perceptions that he was both a transformational and charismatic leader. Indeed, during the campaign, he frequently talked about the need to transform the way the United States addressed issues such as health care, education, and foreign policy. And his personal charisma undoubtedly attracted support from many people as well.

Transformational Leadership

Transformational leadership focuses on the importance of leading for change (as opposed to leading during a period of stability). According to this view, much of what a leader does involves carrying out what might be thought of as basic management "transactions"—assigning work, evaluating performance, making decisions, and so forth. Occasionally, however, the leader has to engage in transformational leadership to initiate and manage major change, such as managing a merger, creating a new work team, or redefining the organization's culture.

Thus, **transformational leadership** is the set of abilities that allows a leader to recognize the need for change, to create a vision to guide that change, and to execute the change effectively. Some experts believe that change is such a vital organizational function that even successful firms need to change regularly to avoid becoming

---

Behavioral Approach to Leadership focused on determining what behaviors are employed by leaders

Task-Focused Leader Behavior leader behavior focusing on how tasks should be performed in order to meet certain goals and to achieve certain performance standards

Employee-Focused Leader Behavior leader behavior focusing on satisfaction, motivation, and well-being of employees

Situational Approach to Leadership assumes that appropriate leader behavior varies from one situation to another

Transformational Leadership the set of abilities that allows a leader to recognize the need for change, to create a vision to guide that change, and to execute the change effectively

complacent and stagnant. In contrast, **transactional leadership** is essentially the same as management in that it involves routine, regimented activities. Only a leader with tremendous influence can hope to perform both functions successfully. Some experts believe that change is such a vital organizational function that even successful firms need to change regularly to avoid becoming complacent and stagnant; accordingly, leadership for change is extremely important.

Some leaders are able to adopt either transformational or transactional perspectives, depending on their circumstances. For instance, Rupert Murdoch, CEO of News Corp., has a long history of transforming the media properties he acquires in order to expand their reach and turn a profit. Early in his career Murdoch relaunched *The Sun*, a British daily newspaper, as a tabloid notorious for its sensationalistic focus on sex. On the other hand, he has generally avoided retooling another of his British acquisitions, the well-regarded *Times*. When he purchased the struggling *Wall Street Journal* in 2007, he pledged to remain a hands-off manager. In the months since, the paper's signature coverage of U.S. business news has decreased to make room for increased coverage of politics and foreign events, and it remains to be seen how Murdoch will balance transformational and transactional leadership at the *Journal*.[3]

Charismatic Leadership

Charismatic leadership is a type of influence based on the leader's charisma, a form of interpersonal attraction that inspires support and acceptance. Charismatic leaders are likely to have a lot of confidence in their beliefs and ideals and a strong need to influence people. They also tend to communicate high expectations about follower performance and to express confidence in their followers. Many of the most influential leaders in history have been extremely charismatic, including entrepreneurs Mary Kay Ash, Steve Jobs, and Ted Turner; civil rights leader Martin Luther King, Jr.; and Pope John Paul II. Unfortunately, charisma can also empower leaders in other directions. Adolf Hitler, for instance, had strong charismatic qualities.

Most experts today acknowledge three crucial elements of charismatic leadership:[4]

1 Charismatic leaders *envision* likely future trends and patterns, set high expectations for themselves and for others, and behave in ways that meet or exceed those expectations.

2 Charismatic leaders *energize* others by demonstrating personal excitement, personal confidence, and consistent patterns of success.

3 Charismatic leaders *enable* others by supporting them, empathizing with them, and expressing confidence in them.

Charismatic leadership ideas are quite popular among managers today and are the subject of numerous books and articles.[5] Unfortunately, few studies have specifically attempted to test the meaning and impact of charismatic leadership. Lingering ethical concerns about charismatic leadership also trouble some people. They stem from the fact that some charismatic leaders inspire such blind faith in their followers that they may engage in inappropriate, unethical, or even illegal behaviors just because the leader instructed them to do so. This tendency likely played a role in the unwinding of both Enron and Arthur Andersen, as people followed orders from their charismatic bosses to hide information, shred documents, and mislead investigators.

Taking over a leadership role from someone with substantial personal charisma is also a challenge. For instance, the immediate successors to very successful and charismatic athletic coaches like Vince Lombardi (Green Bay Packers) and Phil Jackson (Chicago Bulls) each failed to measure up to their predecessors' legacies and were subsequently fired.

Special Issues in Leadership

5 Identify and discuss leadership substitutes and neutralizers.

Another interesting perspective on leadership focuses on *alternatives* to leadership. In some cases, certain factors may actually *substitute* for leadership, making actual leadership unnecessary or irrelevant. In other cases, factors may exist that *neutralize* or negate the influence of a leader even when that individual is attempting to exercise leadership.

Leadership Substitutes

Leadership substitutes are individual, task, and organizational characteristics that tend to outweigh the need for a leader to initiate or direct employee performance. In other words, if certain factors are present, the employee will perform his or her job capably, without the direction of a leader. Table 9.1 identifies several basic leadership substitutes.

Consider, for example, what happens when an ambulance with a critically injured victim screeches to the door of a hospital emergency room. Do the ER employees stand around waiting for someone to take control and instruct them on what to do? The answer is no—they are highly trained and well-prepared professionals who know how to respond and work together as a team without someone playing the role of leader. When a U.S. Airways flight crashed into the Hudson River in 2009, all members of the flight crew knew exactly what to do, without waiting for orders. As a result of their effective and prompt actions, a disaster was averted, and all passengers on the plane were quickly rescued.

Leadership Neutralizers

In other situations, even if a leader is present and attempts to engage in various leadership behaviors, those behaviors may be rendered ineffective—or neutralized—by various factors that can be called **leadership neutralizers.** Suppose, for example, that

TABLE 9.1 Leadership Substitutes and Neutralizers	
Individual factors	• Individual professionalism • Individual ability, knowledge, and motivation • Individual experience and training • Indifference to rewards
Job factors	• Structured/automated • Highly controlled • Intrinsically satisfying • Embedded feedback
Organization factors	• Explicit plans and goals • Rigid rules and procedures • Rigid reward system not tied to performance • Physical distance between supervisor and subordinate
Group factors	• Group performance norms • High level of group cohesiveness • Group interdependence

Transactional Leadership comparable to management, it involves routine, regimented activities

Charismatic Leadership type of influence based on the leader's personal charisma

Leadership Substitutes individual, task, and organizational characteristics that tend to outweigh the need for a leader to initiate or direct employee performance

Leadership Neutralizers factors that may render leader behaviors ineffective

MANAGING IN TURBULENT TIMES

No More Secrets?

As the public faces of their companies, CEOs are subject to intense scrutiny and take the heat from critics and consumer advocates for any company fault or misdeed. As a result, many CEOs take a very cautious and calculated approach to communicating with consumers. Many companies have strict guidelines regarding employees' blogging and reporting on internal issues. This kind of closed-doors approach keeps competitors in the dark and presumably minimizes public scrutiny.

However, a realistic evaluation of today's limitless capacity for information dissemination might lead a CEO to doubt the effectiveness of this policy. Some CEOs have embraced a philosophy of accessibility. In lieu of a carefully worded press release, they are using blogs and websites like YouTube to personally deliver messages to the public. In a YouTube video, the CEO of Jet Blue apologized to passengers who had been trapped for hours in planes grounded by bad weather, and Microsoft now allows its engineers to write about current projects in blogs. Glenn Kelman, CEO of the real estate brokerage firm Redfin, started a blog to air his frustrations regarding real estate sales practices that he judged unfair to the consumer. His blog elicited angry responses in the comments section, to which he posted his own rebuttals. Redfin's customer base expanded, suggesting that Kelman's personal approach made his sympathy for the consumer more believable.

A strategy of transparency may have a humanizing effect on a company, making it more sympathetic to consumers who feel alienated by the trend toward an increasingly automated customer service experience. All firms have flaws and commit errors, and an admission of culpability, frustration, or weakness can make a company more relatable. Responsive, accessible CEOs may not be able to prevent criticism or scrutiny, but they may take a little air out of free-swinging

Comstock/Thinkstock

critics used to hammering faceless offenders. Occasionally, the CEO may even beat the critics to the punch. And, indeed, people today are increasingly expecting managers to be forthright and candid when problems arise. Some employees of a national pizza chain recently made a disgusting video in which they were shown appearing to add unsavory ingredients to pizzas. When this video attracted national attention after it was posted on YouTube, the company did not respond for several days. Many critics were angered by the lack of response, and in the eyes of some experts the public damage was greater than if the firm had responded immediately. So, the challenge for managers during turbulent times is to find the right blend of timely candor and considered deliberation. And sometimes, only the leader's instincts can serve as a guide.[6]

MyBizLab

a relatively new and inexperienced leader is assigned to a work group composed of very experienced employees with long-standing performance norms and a high level of group cohesiveness. The norms and cohesiveness of the group may be so strong that there is nothing the new leader can do to change things.

In addition to group factors, elements of the job itself may also limit a leader's ability to "make a difference." Consider, for example, employees working on a moving assembly line. Employees may only be able to work at the pace of the moving line, so performance quantity and quality are constrained by the speed of the line and simplicity of each individual task.

Finally, organizational factors can also neutralize at least some forms of leader behavior. Suppose a new leader is accustomed to using merit pay increases as a way to motivate people. But in his or her new job, pay increases are dictated by union contracts and are based primarily on employee seniority and cost of living. The leader's previous approach to motivating people would be neutralized, and new approaches would have to be identified.

The Changing Nature of Leadership

6 Discuss leaders as coaches and examine gender and cross-cultural issues in leadership.

Various alternatives to leadership aside, many settings still call for at least some degree of leadership, although the nature of that leadership continues to evolve. Among the recent changes in leadership that managers should recognize are the increasing role of *leaders as coaches* as well as *gender and cross-cultural patterns* of leader behavior.

Leaders as Coaches

We noted in Chapter 6 that many organizations today are using teams. Many other organizations are attempting to become less hierarchical—that is, to eliminate the old-fashioned command-and-control mentality often inherent in bureaucratic organizations and to motivate and empower individuals to work independently. In each case, the role of leaders is also changing. Whereas leaders were once expected to control situations, direct work, supervise people, closely monitor performance, make decisions, and structure activities, many leaders today are being asked to change how they manage people. Perhaps the best description of this new role is for the leader to become a *coach* instead of an *overseer*.[7]

From the standpoint of a business leader, a coaching perspective would call for the leader to help select and train team members and other new employees, to provide some general direction, and to help the team get the information and other resources it needs. Coaches from different teams may play important roles in linking the activities and functions of their respective teams. Some leaders may function as *mentors*, helping less experienced employees learn the ropes and better preparing them to advance within the organization; they may also help resolve conflicts among team members and mediate other disputes that arise. But beyond these activities, the leader keeps a low profile and lets the group get its work done with little or no direct oversight, just as during a game an athletic coach trusts his or her players to execute the plays successfully.

Gender and Leadership

Another factor that is clearly altering the face of leadership is the growing number of women advancing to higher levels in organizations. Given that most leadership theories and research studies have focused on male leaders, developing a better understanding of how women lead is clearly an important next step. Some early observers, for instance, predicted that (consistent with prevailing stereotypes) female leaders would be relatively warm, supportive, and nurturing as compared to their male counterparts. But research suggests that female leaders are not necessarily more nurturing or supportive than male leaders. Likewise, male leaders are not systematically harsher, more controlling, or more task focused than female leaders.

The one difference that has arisen in some cases is that women may be slightly more democratic in making decisions, whereas men have a tendency to be more autocratic.[8] However, much more work needs to be done in order to better understand the dynamics of gender and leadership. In the meantime, high-profile and successful female leaders, such as Andrea Jung (CEO of Avon Products) and Angela Merkel (chancellor of Germany), continue to demonstrate the effectiveness with which women can be exceptional leaders.

Cross-Cultural Leadership

Another changing perspective on leadership relates to cross-cultural issues. In this context, *culture* is used as a broad concept to encompass both international differences and diversity-based differences within one culture. For instance, Japan is generally characterized by *collectivism* (group before individual), whereas the United

States is based more on *individualism* (individual before group). So when a Japanese firm sends an executive to head up the firm's operation in the United States, that person will likely find it necessary to recognize the importance of individual contributions and rewards and the differences in individual and group roles that exist in Japanese and U.S. businesses.

Similarly, cross-cultural factors also play a growing role in organizations as their workforces become more diverse. As African Americans, Asian Americans, Hispanics, and members of other ethnic groups achieve leadership positions, it may be necessary to reassess how applicable current theories and models of leadership are when applied to an increasingly diverse pool of leaders.

7 Describe strategic leadership, ethical leadership, and virtual leadership.

Emerging Issues in Leadership

Finally, there are also three emerging issues in leadership that warrant discussion. These issues are *strategic leadership*, *ethical leadership*, and *virtual leadership*.

Strategic Leadership

Strategic leadership is a new concept that explicitly relates leadership to the role of top management. **Strategic leadership** is a leader's ability to understand the complexities of both the organization and its environment and to lead change in the organization so as to enhance its competitiveness.

To be effective as a strategic leader, a manager needs to have a thorough and complete understanding of the organization—its history, its culture, its strengths, and its weaknesses. In addition, the leader needs a firm grasp of the organization's external environment. This needs to include current business and economic conditions and circumstances as well as significant trends and issues on the horizon. The strategic leader also needs to recognize the firm's current strategic advantages and shortcomings.

Ethical Leadership

Most people have long assumed that business leaders are ethical people. But in the wake of recent corporate scandals at firms like Enron, Boeing, and AIG, faith in business leaders has been shaken. Perhaps now more than ever, high standards of ethical conduct are being held up as a prerequisite for effective leadership. More specifically, business leaders are being called on to maintain high ethical standards for their own conduct, to unfailingly exhibit ethical behavior, and to hold others in their organizations to the same standards—in short, to practice **ethical leadership.**

The behaviors of top leaders are being scrutinized more than ever, and those responsible for hiring new leaders for a business are looking more closely at the backgrounds of those being considered. And the emerging pressures for stronger corporate governance models are likely to further increase the commitment to select only those individuals with high ethical standards for leadership positions in business and to hold them more accountable than in the past for both their actions and the consequences of those actions.

Virtual Leadership

Finally, **virtual leadership** is also emerging as an important issue for organizations. In earlier times, leaders and their employees worked together in the same physical location and engaged in face-to-face interactions on a regular basis. But in today's world, both leaders and their employees may work in locations that are far from one another. Such arrangements might include people telecommuting from a home office one or two days a week to people actually living and working far from company headquarters.

Increasingly, then, communication between leaders and their subordinates happens largely by telephone and e-mail. One implication may be that leaders in these situations must work harder at creating and maintaining relationships with their employees that go beyond words on a computer screen. While nonverbal communication, such as

ENTREPRENEURSHIP AND NEW VENTURES

An Apple a Day

As CEO of Apple Inc., Steve Jobs developed a reputation for brilliance, originality, and charm. His leadership style was criticized as well. One industry observer portrayed Jobs as intimidating and power hungry, while others said he commanded "a cult-like following from employees and consumers." Yet Jobs was clearly a leader who could deliver success in businesses that are evolving, highly technical, and demanding. Writer Steven Berglas says, "Jobs, the *enfant terrible* widely reputed to be one of the most aggressive egotists in Silicon Valley, has an unrivaled track record when it comes to pulling development teams through start-ups."

But how did Jobs's charisma, confidence, and vision shape his leadership style during times of prosperity and success? In a recent interview, Jobs discussed how his passion and focus enable the company to succeed in any type of situation or environment. "Lots of companies have tons of great engineers and smart people," said Jobs. "But ultimately, there needs to be some gravitational force that pulls it all together....That's what was missing at Apple for a while. There were bits and pieces of interesting things floating around, but not that gravitational pull."

Before his recent death, Jobs was riding high, as he focused on bringing Apple's unique blend of hi-tech gadgetry and cool design to applications reaching far beyond the computers that first made his fortune. The company has released several versions of the iPod, its hugely popular digital music player, supported by Apple's online music store, iTunes. The iPhone, a mobile phone that connects to the Internet, was named 2007's Invention of the Year by *TIME Magazine*. And Jobs's confidence and excitement for the future was always growing. "Apple is doing the best work in its history," he said, "and there's a lot more coming."[9]

MyBizLab

Ryan Anson/AFP/Getty Images/Newscom

smiles and handshakes, may not be possible online, managers can instead make a point of adding a few personal words in an e-mail (whenever appropriate) to convey appreciation, reinforcement, or constructive feedback.

Leadership, Management, and Decision Making

8 Relate leadership to decision making and discuss both rational and behavioral perspectives on decision making.

We noted earlier the differences and similarities between managing and leading. **Decision making** is another important related concept. Indeed, decision making is a fundamental component of both leadership and management—managers and leaders must frequently make decisions.

Strategic Leadership leader's ability to understand the complexities of both the organization and its environment and to lead change in the organization so as to enhance its competitiveness

Ethical Leadership leader behaviors that reflect high ethical standards

Virtual leadership leadership in settings where leaders and followers interact electronically rather than in face-to-face settings

Decision Making choosing one alternative from among several options

Figure 9.3 Steps in the Rational Decision-Making Process
Source: From GRIFFIN. *Management* 8e. © 2005 South-Western, a part of Cengage Learning, Inc. Reproduced by permission. www.cengage.com/permissions.

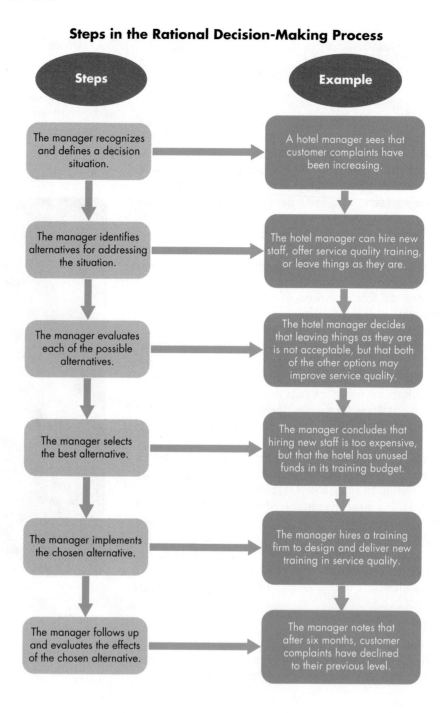

Steps in the Rational Decision-Making Process

Steps

Example

Steps	Example
The manager recognizes and defines a decision situation.	A hotel manager sees that customer complaints have been increasing.
The manager identifies alternatives for addressing the situation.	The hotel manager can hire new staff, offer service quality training, or leave things as they are.
The manager evaluates each of the possible alternatives.	The hotel manager decides that leaving things as they are is not acceptable, but that both of the other options may improve service quality.
The manager selects the best alternative.	The manager concludes that hiring new staff is too expensive, but that the hotel has unused funds in its training budget.
The manager implements the chosen alternative.	The manager hires a training firm to design and deliver new training in service quality.
The manager follows up and evaluates the effects of the chosen alternative.	The manager notes that after six months, customer complaints have declined to their previous level.

Rational Decision Making

Managers and leaders should strive to be rational in making decisions. Figure 9.3 shows the steps in the rational decision-making process.

Recognizing and Defining the Decision Situation The first step in rational decision making is recognizing that a decision is necessary—that is, there must be some stimulus or spark to initiate the process. The stimulus for a decision may be either positive or negative. Managers who must decide how to invest surplus funds, for example, face a positive decision situation. A negative financial stimulus could involve having to trim budgets because of cost overruns.

Inherent in making such a decision is the need to define precisely what the problem is. Consider the situation currently being faced in the international air travel industry. Because of the growth of international travel related to business, education, and tourism, global carriers need to increase their capacity. Because most major international airports are already operating at or near capacity, adding a significant number of new flights to existing schedules is not feasible. As a result, the most logical alternative is to increase capacity on existing flights. Thus, Boeing and Airbus, the world's only manufacturers of large commercial aircraft, recognized an important opportunity and defined their decision situations as how best to respond to the need for increased global travel capacity.[10]

Identifying Alternatives   Once the decision situation has been recognized and defined, the second step is to identify alternative courses of effective action. Developing both obvious, standard alternatives and creative, innovative alternatives is useful. In general, the more important the decision, the more attention is directed to developing alternatives. Although managers should seek creative solutions, they must also recognize that various constraints often limit their alternatives. Common constraints include legal restrictions, moral and ethical norms, and constraints imposed by the power and authority of the manager, available technology, economic considerations, and unofficial social norms. After assessing the question of how to increase international airline capacity, Boeing and Airbus identified three different alternatives: They could independently develop new large planes, they could collaborate in a joint venture to create a single new large plane, or they could modify their largest existing planes to increase their capacity.

Evaluating Alternatives   The third step in the decision-making process is evaluating each of the alternatives. Some alternatives may not be feasible because of legal or financial barriers. Limited human, material, and information resources may make other alternatives impractical. Managers must thoroughly evaluate all the alternatives in order to increase the chances that the alternative finally chosen will be successful. For example, Airbus felt it would be at a disadvantage if it tried simply to enlarge its existing planes because the Boeing 747 was at the time already the largest aircraft being made and could readily be expanded to remain the largest. Boeing, meanwhile, was seriously concerned about the risk inherent in building a new and even larger plane, even if it shared the risk with Airbus as a joint venture.

Selecting the Best Alternative   Choosing the best available alternative is the real crux of decision making. Even though many situations do not lend themselves to objective, mathematical analysis, managers and leaders can often develop subjective estimates and weights for choosing an alternative. Decision makers should also remember that finding multiple acceptable alternatives may be possible; selecting just one alternative and rejecting all the others might not be necessary. For example, Airbus proposed a joint venture with Boeing. Boeing, meanwhile, decided that its best course of action was to modify its existing 747 to increase its capacity. As a result, Airbus decided to proceed on its own to develop and manufacture a new jumbo jet. Boeing then decided that in addition to modifying its 747, it would develop a new plane to offer as an alternative, albeit one not as large as the 747 or the proposed Airbus plane.

Implementing the Chosen Alternative   After an alternative has been selected, managers and leaders must put it into effect. Boeing set its engineers to work expanding the capacity of its 747 by adding 30 feet to the plane's body; the firm also began developing another plane intended for international travel, the 787. Airbus engineers, meanwhile, developed design concepts for a new jumbo jet equipped with escalators and elevators and capable of carrying 655 passengers. Airbus's development costs alone were estimated to exceed $12 billion.

Managers must also consider people's resistance to change when implementing decisions. The reasons for such resistance include insecurity, inconvenience, and fear of the unknown. Managers should anticipate potential resistance at various stages of the implementation process. However, even when all alternatives have been evaluated as precisely as possible and the consequences of each alternative have been weighed, unanticipated consequences are still likely. Employees may resist or protest change; they may even quit rather than agree to it. Other factors, such as unexpected cost increases, a less-than-perfect fit with existing organizational subsystems, or unpredicted effects on cash flow or operating expenses, could develop after implementation has begun. Both Boeing and Airbus were plagued by production delays that pushed back delivery of their respective aircrafts by years and could end up costing each company billions of dollars. Airbus got its plane to market first (it began flying in late 2007), but profits have been pushed far into the future as the global recession of 2008–2010 caused many airlines to cancel or delay orders for several years.

Following Up and Evaluating the Results   The final step in the decision-making process requires that managers and leaders evaluate the effectiveness of their decision—that is, they should make sure that the chosen alternative has served its original purpose. If an implemented alternative appears not to be working, they can respond in several ways. Another previously identified alternative (the original second or third choice, for instance) could be adopted. Or they might recognize that the situation was not correctly defined to begin with and start the process all over again. Finally, managers and leaders might decide that the original alternative is in fact appropriate but either has not yet had time to work or should be implemented in a different way.

At this point, both Boeing and Airbus are nearing the crucial period when they will learn whether they made good decisions. Airbus's A380 made its first commercial flight in 2007, though delays continue to push back its production schedule. The plane has also been hampered by technical problems. Meanwhile, Boeing's 787 faced numerous delays, and widespread use of the plane is not unexpected until at least 2012. The expanded 747 was launched on schedule, however, and was in service in 2011. Most airlines have been willing to wait patiently for the 787s, which are designed to be much more fuel efficient than other international airplanes. Given the dramatic surge in fuel costs in recent years, a fuel-efficient option like the 787 could be an enormous success. Indeed, Airbus has begun developing its own fuel-efficient jet, the A350.[11]

Behavioral Aspects of Decision Making

If all decision situations were approached as logically as described in the previous section, more decisions would prove successful. Yet decisions are often made with little consideration for logic and rationality. Some experts have estimated that U.S. companies use rational decision-making techniques less than 20 percent of the time. Of course, even when organizations try to be logical, they sometimes fail. For example, when Starbucks opened its first coffee shops in New York, it relied on scientific marketing research, taste tests, and rational deliberation in making a decision to emphasize drip over espresso coffee. However, that decision proved wrong, as it became clear that New Yorkers strongly preferred the same espresso-style coffees that were Starbucks mainstays in the West. Hence, the firm had to reconfigure its stores hastily to meet customer preferences.

On the other hand, sometimes a decision made with little regard for logic can still turn out to be correct.[12] Important ingredients in how these forces work are behavioral aspects of decision making. These include *political forces*, *intuition*, *escalation of commitment*, and *risk propensity*.

Political Forces in Decision Making   Political forces contribute to the behavioral nature of decision making. One major element of politics, *coalitions*, is especially relevant to decision making. A **coalition** is an informal alliance of individuals or groups formed to achieve a common goal. This common goal is often a preferred decision alternative. For example, coalitions of stockholders frequently band together to force a board of directors to make a certain decision.

The New York Yankees once contacted three major sneaker manufacturers—Nike, Reebok, and Adidas—and informed them that they were looking to make a sponsorship deal. While Nike and Reebok were carefully and rationally assessing the possibilities, managers at Adidas quickly realized that a partnership with the Yankees made a lot of sense for them. They responded very quickly to the idea and ended up hammering out a contract while the competitors were still analyzing details.[13]

When these coalitions enter the political arena and attempt to persuade lawmakers to make decisions favorable to their interests, they are called *lobbyists*. Lobbyists may also donate money to help elect a candidate who is more likely to pursue their agendas. A recurring theme in U.S. politics is the damaging influence these special interest groups have on politicians, who may feel unduly obligated to favor campaign donors when making decisions.

Intuition   **Intuition** is an innate belief about something, often without conscious consideration. Managers sometimes decide to do something because it "feels right" or they have a hunch. This feeling is usually not arbitrary, however. Rather, it is based on years of experience and practice in making decisions in similar situations. Such an inner sense may help managers make an occasional decision without going through a full-blown rational sequence of steps.

That said, all managers, but most especially inexperienced ones, should be careful not to rely too heavily on intuition. If rationality and logic are continually flouted for "what feels right," the odds are that disaster will strike one day.

Escalation of Commitment   Another important behavioral process that influences decision making is **escalation of commitment** to a chosen course of action. In particular, decision makers sometimes make decisions and then become so committed to the course of action suggested by that decision that they stay with it, even when it appears to have been wrong.[14] For example, when people buy stock in a company, they sometimes refuse to sell it even after repeated drops in price. They choose a course of action—buying the stock in anticipation of making a profit—and then stay with it even in the face of increasing losses. Moreover, after the value drops they may rationalize that they can't sell at such a low price because they will lose money.

Risk Propensity and Decision Making   The behavioral element of **risk propensity** is the extent to which a decision maker is willing to gamble when making a decision. Some managers are cautious about every decision they make. They try to adhere to the rational model and are extremely conservative in what they do. Such managers are more likely to avoid mistakes, and they infrequently make decisions that lead to big losses. Others are extremely aggressive in making decisions and willing to take risks.[15] They rely heavily on intuition, reach decisions quickly, and often risk big investments on their decisions. As in gambling, these managers are more likely than their conservative counterparts to achieve big successes with their decisions; they are also more likely to incur greater losses.[16] The organization's culture is a prime ingredient in fostering different levels of risk propensity.

Coalition an informal alliance of individuals or groups formed to achieve a common goal

Intuition an innate belief about something, often without conscious consideration

Escalation of Commitment condition in which a decision maker becomes so committed to a course of action that she or he stays with it even when it appears to have been wrong

Risk Propensity extent to which a decision maker is willing to gamble when making a decision

Toru Yamanaka/AFP/Getty Images/Newscom

Continued from page 222

Stemming the Tide

Not surprisingly, Microsoft chairman Bill Gates integrates the role of his assistant into a high-tech information-organizing system:

> For example, he uses three computer monitors on his desk, integrated to form a single desktop. This allows him to drag items from one screen to another. The screen on his left is his email inbox, listing all of the items he has received. He uses his assistant to screen his incoming emails, so he only gets about a 100 or so per day.
>
> The filter on his inbox allows him to directly receive emails from people he has previously corresponded with from Microsoft, Intel, HP, other key Microsoft business partners, and his personal contacts. All others are directed to his assistant.
>
> The screen in the center of his desk opens the email that he selects to read and respond to. And the screen to his right displays his browser. This allows him to see new email that arrives (on his left) while he is reading and responding to another email (in the center). Further, if he needs to bring up a link related to his email he can do so (on the right) while he still sees the original email.

Of course, not all leaders have access to the same technology employed by Bill Gates. Most must still manage their time using mainstream techniques—delegation and staff support, for example. But for those leaders willing to work at it, most find they can effectively deal with the demands of their job and lead their organizations to success.

QUESTIONS FOR DISCUSSION

1 What does this case illustrate about the nature of leadership?
2 What does this case illustrate about the situational nature of leadership?
3 In what ways has information technology changed the work of leaders?
4 How do you think the work of leaders will change in the future?

SUMMARY OF LEARNING OBJECTIVES   MyBizLab

1. **Define *leadership* and distinguish it from management. (pp. 222–223)**
Leadership refers to the processes and behaviors used by someone to motivate, inspire, and influence the behaviors of others. While leadership and management are often related, they are not the same thing. Leadership involves such things as developing a vision, communicating that vision, and directing change. Management, meanwhile, focuses more on outlining procedures, monitoring results, and working toward outcomes.

2. **Summarize early approaches to the study of leadership. (pp. 223–224)**
The *trait approach to leadership* focused on identifying the traits of successful leaders. The earliest researchers believed that important leadership traits included intelligence, dominance, self-confidence, energy, activity (versus passivity), and knowledge about the job. More recent researchers have started to focus on traits such as emotional intelligence, drive, honesty and integrity, self-confidence, and charisma. The *behavioral approach* identified two basic and common leader behaviors: *task-focused* and *employee-focused* behaviors.

3. **Discuss the concept of situational approaches to leadership. (pp. 224–225)**
The *situational approach to leadership* proposes that there is no single best approach to leadership. Instead, situational factors influence the approach to leadership that is most effective. This approach was proposed as a continuum of leadership behavior, ranging from having the leader make decisions alone to having employees make decisions with minimal guidance from the leader. Each point on the continuum is influenced by *characteristics of the leader, his or her subordinates*, and the *situation*.

4. **Describe transformational and charismatic perspectives on leadership. (pp. 225–226)**
Transformational leadership (as distinguished from *transactional leadership*) focuses on the set of abilities that allows a leader to recognize the need for change, to create a vision to guide that change, and to execute the change effectively. *Charismatic leadership* is influence based on the leader's personal charisma. The basic concept of charisma suggests that charismatic leaders are likely to have self-confidence, confidence in their beliefs and ideals, and a need to influence people. They also tend to communicate high expectations about follower performance and to express confidence in their followers.

5. **Identify and discuss leadership substitutes and neutralizers. (pp. 227–228)**
Leadership substitutes are individual, task, and organizational factors that tend to outweigh the need for a leader to initiate or direct employee performance. In other words, if certain factors are present, the employee will perform his or her job without the direction of a leader. Even if a leader attempts to engage in leadership behaviors, there exist *leadership neutralizers* that may render the leader's efforts ineffective. Such neutralizers include group cohesiveness as well as elements of the job itself.

6. **Discuss leaders as coaches and examine gender and cross-cultural issues in leadership. (pp. 229–230)**
Many organizations expect their leaders to play the role of *coach*—to select team members, provide direction, train and develop, but otherwise allow the group to function autonomously. Another factor that is altering the face of leadership is the number of women advancing to higher levels. While there appear to be few differences between men and women leaders, the growing number of women leaders suggests a need for more study. Another changing perspective on leadership relates to cross-cultural issues. In this context, *culture* encompasses international differences and diversity-based differences within one culture.

7. **Describe strategic leadership, ethical leadership, and virtual leadership. (pp. 230–231)**
Strategic leadership is the leader's ability to lead change in the organization so as to enhance its competitiveness. Business leaders are also being called on to practice *ethical leadership*—that is, to maintain high ethical standards for their own conduct, and to hold others in their organizations to the same standards. As more leaders and employees work in different settings, a better understanding of *virtual leadership* is also becoming more important.

8. **Relate leadership to decision making and discuss both rational and behavioral perspectives on decision making. (pp. 231–235)**
Decision making—choosing one alternative from among several options—is a critical management and leadership skill. The *rational perspective* prescribes a logical process for making decisions. It involves six steps (1) recognizing and defining the decision situation, (2) identifying alternatives, (3) evaluating alternatives, (4) selecting the best alternative, (5) implementing the chosen alternative, and (6) following up and evaluating the results. The *behavioral perspective* acknowledges that things like *political forces, intuition, escalation of commitment*, and *risk propensity* are also important aspects of decision making.

KEY TERMS   MyBizLab

behavioral approach to leadership
(p. 224)
charismatic leadership (p. 226)
coalition (p. 234)
decision making (p. 231)
employee-focused leader behavior (p. 224)
escalation of commitment (p. 235)

ethical leadership (p. 230)
intuition (p. 235)
leadership (p. 222)
leadership neutralizers (p. 227)
leadership substitutes (p. 227)
risk propensity (p. 235)
situational approach to leadership (p. 224)

strategic leadership (p. 230)
task-focused leader behavior
(p. 224)
trait approach to leadership (p. 223)
transactional leadership (p. 226)
transformational leadership (p. 225)
virtual leadership (p. 230)

QUESTIONS AND EXERCISES

QUESTIONS FOR REVIEW

1. What are the basic differences between management and leadership?
2. Summarize the basic premises underlying the trait, behavioral, and situational approaches to leadership.
3. What are leadership substitutes and neutralizers?
4. List and briefly explain the steps in rational decision making.

QUESTIONS FOR ANALYSIS

5. Identify five people you would consider to be excellent leaders. Explain why you feel that way about each.
6. What factors are present in your job that motivate you to perform without the direction of a leader? Are there factors that neutralize the efforts of your leader?
7. The impact of virtual leadership is likely to grow in the future. As a potential "follower" in a virtual leadership situation, what issues would be of most concern to you? What would the issues be from the perspective of the "leader" role in such a situation?
8. Identify and discuss examples of how your decision making has been affected by at least two of the behavioral processes noted in the chapter.

APPLICATION EXERCISES

9. Interview a senior manager at a local company. Ask that manager if he or she believes that leadership can be taught. What are the key implications of his or her position?
10. Review the running example in the textbook regarding the decisions made by Airbus and Boeing regarding new long-haul aircraft. Research the most current information available about the status of both planes. Based on the information you have available, which firm seems to have made the best decision?

BUILDING YOUR BUSINESS SKILLS

Learning to Lead

Goal
To encourage you to appreciate your own strengths and weaknesses as they relate to critical leadership skills.

Background Information
While not all experts agree, most believe that businesses can teach their managers to become more effective leaders. Indeed, most large businesses devote considerable resources to identifying those managers with the most leadership potential and providing training and development opportunities for those managers to enhance and refine their leadership skills. One major U.S. energy company, for instance, has identified the following traits, characteristics, and skills as reflecting how it sees leadership:

- Personal integrity
- Decision-making skills
- Interpersonal skills
- Communication skills
- Strategic thinking skills
- Global awareness skills
- Financial management skills

Method
Step 1
Working alone or with classmates (as directed by your instructor), develop or describe indicators and measures a business could use to assess each of these traits, characteristics, and skills in managers so as to most effectively select those with the strongest potential for leadership. That is, describe how you would go about selecting managers for special leadership training and development.

Step 2
Working alone or with classmates (again, as directed by your instructor), develop or describe the techniques and methods that might potentially serve to best enhance the traits, characteristics, and skills noted above. That is, having chosen those managers with the strongest potential for growth as leaders, describe how you would go about teaching and developing those individuals so as to enhance their leadership potential and capability.

FOLLOW-UP QUESTIONS

1. Comment on the traits, characteristics, and skills used by the energy company. Do you agree or disagree that these would differentiate between those who might be described as both managers and leaders versus those best described simply as managers? Are there others you might include?
2. How simple or easy would you expect it to be to select managers for leadership and development at this company?
3. Do you believe that leadership can be taught? What are the assumptions underlying your answer?
4. If you personally were selected for a program such as this, what would you expect to encounter during the training and development? What would you expect to be different after the training and development were complete?

EXERCISING YOUR ETHICS: INDIVIDUAL EXERCISE

Exercising Charisma

The Situation

Assume that you are the owner and CEO of a small but growing business. You see yourself as a mild and laid-back kind of person—one that is honest and effective as a manager, but not necessarily someone who strongly inspires and motivates others. This has never been a barrier to your success. You have made excellent decisions since founding your company and are respected by both your employees and the firm's external stakeholders.

Because your business is growing, about a year ago you found it necessary to hire some additional managers. One of these has been increasingly causing you concern. The manager in question, Bill Jackson, is a dynamic and charismatic person—all of the things you are not. Indeed, these qualities have already made him enormously liked by most people in the business. So far, though, Jackson has not really distinguished himself as a manager. He basically makes reasonable decisions and understands how to run his unit, but does not seem to be a real strategic thinker.

The Dilemma

A new competitor has just entered your market area. While you do not see this as a major long-term threat, you have decided that you need for your business to "tighten its belt" a bit. You anticipate, for example, that your business revenues will shrink a bit this year (due to the new company) but will likely start to grow again within a year or so. Your senior financial manager has convinced you that the best course of action would be to terminate one of the newer managers you hired last year.

Your inclination is to terminate Jackson. The basis for this is your concern for how others in the business see him. For example, if you were to decide to retire (which you may want to do in a few years), you suspect there would be a strong and immediate groundswell of support for appointing Jackson as the CEO to take your place. You truly believe that this support would be based on his charisma and dynamic personality, but you also think that while he would be an adequate replacement, there are others in the business who would do a better job actually managing the firm. But given Jackson's enormous popularity, anyone else picked to replace you would at least initially have to work hard to overcome skepticism and disappointment. You are leaning toward terminating Jackson.

QUESTIONS TO ADDRESS

1. What are the ethical issues in this situation?
2. What do you think most managers would do in this situation?
3. What would you do?

EXERCISING YOUR ETHICS: TEAM EXERCISE

Forcing the Hand

The Situation

The Edda Corporation is a large manufacturing company that is assessing the market potential of four new products it has acquired the rights to produce.

The Dilemma

After some preliminary discussions, it seems apparent that two of the new products have market potential, but the others do not. However, the company's CEO, Lucy Shaw, wants to produce all the new products. After all, she is the one who approved the costly acquisition of rights, and it is she who will have to explain to the board of directors why some of the products she approved do not, after all, have market potential. But it is also she who will be accountable if the products are all manufactured but end up performing poorly.

Edda Corporation's top managers have identified several options:

1. Approve all four products for production
2. Be completely frank and recommend approval of only two of the products.
3. Form a coalition with a team of engineers and work toward a proposal to modify the two less attractive products. The management team thinks this is viable, but it will also add some costs for product development and delay product introduction for about six months.

Team Activity

Assemble a group of four students and assign each group member to one of the following roles:

- Lucy Shaw (CEO)
- A member of the top management team
- An Edda Corporation stockholder
- A member of the Edda Corporation board of directors

ACTION STEPS

1 Before hearing any of your group's comments on this situation, and from the perspective of your assigned role, which option do you think is best for the company? Write down the reasons for your position.

2 Before hearing any of your group's comments on this situation, and from the perspective of your assigned role, what are the underlying ethical issues, if any, in this situation? Write down the issues.

3 Gather your group together and reveal, in turn, each member's comments on the three options. Next, reveal the ethical issues listed by each member.

4 Appoint someone to record main points of agreement and disagreement within the group. How do you explain the results? What accounts for any disagreement?

5 From an ethical standpoint, what does your group conclude is the most appropriate action that should have been taken by the Edda Corporation in this situation?

6 Develop a group response to the following question: Regardless of your current opinion of Lucy Shaw as a leader, what actions on her part now would cause you to think less of her as a leader? What actions would cause you to think more of her as a leader?

VIDEO EXERCISE   MyBizLab

Southwest

Learning Objectives

The purpose of this video is to help you:

1 Differentiate between task- and employee-focused behavior.

2 Identify the characteristics of transformational and charismatic leaders.

3 Describe the rational decision making process.

Synopsis

Southwest Airlines is a relative newcomer to the airline industry, having been around only 40 years. However, they are an industry leader in customer service, innovation, and price performance. In many ways, the organization reflects the values of its founders, Rollin King and Herb Kelleher. King and Kelleher were more than managers; they were leaders. Over the years, Southwest has demonstrated the ability to develop unique solutions to problems and to exceed the expectations of their customers and industry analysts. Many years ago, Southwest implemented an innovative solution to assigning seats to customers and loading the airplane. Rather than having reserved seating, customers were assigned to seating groups and allowed to select their seats as the entered the plane. Surprisingly, this method resulted in quicker turnaround times for planes and improved on-time performance. Over the years, this model has been modified to address customer concerns by continuing to evaluate every alternative and adopting innovative solutions.

DISCUSSION QUESTIONS

1 What is the difference between management and leadership? Does the CEO of Southwest need to be a manager, a leader, or both?

2 Managers may exhibit task- or employee-focused behavior. Describe the types of decisions or activities where managers at Southwest likely exhibit task-focused behavior.

3 Describe the types of decisions or activities where managers at Southwest likely exhibit employee-focused behavior.

4 How were Herb Kelleher and Rollin King transformational leaders? How was their style different from typical transactional leadership?

5 The rational decision making process can be describe as having six steps. List the six steps and describe how each step relates to Southwest's decision to have open seating.

Online Exploration

While most people visit Southwest's website www.southwest.com to book travel, the site is also a source of insight into the company and its culture. At the bottom of the home page, click on the link on the left for the company's mission statement. Do a little additional exploration to understand the company's values and culture. You should also read the message from the CEO, Gary Kelly. What does the company's website reveal about the leadership style at Southwest? Be sure to provide several specific examples.

END NOTES

[1] Geoffrey Colvin, "Catch a Rising Star," *Fortune*, February 6, 2006, http://money.cnn.com on March 15, 2011; Bill Gates, "How I Work," *Fortune*, April 7, 2006, http://money.cnn.com on March 15, 2011; Colvin, "Star Power," *Fortune*, January 30, 2006, http://money.cnn.com on March 15, 2011; Jerry Useem, "Making Your Work Work for You," *Fortune*, March 15, 2006, http://money.cnn.com on March 15, 2011.

[2] See John Kotter, "What Leaders Really Do," *Harvard Business Review*, December 2001, 85–94.

[3] David Gunzareth, "Murdoch, Rupert K.," The Museum of Broadcast Communications (May 27, 2008), at http://www.museum.tv/archives/etv/M/htmlM/murdochrupe/murdochrupe.htm; Johnnie L. Roberts, "Murdoch, Ink.," *Newsweek*, April 28, 2008 (May 27, 2008), at http://www

.newsweek.com/id/132852; BBC News, "Murdoch: I Decide Sun's Politics," November 24, 2007 (May 27, 2008), at http://news.bbc.co.uk/2/hi/uk_news/7110532.stm; Mark Jurkowitz, "How Different Is Murdoch's New *Wall Street Journal*?" April 23, 2008 (May 27, 2008), at http://journalism.org/node/10769; Richard Siklos and Andrew Ross Sorkin, "Murdoch on Owning the *Wall Street Journal*," *The New York Times*, May 4, 2007 (May 27, 2008), at http://www.nytimes.com/2007/05/04/business/media/04murdoch.html?pagewanted=print.

[4] David A. Waldman and Francis J. Yammarino, "CEO Charismatic Leadership: Levels-of-Management and Levels-of-Analysis Effects," *Academy of Management Review*, 1999, vol. 24, no. 2, 266–285.

[5] Jane Howell and Boas Shamir, "The Role of Followers in the Charismatic Leadership Process: Relationships and Their Consequences," *Academy of Management Review*, January 2005, 96–112.

[6] Clive Thompson, "The See-Through CEO," *Wired*, March 2007 (July 2, 2008), at http://www.wired.com/wired/archive/15.04/wired40_ceo.html.

[7] J. Richard Hackman and Ruth Wageman, "A Theory of Team Coaching," *Academy of Management Review*, April 2005, 269–287.

[8] "How Women Lead," *Newsweek*, October 24, 2005, 46–70.

[9] Steven Berglas, "What You Can Learn from Steve Jobs," http://www.inc.com; "Apple's Bold Swim Downstream," *BusinessWeek*, January 24, 2006, 32–35; "The Seed of Apple's Innovation," *BusinessWeek*, October 12, 2005, 86–87; Alan Deutschman, *The Second Coming of Steve Jobs* (New York: Broadway Publishing, 2001); Brent Schlender, "How Big Can Apple Get?" *Fortune*, February 21, 2005, 122–128; "Steve Jobs' Magic Kingdom," *BusinessWeek*, February 6, 2006, 62–69 (source of quote); Lev Grossman, "Invention of the Year: The iPhone," *Time*, October 31, 2007 (May 27, 2008), at http://www.time.com/time/business/article/0,8599,1678581,00.html.

[10] Jerry Useem, "Boeing vs. Boeing," *Fortune*, October 2, 2000, 148–160; "Airbus Prepares to 'Bet the Company' As It Builds a Huge New Jet," *Wall Street Journal*, November 3, 1999, A1, A10.

[11] "Accommodating the A380," *Wall Street Journal*, November 29, 2005, B1; "Boeing Roars Ahead," *BusinessWeek*, November 7, 2005, 44–45; "Boeing's New Tailwind," *Newsweek*, December 5, 2005, 45; Judith Crown, "Even More Boeing 787 Delays?" *BusinessWeek*, April 4, 2008 (May 27, 2008), at http://www.businessweek.com/bwdaily/dnflash/content/apr2008/db2008043_948354.htm?campaign_id=rss_daily; Aaron Karp, *ATW Daily News*, April 9, 2008 (May 27, 2008), at http://www.atwonline.com/news/story.html?storyID=12338; "Airbus: New Delays for A380 Deliveries," CNNMoney.com, May 13, 2008 (May 27, 2008), at http://money.cnn.com/2008/05/13/news/international/airbus_delay.ap/index.htm?postversion=2008051304; "Airbus A380 Delays Not Disclosed for Months," MSNBC.com, May 29, 2007 (May 27, 2008), at http://www.msnbc.msn.com/id/18918869/.

[12] "Making Decisions in Real Time," *Fortune*, June 26, 2000, 332–334; see also Malcolm Gladwell, *Blink* (New York: Little, Brown, 2005).

[13] Charles P. Wallace, "Adidas—Back in the Game," *Fortune*, August 18, 1997, 176–182.

[14] Barry M. Staw and Jerry Ross, "Good Money After Bad," *Psychology Today*, February 1988, 30–33; D. Ramona Bobocel and John Meyer, "Escalating Commitment to a Failing Course of Action: Separating the Roles of Choice and Justification," *Journal of Applied Psychology*, vol. 79, 1994, 360–363.

[15] Gerry McNamara and Philip Bromiley, "Risk and Return in Organizational Decision Making," *Academy of Management Journal*, vol. 42, 1999, 330–339.

[16] See Brian O'Reilly, "What It Takes to Start a Startup," *Fortune*, June 7, 1999, 135–140, for an example.

10 Human Resource Management and Labor Relations

A Unique Partnership Drives Nucor Steel

For the most part, the watchwords in U.S. business during the 2008–2010 recession were cutting payroll, reducing headcount, and eliminating jobs. But one company—Nucor, the country's largest steelmaker, still has *all* its jobs. Hit by a 50-percent plunge in output that had begun in September 2008, the U.S. steel industry had laid off some 10,000 workers by January 2009, and the United Steelworkers union was expecting the number to double before the recession came to an end. As of the end of 2010, however, Nucor had refused to follow suit in laying anyone off. At its 11 U.S. facilities, Nucor employees have been rewriting safety manuals, getting a head start on maintenance jobs, mowing the lawns, and cleaning the bathrooms—but they're still drawing paychecks. "Financially," says one employee at the company's facility in Crawfordsville, Indiana, "Nucor workers are still better off than most."

As far as top management is concerned, the company's ability to weather the recent economic crisis was based on several factors, most importantly, the firm's employees and culture. What's that culture like? It originated in the 1960s as the result of policies established by Ken Iverson, who brought a radical perspective on how to manage a company's human resources to the job of CEO. Iverson figured that workers would be much more productive if an employer went out

After reading this chapter, you should be able to:

1 Define *human resource management* and explain how managers plan for their organization's human resource needs.
2 Identify the tasks in staffing a company and discuss ways in which organizations select new employees.
3 Describe how managers develop the workforce in their organization through training and performance appraisal.
4 Describe the main components of a compensation system and describe some of the key legal issues involved in hiring, compensating, and managing workers in today's workplace.
5 Discuss the legal context of human resource management and identify the contemporary legal issues.
6 Discuss workforce diversity, the management of knowledge workers, and the use of a contingent workforce as important changes in the contemporary workplace.
7 Explain why workers organize into labor unions.
8 Describe the collective bargaining process.

of its way to share authority with them, respect what they accomplished, and compensate them as handsomely as possible. Today, the basics of the company's HR model are summed up in its "Employee Relations Principles":

1 Management is obligated to manage Nucor in such a way that employees will have the opportunity to earn according to their productivity.

2 Employees should feel confident that if they do their jobs properly, they will have a job tomorrow.

3 Employees have the right to be treated fairly and must believe that they will be.

4 Employees must have an avenue of appeal when they believe they are being treated unfairly.

The Iverson approach is based on motivation, and the key to that approach is a highly original

H. Mark Weidman Photography/Alamy

WHAT'S IN IT FOR ME?

Effectively managing human resources is the lifeblood of organizations. A firm that handles this activity has a much better chance for success than does a firm that simply goes through the motions. By understanding the material in this chapter, you'll be better able to understand (1) the importance of properly managing human resources in a unit or business you own or supervise and (2) why and how your employer provides the working arrangements that most directly affect you.

We start this chapter by explaining how managers plan for their organization's human resource needs. We'll also discuss ways in which organizations select, develop, and appraise employee performance and examine the main components of a compensation system. Along the way, we'll look at some key legal issues involved in hiring, compensating, and managing workers in today's workplace and discuss workforce diversity. Finally, we'll explain why workers organize into labor unions and describe the collective bargaining process. Let's get started with some basic concepts of human resource management.

MyBizLab Where you see MyBizLab in this chapter, go to www.mybizlab.com for additional activities on the topic being discussed.

pay system. Step 1, which calls for base pay below the industry average, probably doesn't seem like a promising start, but the Nucor compensation plan is designed to get better as the results of the work get better. If a shift, for example, can turn out a defect-free batch of steel, every worker is entitled to a bonus that's paid weekly and that can potentially triple his or her take-home pay. In addition, there are one-time annual bonuses and profit-sharing payouts. In 2005, for instance, Nucor had an especially good year: It shipped more steel than any other U.S. producer, and net income hit $1.3 billion, up from $311 million in 2000. The average steelworker took home $79,000 in base pay and weekly bonuses, plus a $2,000 year-end bonus and an average of $18,000 in profit-sharing money.

The system, however, cuts both ways. Take that defect-free batch of steel, for example. If there's a problem with a batch, workers on the shift obviously don't get any weekly bonus. And that's if they catch the problem before the batch leaves the plant. If it reaches the customer, they may *lose* up to three times what they would have received as a bonus. "In average-to-bad years," adds HR vice president James M. Coblin, "we earn less than our peers in other companies. That's supposed to teach us that we don't want to be average or bad. We want to be good." During fiscal 2009, total pay at Nucor was down by about 40 percent.

Everybody in the company, from janitors to the CEO, is covered by some form of incentive plan tied to various goals and targets. We've just described the Production Incentive Plan, which covers operating and maintenance workers and supervisors and which may boost base salaries by 80 percent to 150 percent. Bonuses for department managers are based on a return-on-assets formula tied to divisional performance, as are bonuses under the Non-Production and Non-Department–Manager Plan, which covers everyone, except senior officers, not included in either of the first two plans; bonuses under both manager plans may increase base pay by 75 percent to 90 percent. Senior officers don't work under contracts or get pension or retirement plans, and their base salaries are below industry average. In a world in which the typical CEO makes more than 400 times what a factory worker makes, Nucor's CEO makes considerably less. In the banner year of 2005, for example, his combined salary and bonus (about $2.3 million) came to 23 times the total taken home by the average Nucor factory worker. His bonus and those of other top managers are based on a ratio of net income to stockholder's equity.[1]

Our opening story continues on page 262.

The Foundations of Human Resource Management

1 Define *human resource management* and explain how managers plan for their organization's human resource needs.

Human resource management (HRM) is the set of organizational activities directed at attracting, developing, and maintaining an effective workforce.

The Strategic Importance of HRM

Human resources (or *personnel*, as the department is sometimes called) has a substantial impact on a firm's bottom-line performance. Consequently, the chief HR executive of most large businesses is a vice president directly accountable to the CEO, and many firms are developing strategic HR plans that are integrated with other strategic planning activities.

HR Planning

As you can see in Figure 10.1, the starting point in attracting qualified human resources is planning. Specifically, HR planning involves job analysis and forecasting the demand for, and supply of, labor.

MyBizLab

Gain hands-on experience through an interactive, real-world scenario. This chapter's simulation entitled Human Resource Management is located at www.mybizlab.com.

Job Analysis   **Job analysis** is a systematic analysis of jobs within an organization; most firms have trained experts who handle these analyses. A job analysis results in two things:

- The **job description** lists the duties and responsibilities of a job; its working conditions; and the tools, materials, equipment, and information used to perform it.
- The **job specification** lists the skills, abilities, and other credentials and qualifications needed to perform the job effectively.

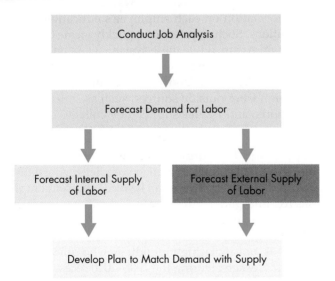

Figure 10.1 **The HR Planning Process**

Job analysis information is used in many HR activities. For instance, knowing about job content and job requirements is necessary to develop appropriate selection methods, to create job-relevant performance appraisal systems, and to set equitable compensation rates.

Forecasting HR Demand and Supply   After managers comprehend the jobs to be performed within an organization, they can start planning for the organization's future HR needs. The manager starts by assessing trends in past HR usage, future organizational plans, and general economic trends.

Forecasting the supply of labor is really two tasks:

1 Forecasting *internal supply*—the number and type of employees who will be in the firm at some future date.

2 Forecasting *external supply*—the number and type of people who will be available for hiring from the labor market at large.

Replacement Charts   At higher levels of an organization, managers plan for specific people and positions. The technique most commonly used is the **replacement chart,** which lists each important managerial position, who occupies it, how long that person will probably stay in it before moving on, and who is now qualified or soon will be qualified to move into it. (In most firms, of course, this information is computerized today.) This technique allows ample time to plan developmental experiences for people identified as potential successors for critical managerial jobs. Halliburton, for instance, has a detailed replacement system that the firm calls its Executive Succession System (ESS). When a manager has his or her performance reviewed each year, notations are placed in the system about the person's readiness for promotion, potential positions for promotion, and what development activities are needed in order to prepare the individual for promotion. Other managers throughout the firm can access the system whenever they have vacant positions available.

Skills Inventories   To facilitate both planning and identifying people for transfer or promotion, some organizations also have **employee information systems (skills inventories)** that contain information on each employee's education, skills, work experience, and career aspirations. Such a system can quickly locate every employee who is qualified to fill a position. Again, while these systems were once handled with charts and files they are almost always in electronic form today.

Forecasting the external supply of labor is a different problem altogether. Planners must rely on information from outside sources, such as state employment commissions, government reports, and figures supplied by colleges on the numbers of students in major fields.

Matching HR Supply and Demand   After comparing future demand and internal supply, managers can make plans to manage predicted shortfalls or overstaffing. If a shortfall is predicted, new employees can be hired, present employees can be retrained and transferred into understaffed areas, individuals approaching retirement can be convinced to stay on, or labor-saving or productivity-enhancing systems can be installed. If overstaffing is expected to be a problem, the main options are transferring the extra employees, not replacing individuals who quit, encouraging early retirement, and laying off workers. During the 2008–2010 recession, many firms found it necessary to reduce the size of their workforces through layoffs. Others accomplished the same thing by reducing the number of hours their employees worked.

2 Identify the tasks in staffing a company and discuss ways in which organizations select new employees.

Staffing the Organization

When managers have determined that new employees are needed, they must then turn their attention to recruiting and hiring the right mix of people. This involves two processes: acquiring staff from outside the company and promoting staff from within. Both external and internal staffing, however, start with effective *recruiting*.

Recruiting Human Resources

Recruiting is the process of attracting qualified persons to apply for the jobs that are open.

Internal Recruiting

Internal recruiting means considering present employees as candidates for openings. Promotion from within can help build morale and keep high-quality employees from leaving. For higher-level positions, a skills inventory system may be used to identify internal candidates, or managers may be asked to recommend individuals to be considered.

External Recruiting

External recruiting involves attracting people outside the organization to apply for jobs. External recruiting methods include posting jobs on the company website or other job sites, such as Monster.com; holding campus interviews for potential college recruits; using employment agencies or executive search firms to scout out potential talent; seeking referrals by present employees; advertising in print publications; and hiring "walk-ins" (unsolicited applicants).

Selecting Human Resources

Once the recruiting process has attracted a pool of applicants, the next step is to select someone to hire. The intent of the selection process is to gather from applicants the information that will predict job success and then to hire the candidates likely to be most successful.

Application Forms

The first step in selection is usually asking the candidate to fill out an application. An application form is an efficient method of gathering information about the applicant's previous work history, educational background, and other job-related demographic data. Application forms are seldom used for upper-level jobs; candidates for such positions usually provide the same information on their résumé. Most applications for larger firms are now prepared electronically and submitted at the firm's website.

Tests

Employers sometimes ask candidates to take tests during the selection process. Tests of ability, skill, aptitude, or knowledge relevant to a particular job are usually the best predictors of job success, although tests of general intelligence or personality are occasionally useful as well. Some companies use a test of the "big five" personality dimensions discussed in Chapter 8 to predict success.

Interviews

Interviews are a very popular selection device, although they are sometimes a poor predictor of job success. For example, biases inherent in the way people perceive and judge others on first meeting affect subsequent evaluations. Interview validity can be improved by training interviewers to be aware of potential biases and by tightening the structure of the interview. In a structured interview, questions are written in advance, and all interviewers follow the same question list with each candidate. For interviewing managerial or professional candidates, a somewhat less structured approach can be used. Although question areas and information-gathering objectives are still planned in advance, specific questions vary with the candidates' backgrounds. Sometimes, companies are looking for especially creative employees and may try to learn more about the individual's creativity during an interview.

Replacement Chart list of each management position, who occupies it, how long that person will likely stay in the job, and who is qualified as a replacement

Employee Information System (Skills Inventory) computerized system containing information on each employee's education, skills, work experiences, and career aspirations

Recruiting process of attracting qualified persons to apply for jobs an organization is seeking to fill

Internal Recruiting considering present employees as candidates for openings

External Recruiting attracting persons outside the organization to apply for jobs

ENTREPRENEURSHIP AND NEW VENTURES

Moving People to Move Movies

Selling movies to consumers is a dynamic and challenging industry today. The market is evolving so rapidly that even the basic business model, product, and technology are unresolved. Is streaming media the right way to deliver content? Are movies best viewed on a television, PC monitor, PDA, or cell phone? Should the consumer rent the content or own it? What is the role of advertising? Netflix is one of the companies at the forefront of addressing these questions.

In order to cope with the many complex issues the company faces, Netflix CEO and founder Reed Hastings recruited a team of top performers in fields as diverse as marketing, content management, and website operations. Then the company had to find a way to motivate these stars to fulfill their potential. Netflix uses monetary rewards as a motivator. "We're unafraid to pay high," says Hastings. However, the company achieves its greatest results by focusing on employee needs.

One important set of needs that Netflix fulfills is the desire to work with friends, be part of a team, and belong. Employees recommend people they've enjoyed working with at other jobs. The atmosphere is casual and collaborative. However, the company avoids patronizing its employees. As Michelle Conlin of *BusinessWeek* puts it, "Netflix is no frat party with beer bashes and foosball tables." The Netflix values statement says, "The benefit of a high-performance culture is that you work with consistently outstanding colleagues, which is exhilarating. We're a high-performance team, not a family. A strong family is together forever, no matter what. A strong company, on the other hand, is more like a professional sports team, which is built to win."[2]

Netflix works to fulfill employees' needs for esteem by providing an employer that is well liked. The job pages of the company's website say, "It is satisfying to work at a company that people love. We're ranked number one in customer satisfaction across the entire Internet, narrowly besting such great companies as Apple and Amazon."

Another set of fulfilled needs is related to employees' passion to achieve. The "best in class" personnel at this firm of just 400 workers are attracted by the opportunity to have a significant impact on a successful and ever-changing company. Before founding Netflix, Hastings started Pure Software. At first the start-up was an exciting place to work, but it became more humdrum and bureaucratic as it grew. When Pure was sold to IBM, Hastings vowed to never repeat that mistake. The Netflix values statement summarizes Hastings's viewpoint, saying, "Rules inhibit creativity and entrepreneurship, leading to a lack of innovation. Our solution to increased complexity is to increase talent density. Great people make great judgment calls, despite ambiguity. We believe in freedom and responsibility, not rules."

Clearly, the Netflix motivation scheme is not for everyone. "At most companies, average performers get an average raise," says Hastings. "At Netflix, they get a generous severance package." However, the company is doing a good job of motivating stellar workers. Netflix is depending on wringing maximum performance from those workers to win competitive advantage over top competitors such as Apple, Blockbuster, and Amazon.

MyBizLab

Michael Tercha/MCT/Newscom

Other Techniques Organizations also use other selection techniques that vary with circumstances. Polygraph tests, once popular, are declining in popularity. On the other hand, organizations occasionally require applicants to take physical exams (being careful that their practices are consistent with the Americans with Disabilities Act). More organizations are using drug tests, especially in situations in which drug-related performance problems could create serious safety hazards. Some organizations also run credit checks on prospective employees. Reference checks with previous employers are also used, but have been shown to have limited value because individuals are likely to only provide the names of references that will give them positive recommendations.

Developing the Workforce

3 Describe how managers develop the workforce in their organization through training and performance appraisal.

After a company has hired new employees, it must acquaint them with the firm and their new jobs. Managers also take steps to train employees and to further develop necessary job skills. In addition, every firm has some system for performance appraisal and feedback.

Training

As its name suggests, **on-the-job training** occurs while an employee is at work. **Off-the-job training** takes place at locations away from a work site. This approach offers a controlled environment and allows focused study without interruptions. Training is a necessary practice if the organization wants to maintain a qualified and effective workforce. Moreover, many employees see training as a benefit—it allows them to keep their job skills current and to learn new skills to prepare them for the jobs of tomorrow.

A variation of off-site training is **vestibule training,** which takes place in simulated work environments that make the off-the-job training more realistic; increasingly, these simulations are computerized or web-based. American Airlines, for example, trains flight attendants at a vestibule training site that resembles the interior cabin of an airplane; it also uses simulation software to help acquaint its pilots with new instrumentation that is added to its aircraft.[3]

Performance Appraisal

Performance appraisals are designed to show workers precisely how well they are doing their jobs. Typically, the appraisal process involves a written assessment issued on a regular basis. As a rule, however, the written evaluation is only one part of a multistep process.

The appraisal process begins when a manager defines performance standards for an employee. The manager then observes the employee's performance. For some jobs, a rating scale like the abbreviated one in Figure 10.2 is useful in providing a basis for comparison. Comparisons drawn from such scales form the basis for written appraisals and for decisions about raises, promotions, demotions, and firings. The process is completed when the manager and employee meet to discuss the appraisal.

Compensation and Benefits

4 Describe the main components of a compensation system and describe some of the key legal issues involved in hiring, compensating, and managing workers in today's workplace.

People who work for a business expect to be paid, and most workers today also expect certain benefits from their employers. Indeed, a major factor in retaining skilled workers is a company's **compensation system**—the total package of rewards that it offers employees in return for their labor. Finding the right combination of compensation elements is always complicated by the need to make employees feel valued, while holding down company costs.

On-the-Job Training training, sometimes informal, conducted while an employee is at work

Off-the-Job Training training conducted in a controlled environment away from the work site

Vestibule Training off-the-job training conducted in a simulated environment

Performance Appraisal evaluation of an employee's job performance in order to determine the degree to which the employee is performing effectively

Compensation System total package of rewards that organizations provide to individuals in return for their labor

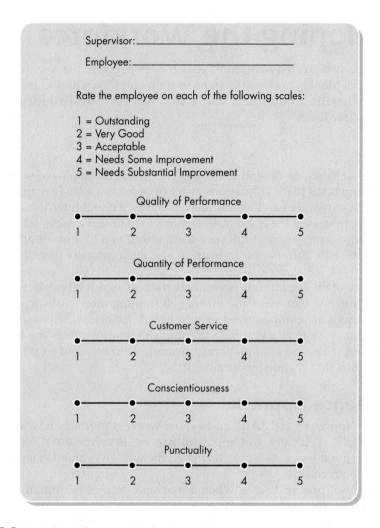

Figure 10.2 **Sample Performance Evaluation Form**

Wages and Salaries

Wages and salaries are the dollar amounts paid to employees for their labor. **Wages** are paid for time worked; for example, if your job pays you $8 an hour, that is your wage. A **salary,** on the other hand, is paid for performing a job. A salaried executive earning $100,000 per year is paid to achieve results even if that means working 5 hours one day and 15 the next. Salaries are usually expressed as an amount paid per month or year.

In setting wage and salary levels, a company may start by looking at its competitors' levels. Firms must also decide how their internal wage and salary levels will compare for different jobs. Although two employees may do exactly the same job, the employee with more experience may earn more.

The recession of 2008–2010 prompted some firms to reduce the wages and salaries they were paying in order to lower costs. For example, Hewlett-Packard reduced the salaries of all but its top performers by amounts ranging from 2.5 to 20 percent. CareerBuilder.com reduced all employee pay but also began giving all employees Friday afternoons off.

Incentive Programs

As we discussed in Chapter 8, studies have shown that beyond a certain point, more money will not produce better performance. Money motivates employees only if it is tied directly to performance. The most common method of establishing this link is the use of **incentive programs**—special pay programs designed to motivate high performance. Some programs are available to individuals, whereas others are distributed on a companywide basis.

Individual Incentives

A sales bonus is a typical incentive. Employees receive a **bonus**—special payments above their salaries—when they sell a certain number or certain dollar amount of goods for the year. Employees who fail to reach this goal earn no bonuses. **Merit salary systems** link pay raises to performance levels in nonsales jobs.

Executives commonly receive stock options as incentives. Halliburton CEO David Lesar, for example, can buy several thousand shares of company stock each year at a predetermined price. If his managerial talent leads to higher profits and stock prices, he can buy the stock at a price lower than the market value for which, in theory, he is largely responsible. He is then free to sell the stock at market price, keeping the profits for himself.

A newer incentive plan is called **pay for performance** (or **variable pay**). In essence, middle managers are rewarded for especially productive output—for producing earnings that significantly exceed the cost of bonuses. The number of variable pay programs in the United States has been growing consistently for the last decade, and most experts predict that they will continue to grow in popularity. Many firms say that variable pay is a better motivator than merit raises because the range between generous and mediocre merit raises is usually quite small.

Companywide Incentives

Some incentive programs apply to all the employees in a firm. Under **profit-sharing plans,** for example, profits earned above a certain level are distributed to employees. Also, **gainsharing plans** distribute bonuses to employees when a company's costs are reduced through greater work efficiency. **Pay-for-knowledge plans** pay workers to learn new skills and to become proficient at different jobs.

Benefits Programs

Benefits—compensation other than wages and salaries and other incentives offered by a firm to its workers—account for an increasing percentage of most compensation budgets. Most companies are required by law to pay tax for Social Security retirement benefits and provide **workers' compensation insurance** (insurance for compensating workers injured on the job). Most businesses also provide health, life, and disability insurance for their workers, as well as paid time off for vacations and holidays. Many also allow employees to use payroll deductions to buy stock at discounted prices. Counseling services for employees with alcohol, drug, or emotional problems are also becoming more common, as are on-site child-care centers. Some companies even provide reduced membership fees at gyms and health clubs, as well as insurance or other protection for identity theft.[4]

Retirement Plans

Retirement plans (or pension plans) constitute another important—and sometimes controversial—benefit that is available to many

---

Wages compensation in the form of money paid for time worked

Salary compensation in the form of money paid for discharging the responsibilities of a job

Incentive Program special compensation program designed to motivate high performance

Bonus individual performance incentive in the form of a special payment made over and above the employee's salary

Merit Salary System individual incentive linking compensation to performance in nonsales jobs

Pay for Performance (Variable Pay) individual incentive that rewards a manager for especially productive output

Profit-Sharing Plan incentive plan for distributing bonuses to employees when company profits rise above a certain level

Gainsharing Plan incentive plan that rewards groups for productivity improvements

Pay-for-Knowledge Plan incentive plan to encourage employees to learn new skills or become proficient at different jobs

Benefits compensation other than wages and salaries

Workers' Compensation Insurance legally required insurance for compensating workers injured on the job

employees. Most company-sponsored retirement plans are set up to pay pensions to workers when they retire. In some cases, the company contributes all the money to the pension fund. In others, contributions are made by both the company and employees. In recent years, some companies have run into problems because they have not set aside enough money to cover the retirement funds they have agreed to provide. Both FedEx and Goodyear, for instance, recently announced that they were freezing their pension programs in order to transition workers to riskier 401(k)s, in which payroll deductions are invested in stocks and other non-guaranteed funds.[5] This trend increased during the 2008–2010 recession. For example, 16 major U.S. employers stopped contributing to employee retirement accounts, and several more followed suit in 2010. Among these were Anheuser-Busch, Wells-Fargo, and Saks.

Containing the Costs of Benefits   As the range of benefits has increased, so has concern about containing the costs of these benefits. Many companies are experimenting with cost-cutting plans while still attracting and retaining valuable employees. One approach is the **cafeteria benefits plan.** A certain dollar amount of benefits per employee is set aside so that each employee can choose from a variety of alternatives.

Another area of increasing concern is health care costs. Medical expenses have increased insurance premiums, which have increased the cost to employers of maintaining benefits plans. Many employers are looking for new ways to cut those costs. One increasingly popular approach is for organizations to create their own networks of health care providers. These providers agree to charge lower fees for services rendered to employees of member organizations. In return, they enjoy established relationships with large employers and, thus, more clients and patients. Insurers also charge less to cover the employees of network members because they make lower reimbursement payments.

The Legal Context of HRM

5 Discuss the legal context of human resource management and identify the contemporary legal issues.

Federal law and judicial review heavily influence HRM as much or more than any area of business. In this section, we summarize some of the most important and far-reaching areas of HR regulation.

Equal Employment Opportunity

The basic goal of all **equal employment opportunity** regulation is to protect people from unfair or inappropriate discrimination in the workplace.[6] Let's begin by noting that discrimination in itself is not illegal. Whenever one person is given a pay raise and another is not, for example, the organization has made a decision to distinguish one person from another. As long as the basis for this discrimination is purely job related (made, for example, on the basis of performance or seniority) and is applied objectively and consistently, the action is legal and appropriate. Problems arise when distinctions among people are not job related. In such cases, the resulting discrimination is illegal.

Protected Classes in the Workplace   To combat illegal discrimination, laws have been passed to protect various classes of individuals. A **protected class** consists of all individuals who share one or more common characteristics as indicated by a given law. The most common criteria for defining protected classes include race, color, religion, gender, age, national origin, disability status, and status as a military veteran.[7] One recent illustration of this protection is the Americans with Disabilities Act of 1990. This law requires employers to not discriminate on the basis of physical limitations and to provide reasonable work-related modifications to help disabled individuals do their jobs.

Enforcing Equal Employment Opportunity The enforcement of equal opportunity legislation is handled by two agencies. The **Equal Employment Opportunity Commission (EEOC)** is a division of the Department of Justice. It was created by

Title VII of the 1964 Civil Rights Act and has specific responsibility for enforcing Title VII, the Equal Pay Act, and the Americans with Disabilities Act.

The other agency charged with monitoring equal employment opportunity legislation is the *Office of Federal Contract Compliance Programs (OFCCP)*. The OFCCP is responsible for enforcing executive orders that apply to companies doing business with the federal government. A business with government contracts must have on file a written **affirmative action plan**—that is, a written statement of how the organization intends to actively recruit, hire, and develop members of relevant protected classes.

Legal Issues in Compensation   As noted earlier, most employment regulations are designed to provide equal employment opportunity. Some legislation, however, deals with other issues such as compensation. For example, the Fair Labor Standards Act (passed in 1938) established a minimum hourly wage, whereas the Employee Retirement Income Security Act of 1974 sets standards by which companies must manage pension funds.

Contemporary Legal Issues in HRM

In addition to these established areas of HR legal regulation, several emerging legal issues will likely become more important in the future. These include employee safety and health, various emerging areas of discrimination law, employee rights, and employment at will.

Employee Safety and Health   The **Occupational Safety and Health Act of 1970 (OSHA)** is the single most comprehensive piece of legislation ever passed regarding worker safety and health. OSHA holds that every employer has an obligation to furnish each employee with a place of employment that is free from hazards that cause or are likely to cause death or physical harm. It is generally enforced through inspections of the workplace by OSHA inspectors. Serious or willful and repeated violations may incur fines up to $10,000 per incident.

Emerging Areas of Discrimination Law   Managers must also be familiar with several emerging areas of discrimination law.

AIDS in the Workplace   Although AIDS is considered a disability under the Americans with Disabilities Act of 1990, the AIDS situation itself is severe enough that it warrants special attention. Employers cannot legally require an HIV test or any other medical examination as a condition for making an offer of employment. Organizations must accommodate or make a good-faith effort to accommodate individuals with HIV, maintain the confidentiality of all medical records, and try to educate coworkers about AIDS.

Sexual Harassment   **Sexual harassment** is defined by the EEOC as unwelcome sexual advances in the work environment. If the conduct is indeed unwelcome and occurs with sufficient frequency to create an abusive work environment, the employer is responsible for changing the environment by warning, reprimanding, or perhaps firing the harasser.[8]

Cafeteria Benefits Plan benefit plan that sets limits on benefits per employee, each of whom may choose from a variety of alternative benefits

Equal Employment Opportunity legally mandated nondiscrimination in employment on the basis of race, creed, sex, or national origin

Protected Class set of individuals who by nature of one or more common characteristics is protected under the law from discrimination on the basis of that characteristic

Equal Employment Opportunity Commission (EEOC) federal agency enforcing several discrimination-related laws

Affirmative Action Plan written statement of how the organization intends to actively recruit, hire, and develop members of relevant protected classes

Occupational Safety and Health Act of 1970 (OSHA) federal law setting and enforcing guidelines for protecting workers from unsafe conditions and potential health hazards in the workplace

Sexual Harassment making unwelcome sexual advances in the workplace

MANAGING IN TURBULENT TIMES

In Good Times and Bad

Sometimes the worst brings out the best in both people and businesses. When Hurricane Katrina struck the Gulf Coast in 2005, for instance, millions of people lost everything they had, and to make matters worse, the response of the federal government was fraught with bureaucratic blundering. Fortunately, many businesses stepped forward to come to the aid of Katrina victims. Dozens of companies, including Apple, Citigroup, Enterprise Rent-a-Car, and the Gap, made contributions of $1 million, and some gave much more, with Wal-Mart's $17 million topping the list.

Some employers made funds available to match employee contributions, and other firms donated goods or services. Abbott donated infant formula, and AT&T donated calling cards. Clorox supplied 50,000 gallons of bleach to aid in removing mold. Albertson's donated $9 million in food, and pharmaceutical firms furnished medicines. Some companies made more unusual offers. A few banks, for example, offered home equity loans, even for homes that weren't habitable. DIRECTV launched a Hurricane Katrina information channel. KB Home, a national builder, committed to building thousands of new houses.

The outpouring of support went a long way toward helping New Orleans residents and other Gulf Coast residents rebuild shattered lives. That support, however, took forms other than corporate financial resources: In many cases, it took the form of corporate human resources. Consider the response of Entergy, the country's third-largest electric utility, which serves 2.7 million customers in the Gulf Coast region. When Katrina hit, more than 1 million Entergy customers were left without power—including 1,500 Entergy employees. CEO Wayne Leonard immediately began organizing repair efforts, but his goal was to restore more than electricity. Leonard firmly believes that he and his employees "do a lot more than make electricity and money. We cool [people's] homes in the summer and warm their homes in the winter. We allow people to cook their food. We clean the environment and educate their children."

Using optimistic (and sometimes emotional) e-mails, Leonard motivated Entergy employees by appealing to a company culture based on his conviction that the people who work for an organization "want to know that what they do makes a difference." "We have a great passion for the difference we make in other people's lives," he told his workforce." "We provide a commodity that sustains life." Working 16-hour days, Entergy crews had restored power to 550,000 people by the end of the first week, and by the end of September, nearly every Entergy customer had electricity. In the third week of September, when Hurricane Rita followed hard on the heels of Katrina, knocking out power to 750,000 customers, Entergy employees—many of whom had

Jeff Greenberg/Alamy

barely had time to check up on their own families—were back at work with the same levels of commitment and teamwork.

Employees were also a major focus of disaster response at the Domino Sugar refinery located in St. Bernard Parish, east of New Orleans. Virtually the entire parish was flooded, leaving most of the plant's 332 employees homeless. At the refinery itself, floodwaters melted 6.5 million pounds of sugar into huge lakes of sugar syrup. Because 19 percent of the nation's sugar supply comes through the St. Bernard facility, it was imperative for officials to get it up and running again as quickly as possible. "We can fix anything," says VP for operations Mickey Seither. "We can rebuild everything. But," he adds, "if we don't have employees, it's for naught." From the outset, Seither recalls, "we decided the one thing we have to really concentrate on is fixing the situation that our employees are in."

So Domino managed to get 200 mobile homes from the Federal Emergency Management Agency within two weeks and immediately set up a mobile home park on the grounds of the refinery. Other companies in the area also set up mobile home parks, but Domino was the only employer to house employees' families as well. Not every household was comfortable, but each mobile home had hot water and a microwave for cooking. Said one worker who lived in 28-foot mobile home with his wife and five children, "We, as employees, appreciate it because, if not, we'd be ... at my brother-in-law's house with 15 people." Within 6 months, the refinery was operating at nearly full capacity, providing 300 well-paying jobs and working to function as a catalyst for further recovery in the parish. During the entire period, according to the company, not one employee lost an hour of pay.

MyBizLab

The courts have defined two types of sexual harassment:

1 In cases of **quid pro quo harassment**, the harasser offers to exchange something of value for sexual favors. A male supervisor, for example, might tell or suggest to a female subordinate that he will recommend her for promotion or give her a raise in exchange for sexual favors.

2 The creation of a **hostile work environment** is a subtler form of sexual harassment. A group of male employees who continually make off-color jokes and lewd comments and perhaps decorate the work environment with inappropriate photographs may create a hostile work environment for a female colleague, who may become uncomfortable working in that environment.

In recent years, the concept of harassment has been expanded to encompass unwelcome or inappropriate behaviors regarding ethnicity, religion, and age.

Employment at Will The concept of **employment at will** holds that both employer and employee have the mutual right to terminate an employment relationship at any time for any reason, with or without advance notice to the other. Over the last two decades, however, terminated employees have challenged the employment-at-will doctrine by filing lawsuits against former employers on the grounds of wrongful discharge.

In the last several years, such suits have put limits on employment-at-will provisions in certain circumstances. In the past, for example, organizations were guilty of firing employees who filed workers' compensation claims or took "excessive" time off to serve on jury duty. More recently, however, the courts have ruled that employees may not be fired for exercising rights protected by law.

The Patriot Act In response to the terrorist attacks of September 11, 2001, the U.S. government passed legislation that increases its powers to investigate and prosecute suspected terrorists. This legislation, known as the Patriot Act, has several key implications for HRM. For instance, certain "restricted" individuals (including ex-convicts and aliens from countries deemed by the State Department to have "repeatedly provided support for acts of international terrorism") are ineligible to work with potentially dangerous biological agents. More controversial are sections granting government investigators access to previously confidential personal and financial records.

New Challenges in the Changing Workplace

6 Discuss workforce diversity, the management of knowledge workers, and the use of a contingent workforce as important changes in the contemporary workplace.

In addition to the challenges we have already considered, HR managers face several new challenges reflecting the changing economic and social environments of business.

Managing Workforce Diversity

One extremely important set of HR challenges centers on **workforce diversity**—the range of workers' attitudes, values, beliefs, and behaviors that differ by gender, race, age, ethnicity, physical ability, and other relevant characteristics. In the past, organizations tended to work toward homogenizing their workforces, getting everyone to think and behave in similar ways. Partly as a result of affirmative action efforts, however, many U.S. organizations are now creating more diverse workforces than ever before.

Quid Pro Quo Harassment form of sexual harassment in which sexual favors are requested in return for job-related benefits

Hostile Work Environment form of sexual harassment deriving from off-color jokes, lewd comments, and so forth

Employment at Will principle, increasingly modified by legislation and judicial decision, that organizations should be able to retain or dismiss employees at their discretion

Workforce Diversity the range of workers' attitudes, values, beliefs, and behaviors that differ by gender, race, age, ethnicity, physical ability, and other relevant characteristics

Figure 10.3 Distribution of the labor force by race 1990-2050
Source: http://www.dol.gov/asp/media/reports/workforce2007/ADW2007_Full_Text.pdf (p. 38). U.S. Department of Labor, "America's Dynamic Workforce," (August 2007), p. 38, at http://www.dol.gov/asp/media/reports/workforce2007/ADW2007_Full_Text.pdf.

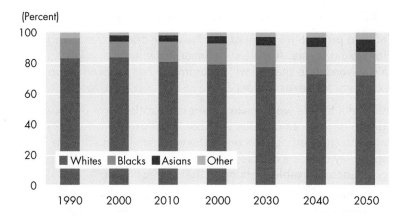

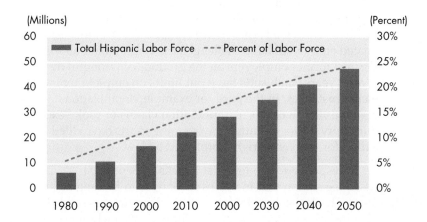

Figure 10.3 projects the racial and ethnic composition of the U.S. workforce through 2050. The picture is clearly one of increasing diversity. The number of white Americans as a percentage of the total workforce is declining steadily, offset by increases in every other racial group. Most striking are the growing numbers of people of Hispanic origin (who may be members of any racial group). By 2050 the U.S. Department of Labor estimates that nearly a quarter of the workforce will be Hispanic.

Today, organizations are recognizing that diversity can be a competitive advantage. For example, by hiring the best people available from every single group rather than hiring from just one or a few groups, a firm can develop a higher-quality labor force. Similarly, a diverse workforce can bring a wider array of information to bear on problems and can provide insights on marketing products to a wider range of consumers.

Managing Knowledge Workers

Traditionally, employees added value to organizations because of what they did or because of their experience. In the information age, however, many employees add value because of what they *know*.

The Nature of Knowledge Work   Employees who add value because of what they know are usually called **knowledge workers.** Knowledge workers—including computer scientists, engineers, physical scientists, and game developers—typically require extensive and highly specialized training; once they are on the job, retraining and training updates are critical to prevent their skills from becoming obsolete. It has been suggested, for example, that the half-life of a technical education in engineering is about three years.

A firm's failure to update the skills of its knowledge workers will not only result in the loss of competitive advantage, it will also increase the likelihood that those workers will go to other firms that are more committed to updating their skills. Hence, HR managers must ensure that the proper training is prepared to enable knowledge workers to stay current while also making sure they are compensated at market rates.

Contingent and Temporary Workers

A final contemporary HR issue of note involves the growing use of contingent and temporary workers. Many employers use contingent and temporary workers to increase their flexibility and, in most cases, lower their costs.

Trends in Contingent and Temporary Employment   A **contingent worker** is a person who works for an organization on something other than a permanent or full-time basis. Categories of contingent workers include independent contractors, on-call workers, temporary employees (usually hired through outside agencies), and contract and leased employees. Another category is part-time workers. In recent years there has been an explosion in the use of such workers by organizations. For instance, in 2010 about 12 percent of employed U.S. workers fell into one of these categories, up from 10 percent in 2008.

Managing Contingent and Temporary Workers   One key to managing contingent workers effectively is careful planning and analysis. Rather than having to call in workers sporadically, and with no prior notice, organizations try to bring in specified numbers of workers for well-defined periods of time. Firms should also be able to document the labor-cost savings of using contingent workers.

A second key is recognizing what can and cannot be achieved by using contingent and temporary workers. For instance, these workers may lack the firm-specific knowledge to perform as effectively as a permanent employee would perform. They are also less committed to the organization and less likely to engage in organizational citizenship behaviors.

Finally, managers must make decisions about how to integrate contingent workers into the organization. These decisions may be as simple as whether to invite contingent workers to the holiday party, or they may be more complicated, such as whether to grant contingent workers access to such employee benefits as counseling services and child care.

Dealing with Organized Labor

7 Explain why workers organize into labor unions.

A **labor union** is a group of individuals working together to achieve shared job-related goals, such as higher pay, shorter working hours, more job security, greater benefits, or better working conditions. **Labor relations** refers to the process of dealing with employees who are represented by a union.

Unionism Today

In the years immediately following World War II and continuing through the mid-1960s, most unions routinely won certification elections. In recent years, however, labor unions have been winning certification less than 50 percent of the times that workers are called upon to vote. As a result, although millions of workers still belong

Knowledge Workers employees who are of value because of the knowledge they possess

Contingent Worker employee hired on something other than a full-time basis to supplement an organization's permanent workforce

Labor Union group of individuals working together to achieve shared job-related goals, such as higher pay, shorter working hours, more job security, greater benefits, or better working conditions

Labor Relations process of dealing with employees who are represented by a union

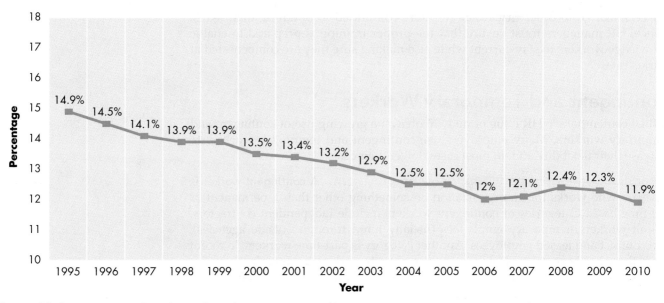

Figure 10.4 **Percentage of Workers Who Belong to Unions: 1995–2010**
Source: U.S. Department of Labor, Bureau of Labor Statistics, www.aflcio.org/joinaunion/why/uniondifference/uniondiff11.cfm.

to unions, union membership as a percentage of the total workforce has steadily declined. In 2007, only 12.1 percent of U.S. workers belonged to a labor union, down from 20.1 percent in 1983, when the U.S. Department of Labor first began compiling data.[9] As the recession of 2008–2010 began to increase fears about unemployment and wage cuts, union membership began to increase again, albeit only slightly. By 2010 it had dropped again, falling below pre-recession levels. These trends are shown in Figure 10.4.

The Future of Unions   Even though several of its members withdrew from the parent organization in 2005, the American Federation of Labor and Congress of Industrial Organizations (AFL-CIO), as well as independent major unions such as the Teamsters and the National Education Association (NEA), still play a major role in U.S. business. Unions in the traditional strongholds of goods-producing industries continue to wield considerable power as well. The United Auto Workers (UAW) was for decades one of the largest unions in the United States. But it, too, seems to be entering a period of decline. The traumas experienced by the U.S. auto industry in 2008–2009, for instance, required the UAW to make many major concessions in order to help Ford, DaimlerChrysler, and General Motors survive. In addition, auto plant closures will dramatically reduce the number of auto jobs in the years to come.

Another issue affecting the future of unionism is the geographic shift in the U.S. economy. For the most part unionism in the United States started in the north and midwest regions and in cities like Detroit, Pittsburgh, Cleveland, St. Louis, and Chicago. But over the past several decades there has been a pronounced shift as businesses have moved their operations to the south and southwest, areas that do not have a strong union heritage. For instance, Nucor Steel, profiled in our opening case, locates its facilities in smaller communities in the southern United States in part because it knows these workers are not prone to unionization.

8 Describe the collective bargaining process.

Collective Bargaining

The power of unions comes from collective action—forcing management to listen to the demands of all workers rather than to just the few who speak out. **Collective bargaining** is the process by which labor and management negotiate conditions of employment for union-represented workers and draft a labor contract.

Reaching Agreement on Contract Terms

The collective bargaining process begins when the union is recognized as the exclusive negotiator for its members and union leaders meet with management representatives to agree on a contract. By law, both parties must sit down at the bargaining table and negotiate in good faith. Figure 10.5 shows what is called the "bargaining zone." For instance, in theory employers want to pay as little as possible; they will generally pay more than the minimum, but there is also some upper limit beyond which they will not pay. Likewise, unions want the highest pay possible but expect to get less. But they too have a limit beyond which they will not go.

For example, suppose the barganing issue is pay increases. The employer may initially propose a pay increase of 2 percent but (secretly) be willing to offer up to 6 percent. However, under no circumstances can it afford to pay more than 8 percent. The union, meanwhile, may initially demand a 10 percent increase but (secretly) be willing to accept as little as 4 percent. Assuming each party negotiates in good faith and is willing to make concessions to the other, the real bargaining zone falls between the union minimum (4 percent) and the employer maximum (6 percent). The real outcome will then depend on such things as other items being negotiated and the skills of the respective negotiators.

Sometimes, this process goes quite smoothly. At other times, the two sides cannot agree. For instance, the example above should result in an agreement since the union minimum and the employer maximum provide a bargaining zone. But if the union demands no less than, say 8 percent and the employer is unwilling to give more than a 4 percent increase, there is no bargaining zone. Resolving the impasse depends in part on the nature of the contract issues, the willingness of each side to use certain tactics, such as strikes, and the prospects for mediation or arbitration.

Contract Issues

The labor contract itself can address an array of different issues. Issues that are typically most important to union negotiators include *compensation*, *benefits*, and *job security*. Certain management rights, such as control over hiring policies and work

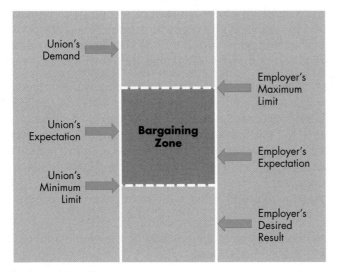

Figure 10.5 **The Bargaining Zone**

Collective Bargaining process by which labor and management negotiate conditions of employment for union-represented workers

assignments, are also negotiated in most bargaining agreements. Other possible issues might include such specific details as working hours, overtime policies, rest period arrangements, differential pay plans for shift employees, the use of temporary workers, grievance procedures, and allowable union activities (dues collection, union bulletin boards, and so forth).

Compensation   Compensation includes both current and future wages. One common tool for securing wage increases is a **cost-of-living adjustment (COLA)**. Most COLA clauses tie future raises to the *Consumer Price Index (CPI)*, a government statistic that reflects changes in consumer purchasing power. Almost half of all labor contracts today include COLA clauses.

A union might be uncomfortable with a long-term contract based solely on COLA wage increases. One solution is a **wage reopener clause,** which allows wage rates to be renegotiated at preset times during the life of the contract.

Benefits   Employee benefits are also an important component in most labor contracts. Unions typically want employers to pay all or most of the costs of insurance for employees. Other benefits commonly addressed during negotiations include retirement benefits, paid holidays, and working conditions. Due to surging health care costs, employee health insurance premiums have become a major point of contention in recent years. For example, many employees have much larger co-pays today when they visit their doctor than was the case a few years ago. (A *co-pay* is the dollar amount a patient pays to the doctor; insurance then pays the remainder.)

Job Security   Job security also remains an important agenda item in many bargaining sessions today. In some cases, a contract may dictate that if the workforce is reduced, seniority will be used to determine which employees keep their jobs. Unions are setting their sights on preserving jobs for workers in the United States in the face of business efforts to outsource production in some sectors to countries where labor costs are cheaper. For example, the AFL-CIO has been an outspoken opponent of efforts to normalize trade relations with China, fearing that more businesses might be tempted to move jobs there to take advantage of lower wage levels.

When Bargaining Fails

An impasse occurs when, after a series of bargaining sessions, management and labor have failed to agree on a new contract or a contract to replace an agreement that is about to expire. Although it is generally agreed that both parties suffer when an impasse is reached and some action by one part against the other is taken, each side can use several tactics to support its cause until the impasse is resolved.

Union Tactics   Historically, one of the most common union tactics has been the **strike,** which occurs when employees temporarily walk off the job and refuse to work. The number of major strikes in the U.S. has steadily declined over the past few decades. From 1960 to 1980, for example, an average of 281 strikes occurred per year. In the 1980s there was an average of 83 major strikes per year; in the 1990s this figure fell to an average of 35 per year. And between 2000 and 2009 there was an average of 20 major strikes per year.[10]

To support a strike, a union faced with an impasse has recourse to additional legal activities:

- In **picketing,** workers march at the entrance to the employer's facility with signs explaining their reasons for striking.

- A **boycott** occurs when union members agree not to buy the products of a targeted employer. Workers may also urge consumers to boycott the firm's products.

- Another alternative to striking is a **work slowdown.** Instead of striking, workers perform their jobs at a much slower pace than normal. A variation is the *sickout,* during which large numbers of workers call in sick.

Management Tactics   Like workers, management can respond forcefully to an impasse with the following:

- **Lockouts** occur when employers deny employees access to the workplace. Lockouts are illegal if they are used as offensive weapons to give management a bargaining advantage. However, they are legal if management has a legitimate business need (for instance, avoiding a buildup of perishable inventory). When the National Football League failed to reach a new contract agreement with its player's union in 2011, the league owners imposed a lockout until an agreement was reached.

- A firm can also hire temporary or permanent replacements called **strikebreakers.** However, the law forbids the permanent replacement of workers who strike because of unfair practices. In some cases, an employer can obtain legal injunctions that either prohibit workers from striking or prohibit a union from interfering with its efforts to use replacement workers.

Mediation and Arbitration   Rather than wield these often unpleasant weapons against one another, labor and management can agree to call in a third party to help resolve the dispute:

In **mediation,** the neutral third party (the mediator) can suggest, but cannot impose, a settlement on the other parties.

In **arbitration,** the neutral third party (the arbitrator) dictates a settlement between the two sides, which have agreed to submit to outside judgment. In some disputes, such as those between the government and public employees, arbitration is compulsory, or required by law.

Managing an organization's human resources is both a complex and an important undertaking. Most businesses can buy the same equipment and use the same technology as their competitors. But differences in employee talent and motivation are not easily copied. Consequently, most well-managed companies today recognize the value provided by their employees and strive to ensure that the HR function is managed as efficiently and effectively as possible.

Cost-Of-Living Adjustment (COLA) labor contract clause tying future raises to changes in consumer purchasing power

Wage Reopener Clause clause allowing wage rates to be renegotiated during the life of a labor contract

Strike labor action in which employees temporarily walk off the job and refuse to work

Picketing labor action in which workers publicize their grievances at the entrance to an employer's facility

Boycott labor action in which workers refuse to buy the products of a targeted employer

Work Slowdown labor action in which workers perform jobs at a slower than normal pace

Lockout management tactic whereby workers are denied access to the employer's workplace

Strikebreaker worker hired as a permanent or temporary replacement for a striking employee

Mediation method of resolving a labor dispute in which a third party suggests, but does not impose, a settlement

Arbitration method of resolving a labor dispute in which both parties agree to submit to the judgment of a neutral party

H. Mark Weidman Photography/Alamy

Continued from page 244

Getting the Steel Out the Door

Nucor needs just four incentive plans because of an unusually flat organizational structure—another Iverson innovation. There are just four layers of personnel between a janitor and senior management: general managers, department managers, line supervisors, and hourly personnel. Most operating decisions are made at the divisional level or lower, and the company is known for its tolerance of honest mistakes made in the line of decision-making duty. The Nucor website quotes an unnamed executive as saying, "Workers excel here because they are allowed to fail," and goes on to explain that the occasional misstep is considered a good trade-off for the benefits of initiative and idea sharing: "Nucor managers at all levels encourage their employees to try out their new ideas. Sometimes the ideas work out, sometimes they don't. But this freedom to try helps give Nucor one of the most creative, get-it-done workforces in the world."

The Nucor system works not only because employees share financial risks and benefits but because, in sharing risks and benefits, they're a lot like owners. And people who think like owners are a lot more likely to take the initiative when decisions have to be made or problems solved. What's more, Nucor has found that teamwork is a good incubator for initiative as well as idea sharing. John J. Ferriola, who managed the Nucor mill in Hickman, Arkansas, before becoming chief operating officer, remembers an afternoon in March 2006 when the electrical grid at his facility went down. His electricians got on the phone to three other company electricians, one in Alabama and two in North Carolina, who dropped what they were doing and went straight to Arkansas. Working 20-hour shifts, the joint team had the plant up and running again in three days (as opposed to an anticipated full week). There was nothing in it (at least financially) for the visiting electricians, but they knew that maintenance personnel get no bonuses when equipment in their facility isn't operating. "At Nucor," says one frontline supervisor, "we're not 'you guys' and 'us guys.' It's all of us guys. Wherever the bottleneck is, we go there, and everyone works on it."

Nucor also likes to see teamwork—cooperation and idea sharing—combined with a little productive competition. Plant managers often set up contests between shifts to improve efficiency, output, or safety, but sometimes the effort of a work group to give itself a competitive edge can be taken to another level. In 2002, the Nucor plant in Crawfordsville, Indiana, was a pioneer in the development of an innovative process called thin-strip steel casting, and as of 2008, it was still setting records for continuous output from the process. The facility, however, isn't located near any major waterway and is thus at a disadvantage when it comes to transportation costs, especially when fuel prices are high. So General Manager Ron Dickerson and his employees collaborated on a plan not only to get around the problem but to increase profitability at the same time. Because it was too expensive for them to ship sheet steel as wide as that regularly made by competitors (including other Nucor-owned plants), Crawfordsville management and workers campaigned for the opportunity to shift the plant's focus to other types of steel.

It was a risky proposition, but today Crawfordsville turns out 160 different grades of steel. Some of them present manufacturing difficulties that employees have had to solve over time, but making the new processes work meant more orders for the plant and more hours for its employees. By the first quarter of 2008, the plant was setting production and shipment records. "We're continually expanding product ranges and the types of steel we make," says Dickerson, who continues to look forward, particularly to the opportunity to apply the Nucor brand of employee initiative to new technologies. "Nucor has a couple of other things going on," he notes, "and it's not yet decided where they'll make an investment. [But] Crawfordsville is known for successful startups, so I'm hoping we get some of these new technologies."

QUESTIONS FOR DISCUSSION

1   Instead of a system of individual performance appraisals, Nucor appraises employee performance according to division-wide quality, productivity, and profitability goals and targets. What are the advantages and disadvantages of this approach?

2   Identify the incentives—both financial and non-financial—that Nucor uses to motivate employees.

3   How does Nucor's flat organizational structure contribute to the success of its compensation system?

4   Many firms today use temporary, part-time, or virtual workers to reduce costs and gain flexibility. Nucor has never taken this route. Should management consider it in the future? Why or why not?

5   Nucor's CEO believes that when the economy turns around, Nucor will be "first out of the box" in the steel industry. What reasons does he have for being so optimistic?

SUMMARY OF LEARNING OBJECTIVES   MyBizLab

1.   **Define** *human resource management* **and explain how managers plan for their organization's human resource needs. (pp. 245–246)**
Human resource management (HRM) is the set of organizational activities directed at attracting, developing, and maintaining an effective workforce. *Job analysis* is a systematic analysis of jobs within an organization resulting in two things: a *job description* and a *job specification*. Managers must plan for future HR needs by assessing past trends, future plans, and general economic trends. Forecasting labor supply is really two tasks: (a) *forecasting internal supply* and (b) *forecasting external supply*. The next step in HR planning is matching HR supply and demand.

2.   **Identify the tasks in staffing a company and discuss ways in which organizations select new employees. (pp. 246–248)**
Staffing an organization means recruiting and hiring the right mix of people. *Recruiting* is the process of attracting qualified persons to apply for open jobs, either from within the organization or from outside the organization. The next step is the *selection process*—gathering information that will predict applicants' job success and then hiring candidates. Common selection techniques include application forms; tests of ability, aptitude, or knowledge; and interviews.

3.   **Describe how managers develop the workforce in their organization through training and performance appraisal. (p. 249)**
New employees must be trained and allowed to develop job skills. *On-the-job training* occurs while the employee is at work. *Off-the-job training* takes place off-site where controlled environments allow focused study. Some firms use *vestibule training*—off-the-job training in simulated work environments. In larger firms, *performance appraisals* show how well workers are doing their jobs.

4.   **Describe the main components of a compensation system and describe some of the key legal issues involved in hiring, compensating, and managing workers in today's workplace. (pp. 249–252)**
A *compensation system* is the total package of rewards that a firm offers employees in return for their labor. Although *wages* and *salaries* are key parts of all compensation systems,

most also include incentives and employee benefits programs. Beyond a certain point, money motivates employees only when tied directly to performance. One way is to use *incentive programs*—special pay programs designed to motivate performance. *Benefits*—compensation other than wages and salaries—account for a large percentage of compensation budgets. The law requires most companies to provide social security benefits and *workers' compensation insurance*. Most companies provide health, life, and disability insurance; retirement plans pay pensions to workers when they retire.

5.   **Discuss the legal context of human resource management and identify the contemporary legal issues. (pp. 252–255)**
HR management is influenced by the law. One area of HR regulation is *equal employment opportunity*—regulation to protect people from discrimination in the workplace. Because illegal discrimination is based on a prejudice about classes of individuals, laws protect various classes. A *protected class* consists of individuals who share one or more common characteristics as indicated by a given law (such as race, color, religion, gender, age, national origin, and so forth).

6.   **Discuss workforce diversity, the management of knowledge workers, and the use of a contingent workforce as important changes in the contemporary workplace. (pp. 255–257)**
Workforce diversity refers to the range of workers' attitudes, values, beliefs, and behaviors that differ by gender, race, age, ethnicity, physical ability, and other relevant characteristics. Employees who add value because of what they know are usually called *knowledge workers*, and managing them skillfully helps to determine which firms will be successful in the future. *Contingent workers*, including independent contractors, on-call workers, temporary employees, contract and leased employees, and part-time employees, work for organizations on something other than a permanent or full-time basis.

7.   **Explain why workers organize into labor unions. (pp. 257–258)**
A *labor union* is a group of individuals working together to achieve shared job-related goals. *Labor relations* refers to the process of dealing with employees represented by a union.

8. Describe the collective bargaining process. **(pp. 258–261)** The *collective bargaining* cycle begins when union leaders and management meet to agree on a contract. Each presents its demands, and then the two sides identify a *bargaining zone*. When a compromise is reached, the agreement is voted on by union members.

An *impasse* occurs when management and labor fail to agree on a contract. The most important union tactic is the *strike*. Unions may also use *picketing*. Under a *boycott*, union members agree not to buy the products of a targeted employer. During a *work slowdown*, workers perform their jobs at a much slower pace than normal. During a *sickout*, large numbers of workers call in sick. Management may resort to *lockouts*—denying employees access to the workplace. Labor and management can call in a third party to help resolve the dispute. Common options include *mediation, voluntary arbitration,* and *compulsory arbitration*.

KEY TERMS MyBizLab

affirmative action plan (p. 253)
arbitration (p. 261)
benefits (p. 251)
bonus (p. 251)
boycott (p. 260)
cafeteria benefits plan (p. 252)
collective bargaining (p. 258)
compensation system (p. 249)
contingent worker (p. 257)
cost-of-living adjustment (COLA) (p. 260)
employee information system (skills inventory) (p. 246)
employment at will (p. 255)
equal employment opportunity (p. 252)
Equal Employment Opportunity Commission (EEOC) (p. 252)
external recruiting (p. 247)
gainsharing plan (p. 251)
hostile work environment (p. 255)

human resource management (HRM) (p. 245)
incentive program (p. 250)
internal recruiting (p. 247)
job analysis (p. 245)
job description (p. 245)
job specification (p. 245)
knowledge workers (p. 256)
labor relations (p. 257)
labor union (p. 257)
lockout (p. 261)
mediation (p. 261)
merit salary system (p. 251)
Occupational Safety and Health Act of 1970 (OSHA) (p. 253)
off-the-job training (p. 249)
on-the-job training (p. 249)
pay for performance (or variable pay) (p. 251)
pay-for-knowledge plan (p. 251)

performance appraisal (p. 249)
picketing (p. 260)
profit-sharing plan (p. 251)
protected class (p. 252)
quid pro quo harassment (p. 255)
recruiting (p. 247)
replacement chart (p. 246)
salary (p. 250)
sexual harassment (p. 253)
strike (p. 260)
strikebreaker (p. 261)
vestibule training (p. 249)
wage reopener clause (p. 260)
wages (p. 250)
work slowdown (p. 260)
workers' compensation insurance (p. 251)
workforce diversity (p. 255)

QUESTIONS AND EXERCISES

QUESTIONS FOR REVIEW

1. What are the advantages and disadvantages of internal and external recruiting? Under what circumstances is each more appropriate?
2. Why is the formal training of workers so important to most employers? Why don't employers simply let people learn about their jobs as they perform them?
3. What different forms of compensation do firms typically use to attract and keep productive workers?
4. Why do workers in some companies unionize whereas workers in others do not?

QUESTIONS FOR ANALYSIS

5. What are your views on drug testing in the workplace? What would you do if your employer asked you to submit to a drug test?

6. Workers at Ford, GM, and Chrysler are represented by the UAW. However, the UAW has been much less successful in its attempts to unionize U.S. workers employed at Toyota, Nissan, and Honda plants in the United States. Why do you think this is so?
7. What training do you think you are most likely to need when you finish school and start your career?
8. How much will benefit considerations affect your choice of an employer after graduation?

APPLICATION EXERCISES

9. Interview an HR manager at a local company. Focus on a position for which the firm is currently recruiting applicants and identify the steps in the selection process.
10. Interview the managers of two local companies, one unionized and one nonunionized. Compare the wage and salary levels, benefits, and working conditions of employees at the two firms.

BUILDING YOUR BUSINESS SKILLS

A Little Collective Brainstorming

Goal
To help you understand why some companies unionize and others do not.

Background Information
You've been working for the same nonunion company for five years. Although there are problems in the company, you like your job and have confidence in your ability to get ahead. Recently, you've heard rumblings that a large group of workers wants to call for a union election. You're not sure how you feel about this because none of your friends or family are union members.

Method

Step 1
Come together with three other "coworkers" who have the same questions as you. Each person should target two companies to learn about their union status. Avoid small businesses. Choose large corporations such as General Motors, Intel, and Sears. As you investigate, answer the following questions:

- Is the company unionized?
- Is every worker in the company unionized, or just selected groups of workers? Describe the groups.
- If a company is unionized, what is the union's history in that company?
- If a company is unionized, what are the main labor-management issues?
- If a company is unionized, how would you describe the current status of labor-management relations? For example, is it cordial or strained?
- If a company is not unionized, what factors are responsible for its nonunion status? To learn the answers to these questions, contact the company, read corporate annual reports, search the company's website, contact union representatives, or do research on a computerized database.

Step 1
Go to the website of the AFL-CIO (www.aflcio.org) to learn more about the current status of the union movement. Then with your coworkers, write a short report about the advantages of union membership.

Step 1
Research the disadvantages of unionization. A key issue to address is whether unions make it harder for companies to compete in the global marketplace.

FOLLOW-UP QUESTIONS
1. Based on everything you learned, are you sympathetic to the union movement? Would you want to be a union member?
2. Are the union members you spoke with or read about satisfied or dissatisfied with their union's efforts to achieve better working conditions, higher wages, and improved benefits?
3. What is the union's role when layoffs occur?
4. Based on what you learned, do you think the union movement will stumble or thrive in the years ahead?

EXERCISING YOUR ETHICS: INDIVIDUAL EXERCISE

Operating Tactically

The Situation
Assume that you work as a manager for a medium-sized, nonunion company that is facing its most serious union-organizing campaign in years. Your boss, who is determined to keep the union out, has just given you a list of things to do in order to thwart the efforts of the organizers. For example, he has suggested each of the following tactics:

- Whenever you learn about a scheduled union meeting, you should schedule a "worker appreciation" event at the same time. He wants you to offer free pizza and to give cash prizes, which winners have to be present to receive.
- He wants you to look at the most recent performance evaluations of the key union organizers and to terminate the one with the lowest overall evaluation based on the "need to lower costs."
- He wants you to make an announcement that the firm is seriously considering such new benefits as on-site child care, flexible work schedules, telecommuting options, and exercise facilities. Although you know that the firm is indeed looking into these benefits, you also know that, ultimately, your boss will provide far less lavish benefits than he wants you to intimate.

The Dilemma
When you questioned the ethics—and even the legality—of these tactics, your boss responded by saying, "Look, all's fair in love and war, and this is war." He went on to explain that he was seriously concerned that a union victory might actually shut down the company's domestic operations altogether, forcing it to move all of its production capacities to lower-cost foreign plants. He concluded by saying that he was really looking out for the employees, even if he had to play hardball to help them. You easily see through his hypocrisy, but you also recognize some potential truth in his warning: If the union wins, jobs may actually be lost.

QUESTIONS TO ADDRESS
1 What are the ethical issues in this situation?
2 What are the basic arguments for and against extreme measures to fight unionization efforts?
3 What do you think most managers would do in this situation? What would you do?

EXERCISING YOUR ETHICS: TEAM EXERCISE

Handling the Layoffs

The Situation
The CEO of a moderate-sized company is developing a plan for laying off some members of the company workforce. He wants each manager to rank his or her employees according to the order in which they should be laid off, from first to last.

The Dilemma
One manager has just asked for help. He is new to his position and has little experience to draw from. The members of the manager's team are as follows:
- Tony Jones: white male, 10 years with the company, average performer, reportedly drinks a lot after work
- Amanda Wiggens: white female, very ambitious, 3 years with company, above-average performer, puts in extra time at work; is known to be abrasive when dealing with others
- Jorge Gonzalez: Latino, 20 years with the company, average performer, was laid off before but then called back when business picked up
- Dorothy Henderson: white female, 25 years with company, below-average performer, has filed five sexual harassment complaints in last 10 years
- Wanda Jackson: African American female, 8 years with company, outstanding performer, is rumored to be looking for another job

- Jerry Loudder: white male, single parent, 5 years with company, average performer
- Martha Strawser: white female, 6 years with company, excellent performer but spotty attendance, is putting husband through college

Team Activity
Assemble a group of four students. Your group has agreed to provide the manager with a suggested rank ordering of the manager's employees.

ACTION STEPS
1 Working together, prepare this list, ranking the manager's employees according to the order in which they should be laid off, from first to last.
2 As a group, discuss the underlying ethical issues in this situation and write them down.
3 As a group, brainstorm any legal issues involved in this situation and write them down.
4 Do the ethical and legal implications of your choices always align?
5 Do the ethical and performance implications of your choices always align?

CRAFTING A BUSINESS PLAN

Part 3: People in Organizations

Goal of the Exercise
At this point, your business has an identity and you've described the factors that will affect your business and how you will operate it. Part 3 of the business plan project asks you to think about your employees, the jobs they will be performing, and the ways in which you can lead and motivate them.

Exercise Background: Part 3 of the Business Plan
To complete this part of the plan, you need to refer back to the organizational chart that you created in Part 2. In this part of the business plan exercise, you'll take the different job titles you created in the organizational chart and give thought to the *skills* that employees will need to bring to the job *before* they begin. You'll also consider *training* you'll need to provide *after* they are hired, as well as how you'll compensate your employees. Part 3 of the business plan also asks you to consider how you'll lead your employees and keep them happy and motivated.

Your Assignment

Step 1
Open the *Business Plan* file you began working on in Parts 1 and 2.

Step 1
For the purposes of this assignment, you will answer the questions in "Part 3: People in Organizations:"
1 What do you see as the "corporate culture" of your business? What types of employee behaviors, such as organizational citizenship, will you expect?

Hint: Will your business demand a casual environment or a more professional environment? Refer to the discussion on employee behavior in Chapter 8 for information on organizational citizenship and other employee behaviors.
2 What is your philosophy on leadership? How will you manage your employees day-to-day?
Hint: Refer to the discussion on leadership in Chapter 9, to help you formulate your thoughts.
3 Looking back at your organizational chart in Part 2, briefly create a job description for each team member.
Hint: As you learned in Chapter 10, a job description lists the duties and responsibilities of a job; its working conditions; and the tools, materials, equipment, and information used to perform it. Imagine your business on a typical day. Who is working and what is each person's responsibilities?
4 Next, create a job specification for each job, listing the skills and other credentials and qualifications needed to perform the job effectively.
Hint: As you write your job specifications, consider what you would write if you were making an ad for the position. What would the new employee need to bring to the job in order to qualify for the position?
5 What sort of training, if any, will your employees need once they are hired? How will you provide this training?
Hint: Refer to the discussion of training in Chapter 10. Will you offer your employees on-the-job training? Off-the-job training? Vestibule training?
6 A major factor in retaining skilled workers is a company's compensation system—the total package of rewards that it offers

employees in return for their labor. Part of this compensation system includes wages/salaries. What wages or salaries will you offer for each job? Why did you decide on that pay rate? *Hint*: Refer to Chapter 10 for more information on forms of compensation. You may also want to check out sites like www.salary.com, which includes a salary wizard you can use to determine how much people with different job titles are making in your area and across the United States.

7 As you learned in Chapter 10, incentive programs are special programs designed to motivate high performance. What incentives will you use to motivate your workforce?

Hint: Be creative and look beyond a simple answer, such as giving pay increases. Ask yourself, who are my employees and what is important to them? Refer to Chapter 10 for more information on the types of incentives you may want to consider.

Note: Once you have answered the questions, save your Word document. You'll be answering additional questions in later chapters.

VIDEO EXERCISE   MyBizLab

Patagonia

Learning Objectives

The purpose of this video is to help you:

1 Understand how a company's human resource management system supports the company's mission.

2 Identify how a company can use recruitment and selection to find the best employees.

3 Describe the components of a company's compensation system.

Synopsis

Patagonia is a company with environmentalism at its core. Founder Yvon Chouinard became interested in rock climbing as a teenager and began forging pitons in his parents' backyard. This hobby has grown into an international business that still reflects Yvon's sense of adventure and love of the great outdoors. The company's mission statement reflects these values: *Build the best product, cause no unnecessary harm, use business to inspire and implement solutions to the environmental crisis*. Patagonia's products, from clothing to climbing supplies, are recognized for their quality and environmentally conscious production. *Fortune* magazine has recognized Patagonia year after year as one of the 100 best places to work. The company exhibits a high level of social responsibility, taking care of employees with on-site child care centers and flexible work hours and through a sustained program of donating 1 percent of sales or 10 percent of products (whichever is greater) to environmental causes.

DISCUSSION QUESTIONS

1 Yvon Chouinard's mantra is "Let my people surf." What does this mean to Patagonia and its employees?

2 Patagonia has been recognized for its family-friendly policies? Describe a few of these policies as highlighted in the video. What are the benefits to the company and its employees?

3 How does the hiring process at Patagonia differ from the procedures used by most organizations? How does this process support the company's values and work style?

4 Although Patagonia is considered a great place to work, the company is not a pay leader, often paying slightly less than average wages to employees. Describe Patagonia's compensation system.

5 What motivates employees to work for Patagonia?

Online Exploration

After watching this video, you probably want to know more about Patagonia. Visit the company's website (www.patagonia.com), scrolling to the bottom of the home page. Click on Company Info, where you will find a detailed history of the company as well as information about jobs. Clicking on the Jobs link, you can view available jobs at the company's Ventura, California, headquarters as well as other locations. Click on the available jobs to view a job description for each opening. How do these job descriptions reflect the company's values?

END NOTES

[1] "Employee Relations Principles," NUCOR Corporation; "Pain, but No Layoffs at Nucor," *BusinessWeek*, March 26, 2009, www.businessweek.com on March 25, 2011; Byrnes with Michael Arndt, "The Art of Motivation," *BusinessWeek*, May 1, 2006, www.businessweek.com on March 26, 2011; "About Us," Nucor website, www.nucor.com on April 2, 2011; "Nucor Reports Record Results for 2008," Reuters, January 27, 2009, www.reuters.com on April 2, 2011; Kathy Mayer, "Nucor Steel: Pioneering Mill in Crawfordsville Celebrates 20 Years and 30 Million Tons," *AllBusiness*, September 1, 2008, www.allbusiness.com on April 3, 2011.

[2] "NetFlix Takes Off," *BusinessWeek*, April 25, 2009, p. 47.

[3] Lathryn Tyler, "Taking E-Learning to the Next Level," *HRMagazine*, February 2005, 56–61.

[4] "Some Employers Offer ID Theft Coverage," *USA Today*, September 12, 2005, 1B.

[5] "FedEx, Goodyear Make Big Pension Plan Changes," *Workforce Management* (March 1, 2007), at http://www.workforce.com/section/00/article/24/77/95.html.

[6] Henry R. Cheeseman, *Business Law: Ethical, International, and E-Commerce Environment*, 8th ed. (Upper Saddle River, NJ: Prentice Hall, 2010), Chapter 41.

[7] Angelo DeNisi and Ricky Griffin, *HRM*, (Cincinnati: Cengage, 2012).

[8] Ibid.

[9] U.S. Department of Labor, Bureau of Labor Statistics, at http://www.bls.gov/news.release/union2.nr0.htm, accessed March 22, 2011.

[10] U.S. Department of Labor, Bureau of Labor Statistics, at http://www.bls.gov/news.release/pdf/wkstp.pdf, accessed March 22 2011.

11 Marketing Processes and Consumer Behavior

Starbucks Brews a New Marketing Mix

For lovers of upscale coffee products, Starbucks has long been the standout brand with a premium image as the "home of affordable luxury." With its well-established line of tasty lattes and Frappuccinos—some priced above $4 and all presented by service-savvy baristas—Starbucks gained great popularity in the connoisseur coffee market. Seeking to tap the market's full potential, Chairman and CEO Howard Schultz spearheaded an ambitious expansion dream for 40,000 retail outlets globally, creating a massive network of stores dispensing Starbucks products, along with an infusion of Starbucks's "romance, warmth and theater," to millions of coffee gourmets. All of that changed, however, with the sting of the 2008–2010 recession.

To stay afloat, Starbucks is reconsidering all aspects of its marketing strategy, including downsizing the distribution network of retail stores, refashioning its line of products and prices, and promoting a repositioned Starbucks image. The new strategy—presenting Starbucks as being more affordable—reflects the company's tighter budget and realignment with the target market, as consumers adjust to the realities of a down-turning economy. Instead of adding 2,500 locations annually, hundreds of the once-17,000 locations have been closed, including stores in areas such as Florida and California that have seen widespread home foreclosures. And fewer of the planned new stores have opened. The strategy also refocuses its products back onto what made Starbucks great—coffee—instead of side-tracking into movies and music. New entries in the product mix include a line of instant

After reading this chapter, you should be able to:

1 Explain the concept of marketing and identify the five forces that constitute the external marketing environment.
2 Explain the purpose of a marketing plan and identify the four components of the marketing mix.
3 Explain market segmentation and how it is used in target marketing.
4 Describe the key factors that influence the consumer buying process.
5 Discuss the three categories of organizational markets.
6 Explain the definition of a product as a value package and classify goods and services.
7 Describe the key considerations in the new product development process, and explain the importance of branding and packaging.
8 Discuss the marketing mix as it applies to international and small business.

coffee (once shunned by Starbucks). In a competitive response to McDonald's (with its own specialty coffee drinks) and Dunkin' Donuts, Starbucks has presented a newer line of recession-friendly value meals, including a choice of breakfast sandwich paired with a coffee product, at a reduced-price savings of as much as $1.20. To keep its customers and bolster sales, the company launched Starbucks Card Rewards, a customer loyalty promotion that gets you free coffee refills and other extras, all to support the affordability image.[1]

Will it work? Can Starbucks reposition the brand so it appeals to the convenience market without tarnishing the company's premium image? Some observers note that the new approach may attract some cost-conscious customers at the same time that it alienates others in the coffee connoisseur segment. It's a marketing risk that Starbucks is taking.

Our opening story continues on page 292.

Our opening story continues on page 292.

WHAT'S IN IT FOR ME?

Adjusting its marketing strategy is an example of how a company can apply marketing basics in an innovative way to appeal to the forces of the external marketing environment. This chapter discusses these basics along with the marketing plan and components of the marketing mix, as well as target marketing and market segmentation. It also explores key factors that influence consumer and organizational buying processes, as well as how new products are developed and how they are defined by branding and packaging. By grasping the marketing methods and ideas in this chapter, you will not only be better prepared as a marketing professional, but also as an informed consumer.

MyBizLab Where you see MyBizLab in this chapter, go to **www.mybizlab.com** for additional activities on the topic being discussed.

Richard Levine/Alamy

1 Explain the concept of marketing and identify the five forces that constitute the external marketing environment.

What Is Marketing?

What comes to mind when you think of marketing? Most of us think of marketing as advertisements for detergents, social networking, and soft drinks. Marketing, however, encompasses a much wider range of activities. The American Marketing Association defines **marketing** as "an organizational function and a set of processes for creating, communicating, and delivering value to customers and for managing customer relationships in ways that benefit the organization and its stakeholders."[2] To see this definition in action we'll continue this chapter by looking at some marketing basics, including the ways marketers build relationships with customers. We'll then examine forces that constitute the external marketing environment, followed by the marketing plan, the components of the marketing mix, and we'll discuss market segmentation and how it is used in target marketing. We'll then look at key factors that influence the buying processes of consumers and industrial buyers. Finally, we'll explore how new products are developed and see how branding and packaging help establish their identity in the marketplace.

Delivering Value

What attracts buyers to one product instead of another? Although our desires for the many goods and services available to us may be unbounded, limited financial resources force most of us to be selective. Accordingly, customers buy products that offer the best value when it comes to meeting their needs and wants.

Value and Benefits   The **value** of a product compares its benefits with its costs. Benefits include not only the functions of the product, but also the emotional satisfaction associated with owning, experiencing, or possessing it. But every product has costs, including sales price, the expenditure of the buyer's time, and even the emotional costs of making a purchase decision. A satisfied customer perceives the benefits derived from the purchase to be greater than its costs. Thus, the simple but important ratio for value is derived as follows:

$$\text{Value} = \frac{\text{Benefits}}{\text{Costs}}$$

The marketing strategies of leading firms focus on increasing value for customers. Marketing resources are deployed to add benefits and decrease costs of products to provide greater value. To satisfy customers, a company may:

- Develop an entirely new product that performs better (provides greater performance benefits) than existing products;

- Keep a store open longer hours during a busy season (adding the benefit of greater shopping convenience);

- Offer price reductions (the benefit of lower costs).

- Offer information that explains how a product can be used in new ways (the benefit of new uses at no added cost).

Value and Utility   To understand how marketing creates value for customers, we need to know the kind of benefits that buyers get from a firm's goods or services. As we discussed in Chapter 7, those benefits provide customers with **utility**—the ability of a product to satisfy a human want or need. Marketing strives to provide four kinds of utility in the following ways:

- *Form utility.* Marketing has a voice in designing products with features that customers want.

- *Time utility.* Marketing creates a time utility by providing products when customers will want them.

- *Place utility.* Marketing creates a place utility by providing products where customers will want them.

- *Possession utility.* Marketing creates a possession utility by transferring product ownership to customers by setting selling prices, setting terms for customer credit payments, if needed, and providing ownership documents.

Because they determine product features, and the timing, place, and terms of sale that provide utility and add value for customers, marketers must understand customers' wants and needs. Their methods for creating utility are described in this and the following chapter.

Goods, Services, and Ideas

The marketing of tangible goods is obvious in everyday life. It applies to two types of customers: those who buy consumer goods and those who buy industrial goods. Think of the products that you bought the last time you went to the mall or the grocery store or on the Internet. In a department store an employee asks if you'd like to try a new cologne. A pharmaceutical company proclaims the virtues of its new cold medicine. Your local auto dealer offers an economy car at an economy price. These products are all **consumer goods:** tangible goods that you, the consumer, may buy for personal use. Firms that sell goods to consumers for personal consumption are engaged in consumer marketing, also known as B2C (business-to-consumer) marketing.

Marketing also applies to **industrial goods:** physical items used by companies to produce other products. Surgical instruments and bulldozers are industrial goods, as are such components and raw materials as integrated circuits, steel, and plastic. Firms that sell goods to other companies are engaged in industrial marketing, also known as B2B (business-to-business) marketing.

But marketing techniques are also applied to **services**—products with intangible (nonphysical) features, such as professional advice, timely information for decisions, or arrangements for a vacation. Service marketing—the application of marketing for services—continues to be a major growth area in the United States. Insurance companies, airlines, public accountants, and health clinics all engage in service marketing, both to individuals (consumer markets) and to other companies (industrial markets). Thus, the terms consumer marketing and industrial marketing include services as well as goods.

Finally, marketers also promote ideas. Ads in theaters, for example, warn us against copyright infringement and piracy. Other marketing campaigns may stress the advantages of avoiding fast foods, texting while driving, or quitting smoking—or they may promote a political party or candidate.

Relationship Marketing and Customer Relationship Management

Although marketing often focuses on single transactions for products, services, or ideas, marketers also take a longer-term perspective. Thus, **relationship marketing** emphasizes building lasting relationships with customers and suppliers. Stronger relationships—including stronger economic and social ties—can result in greater long-term satisfaction, customer loyalty, and customer retention.[3] Starbucks's Card Rewards attracts return customers with free coffee refills and other extras. Similarly, commercial banks offer economic incentives to encourage longer lasting relationships.

Marketing organizational function and a set of processes for creating, communicating, and delivering value to customers, and for managing customer relationships in ways that benefit the organization and its stakeholders.

Value relative comparison of a product's benefits versus its costs

Utility ability of a product to satisfy a human want or need

Consumer Goods physical products purchased by consumers for personal use

Industrial Goods physical products purchased by companies to produce other products

Services products having nonphysical features, such as information, expertise, or an activity that can be purchased

Relationship Marketing marketing strategy that emphasizes building lasting relationships with customers and suppliers

Long-time customers who purchase a certain number of the bank's products (for example, checking accounts, savings accounts, and loans) accumulate credits toward free or reduced-price products or services, such as free investment advice.

Customer Relationship Management   Like many other marketing areas, the ways that marketers go about building relationships with customers have changed dramatically. **Customer relationship management (CRM)** is an organized method that an enterprise uses to build better information connections with clients, so that stronger enterprise-client relationships are developed. The power of Internet communications coupled with the ability to gather and assemble information on customer preferences allows marketers to better predict what clients will want and buy. The compiling and storage of customers' data, known as *data warehousing*, provides the raw materials from which marketers can extract information that enables them to find new clients. It also identifies their best customers who can then be posted on upcoming new products, and supplied with special information such as post-purchase service reminders. *Data mining* automates the massive analysis of data by using computers to sift, sort, and search for previously undiscovered clues about what customers look at, react to, and how they might be influenced. The hoped-for result is a clearer picture of how marketing, knowing a client's preferences, can more effectively use its resources to better satisfy those particular needs, thereby building closer, stronger relationships with customers.[4]

Toronto-based Fairmont Resort Hotels, for example, first used data mining to rebuild its customer-relations package by finding out what kinds of vacations their customers prefer, and then placed ads where they were more likely to reach those customers. When data mining revealed the worldwide destinations of Fairmont customers, it helped determine Fairmont's decision to buy their customers' number-one preference—the Savoy in London.[5] More recently, Fairmont's enhanced CRM is attracting new guests, along with heightening relationships and loyalty among existing clients, through web-based promotions and incentives. Using profiles of guest information, Fairmont identifies target traveler segments and supplies travelers with personalized price discounts and special hotel services.[6] We'll discuss data warehousing and data mining in more detail in Chapter 13.

The Marketing Environment

Marketing strategies are not determined unilaterally by any business—rather, they are strongly influenced by powerful outside forces. As you see in Figure 11.1, every marketing program must recognize the factors in a company's *external environment*, which is everything outside an organization's boundaries that might affect it. In this section we'll discuss how these external forces affect the marketing environment in particular.

Political-Legal Environment   Political activities, both global and domestic, have profound effects on marketing. For example, environmental legislation has determined the destinies of entire industries. The political push for alternative energy sources is creating new markets and products for emerging companies such as India's Suzlon Energy Limited (large wind turbines), wind-powered electric generators by Germany's Nordex AG, and wind farms and power plants by Spain's Gamesa Corporation. Marketing managers try to maintain favorable political and legal environments in several ways. To gain public support for products and activities, marketers use ad campaigns to raise public awareness of important issues. Companies contribute to political candidates and frequently support the activities of political action committees (PACs) maintained by their respective industries.

Sociocultural Environment   Changing social values force companies to develop and promote new products for both individual consumers and industrial customers. Just a few years ago, organic foods were available only in specialty food stores like Whole Foods. Today, in response to a growing demand for healthy foods, Target's Archer Farms product line brings affordable organic food to a much larger audience. New industrial products, too, reflect changing social values: A growing number of wellness programs are available to companies for improving employees' health. Quest Diagnostics, for

Figure 11.1 The External Marketing Environment

example, a B2B company, supplies a "Blueprint for Wellness" service that assesses employee health-care risks in client companies and recommends programs for reducing those risks. This and other trends reflect the values, beliefs, and ideas that shape society.

Technological Environment   New technologies create new goods and services. New products make existing products obsolete, and many products change our values and lifestyles. In turn, lifestyle changes often stimulate new products not directly related to the new technologies themselves. Cell phones and PDAs, for example, facilitate business communication just as pre-packaged meals provide convenience for busy household cooks. Both kinds of products also free up time for recreation and leisure.

Economic Environment   Because they determine spending patterns by consumers, businesses, and governments, economic conditions influence marketing plans for product offerings, pricing, and promotional strategies. Marketers are concerned with such economic variables as inflation, interest rates, and recession. Thus, they monitor the general business cycle to anticipate trends in consumer and business spending.

Marketing strategies are strongly influenced by powerful outside forces. For example, new technologies create new products, such as the cell phone "gas station" shown here. These recharging stations enable customers to recharge their mobile devices just as they would refuel their cars. The screens at the stations also provide marketers with a new way to display ads to waiting customers.

The interconnected global economy has become an increasingly important concern for marketers worldwide—for example, in 2008, rising oil prices broke records on an almost daily basis. Fed up with gas prices, U.S. drivers drove less, decreasing the demand and prices for gasoline. As the global economy continued to sour, the Canadian government demanded its automakers reduce production costs and auto prices to qualify for the government's bailout fund. Meanwhile, the continuing U.S. housing crisis is leaving many former homeowners awash in debt they cannot afford

Customer Relationship Management (CRM)
organized methods that a firm uses to build
better information connections with clients,
so that stronger company-client relationships are developed

MANAGING IN TURBULENT TIMES

Feeling the Pressure for "Green"

Today's marketers are struggling with pressures from several outside forces: The political-legal, sociocultural, technological, and economic environments are all pushing for change. Industries ranging from autos to energy to housing are grappling with a common environmental theme: green. Public sentiment turned decidedly toward alternatives to gas-guzzling cars. Home buyers, too, want energy-efficient heating and cooling, such as geothermal heat, in their next home. Environmentalists are pushing for alternative energy sources, notably wind and solar power, to replace fossil fuels. Local utilities are offering incentives for construction using environmentally sensitive building designs to conserve energy. Purchases of tiny-size houses are growing. Solar-powered wells are replacing mechanical windmills on farms. In Washington, the Obama administration and Congress are struggling to reverse severe economic conditions and meet commitments for a cleaner environment using energy-saving technologies.

These outside pressures present challenges to all areas of marketing, from identifying the new target markets, to designing new products for those markets and, in some cases, finding technologies to make those products. Success depends on coordinating the various marketing activities—making them compatible with one another. Marketers need to present a convincing rationale for a product's pricing and demonstrate how the product provides the benefits sought by the target markets. Distribution methods—delivering products and after-services to customers—have to match up with promises in the promotional message so that, together, the marketing activities provide a persuasive package that delivers the desired value and benefits. Further, this integrated marketing strategy must be coordinated with financial management and production operations to provide timely customer satisfaction.

The marketing blueprint for Toyota's Prius automobile utilized an integrated marketing mix for meeting the challenge of *going green*. While developing the fuel-efficient hybrid

David Koscheck/Shutterstock

technology, Toyota identified niche target markets of users in some 40 countries and determined a price range compatible with the company's performance reliability and quality reputation. Promotion in the U.S. market started two years before the car was released so customers could view and purchase a Prius. One pre-launch promotion involved teaming up with the Sierra Club; in addition, lending the Prius to environmentally sensitive Hollywood superstars provided exposure and allowed car testing in the target market. The main ad campaign to general audiences emphasized that consumers can still have speed and comfort along with environmental friendliness. And pre-orders were delivered on time to buyers. As a result, the Prius is the most successful hybrid automobile in the United States and the rest of the world.[7]

MyBizLab

to repay. As a result, money-strapped consumers have shifted to used cars (instead of new) and to down-sized, more modest housing. This product shift by consumers affects all areas of marketing—target markets, pricing, promotion, and distribution—for cars, fuel, and housing.[8]

Competitive Environment   In a competitive environment, marketers must convince buyers that they should purchase one company's products rather than those of some other seller. Because both consumers and commercial buyers have limited resources, every dollar spent on one product is no longer available for other purchases. Each marketing program, therefore, seeks to make its product the most attractive. Expressed in business terms, a failed program loses the buyer's dollar forever (or at least until it is time for the next purchase decision).

To promote products effectively, marketers must first understand which of three types of competition they face:

- **Substitute products** may not look alike or they may seem very different from one another, but they can fulfill the same need. For example, your cholesterol level may be controlled with either of two competing products: a physical fitness program or a drug regimen. The fitness program and the drugs compete as substitute products.

- **Brand competition** occurs between similar products and is based on buyers' perceptions of the benefits of products offered by particular companies. For Internet searches do you turn to the Google, Bing, or Yahoo search engine? Brand competition is based on users' perceptions of the benefits offered by each product.

- **International competition** matches the products of domestic marketers against those of foreign competitors. The intensity of international competition has been heightened by the formation of alliances, such as the European Union and NAFTA. In 2009 the U.S. Air Force opened bidding to foreign manufacturers for three new planes to replace the existing Presidential Air Force One fleet (made by Boeing). If Europe's Airbus had won the contract it would have been the first time a U.S. President has flown in a non-U.S. made Air Force One.[9] Instead, however, Airbus withdrew from bidding, leaving Boeing the sole competitor.

Having identified the kind of competition, marketers can then develop a strategy for attracting more customers.

Strategy: The Marketing Mix

2 Explain the purpose of a marketing plan and identify the four components of the marketing mix.

A company's **marketing managers** are responsible for planning and implementing all the activities that result in the transfer of goods or services to its customers. These activities culminate in the **marketing plan**—a detailed strategy for focusing marketing efforts on customers' needs and wants. Therefore, marketing strategy begins when a company identifies a customer need and develops a product to meet it. Starbucks's revised strategy in our opening case, for example, recognizes consumers' needs for more affordable coffee products in a down-turned economy.

In planning and implementing strategies, marketing managers develop the four basic components (often called the "Four Ps") of the **marketing mix:** product, pricing, place, and promotion.

Product

Marketing begins with a **product**—a good, a service, or an idea designed to fill a customer's need or want. Conceiving and developing new products is a constant challenge for marketers, who must always consider the factor of change—changing technology, changing wants and needs of customers, and changing economic conditions. Meeting these changing conditions often means changing existing products—such as Starbucks's introduction of its new line of instant coffee—to keep pace with emerging markets and competitors.

Product Differentiation Producers often promote particular features of products in order to distinguish them in the marketplace. **Product differentiation** is the creation of a feature or image that makes a product differ enough from existing products to attract customers. For example, Jann Wenner started *Rolling Stone* magazine in 1967, and it's been the cash cow of Wenner Media ever since. In 1985, however, Wenner bought *US*

Substitute Product product that is dissimilar from those of competitors but that can fulfill the same need

Brand Competition competitive marketing that appeals to consumer perceptions of benefits of products offered by particular companies

International Competition competitive marketing of domestic products against foreign products

Marketing Manager manager who plans and implements the marketing activities that result in the transfer of products from producer to consumer

Marketing Plan detailed strategy for focusing marketing efforts on consumers' needs and wants

Marketing Mix combination of product, pricing, promotion, and place (distribution) strategies used to market products

Product good, service, or idea that is marketed to fill consumers' needs and wants

Product Differentiation creation of a product feature or product image that differs enough from existing products to attract customers

Frances M. Roberts/Newscom

Wenner Media Chair and CEO Jann Wenner (above) is hoping that his strategy for greater differentiation between his *Us Weekly* magazine and rival *People* will continue to pay off. *People* is news driven, reporting on ordinary people as well as celebrities, whereas *Us Weekly* features more coverage of celebrity sex and glitter.

magazine and set out to compete with *People.* Wenner's strategy calls for greater differentiation between the two products. *People* is news driven, reporting on ordinary people as well as celebrities, and Wenner has punched up *Us Weekly* with more coverage of gossipy celebrity sex and glitter. So far, he hasn't been as successful as some expected: *People* reaches 3.7 million readers, *Us Weekly* about 1.9 million.[10]

Pricing

The **pricing** of a product—selecting the best price at which to sell it—is often a balancing act. On the one hand, prices must support a variety of costs—operating, administrative, research costs, and marketing costs. On the other hand, prices can't be so high that customers turn to competitors. Successful pricing means finding a profitable middle ground between these two requirements. By offering a reduced-price savings for its breakfast meals, Starbucks is promoting its affordability image.

Both low-and high-price strategies can be effective in different situations. Low prices, for example, generally lead to larger sales volumes. High prices usually limit market size but increase profits per unit. High prices may also attract customers by implying that a product is of high quality. We discuss pricing in more detail in Chapter 12.

Place (Distribution)

In the marketing mix, **place** refers to **distribution.** Placing a product in the proper outlet—for example, a retail store—requires decisions about several activities, all of which are concerned with getting the product from the producer to the consumer. Decisions about warehousing and inventory control are distribution decisions, as are decisions about transportation options.

Firms must also make decisions about the *channels* through which they distribute products. Many manufacturers, for example, sell goods to other companies that, in turn, distribute them to retailers. Others sell directly to major retailers, such as Target and Sears. Still others sell directly to final consumers. We explain distribution decisions further in Chapter 12.

Promotion

The most visible component of the marketing mix is no doubt **promotion,** which refers to techniques for communicating information about products. The most important promotional tools include advertising, personal selling, sales promotions, publicity/public relations, and direct or interactive marketing. Promotion decisions are discussed further in Chapter 12.

Blending It All Together: Integrated Strategy

An **integrated marketing strategy** ensures that the Four Ps blend together so that they are compatible

Richard Levine/Alamy

American Eagle Outfitters (AEO) is a chain of more than 900 stores specializing in clothes, accessories, and personal care products designed to appeal to a demographic consisting of girls and guys ages 15 to 25. In 2006, the brand expanded its line with Aerie, a chain of standalone stores in the U.S. and Canada, and an online store, that sell girls' intimates, workout wear, and Aerie's Dormwear—a collection of leggings, hoodies, and fashionable sweats appropriate for lounging in the dorm or wearing to a morning class.

with one another and with the company's non-marketing activities as well. As an example, Toyota has become the world's largest automaker: Its nearly 30-year auto superiority, even with its massive product recalls in 2008–2009, stems from a coherent marketing mix that is tightly integrated with its production strategy. Offering a relatively small number of different models, Toyota targets auto customers that want high quality, excellent performance reliability, and moderate prices (a good value for the price). With a smaller number of different models than U.S. automakers, fewer components and parts are needed, purchasing costs are lower, and less factory space is required for inventory and assembly in Toyota's lean production system. Lean production's assembly simplicity yields higher quality, the factory's cost savings led to lower product prices, and speedy production gives shorter delivery times in Toyota's distribution system. Taken together, this integrated strategy is completed when Toyota's advertising communicates its message of industry-high customer satisfaction.[11]

Target Marketing and Market Segmentation

3 Explain market segmentation and how it is used in target marketing.

Marketers have long known that products cannot be all things to all people. The emergence of the marketing concept and the recognition of customers' needs and wants led marketers to think in terms of **target markets**—groups of people or organizations with similar wants and needs and who can be expected to show interest in the same products. Selecting target markets is usually the first step in the marketing strategy.

Target marketing requires **market segmentation**—dividing a market into categories of customer types or "segments." Once they have identified segments, companies may adopt a variety of strategies. Some firms market products to more than one segment. General Motors, for example, once offered automobiles with various features and at various price levels. GM's past strategy was to provide an automobile for nearly every segment of the market. The financial crisis, however, has forced GM's changeover to fewer target markets and associated brands by closing Saturn, phasing out Pontiac, and selling or shutting down Hummer and Saab.

In contrast, some businesses offer a narrower range of products, such as Ferrari's high-priced sports cars, aiming at just one segment. Note that segmentation is a strategy for analyzing consumers, not products. Once a target segment is identified, the marketing of products for that segment begins. The process of fixing, adapting, and communicating the nature of the product itself is called **product positioning**.

Identifying Market Segments

By definition, members of a market segment must share some common traits that affect their purchasing decisions. In identifying consumer segments, researchers look at several different influences on consumer behavior. Here are five of the most important variables:

Pricing process of determining the best price at which to sell a product

Place (Distribution) part of the marketing mix concerned with getting products from producers to consumers

Promotion aspect of the marketing mix concerned with the most effective techniques for communicating information about products

Integrated Marketing Strategy strategy that blends together the Four Ps of marketing to ensure their compatibility with one another and with the company's non-marketing activities as well

Target Market group of people who have similar wants and needs and can be expected to show interest in the same products

Market Segmentation process of dividing a market into categories of customer types, or "segments"

Product Positioning process of fixing, adapting, and communicating the nature of a product

Geographic Segmentation   Many buying decisions are affected by the places people call home. Urban residents don't need agricultural equipment, and sailboats sell better along the coasts than on the Great Plains. **Geographic variables** are the geographic units, from countries to neighborhoods, that may be considered in a segmentation strategy. McDonald's restaurants in Germany, in contrast to those in the United States, offer beer on the menu. Pharmacies in Jackson Hole, Wyoming, sell firearms that are forbidden in Chicago.

Demographic Segmentation   **Demographic variables** describe populations by identifying traits, such as age, income, gender, ethnic background, marital status, race, religion, and social class, as detailed in Table 11.1. Depending on the marketer's purpose, a demographic segment can be a single classification (ages 20–34) or a combination of categories (ages 20–34, married without children, earning $25,000–$44,999 a year).

For example, Hot Topic is a California-based chain that specializes in clothes, accessories, and jewelry designed to appeal to the Generation Y and Millennials—a demographic consisting of American consumers between 13 and 17. The theme is pop culture music—anything from rock and rockabilly to rave and acid rap—because it's the biggest influence on the demographic's fashion tastes.

Geo-Demographic Segmentation   **Geo-demographic variables** are a combination of geographic and demographic traits and is becoming the most common segmentation tool. An example would be Young Urban Professionals—well educated, 25- to 34-year-olds with high paying professional jobs living in the "downtown" zip codes of major cities. Segmentation is more effective because the greater number of variables defines the market more precisely.

Psychographic Segmentation   Markets can also be segmented according to such **psychographic variables** as lifestyles, interests, and attitudes. For example, Burberry, whose raincoats have been a symbol of British tradition since 1856, has repositioned itself as a global luxury brand, like Gucci and Louis Vuitton. The strategy calls for attracting a different type of customer—the top-of-the-line, fashion-conscious individual—who shops at stores like Neiman Marcus and Bergdorf Goodman. Psychographics are particularly important to marketers because, unlike demographics and geographics, they can be changed by marketing efforts. For example, Polish companies have overcome consumer resistance by promoting the safety and desirability of using credit cards rather than depending on solely using cash.[12]

Behavioral Segmentation   **Behavioral variables** include such areas as heavy users (buy in bulk, the key to Sam's and Costco); situation buyers (Halloween is now the second largest "holiday" in terms of spending)[13]; or specific purpose (All Free is a new detergent for people who have skin reactions to additives in other detergents).

TABLE 11.1	**Demographic Variables**
Age	Under 5, 5–11, 12–19, 20–34, 35–49, 50–64, 65+
Education	Grade school or less, some high school, graduated high school, some college, college degree, advanced degree
Family Life Cycle	Young single, young married without children, young married with children, older married with children under 18, older married without children under 18, older single, other
Family Size	1, 2–3, 4–5, 6+
Income	Under $15,000, $15,000–$24,999, $25,000–$50,000, $50,000–$100,000, over $100,000
Nationality	African, American, Asian, British, Eastern European, French, German, Irish, Italian, Latin American, Middle Eastern, Scandinavian
Race	Native American, Asian, African American, Caucasian
Religion	Buddhist, Catholic, Hindu, Jewish, Muslim, Protestant
Sex	Male, female

Understanding Consumer Behavior

4 Describe the key factors that influence the consumer buying process.

Although marketing managers can tell us what features people want in a new refrigerator, they cannot tell us why they buy particular refrigerators. What desire are consumers fulfilling? Is there a psychological or sociological explanation for why they purchase one product and not another? These questions and many others are addressed in the study of **consumer behavior**—the study of the decision process by which people buy and consume products.

Influences on Consumer Behavior

To understand consumer behavior, marketers draw heavily on such fields as psychology and sociology. The result is a focus on four major influences on consumer behavior: *psychological, personal, social,* and *cultural.* By identifying which influences are most active in certain circumstances, marketers try to explain consumer choices and predict future buying behavior.

- Psychological influences include an individual's motivations, perceptions, ability to learn, and attitudes.

- Personal influences include lifestyle, personality, and economic status.

- Social influences include family, opinion leaders (people whose opinions are sought by others), and such reference groups as friends, coworkers, and professional associates.

- Cultural influences include culture (the way of living that distinguishes one large group from another), subculture (smaller groups with shared values), and social class (the cultural ranking of groups according to such criteria as background, occupation, and income).

Although these factors can have a strong impact on a consumer's choices, their effect on actual purchases is sometimes weak or negligible. Some consumers, for example, exhibit high **brand loyalty**—they regularly purchase products, such as McDonald's foods, because they are satisfied with their performance. Such people are less subject to influence and stick with preferred brands.[14] On the other hand, the clothes you wear, the social network you choose, and the way you decorate your room, often reflect social and psychological influences on your consumer behavior.

The Consumer Buying Process

Students of consumer behavior have constructed various models to help show how consumers decide to buy products. Figure 11.2 presents one such model. At the core of this and similar models is an awareness of the many influences that lead to consumption. Ultimately, marketers use this information to develop marketing plans.

Geographic Variables geographic units that may be considered in developing a segmentation strategy

Demographic Variables characteristics of populations that may be considered in developing a segmentation strategy

Geo-Demographic VariableS combination of geographic and demographic traits used in developing a segmentation strategy

Psychographic Variables consumer characteristics, such as lifestyles, opinions, interests, and attitudes that may be considered in developing a segmentation strategy

Behavioral Variables behavioral patterns displayed by groups of consumers and that are used in developing a segmentation strategy

Consumer Behavior study of the decision process by which people buy and consume products

Brand Loyalty pattern of regular consumer purchasing based on satisfaction with a product's performance

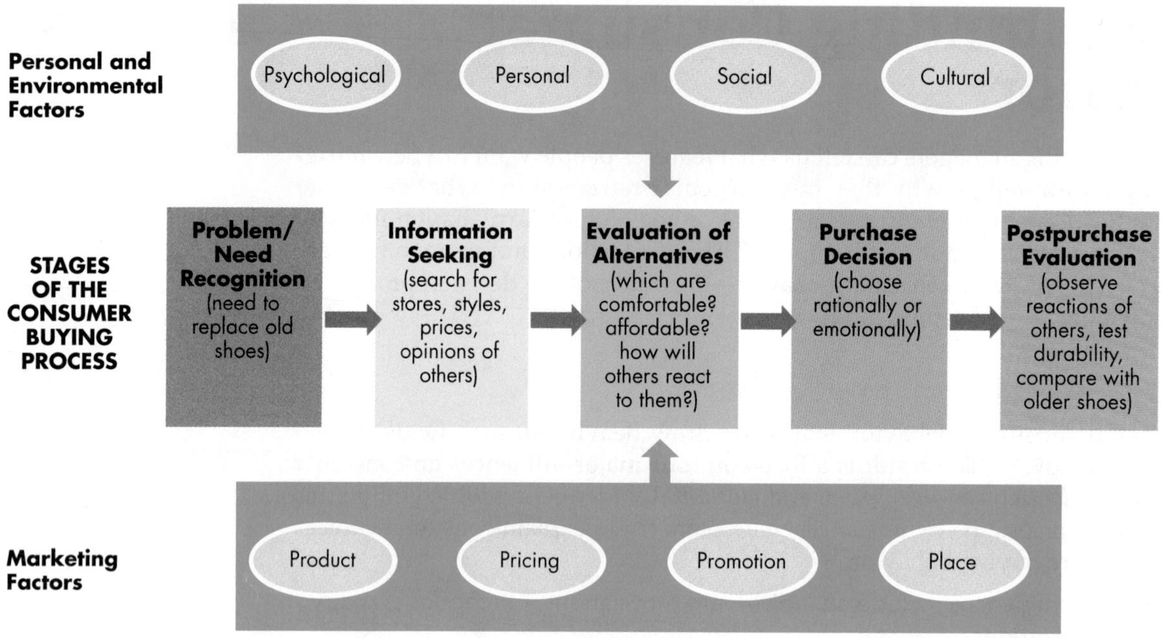

Figure 11.2 The Consumer Buying Process

Problem/Need Recognition   This process begins when the consumer recognizes a problem or need. Need recognition also occurs when you have a chance to change your buying habits. When you obtain your first job after graduation, your new income may let you buy things that were once too expensive for you. You may find that you need professional clothing, apartment furnishings, and a car. Bank of America and Citibank cater to such shifts in needs when they market credit cards to college students.

Information Seeking   Having recognized a need, consumers often seek information. The search is not always extensive, but before making major purchases, most people seek information from personal sources, public sources, and experience. From this information search, consumers develop an **evoked set** or **consideration set,** which is the group of products they will consider buying.

Evaluation of Alternatives   If someone is in the market for skis, they probably have some idea of who makes skis and how they differ. By analyzing product attributes (price, prestige, quality) of the consideration set, consumers compare products before deciding which one best meets their needs.

Purchase Decision   Ultimately, consumers make purchase decisions. "Buy" decisions are based on rational motives, emotional motives, or both. **Rational motives** involve the logical evaluation of product attributes: cost, quality, and usefulness. **Emotional motives** involve nonobjective factors and include sociability, imitation of others, and aesthetics. For example, you might buy the same brand of jeans as your friends to feel accepted in a certain group, not because your friends happen to have the good sense to prefer durable, comfortably priced jeans.

Postpurchase Evaluation   Marketing does not stop with the sale of a product. What happens after the sale is important. Marketers want consumers to be happy after buying products so that they are more likely to buy them again. Because consumers do not want to go through a complex decision process for every purchase, they often repurchase products they have used and liked. Not all consumers are satisfied with their purchases. These buyers are not likely to purchase the same product(s) again and are much more apt to broadcast their experiences than are satisfied customers.

Organizational Marketing and Buying Behavior

5 Discuss the three categories of organizational markets.

In the consumer market, buying and selling transactions are visible to the public. Equally important, though far less visible, are organizational (or commercial) markets. Marketing to organizations that buy goods and services used in creating and delivering consumer products involves various kinds of markets and buying behaviors different from those in consumer markets.

Business Marketing

Business marketing involves organizational or commercial markets that fall into three B2B categories: industrial, reseller, and government/institutional markets. Taken together, the B2B markets do over $25 trillion in business annually—more than two times the amount done in the U.S. consumer market.[15]

Industrial Market   The **industrial market** includes businesses that buy goods to be converted into other products or that are used up during production. It includes farmers, manufacturers, and some retailers. For example, clockmaking company Seth Thomas buys electronics, metal components, and glass from other companies to make clocks for the consumer market. The company also buys office supplies, tools, and factory equipment—items never seen by clock buyers—that are used during production.

Reseller Market   Before products reach consumers, they pass through a **reseller market** consisting of intermediaries, including wholesalers and retailers, that buy and resell finished goods. For example, as a leading distributor of parts and accessories for the pleasure boat market, Coast Distribution System buys lights, steering wheels, and propellers and resells them to marinas and boat-repair shops.

Government and Institutional Market   In addition to federal and state governments, there are some 87,000 local governments in the United States. State and local governments annually spend nearly $7 trillion for durable goods, nondurables, services, and construction.[16] The **institutional market** consists of nongovernmental organizations, such as hospitals, churches, museums, and charities, that also use supplies and equipment as well as legal, accounting, and transportation services.

B2B Buying Behavior

In some respects, organizational buying behavior bears little resemblance to consumer buying practices. Differences include the buyers' purchasing skills and an emphasis on buyer-seller relationships.

Differences in Buyers   Unlike most consumers, organizational buyers purchase in large quantities, and are professional, specialized, and well informed.

- Industrial buyers buy in bulk or large quantities. Because of this fact, and with so much money at stake, the following are also characteristics of organizational buyers.

Evoked Set (or Consideration Set) group of products consumers will consider buying as a result of information search

Rational Motives reasons for purchasing a product that are based on a logical evaluation of product attributes

Emotional Motives reasons for purchasing a product that are based on nonobjective factors

Industrial Market organizational market consisting of firms that buy goods that are either converted into products or used during production

Reseller Market organizational market consisting of intermediaries that buy and resell finished goods

Institutional Market organizational market consisting of such nongovernmental buyers of goods and services as hospitals, churches, museums, and charitable organizations

- As professionals, B2B buyers are trained in methods for negotiating purchase terms. Once buyer-seller agreements have been reached, they also arrange formal contracts.

- As a rule, industrial buyers are company specialists in a line of items and are often experts about the products they buy. As one of several buyers for a large bakery, for example, you may specialize in food ingredients. Another buyer may specialize in baking equipment (industrial ovens and mixers), whereas a third may buy office equipment and supplies.

Differences in the Buyer-Seller Relationship Consumer-seller relationships are often impersonal, short-lived, one-time interactions. In contrast, B2B situations often involve frequent and enduring buyer-seller relationships. The development of a long-term relationship provides each party with access to the technical strengths of the other as well as the security of knowing what future business to expect. Thus, a buyer and a supplier may form a design team to create products to benefit both parties. Accordingly, industrial sellers emphasize personal selling by trained representatives who understand the needs of each customer.

What Is a Product?

6 Explain the definition of a product as a value package and classify goods and services.

In developing the marketing mix for any product, whether goods or services, marketers must consider what customers really want when they purchase products. Only then can these marketers plan strategies effectively.

The Value Package

Whether it is a physical good, a service, or some combination of the two, customers get value from the various benefits, features, and even intangible rewards associated with a product. **Product features** are the qualities, tangible and intangible, that a company builds into its products, such as a 12-horsepower motor on a lawnmower. However, as we discussed earlier, to attract buyers, features must also provide benefits: The lawnmower must produce an attractive lawn. The owner's pleasure in knowing that the mower is nearby when needed is an intangible reward.

Today's customer regards a product as a bundle of attributes—benefits and features—that, taken together, marketers call the **value package.** Increasingly, buyers expect to receive products with greater value—with more benefits and features at reasonable costs—so firms must compete on the basis of enhanced value packages. Consider, for example, the possible attributes in a personal computer value package:

- Easy access to understandable prepurchase information

- Features, such as wireless capability

- Attractive color and design

- Useful software packages

- Attractive prices

- Fast, simple ordering via the Internet

- Secure credit card purchasing

- Assurance of speedy delivery

- Warranties

- Easy access to technical support

Although the computer includes physical *features*—processing devices and other hardware—many items in the value package are services or intangibles that, collectively, add value by providing *benefits* that increase the customer's satisfaction. Reliable data processing is certainly a benefit, but so too are speedy delivery and easy access to technical support. Top-performing companies find that the addition of a new service often pleases customers far beyond the cost of providing it. Just making the purchase transaction faster and more convenient, for example, adds value by sparing customers long waits and cumbersome paperwork.

Classifying Goods and Services

We can classify products according to expected buyers, who fall into two groups: buyers of consumer products and buyers of organizational products. As we saw earlier in this chapter, the consumer and industrial buying processes differ significantly. Similarly, marketing products to consumers is vastly different from marketing products to companies and other organizations.

Classifying Consumer Products Consumer products are commonly divided into three categories that reflect buyer behavior: **convenience goods and services, shopping goods and services,** and **specialty goods and services.** These are outlined in Table 11.2.

Classifying Organizational Products Depending on how much they cost and how they will be used, organizational products can be divided into three categories: **production items, expense items,** and **capital items.** These are explained in Table 11.3.

TABLE 11.2	Categories of Consumer Products	
Category	**Description**	**Examples**
Convenience goods and services	• Consumed rapidly and regularly • Inexpensive • Purchased often and with little input of time and effort	• Milk • Newspaper • Fast food
Shopping goods and services	• Purchased less often • More expensive • Consumers may shop around and compare products based on style, performance, color, price, and other criteria.	• Television set • Tires • Car insurance
Specialty goods and services	• Purchased infrequently • Expensive • Consumer decides on a precise product and will not accept substitutions and spends a good deal of time choosing the "perfect" item.	• Jewelry • Wedding gown • Catering

Product Features tangible and intangible qualities that a company builds into its products

Value Package product marketed as a bundle of value-adding attributes, including reasonable cost

Convenience Good/Convenience Service inexpensive good or service purchased and consumed rapidly and regularly

Shopping Good/Shopping Service moderately expensive, infrequently purchased good or service

Specialty Good/Specialty Service expensive, rarely purchased good or service

Production Item industrial product purchased and used directly in the production process that creates other goods or services

Expense Item industrial product purchased and consumed within a year by firms producing other products

Capital Item expensive, long-lasting, infrequently purchased industrial product, such as a building, or industrial service, such as a long-term agreement for data warehousing services

TABLE 11.3   Organizational Products

Category	Description	Examples
Production items	• Goods or services used directly in the production process	• Loads of tea processed into tea bags • Information processing for real-time production
Expense items	• Goods or services that are consumed within a year by firms producing other goods or supplying other services	• Oil and electricity for machines • Building maintenance • Legal services
Capital items	• Permanent (expensive and long-lasting) goods and services • Life expectancy of more than a year • Purchased infrequently so transactions often involve decisions by high-level managers	• Buildings (offices, factories) • Fixed equipment (water towers, baking ovens) • Accessory equipment (computers, airplanes)

The Product Mix

The group of products that a company makes available for sale, whether consumer, industrial, or both, is its **product mix.** Black & Decker, for example, makes toasters, vacuum cleaners, electric drills, and a variety of other appliances and tools. 3M makes everything from Post-it Notes to laser optics.

Product Lines   Many companies begin with a single product. Over time, they find that the initial product fails to suit every customer shopping for the product type. To meet market demand, they introduce similar products—such as flavored coffees and various roasts—designed to reach more customers. For example, Starbucks stores expanded the line of coffees by adding various Italian-style espresso beverages that include mochas, cappucinos, and lattes—hot and iced—and flavored blended cremes. A group of products that are closely related because they function in a similar manner (e.g., flavored coffees) or are sold to the same customer group (e.g., stop-in coffee drinkers) who will use them in similar ways is a **product line.**

Companies may extend their horizons and identify opportunities outside existing product lines. The result—multiple (or diversified) product lines—is evident at Starbucks. Beyond just serving beverages to customers at coffee bars, Starbucks has lines of home-brewing equipment, supermarket products, music products, and industry services. Multiple product lines allow a company to grow rapidly and can help offset the consequences of slow sales in any one product line.

7   Describe the key considerations in the new product development process, and explain the importance of branding and packaging.

Developing New Products

To expand or diversify product lines—in fact, just to survive—firms must develop and introduce streams of new products. Faced with competition and shifting customer preferences, no firm can count on a single successful product to carry it forever.

The New Product Development Process

For many years, the growing demand for improved health care has stimulated the development of new dietary supplements, heart medicines, and other pharmaceuticals. However, companies that develop and sell these products face a big problem: It costs well over $100 million, sometimes over $1 billion, and can take as long as 8 to 10 years to get a new product through the approval process at the U.S. Food and Drug Administration (FDA).

Testing, both for FDA approval and for marketing, can be the most time-consuming stage of development. For example, Merck & Co. is developing an experimental heart drug—called anacetrapib—to raise levels of good cholesterol, thereby reducing the risk of heart attack. Years of laboratory work were followed by a lengthy test study using 1,600 patients, and the results of that study must undergo further analysis. Thereafter, a major 30,000-patient study beginning in 2011 must be completed before the drug may be deemed ready for approval and use sometime after 2015.[17] If successful, Merck could cash in on the growth of the cholesterol-lowering drug market, but it requires an immense amount of time, patience, money, and risk of failure.

Product development is a long and expensive process, and like Merck & Co., many firms have research and development (R&D) departments for exploring new product possibilities. Why do they devote so many resources to exploring product possibilities, rejecting many seemingly good ideas along the way? First, high *mortality rates* for new ideas mean that only a few new products reach the market. Second, for many companies, *speed to market* with a product is as important as care in developing it.

Product Mortality Rates

It is estimated that it takes 50 new product ideas to generate one product that finally reaches the market. Even then, only a few of these survivors become successful products. Many seemingly great ideas have failed as products. Creating a successful new product has become increasingly difficult—even for the most experienced marketers. Why? The number of new products hitting the market each year has increased dramatically; more than 180,000 new household, grocery, and drugstore items are introduced annually. In 2009 the U.S. consumer packaged goods industry alone launched 45,000 new products (foods, beverages, school supplies, and other nonfood products).[18] At any given time, however, the average North American supermarket carries a total of only 45,000 different items. Because of lack of space and customer demand, about 9 out of 10 new products will fail. Those with the best chances are innovative and deliver unique benefits. The single greatest factor in product failure is the lack of significant difference (i.e., the new product is a "me-too" product). Some prominent examples of this are Mr. Pibb versus Dr. Pepper, which while still on the market is an "also-ran," and Burger King's Big King, their answer to the Big Mac.

Speed to Market   The more rapidly a product moves from the laboratory to the marketplace, the more likely it is to survive. By introducing new products ahead of competitors, companies establish market leadership. They become entrenched in the market before being challenged by newer competitors. For example, sales of Apple's new iPad surged after its introduction in early 2010, and estimates are that more than 13 million units were sold by year end. Industry observers expect nearly every other company in the industry will try to come out with competing products beginning later in 2011, but the iPad's visibility and popularity make it a formidable market leader. How important is **speed to market** (or *time compression*)—that is, a firm's success in responding rapidly to customer demand or market changes? One study reports that a product that is only three months late to market (three months behind the leader) loses 12 percent of its lifetime profit potential. At six months, it will lose 33 percent.

Product Life Cycle

When a product reaches the market, it enters the **product life cycle (PLC)**: a series of stages through which it passes during its commercial life. Depending on the product's ability to attract and keep customers, its PLC may be a matter of months, years,

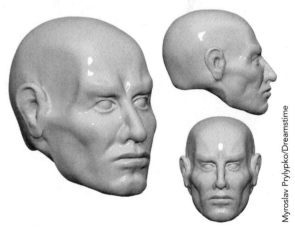

Myroslav Prylypko/Dreamstime

Designers used to create products, such as this head for a human-like toy, by sculpting models out of clay. Now they use "rapid prototyping," a technology that allows several employees to work simultaneously on 3D digital/visual "models" that can be e-mailed to clients for instant review. It now takes days, or just hours, instead of weeks to make an initial sculpture.

Product Mix group of products that a firm makes available for sale

Product Line group of products that are closely related because they function in a similar manner or are sold to the same customer group who will use them in similar ways

Speed To Market strategy of introducing new products to respond quickly to customer or market changes

Product Life Cycle (PLC) series of stages in a product's commercial life

or decades. Strong, mature products (such as Clorox bleach and H&R Block tax preparation) have had long productive lives.

Stages in the PLC   The life cycle for both goods and services is a natural process in which products are born, grow in stature, mature, and finally decline and die. Look at the two graphics in Figure 11.3. In Figure 11.3(a), the four phases of the PLC are applied to several products with which you are familiar:

Introduction. This stage begins when the product reaches the marketplace. Marketers focus on making potential customers aware of the product and its benefits. Extensive development, production, and sales costs erase all profits.

Growth. If the new product attracts enough customers, sales start to climb rapidly. Marketers lower price slightly and continue promotional expenditures to increase sales. The product starts to show a profit as revenues surpass costs, and other firms move rapidly to introduce their own versions.

Maturity. Sales growth starts to slow. Although the product earns its highest profit level early in this stage, increased competition eventually forces price-cutting, increasing advertising and promotional expenditures, and lower profits. Toward the end of the stage, sales start to fall.

Figure 11.3 Products in the Life Cycle: (a) Phases and (b) Profit (or Loss)
Source: Adapted from Jay Heizer and Barry Render, *Operations Management*, 7th ed. (Upper Saddle River, NJ: Prentice Hall, 2004), 157.

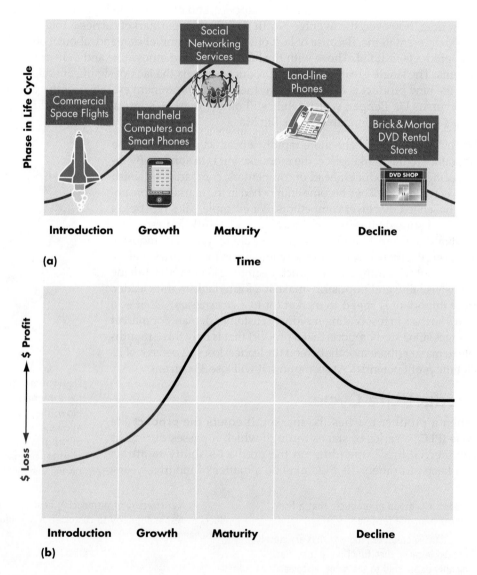

Decline. Sales and profits continue to fall, as new products in the introduction stage take away sales. Firms end or reduce promotional support (ads and sales-people), but may let the product linger to provide some profits.

Figure 11.3(b) plots the relationship of the PLC to a product's typical profits (in black) or losses (in red). Although the early stages of the PLC often show financial losses, increased sales for successful products recover earlier losses and continue to generate profits until the decline stage. For many products, profitable life spans are short—thus, the importance placed by so many firms on the constant replenishment of product lines.

Identifying Products

Marketers must also identify products so that consumers recognize them. Two important tools for this task are branding and packaging.

Branding Products   Coca-Cola is the best-known brand in the world. Some Coke executives claim that if all the company's other assets were obliterated, they could go to the bank and borrow $100 billion on the strength of the brand name alone. Indeed, Interbrand, the brand-ranking firm, says the Coke brand in 2010 was worth over $70 billion in terms of revenue generation from its ability to create demand for the product. Industry observers regard brands as a company's most valuable asset.[19] **Branding** is a process of using names and symbols, like Coca-Cola or McDonald's golden arches, to communicate the qualities of a particular product made by a particular producer. Brands are designed to signal uniform quality; customers who try and like a product can return to it by remembering its name or its logo.

Several benefits result from successful branding, including brand loyalty and **brand awareness**—the brand name that first comes to mind when you consider a particular product category. What company, for example, comes to mind when you need to ship a document a long way on short notice? For many people, FedEx has the necessary brand awareness.

Gaining Brand Awareness   The expensive, sometimes fierce struggle for brand recognition is perhaps nowhere more evident than in branding battles among dot-com firms. Collectively, the top Internet brands—Google (ranked fourth), eBay (forty-third), and Amazon.com (thirty-sixth)—spend billions a year, even though only Google, Amazon, and eBay have cracked the ranks of the top 50 global brands.[20] Moreover, the mounting costs of establishing a brand identity mean that many more would-be e-businesses do and will probably fail.

With its growing importance in nearly every industry, marketers are finding more effective, less expensive ways to gain brand awareness. Recent successes have been found with several methods, including product placements, buzz marketing, viral marketing, and social networking.

Product Placements   Television commercials can be a real turnoff for many viewers, but entertainment programming gets our full attention. And that's when marketers are turning up the promotional juice with **product placement**—a promotional tactic for brand exposure in which characters in television, film, music, magazines, or video games use a real product with a brand visible to viewers.

Branding process of using symbols to communicate the qualities of a product made by a particular producer

Brand Awareness extent to which a brand name comes to mind when a consumer considers a particular product category

Product Placement a promotional tactic for brand exposure in which characters in television, film, music, magazines, or video games use a real product with its brand visible to viewers

Product placements are effective because the message is delivered in an attractive setting that holds the customer's interest. When used in successful films and TV shows, the brand's association with famous performers is an implied celebrity endorsement. The idea is to legitimize the brand in the mind of the customer. In all, nearly $5 billion is spent annually on product placements, especially in television, and major marketers are putting more into product placements instead of television advertisements. A Minute Maid beverage and Clorox make appearances in the hit movie *Madea Goes to Jail*, while the new Mini Cooper brand was launched in the movie, *The Italian Job*. In print placements, Hewlett-Packard computers appear in the photo layouts in the IKEA catalog. Television placements are widespread, including Hyundai in *Leverage* and *Burn Notice*, and are especially effective as digital video recorders (DVRs) remain popular. Viewers can use their DVRs to skip commercials in recorded shows, but product placements are unavoidable.

Buzz Marketing   One method for increasing brand awareness is **buzz marketing** which relies on word-of-mouth to spread "buzz" about a particular product or idea. Buzz marketing agencies provide volunteer participants with new products to try and ask them to share the buzz with their friends, family, coworkers, and others in their social network. Here's the key—most companies running word-of-mouth campaigns require full disclosure, which means the participants should let people know they are participating in a campaign. This is essential so that those on the receiving end of the "buzz" don't feel tricked or taken advantage of.

Viral Marketing and Social Networking   **Viral marketing** is the new form of buzz marketing that relies on social networking on the Internet to spread information like a "virus" from person to person. Messages about new cars, sports events, and numerous other goods and services flow via networks among potential customers who pass the information on to others. Using various social network formats—games, contests, chat rooms, blogs, and bulletin boards—marketers encourage potential customers to try out products and tell other people about them. Marketers—including such giants as Bank of America, McDonald's, eBay, and Cisco—are using **corporate blogs** increasingly for public relations, branding, and otherwise spreading messages that stimulate chat about products to target markets.[21] Many major consumer companies now have their own Facebook page.

How effective can it be? Viral marketing can lead to consumer awareness faster and with wider reach than traditional media messages—and at a lower cost. It works for two reasons. First, people rely on the Internet for information that they used to get from newspapers, magazines, and television. Equally important, however, is the interactive element: The customer becomes a participant in the process of spreading the word by forwarding information to other Internet users. Success of the movie *Avatar* is credited to 20th Century Fox's use of pre-release viral tactics for stimulating public awareness of the blockbuster movie.

Types of Brand Names   Just about every product has a brand name. Generally, different types of brand names—national, licensed, or private—increase buyers' awareness of the nature and quality of competing products. When customers are satisfied with a product, marketers try to build brand loyalty among the largest possible segment of repeat buyers.

National Brands   **National brands** are produced by, widely distributed by, and carry the name of the manufacturer. These brands are often widely recognized by customers because of national advertising campaigns, and they are, therefore, valuable assets. Because the costs of developing a national brand are high, some companies use a national brand on several related products, called **brand extension**. Procter & Gamble now markets Ivory Shampoo, capitalizing on the name of its bar soap and dishwashing liquid. While cost efficient, this can sometimes dilute the original brand's effectiveness. Coors Light Beer now outsells original Coors Beer.

Licensed Brands   We have become used to companies (and even personalities) selling the rights to put their names on products. These are called **licensed brands.**

For example, the popularity of auto racing is generating millions in revenues for the NASCAR brand, which licenses its name on car accessories, ladies and men's apparel, headsets, and countless other items with the names of popular drivers such as Martin, Johnson, Stewart, and Edwards. Harley-Davidson's famous logo—emblazoned on boots, eyewear, gloves, purses, lighters, and watches—brings the motorcycle maker more than $200 million annually. Along with brands such as Coors and Ferrari, licensing for character-based brands—Tinker Bell, Mickey Mouse, and other Disney characters—are equally lucrative. Marketers exploit brands because of their public appeal—the image and status that customers hope to gain by associating with them.

Private Brands   When a wholesaler or retailer develops a brand name and has a manufacturer put it on a product, the resulting name is a **private brand** (or **private label**). Sears, which carries such lines as Craftsman tools, Canyon River Blues denim clothing, and Kenmore appliances, is a well-known seller of private brands.

Packaging Products   With a few exceptions, products need some form of **packaging** to reduce the risk of damage, breakage, or spoilage, and to increase the difficulty of stealing small products. A package also serves as an in-store advertisement that makes the product attractive, displays the brand name, and identifies features and benefits. Also, packaging features, such as no-drip bottles of Clorox bleach, add utility for consumers.

The International Marketing Mix

8 Discuss the marketing mix as it applies to international and small business.

Marketing internationally means mounting a strategy to support global business operations. Foreign customers, for example, differ from domestic buyers in language, customs, business practices, and consumer behavior. If they go global, marketers must reconsider each element of the marketing mix—product, pricing, place, and promotion.

International Products

Some products can be sold abroad with virtually no changes. Coca-Cola and Marlboro are the same in Peoria, Illinois, and Paris, France. In other cases, U.S. firms have had to create products with built-in flexibility—for example, an electric shaver that is adaptable to either 120- or 230-volt outlets, so travelers can use it in both U.S. and European electrical outlets. Frequently, however, domestic products require a major redesign for buyers in foreign markets. To sell computers in Japan, for example, Apple had to develop a Japanese-language operating system.

International Pricing

When pricing for international markets, marketers must consider the higher costs of transporting and selling products abroad. For example, because of the higher costs of buildings, rent, equipment, and imported meat, a McDonald's Big Mac costs more in Switzerland than in the United States.

Buzz Marketing promotional method that relies on word of mouth to create buzz about products and ideas

Viral Marketing type of buzz marketing that relies on the Internet to spread information like a "virus" from person to person about products and ideas

Corporate Blogs comments and opinions published on the web by or for an organization to promote its activities

National Brand brand-name product produced by, widely distributed by, and carrying the name of a manufacturer

Brand Extension a company's use of a national brand on several additional related products

Licensed Brand brand-name product for whose name the seller has purchased the right from an organization or individual

Private Brand (Private Label) brand-name product that a wholesaler or retailer has commissioned from a manufacturer

Packaging physical container in which a product is sold, advertised, or protected

Indranil Kishor/Majority World/Photoshot

Before creating an international ad like this Chinese advertisement for Coca-Cola, it is crucial to research what disparities, such as meaning of words, traditions, and taboos, exist between different societies. For example, German manufacturers of backpacks label them as "body bags," not terribly enticing to the U.S. consumer. Can you guess why Gerber baby food is not sold in France? The French translation of Gerber is "to vomit"! Effective marketing does not just involve knowledge of culture abroad, but also requires a general sensitivity to social trends and language.

International Distribution

In some industries, delays in starting new international distribution networks can be costly. Therefore, companies with existing distribution systems often enjoy an advantage. Many companies have avoided time delays by buying existing businesses with already-established distribution and marketing networks. Procter & Gamble, for example, bought Revlon's Max Factor and Betrix cosmetics, both of which have distribution and marketing networks in foreign markets. And many times, distribution methods used in the United States don't fit in international markets. For example, in Europe, Breathe Right Nasal Strips are identified as "medicinal" and must be sold in pharmacies.

International Promotion

Occasionally, a good ad campaign is a good campaign just about anywhere. Quite often, however, U.S. promotional tactics do not succeed in other countries. Many Europeans believe that a product must be inherently shoddy if a company resorts to any advertising, particularly the American hard-sell variety.

International marketers are ever more aware of cultural differences that can cause negative reactions to improperly advertised products. Some Europeans, for example, are offended by TV commercials that show weapons or violence. Meanwhile, cigarette commercials that are banned from U.S. television thrive in many Asian and European markets. Product promotions must be carefully matched to local customs and cultural values.

Because of the need to adjust the marketing mix, success in international markets is hard won. But whether a firm markets in domestic or international markets, the basic principles of marketing still apply; only their implementation changes.

Small Business and the Marketing Mix

Many of today's largest firms were yesterday's small businesses. Behind the success of many small firms lies a skillful application of the marketing concept and an understanding of each element in the marketing mix.

Small-Business Products   Some new products and firms are doomed at the start because few customers want or need what they have to offer. Many fail to estimate realistic market potential, and some offer new products before they have clear pictures of their target segments. In contrast, a thorough understanding of what customers want has paid off for many small firms. Take, for example, the case of Little Earth Productions, Inc., a company that makes fashion accessories, such as handbags. Originally, the company merely considered how consumers would use its handbags. But after examining shopping habits, Little Earth Productions redesigned for better in-store display. Because stores can give handbags better visibility by hanging them instead of placing them on floors or low countertops, Little Earth Productions added small handles specifically for that purpose.

ENTREPRENEURSHIP AND NEW VENTURES

Social Networking for Job Opportunities in Tough Times

If you're out of work, looking for a job, and wondering where to turn, help is as close as your PC or iPod. While troubled times have dampened demand for many products, others are getting a boost. Service products such as social networking sites are an example. While popular entertainment sites—including Facebook and MySpace—began as cyber highways for recreational and friendship interactions, social networking is no longer just for entertainment. In today's economy, there's a different kind of traffic—professional networking for career transition—among the list of cyber networking products for job-hunting assistance.

LinkedIn, started by five co-founders in the living room of Reid Hoffman in 2002, is an example of an interconnected network that now serves professionals in 200 countries and some 170 industries. Officially founded in 2003, this Mountain View, California, start-up had 4,500 members in the network after just one month. Today, profiles from more than 85 million members include executives from all *Fortune 500* companies. Users can post résumés, search companies, and find job openings. The Linkedin jobs directory allows users choices for searching by industry, or by job function, geographic region, job title, or by company. However, the key attraction of the network is personal connections: One member knows other LinkedIn users, who link with still others, and so on as information flows to those looking for good candidates until they find a word-of-mouth prospect that looks good. The system is based on trusted relationships and connections, and it works: LinkedIn is the world's largest business network, and it connects a huge pool of talent that keeps on growing.

In addition to professionals looking for jobs, there are also business members, some searching for prospective employees, industry experts, potential clients, or new business opportunities. Others are interested in sharing the latest business developments within their networks of contacts. LinkedIn Open Groups, for example, consists of specialty network-groups of businesses focused on particular industries, including Social Media Marketing, or Finance and Accounting Professionals, or Business in Japan, to name just three of many. Group members may share industry-specific information on performance-enhancing practices, legal issues, current events, and even participate in determining new directions for their industry. LinkedIn's further growth depends on the value it provides for meeting its members' needs for professional fulfillment.[22]

MyBizLab

Vika Sabo/Alamy

Small-Business Pricing Haphazard pricing can sink a firm with a good product. Small-business pricing errors usually result from a failure to estimate operating expenses accurately. Owners of failing businesses have often been heard to say, "I didn't realize how much it costs to run the business!" But when small businesses set prices by carefully assessing costs, many earn satisfactory profits.

Small-Business Distribution The ability of many small businesses to attract and retain customers depends partly on the choice of location, especially for new service businesses.

In distribution as in other aspects of the marketing mix, however, smaller companies may have advantages over larger competitors. A smaller company may be able to address customers' needs more quickly and efficiently with an added personal touch. Everex Systems, Inc. of Fremont, California, designs and sells computers to wholesalers and dealers through a system that the company calls *zero response time*. Because Everex Systems is small and flexible, phone orders can be reviewed every two hours and factory assembly adjusted to match demand.

Small-Business Promotion Successful small businesses plan for promotional expenses as part of start-up costs. Some hold down costs by using less expensive promotional methods, like publicity in local newspapers. Other small businesses identify themselves and their products with associated groups, organizations, and events. Thus, a crafts gallery might join with a local art league to organize public showings of their combined products.

Richard Levine/Alamy

Continued from page 269

Can Starbucks Have the Best of Both Markets—Luxury AND Affordability?

Howard Schultz, Starbucks CEO, admits that the recession is propelling not only economic behavior, but social behavior as well. Among the recession's belt-tightening behaviors are consumers' purchasing habits, including their choices for coffee products. Convenience and affordability have moved to the forefront with coffee-drinkers, and Starbucks wants to show it is moving with them with lower prices and more value packages. Can the prestige-oriented Starbucks brand fend off competitors, including McDonald's, with its already-established image for affordability and convenience? Even at its Seattle home base, Starbucks officials may have blanched at an aggressive McDonald's billboard ad with its pointed broadside about coffee-drink prices: "Four bucks is dumb."

In addition to its upscale coffee houses, Starbucks can also be found at non-traditional locations as part of its "convenience and affordability" movement, as seen here.

B Christopher/Alamy

Part of its repositioning, then, involves changing any misperceptions that may linger among coffee consumers, especially regarding Starbucks's luxury image with upscale coffees and prices. Starting in-house, the company's baristas are being trained to communicate to consumers that its prices are affordable: 90 percent of the drinks cost less than $4, with an average drink price under $3. And the new value-pricing with meals drives prices even lower: At $3.95, you can get a 12 ounce coffee with a breakfast sandwich. Are the company's promotional efforts working? One report in 2009 indicates that while Starbucks's prices remain higher than McDonald's, the gap has narrowed since 2007.[23] But pricing is only one factor that can turn around decreasing sales and reverse a recent profitability shrinkage of nearly 70 percent. That's why Starbucks continues to revise its distribution network globally—to reduce operating costs by closing hundreds of existing stores and opening fewer new ones.[24]

QUESTIONS FOR DISCUSSION

1 What forces in the external environment are influencing the changes in Starbucks's marketing strategy? Explain.

2 How are the components of Starbucks's marketing mix being used for implementing the new marketing strategy?

3 Identify the main factors favoring success for Starbucks's crossover into the affordability market. What prominent factors suggest major problems or even failure for this crossover attempt?

4 Applying this chapter's definition of product value to Starbucks's plans, what are the benefits in Starbucks's affordability offerings? What are the costs?

5 In what ways, if any, does Starbucks's plan for closing some existing stores and opening fewer new ones have any impact on the product value of its new affordability products and its more-established luxury products?

SUMMARY OF LEARNING OBJECTIVES   MyBizLab

1. **Explain the concept of marketing and identify the five forces that constitute the external marketing environment. (pp. 270–275)**
   Marketing is responsible for creating, communicating, and delivering value and satisfaction to customers at a profit. Marketing manages customer relationships to benefit the organization and its stakeholders. After identifying customers' needs and wants, it develops plans to satisfy them by creating products, establishing their prices, methods for distributing them, and ways for promoting them to potential customers. Marketing is successful if satisfied buyers perceive that the benefits derived from each purchase outweigh its costs, and if the firm, in exchange for providing the products, meets its organizational goals. Five outside factors comprise a company's external environment and influence its marketing programs: (1) *political and legal actions*, (2) *sociocultural factors*, (3) *technological changes*, (4) *economics*, and (5) *competition*.

2. **Explain the purpose of a marketing plan and identify the four components of the marketing mix. (pp. 275–277)**
   The *marketing plan* is a detailed strategy for focusing marketing efforts on meeting consumer needs and wants. The plan defines the organization's marketing goals, and identifies all the activities for reaching those goals, that will result in the successful transfer of goods and services to its customers. In planning and implementing strategies, marketing managers focus on the four elements (Four Ps) of the *marketing mix*: (1) *products* for consumers, (2) *pricing* of products, (3) *place (distribution)* of products to consumers, and (4) *promotion* of products.

3. **Explain market segmentation and how it is used in target marketing. (pp. 277–278)**
   Marketers think in terms of *target markets*—groups of people or organizations with similar wants and needs and who can be expected to show interest in the same products. Target marketing requires *market segmentation*—dividing a market into categories of customer types or "segments." Members of a market segment must share some common traits that influence purchasing decisions. Once they identify segments, companies adopt a variety of strategies for attracting customers in one or more of the chosen target segments. The following are five variables used for segmentation: (1) *Geographic variables* are the geographical units that may be considered in developing a segmentation strategy. (2) *Demographic variables* describe populations by identifying such traits as age, income, gender, ethnic background, and marital status. (3) *Geo-demographic variables* combine demographic variables with geographic variables, such as an age category coupled with urban areas. (4) *Psychographic variables* include lifestyles, interests, and attitudes. (5) *Behavioral variables* include categories of behavioral patterns such as online consumers or large-volume buyers.

4. **Describe the key factors that influence the consumer buying process. (pp. 279–280)**
   One consumer behavior model considers five influences that lead to consumption: (1) *Problem/need recognition*: The buying process begins when the consumer recognizes a problem or need. (2) *Information seeking*: Having recognized a need, consumers seek information. The information search leads to an evoked set (or consideration set)—a group of products they will consider buying. (3) *Evaluation of alternatives*: By analyzing product attributes (price, prestige, quality) of the consideration set, consumers compare products to decide which product best meets their needs. (4) *Purchase decision*: "Buy" decisions are based on rational motives, emotional motives, or both. *Rational motives* involve the logical evaluation of product attributes, such as cost, quality, and usefulness. *Emotional motives* involve nonobjective factors and include sociability, imitation of others, and aesthetics. (5) *Postpurchase evaluations*: Consumers continue to form opinions after their purchase. Marketers want consumers to be happy after the consumption of products so that they are more likely to buy them again.

5. **Discuss the three categories of organizational markets. (pp. 281–282)**
   (1) The *industrial market* consists of businesses that buy goods to be converted into other products or that are used during production. It includes farmers, manufacturers, and some retailers. (2) Before products reach consumers, they pass through a *reseller market* consisting of intermediaries—wholesalers and retailers—that buy finished goods and resell them. (3) The *government and institutional market* includes federal, state, and local governments, and nongovernmental buyers—hospitals, churches, and charities—that purchase goods and services needed for serving their clients. Taken together, these organizational markets do more than two times the business annually than that of the U.S. consumer markets.

6. **Explain the definition of a product as a value package and classify goods and services. (pp. 282–284)**
   Customers buy products to receive value that satisfies a want or a need. Thus, a successful product is a *value package*—a bundle of attributes that, taken together, provides the right features and offers the right benefits that satisfy customers' wants and needs. *Features* are the qualities, tangible and intangible, that are included with the product. To be satisfying, features must provide *benefits* that allow customers to achieve the end results they want. The value package has services and features that add value by providing benefits that increase the customer's satisfaction.
   Products (both goods and services) can be classified according to expected buyers as either *consumer products* or *organizational products*. *Convenience products* are inexpensive consumer goods and services that are consumed rapidly and regularly. *Shopping products* are more expensive and are purchased less often than convenience products. *Specialty products* are extremely important and expensive goods and services. *Organizational products* are classified as either *production items*, *expense items* or *capital items*. Production items are goods and services used directly in the production process. *Expense items* are goods or services consumed within a year to produce other products. *Capital items* are expensive and long-lasting goods and services that have expected lives of several years.

7. **Describe the key considerations in the new product development process, and explain the importance of branding and packaging. (pp. 284–289)**
   To expand or diversify product lines, new products must be developed and introduced. Many firms have research and development (R&D) departments for continuously exploring new product possibilities because high mortality rates for new ideas result in only a few new products reaching the market. Even then, only a few of these survivors become successful products. *Speed to market*—how fast a firm responds with new products or market

changes—determines a product's profitability and success. A continuous product development process is necessary because every product has a *product life cycle*—a series of stages through which it passes during its commercial life. The development of new products, then, is the source for renewal of the firm's product offerings in the marketplace.

Branding and packaging identify products so that consumers recognize them. Branding is the use of names and symbols, like Coca-Cola or McDonald's golden arches, to communicate the qualities of a particular product made by a particular producer. The goal in developing a brand is to distinguish a product from others so that consumers develop a preference for that particular brand name. Most products need some form of *packaging*—a physical container in which it is sold, advertised, or protected. A package makes the product attractive, displays the brand name, and identifies features and benefits. It also reduces the risk of damage, breakage, or spoilage, and it lessens the likelihood of theft.

8. **Discuss the marketing mix as it applies to international and small business. (pp. 289–291)**
   In going *global*, marketers must reconsider each element of the marketing mix—product, pricing, place, and promotion—because foreign customers differ from domestic buyers in language, customs, business practices, and consumer behavior. While some products can be sold abroad with virtually no changes, others require major redesign. Pricing must consider differences in the costs of transporting and selling products abroad. Delays in starting international distribution networks can be costly, so companies with existing distribution systems enjoy an advantage. Often, U.S. promotional tactics do not succeed in other countries, so promotional methods must be developed and matched to local customs and cultural values.

   Each element in the marketing mix can determine success or failure for any *small business*. Many *products* are failures because consumers don't need what they have to offer. A realistic market potential requires getting a clearer picture of what target segments want. Small-business pricing errors usually result from a failure to estimate operating expenses accurately. By carefully assessing costs, prices can be set to earn satisfactory profits. Perhaps the most crucial aspect of *place*, or distribution, is location because it determines the ability to attract customers. Although *promotion* can be expensive and is essential for small businesses, costs can be reduced by using less expensive promotional methods. Local newspaper articles and television cover business events, thus providing free public exposure.

KEY TERMS   MyBizLab

behavioral variables (p. 278)
brand awareness (p. 287)
brand competition (p. 275)
brand extension (p. 288)
brand loyalty (p. 279)
branding (p. 287)
buzz marketing (p. 288)
capital item (p. 283)
consumer behavior (p. 279)
consumer goods (p. 271)
convenience good/convenience service (p. 283)
corporate blogs (p. 288)
customer relationship management (CRM) (p. 272)
demographic variables (p. 278)
emotional motives (p. 280)
evoked set (or consideration set) (p. 280)
expense item (p. 283)
geo-demographic variables (p. 278)
geographic variables (p. 278)

industrial goods (p. 271)
industrial market (p. 281)
institutional market (p. 281)
integrated marketing strategy (p. 276)
international competition (p. 275)
licensed brand (p. 288)
market segmentation (p. 277)
marketing (p. 270)
marketing manager (p. 275)
marketing mix (p. 275)
marketing plan (p. 275)
national brand (p. 288)
packaging (p. 289)
place (distribution) (p. 276)
pricing (p. 276)
product (p. 275)
product differentiation (p. 275)
product features (p. 282)
product life cycle (PLC) (p. 285)
product line (p. 284)

product mix (p. 284)
product placement (p. 287)
product positioning (p. 277)
production item (p. 283)
promotion (p. 276)
psychographic variables (p. 278)
rational motives (p. 280)
relationship marketing (p. 271)
reseller market (p. 281)
services (p. 271)
shopping good/shopping service (p. 283)
specialty good/specialty service (p. 283)
speed to market (p. 285)
substitute product (p. 274)
target market (p. 277)
utility (p. 270)
value (p. 270)
value package (p. 282)
viral marketing (p. 288)

QUESTIONS AND EXERCISES

QUESTIONS FOR REVIEW

1. What are the key similarities and differences between consumer buying behavior and B2B buying behavior?
2. Why and how is market segmentation used in target marketing?
3. What are the various classifications of consumer and industrial products? Give an example of a good and a service for each category other than those discussed in the text.

4. How is the concept of the value package useful in marketing to consumers and industrial customers?

QUESTIONS FOR ANALYSIS

5. Select an everyday product (personal fitness training, CDs, dog food, cell phones, or shoes, for example). Show how different versions of your product are aimed toward different market segments. Explain how the marketing mix differs for each segment.

6. Select a second everyday product and describe the consumer buying process that typically goes into its purchase.

7. Consider a service product, such as transportation, entertainment, or health care. What are some ways that more customer value might be added to this product? Why would your improvements add value for the buyer?

8. How would you expect the branding and packaging of convenience, shopping, and specialty goods to differ? Why? Give examples to illustrate your answers.

APPLICATION EXERCISES

9. Identify a company with a product that interests you. Consider ways the company could use customer relationship management (CRM) to strengthen relationships with its target market. Specifically, explain your recommendations on how the company can use each of the four basic components of the marketing mix in its CRM efforts.

10. Select a product made by a foreign company and sold in the United States. What is the product's target market? What is the basis on which the target market is segmented? Do you think that this basis is appropriate? How might another approach, if any, be beneficial? Why?

11. Choose a product that could benefit from word-of-mouth buzz marketing. Then create a marketing campaign kit for participants to spread the word about this product.

BUILDING YOUR BUSINESS SKILLS

Dealing with Variables

Goal
To encourage you to analyze the ways in which various market segmentation variables affect business success.

Background Information
You and four partners are thinking of purchasing a heating and air conditioning (H/AC) dealership that specializes in residential applications priced between $2,000 and $40,000. You are now in the process of deciding where that dealership should be located. You are considering four locations: Miami, Florida; Westport, Connecticut; Dallas, Texas; and Spokane, Washington.

Method

Step 1
Working with your partnership group, examine some business information sources to learn how H/AC makers market residential products. Check for articles in the *Wall Street Journal, Business Week, Fortune*, and other business publication sources.

Step 2
Continue your research by focusing on the specific marketing variables that define each prospective location. Check Census Bureau and Department of Labor data at your library and on the Internet and contact local chambers of commerce (by phone and via the Internet) to learn about the following factors for each location:

1. Geography
2. Demography (especially age, income, gender, family status, and social class)
3. Geo-demographic information
4. Psychographic factors (lifestyles, interests, and attitudes)
5. Behavioral patterns of consumers

Step 3
As a group, determine which location holds the greatest promise as a dealership site. Base your decision on your analysis of market segment variables and their effects on H/AC sales.

FOLLOW-UP QUESTIONS

1. Which location did you choose? Describe the segmentation factors that influenced your decision.
2. Identify the two most important variables that you believe will affect the dealership's success. Why are these factors so important?
3. Which factors were least important? Why?
4. When equipment manufacturers advertise residential H/AC products, they often show them in different climate situations (winter, summer, or high-humidity conditions). Which market segments are these ads targeting? Describe these segments in terms of demographic and psychographic characteristics.

EXERCISING YOUR ETHICS: INDIVIDUAL EXERCISE

Driving a Legitimate Bargain

The Situation
A firm's marketing methods are sometimes at odds with the consumer's buying process. This exercise illustrates how ethical issues can become entwined with personal selling activities, product pricing, and customer relations.

The Dilemma
In buying his first new car, Matt visited showrooms and websites for every make of SUV. After weeks of reading and test-driving, he settled on a well-known Japanese-made vehicle with a manufacturer's suggested retail price of $37,500 for the 2011 model. The price included accessories and options that Matt considered essential. Because he planned to own the car for at least five years, he was willing to wait for just the right package rather than accept a lesser-equipped car already on the lot. Negotiations with Gary, the sales representative, continued for two weeks. Finally, a sales contract was signed for $33,600, with delivery due no more than two or three months later if the vehicle had to be special-ordered from the factory and earlier if Gary found the exact car when he searched other dealers around the country. On April 30, to close the deal, Matt had to write a check for $1,000.

Matt received a call on June 14 from Angela, Gary's sales manager: "We cannot get your car before October," she reported, "so it will have to be a 2012 model. You will have to pay the 2012 price." Matt replied that the agreement called for a stated price and delivery deadline for 2011, pointing out that money had exchanged hands for the contract. When asked what the 2012 price would be, Angela responded that it had not yet been announced. Angrily, Matt replied that he would be foolish to agree now on some unknown future price. Moreover, he didn't like the way the dealership was treating him. He told Angela to send him back everything he had signed; the deal was off.

QUESTIONS TO ADDRESS

1 Given the factors involved in the consumer buying process, how would you characterize the particular ethical issues in this situation?

2 From an ethical standpoint, what are the obligations of the sales representative and the sales manager regarding the pricing of the product in this situation?

3 If you were responsible for maintaining good customer relations at the dealership, how would you handle this matter?

EXERCISING YOUR ETHICS: TEAM EXERCISE

Cleaning Up in Sales

The Situation

Selling a product—whether a good or a service—requires the salesperson to believe in it, to be confident of his or her sales skills, and to keep commitments made to clients. Because so many people and resources are involved in delivering a product, numerous uncertainties and problems can give rise to ethical issues. This exercise encourages you to examine some of the ethical issues that can surface in the selling process for industrial products.

The Dilemma

Along with 16 other newly hired graduates, Denise Skilsel has just completed the sales training program for a new line of high-tech machinery that Cleaning Technologies Corporation (CTC) manufactures for industrial cleaners. As a new salesperson, Denise is eager to meet potential clients, all of whom are professional buyers for companies—such as laundries and dry cleaners, carpet cleaners, and military cleaners—that use CTC products or those of competitors. Denise is especially enthusiastic about several facts that she learned during training: CTC's equipment is the most technically advanced in the industry, carries a 10-year performance guarantee, and is safe—both functionally and environmentally.

The first month was difficult but successful: In visits to seven firms, Denise successfully closed three sales, earning large commissions (pay is based on sales results) as well as praise from the sales manager. Moreover, after listening to her presentations, two more potential buyers had given verbal commitments and were about to sign for much bigger orders than any Denise had closed to date. As she was catching her flight to close those sales, Denise received two calls—one from a client and one from a competitor. The client, just getting started with CTC equipment, was having

some trouble: Employees stationed nearby were getting sick when the equipment was running. The competitor told Denise that the U.S. Environmental Protection Agency (EPA) had received complaints that CTC's new technology was environmentally unsafe because of noxious emissions.

Team Activity

Assemble a group of four students and assign each group member to one of the following roles:

- Denise: CTC salesperson (employee)
- CTC sales manager (employer)
- CTC customer
- CTC investor

ACTION STEPS

1 Before hearing any of your group's comments on this situation, and from the perspective of your assigned role, what do you recommend Denise should say to the two client firms she is scheduled to visit? Write down your recommendation.

2 Gather your group together and reveal, in turn, each member's recommendation.

3 Appoint someone to record main points of agreement and disagreement within the group. How do you explain the results? What accounts for any disagreement?

4 Identify any ethical issues involved in group members' recommendations. Which issues, if any, are more critical than others?

5 From an ethical standpoint, what does your group finally recommend Denise should say to the two client firms she is scheduled to visit? Explain your result.

6 From the standpoint of customer relationship management, identify the advantages and drawbacks resulting from your recommendations.

VIDEO EXERCISE   MyBizLab

DC Shoes

Learning Objectives

The purpose of this video is to help you:

1 Understand the importance of branding.

2 Describe how market segmentation is used to create a target market for a product.

3 Discuss the components of the value package.

Synopsis

DC Shoes is a manufacturer and distributor of clothing and accessories for extreme sports enthusiasts. Founded in 1993 by rally racer Ken Block and skateboarder Damon Way, DC Shoes sells products for skateboarding, snowboarding, surfing, motocross, and BMX. The company's media arm, DC Films, produces high

quality videos that define and sustain the brand. Video shorts produced by DC Films often feature the company's products, but that is only the beginning. The films highlight extreme sports athletes and embody the lifestyle and priorities of their target market.

DISCUSSION QUESTIONS

1 Describe DC Shoes's target market in terms of age, gender, and lifestyle. How does the company's marketing mix appeal to this target market?

2 What are the components of DC Shoes's value package?

3 How does DC Shoes use its media arm, DC Films, to attract and retain customers?

4 How does DC Shoes differentiate themselves from their competition?

5 Recently, DC Shoes signed skateboarder Chris Cole. How did DC Shoes use buzz marketing before the announcement?

Online Exploration

DC Shoes has a multimedia approach to building its brand. Go to YouTube (www.youtube.com) and search for "DC Shoes" to find the company's YouTube channel. View a sample of the hundreds of videos, paying particular attention to the videos introducing Chris Cole. How does DC Shoes use YouTube and social media to build and define the brand? How is YouTube particularly suited to the company's target market?

END NOTES

[1] Janet Adamy, "At Starbucks, a Tall Order for New Cuts, Store Closures," *Wall Street Journal*, January 29, 2009, pp. B1, B4; Associated Press, "Want Fries with That?" *Columbia Daily Tribune*, February 3, 2009, p. 6B; Rick Wartzman, "A Marketing Spill on Starbucks' Hands," *BusinessWeek*, February 20, 2009, at http://www.businessweek.com/managing/content/feb2009/ca20090220_819348.htm; Michael Arndt, "McDonald's Specialty Coffee Kick," May 14, 2008, at http://www.businessweek.com/bwdaily/dnflash/content/may2008/db20080514_138620.htm; Associated Press, "Starbucks to Sell Value-Meal Pairings for $3.95," *MSNBC.com*, February 9, 2009, at http://www.msnbc.msn.com/id/29099087.

[2] American Marketing Association, "Marketing Definitions" (December 1, 2010), at http://www.marketingpower.com.

[3] Philip Kotler and Gary Armstrong, *Principles of Marketing*, 12th ed. (Upper Saddle River, NJ: Prentice Hall, 2008), 7.

[4] "CRM (customer relationship management)," *TechTarget.com*, accessed Dec. 8, 2010 at http://searchcrm.techtarget.com/definition/CRM ; "Customer Relationship Management," *Wikipedia*, accessed Dec. 8, 2010 at http://en.wikipedia.org/wiki/Customer_relationship_management

[5] Poonam Khanna, "Hotel Chain Gets Personal with Customers," *Computing Canada*, April 8, 2005, page 18.

[6] "Fairmont Hotels & Resorts: Website Development and Enhanced CRM," *accenture*, accessed Dec. 8, 2010 at http://www.accenture.com/Global/Services/By_Industry/Travel/Client_Successes/FairmontCrm.htm

[7] "Tiny House Purchases See Big Growth," *Columbia Daily Tribune*, December 4, 2010, page 11; "Solar Wells Displace Windmills on Range," Columbia Daily Tribune, July 22, 2010. Page 8B; Shawn McCarthy and Greg Keenan, "Ottawa Demands Lower Auto Worker Costs," *The Globe and Mail*, January 19, 2009, at http://v1business.theglobeandmail.com/servlet/story/RTGAM.20090119.wrautos19/BNStory/Business; Gail Edmondson, Ian Rowley, Nandini Lakshman, David Welch, and Dexter Roberts, "The Race to Build Really Cheap Cars," *BusinessWeek*, April 23, 2007, at http://www.businessweek.com/magazine/content/07_17/b4031064.htm; McClatchy Newspapers (Las Vegas), "Downsizing to 'Right-Sizing,'" *Columbia Daily Tribune: Saturday Business*, January 31, 2009, page 10; Jim Henry, "Prius Hybrid Aimed Small, Stood Tall," *Automotive News*, October 29, 2007, page 150 (3 pages) at http://www.autonews.com/apps/pbcs.dll/article?AID=/20071029/ANA06/710290326/1078&Profile=1078#; Burrelles Luce, "Hitting the Right Note: Best Practices for Corporate Social Responsibility (CSR) Marketing," *E-Newsletter*, July 2007, at http://luceonline.us/newsletter/default_july07.php.

[8] Shawn McCarthy and Greg Keenan, "Ottawa Demands Lower Auto Worker Costs," *The Globe and Mail*, January 19, 2009, at http://v1business.theglobeandmail.com/servlet/story/RTGAM.20090119.wrautos19/BNStory/Business; McClatchy Newspapers, "Lemons into Lemonade," *Columbia Daily Tribune*, February 2, 2009, page 7B.

[9] McClatchy Newspapers, "Airbus to Be Allowed to Bid to Replace Air Force One," *Columbia Daily Tribune*, January 25, 2009, page 4D.

[10] "Largest U.S. Magazines by Circulation: 2008," *nyjobsource.com* at www.nyjobsource.com/magazines.html

[11] Steve Schifferes, "The Triumph of Lean Production," *BBC News*, February 27, 2007, at http://news.bbc.co.uk/2/hi/business/6346315stm.

[12] "Financial Cards in Poland," Euromonitor International, (May 2008), at http://www.euromonitor.com/Consumer_Finance_in_Poland.

[13] "Halloween spending improves as shoppers hunt for deals," *USA TODAY*, (October 30, 2010) at http://www.usatoday.com/money/industries/retail/2010-10-30-halloween-sales_N.htm

[14] "2008 Brand Keys Customer Loyalty Engagement Index," (March 18, 2008), at http://www.brandkeys.com/awards/cli08.cfm.

[15] *U.S. Department of Commerce, Statistical Abstract of the United States: 2009* (Washington, DC: Bureau of the Census, 2008), Tables No. 413, 1006, and 1016; *National Income and Products Account Table*, Table 1.1.5 Gross Domestic Product, February 27, 2009 at http://www.bea.gov/national/index.htm.

[16] Ibid.

[17] Ron Winslow, "Cholesterol Drug Advances," *The Wall Street Journal*, November 18, 2010, pages B1–2.

[18] "Food Marketing System in the U.S.: New Product Introductions," *USDA Economic Research Service*, May 21, 2010, accessed at http://www.ers.usda.gov/Briefing/FoodMarketingSystem/new_product.htm

[19] "BP's Brand Value Sinks with Oil Spill," *Columbia Daily Tribune*, September 16, 2010, accessed at http://www.columbiatribune.com/news/2010/sep/16/bps-brand-value-sinks-with-oil-spill/

[20] "Best Global Brands 2010," *Interbrand*, accessed at http://www.interbrand.com/en/knowledge/best-global-brands/best-global-brands-2008/best-global-brands-2010.aspx

[21] Judy Strauss, Adel El-Ansary, and Raymond Frost, *E-Marketing*, 5th ed. (Upper Saddle River, NJ: Prentice Hall, 2007); "Ten Corporate Blogs Worth Reading," February 19, 2009, at http://www.blogtrepreneuer.com/2009/02/19/ten-corporate-blogs-worth-reading/.

[22] McClatchy Newspapers (Minneapolis), "Social Networking Sites Make Powerful Job-Hunting Tools," *Columbia Daily Tribune*, January 21, 2009, 7B; Press Release, "LinkedIn Launches New Tools to Boost HR Professionals' Efficiency as Responses to Job Postings Double in Challenging Economy," February 2, 2009, at http://press.linkedin.com/linkedin-new-hr-tools; *Linkedin.com*, accessed on December 29, 2010 at http://www.linkedin.com.

[23] Janet Adamy, "Starbucks Plays Common Joe," *The Wall Street Journal*, February 9, 2009, accessed at http://online.wsj.com/article/SB123413848760761577.

[24] Wendy Stueck, "Hold the Frappucino, Starbucks is Retrenching Globally," *ScrippsNews*, April 16, 2009, accessed at http://www.scrippsnews.com/node/42556; Claire Cain Miller, "Starbucks to Close 300 Stores and Open Fewer New Ones," *The New York Times*, January 29, 2009, accessed at http://www.nytimes.com/2009/01/29/business/29sbux.html.

12 Pricing, Distributing, and Promoting Products

iTunes Is It

In 2010, iTunes continued as the number-one music retailer in the United States, with 28 percent of all music purchased by U.S. consumers. Since its beginning, Apple's giant storehouse of digital music has sold over 10 billion songs to more than 100 million customers and holds more than 70 percent of the market share for global digital downloads.

Apple has perfected the art of creating a buzz by coupling iTunes's massive music library with stylish, must-have gadgets like the iPad, iPod, and iPhone. TV and online ads feature products showing off their ground-breaking functionality to the soundtracks of songs so infectious you can hardly resist shelling out $0.69 (for some songs), $0.99 (for most), or $1.29 (top hits) each for them at the iTunes music store. That three-tier (or "variable") pricing policy was part of former Apple CEO Steve Jobs's plan to keep a customer base of loyal purchasers from resorting to piracy. He criticized the "greedy" music industry for its push to raise digital download prices. But don't assume that Jobs was all generosity—his contentment with a relatively meager profit from the iTunes music store was more than made up for by the billions of dollars Apple rakes in each year from sales of its own iTunes-compatible MP3 players.[1]

iTunes has also capitalized on the fastest method of product delivery—high-speed Internet—and the tech savvy of its target teen market. The result has

After reading this chapter, you should be able to:

1 Identify the various pricing objectives that govern pricing decisions, and describe the price-setting tools used in making these decisions.
2 Discuss pricing strategies that can be used for different competitive situations and identify the pricing tactics that can be used for setting prices.
3 Explain the meaning of *distribution mix* and identify the different channels of distribution.
4 Describe the role of wholesalers and explain the different types of retailing.
5 Describe the role of e-intermediaries and explain how online shopping agents and online retailers add value for advertisers and consumers on the Internet.
6 Describe the major activities in the physical distribution process.
7 Identify the important objectives of promotion, discuss the considerations in selecting a promotional mix, and discuss advertising promotions.
8 Outline the tasks involved in personal selling, describe the various types of sales promotions, and distinguish between publicity and public relations.

been that fewer than 48 percent of U.S. teens didn't purchase a single CD in 2008 (compared to 38 percent the year before) and brick-and-mortar retailers like Walmart have reduced the amount of physical store space devoted to CDs.[2] As gadgets and software become increasingly affordable and user-friendly, teens aren't the only demographic flooding the market. Baby Boomers can tap into iTunes's increasing supply of classic music titles to replace their worn-out vinyl, including, beginning with the Christmas season 2010, the complete Beatles catalog. iTunes shoppers of all ages, including older generations, can download books and informational podcasts through iTunes U, a distribution system which offers downloadable lectures, films, and other educational programs.

Our opening story continues on page 320.

WHAT'S IN IT FOR ME?

To become the number-one retailer in any market takes a solid understanding of how best to set prices to achieve profit and market share objectives, and how to promote and distribute products to customers. This chapter also describes different types of wholesalers, retailers, and intermediaries, as well as how the online marketplace has changed the nature of how companies do business. By understanding this chapter's methods for pricing, distributing, and promoting products, you'll have a clearer picture of how to sort out and identify the different kinds of people that are targeted by various companies, products, and advertising campaigns. You'll also be prepared to evaluate a company's marketing programs, distribution methods, and competitive potential.

MyBizLab Where you see MyBizLab in this chapter, go to **www.mybizlab.com** for additional activities on the topic being discussed.

Jim Goldstein/Alamy

As we saw in Chapter 11, product development managers decide what products a company will offer to its customers. In this chapter, we'll look at three of the Four *P*s of the marketing mix. We'll start this chapter by looking at the concept of *pricing* and the price-setting tools used in making pricing decisions. We'll then look at *place*—the distribution mix and the different channels and methods of distribution. We'll then look at *promotion* and discuss the considerations in selecting a promotional mix. Finally, we'll discuss the tasks involved in personal selling and various types of sales promotions.

1 Identify the various pricing objectives that govern pricing decisions, and describe the price-setting tools used in making these decisions.

Determining Prices

The second major component of the marketing mix is **pricing**—determining what the customer pays and the seller receives in exchange for a product. Setting prices involves understanding how they contribute to achieving the firm's sales objectives.

Pricing to Meet Business Objectives

eBay, the popular Internet auction site, has a straightforward pricing structure that's a consumer favorite: Let buyers make offers until a price is finally settled. While eBay sellers hope for a high price, they sometimes are willing to give up some profit in return for a quick sale. Unfortunately, the eBay pricing model, one-on-one price setting, isn't feasible for all companies with lots of customers and products. **Pricing objectives** are the goals that sellers hope to achieve in pricing products for sale. Some companies have *profit-maximizing pricing objectives*, while others have *market share pricing objectives*. Pricing decisions are also influenced by the need to compete in the marketplace, by social and ethical concerns, and even by corporate image. Most recently we've seen how prices of financial products—loans and other borrowing—are determined by the government's persuasion and its control of interest rates in times of crisis.

Profit-Maximizing Objectives   The seller's pricing decision is critical for determining the firm's revenue, which is the selling price times the number of units sold.

$$\text{Revenue} = \text{Selling price} \times \text{Units sold}$$

Companies that set prices to maximize profits want to set the selling price to sell the number of units that will generate the highest possible total profits. If a company sets prices too low, it will probably sell many units but may miss out on additional profits on each unit (and may even lose money on each exchange). If a company sets prices too high, it will make a large profit on each item but will sell fewer units. Again, the firm loses money, and it may also be left with excess inventory.

In calculating profits, managers weigh sales revenues against costs for materials and labor, as well as capital resources (plant and equipment) and marketing costs (such as maintaining a large sales staff). To use these resources efficiently, many firms set prices to cover costs and achieve a targeted level of return for owners.

Market Share (Market Penetration) Objectives   In the long run, a business must make a profit to survive. Because they are willing to accept minimal profits, even losses, to get buyers to try products, companies may initially set low prices for new products to establish **market share** (or **market penetration**)—a company's percentage of the total industry sales for a specific product type.

MyBizLab

Gain hands-on experience through an interactive, real-world scenario. This chapter's simulation entitled Pricing Strategies and Objectives is located at **www.mybizlab.com.**

Price-Setting Tools

Whatever a company's objectives, managers like to measure the potential impact before deciding on final prices. Two tools used for this purpose are *cost-oriented pricing* and *breakeven analysis*. Although each can be used alone, both are often used because they provide different kinds of information for determining prices that will allow the company to reach its objectives.

Cost-Oriented Pricing

Cost-oriented pricing considers a firm's desire to make a profit and its need to cover production costs.

$$\text{Selling price} = \text{Seller's costs} + \text{Profit}$$

A video store manager would price DVDs by calculating the cost of making them available to shoppers. Thus, price would include the costs of store rent, employee wages, utilities, product displays, insurance, and the DVD manufacturer's price.

If the manufacturer's price is $8 per DVD and the store sells DVDs for $8, the store won't make any profit. Nor will it make a profit if it sells DVDs for $8.50 each—or even $10 or $11. To be profitable, the company must charge enough to cover product and other costs. Together, these factors determine the **markup**—the amount added to an item's purchase cost to sell it at a profit. In this case, a reasonable markup of $7 over the purchase cost means a $15 selling price. The following equation calculates the markup percentage and determines what percent of every dollar of revenue is gross profit:

$$\text{Markup percentage} = \frac{\text{Markup}}{\text{Sales price}} \times 100\%$$

For our DVD retailer, the markup percentage is 46.7:

$$\text{Markup percentage} = \frac{\$7}{\$15} \times 100\% = 46.7\%$$

Out of every $1.00 taken in, $0.467 will be gross profit. Out of gross profit, the store must still pay rent, utilities, insurance, and all other costs.

For experienced price setters, an even simpler method uses a standard cost-of-goods percentage to determine the markup amount. Many retailers, for example, use 100 percent of cost-of-goods as the standard markup. If the manufacturer's price is $8 per DVD, the markup (100 percent) is also $8, so the selling price is $16.

Breakeven Analysis: Cost-Volume-Profit Relationships

Using cost-oriented pricing, a firm will cover **variable costs**—costs that change with the number of units of a product produced and sold, such as raw materials, sales commissions, and shipping. Firms also need to pay **fixed costs**—costs, such as rent, insurance, and utilities, that must be paid *regardless of the number of units produced and sold*.

Costs, selling price, and the number of units sold determine how many units a company must sell before all costs, both variable and fixed, are covered, and it begins to make a profit. **Breakeven analyses** assess costs versus revenues for various sales volumes and show, at any particular selling price, the amount of loss or profit for each possible volume of sales.

If you were the manager of a video store, how would you determine how many DVDs you needed to sell to break even? We know that the *variable cost*

Pricing process of determining what a company will receive in exchange for its products

Pricing Objectives the goals that sellers hope to achieve in pricing products for sale

Market Share (or Market Penetration) company's percentage of the total industry sales for a specific product type

Cost-Oriented Pricing pricing that considers the firm's desire to make a profit and its need to cover production costs

Markup amount added to an item's purchase cost to sell it at a profit

Variable Cost cost that changes with the quantity of a product produced and sold

Fixed Cost cost that is incurred regardless of the quantity of a product produced and sold

Breakeven Analysis for a particular selling price, assessment of the seller's costs versus revenues at various sales volumes

Using low-cost, direct-to-consumer selling and market share pricing, Dell profitably dominated the personal computer market, while its competitors—Apple, IBM, Compaq, and Hewlett-Packard—sold through retailers, adding extra costs that prevented them from matching Dell's low prices. Competitors have switched to direct-to-consumer sales, but Dell is strongly anchored as the industry's number-two PC seller (after HP).

Richard Levine/Alamy

of buying each DVD from the manufacturer is $8. This means that the store's annual variable costs depend on how many DVDs are sold—the number of DVDs sold times the $8 cost for each DVD. Say that *fixed costs* for keeping the store open for one year are $100,000 (no matter how many DVDs are sold). At a selling price of $15 each, how many DVDs must be sold *so that total revenues exactly cover both* fixed and variable costs? The answer is the **breakeven point,** which is 14,286 DVDs:

$$\text{Breakeven point (in units)} = \frac{\text{Total Fixed Cost}}{\text{Price } - \text{ Variable Cost}}$$

$$= \frac{\$100,000}{\$15 - \$8} = 14,286 \text{ DVDs}$$

Look at Figure 12.1. If the store sells fewer than 14,286 DVDs, it loses money for the year. If sales go over 14,286, profits grow by $7 for each additional DVD. If the store sells exactly 14,286 DVDs, it will cover all its costs but earn zero profit.

Figure 12.1 Breakeven Analysis

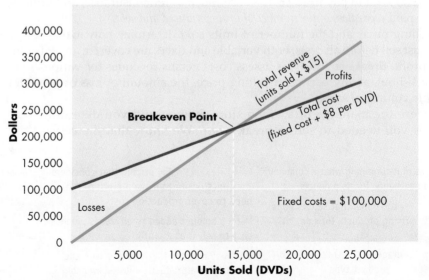

Zero profitability at the breakeven point can also be seen by using the profit equation:

$$\text{Profit} = \frac{\text{Total}}{\text{Revenue}} - \left(\begin{array}{ccc} \text{Total} & & \text{Total} \\ \text{Fixed} & + & \text{Variable} \\ \text{Cost} & & \text{Cost} \end{array}\right)$$

$$= (14{,}286 \text{ DVDs} \times \$15) - (\$100{,}000 \text{ Fixed Cost}$$

$$+ [14{,}286 \text{ DVDs} \times \$8 \text{ Variable Cost}])$$

$$\$0 = (\$214{,}290) - (\$100{,}00 + \$114{,}288)$$

(rounded to the nearest whole DVD)

Pricing Strategies and Tactics

2 Discuss pricing strategies that can be used for different competitive situations and identify the pricing tactics that can be used for setting prices.

The pricing tools discussed in the previous section help managers set prices on specific goods. They do not, however, help them decide on pricing philosophies for diverse competitive situations. In this section, we discuss pricing *strategy* (pricing as a planning activity) and some basic pricing *tactics* (ways in which managers implement a firm's pricing strategies).

Pricing Strategies

Pricing is an extremely important element in the marketing mix, as well as a flexible marketing tool: it is certainly easier to change prices than to change products or distribution channels. This section will look at how pricing strategies can result in widely differing prices for very similar products.

Pricing Existing Products   A firm has three options for pricing existing products:

1 Pricing above prevailing market prices for similar products to take advantage of the common assumption that higher price means higher quality

2 Pricing below market prices while offering a product of comparable quality to higher-priced competitors

3 Pricing at or near market prices

Godiva chocolates and Patek Phillipe watches price high by promoting prestige and quality images. In contrast, both Budget and Dollar car-rental companies promote themselves as low-priced alternatives to Hertz and Avis. Pricing below prevailing market price works if a firm offers a product of acceptable quality while keeping costs below those of higher-priced competitors.

Pricing New Products   When introducing new products, companies must often choose between very high prices or very low prices. **Price skimming**—setting an initial high price to cover development and introduction costs and generate a large profit on each item sold—works only if marketers can convince customers that a new product is truly different from existing products and there is no foreseeable major competition on the horizon. Apple's iPod is a good example. With no strong competitors entering the market for several years, Apple was able to maintain a high retail price with little discounting, even at Walmart. In contrast, **penetration pricing**—setting an

Breakeven Point sales volume at which the seller's total revenue from sales equals total costs (variable and fixed) with neither profit nor loss

Price Skimming setting an initially high price to cover new product costs and generate a profit

Penetration Pricing setting an initially low price to establish a new product in the market

initial low price to establish a new product in the market—seeks to create customer interest and stimulate trial purchases. This is the best strategy when introducing a product which has or expects to have competitors very quickly. Gillette uses this strategy on nearly all of their new shaving systems to make sure the product receives a high early adoption rate.

Startup firms often use one-price, fixed pricing for launching new products. Carbonite, Inc., started its online backup service in 2006 with "one-flat-low price," no matter how much space you needed to back up your PC files.[3] To date the company has backed up more than 80 billion files, using a $54.95-per-year one-price strategy. The initial policy of Apple's iTunes was to use one low price per song, $0.99, to attract and build a customer base in the first five years. In 2009, with 75 million customers, the three-tier pricing, discussed in our opening story, was adopted to reflect differences in value among songs. Older or obscure tunes of lesser value are priced at $0.69, while current hot songs are priced at $1.29, and still others sell for $0.99.

Fixed Versus Dynamic Pricing for Online Business   The digital marketplace has introduced a highly variable pricing system as an alternative to conventional fixed pricing for both consumer and business-to-business (B2B) products. At present, fixed pricing is still the most common option for cybershoppers. E-tail giant Amazon.com has maintained this practice as its pricing strategy for its millions of retail items. In contrast, dynamic pricing, like eBay's auction bidding, uses flexibility between buyers and sellers in setting a price and uses the web to instantly notify millions of buyers of product availability and price changes.

Another kind of dynamic pricing—the reverse auction—allows sellers to alter prices privately on an individual basis. At Priceline.com, for example, consumers set a price (below the published fixed price) they are willing to pay for airfare (or a rental car or a hotel room); then an airline can complete the sale by accepting the bid price. For B2B purchases, MediaBids.com uses reverse advertising auctions to sell ad space. A company will notify MediaBids that it is going to spend $1,000 for advertising. Publications then use their ad space as currency to place bids for the advertising dollars. The company can then accept the bid that offers the most ad exposure in the best publication.[4]

Pricing Tactics

Regardless of its pricing strategy, a company may adopt one or more *pricing tactics*. Companies selling multiple items in a product category often use **price lining**—offering all items in certain categories at a limited number of prices. A department store, for example, might predetermine $175, $250, and $400 as the *price points* for men's suits, so all men's suits would be set at one of these three prices. This allows the store to have a suit for all of the different customer segments it hopes to attract. Grocery stores utilize this strategy as well; for example, in canned goods they will carry a national brand, a store brand and a generic brand.

Psychological pricing takes advantage of the fact that

Ian Dagnall/Alamy

Dynamic pricing, with online bidding screens on the wall, is a mainstream feature of this salesroom for the British Car Auctions (BCA) site in Brighouse, West Yorkshire, UK.

customers are not completely rational when making buying decisions. One type, **odd-even pricing,** is based on the theory that customers prefer prices that are not stated in even dollar amounts. Thus, customers regard prices of $1,000, $100, $50, and $10 as significantly higher than $999.95, $99.95, $49.95, and $9.95, respectively. Finally, sellers must often resort to price reductions—**discounts**—to stimulate sales.

The Distribution Mix

In addition to a good product mix and effective pricing, the success of any product also depends on its **distribution mix**—the combination of distribution channels by which a firm gets products to end users. In this section, we look at intermediaries and different kinds of distribution channels. Then we discuss some benefits consumers reap from services provided by intermediaries.

3 Explain the meaning of *distribution mix* and identify the different channels of distribution.

Intermediaries and Distribution Channels

Once called *middlemen*, **intermediaries** help to distribute goods, either by moving them or by providing information that stimulates their movement from sellers to customers. **Wholesalers** are intermediaries who sell products to other businesses for resale to final consumers. **Retailers** sell products directly to consumers.

Distribution of Goods and Services   A **distribution channel** is the path a product follows from producer to end user. Figure 12.2 shows how four popular distribution channels can be identified according to the channel members involved in getting products to buyers.

Channel 1: Direct Distribution In a **direct channel,** the product travels from the producer to the consumer or organizational buyer without intermediaries. Avon, Dell, GEICO, and Tupperware, as well as many online companies, use this channel. Most

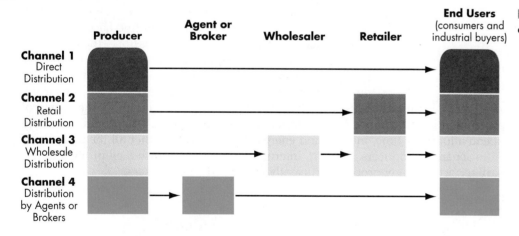

Figure 12.2 **Channels of Distribution**

Price Lining setting a limited number of prices for certain categories of products

Psychological Pricing pricing tactic that takes advantage of the fact that consumers do not always respond rationally to stated prices

Odd-Even Pricing psychological pricing tactic based on the premise that customers prefer prices not stated in even dollar amounts

Discount price reduction offered as an incentive to purchase

Distribution Mix combination of distribution channels by which a firm gets its products to end users

Intermediary individual or firm that helps to distribute a product

Wholesaler intermediary who sells products to other businesses for resale to final consumers

Retailer intermediary who sells products directly to consumers

Distribution Channel network of interdependent companies through which a product passes from producer to end user

Direct Channel distribution channel in which a product travels from producer to consumer without intermediaries

Keith Dannemiller/ZUMA Press/Newscom

At this plant of an electrical components supplier, this employee assembles electrical systems according to a process that meets the requirements for their industrial customers. The finished assemblies are shipped from the plant to customers' facilities, illustrating a direct (producer to customer) channel of distribution.

business goods, especially those bought in large quantities, are sold directly by the manufacturer to the industrial buyer.

Channel 2: Retail Distribution In Channel 2, producers distribute consumer products through retailers. Goodyear, for example, maintains its own system of retail outlets. Levi's has its own outlets but also produces jeans for other retailers. Large outlets, such as Walmart, buy merchandise directly from producers. Many industrial buyers, such as businesses buying office supplies at Staples, rely on this channel.

Channel 3: Wholesale Distribution Once the most widely used method of nondirect distribution, Channel 2 requires a large and costly amount of floor space for storing and displaying merchandise. Wholesalers relieve the space problem by storing merchandise and restocking store displays frequently. With approximately 90 percent of its space used to display merchandise and only 10 percent left for storage and office facilities, the combination convenience store/gas station's use of wholesalers is an example of Channel 3.

Channel 4: Distribution by Agents or Brokers Sales agents or brokers represent producers and receive commissions on the goods they sell to consumers or industrial users. **Sales agents,** including many travel agents, generally deal in the related product lines of a few producers, such as tour companies, to meet the needs of many customers. **Brokers,** in such industries as real estate and stock exchanges, match numerous sellers and buyers as needed to sell properties, often without knowing in advance who they will be.

The Pros and Cons of Nondirect Distribution One downfall of nondirect distribution is higher prices: The more members in the channel—the more intermediaries making a profit by charging a markup or commission—the higher the final price. Intermediaries, however, can provide *added value* by providing time-saving information and making the right quantities of products available where and when consumers need them. Figure 12.3 illustrates the problem of making chili without the benefit of a common intermediary—the supermarket. As a consumer, you would obviously spend a lot more time, money, and energy if you tried to gather all the ingredients from separate producers. In short, intermediaries exist because they provide necessary services that get products efficiently from producers to users.

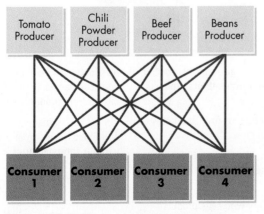
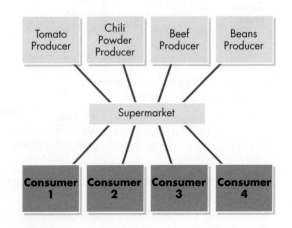

Figure 12.3 **The Value-Adding Intermediary**

Wholesaling

4 Describe the role of wholesalers and explain the different types of retailing.

The roles differ among the various intermediaries in distribution channels. Most wholesalers are independent operations that buy products from manufacturers and sell them to various consumers or other businesses. They usually provide storage, delivery, and additional value-adding services, including credit, marketing advice, and merchandising services, such as marking prices and setting up displays.

Unlike wholesalers, agents and brokers do not own their merchandise. Rather, they serve as sales and merchandising arms for producers or sellers who do not have their own sales forces. The value of agents and brokers lies in their knowledge of markets and their merchandising expertise. They show sale items to potential buyers and, for retail stores, they provide such services as shelf and display merchandising and advertising layout. They remove open, torn, or dirty packages; arrange products neatly; and generally keep goods attractively displayed.

Retailing

There are more than 3 million brick-and-mortar retail establishments in the United States. Many consist only of owners and part-time help. Indeed, over one-half of the nation's retailers account for less than 10 percent of all retail sales. Retailers also include huge operations, such as Walmart, the world's largest corporate employer, and Home Depot. Although there are large retailers in many other countries—Metro in Germany, Carrefour in France, and Daiei in Japan—most of the world's largest retailers are U.S. businesses.

Types of Brick-and-Mortar Retail Outlets

U.S. retail operations vary widely by type as well as size. They can be classified by their pricing strategies, location, range of services, or range of product lines. Choosing the right types of retail outlets is a crucial aspect of distribution strategy. This section describes U.S. retail stores by using three classifications: *product-line retailers*, *bargain retailers*, and *convenience stores*.

Product Line Retailers   Retailers featuring broad product lines include **department stores,** which are organized into specialized departments: shoes, furniture, women's petite sizes, and so on. Stores are usually large, handle a wide range of goods, and offer a variety of services, such as credit plans and delivery. Similarly, **supermarkets** are divided into departments of related products: food products, household products, and so forth. They stress low prices, self-service, and wide selection.

In contrast, **specialty stores,** like Lids—a retailer selling athletic fashion headwear—are small, serve specific market segments with full product lines in narrow product fields, and often feature knowledgeable sales personnel.

Bargain Retailers   **Bargain retailers** carry wide ranges of products at low prices. **Discount houses** began by selling large numbers of items at substantial price reductions to cash-only customers. As name-brand items became more common, they offered better product assortments while still transacting cash-only sales in low-rent

---

Sales Agent independent intermediary who generally deals in the related product lines of a few producers and forms long-term relationships to represent those producers and meet the needs of many customers

Broker independent intermediary who matches numerous sellers and buyers as needed, often without knowing in advance who they will be

Department Store large product-line retailer characterized by organization into specialized departments

Supermarket large product-line retailer offering a variety of food and food-related items in specialized departments

Specialty Store retail store carrying one product line or category of related products

Bargain Retailer retailer carrying a wide range of products at bargain prices

Discount House bargain retailer that generates large sales volume by offering goods at substantial price reductions

ENTREPRENEURSHIP AND NEW VENTURES

A 'Helping Hand' for Professional Inspiration: wowOwow!

The five founders of a new social networking service in 2008 had no idea that wowOwow.com would reinvigorate the talents of midlife professionals into new, more promising careers in the economic downturn. After just two years, its inspiring content led to the website's selection as one of *Forbes.com*'s "Top 100 websites for Women" in 2010. The site's business concept is simple: (a) Women over 40 enjoy social networking but with different interests than the younger crowd. (b) The fame and sophistication of its founders' personal lives, interests, and experiences is an attraction for the target audience. Plus, a contributing cast, including Whoopi Goldberg, Candice Bergen, and Lily Tomlin, provides added punch. (c) The $1 million start-up investment is shared equally among its media-savvy founders; all are pace-setting veteran businesswomen: Lesley Stahl (broadcast journalist), Mary Wells (advertising executive), Joni Evans (publishing executive), Peggy Noonan (political commentator), and Liz Smith (gossip columnist). (d) Branding—the distinctive wowOwow.com (for Women on the web)—signifies the site's mature audience and its goal of sharing professional and personal experiences to encourage one another and to make the world better. (e) The price is right for social networkers: Sign-up is free. Revenues from advertisers will be firmed up later, after wowOwow demonstrates that it can attract a massive audience: Grow the audience, and advertisers will come. (f) Publicity gives wowOwow's message a powerful boost, including interviews on National Public Radio, prominent articles in *The New York Times* and *The Los Angeles Times*, and television features on NBC's *Today Show*.

The surprising career-change twist came with wowOwow. com's Executive Intern Program, begun in late 2008. It's not for newcomer youth interns but, rather, for experienced businesswomen with marketable skills, who, in the business downturn, especially in media industries, need new skills leading to another job. With more and more newspapers and magazines moving online, newer print-web skills are required, while traditional print media personnel are being displaced. That was the situation for the first intern (unpaid), who at age 55 started listening, watching, and learning by doing and asking for help from much younger tech-savvy web writers at WOW's offices. She learned new skills in writing URLs, tags, headlines, subheads, and links in story development for wowOwow. com content. Positive buzz created by the internship program confirms that wowOwow's social network endorses the site's goal of sharing professional and personal experiences to encourage others and to make the world better.[5]

MyBizLab

Patrick McMullan Co/SIPA/Newscom

facilities. As they became firmly entrenched, they began moving to better locations, improving decor, selling better-quality merchandise at higher prices, and offering services such as credit plans and noncash sales.

Catalog showrooms mail catalogs to attract customers into showrooms to view display samples, place orders, and wait briefly while clerks retrieve orders from attached warehouses. **Factory outlets** are manufacturer-owned stores that avoid wholesalers and retailers by selling merchandise directly from factory to consumer. **Wholesale clubs,** like Costco, offer large discounts on a wide range of brand-name merchandise to customers who pay annual membership fees.

Convenience Stores   **Convenience store** chains, such as 7-Eleven and Circle K stores, stress easily accessible locations, extended store hours, and speedy service. They differ from most bargain retailers in that they do not feature low prices.

Nonstore Retailing

Some of the largest retailers sell all or most of their products without brick-and-mortar stores. Certain types of products—snack foods, pinball, jukeboxes, pool, and cigarettes—sell well from card- and coin-operated machines. For all products, global annual sales through vending are projected to reach nearly $200 billion by 2015. Still, vending machine sales make up less than 1 percent of all U.S. retail sales.[6]

Nonstore retailing also includes **direct-response retailing,** in which firms contact customers directly to inform them about products and to receive sales orders. **Mail order** (or **catalog marketing**) is a popular form of direct-response retailing practiced by Crate & Barrel and Land's End. Less popular in recent years due to do-not-call registries, outbound **telemarketing** uses phone calls to sell directly to consumers. However, telemarketing also includes inbound toll-free calls which most catalog and other retail stores make available. Finally, more than 600 U.S. companies, including Mary Kay cosmetics, use **direct selling** to sell door-to-door or through home-selling parties. Avon Products, the world's largest direct seller, has 6 million door-to-door sales representatives in more than 100 countries.[7]

The Role of E-Intermediaries

The ability of e-commerce to bring together millions of widely dispersed consumers and businesses has changed the types and roles of intermediaries. **E-intermediaries** are Internet-based channel members who perform one or both of two functions: (1) They collect information about sellers and present it to consumers, or (2) they help deliver Internet products to buyers. We will examine two types of e-intermediaries: *shopping agents* and *e-retailers*.

5   Describe the role of e-intermediaries and explain how online shopping agents and online retailers add value for advertisers and consumers on the Internet.

Online Shopping Agents

Shopping agents (e-agents), like PriceSCAN.com, help Internet shoppers by gathering and sorting information. Although they don't take possession of products, they know which websites and stores to visit, give accurate comparison prices, identify product features, and help customers complete transactions by presenting information in a usable format.

Electronic Retailing

Over 85 percent of the world's online population—over 1 billion consumers—have made purchases on the Internet. iTunes has outsold brick-and-mortar music retailers, and Amazon.com is the world's largest online retailer, with annual sales of $24 billion.[8]

Catalog Showroom bargain retailer in which customers place orders for catalog items to be picked up at on-premises warehouses

Factory Outlet bargain retailer owned by the manufacturer whose products it sells

Wholesale Club bargain retailer offering large discounts on brand-name merchandise to customers who have paid annual membership fees

Convenience Store retail store offering easy accessibility, extended hours, and fast service

Direct-Response Retailing form of nonstore retailing in which firms directly interact with customers to inform them of products and to receive sales orders

Mail Order (Catalog Marketing) form of nonstore retailing in which customers place orders for catalog merchandise received through the mail

Telemarketing form of nonstore retailing in which the telephone is used to sell directly to consumers

Direct Selling form of nonstore retailing typified by door-to-door sales

E-Intermediary Internet distribution channel member that assists in delivering products to customers or that collects information about various sellers to be presented to consumers

Shopping Agent (E-Agent) e-intermediary (middleman) in the Internet distribution channel that assists users in finding products and prices but does not take possession of products

TABLE 12.1   **Leading Online Retailers in Selected Consumer Products Categories***

Consumer Product Category	Online Retailer
Mass Merchandise	Amazon.com
Video and Audio Entertainment	Netflix Inc.
Computers and Electronics	Apple Inc.
Office Supplies	Staples Inc.
Home Repair and Improvement	W.W. Grainger Inc.
Apparel and Accessories	Victoria's Secret
Health and Beauty	Amway Global
Home Furnishings and Housewares	Williams-Sonoma Inc.
Toys	Toys "R" Us Inc.
Sporting Goods	Cabela's Inc.

*Based on "Top 500 Guide," Internet Retailer (2011), at http://www.internetretailer.com/top500/list/.

Electronic retailing (online retailing) allows sellers to inform, sell to, and distribute to consumers via the web. Some of the largest U.S. "e-tailers" for selected products are shown in Table 12.1. In addition to large companies, millions of small businesses around the globe have their own websites.

Electronic Catalogs   **E-catalogs** use online displays of products to give millions of retail and business customers instant access to product information. The seller avoids mail distribution and printing costs, and once an online catalog is in place, there is little cost in maintaining and accessing it. About 90 percent of all catalogers are now on the Internet, with sales via websites accounting for nearly 50 percent of all catalog sales.[9]

Electronic Storefronts and Cybermalls   Each seller's website is an **electronic storefront** (or *virtual storefront*) from which shoppers collect information about products and buying opportunities, place orders, and pay for purchases. Producers of large product lines, such as Dell, dedicate storefronts to their own product lines. Other sites, such as Newegg.com, which offers computer and other electronics equipment, are category sellers whose storefronts feature products from many manufacturers.

Search engines like Yahoo! serve as **cybermalls**—collections of virtual storefronts representing diverse products and offering speed, convenience, 24-hour access, and efficient searching. After entering a cybermall, shoppers can navigate by choosing from a list of stores (L.L. Bean or Macy's), product listings (computers or MP3 players), or departments (apparel or bath/beauty).

Interactive and Video Retailing   Today, both retail and B2B customers interact with multimedia sites using voice, graphics, animation, film clips,

James Atoa/Everett/Photoshot

Wolfgang Puck products are distributed regularly through QVC and HSN television networks. The chef's name-brand kitchen appliances and cookware are also marketed through such online outlets as eBay and Shopping.com, as well as the QVC and HSN websites.

and access to live human advice. As an example of **interactive retailing,** LivePerson.com is a leading provider of real-time sales and customer service that allows customers to enter a live chat room with a service operator who can answer their specific product questions.

Video retailing, a long-established form of interactive marketing, lets viewers shop at home from channels on their TVs. QVC, for example, displays and demonstrates products and allows viewers to phone in or e-mail orders, and is available on Facebook, YouTube, and Twitter.

Physical Distribution

6 Describe the major activities in the physical distribution process.

Physical distribution refers to the activities needed to move products from manufacturer to customer and includes *warehousing* and *transportation operations*. Its purpose is to make goods available when and where customers want them, keep costs low, and provide services to satisfy customers. Because of its importance for customer satisfaction, some firms have adopted distribution as their marketing strategy of choice.

Consider, for example, the distribution system of National Semiconductor, one of the world's largest microchip makers. Finished microchips are produced in plants around the world and shipped to hundreds of customers, such as IBM, Toshiba, and Hewlett-Packard, which also run factories around the globe. Chips originally traveled 20,000 different routes on as many as 12 airlines and sat waiting at one location after another—on factory floors, at customs, in distributors' facilities, and in warehouses—before reaching customers. National has streamlined the system and now airfreights chips worldwide from a single center in Singapore. Every activity—storage, sorting, and shipping—is run by FedEx. By outsourcing the activities, National's distribution costs have fallen, delivery times have been reduced by half, and sales have increased.

Warehousing Operations

Storing, or **warehousing,** is a major part of distribution management. In selecting a strategy, managers must keep in mind both the different characteristics and costs of warehousing operations. **Private warehouses** are owned by a single manufacturer, wholesaler, or retailer that deals in mass quantities and needs regular storage. Most are run by large firms that deal in mass quantities and need regular storage. J. C. Penney, for example, maintains its own warehouses to facilitate the movement of products to its retail stores.

Independently owned and operated **public warehouses,** which rent to companies only the space they need, are popular with firms needing storage only during peak periods and with manufacturers who need multiple storage locations to get products to multiple markets.

Electronic Retailing (Online Retailing) nonstore retailing in which information about the seller's products and services is connected to consumers' computers, allowing consumers to receive the information and purchase the products in the home

E-Catalog nonstore retailing in which the Internet is used to display products

Electronic Storefront commercial website at which customers gather information about products and buying opportunities, place orders, and pay for purchases

Cybermall collection of virtual storefronts (business websites) representing a variety of products and product lines on the Internet

Interactive Retailing nonstore retailing that uses a website to provide real-time sales and customer service

Video Retailing nonstore retailing to consumers via home television

Physical Distribution activities needed to move a product efficiently from manufacturer to consumer

Warehousing physical distribution operation concerned with the storage of goods

Private Warehouse warehouse owned by and providing storage for a single company

Public Warehouse independently owned and operated warehouse that stores goods for many firms

Joseph Sibilsky/Alamy

Specializing in long-haul shipping, U.S. Xpress Enterprises employs over 3,000 drivers to operate a fleet of 9,000 trucks and 26,000 trailers. Trucks have satellite capabilities, anti-collision radar, vehicle-detection sensors, computers for shifting through 10 speeds, and roomy cabs with sleepers, refrigerators, and microwaves.

Non-Physical Storage The digital age brings with it massive quantities of data that need to be safely stored, preserved, organized, and accessible to users. Many companies, to protect their valuable data resources, rely on remote off-site digital storage services as a safety net. Home users, too, use daily online backup services, such as *Carbonite Backup* and *SOS Online Backup*, to protect against losing data when their computers crash. In the event of any physical catastrophe—floods, fires, earthquakes—at the client's facility, data can be restored online from the backup system.[10]

Transportation Operations

Physically moving a product creates the highest cost many companies face. In addition to transportation methods, firms must also consider the nature of the product, the distance it must travel, the speed with which it must be received, and customer wants and needs.

Transportation Modes   Differences in cost among the major transportation modes—trucks, railroads, planes, digital transmission, water carriers, and pipelines—are usually most directly related to delivery speed.

Trucks With more than 3 million drivers, trucks haul more than two-thirds of all tonnage carried by all modes of U.S. freight transportation. The advantages of trucks include flexibility for any-distance distribution, fast service, and dependability. Increasing truck traffic, however, is raising safety and courtesy concerns.

Planes Air is the fastest and most expensive mode of transportation for physical goods. Airfreight customers benefit from lower inventory costs by eliminating the need to store items that might deteriorate. Shipments of fresh fish, for example, can be picked up by restaurants each day, avoiding the risk of spoilage from packaging and storing.

Digital Transmission iTunes's transportation mode of choice, online transmission, discussed in our opening story, is newer, faster, and less expensive than all other modes. It is also restricted to products—such as music, images, movies, and software—that exist as digital bits that can be transmitted over communication channels.

Water Carriers Aside from digital transmission, water is the least expensive mode but, unfortunately, also the slowest. Networks of waterways—oceans, rivers, and lakes—let water carriers reach many areas throughout the world. Boats and barges are used mostly for moving bulky products (such as oil, grain, and gravel).

Railroads Railroads can economically transport high-volume, heavy, bulky items, such as cars, steel, and coal. However, their delivery routes are limited by fixed, immovable rail tracks.

Pipelines Pipelines are slow and lack flexibility and adaptability, but for specialized products, like liquids and gases, they provide economical and reliable delivery.

Distribution through Supply Chains as a Marketing Strategy

Instead of just offering advantages in product features, quality, price, and promotion, many firms have turned to supply chains that depend on distribution as a cornerstone of business strategy. This approach means assessing, improving, and integrating the entire stream of activities—upstream suppliers, wholesaling, warehousing,

MANAGING IN TURBULENT TIMES

Getting a Stimulus Boost with Pricing and Promotion

The past three years have been difficult for consumers, employees, and companies. "We're not trying to make a profit; we just want to cover costs and keep our employees." This broadcast message illustrates how a construction company is using reduced pricing coupled with coordinated advertising promotions to stimulate demand in a slow economy. Unusual marketing conditions sometimes call for uncommon actions, including changes in pricing and promotions for attracting customers in different ways than usual. Some of these methods seem simple and straightforward, but others are downright creative and unique.

Price discounts and free shipping are among the ordinary pricing attractions, but even those won't work without integrated promotions that get the cost-savings message to customers. Online B2B clothing wholesaler Apparelus.com offers free shipping to clothing merchants, as does retailer LLBean.com, with its wide-ranging line of consumer products. Both, however, highlight free shipping in Internet marketing campaigns that can also include online chats for stimulating buzz that informs customers about the cost savings.[11]

Auto dealers, too, are adopting newer, more radical tactics, with promotions that shift costs, such as increasing gasoline prices, from customers to the dealers: "Buy a new car now, and if gas prices exceed $2, we'll pay the gas bill." Even more extreme, as a safety net against rising job losses, in 2009 Ford and General Motors announced protection when customers buy a new vehicle and then lose their job. Ford will make monthly payments up to $700 for up to one year. GM will cover payments up to $500 per month for up to nine months. Hyundai Motor Co. allows buyers to return a new car within a year due to the buyer's job loss and, in the event of a layoff, Hyundai will make payments for up to three months. All of these offers are coordinated with advertising promotions—on radio,

Laura Gangi Pond/Shutterstock

television, and the Internet—along with public relations and widespread publicity to boost sagging auto sales.[12]

Want to take a vacation, but your portfolio's gone south in the stock-market downfall? It's too late now, but Elite Island Resorts may have had the answer you needed. In December 2008 and January 2009 you could have booked a deluxe Caribbean vacation by paying up to $5,000 per room with stock instead of credit cards. Elite Island promoted the unique "Roll Back Your Stock's Value" offer, accepting a list of some 100 stocks at their higher mid-2008 market values for payment. For example, Elite Island accepted American Express at its earlier value of $40 per share although its value at the time had fallen to less than $22, and Goldman Sachs at $177 although its current value at the time was less than $72. By transferring the stock as payment, the resort was betting that the stock would eventually regain its value, and customers enjoyed the same price benefit as when their portfolio had been more valuable.[13]

MyBizLab

transportation, delivery, and follow-up services—involved in getting products to customers.

Combining JIT and Supply Chains for Competitive Advantage   Since the 1960s, starting with Toyota in Japan, the industrial world has seen the rise of the Just-in-Time (JIT) inventory system, discussed in Chapter 7. Used for quality improvement and cost savings, it was primarily adopted by U.S. manufacturing firms coming by way of Ford Motor Company in the early 1980s. Along with JIT, the past twenty years have seen dramatic improvements in supply chain technology and management, and its adoption by the retail sector. In the decade of the eighties, Walmart decided to build their own distribution system utilizing the best practices of both Just-in-Time and supply chains instead of the industry practice of relying on outside freight haulers and wholesalers. Let's look at how this has enabled Walmart to dominate their competition and made them the leading retailer in the world:

You are shopping at Walmart and decide to pick up a *Mr. Coffee* 8-cup coffeemaker. When you check out, the scanner reads the bar code on the box and Walmart's inventory system is updated instantly, showing that a replacement coffeemaker is needed on the shelf; the replacement comes from "in the back" at that store, where the remaining on-hand supply count is reduced in Walmart's computer system. Once the back-room supply dwindles to its automatic triggering number, Walmart's distribution warehouse receives a digital signal notifying that this store needs more *Mr. Coffee* 8-cup coffeemakers. At the same time, the computer system also notifies the manufacturer that Walmart's distribution warehouse needs a replenishment supply—a predetermined number of the coffeemakers. The manufacturer's suppliers, too, are notified, and so on, continuing upstream with information that enables faster resupply coordination throughout the supply chain. Walmart's data mining system determines the reorder number for every product based on sales (daily, weekly, and even by time of the year). Because of Walmart's constant rapid restocking from upstream sources, its store shelves are re-supplied without having to keep large inventories in its warehouses and retail stores, thus reducing inventory costs and providing lower prices.

Walmart's JIT system has allowed it to achieve as low as a 2-day turnaround from manufacturer to the store shelf, thus providing cost control and product availability. It maintains lower levels of inventory, meets customer demand, and keeps the lowest prices in the retail industry. Another retailer that has been able to adopt this method on a similar scale and compete effectively with Walmart (but only in groceries) is the H-E-B Grocery Company's chain of stores in Texas. Its data mining software can evaluate what products are purchased when, and with what other products (so, for example, they know to have tamales available at Christmas with coupons for enchilada sauce), and use this information for forecasting upcoming demand.

The Importance of Promotion

7 Identify the important objectives of promotion, discuss the considerations in selecting a promotional mix, and discuss advertising promotions.

Promotion refers to techniques for communicating information about products and is part of the *communication mix*—the total message any company sends to customers about its product. Promotional techniques, especially advertising, must communicate the uses, features, and benefits of products, and marketers use an array of tools for this purpose.

Promotional Objectives

The ultimate objective of any promotion is to increase sales. In addition, marketers may use promotion to *communicate information, position products, add value,* and *control sales volume.*

As we saw in Chapter 11, **positioning** is the process of establishing an easily identifiable product image in the minds of consumers by fixing, adapting, and communicating the nature of the product itself. First, a firm must identify which market segments are likely to purchase its product and how its product measures up against competitors. Then, it can focus on promotional choices for differentiating its product and positioning it in the minds of the target audience. As an example, when I say, "Ketchup," most people respond with…Heinz. "The Ultimate Driving machine" is…BMW. This is successful positioning.

Promotional mixes are often designed to communicate a product's *value-added benefits* to distinguish it from the competition. Mercedes automobiles and Ritz-Carlton Hotels, for example, promote their products as upscale goods and services featuring high quality, style, and performance, all at a higher price.

The Promotional Mix

Five of marketing's most powerful promotional tools are *advertising, personal selling, sales promotions, direct* or *interactive marketing*, and *publicity and public relations*. The best combination of these tools—the best **promotional mix**—depends on many factors. The most important is the target audience. As an example, two generations from now, 25 percent of the U.S. workforce will be Hispanic. With 50 million Hispanic Americans, the rise in Latinos' disposable income has made them a potent economic force, and marketers are scrambling to redesign and promote products to appeal to them. Spanish-language media is one obvious outlet: The audience for programming from Univision, the biggest Spanish-language media company in the United States—with television, radio, music, and Internet—has ballooned by over 50 percent since 2001 to become the number five TV network in the United States.[14]

The Target Audience: Promotion and the Consumer Decision Process   In establishing a promotional mix, marketers match promotional tools with the five stages in the buyer decision process:

1 When consumers first recognize the need to make a purchase, marketers use advertising and publicity, which can reach many people quickly, to make sure buyers are aware of their products.

2 As consumers search for information about available products, advertising and personal selling are important methods to educate them.

3 Personal selling can become vital as consumers compare competing products. Sales representatives can demonstrate product quality, features, benefits, and performance in comparison with competitors' products.

4 When buyers are ready to purchase products, sales promotion can give consumers an incentive to buy. Personal selling can help by bringing products to convenient purchase locations.

5 After making purchases, consumers evaluate products and note (and remember) their strengths and deficiencies. At this stage, advertising and personal selling can remind customers that they made wise purchases.

Figure 12.4 summarizes the effective promotional tools for each stage in the consumer buying process.

Stage of the Consumer Buying Process	Problem (Need) Recognition	Information Seeking	Evaluation of Alternatives	Purchase Decisions	Postpurchase Evaluation
Most Effective Promotional Tool	Advertising; Publicity	Advertising; Personal Selling	Personal Selling	Sales Promotion; Personal Selling	Advertising; Personal Selling

Figure 12.4 **The Consumer Buying Process and the Promotional Mix**

Promotion aspect of the marketing mix concerned with the most effective techniques for communicating information about and selling a product

Positioning process of establishing an identifiable product image in the minds of consumers

Promotional Mix combination of tools used to promote a product

Figure 12.5 Top 10 U.S. National Advertisers
Source: "TNS Media Intelligence Reports U.S. Advertising Expenditures Grew 0.2 Percent in 2007," TNS Media Intelligence, March 25, 2008, at *http:// www .tns-mi.com/news/03252008 .htm;* "2007 U.S. Advertising Expenditures Wrap-up: Spend Up Just 0.2%," at *http://www.marketingcharts .com/ television/tns-issues-2007- usadvertising-expenditures-wrap-upspend- up-just-02-3952/.*

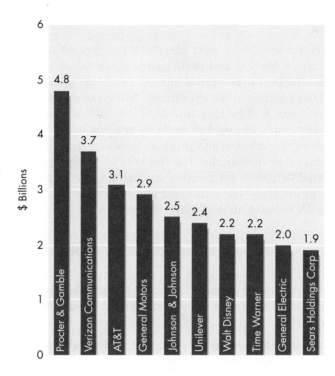

Advertising Promotions

Advertising is paid, nonpersonal communication by which an identified sponsor informs an audience about a product. In 2008, U.S. firms spent $280 billion on advertising—nearly $28 billion of it by just 10 companies.[15] Figure 12.5 shows U.S. advertising expenditures for the top-spending firms. Let's take a look at the different types of advertising media, noting some of the advantages and limitations of each.

Advertising Media Consumers tend to ignore the bulk of advertising messages that bombard them; they pay attention to what interests them. Moreover, the advertising process is dynamic, reflecting the changing interests and preferences of both customers and advertisers. A 2008 customer survey, for example, reports that mail ads are rated as most irritating and boring, while newspaper and magazine ads are least annoying. Yet, while newspaper ads are rated as more informative and useful than some other media, advertisers continue to shift away, using instead more online, cell phone, and PDA advertising because newsprint readership (the audience) is dwindling.[16]

Real-Time Ad Tracking Advertisers always want better information about who looks at ads and for how long. Which target audiences and demographics are more attracted to various ad contents? Accurate ad-watching behavior of shoppers in malls, theaters, and grocery stores is on the increase with assistance from high-tech real-time surveillance. As passing consumers watch ads on video screens, cameras watch the shoppers, while software analyzes the viewers' demographics and reactions to various ad contents and formats. The makers of the tracking system claim accuracy of up to 90 percent for determining gender, approximate age, and ethnicity. Once perfected, the system might measure your demographics, identify you with a target audience, then instantly change the presentation to a preferred product and visual format to attract and hold your attention.[17] Marketers must find out, then, who their customers are, which media they pay attention to, what messages appeal to them, and how to get their attention. Thus, marketers use several different **advertising media**—specific communication devices for carrying a seller's message to potential customers. The combination of media through which a company advertises is called its **media mix.** Table 12.2 shows the relative sizes of media usage and their strengths and weaknesses.

TABLE 12.2   Total U.S. Media Usage, Strengths, and Weaknesses

Advertising Medium	Percentage* of Advertising Outlays	Strengths	Weaknesses
Television	32%	Program demographics allow for customized ads Large audience	Most expensive
Direct mail	24%	Targeted audience Personal messages Predictable results	Easily discarded Environmentally irresponsible
Internet	15%	Targeted audience Measurable success	Nuisance to consumers Easy to ignore
Newspapers	10%	Broad coverage Ads can be changed daily	Quickly discarded Broad readership limits ability to target specific audience
Radio	9%	Inexpensive Large audience Variety of ready market segmentation	Easy to ignore Message quickly disappears
Magazines	8%	Often reread and shared Variety of ready market segmentation	Require advanced planning Little control over ad placement
Outdoor	2%	Inexpensive Difficult to ignore Repeat exposure	Presents limited information Little control over audience

A combination of additional unmeasured media such as yellow pages, catalogs, special events, sidewalk handouts, ads on transport vehicles, skywriting, movies, and door-to-door communications, are not included.

*Estimated. Based on the following sources: "U.S. Ad Spending Grew 6.5% in 2010 as Auto Surged and Pharma Hit a Low," Advertising Age, March 17, 2011, at http://adage.com/article/mediaworks/u-s-ad-spending-grew-6-5-2010-auto-rose-pharma-fell/149436/; "Online Ad spending Passes Print Advertising," Sweet Spot Marketing, January 17, 2011, at http://www.sweetspotmarketing.com/news/online-ad-spend-passes-print/; "U.S. Advertising Revenue, By Medium," Business Insider, October 27, 2009, at http://www.businessinsider.com/us-advertising-spending-by-medium-2009-10; "Ad Spending Continues 2009 Spiral, Forecasts Slightly Better for 2010," March 13, 2009, Marketing Charts, at http://www.marketingcharts.com/television/ad-spending-continues-2009-spiral-forecasts-slightly-better-for-2010-8306/jack-myers-media-business-report-projected-change-ad-spending-2009jpg/.

Personal Selling

In the oldest and most expensive form of sales, **personal selling,** a salesperson communicates one-on-one with potential customers to identify their needs and align them with the product. Salespeople gain credibility by investing a lot of time getting acquainted with potential customers and answering their questions.

Salespeople must be adept at performing three basic tasks of personal selling. In **order processing,** a salesperson receives an order and sees to its handling and delivery. Route salespeople, who call on regular customers to check inventories, are

8 Outline the tasks involved in personal selling, describe the various types of sales promotions, and distinguish between publicity and public relations.

Advertising promotional tool consisting of paid, nonpersonal communication used by an identified sponsor to inform an audience about a product

Advertising Media variety of communication devices for carrying a seller's message to potential customers

Media Mix combination of advertising media chosen to carry a message about a product

Personal Selling promotional tool in which a salesperson communicates one-on-one with potential customers

Order Processing personal-selling task in which salespeople receive orders and see to their handling and delivery

often order processors. With the customer's consent, they may decide on the sizes of reorders, fill them directly from their trucks, and even stock shelves. In other situations, however, when potential customers are not aware that they need or want a product, **creative selling** involves providing information and demonstrating product benefits to persuade buyers to complete a purchase. Creative selling is crucial for industrial products and high-priced consumer products, such as cafeteria-management services and cars, for which buyers comparison shop. Finally, a salesperson may use **missionary selling** to promote a company and its products rather than simply to close a sale. Pharmaceutical companies often use this method to make doctors aware of the company and its products so they will recommend the company's products to others. Depending on the product and company, sales jobs usually require individuals to perform all three tasks—order processing, creative selling, and missionary selling—to some degree.

Sales Promotions

Sales promotions are short-term promotional activities designed to encourage consumer buying, industrial sales, or cooperation from distributors. They can increase the likelihood that buyers will try products, enhance product recognition, and increase purchase size and sales revenues.

Types of Sales Promotions   Most consumers have taken part in a variety of sales promotions such as free *samples* (giveaways), which let customers try products without risk, and **coupon** promotions, which use certificates entitling buyers to discounts in order to encourage customers to try new products, lure them away from competitors, or induce them to buy more of a product. **Premiums** are free or reduced-price items, such as pencils, coffee mugs, and six-month low-interest credit cards, given to consumers in return for buying a specified product. *Contests* can boost sales by rewarding high-producing distributors and sales representatives with vacation trips to Hawaii or Paris. Consumers, too, may win prizes by entering their cats in the Purina Cat Chow calendar contest, for example, by submitting entry blanks from the backs of cat-food packages.

To grab customers' attention in stores, companies use **point-of-sale (POS) displays** at the ends of aisles or near checkout counters to ease finding products and to eliminate competitors from consideration. In addition to physical goods, POS pedestals also provide services, namely information for consumers. Bank lobbies and physicians' waiting rooms, for example, have computer-interactive kiosks inviting clients to learn more about bank products and educational information about available treatments on consumer-friendly touch-screen displays. For B2B promotions, industries sponsor **trade shows** where companies rent booths to display and demonstrate products to customers who have a special interest or who are ready to buy.

Direct (or Interactive) Marketing

Direct (or interactive) marketing is one-on-one nonpersonal selling and now makes up 54 percent of all promotional spending in the United States.[18] It includes the nonstore retailers (catalogs, telemarketing, home video shopping), direct mail, direct response advertising (such as infomercials and direct response magazine and newspaper ads), and most important, the Internet. When used by B2B businesses, direct marketing is primarily lead generation so a salesperson can close the sale where interest has been shown. In B2C businesses, it has primarily a selling goal. The advantage of direct marketing is that you can target the message to the individual and you can measure the results. For example, Amazon knows when you sign in who you are and what you have purchased in the past and makes recommendations based on your purchases. By selecting a certain title, they can suggest other titles that other buyers of your selection have also purchased and in that way, increase the sale to you.

The Internet has enhanced traditional direct marketing methods, especially direct mail. By using *permission marketing*, a form of e-mail where the consumer gives a company permission to contact them, a list of customers' e-mails is compiled and they are regularly contacted with special offers and deals based on their past purchases. The e-mail is coming from a company the consumer has experience with and has agreed to receive their messages, and it contains a direct link to the company's website and the sale item. Companies such as Amazon, Dell, Office Depot, and others have used this direct marketing method and technology very successfully.

Publicity and Public Relations

Publicity is information about a company, a product, or an event transmitted by the general mass media to attract public attention. While publicity is free, marketers have no control over the content media reporters and writers disseminate, and because it is presented in a news format, consumers often regard it as objective and credible. In 2005, for example, U.S. fast-food patrons were horrified when a customer said she found a human fingertip in a bowl of Wendy's chili. The publicity nightmare immediately bruised the food chain's reputation and cost about $15 million in lost sales in just six weeks. [19]

In contrast to publicity, **public relations** is company-influenced information that seeks either to build good relations with the public—by publicizing the company's charitable contributions, for example—or to deal with unfavorable events. In the Wendy's case, CEO Jack Schuessler's public relations response was decisive and focused: protect the brand and tell the truth. That meant there would be no payoff or settlement to keep it out of the news. Instead, Wendy's enlisted cooperation with the health department and police, did visual inspections, polygraphed employees, publicly announced a hotline for tips, and offered a reward for information, all leading to the conclusion that the reported episode was a hoax. Energetic public relations was an effective promotional tool for clearing the Wendy's name and preserving the company's reputation. [20]

Creative Selling personal-selling task in which salespeople try to persuade buyers to purchase products by providing information about their benefits

Missionary Selling personal-selling task in which salespeople promote their firms and products rather than try to close sales

Sales Promotion short-term promotional activity designed to encourage consumer buying, industrial sales, or cooperation from distributors

Coupon sales-promotion technique in which a certificate is issued entitling the buyer to a reduced price

Premium sales-promotion technique in which offers of free or reduced-price items are used to stimulate purchases

Point-of-Sale (POS) Display sales-promotion technique in which product displays are located in certain areas to stimulate purchase or to provide information on a product

Trade Show sales-promotion technique in which various members of an industry gather to display, demonstrate, and sell products

Direct (or Interactive) Marketing one-on-one nonpersonal selling by nonstore retailers and B2B sellers using direct contact with prospective customers, especially via the Internet

Publicity promotional tool in which information about a company, a product, or an event is transmitted by the general mass media to attract public attention

Public Relations company-influenced information directed at building goodwill with the public or dealing with unfavorable events

Jim Goldstein/Alamy

Continued from page 299

At Apple, iTunes Means Mu$ic

Will it be Lady GaGa? Or could it be Black Eyed Peas, Ke$ha, or Taylor Swift? No... can you believe...it's Johnny Cash's 1958 hit song, "Guess Things Happen That Way"! That was the milestone 10 billionth download for Apple's iTunes in early 2010 by 71-year-old Louis Sulcer using his iPod Nano. Along with his favorite song, the Woodstock, Georgia, grandfather of nine received a $10,000 iTunes gift card and a telephone greeting from Steve Jobs. While Mr. Sulcer isn't the typical customer, he represents the broadening iTunes audience that could download the next 10 billion, perhaps even faster than the first. The driving force behind song sales has been the number of iPods, totaling some 250 million sold as of early 2010, and that number keeps growing. Add to that the more-than 6 million iPads sold soon after its launch in 2010, and the demand for iTunes songs would seem to be accelerating.[21]

A positive indicator for growth is the industry's continuing transition to digital music: The digital format accounted for 40 percent of all industry purchases in 2009, up from 32 percent in 2008. However, some indicators suggest a possible slowdown on the horizon. Total music purchases grew by only 2 percent in 2009, down from 10 percent in 2008. The industry's digital album sales were up 16 percent in 2009, but that was only half the 2008 growth of 32 percent. And for Apple in particular, recent iTunes price increases seemed to hurt sales rankings for several popular songs. Forty of the Top 100 songs were repriced upward from $0.99 to $1.29, while the other 60 remained at $0.99. The next day, the 40 higher-priced songs lost an average of over 5.0 chart positions; the 60 songs priced at $0.99 gained an average of 2.5 chart positions. Similar changes continued in the days that followed. Meanwhile, a major competitor—Amazon.com—continues with its one-price policy, set at $0.99. The longer-term effects on iTunes sales remain to be determined by competition, consumer tastes, and other industry trends.[22]

QUESTIONS FOR DISCUSSION

1 Consider the distribution channel for iTunes music products versus the channels used by brick-and-mortar retail music stores. What are the advantages and disadvantages of those channels?

2 What is (are) iTunes's target market(s)? What factors in the marketing environment, if any, are likely to change the target market(s) over the next few years?

3 What kind of promotional mix(es) would you recommend as most effective for reaching iTunes's current target market(s)?

4 In what ways might Apple benefit by jointly advertising its music products together with its digital-music-player products?

5 Would you advise iTunes to continue with the three-tier pricing system for music products or, instead, return to a one-price policy? Explain.

SUMMARY OF LEARNING OBJECTIVES MyBizLab

1. **Identify the various pricing objectives that govern pricing decisions, and describe the price-setting tools used in making these decisions. (pp. 300–303)**
Two major pricing objectives are (1) *Pricing to maximize profits*: Set the price to sell the number of units that will generate the highest possible total profits. With prices set too low, the seller misses the chance to make additional profits on each of the many units sold. With prices set too high, a larger profit will be made on each unit, but fewer units will be sold. (2) *Market share objectives*: Pricing is used for establishing market share. The seller is willing to accept minimal profits, even losses, to get buyers to try products. Two basic tools are used: (1) *Cost-oriented pricing* begins by determining total costs for making products available to shoppers, then a figure for profit is added in to arrive at a selling price. (2) *Breakeven analysis* assesses total costs versus revenues for various sales volumes. It shows, at each possible sales volume, the amount of loss or profit for any chosen sales price. It also shows the *breakeven point*: the number of sales units for total revenue to equal total costs.

2. **Discuss pricing strategies that can be used for different competitive situations and identify the pricing tactics that can be used for setting prices. (pp. 303–305)**
Pricing for existing products can be set above, at, or below market prices for similar products. High pricing is often interpreted as meaning higher quality and prestige, while low pricing may attract greater sales volume. Strategies for new products include *price skimming*—setting an initially high price to cover costs and generate a profit—and *penetration pricing*—setting a low price to establish a new product in the market. Strategies for e-businesses include dynamic versus fixed pricing. *Dynamic pricing* establishes individual prices by real-time interaction between the seller and each customer on the Internet. *Fixed pricing* is the traditional one-price-for-all arrangement.

Three tactics are often used for setting prices: (1) With *price lining*, any product category (such as lady's shoes) will be set at three or four price levels, and all shoes will be priced at one of those levels. (2) *Psychological pricing* acknowledges that customers are not completely rational when making buying decisions, as with *odd-even pricing* where customers regard prices such as $10 as being significantly higher than $9.95. (3) *Discount pricing* uses price reductions to stimulate sales.

3. **Explain the meaning of *distribution mix* and identify the different channels of distribution. (pp. 305–306)**
The combination of distribution channels for getting products to end users—consumers and industrial buyers—is the *distribution mix*. *Intermediaries* help to distribute a producer's goods by moving them from sellers to customers: *Wholesalers* sell products to other businesses, which resell them to final users. *Retailers*, *sales agents*, and *brokers* sell products directly to end users. In the simplest of four distribution channels, the producer sells directly to users. Channel 2 includes a retailer, Channel 3 involves both a retailer and a wholesaler, and Channel 4 includes an agent or broker.

4. **Describe the role of wholesalers and explain the different types of retailing. (pp. 307–309)**
Wholesalers provide a variety of services—delivery, credit arrangements, and product information—to buyers of products for resale or business use. In buying and reselling an assortment of products, wholesalers provide storage, marketing advice, and assist customers by marking prices and setting up displays. *Retail stores* range from broad product-line department stores and supermarkets, to small specialty stores for specific market segments seeking narrow product lines. With all retail stores, there is always an intermediary that moves products from producers to users. Various kinds of nonstore retailing include *direct-response retailing*, *mail order* (or *catalog marketing*), *telemarketing*, and *direct selling*. Electronic retailing includes e-catalogs, electronic storefronts, cybermalls, and interactive and video retailing. Many nonstore retailers do not use intermediaries but, instead, use direct-to-consumer contact by the producer.

5. **Describe the role of e-intermediaries and explain how online shopping agents and online retailers add value for advertisers and consumers on the Internet. (pp. 309–311)**
E-intermediaries are Internet-based channel members who perform one or both of two functions: (1) They collect information about sellers and present it to consumers, and (2) they help deliver Internet products to buyers. Two prominent types of e-intermediaries are shopping agents and electronic retailers: (1) *Shopping agents* (*e-agents*) help online consumers by gathering and sorting information (such as comparison prices and product features) for making purchases. They add value for sellers by listing sellers' web addresses for consumers. (2) *Electronic retailers* interact online with customers and add value by informing, selling to, and distributing products to them. *E-catalogs* are electronic displays that give instant worldwide access to pages of product information. *Electronic storefronts* and *cybermalls* provide collections of virtual storefronts at which Internet shoppers collect information about products, place orders, and pay for purchases.

6. **Describe the major activities in the physical distribution process. (pp. 311–314)**
Physical distribution activities include providing customer services, warehousing, and transportation of products. *Warehouses* provide storage for products, whereas *transportation operations* physically move products from suppliers to customers. Trucks, railroads, planes, water carriers (boats and barges), digital transmission, and pipelines are the major transportation modes used in the distribution process.

7. Identify the important objectives of promotion, discuss the considerations in selecting a promotional mix, and discuss advertising promotions. **(pp. 314–317)**

Although the ultimate goal of any *promotion* is to increase sales, other goals include communicating information, positioning a product, adding value, and controlling sales volume. In deciding on the appropriate *promotional mix*—the best combination of promotional tools (e.g., advertising, personal selling, sales promotions, direct or interactive marketing, public relations), marketers must consider the good or service being offered, characteristics of the target audience, the buyer's decision process, and the promotional mix budget. *Advertising* is paid, nonpersonal communication, by which an identified sponsor informs an audience about a product. Marketers use several different *advertising media*—specific communication devices for carrying a seller's message to potential customers—each having its advantages and drawbacks. The combination of media through which a company advertises is called its *media mix*.

8. Outline the tasks involved in personal selling, describe the various types of sales promotions, and distinguish between publicity and public relations. **(pp. 317–319)**

Personal selling tasks include *order processing*, *creative selling*, and *missionary selling*. *Sales promotions* include *point-of-sale (POS)* displays to attract consumer attention, help them find products in stores and offices, and provide product information. Other sales promotions give purchasing incentives, such as *samples* (customers can try products without having to buy them), *coupons* (a certificate for price reduction), and *premiums* (free or reduced-price rewards for buying products). At *trade shows*, B2B sellers rent booths to display products to industrial customers. *Contests* intend to stimulate sales, with prizes to high-producing intermediaries and consumers who use the seller's products.

Publicity is information about a company, a product, or an event transmitted by the general mass media to attract public attention. Control of the message's content is determined by outside writers and reporters. In contrast to publicity, *public relations* is company-influenced information that seeks to either build good relations with the public or to deal with unfavorable events.

KEY TERMS   MyBizLab

QUESTIONS AND EXERCISES

QUESTIONS FOR REVIEW

1. How does breakeven analysis help managers measure the potential impact of prices?
2. Discuss the goal of price skimming and penetration pricing.
3. Identify the channels of distribution. In what key ways do they differ from one another?
4. Explain how e-agents or e-brokers differ from traditional agents or brokers.
5. Select four advertising media and compare the advantages and disadvantages of each.

QUESTIONS FOR ANALYSIS

6. Suppose that a small publisher selling to book distributors has fixed operating costs of $600,000 each year and variable costs of $3.00 per book. How many books must the firm sell to break even if the selling price is $6.00?
7. Choose two advertising campaigns: one that you think is effective and one that you think is ineffective. What makes one campaign better than the other?

8. Give examples of two products that typify the products sold to shoppers through each form of nonstore retailing. Explain why different products are best suited to each form of nonstore retailing.

APPLICATION EXERCISES

9. Select a product and analyze pricing objectives for it. What information would you want if you were to adopt a profit-maximizing objective or a market share objective?
10. Select a product and identify the media used in its promotion. On the whole, do you think the campaign is effective? Why or why not? If the campaign is not effective, what changes would you suggest to improve it?
11. Identify a company that is a member in a supply chain. Explain how its presence in the chain affects the company's marketing decisions for pricing, promoting, and distributing its products.

BUILDING YOUR BUSINESS SKILLS

Greeting Start-Up Decisions

Goal

To encourage you to analyze the potential usefulness of two promotional methods—personal selling and direct mail—for a start-up greeting card company.

Background Information

You are the marketing adviser for a local start-up company that makes and sells specialty greeting cards in a city of 400,000. Last year's sales totaled 14,000 cards, including personalized holiday cards, birthday cards, and special-events cards for individuals. Although revenues increased last year, you see a way of further boosting sales by expanding into card shops, grocery stores, and gift shops. You see two alternatives for entering these outlets:

Use direct mail to reach more individual customers for specialty cards.

Use personal selling to gain display space in retail stores.

Your challenge is to convince the owner of the start-up company which alternative is the more financially sound decision.

Method

Step 1

Get together with four or five classmates to research the two kinds of product segments: personalized cards and retail store cards. Find out which of the two kinds of marketing promotions will be more effective for each of the two segments. What will be the reaction to each method by customers, retailers, and card-company owners?

Step 2

Draft a proposal to the company owner. Leaving budget and production details to other staffers, list as many reasons as possible for adopting direct mail. Then, list as many reasons as possible for adopting personal selling. Defend each reason. Consider the following reasons in your argument:

- **Competitive environment.** Analyze the impact of other card suppliers that offer personalized cards and cards for sale in retail stores.
- **Expectations of target markets.** Who buys personalized cards and who buys ready-made cards from retail stores?
- **Overall cost of the promotional effort.** Which method, direct mail or personal selling, will be more costly?
- **Marketing effectiveness.** Which promotional method will result in greater consumer response?

FOLLOW-UP QUESTIONS

1. Why do you think some buyers want personalized cards? Why do some consumers want ready-made cards from retail stores?
2. Consider today's easy access to online sources of cards and to software for designing and making cards on home PCs. How does the availability of these resources affect your recommendation?
3. What was your most convincing argument for using direct mail? For using personal selling?
4. Can a start-up company compete in retail stores against industry giants, such as Hallmark and American Greetings?

EXERCISING YOUR ETHICS: INDIVIDUAL EXERCISE

The Chain of Responsibility

The Situation

Because several stages are involved when distribution chains move products from supply sources to end consumers, the process offers ample opportunity for ethical issues to arise. This exercise encourages you to examine some of the ethical issues that can emerge during transactions among suppliers and customers.

The Dilemma

A customer bought an expensive wedding gift at a local store and asked that it be shipped to the bride in another state. Several weeks after the wedding, the customer contacted the bride, who had not confirmed the arrival of the gift. It hadn't arrived. Charging that the merchandise had not been delivered, the customer requested a refund from the retailer. The store manager uncovered the following facts:

- All shipments from the store are handled by a well-known national delivery firm.
- The delivery firm verified that the package had been delivered to the designated address two days after the sale.

- Normally, the delivery firm does not obtain recipient signatures; deliveries are made to the address of record, regardless of the name on the package.

The gift giver argued that even though the package had been delivered to the right address, it had not been delivered to the named recipient. It turns out that, unbeknownst to the gift giver, the bride had moved. It stood to reason, then, that the gift was in the hands of the new occupant at the bride's former address. The manager informed the gift giver that the store had fulfilled its obligation. The cause of the problem, she explained, was the incorrect address given by the customer. She refused to refund the customer's money and suggested that the customer might want to recover the gift by contacting the stranger who received it at the bride's old address.

QUESTIONS TO ADDRESS

1 What are the responsibilities of each party—the customer, the store, the delivery firm—in this situation?
2 From an ethical standpoint, in what ways is the store manager's action right? In what ways is it wrong?
3 If you were appointed to settle this matter, what actions would you take?

EXERCISING YOUR ETHICS: TEAM EXERCISE

A Big Push for Publicity

The Situation

J Company is known as a "good citizen" and prides itself on publicity it receives from sponsoring civic programs and other community projects. J Company's executive vice president, Ms. Q, has just been named chairperson of annual fundraising for MAS, a large coalition of community services that depend on voluntary donations. In the highly visible chairperson's role, Ms. Q has organized the support of officials at other firms to ensure that the fundraising target is met or surpassed.

The Dilemma

Ms. Q began a J Company meeting of 30 department managers to appeal for 100 percent employee participation in MAS giving in the fundraising drive: "We will have 100 percent participation here." As follow-up the week before the drive officially started, Ms. Q met with each manager, saying: "I expect you to give your fair share and for you to ensure that all your employees do likewise. I don't care what it takes, just do it. Make it clear that employees will at least donate cash. Even better, get them to sign up for weekly payroll deductions to the MAS fund because it nets more money than one-time cash donations."

An hour after meeting with Ms. Q, Nathan Smith was both surprised and confused. As a newly appointed department manager, he was unsure how to go about soliciting donations from his 25 employees. Remembering Ms. Q's comment, "I don't care what it takes, just do it," Nathan wondered what to do if someone

did not give. Personally, too, he was feeling uneasy. How much should he give? With his family's pressing financial needs, he would rather not give money to MAS. He began to wonder if his donation to MAS would affect his career at J Company.

Team Activity

Assemble a group of four to five students and assign each group member to one of the following roles:
- Nathan Smith (employee)
- Ms. Q (employer)
- Director of MAS (customer)
- J Company stockholder (investor)
- J Company CEO (use this role only if your group has at least five members)

ACTION STEPS

1 Before hearing any of your group's comments, and from the perspective of your assigned role, do you think there are any *ethical issues* with J Company's fundraising program? If so, write them down.
2 Before hearing any of your group's comments, and from the perspective of your assigned role, are any *problems* likely to arise from J Company's fundraising program? If so, write them down.
3 Together with your group, share the ethical issues you identified. Then, share the potential problems you listed. Did the different roles you were assigned result in different ethical issues and problems?

4 For the various ethical issues that were identified, decide as a group which one is the most important for J Company to resolve. Likewise, for potential problems that were identified, which is the most important one for J Company?

5 From an ethical standpoint, what does your group recommend be done to resolve the most important ethical issue? How should the most important problem be resolved? Identify the advantages and drawbacks of your recommendations.

VIDEO EXERCISE   MyBizLab

Joby

Learning Objectives

The purpose of this video is to help you:
1 Describe the objectives of promotion.
2 Understand the importance of positioning in the marketing of a product.
3 Explain the role of trade shows and publicity in the promotional mix.

Synopsis

Joby is a San Francisco–based company that manufactures camera and phone accessories. Founded in the 2005, the company has experienced rapid growth on a limited promotional budget. Recognizing that traditional camera tripods were unsuited to many settings, Joby created the GorillaPod, which allows cameras to be mounted in almost any environment through the use of flexible arms. Joby expanded its product mix with the GorillaMobile line of mobile phone accessories and the GorillaTorch line of spotlights. Joby has developed a loyal following with their ever-expanding line of innovative products, heavy use of trade shows, and intensive presence on social media sites. Joby's operations have expanded to an international market, with offices in Switzerland, Japan, Singapore, and China.

DISCUSSION QUESTIONS

1 What are the objectives of promotion? How do each apply to Joby?
2 How has Joby positioned itself in the market?
3 Joby's promotional strategy has de-emphasized television advertising. Why did the company make this decision? Do you think that this will limit sales?
4 How does Joby use publicity to promote their products? Has this been effective?
5 What role do trade shows play in Joby's promotional strategy?

Online Exploration

The Joby website (www.joby.com) provides great insight into Joby's products and marketing mix. You can begin your exploration by finding out more about the company's product lines, focusing on how the company has adapted their initial technology to a wide range of applications. By clicking on the Store Link, you can view prices for each of their products. How do prices for Joby products compare to more traditional tripods and spotlights? Finally, you can gain insight into the company's use of publicity by scrolling to the bottom of the page and clicking on "About Joby". Pay particular attention to the press releases, trade shows, and social media information to understand Joby's promotional strategy. Briefly summarize the company's promotional strategy after viewing these links.

Using low-cost, direct-to-consumer selling and market share pricing, Dell profitably dominated the personal computer market, while its competitors—Apple, IBM, Compaq, and Hewlett-Packard—sold through retailers, adding extra costs that prevented them from matching Dell's low prices. Competitors have switched to direct-to-consumer sales, but Dell is strongly anchored as the industry's number-two PC maker (after Hewlett-Packard).

Roy Cooper scours the markets of Quito, Ecuador, for tapestries, baskets, and religious relics. He then sells them on the Internet, usually at substantial markups, by privately negotiating prices with buyers.

At the plant of the world's largest auto parts supplier, Delphi Automotive Systems, Jessica V. Prince assembles fuel pumps according to a process that she helped engineers and consultants design. The auto parts are shipped from the plant to an auto manufacturer, illustrating a direct (producer to consumer) channel of distribution.

Commenting on potential contributions by mature women, cofounder Liz Smith says, "A long time ago, Margaret Mead, the great anthropologist, said that there was nothing to equal the power of the menopausal woman. And I think she is right."

QVC host Bob Bowersox is getting ready to offer bedding made by Northern Lights, which distributes regularly through the TV home-shopping channel. Northern Lights markets through such electronic-retailing outlets as eBay and Shopping.com as well as QVC, which also sells online through its website and through six outlet stores.

Specializing in long-haul shipping, U.S. Xpress Enterprises employs nearly 6,000 drivers to operate 5,300 trucks and 12,000 trailers. Trucks have satellite capabilities, anticollision radar, vehicle-detection sensors, computers for shifting through 10 speeds, and roomy cabs with sleepers, refrigerators, and microwaves.

END NOTES

[1] Apple Inc., *Form 10-K* (October 27, 2010), accessed at http://www.apple.com/investor/; Glenn Peoples, "iTunes Price Changes Hurt Some Rankings," *Billboard.biz*, April 10, 2009 at http://www.billboard.biz/bbbiz/content_display/industry/news/e3i7917210cb575a9b91b4543e3d671922a ; Edward Christman, "UPDATE: First Half 2010 Sales Recap: Lady Antebellum, UMG Lead the Way," *Billboard.biz*, July 7, 2010 at http://www.billboard.biz/bbbiz/content_display/industry/news/e3ic639ed027f3e13c9f62b3cb6e00e1f0e.

[2] Jim Dalrymple, "Apple now number 2 music retailer in the U.S.," *Network World* (February 26, 2008), at http://www.networkworld.com/news/2008/022608-apple-now-number-2-music.html; "iTunes Increasing Its Dominance," Telecom (April 30, 2008), at http://web20.telecomtv.com/pages/?newsid=43081&id=e9381817-0593-417a-8639-c4c53e2a2a10&view=news; Chris Maxcer, "iTunes Tops Music Vendor Charts," *E-Commerce Times* (April 4, 2008), at ; "Amazon Ties Walmart as Second-Ranked U.S. Music Retailer, Behind Industry-Leader iTunes," The *NBD Group* (*press release*), May 26, 2010, accessed at http://www.npd.com/press/releases/press_100526.html.

[3] "About Carbonite," at http://www.carbonite.com/en/about/company/our-story.

[4] "Reverse Auction," *Encyclopedia of Management. 2009. Encyclopedia.com.* (January 16, 2011). http://www.encyclopedia.com/doc/1G2-3273100254.html; MediaBids.com, at http://www.mediabids.com/.

[5] Meghan Casserly and Jenna Goudreau, "Top 100 websites for Women," *Forbes.com*, June 23, 2010, at http://www.forbes.com/2010/06/23/100-best-womens-blogs-forbes-woman-time-websites.html; "Wowowow.com Gives a Voice to Mature Women," *TimesOnline*, April 6, 2008, at http://technology.timesonline.co.uk/tol/news/tech_and_web/the_web/article3662890.ece; Stephanie Rosenbloom, "Boldface in Cyberspace: It's a Woman's Domain," *The New York Times*, March 6, 2008, at http://www.nytimes.com/2008/03/06/fashion/06WOW.html; Geraldine Baum, "It's Web 101 for This Experienced Intern," *Los Angeles Times: Article Collections*, March 6, 2009, at http://articles.latimes.com/2009/mar/06/nation/na-senior-intern6; Asa Aarons, "'On the Job' Training Takes on New Meaning," *NY1.com*, March 23, 2009, at http://www.ny1.com/?ArID=96052.

[6] "Vending Machines: A Global Strategic Business Report," *CompaniesAndMarkets.com: Market Report*, September 1, 2010, at http://www.companiesandmarkets.com/Market-Report/vending-machines-a-global-strategic-business-report-companiesandmarkets.com.

[7] *AVON 2009 Annual Report*, at http://phx.corporate-ir.net/phoenix.zhtml?c=90402&p=irol-irhome.

[8] *YAHOO! FINANCE*, January 16, 2011, at http://finance.yahoo.com/q/is?annual&s=amzn.

[9] Melissa Dowling, "Online Sales Continue to Climb," *Multichannel Merchant* (March 1, 2008), at http://www.multichannelmerchant.com/ecommerce/archive/online_sales_continue/.

[10] Michael Muchmore, "The Best Online Backup Services," *PC Magazine*, October 28, 2010, at http://www.pcmag.com/article2/0,2817,2288745.asp.

[11] "Highlight Free Shipping Offers in Online Marketing Campaigns," *ClickThrough Search Engine Marketing Services*, February 16, 2009, at http://www.click-through-marketing.com/highlight-free-shipping-offers-in-online-marketing-campaigns/19027764/; "Free Shipping Strategies Gain Retailers Loyal Customers," *ManageSmarter*, July 30, 2010, at http://www.salesandmarketing.com/article/free-shipping-strategies-gain-retailers-loyal-customers.

[12] "Ford, GM to Cover Car Payments if Buyer Loses Job," *Bloomberg News*, March 31, 2009, at http://www.chron.com/disp/story.mp/business/6351277.html.

[13] "Use Those stocks to Pay for a Caribbean Vacation-at July 2008 Market Prices!," *Travel4People.com*, at http://www.travel4people.com/index.php?view=article&catid=1%3Anews1&id=314%3Ause-those-stocks-to-pay-for-a-caribbean-vacation-at-july-market-prices&tmpl=component&print=1&layout=default&page=&option=com_content&Itemid=49.

[14] Steve McClellan, "Univision's Spanish Conquest: Aiming to Become the Top Broadcast Network," *ADWEEK*, October 24, 2010, at http://www.adweek.com/aw/content_display/news/media/e3i1c1499752deb3a604fc967b1603c1946.

[15] "100 Leading National Advertisers," *Docstoc*, accessed January 14, 2011 at http://www.docstoc.com/docs/8385834/100-Leading-National-Advertisers-US; "U.S. Advertising Revenue, By Medium," *Business Insider*, October 27, 2009, at http://www.businessinsider.com/us-advertising-spending-by-medium-2009-10.

[16] Nat Ives, "Consumers Are Bugged By Many Ads," *Advertising Age*, December 1, 2008, page 6.

[17] "Ads Now Watching Shoppers," *Columbia Daily Tribune* (Associated Press), February 3, 2009, page 7B.

[18] "DMA's Power of Direct Marketing Report Finds DM AdExpenditures Climb to Over 54% of All Advertising Expenditures," *Direct Marketing Association*, October 19, 2009, at http://www.thedma.org/cgi/dispannouncements?article=1335.

[19] Associated Press, "New Arrest in Wendy's Finger Case," MSNBC.com (May 19, 2005), at http://www.msnbc.msn.com/id/7844274.

[20] Ron Insana, "Wendy's Knew from Start Story Was a Hoax," *USA Today* (June 5, 2005), at http://www.usatoday.com/money/companies/management/2005-06-05-insana-wendys_x.htm.

[21] "Apple Marks 10 Billionth Song Download," *CBSNews.com*, February 26, 2010 at http://www.cbsnews.com/stories/2010/02/26/earlyshow/leisure/gamesgadgetsgizmos/main6246268.shtml.

22 "Apple Hits 10 Billion Songs Sold—But What's Happening to Music Sales Growth?" *guardian.co.uk Technology Blog*, February 25, 2010 at http://www.guardian.co.uk/technology/blog/2010/feb/25/apple-ten-billion-songs-itunes-analysis; Glenn Peoples, "iTunes Price Changes Hurt Some Rankings," *Billboard.biz*, April 10, 2009 at http://www.billboard.biz/bbbiz/content_display/ industry/news/e3i7917210cb575a9b91b4543e3d6719 22a; Todd Martens, "Overall Music Sales Hit an All-Time High in 2009; Taylor Swift's 'fearless' is the Year's Top-Selling Album," *Pop & Hiss, The L.A. Times Music Blog: Los Angeles Times/Entertainment*, January 6, 2010 at http://latimesblogs.latimes.com/music_blog/2010/01/overall-music-purchases-hit-an-alltime-high-in-2009.html.

13 Information Technology for Business

Online Pirates Feast on Economic Downturn

" *S tart a 'work-at-home' job as an 'international sales representative' or a 'shipping manager,' with excellent pay. Simply open a new bank account in your name, accept money transfers into the account, then forward the money to our customers at locations around the globe."* For out-of-work computer users, this e-mail message can be quite appealing. In reality, the victim is tricked into becoming a "mule" in a money-laundering racket. The new "employee" provides anonymous racketeers a safe way to launder stolen or otherwise illegal money. As Internet money transfers arrive, the mule relays them (illegally) to a global network of recipient racketeers. With rising unemployment, the volume of mule e-mails is growing; more job-seekers seem willing to take the risk of being arrested.

Financial fears are a boon to scammers, as businesses and consumers grasp at schemes that are ordinarily ignored. Fake websites, mobile devices, and Internet-based phones boast high-paying jobs, low-cost loans, and can't-miss lotteries. Text messages, saying victims' credit cards have been deactivated, lure bank customers into relaying account information. Internet-based phone users receive fake caller IDs of real hospitals, government agencies, banks, and other businesses in a new form of telephone phishing that talks victims into revealing personal information. Perhaps most impressive, cyber-thieves

> *After reading this chapter, you should be able to:*
>
> 1 Discuss the impacts information technology has had on the business world.
> 2 Identify the IT resources businesses have at their disposal and how these resources are used.
> 3 Describe the role of information systems, the different types of information systems, and how businesses use such systems.
> 4 Identify the threats and risks information technology poses on businesses.
> 5 Describe the ways in which businesses protect themselves from the threats and risks information technology poses.

are using marketing techniques—most notably "targeting"—to reach specific audiences. Also known as "spear phishing," with targeting, scammers do research to identify wealthy individuals, families, and professional money managers. Victims receive friendly-sounding e-mails containing contaminated attachments that, once opened, infect their computers, exposing bank account and other identity information to scammers. While computer security devices—spam filters, data encryption, firewalls, and anti-virus software—catch a vast number of intrusions, the threat remains.[1]

Our opening story continues on page 350.

WHAT'S IN IT FOR ME?

Protecting against cyber-attacks is an extreme example of the way the Internet and related technologies are reshaping the business landscape. But even the most traditional businesses must change with the times, whether those times are defined by paper and pencil, telephone and fax machine, or digital language translators and smartphones. Indeed, it may seem like the times are changing more rapidly with each passing year, and it is in this context that our discussion of the various kinds of information technology, their functions, and the benefits and risks associated with each assumes particular importance. By understanding the material in this chapter, you'll have a clearer picture of how technology is used by and affects business, and how you can use it to your best advantage.

MyBizLab Where you see MyBizLab in this chapter, go to **www.mybizlab.com** for additional activities on the topic being discussed.

Dave Pilibosian/iStockphoto.com

Discuss the impacts information technology has had on the business world.

IT Impacts

The effect of **Information technology (IT)** on business has been immeasurable. In fact, IT—the various appliances and devices for creating, storing, exchanging, and using information in diverse modes, including visual images, voice, multimedia, and business data—has altered the very structure of business organizations, radically changing the way employees and customers interact. We see ads all the time for the latest cell phones, iPads, laptops, PDAs, and smartphones, and most of us connect daily to the Internet. E-mail has become a staple in business, and even such traditionally "low-tech" businesses as nail salons and garbage collection companies are becoming dependent on the Internet, computers, and networks. As consumers, we interact with databases every time we withdraw money from an ATM, order food at McDonalds, or check on the status of a package at UPS.com. Technology and its effects are evident everywhere.

E-commerce (short for *electronic commerce*)—the use of the Internet and other electronic means for retailing and business-to-business transactions—has created new market relationships around the globe. In this section, we'll look at how businesses are using IT to bolster productivity, improve operations and processes, create new opportunities, and communicate and work in ways not possible before.

Creating Portable Offices: Providing Remote Access to Instant Information

IT appliances such as BlackBerry® smartphones, Nokia smartphones, and others feature wireless Internet access and PC-style office applications, saving businesses time and travel expenses by enabling employees, customers, and suppliers to communicate from any location. IT's mobile messaging capabilities mean that a geographic separation between the workplace and headquarters is more common. Employees no longer work only at the office or the factory, nor are all of a company's operations performed at one place; employees take the office with them. When using such devices, off-site employees have continuous access to information, instead of being forced to be at a desk to access their files and the Internet. Client project folders, e-mail, and voice messaging are accessible from any location. Such benefits have attracted 55 million enthusiastic subscribers to BlackBerry® smartphones, making it a leader in the handheld wireless industry until losing its top spot to the iPad.[2]

Enabling Better Service by Coordinating Remote Deliveries

Meanwhile, with access to the Internet, company activities may be geographically scattered but remain coordinated through a networked system that provides better service for customers. Many businesses, for example, coordinate activities from one centralized location, but their deliveries flow from several remote locations, often at lower cost. When you order furniture—for example, a chair, a sofa, a table, and two lamps—from an Internet storefront, the chair may come from a warehouse in Philadelphia and the lamps from a manufacturer in California; the sofa and table may be shipped direct from different suppliers in North Carolina. Beginning with the customer's order, activities are coordinated through the company's network, as if the whole order were being processed at one place. This avoids the expensive in-between step of first shipping all the items to a central location.

Creating Leaner, More Efficient Organizations

Networks and technology are also leading to leaner companies with fewer employees and simpler structures. Because networks enable firms to maintain information linkages among both employees and customers, more work and

customer satisfaction can be accomplished with fewer people. Bank customers dial into a 24-hour information system and monitor their accounts without employee assistance. Instructions that once were given to assembly workers by supervisors are now delivered to workstations electronically. IT communications provide better use of employee skills and greater efficiencies from physical resources. For example, truck drivers used to return to a shipping terminal to receive instructions from supervisors on reloading freight for the next delivery. Today, one dispatcher using IT has replaced several supervisors. Instructions to the fleet arrive on electronic screens in trucks on the road so drivers know in advance the next delivery schedule, while satellite navigation services, such as the XM NavTraffic, alert drivers of traffic incidents ahead so they can reroute to avoid delivery delays.[3]

Barack Obama's Blackberry uses an encrypted system for secure messaging with advisors and colleagues.

Enabling Increased Collaboration

Collaboration among internal units and with outside firms is greater when firms use collaboration (collaborative) software and other IT communications devices, which we'll discuss later in this chapter. Companies are learning that complex problems can be better solved through IT-supported collaboration, either with formal teams or spontaneous interaction among people and departments. The design of new products, for example, was once an engineering responsibility. Now it is a shared activity using information from people in marketing, finance, production, engineering, and purchasing who, collectively, determine the best design. For example, the design of Boeing's 787 Dreamliner aircraft is the result of collaboration, not just among engineers, but also from passengers (who wanted electric outlets to recharge personal electronic devices), cabin crews (who wanted more bathrooms and wider aisles), and air-traffic controllers (who wanted larger, safer air brakes).

Enabling Global Exchange

The global reach of IT is enabling business collaboration on a scale that was unheard of before. Consider Lockheed Martin's contract for designing and supplying thousands of Joint Strike Fighters in different versions for the United States, Britain, Italy, Denmark, Canada, and Norway. Lockheed can't do the job alone— over the project's 20-year life, more than 1,500 firms will supply everything from radar systems to engines to bolts. In just the startup phase, Lockheed collaborated with Britain's BAE Systems along with more than 70 U.S. and 18 international subcontractors at some 190 locations, including an Australian manufacturer of aviation communications and a Turkish electronics supplier. In all, 40,000 remote computers are collaborating on the project using Lockheed's Internet-based system. Web collaboration on a massive scale is essential for coordinating design, testing, and construction while avoiding delays, holding down costs, and maintaining quality.[4]

Information Technology (IT) various appliances and devices for creating, storing, exchanging, and using information in diverse modes, including visual images, voice, multimedia, and business data

E-commerce use of the Internet and other electronic means for retailing and business-to-business transactions

Improving Management Processes

IT has also changed the nature of the management process. The activities and methods of today's manager differ significantly from those that were common just a few years ago. At one time, upper-level managers didn't concern themselves with all of the detailed information filtering upward from the workplace because it was expensive to gather, slow in coming, and quickly became out of date. Workplace management was delegated to middle and first-line managers.

With databases, specialized software, and networks, however, instantaneous information is accessible and useful to all levels of management. For example, consider *enterprise resource planning (ERP)*: an information system for organizing and managing a firm's activities across product lines, departments, and geographic locations. The ERP stores real-time information on work status and upcoming transactions and notifies employees when action is required if certain schedules are to be met. It coordinates internal operations with activities of outside suppliers and notifies customers of upcoming deliveries and billings. Consequently, more managers use it routinely for planning and controlling company-wide operations. Today, a manager at Hershey Foods, for example, uses ERP to check on the current status of any customer order for Kisses or strawberry Twizzlers, inspect productivity statistics for each workstation, and analyze the delivery performance on any shipment. Managers can better coordinate company-wide performance. They can identify departments that are working well together and those that are lagging behind schedule and creating bottlenecks.

Providing Flexibility for Customization

IT advances also create new manufacturing capabilities that enable businesses to offer customers greater variety, customizable options, and faster delivery cycles. Whether it's an iPhone app or a Rawlings baseball glove, today's design-it-yourself world is possible through fast, flexible manufacturing using IT networks. At Ponoko. com you can design and make just about anything, from electronics to furniture. Buyers and materials suppliers, meeting electronically, have rapidly generated thousands of product designs online. The designs can be altered to suit each buyer's tastes. Similarly, at San Francisco–based Timbuk2's website, you can "build your own" custom messenger bag at different price levels with your choice of size, fabric, color combination, accessories, liner material, strap, and even left- or right-hand access.[5] This principle is called **mass-customization**: Although companies produce in large volumes, IT allows each item to feature the unique options the customer prefers. With IT, the old standardized assembly line has become quickly adaptable because workers have instantaneous access to assembly instructions for all the product options, and equipment can be changed quickly for each customer's order.

As shown in Figure 13.1, flexible production and speedy delivery depend on an integrated network of information to coordinate all the activities among customers, manufacturers, suppliers, and shippers.

Providing New Business Opportunities

Not only is IT improving existing businesses, it is creating entirely new businesses where none existed before. For big businesses, this means developing new products, offering new services, and reaching new clients. Only a few years ago, today's multibillion-dollar behemoth known as Google was a fledgling search engine. That company boasts not just a search engine but hundreds of services including virtual maps, YouTube video, instant messaging, e-mail, and online software services such as photo editing and document creation.

The IT landscape has also presented small-business owners with new e-business opportunities. Consider Richard Smith. His love for stamp collecting began at age seven. Now, some 50 years after saving that first stamp, he's turned his hobby into a profitable eBay business. Each day begins at the PC in his home office, scanning eBay's listings for items available and items wanted by sellers and buyers around the world. With more than 3,000 sales transactions to date, Richard maintains a perfect

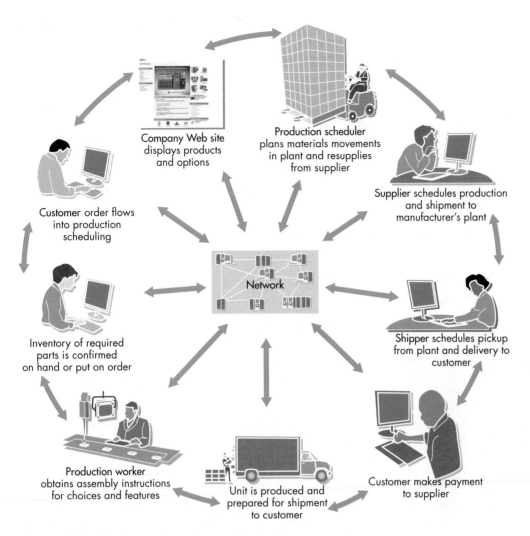

Figure 13.1 **Networking for Mass Customization**

customer rating and recently earned more than $4,000 on a single eBay transaction. More than 600 online marketplaces allow entrepreneurs to sell directly to consumers, bypassing conventional retail outlets, and enable B2B selling and trading with access to a worldwide customer base. To assist start-up businesses, eBay's services network is a ready-made online business model, not just an auction market. Services range from credit financing to protection from fraud and misrepresentation, information security, international currency exchanges, and post-sales management. These features enable users to complete sales transactions, deliver merchandise, and get new merchandise for future resale, all from the comfort of their own homes. Many eBay users, like Richard Smith, have carved profitable new careers.

Improving the World and Our Lives

Can advancements in IT really make the world a better place? The development of smartphones and other electronic devices has certainly brought enjoyment and convenience to the everyday lives of millions of people around the globe. Extending technology beyond earlier cell phones and PCs, new technologies provide access to endless choices of *apps* (shorthand for *application software*), allowing each user to "build it your way," depending on what you want your device to do and how you'll be using it. Apps

Mass-Customization principle in which companies produce in large volumes, but each item features the unique options the customer prefers

Social Networking as a Service The many forms of social media—blogs, chats, and networks such as LinkedIn, Twitter, and Facebook—are no longer just playthings for gossips and hobbyists. They're also active tools for getting a job. With the economic meltdown, millions of job seekers have turned to online networking—tapping leads from friends, colleagues, and acquaintances—for contacts with companies that may be hiring. Peers and recruiters are networking using electronic discussion forums and bulletin boards at websites of professional associations and trade groups, technical schools, and alumni organizations. Some social sites provide occupation-specific career coaching and job tips: Scientists are connecting with Epernicus, top managers use Meet the Boss, and graduate students are connecting with Graduate Junction.[6]

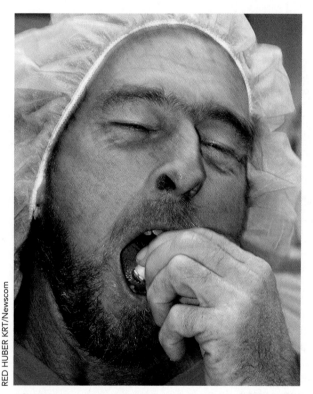

After this capsule is swallowed, the camera inside it can transmit almost 50,000 images during its eight-hour journey through the digestive tract.

for computers and smartphones include *programs* for learning languages, music, work, games, traveling, art, and almost any other area of interest. Just two years after its opening, Apple's App Store had supplied over 10 billion app downloads worldwide to users of Macs, iPhones, iPads, and iPod touches.

Organizations, too, including hospitals and medical equipment companies are embracing IT advancements to provide better services. For example, when treating combat injuries, surgeons at Walter Reed Army Medical Center rely on high-tech imaging systems that convert two-dimensional photographs of their patients' anatomies into three-dimensional physical models for presurgical planning. These 3-D mockups of shoulders, femurs, and facial bones give doctors the opportunity to see and feel the anatomy as it will be seen in the operating room, before they even use their scalpels. Meanwhile, pill-sized cameras that patients swallow are providing doctors with images of the insides of the human body, helping them to make better diagnoses for such ailments as ulcers and cancer.[7]

IT Building Blocks: Business Resources

Businesses today have a wide variety of IT resources at their disposal. In addition to the Internet and e-mail, these include communications technologies, networks, hardware devices, and software, as shown at technology media sites such as Techweb.com.

The Internet and Other Communication Resources

2 Identify the IT resources businesses have at their disposal and how these resources are used.

The **Internet** is a gigantic system of interconnected computer networks belonging to millions of collaborating organizations and agencies—government, business, academic, and public—linked together by voice, electronic, and wireless technologies.[8] Computers within the networks are connected by various communications protocols, or standardized coding systems, such as the **hypertext transfer protocol (HTTP)**—which is used for the **World Wide Web,** a branch of the Internet consisting of interlinked hypertext documents, or web pages. Other protocols serve a variety of purposes such as sending and receiving e-mail. The World Wide web and its protocols provide the common language that allows information sharing on the Internet. For thousands of businesses, the Internet has replaced the telephone, fax machine, and standard mail as the primary communications tool.

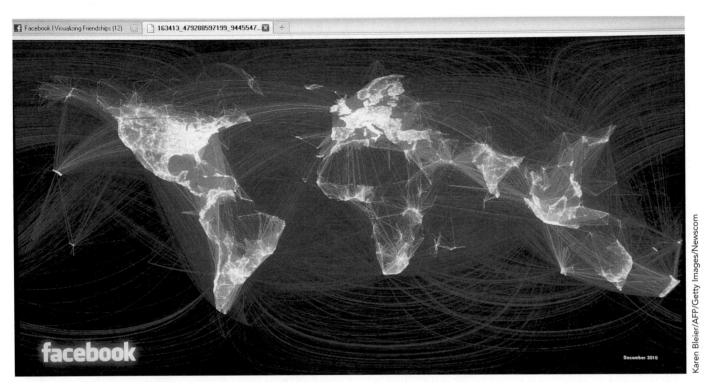

In this map of the Internet, from The Opte Project, each line represents a connection between computers or other network devices.

The Internet has spawned a number of other business communications technologies, including *intranets, extranets, electronic conferencing*, and *VSAT satellite communications*.

Intranets Many companies have extended Internet technology by maintaining internal websites linked throughout the firm. These private networks, or **intranets,** are accessible only to employees and may contain confidential information on benefits programs, a learning library, production management tools, or product design resources. The Ford Motor Company's intranet is accessible to 200,000 people daily at workstations in Asia, Europe, and the United States. It contains private information on Ford's employee benefits, production management tools, and product design resources. Sharing information on engineering, distribution, and marketing has reduced the lead time for getting new models into production and has shortened customer delivery times.[9]

Extranets **Extranets** allow outsiders limited access to a firm's internal information network. The most common application allows buyers to enter a system to see which products are available for sale and delivery, thus providing convenient product-availability information. Industrial suppliers are often linked into customers' information networks so that they can see planned production schedules and prepare supplies for customers' upcoming operations. The extranet at Chaparral

Internet gigantic system of interconnected computer networks linked together by voice, electronic, and wireless technologies

Hypertext Transfer Protocol (HTTP) communications protocol used for the World Wide Web, in which related pieces of information on separate web pages are connected using hyperlinks

World Wide Web branch of the Internet consisting of interlinked hypertext documents, or web pages

Intranet organization's private network of internally linked websites accessible only to employees

Extranet system that allows outsiders limited access to a firm's internal information network

Steel Company, for example, lets customers shop electronically through its storage yards and gives them electronic access to Chaparral's planned inventory of industrial steel products.

Electronic Conferencing   **Electronic conferencing** allows groups of people to communicate simultaneously from various locations via e-mail, phone, or video, thereby eliminating travel time and saving money. One form, called *dataconferencing*, allows people in remote locations to work simultaneously on one document. *Videoconferencing* allows participants to see one another on video screens while the conference is in progress. For example, Lockheed Martin's Joint Strike Fighter project, discussed earlier, uses Internet collaboration systems with both voice and video capabilities. Although separated by oceans, partners can communicate as if they were in the same room for redesigning components and production schedules. Electronic conferencing is attractive to many businesses because it eliminates travel and saves money.

VSAT Satellite Communications   Another Internet technology businesses use to communicate is **VSAT satellite communications.** VSAT (short for *very small aperture terminal*) systems have a transmitter-receiver (*transceiver*) that sits outdoors with a direct line of sight to a satellite. The hub—a ground-station computer at the company's headquarters—sends signals to and receives signals from the satellite, exchanging voice, video, and data transmissions. An advantage of VSAT is privacy. A company that operates its own VSAT system has total control over communications among its facilities, no matter their location, without dependence on other companies. A firm might use VSAT to exchange sales and inventory information, advertising messages, and visual presentations between headquarters and store managers at remote sites. For example, stores in Minneapolis, London, and Boston might communicate with headquarters in New York, sending and receiving information via a satellite, as shown in Figure 13.2.

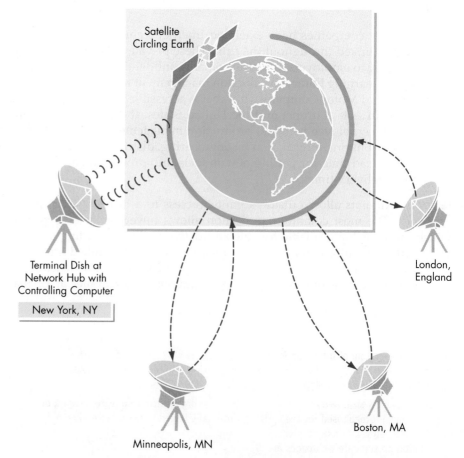

Figure 13.2 **A VSAT Satellite Communication Network**

Networks: System Architecture

A **computer network** is a group of two or more computers linked together, either hard-wired or wirelessly, to share data or resources, such as a printer. The most common type of network used in businesses is a **client-server network.** In client-server networks, *clients* are usually the laptop or desktop computers through which users make requests for information or resources. *Servers* are the computers that provide the services shared by users. In big organizations, servers are usually assigned a specific task. For example, in a local university or college network, an *application server* stores the word-processing, spreadsheet, and other programs used by all computers connected to the network. A *print server* controls the printers, stores printing requests from client computers, and routes jobs as the printers become available. An *e-mail server* handles all incoming and outgoing e-mail. With a client-server system, users can share resources and Internet connections—and avoid costly duplication.

Networks can be classified according to geographic scope and means of connection (either wired or wireless).

Wide Area Networks (WANs)
Computers that are linked over long distances—statewide or even nationwide—through telephone lines, microwave signals, or satellite communications make up what are called **wide area networks (WANs).** Firms can lease lines from communications vendors or maintain private WANs. Walmart, for example, depends heavily on a private satellite network that links thousands of U.S. and international retail stores to its Bentonville, Arkansas, headquarters.

Local Area Networks (LANs)
In **local area networks (LANs),** computers are linked in a smaller area such as an office or a building. For example, a LAN unites hundreds of operators who enter call-in orders at TV's Home Shopping Network facility. The arrangement requires only one computer system with one database and one software system.

Wireless Networks
Wireless networks use airborne electronic signals to link network computers and devices. Like wired networks, wireless networks can reach across long distances or exist within a single building or small area. For example, the BlackBerry® smartphones system shown in Figure 13.3 consists of devices that send and receive transmissions on the **wireless wide area networks (WWANs)** of more than 100 service providers—such as Cellular One (United States), T-Mobile (United Kingdom and United States), and Vodafone Italia (Italy)—in countries throughout the world. The wireless format that the system relies on to control wireless messaging is supplied by Research In Motion® (RIM®), the company that makes the BlackBerry® smartphone, and is installed on the user-company's computer. A *firewall* provides privacy protection. We'll discuss firewalls in more detail later in the chapter.

Wi-Fi
You've no doubt heard of "hotspots"—nearly 1 million locations worldwide, such as coffee shops, hotels, airports, and cities that provide wireless Internet connections for people on the go. Each hotspot, or **Wi-Fi** (a play on audio recording term Hi-Fi) access point, uses its own small network, called a **wireless local area network (wireless LAN or WLAN).** Although wireless service is free at some hotspots, others charge a fee—a daily or hourly rate—for the convenience of Wi-Fi service.

Electronic Conferencing IT that allows groups of people to communicate simultaneously from various locations via e-mail, phone, or video

VSAT Satellite Communications network of geographically dispersed transmitter-receivers (transceivers) that send signals to and receive signals from a satellite, exchanging voice, video, and data transmissions

Computer Network group of two or more computers linked together by some form of cabling or by wireless technology to share data or resources, such as a printer

Client-Server Network common business network in which **clients** make requests for information or resources and **servers** provide the services

Wide Area Network (WAN) computers that are linked over long distances through telephone lines, microwave signals, or satellite communications

Local Area Network (LAN) computers that are linked in a small area, such as all of a firm's computers within a single building

Wireless Wide Area Network (WWAN) network that uses airborne electronic signals instead of wires to link computers and electronic devices over long distances

Wi-Fi technology using a wireless local area network

Wireless Local Area Network (Wireless Lan or Wlan) local area network with wireless access points for PC users

Figure 13.3 Core Components in BlackBerry Wireless Internet Architecture

Source: Major modifications of diagrams at the BlackBerry Web site, modified from Research in Motion, Limited, technical images, at http://www.blackberry.com/images/technical/bes_exchange_architecture.gif. BlackBerry®, RIM®, Research In Motion® y las marcas comerciales, los nombres y los logos relacionados son propiedad de Research In Motion Limited y están registrados y/o se utilizan en los Estados Unidos y en otros países. Uso bajo licencia de Research In Motion Limited.

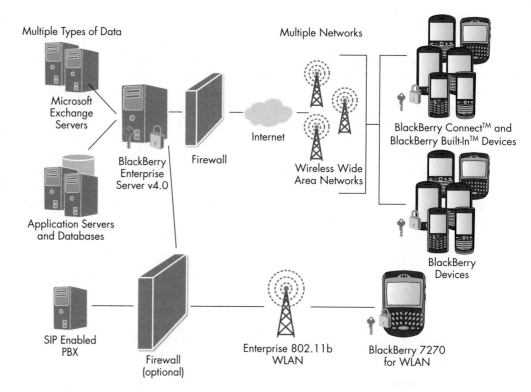

The benefit of Wi-Fi is that its millions of users are not tethered to a wire for accessing the Internet. Employees can wait for a delayed plane in the airport and still be connected to the Internet through their wireless-enabled laptops or other devices. However, as with every technology, Wi-Fi has limitations, including a short range of distance. This means that your laptop's Internet connection can be severed if you move farther than about 300 feet from the hotspot. In addition, thick walls, construction beams, and other obstacles can interfere with the signals sent out by the network. So, while a city may have hundreds of hotspots, your laptop must remain near one to stay connected. *WiMAX (Worldwide Interoperability for Microwave Access)*, the next step in wireless advancements, improves this distance limitation with its wireless range of up to 30 miles.

Hardware and Software

Any computer network or system needs **hardware**—the physical components, such as keyboards, monitors, system units, and printers. In addition to the laptops, desktop computers, and BlackBerry® smartphones mentioned earlier, *handheld computers* and smartphones are also used often in businesses. For example, Target employees roam the store aisles using handhelds to identify, count, and order items; track deliveries; and update backup stock at distribution centers to keep store shelves replenished with merchandise.

The other essential in any computer system is **software**: programs that tell the computer how to function. Software includes *system software*, such as Microsoft Windows 7 for PCs, which tells the computer's hardware how to interact with the software, what resources to use, and how to use them. It also includes *application software* (apps) such as Microsoft's Live Messenger and Photo Gallery, which are programs that meet the needs of specific users. Some application programs are used to address such common, long-standing needs as database management and inventory control, whereas others have been developed for a variety of specialized tasks ranging from mapping the oceans' depths to analyzing the anatomical structure of the human body. For example, IBM's Visualization Data Explorer software uses data from field samples to model the underground structure of an oil field. The imagery in Figure 13.4, for example, provides engineers with better information on oil location and reduces the risk of their hitting less productive holes.

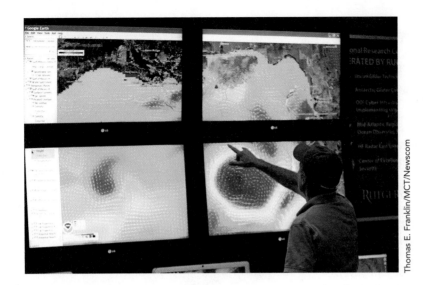

Thomas E. Franklin/MCT/Newscom

Figure 13.4 3-D computer modeling software gives engineers a better idea of where oil might be located

Finally *groupware*—software that connects group members for e-mail distribution, electronic meetings, message storing, appointments and schedules, and group writing—allows people to collaborate from their own desktop PCs, even if they're remotely located. It is especially useful when people work together regularly and rely heavily on information sharing. Groupware systems include IBM Lotus Sametime and Novell GroupWise.

Information Systems: Harnessing the Competitive Power of IT

3 Describe the role of information systems, the different types of information systems, and how businesses use such systems.

Business today relies on information management in ways that no one could foresee a decade ago. Managers now treat IT as a basic organizational resource for conducting daily business. At major firms, every activity—designing services, ensuring product delivery and cash flow, and evaluating personnel—is linked to *information systems*. An **information system (IS)** uses IT resources that enable managers to take **data**—raw facts and figures that, by themselves, may not have much meaning—and turn those data into **information**—the meaningful, useful interpretation of data. Information systems also enable managers to collect, process, and transmit that information for use in decision making.

One company well-known for its strategic use of information systems is Walmart. The nerve center for company operations is a centralized IS in Bentonville, Arkansas. The IS drives costs down and raises efficiency because the same methods and systems are applied for all 9,000-plus stores in 15 countries. Data on the billions of

---

Hardware physical components of a computer network, such as keyboards, monitors, system units, and printers

Software programs that tell the computer how to function, what resources to use, how to use them, and application programs for specific activities

Information System (IS) system that uses IT resources to convert data into information and to collect, process, and transmit that information for use in decision making

Data raw facts and figures that, by themselves, may not have much meaning

Information meaningful, useful interpretation of data

MANAGING IN TURBULENT TIMES

When Cash Gets Scarce, Businesses Switch to Internet Bartering

For many companies, the economic downturn involves tighter credit, a drop in sales revenues, and a shortage of cash for doing business. Without cash and credit, companies can't buy the materials, services, and supplies needed to produce products for customers, so business prospects grow even dimmer. Or do they? Enter an unexpected liberator—bartering. This ancient trade practice survives even today, but in an Internet-enhanced form with global reach and instantaneous access to a vast network of swap agreements. And best of all, it can be done without cash: For example, Firm A provides an advertising program for Firm B that, in return, has vacant building space needed by Firm A. Thus, the needs of both are met, and a cashless swap is born. As the recession has deepened, the popularity of bartering is booming. In 2010, BarterQuest.com had more than 50,000 monthly visitors from Australia, USA, and elsewhere. Activity has tripled at U-Exchange.com, where its "Barter 101" gets you started, and you can barter as much as you like at no cost. Overall, the electronically based barter business has grown to a $600 billion industry.[10]

Whether it's B2B or business-to-consumer, online bartering is an efficient way around the recession's credit crunch because it enables companies and individuals to get goods and services without using cash. Restaurants, for example, can trade meals or catering for advertising or for cooking equipment. Bartering can also be a good way to move excessive inventory and get needed benefits in return. An unemployed electrician bartered with homeowners who needed electrical wiring; in return, the homeowners gave up unneeded furniture and laptops that the electrician later sold to make mortgage payments.

Yuri Arcurs/Shutterstock

For avid swappers of services, websites such as PeopleTrading Services.com make it easy for small business owners to find barter matchups with hundreds of kinds of services, ranging from gardeners to songwriters to clergy. As a barter matchmaker, PeopleTradingServices.com posts members' profiles, lists services they trade, and provides a convenient way to contact member professionals online. Along with endless trading possibilities, the cash conservation can be a life-saver for any cash-strapped small business during troubled times.[11]

MyBizLab

sales transactions—time, date, and place—flow to Bentonville. The information system tracks millions of stock-keeping units (SKUs) weekly, enforces uniform reordering and delivery procedures on its suppliers, including 57,000 in the U.S. and 22,000 in China, and regulates the flow of merchandise through its distribution centers and stores.

Beyond the firm's daily operations, information systems are also crucial in planning. Managers routinely use the IS to decide on products and markets for the next 5 to 10 years. The company's vast database enables marketing managers to analyze demographics, and it is also used for financial planning, materials handling, and electronic funds transfers with suppliers and customers.

Walmart, like most businesses, regards its information as a private resource—an asset that's planned, developed, and protected. Therefore, it's not surprising that they have **information systems managers** who operate the systems used for gathering, organizing, and distributing information, just as they have production, marketing, and finance managers. These managers use many of the IT resources we discussed earlier—the Internet, communications technologies, networks, hardware, and software—to sift through information and apply it to their jobs.

Leveraging Information Resources: Data Warehousing and Data Mining

Almost everything you do leaves a trail of information about you. Your preferences in movie rentals, television viewing, Internet sites, and groceries; the destinations of your phone calls, your credit card charges, your financial status; personal information about age, gender, marital status, and even your health are just a few of the items about each of us that are stored in scattered databases. The behavior patterns of millions of users can be traced by analyzing files of information gathered over time from their Internet usage and in-store purchases.

Retailers such as Wal-Mart and Sam's Club rely on data warehousing and mining to keep shelves stocked with in-demand merchandise.

Marc F. Henning/Alamy

The collection, storage, and retrieval of such data in electronic files is called **data warehousing.** For managers, the data warehouse is a goldmine of information about their business. Indeed, Kroger Co., the Ohio-based grocery chain, collects data on customer shopping habits to find ways to gain greater customer loyalty. As part owner of a data-mining firm, Kroger accumulates information from its shopper cards, analyzes the data to uncover shopping patterns, and sends money-saving coupons to regular customers for the specific products they usually buy. Kroger's precision targeting pays off, especially in the recession economy. With a rate of coupon usage up to as much as 50 times the industry average, it's a money-saver for Kroger customers and boosts the company's sales, too.[12]

Data Mining   After collecting information, managers use **data mining**—the application of electronic technologies for searching, sifting, and reorganizing pools of data to uncover useful information. Data mining helps managers plan for new products, set prices, and identify trends and shopping patterns. By analyzing what consumers actually do, businesses can determine what subsequent purchases they are likely to make and then send them tailor-made ads. The *Washington Post*, for example, uses data-mining software to analyze census data and target households likely to respond to sales efforts.[13]

Information Linkages with Suppliers   The top priority for Walmart's IS—improving in-stock reliability—requires integration of Walmart's and suppliers' activities with store sales. That's why P&G, Johnson & Johnson, and other suppliers connect into Walmart's information system to observe up-to-the-minute sales data on individual items, by store. They can use the system's computer-based tools—spreadsheets, sales forecasting, and weather information—to forecast sales demand and plan delivery schedules. Coordinated planning avoids excessive inventories, speeds up deliveries, and holds down costs throughout the supply chain while keeping shelves stocked for retail customers.

Information Systems Managers managers who operate the systems used for gathering, organizing, and distributing information

Data Warehousing the collection, storage, and retrieval of data in electronic files

Data Mining the application of electronic technologies for searching, sifting, and reorganizing pools of data to uncover useful information

ENTREPRENEURSHIP AND NEW VENTURES

Speaking Loud and Clear: A New Voice Technology

IT users for years have sought a natural-sounding voice interface to enhance IT systems with vocal output, beyond traditional print or visual output. Vocal technologies, however, were less than effective, that is until 2005 when Matthew Aylett and Nick Wright formed CereProc (short for Cerebral Processing) in Edinburgh, Scotland.[14] From the outset, the firm has been dedicated to creating better synthetic voices with character and emotion that stimulates listeners with natural-sounding messages. Before CereProc, these lofty goals were prohibitive. Speech experts couldn't create text-to-voice software that sounds realistically conversational, varying tone-of-voice and providing various vocal inflections for different situations. Previous software couldn't adapt incoming text (from word processing or from text messages) into natural voice formats. To attack these challenges CereProc brought together a team of leading speech experts. It also partnered with leading universities and research programs in speech science technology, and in developing new applications and markets for voice output.

The company's main product is CereVoice, an advanced text-to-voice technology available on mobile devices, PCs, servers, and headsets, and that has applications in most any company's products for better synthetic voices. Any computer's existing voice system can be replaced with more natural-sounding speech in a choice of accents, including Southern British English, Scottish, and American that can be sampled with live voice demos at the firm's web-site.[15] Potential applications are endless—kitchen appliances, alarm systems, traffic controllers, automobile appliances, radio broadcasting, telephone messaging, and movies, to name a few. Although consumers may not see the CereVoice label, they will be hearing its various voices often in their everyday lives.

CereProc's Voice Creation service can create a synthesized imitation of a person's voice, including its tones and inflections. That's how noted film critic Roger Ebert got his voice back, four years after losing the ability to speak following cancer-related surgery. CereProc's voice engineers used recordings of Ebert's voice from 40 years of past television broadcasts, capturing individual sounds and identifying various voice characteristics. With meticulous care, specialists then pieced them back together into software that mimics the Pulitzer-Prize winner's earlier voice. Ebert types his comments into a computer that, in turn, converts the text into words that are spoken in his voice. This first-of-its-kind application made a memorable public appearance on the Oprah show, as Roger enthusiastically demonstrated his voice coming from the computer.[16] Beyond its technical success, this project vividly displays a compassionate side in CereProc's business.

MyBizLab

AB5 WENN Photos/Newscom

Types of Information Systems

Employees have a variety of responsibilities and decision-making needs, and a firm's *information system* may actually be a set of several systems that share information while serving different levels of the organization, different departments, or different operations. Because they work on different kinds of problems, managers and their employees have access to the specialized information systems that satisfy their different information needs.

In addition to different types of users, each business *function*—marketing, human resources, accounting, production, or finance—has its own information needs, as do groups working on major projects. Each user group and department, therefore, may need a special IS.

Information Systems for Knowledge Workers   As we discussed in Chapter 10, *knowledge workers* are employees for whom information and knowledge are the raw materials of their work, such as engineers, scientists, and IT specialists who rely on IT to design new products or create new processes. These workers require **knowledge information systems,** which provide resources to create, store, use, and transmit new knowledge for useful applications—for instance, databases to organize and retrieve information, and computational power for data analysis.

Specialized support systems have also increased the productivity of knowledge workers. **Computer-aided design (CAD)** helps knowledge workers—and now ordinary people too, as we saw at the beginning of this chapter—design products ranging from cell phones to jewelry to auto parts by simulating them and displaying them in 3-D graphics. In a more advanced version, known as *rapid prototyping*, the CAD system electronically transfers instructions to a computer-controlled machine that quickly builds a prototype—a physical model—of the newly designed product. The older method—making handcrafted prototypes from wood, plastic, or clay—is replaced with faster, cheaper prototyping.

The 3-D computer model of this dinosaur is constructed from digital scans of fossilized tissue.

In archaeology, CAD is helping scientists uncover secrets hidden in fossils using 3-D computer models of skeletons, organs, and tissues constructed with digital data from CT (computed tomography) scans of dinosaur fossils. From these models, scientists have learned, for example, that the giant apatosaurus's neck curved downward, instead of high in the air as once thought. By seeing how the animals' bones fit together with cartilage, ligaments, and vertebrae, scientists are discovering more about how these prehistoric creatures interacted with their environment.[17]

In a direct offshoot of computer-aided design, **computer-aided manufacturing (CAM)** uses computers to design and control the equipment needed in a manufacturing process. For example, CAM systems can produce digital instructions to control all the machines and robots on a production line. CAD and CAM coupled together (CAD/CAM) is useful to engineers in a manufacturing environment for designing and testing new products and then designing the machines and tools to manufacture the new product.

Information Systems for Managers   Each manager's information activities and IS needs vary according to his or her functional area (accounting or marketing and so forth) and management level. The following are some popular information systems used by managers for different purposes.

Management Information Systems **Management information systems (MIS)** support managers by providing reports, schedules, plans, and budgets that can then be used for making decisions, both short- and long-term. For example, at Walsworth Publishing Company, managers rely on detailed information—current customer orders, staffing schedules, employee attendance, production schedules, equipment status, and materials availability—for moment-to-moment decisions during the day. They require similar information to plan such mid-range activities as personnel

---

Knowledge Information System information system that supports knowledge workers by providing resources to create, store, use, and transmit new knowledge for useful applications

Computer-Aided Design (CAD) IS with software that helps knowledge workers design products by simulating them and displaying them in three-dimensional graphics

Computer-Aided Manufacturing (CAM) IS that uses computers to design and control equipment in a manufacturing process

Management Information System (MIS) computer system that supports managers by providing information—reports, schedules, plans, and budgets—that can be used for making decisions

training, materials movements, and cash flows. They also need to anticipate the status of the jobs and projects assigned to their departments. Many MIS—cash flow, sales, production scheduling, and shipping—are indispensable for helping managers complete these tasks.

For longer-range decisions involving business strategy, Walsworth managers need information to analyze trends in the publishing industry and overall company performance. They need both external and internal information, current and future, to compare current performance data to data from previous years and to analyze consumer trends and economic forecasts.

Decision Support Systems Managers who face a particular kind of decision repeatedly can get assistance from **decision support systems (DSS)**—interactive systems that create virtual business models and test them with different data to see how they respond. When faced with decisions on plant capacity, for example, Walsworth managers can use a capacity DSS. The manager inputs data on anticipated sales, working capital, and customer-delivery requirements. The data flow into the DSS processor, which then simulates the plant's performance under the proposed data conditions. After experimenting with various data conditions, the DSS makes recommendations on the best levels of plant capacity for each future time period.

IT Risks and Threats

4 Identify the threats and risks information technology poses on businesses.

As with other technologies throughout history, IT has attracted abusers set on doing mischief, with severity ranging from mere nuisance to outright destruction. Eager IT users everywhere are finding that even social networking and cell phones have a "dark side"—privacy invasion. Facebook postings of personal information about users can be intercepted and misused by intruders. Beacon caused a public uproar when it published peoples' online purchases publicly on their Facebook newsfeeds. And with cellular technology, some features of Bluetooth connections allow savvy intruders to read a victim's text messages, listen in on live conversations, and even view unwary users' photos.[18]

Businesses, too, are troubled with IT's "dark side." Hackers break into computers, stealing personal information and company secrets, and launching attacks on other computers. Meanwhile, the ease of information sharing on the Internet has proven costly for companies who are having an increasingly difficult time protecting their intellectual property, and viruses that crash computers have cost companies many billions annually. In this section, we'll look at these and other IT risks. In the next section, we'll discuss ways in which businesses are protecting themselves from these risks.

Hackers

Breaking and entering no longer refers merely to physical intrusion. Today, it applies to IT intrusions as well. **Hackers** are cybercriminals who gain unauthorized access to a computer or network, either to steal information, money, or property or to tamper with data. Another common hacker activity is to launch *denial of service (DoS) attacks*. DoS attacks flood networks or websites with bogus requests for information and resources, thereby shutting the networks or websites down and preventing legitimate users from accessing them.

Wireless mooching is a profitable industry for cybercriminals. In just five minutes, a *St. Petersburg Times* (Florida) reporter using a laptop found six unprotected wireless networks that were wide open to outside users.[19] Once inside an unsecured wireless network, hackers can use it to conduct illegal business, such as child pornography or money laundering. When police officers try to track down these criminals, they're long gone, leaving you, the network host, exposed to criminal prosecution.

Of Pirates and Profits Hackers often break into company networks to steal company or trade secrets. But it's not just hackers who are doing the stealing. Because the chances of getting caught seem slim, home users continue, illegally, to download unpaid-for movies, music, and other resources from file-swapping networks. A recent study shows that sound piracy costs the United States $12.5 billion and 71,060 jobs annually. However, these losses also showcase what can happen to businesses who fail to adapt to changes in technology. The recording industry has been reluctant to embrace the Internet as a path for distribution, preferring to prosecute pirates rather than offer them legal online alternatives. On the other hand, Apple has benefitted immensely from its online distribution models, with over 10 billion songs sold—some analysts predict that by 2012 Apple's iTunes music store will account for 28 percent of all music sold throughout the world.[20]

Identity Theft

Once inside a computer network, hackers are able to commit **identity theft,** the unauthorized stealing of personal information (such as Social Security number and address) to get loans, credit cards, or other monetary benefits by impersonating the victim. With up to 10 million victims each year, identity theft is the fastest growing crime in the United States.

Clever crooks get information on unsuspecting victims by digging in trash, stealing mail, or using *phishing* or *pharming* schemes to lure Internet users to bogus websites. For instance, a cybercriminal might send an America Online subscriber an e-mail notifying him or her of a billing problem with his or her account. When the customer clicks on the AOL Billing Center link, he or she is transferred to a spoofed (falsified) web page, modeled after AOL's. The customer then submits the requested information—credit card number, Social Security number, and PIN—into the hands of the thief. Her accounts are soon empty.

Intellectual Property Theft

Nearly every company faces the dilemma of protecting product plans, new inventions, industrial processes, and other **intellectual property**: something produced by the intellect or mind that has commercial value. Its ownership and right to its use may be protected by patent, copyright, trademark, and other means.

Hackers often break into company networks to steal company or trade secrets. But it's not just hackers who are doing the stealing. Because the chances of getting caught seem slim, home users continue, illegally, to download or copy unpaid-for movies, music, and other resources. The Commerce Department estimates that illegal product usage in the global market is costing U.S. companies hundreds of billions annually.

Computer Viruses, Worms, and Trojan Horses

Another IT risk facing businesses is rogue programmers who disrupt IT operations by contaminating and destroying software, hardware, or data files. Viruses, worms, and Trojan horses are three kinds of malicious programs that, once installed, can

---

Decision Support System (DSS) interactive system that creates virtual business models for a particular kind of decision and tests them with different data to see how they respond

Hacker cybercriminal who gains unauthorized access to a computer or network, either to steal information, money, or property or to tamper with data

Identity Theft unauthorized use of personal information (such as Social Security number and address) to get loans, credit cards, or other monetary benefits by impersonating the victim

Intellectual Property something produced by the intellect or mind that has commercial value

shut down any computer system. A *computer virus* exists in a file that attaches itself to a program and migrates from computer to computer as a shared program or as an e-mail attachment. It does not infect the system unless the user opens the contaminated file, and users typically are unaware they are spreading the virus by file sharing. It can, for example, quickly copy itself over and over again, using up all available memory and effectively shutting down the computer.

Worms are a particular kind of virus that travel from computer to computer within networked computer systems, without your needing to open any software to spread the contaminated file. In a matter of days, the notorious Blaster worm infected some 400,000 computer networks, destroying files and even allowing outsiders to take over computers remotely. The worm replicates itself rapidly, sending out thousands of copies to other computers in the network. Traveling through Internet connections and e-mail address books in the network's computers, it absorbs system memory and shuts down network servers, web servers, and individual computers.

Unlike viruses, a *Trojan horse* does not replicate itself. Instead, it most often comes into the computer, at your request, masquerading as a harmless, legitimate software product or data file. Once installed, the damage begins. For instance, it may simply redesign desktop icons or, more maliciously, delete files and destroy information.

Spyware

As if forced intrusion isn't bad enough, Internet users unwittingly invite spies—masquerading as a friendly file available as a giveaway or shared among individual users on their PCs. This so-called **spyware** is downloaded by users that are lured by "free" software. Once installed, it crawls around to monitor the host's computer activities, gathering e-mail addresses, credit card numbers, passwords, and other inside information that it transmits back to someone outside the host system. Spyware authors assemble incoming stolen information to create their own "intellectual property" that they then sell to other parties to use for marketing and advertising purposes or for identity theft.[21]

Spam

Spam—junk e-mail sent to a mailing list or a newsgroup (an online discussion group)—is a greater nuisance than postal junk mail because the Internet is open to the public, e-mail costs are negligible, and massive mailing lists are accessible through file sharing or by theft. Spam operators send unwanted messages ranging from explicit pornography to hate mail to advertisements, and even destructive computer viruses. In addition to wasting users' time, spam also consumes a network's bandwidth, thereby reducing the amount of data that can be transmitted in a fixed amount of time for useful purposes. U.S. industry experts estimate spam's damage in lost time and productivity at more than $140 billion worldwide in 2008 alone.[22]

IT Protection Measures

5 Describe the ways in which businesses protect themselves from the threats and risks information technology poses.

Security measures against intrusion and viruses are a constant challenge. Most systems guard against unauthorized access by requiring users to have protected passwords. Other measures include firewalls, special software, and encryption.

Preventing Unauthorized Access: Firewalls

Firewalls are security systems with special software or hardware devices designed to keep computers safe from hackers. A firewall is located where two networks—for example, the Internet and a company's internal network—meet. It contains two components for filtering incoming data:

- The company's *security policy*—Access rules that identify every type of data that the company doesn't want to pass through the firewall.

- A *router*—A table of available routes or paths; a "traffic switch" that determines which route or path on the network to send each piece of data after it is tested against the security policy.

Only that information that meets the conditions of the user's security policy is routed through the firewall and permitted to flow between the two networks. Data that fail the access test are blocked and cannot flow between the two networks.

Preventing Identity Theft

While foolproof prevention is impossible, steps can be taken to avoid being victimized. A visit to the Identity Theft Resource Center (http://www.idtheftcenter. org) is a valuable first step to get information on everything from scam alerts to victim issues to legislation such as the Fair and Accurate Credit Transactions Act (FACTA). FACTA strengthens identity-theft protections by specifying how organizations must destroy information instead of dropping it in a dumpster. When a company disposes of documents that contain credit or Social Security information, they must be shredded, pulverized, or burned, and all electronic records (in computers and databases) must be permanently removed to keep them out of the hands of intruders.[23]

Preventing Infectious Intrusions: Anti-Virus Software

Combating viruses, worms, Trojan horses, and any other infectious software (collectively known as *malware*) has become a major industry for systems designers and software developers. Installation of any of hundreds of **anti-virus software** products protects systems by searching incoming e-mail and data files for "signatures" of known viruses and virus-like characteristics. Contaminated files are discarded or placed in quarantine for safekeeping.

Many viruses take advantage of weaknesses in operating systems, such as Microsoft Windows, in order to spread and propagate. Network administrators must make sure that the computers on their systems are using the most up-to-date operating system that includes the latest security protection.

Protecting Electronic Communications: Encryption Software

Security for electronic communications is another concern for businesses. Unprotected e-mail can be intercepted, diverted to unintended computers, and opened, revealing the contents to intruders. Protective software is available to guard against those intrusions, adding a layer of security by encoding e-mails so that only intended recipients can open them. An **encryption system** works by scrambling an e-mail message so that it looks like garbled nonsense to anyone who doesn't possess the key.

Spyware program unknowingly downloaded by users that monitors their computer activities, gathering e-mail addresses, credit card numbers, and other information that it transmits to someone outside the host system

Spam junk e-mail sent to a mailing list or a newsgroup

Firewall security system with special software or hardware devices designed to keep computers safe from hackers

Anti-Virus Software product that protects systems by searching incoming e-mails and data files for "signatures" of known viruses and virus-like characteristics

Encryption System software that assigns an e-mail message to a unique code number (digital fingerprint) for each computer so only that computer, not others, can open and read the message

Avoiding Spam and Spyware

To help their employees avoid privacy invasion and to improve productivity, businesses often install anti-spyware and spam-filtering software on their systems. While dozens of anti-spyware products provide protection—software such as Webroot Spy Sweeper and Microsoft Windows Defender—they must be continually updated to keep pace with new spyware techniques.

The federal CAN-SPAM Act of 2003 requires the Federal Trade Commission to shield the public from falsified header information, sexually explicit e-mails that are not so labeled, Internet spoofing (using trickery to make a message appear as if it came from a trusted source), and hijacking of computers through worms or Trojan horses. While it cannot be prevented entirely, spam is abated by many Internet service providers (ISPs) that ban the spamming of ISP subscribers. In a now-classic punishment, an ISP in Iowa was awarded $1 billion in a lawsuit against 300 spammers that jammed the ISP system with an astounding 10 million e-mails a day. Anti-spam groups, too, promote the public's awareness of known spammers. The Spamhaus Project (http://www.spamhaus.org), for example, maintains a list—the Register of Known Spam Operators (ROKSO)—of around 100 professional spammers that are responsible for over 80 percent of spam traffic in North America and Europe.

Ethical Concerns in IT

It is apparent that IT developments and usage are progressing faster than society's appreciation for the potential consequences, including new ethical concerns. Along with IT's many benefits, its usage is creating previously unanticipated problems for which solutions are needed, yet they don't exist. Ease of access to computers, mobile devices, and the Internet, together with messaging capabilities and social networking, promote widespread public exposure about people's private lives, including personal information about how they think and feel. Just how this information should be used, by whom, under what conditions, and with what restrictions, if any, are issues teeming with ethical considerations. Several real-life episodes with ethical implications are shown in Table 13.1. See if you can identify significant ethical issues among the episodes in the table.

TABLE 13.1 Areas for Ethical Concerns in Information Technology and Its Uses

- In a now-classic case of cyber-bullying, a 13-year-old girl hanged herself after being taunted by a hoax message on her MySpace page.
- Secret webcasts of other people's behavior have resulted in embarrassment and even death: A university student, leaving a final message on his Facebook page, jumped from a bridge to his death after other students covertly webcast his sexual activities with another student.
- IT is used increasingly for sending out cries for help. Many college students have posted public messages requesting physical and emotional support. Others, having read those messages, are unsure if they should respond, or not.
- Employers and employees struggle about the extent of personal use of the company's IT. Many employees admit they use social networking and personal e-mailing at work, but should they? Many company's say "no," adding that employees should know that the company has access to all e-mails sent, received, and stored on its IT system.
- States are forming database pools, sharing information to check on suspicious prescription drug activities. Data are gathered on purchases at pharmacies, physicians' prescriptions, and police records to identify drug abuse by individuals and companies within states, and are being shared across state lines.
- Using drug prescription records for marketing purposes, companies collect data from pharmacies that keep track of physicians' histories in prescribing drugs. The companies then use data mining to uncover patterns of physician prescriptions, including the names of drugs and manufacturers. The data-mining companies then sell the resulting information to pharmaceutical manufacturers that can use it for selling their drugs to physicians who are prescribing competitors' drugs.

TABLE 13.1 *Continued*

- A Google engineer created a program that recorded personal information obtained from unsecured wireless networks by dispatching cars in several countries to identify wireless networks and to take photos for use in online mapping. The recordings captured unauthorized personal passwords, e-mails, and website addresses.
- A University of Iowa student flunked out of school due to his uncontrollable addiction to a video game that consumed all his attention.
- The Department of Homeland Security abandoned one of its major data-mining tools for combating terrorism after questions about its compliance with privacy rules. It was discovered that DHS had tested the data-mining program using information about real people, without ensuring the privacy of that information.
- To save money, IT users retrieve and share intellectual property—movies, articles, books, music, industrial information—with others, ignoring copyright, trademark, and patent protections. Written content is often taken from the Internet, inserted into the user's written work and is represented as the user's own original creation without citing its true source.

Dave Pilibosian/iStockphoto.com

Continued from page 329

Online Piracy Means Tougher Economic Times

Cyber cheating in many forms continues its upsurge during economic downturns. In one popular "work-at-home" scam, the unsuspecting victim (the new online "employee") cashes checks sent from the "employer" in a foreign country and gets to keep 10 percent of the cash as a payment for service. The remaining 90 percent is sent via Western Union back to the employer. Because the checks are bogus, they bounce, and the victim must repay the full amounts to the bank. Alerting the public to another scam, SC Johnson, the company that makes household products such as Raid, Windex, and Pledge furniture cleaner, warns of phony online job offers for work-at-home customer service jobs, falsely using the Johnson name. The scammers say the job pays trainees $20 an hour initially, advancing to $25 after training, but employees must first buy some training software—which, of course, they pay for but never receive.

Organizations, too, are victims of cyber con-jobs: Why did U.S. DVD sales fall from $20 billion in 2006 to $14 billion in 2010? One reason is piracy, including simple tactics such as focusing a video camera at the computer screen that's showing the movie. How are international industrial firms gaining competitive advantage in today's tight world economy? Security consultants say that global cyber-attacks originating in China, and known as Night Dragon, are invading computers of oil companies, stealing information on competitive bidding, financing, and operations practices. Some governments, to save money, are actively scamming others, using hackers to steal technology secrets for leading-edge military equipment, including defense systems of other countries. Organizations of all kinds are finding cyber security more difficult as more and more employees use their personal phones and computers for conducting business. Organizational information, then, is more widely dispersed and increasingly susceptible to intrusion via mobile-phone malware, virus-contaminated applications, and links containing spyware sent from text messages.[24]

QUESTIONS FOR DISCUSSION

1 Think about recent spam e-mails you've seen on PCs, and scam messages received via cell phone or smartphone. What kinds of information were the intruders seeking?

2 Continuing with the above question, were you able to identify the e-mails and messages to be "scams" before opening them, or was it later after they were opened that you discovered their real contents?

3 In what ways might the "opened" message from a scammer be harmful to you? To your IT devices and systems?

4 What steps can you take (or have you taken) to protect against such intrusions? What costs would be involved for gaining that protection?

5 Consider the various IT systems you use daily. What kinds of protective devices do they have to protect against invasion by cyber pirates?

SUMMARY OF LEARNING OBJECTIVES   MyBizLab

1. **Discuss the impacts information technology has had on the business world. (pp. 330–334)**
   The growth of IT has changed the very structure of business organizations. Its adoption provides new modes of communication, including portable offices, resulting in the geographic separation of the workplace from headquarters for many employees. By providing instantaneous access to company information, IT has altered the workforces in many companies, enabling them to streamline with fewer employees and simpler structures. It also contributes to greater flexibility in serving customers and enables closer coordination with suppliers. IT's global reach facilitates project collaboration with remote business partners and the formation of new market relationships around the globe. Just as electronic collaboration has changed the way employees interact with each other, IT networks have created new manufacturing flexibility for mass customization, and Internet access has brought new opportunities for small businesses.

2. **Identify the IT resources businesses have at their disposal and how these resources are used. (pp. 334–339)**
   The Internet and the World Wide Web serve computers with information and provide communication flows among networks around the world. For many businesses, the Internet has replaced the telephone, fax machine, and standard mail as the primary communications tool. To support internal communications, many companies maintain internal websites—*intranets*—accessible only to employees. Some firms give limited network access to outsiders via *extranets* for coordination with suppliers and customers. Electronic conferencing allows simultaneous communication among groups from various locations, saving travel time and expenses. *VSAT satellite networks* provide private remote communications for voice, video, and data transmissions. *Computer networks* (wide area networks, local area networks) enable the sharing of information, hardware, software, and other resources over wired or wireless connections. *Hardware* refers to the computer's physical components. *System software* tells computer components and resources what to do. *Application software* includes programs to meet specific user needs, such as groupware with voice and video connections for remote collaboration.

3. **Describe the role of information systems, the different types of information systems, and how businesses use such systems. (pp. 339–344)**
   An *information system (IS)* enables users to create, process, and transmit information for use in decision making. *Knowledge information systems* support knowledge workers by providing resources to create, store, use, and transmit new knowledge for useful applications. *Management information systems (MIS)* support managers by providing reports, schedules, plans, and budgets that can then be used for making decisions at all levels ranging from detailed daily activities to long-range business strategies. The many uses of information systems include experimenting with *decision support systems* to test the effectiveness of potential decisions, data mining to identify shopping trends and to plan for new products, and planning for delivery schedules from suppliers and to customers.

4. **Identify the threats and risks information technology poses on businesses. (pp. 344–346)**
   IT has attracted abusers that do mischief, with severity ranging from mere nuisance to outright destruction, costing companies millions. *Wireless moochers* use victims' networks for illegal activities, exposing the host to criminal prosecution. *Hackers* break into computers, stealing personal information and company secrets, tampering with data, and launching attacks on other computers. Once inside a computer network, hackers are able to commit *identity theft*, the unauthorized stealing of personal information to get loans, credit cards, or other monetary benefits by impersonating the victim. Even the ease of information sharing on the Internet poses a threat: It has proven costly for companies who are having a difficult time protecting their *intellectual property*, such as software products, movies, and music. Another IT risk facing businesses is system shutdown and destruction of software, hardware, or data files by *viruses*, *worms*, and *Trojan horses*. After invading a victim's computer, *spyware* gathers inside information and transmits it to outside spies. *Spam*'s damage, too, is costly in terms of lost time and productivity.

5. **Describe the ways in which businesses protect themselves from the threats and risks information technology poses. (pp. 346–349)**
   Most systems guard against unauthorized access by requiring users to have protected passwords. In addition, many firms rely on *firewalls*, so that only messages that meet the conditions of the company's security policy are permitted to flow through the network. Firms can protect against identity theft by using assistance from advisory sources, such as the Identity Theft Resource Center, and by implementing the identity-theft protection provisions of the federal FACTA rule for maintaining and destroying personal information records. To combat viruses, worms, and Trojan horses, *anti-virus software* products search incoming e-mail and data files for "signatures" of known viruses and virus-like characteristics. Contaminated files are discarded or placed in quarantine for safe-keeping. Additional intrusion protection is available by installing *anti-spyware* and *spam filtering software*. *Encryption* adds security by encoding messages that can be read only by intended recipients.

KEY TERMS   MyBizLab

anti-virus software (p. 347)
client-server network (p. 337)
computer network (p. 337)
computer-aided design (CAD) (p. 343)
computer-aided manufacturing (CAM) (p. 343)
data (p. 339)
data mining (p. 341)
data warehousing (p. 341)
decision support system (DSS) (p. 344)
e-commerce (p. 330)
electronic conferencing (p. 336)
encryption system (p. 347)
extranet (p. 335)

firewall (p. 346)
hacker (p. 344)
hardware (p. 338)
hypertext transfer protocol (HTTP) (p. 334)
identity theft (p. 345)
information (p. 337)
information system (IS) (p. 339)
information systems managers (p. 340)
information technology (IT) (p. 330)
intellectual property (p. 345)
Internet (p. 334)
intranet (p. 335)
knowledge information system (p. 343)

local area network (LAN) (p. 337)
management information system (MIS) (p. 343)
mass-customization (p. 332)
software (p. 338)
spam (p. 346)
spyware (p. 346)
VSAT satellite communications (p. 336)
wide area network (WAN) (p. 337)
Wi-Fi (p. 337)
wireless local area network (p. 337)
wireless wide area network (WWAN) (p. 337)
World Wide Web (p. 334)

QUESTIONS AND EXERCISES

QUESTIONS FOR REVIEW

1. Why must a business manage information as a resource?
2. How can electronic conferencing increase a company's productivity and efficiency?
3. Why do different users in an organization need different kinds of information from the information system?
4. Why have the BlackBerry® smartphones become a popular tool among business people?
5. What is the definition of *intellectual property*? List three examples of intellectual property.

QUESTIONS FOR ANALYSIS

6. Describe how a company might use data warehousing and data mining in its information system to better plan for new products.
7. Aside from the eBay example in this chapter, describe one or more ways that IT presents new business opportunities for small businesses.

8. Give three examples (other than those in this chapter) of how a company can become leaner and more efficient by adopting IT.

APPLICATION EXERCISES

9. Consider your daily activities—as a consumer, student, parent, friend, homeowner or renter, car driver, employee, etc.—and think about the ways that you are involved with IT systems. Make a list of your recent IT encounters and then recall instances in those encounters that you revealed personal information that could be used to steal your identity. Are some encounters on your list riskier than others? Why or why not?
10. Describe the computer network at your school. Identify its components and system architecture. What features either promote or inhibit intrusions from hackers? What features either promote or inhibit intellectual property theft? What features either promote or inhibit computer viruses and spam?

BUILDING YOUR BUSINESS SKILLS

The Art and Science of Point-and-Click Research

Goal
To learn how to use the web to conduct research more effectively.

Background Information
In a survey of nearly 2,000 web users, two-thirds said they used the web to obtain work-related information. With billions of pages of information on the web, the challenge for business users is: how best to find what they're seeking.

Method
You'll need a computer and access to the web to complete this exercise.

Step 1
Get together with three classmates and decide on a business-related research topic. Choose a topic that interests you—for example, "Business Implications of the War in Afghanistan," "Labor Disputes in Professional Sports," or "Marketing Music Lessons to Parents of Young Children."

Step 2
Search the following sites for information on your topic (dividing sites among group members to speed the process):

- Dogpile (www.dogpile.com)
- Excite (www.excite.com)
- Google (www.google.com)
- Yahoo! (www.yahoo.com)

Take notes as you search so that you can explain your findings to other group members.

Step 3

Working as a group, answer the following questions about your collective search:

Which sites were the easiest to use?

Which sites offered the most helpful results? What specific factors made these sites better than the others?

Which sites offered the least helpful results? What were the problems?

Why is it important to learn the special code words or symbols, called *operators*, that target a search? (Operators are words such as *AND*, *OR*, and *NOT* that narrow search queries. For example, using *AND* in a search tells most search engines to look only for sites in which all words appear in the results—American *AND* Management *AND* Association.)

FOLLOW-UP QUESTIONS

Research the differences between *search engines* and *subject directories*. Given your topic, would a search engine or a subject directory be more helpful for your research?

1. Why is it important to learn how to use a search site's Help function?
2. Look into some of the sites' Advanced Search pages. How do these pages affect your searches?
3. How has the web changed the nature of business research?

EXERCISING YOUR ETHICS: INDIVIDUAL EXERCISE

Caught in a Cyber Bind

The Situation

Time pressures to complete project assignments, coupled with easy access to the Internet, can present interesting temptations. This exercise illustrates how ethical issues may arise in using information from the Internet.

The Dilemma

Suppose you are assigned to write a report that requires research into a business problem. In searching the Internet, you find mounds of published articles that discuss the problem, but most of them are complicated write-ups using technical terms that you don't completely understand. As the deadline approaches, you realize that you can't figure out a logical, sensible format for writing the report. You then recall, from conversations with colleagues, two possible solutions for your problem: (1) From the many articles found on the Internet, you can select the best-sounding phrases, sentences, and paragraphs, arrange them into a logical sequence, and piece them together as your final report, or (2) you can hire an Internet report-writing service at $20 per page to write your report. Chances of being detected are slim.

QUESTIONS TO ADDRESS

1. Given the factors in this situation, what, if any, ethical issues exist?
2. Would you adopt either of the two "possible solutions" listed above? Why or Why not?
3. If a friend was confronted with this same situation and asked your opinion, what advice would you offer?

EXERCISING YOUR ETHICS: TEAM EXERCISE

This Game Is Getting Serious

The Situation

Interactive games have become big-time entertainment for millions of enthusiasts playing side by side or among contestants anywhere on the Internet. Amidst the fun, questions can arise about the use of intellectual property and the ownership obligations of gamers. This exercise encourages you to examine some of the ethical issues that can surface in gaming.

The Dilemma

Tracy was enamored with a new adventure-and-strategy game from the moment she bought it. Her favorite character—Goddess Diaphanese—had accumulated overwhelming powers, thanks to Tracy's gaming skills and lots of trial and error, during two months of intense competition. Opponents were consistently overwhelmed by Diaphanese's mystical powers, and her ability to foresee the future, ward off attacks with invincible armor, and elevate her intellect to outsmart opponents in this virtual universe. Tracy's Diaphanese was, in effect, an invincible game character.

Another gamer wanted to buy Tracy's personal version of the game, but she decided instead to list it for sale on a popular Internet auction site. The bid price rose to over 10 times the original game price when Tracy got an e-mail from the manufacturer objecting to her sale of the game, stating that both the game name and the character itself are intellectual properties of the firm. The message insisted that she withdraw the product from auction.

Tracy's response to the company stated that her game cartridge—including the unique version of the powerful Goddess Diaphanese—was not the same product she purchased months earlier but, instead, was entirely different due to months of thoughtful game playing. Accordingly, she was selling her creation—a one-of-a-kind, new product.

Team Activity

Assemble a group of four students and assign each group member to one of the following roles:
- Tracy
- auction winner buying Tracy's version of the game
- manufacturer of the game
- investor/owner of the company that manufactures the game

ACTION STEPS

1 Before hearing any of your group's comments, and from the perspective of your assigned role, write down the ethical issues, if any, that you see in this situation.

2 Before hearing any of your group's comments, what actions do you think your assigned role should have taken in this situation? Write down your recommended actions.

3 Gather your group together and reveal, in turn, each member's comments and recommendations.

4 Appoint someone to record main points of agreement and disagreement within the group. How do you explain the results? What accounts for any disagreement?

5 From an ethical standpoint, what does your group recommend Tracy do?

VIDEO EXERCISE   MyBizLab

ZIPCAR

Learning Objectives

The purpose of this video is to help you:

1 Understand how information technology has influenced business.

2 Describe how businesses use information technology to meet the needs of customers and support profitable operations.

3 Explain the risks, threats, and ethical concerns related to information technology.

Synopsis

ZipCar's business model is built on the European concept of car sharing. From their first location in Cambridge, Massachusetts, ZipCar has expanded to over fifty cities in the United States and United Kingdom and over one hundred college campuses. ZipCar's business model allows members to have the convenience of having a car at their disposal, without the attendant costs of car ownership, such as car payments, insurance, or even gasoline. To become a member, or Zipster, the applicant pays a one-time fee. A variety of plans are available, with the Zipster paying a daily or hourly rate when they use a car. For those with only occasional use, there is also an annual fee. The member can reserve a car through a smart phone application or on their computer. Once the reservation is complete, Zipsters gain access to the cars with a swipe of their ZipCard. Technology allows the company to remotely enable and track the car and even allows the company to disable a car when there is unauthorized access.

DISCUSSION QUESTIONS

1 The text discusses a number of ways that information technology has influenced business. Discuss how at least three of these relate to ZipCar.

2 What technologies allow ZipCar to operate?

3 What type of consumers do you think are most likely to use ZipCar?

4 How is ZipCar especially well suited to college students?

5 What are the ethical concerns related to ZipCar's use of technology?

Online Exploration

ZipCar's website (www.zipcar.com) provides information about how ZipCar meets the needs of individual consumers, businesses, and college students. To find out more about how the technology works, click on "how it works", then "our technology". Briefly describe the steps involved in becoming a Zipster and using a car for the first time.

END NOTES

[1] M. P. McQueen, "Cyber-Scams on the Uptick in Downturn," *The Wall Street Journal*, January 29, 2009, D1, D4; Joseph De Avila, "Beware of Facebook 'Friends' Who May Trash Your Laptop," *The Wall Street Journal*, January 29, 2009, D1, D4; Byron Acohido and Jon Swartz, "Data Scams Have Kicked into High Gear as Markets Tumble," *USAToday*, January 28, 2009, at http://www.usatoday.com/tech/news/computersecurity/2009-01-28-hackers-data-scams_N.htm; Chris Wragge, "FBI Warns of High-Tech Cyber ID Theft," *wcbstv.com*, April 8, 2009, at http://wcbstv.com/local/cyber.criminals.fbi.2.980245.html; Jordan Robertson, "Bad Economy Helps Web Scammers Recruit 'Mules'," *ABC News*, December 9, 2008, at http://abcnews.go.com/print?id=6422327.

[2] "Research in Motion Reports Third Quarter Results," *RIM* (press release), December 16, 2010, at http://www.rim.com/inves- tors/documents/pdf/pressrelease/2011/Q3_press_release.pdf.

[3] See http://www.siriusxm.com/navtraffic/.

[4] "Lockheed Martin Aeronautics: Siemens' PLM Software," *Siemens*, at http://www.plm.automation.siemans.com/en_us/about-us/success/case_s, accessed June 16, 2009.

[5] Laura Northrup, "Timbuk2 Really, Really Wants You to Be Happy with Their Bags," *The Consumerist*, June 5, 2009, at http://www.consumerist.com/2009/06/timbuk2really-really-wants-you-to-be-happy-with-their-bags.html.

[6] David LaGesse, "How to Turn Social Networking into a Job Offer," *U.S. News & World Report*, May 11, 2009, at http://www.usnews.com/money/careers/articles/2009/05/11/how-to-turn-social-networking-into-a-job-offer.html.

[7] 3D Systems, "3D Systems Helps Walter Reed Army Medical Center Rebuild Lives," at http://www.3dsystems.com/

appsolutions/casestudies/walter_reed.asp, accessed June 15, 2009; "Hannah Hickey, "Camera in a Pill Offers Cheaper, Easier Window on Your Insides," UWNews.org (January 24, 2008), at http://uwnews.org/article.asp?articleid=39292.

8 See http://www.internetworldstats.com/stats.htm.

9 "BAN AMRO Mortgage Group Offers OneFee to Ford Motor Company Employees," *Mortgage Mag*, February 14, 2005, at http://www.mortgagemag.com/n/502_003.htm; "An Intranet's Life Cycle," *morebusiness.com* (June 16, 1999), at http://www.morebusiness.com/getting_started/website/d928247851.brc; Sally Ahmed, "Ford Motor Company—Case Study," Ezine Articles, August 18, 2008, at http://ezinearticles.com/?Ford-Motor-Company---Case-Study&id=1420478.

10 Emily Bazar, "Bartering Booms During Economic Tough Times," *USA Today*, February 25, 2009, at http://usatoday.com/tech/webguide/internetlife/2009-02-25-barter_N.htm; Debbie Lombardi, "Bartering Can Boost Your Budget and Business," at http://www.bbubarter.com/news.aspx?NewsID=18, accessed October 27, 2008; Donna Wright, "Hard Times Create Boom of Local Bartering," *BradentonHerald.com*, March 8, 2009, at http://www.bradenton.com/874/v-print/story/1277848.html; "The Advantages of Business Bartering," *U-Exchange.com*, http://www.u-exchange.com/advantages-business-bartering, accessed February 24, 2011.

11 "What Do Bartering Websites Do?" at http://www.peopletradingservices.com, accessed June 8, 2009; "BarterQuest, the Online Bartering Website, Is Out of Beta," *BarterQuest* (press release), January 16, 2010, at http://www.prlog.org/10535364-barterquest-the-online-bartering-website-is-out-of-beta.html.

12 "Kroger Tailors Ads to Its Customers," *Columbia Daily Tribune*, January 12, 2009, 7B.

13 "Data Mining Examples & Testimonials," at http://www.data-mining-software.com/data_mining_examples.htm, accessed 2/24/2011.

14 Glen Brizius, "CereProc: An Example of a Technology Finally Fulfilling Its Potential," Associated Content in Technology, March 16, 2010, at http://www.associatedcontent.com/article/2786052/cereproc_an_example_of_a_technology.html?cat=5.

15 http://www.cereproc.com/en/products

16 Alyson Sheppard, "Giving Roger Ebert a New Voice: Q&A With CereProc," Popular Mechanics, March 8, 2010, at http://www.popularmechanics.com/science/health/prosthetics/rogerebertvoicetech; Hayley Millar, "New Voice for Film Critic," BBC News, March 3, 2010, at http://news.bbc.co.uk/2/hi/uk_news/scotland/edinburgh_and_east/8547645.stm.

17 Jo Marchant, "Virtual Fossils Reveal How Ancient Creatures Lived," *NewScientist*, May 27, 2009, at http://www.newscientist.com/article/mg20227103.500-virtual-fossils-reveal-how-ancient-creatures-lived.html.

18 Matt Warman, "Viruses on Smartphones: Security's New Frontier," *The Telegraph*, February 8, 2011, at http://www.telegraph.co.uk/technology/news/8311214/Viruses-on-smartphones-securitys-new-frontier.html; Jacqui Cheng, "Canadian Group: Facebook "A Minefield of Privacy Invasion," May 30, 2008, at http://arstechnica.com/tech-policy/news/2008/05/canadian-group-files-complaint-over-facebook-privacy.ars; "Cell Phones a Much Bigger Privacy Risk Than Facebook," *Fox News*, February 20, 2009, at http://www.foxnews.com/printer_friendly_story/0,3566,497544,00.html.

19 Alex Leary, "Wi-Fi Cloaks a New Breed of Intruder," *St. Petersburg Times* (July 4, 2005), at http://www.sptimes.com/2005/07/04/State/Wi_Fi_cloaks_a_new_br.shtml.

20 Eliot Van Buskirk, "iTunes Store May Capture One-Quarter of Worldwide Music by 2012," *Wired* (April 27, 2008), at http://www.wired.com/entertainment/music/news/2008/04/itunes_birthday; Christopher Burgess and Richard Power, "How to Avoid Intellectual Property Theft," CIO (July 10, 2006), at http://www.cio.com/article/22837; Hiawatha Bray, "Music Industry Aims to Send in Radio Cops," *Boston Globe* (November 15, 2004), at http://www.boston.com/business/articles/2004/11/15/music_industry_aims_to_send_in_radio_cops/; Ethan Smith and Yukari Iwatani Kane, "Apple Changes Tune on Music Pricing," *The Wall Street Journal*, Jan. 7, 2009, at http://online.wsj.com/article/SB123126062001057765.html.

21 See http://www.webopedia.com/TERM/S/spyware.html.

22 "Ferris Research and Abaca Technology Corporation Hold Anti-Spam Webinar," *NewswireToday*, April 9, 2008, at http://www.newswiretoday.com/news/32531/.

23 Brad Carlson, "Organizations Face New Records-Destruction Rule," *Idaho Business Review* (July 25, 2005), at http://www.idahobusiness.net/archive.htm/2005/07/25/Organizations-face-new-recordsdestruction-rule.

24 Ryan Nakashima, **"**Awards-Screeners a Problem When it Comes to Movie Leaks," *The Seattle Times*, January 30, 2011, at http://seattletimes.nwsource.com/html/living/2014078651_btmhollywoodpiracy31.html?syndication=rss; "Hackers in China Blamed for Cyber-Attacks," *Columbia Daily Tribune*, February 10, 2011, page 5B, and at http://www.columbiatribune.com/news/2011/feb/10/hackers-in-china-blamed-for-cyber-attacks/?news; Mary Ann Milbourn, "Beware of Fake Job Offers," *The Orange County Register*, October 12, 2010, at http://economy.ocregister.com/2010/10/12/beware-of-fake-job-offers/42194/; Richard Eppstein, "Scammers Pop Up During Economic Downturns," *Toledo Biz Insider*, March 4, 2010, at http://www.toledoblade.com/article/20100304/BUSINESS11/100309863/-1/BUSINESS; Matt Warman, "Viruses on Smart-Phones: Security's New Frontier," *The Telegraph*, February 8, 2011, at http://www.telegraph.co.uk/technology/news/8311214/Viruses-on-smartphones-securitys-new-frontier.html.

14 The Role of Accountants and Accounting Information

CSI: Wall Street

In the aftermath of a flurry of financial scandals, many companies are showing an urgent interest in the field of forensic accounting: the use of accounting for legal purposes. The expansion of the forensic accounting field—the Association of Certified Fraud Examiners (ACFE) has experienced a surging membership, reaching 55,000 professionals in 2011—is due to increased vigilance against various kinds of financial scams, including a strong desire on the part of companies to protect themselves from accounting fraud.

Fraud examiners typically begin an investigation of a company by interviewing high-level executives. Team members pursue tips from employees or outsiders, then comb through e-mails, searching for suspicious words and phrases. The combination of interviews and e-mails may lead investigators to specific accounting files or ledger entries. According to Al Vondra, a Certified Fraud Examiner at PricewaterhouseCoopers, some of the most common fraudulent practices involve hiding revenues and expenses under phony categories such as "Total Noncurrent Assets" or "Other Current Liabilities." At India's Satyam Computer Services Ltd., for example, founder and former CEO Ramalinga Raju was arrested after admitting he falsified accounts, thus deceiving investors for years. The government's Serious Fraud Investigation Office is searching to identify collaborators who falsely reported more than $1 billion in cash and assets that didn't exist at India's fourth largest software company.[1]

After reading this chapter, you should be able to:

1 Explain the role of accountants and distinguish between the kinds of work done by public accountants, private accountants, management accountants, and forensic accountants.

2 Explain how the accounting equation is used.

3 Describe the three basic financial statements and show how they reflect the activity and financial condition of a business.

4 Explain the key standards and principles for reporting financial statements.

5 Describe how computing financial ratios can help users get more information from financial statements to determine the financial strengths of a business.

6 Discuss the role of ethics in accounting.

7 Describe the purpose of the International Accounting Standards Board and explain why it exists.

Although accounting scandals have always existed, they spike upward in economic recessions. Data from the ACFE indicate that corporate fraud cases began increasing significantly early in the recent recession, and worldwide fraud losses reached $2.9 trillion in 2009. Fraud-related reports and whistle-blowing at U.S. firms also jumped dramatically in 2009. ACFE members believe the increase stems from heavier financial pressures: When employees feel less secure, they may falsify data to show better performance, or they may take greater risks that need to be covered up to show financial success. Forensic accounting professor Tommie Singleton states, "The cases of fraud will only climb as the country sinks into recession, and with that so will the demand for highly skilled, specialized forensic accountants to help prevent, detect and prosecute those looking to cheat the system."[2]

Our opening story continues on page 378

WHAT'S IN IT FOR ME?

For most of us, the words and ideas in accounting can seem like a foreign language. As we have seen, the specialized terminology can be used to mask fraud and corruption. However, it's also a necessary tool that allows professionals in every industry to analyze growth, understand risk, and communicate complex ideas about a firm's financial health. This chapter will cover the fundamental concepts of accounting and apply them to familiar business situations. By grasping the basic accounting vocabulary you will be able to participate when the conversation turns to the financial matters that constitute so great a part of a firm's daily operations.

MyBizLab Where you see MyBizLab in this chapter, go to **www.mybizlab.com** for additional activities on the topic being discussed.

Johnny Lye/Shutterstock

What Is Accounting, and Who Uses Accounting Information?

Accounting is a comprehensive system for collecting, analyzing, and communicating financial information to a firm's owners and employees, to the public, and to various regulatory agencies. To perform these functions, accountants keep records of taxes paid, income received, and expenses incurred—a process called **bookkeeping**—and they assess the effects of these transactions on business activities. By sorting and analyzing such transactions, accountants can determine how well a business is being managed and how financially strong it is.

Because businesses engage in thousands of transactions, ensuring consistent, dependable financial information is mandatory. This is the job of the **accounting information system (AIS)**—an organized procedure for identifying, measuring, recording, and retaining financial information so that it can be used in accounting statements and management reports. The system includes all of the people, reports, computers, procedures, and resources that are needed to compile financial transactions.[3]

Users of accounting information are numerous:

- *Business managers* use it to develop goals and plans, set budgets, and evaluate future prospects.

- *Employees and unions* use it to plan for and receive compensation and such benefits as health care, vacation time, and retirement pay.

- *Investors and creditors* use it to estimate returns to stockholders, determine growth prospects, and decide whether a firm is a good credit risk.

- *Tax authorities* use it to plan for tax inflows, determine the tax liabilities of individuals and businesses, and ensure that correct amounts are paid on time.

- *Government regulatory agencies* rely on it to fulfill their duties toward the public. The Securities and Exchange Commission (SEC), for example, requires firms to file financial disclosures so that potential investors have valid information about their financial status.

1 Explain the role of accountants and distinguish between the kinds of work done by public accountants, private accountants, management accountants, and forensic accountants.

Gain hands-on experience through an interactive, real-world scenario. This chapter's simulation, entitled OBM and Financial Statements, is located at **www.mybizlab.com.**

Who Are Accountants and What Do They Do?

The **controller,** or chief accounting officer, manages a firm's accounting activities by ensuring that the AIS provides the reports and statements needed for planning, decision making, and other management activities. This range of activities requires different types of accounting specialists. In this section, we begin by distinguishing between the two main fields of accounting: *financial* and *managerial*. Then, we discuss the different functions and activities of *certified public accountants*, *private accountants*, *management accountants*, and *forensic accountants*.

Financial versus Managerial Accounting

In any company, the two fields of accounting—financial and managerial—can be distinguished by the users they serve: those outside the company and those within.[4]

Financial Accounting   A firm's **financial accounting** system is concerned with external information users: consumer groups, unions, stockholders, suppliers, creditors, and government agencies. It prepares reports such as income statements and balance sheets that focus on the activities of the company as a whole rather than on individual departments or divisions.[5]

Managerial Accounting **Managerial (management) accounting** serves internal users. Managers at all levels need information to make departmental decisions, monitor projects, and plan future activities. Other employees also need accounting information. Engineers must know certain costs, for example, before making product or operations improvements, purchasing agents use information on materials costs to negotiate terms with suppliers, and to set performance goals, salespeople need past sales data organized by geographic region.

Certified Public Accountants

Public accountants offer accounting services to the public and are distinguished by their independence from the clients they serve. That is to say, they typically work for an accounting firm providing services for outside client firms in which the public accountant has no vested interest, thus avoiding any potential biases in conducting their professional services. Among public accountants, **certified public accountants (CPAs)** are licensed by a state after passing an exam prepared by the American Institute of Certified Public Accountants (AICPA). Preparation for certification begins with majoring in a college program studying the theory, practices, and legal aspects of accounting. In addition to the CPA exam, certification requires two years of practice in an accounting firm and extensive experience in auditing. Once certified, the CPA can perform services beyond those allowed by non-certified public accountants.[6] Whereas some CPAs work as individual practitioners, many form or join existing partnerships or professional corporations.

CPA Services Virtually all CPA firms, whether large or small, provide auditing, tax, and management services. Larger firms such as Deloitte Touche Tohmatsu and Ernst & Young earn much of their revenue from auditing services, though consulting (management advisory) services constitute a major growth area. Smaller firms earn most of their income from tax and management services.

Auditing An **audit** examines a company's AIS to determine whether financial reports reliably represent its operations.[7] Organizations must provide audit reports when applying for loans, selling stock, or when going through a major restructuring. Independent auditors who do not work for the company must ensure that clients' accounting systems follow **generally accepted accounting principles (GAAP)**, which are formulated by the Financial Accounting Standards Board (FASB) of the AICPA and govern the content and form of financial reports.[8] The auditing of a firm's financial statements is one of the services that can be performed only by a CPA. The Securities and Exchange Commission (SEC) is the U.S. government agency that legally enforces accounting and auditing rules and procedures. Ultimately, the auditor will certify whether the client's reports comply with GAAP.

Sometimes, companies ignore GAAP and accountants fail to disclose violations. Richard Causey (right) was Chief Account Executive at now-bankrupt Enron, and was responsible for the firm's public accounting statements. Pleading guilty to securities fraud, he was sentenced to seven years in prison and forfeited $1.25 million.

Ron Sachs-CNP-PHOTOlink.net/Newscom

Accounting comprehensive system for collecting, analyzing, and communicating financial information

Bookkeeping recording of accounting transactions

Accounting Information System (AIS) organized procedure for identifying, measuring, recording, and retaining financial information for use in accounting statements and management reports

Controller person who manages all of a firm's accounting activities (chief accounting officer)

Financial Accounting field of accounting concerned with external users of a company's financial information

Managerial (Management) Accounting field of accounting that serves internal users of a company's financial information

Certified Public Accountant (CPA) accountant licensed by the state and offering services to the public

Audit systematic examination of a company's accounting system to determine whether its financial reports reliably represent its operations

Generally Accepted Accounting Principles (GAAP) accounting guidelines that govern the content and form of financial reports

Tax Services **Tax services** include assistance not only with tax-return preparation but also with tax planning. A CPA's advice can help a business structure (or restructure) operations and investments and perhaps save millions of dollars in taxes. Staying abreast of tax-law changes is no simple matter. Some critics charge that tax changes have become a full-time vocation among some state and federal legislators who add increasingly complicated laws and technical corrections on taxation each year.

Management Advisory Services As consultants, accounting firms provide **management advisory services** ranging from personal financial planning to planning corporate mergers. Other services include production scheduling, information systems studies, AIS design, and even executive recruitment. The staffs of the largest CPA firms include engineers, architects, mathematicians, and psychologists, all of whom are available for consulting.

Noncertified Public Accountants   Many accountants don't take the CPA exam; others work in the field while getting ready for it or while meeting requirements for state certification. Many small businesses, individuals, and even larger firms rely on these noncertified public accountants for income-tax preparation, payroll accounting, and financial-planning services so long as they abide by local and state laws. Noncertified accountants often put together financial statements that are used in the firm for internal purposes, based on information provided by management. These statements may include a notification that auditing methods were not used in their preparation.

The CPA Vision Project   The recent talent shortage in accounting has led the profession to rethink its culture and lifestyle.[9] With grassroots participation from CPAs, educators, and industry leaders, the AICPA, through its CPA Vision Project, is redefining the role of the accountant for today's world economy. The Vision Project identifies a unique combination of skills, technology, and knowledge—called **core competencies for accounting**—that will be necessary for the future CPA. As Table 14.1 shows, those skills—which include communication, critical thinking, and leadership—go far beyond the ability to "crunch numbers." They include certain communications skills, along with skills in critical thinking and leadership. Indeed, the CPA Vision Project foresees CPAs who combine specialty skills with a broad-based orientation in order to communicate more effectively with people in a wide range of business activities.

TABLE 14.1 Emerging Competencies for Success in Accounting	
Skills in Strategic Thinking and Critical Problem Solving	The accountant can combine data with reasoning and professional knowledge to recognize and help solve critical problems for better strategic action.
Communications, Interpersonal Skills, and Effective Leadership	The accountant can communicate effectively in various business situations using meaningful communications skills that provide interpersonal effectiveness and leadership.
Dedication to Meeting Customer Needs	The accountant surpasses the competition in understanding each client's unique needs, in meeting those needs, and in visualizing the client's future needs.
Ability to Integrate Diverse Information	The accountant can combine financial and other kinds of information to gain new meaning that provides clients with useful insights and understanding for solving problems.
Proficiency with Information Technology	The accountant can use information technology (IT) in performing services for clients, and can identify IT applications that the client can adopt for added value to the business.

Source: Based on "The CPA Vision Project and Beyond," *American Institute of Certified Public Accountants,* at http://www.aicpa.org/RESEARCH/CPAHORIZONS2025/CPAVISIONPROJECT/Pages/CPAVisionProject.aspx, accessed on March 8, 2011.

Private Accountants and Management Accountants

To ensure integrity in reporting, CPAs are always independent of the firms they audit. However, many businesses also hire their own salaried employees—**private accountants**—to perform day-to-day activities.

Private accountants perform numerous jobs. An internal auditor at ConocoPhillips might fly to the North Sea to confirm the accuracy of oil-flow meters on offshore petroleum drilling platforms. A supervisor responsible for $2 billion in monthly payouts to vendors and employees may never leave the executive suite, with duties such as hiring and training, assigning projects, and evaluating performance of accounting personnel. Large businesses employ specialized accountants in such areas as budgeting, financial planning, internal auditing, payroll, and taxation. In small businesses, a single person may handle all accounting tasks.

While private accountants may be either CPAs or noncertified accountants, most are **management accountants** who provide services to support managers in various activities (marketing, production, engineering, and so forth). Many hold the **certified management accountant (CMA)** designation, awarded by the Institute of Management Accountants (IMA), recognizing qualifications of professionals who have passed IMA's experience and examination requirements. With more than 60,000 worldwide members, IMA is dedicated to supporting accounting professionals to create quality internal controls and financial practices in their companies.

Forensic Accountants

The fastest growing area in accounting is **forensic accounting**—the use of accounting for legal purposes.[10] Sometimes known as "the private eyes of the corporate culture," forensic accountants must be good detectives. They look behind the corporate façade instead of accepting financial records at face value. In combining investigative skills with accounting, auditing, and the instincts of a bloodhound, they assist in the investigation of business and financial issues that may have application to a court of law. Forensic accountants may be called upon—by law enforcement agencies, insurance companies, law firms, and business firms—for both investigative accounting and litigation support in crimes against companies, crimes by companies, and civil disagreements. They may conduct criminal investigations of Internet scams and misuse of government funds. Civil cases often require investigating and quantifying claims of personal injury loss due to negligence and analyzing financial issues in matrimonial disputes. Forensic accountants also assist business firms in tracing and recovering lost assets from employee business fraud or theft.

Investigative Accounting   A forensic accountant may be asked to investigate a trail of financial transactions behind a suspected crime, as in a money-laundering scheme or an investment swindle. Try your hand, for example, at "Catch Me If You Can," the popular interactive forensic accounting game sponsored by the AICPA (at **www.StartHereGoPlaces.com).** The forensic accountant, being familiar with the legal concepts and procedures of the case, identifies and analyzes pertinent financial evidence—documents, bank accounts, phone calls, computer records, and people—and presents accounting conclusions and their legal implications. They develop reports, exhibits, and documents to communicate their findings.

Tax Services assistance provided by CPAs for tax preparation and tax planning

Management Advisory Services assistance provided by CPA firms in areas such as financial planning, information systems design, and other areas of concern for client firms

Core Competencies For Accounting the combination of skills, technology, and knowledge that will be necessary for the future CPA

Private Accountant salaried accountant hired by a business to carry out its day-to-day financial activities

Management Accountant private accountant who provides financial services to support managers in various business activities within a firm

Certified Management Accountant (CMA) professional designation awarded by the Institute of Management Accountants in recognition of management accounting qualifications

Forensic Accounting the practice of accounting for legal purposes

Litigation Support   Forensic accountants assist in the application of accounting evidence for judicial proceedings by preparing and preserving evidence for these proceedings. They also assist by presenting visual aids to support trial evidence, by testifying as expert witnesses, and, especially, in determining economic damages in any case before the court. A divorce attorney, for example, may suspect that assets are being understated and request financial analysis by a forensic accountant. A movie producer may need help in determining damages for breach of contract by an actress who quits before the film is completed.

Certified Fraud Examiners   A specific area within forensic accounting—the **Certified Fraud Examiner (CFE)** designation—is administered by the Association of Certified Fraud Examiners. The CFE's activities focus specifically on fraud-related issues: fraud detection, evaluating accounting systems for weaknesses and fraud risks, investigating white-collar crime on behalf of law enforcement agencies, evaluating internal organizational controls for fraud prevention, and expert witnessing. Many CFEs, like Al Vondra from our opening story, find employment in corporations seeking to prevent fraud from within. The CFE examination covers four areas:

1 *Criminology and ethics.* Includes theories of fraud prevention and ethical situations

2 *Financial transactions.* Examines types of fraudulent financial transactions incurred in accounting records

3 *Fraud investigation.* Pertains to tracing illicit transactions, evaluating deception, and interviewing and taking statements

4 *Legal elements of fraud.* Includes rules of evidence, criminal and civil law, and rights of the accused and accuser

Eligibility to take the exam includes both educational and experience requirements. While a minimum of a Bachelor's degree is required, it does not have to be in accounting or any other specific field of study. Candidates without a bachelor's degree, but with fraud-related professional experience, may substitute two years of experience for each year of academic study. Experience requirements for certification include at least two years in any of several fraud-related areas, such as auditing, criminology, fraud investigation, or law.

Federal Restrictions on CPA Services and Financial Reporting: Sarbox

The financial wrongdoings associated with firms such as ImClone Systems, Tyco, WorldCom, Enron, Arthur Andersen, and others have not gone unnoticed in legislative circles. Federal regulations, in particular the **Sarbanes-Oxley Act of 2002 (Sarbox** or **SOX)**, have been enacted to restore public trust in corporate accounting practices.

Sarbox restricts the kinds of nonaudit services that CPAs can provide. Under the Sarbox law, for example, a CPA firm can help design a client's financial information system, but not if it also does the client's auditing. Hypothetically, an unscrupulous accounting firm's audit might intentionally overlook a client's false financial statements if, in return, the client rewards the accounting firm with a contract for lucrative nonaccounting services, such as management consulting. This was a core allegation in the Enron-Arthur Andersen scandal. By prohibiting auditing and nonauditing services to the same client, Sarbox encourages audits that are independent and unbiased.

Sarbox Compliance Requirements   Sarbox imposes new requirements on virtually every financial activity in publicly traded corporations, as well as severe criminal penalties for persons committing or concealing fraud or destroying financial records. CFOs and CEOs, for example, have to pledge that the company's finances are correct and must vouch for the methods and internal controls used to get those numbers. Companies have to provide a system that is safe for all employees—potential whistleblowers—to anonymously report unethical accounting practices and illegal activities without fear of retaliation. Table 14.2 provides brief descriptions of several of Sarbox's many provisions.

TABLE 14.2   Selected Provisions of the Sarbanes-Oxley Act[11]
• Creates a national Accounting Oversight Board that, among other activities, must establish the ethics standards used by CPA firms in preparing audits.
• Requires that auditors retain audit working papers for specified periods of time.
• Requires auditor rotation by prohibiting the same person from being the lead auditor for more than five consecutive years.
• Requires that the CEO and CFO certify that the company's financial statements are true, fair, and accurate.
• Prohibits corporations from extending personal loans to executives and directors.
• Requires that the audited company disclose whether it has adopted a code of ethics for its senior financial officers.
• Requires that the SEC regularly review each corporation's financial statements.
• Prevents employers from retaliating against research analysts who write negative reports.
• Imposes criminal penalties on auditors and clients for falsifying, destroying, altering, or concealing records (10 years in prison).
• Imposes a fine or imprisonment (up to 25 years) on any person who defrauds shareholders.
• Increases penalties for mail and wire fraud from 5 to 20 years in prison.
• Establishes criminal liability for failure of corporate officers to certify financial reports.

The Accounting Equation

2 Explain how the accounting equation is used.

All accountants rely on record keeping to enter and track transactions. Underlying all record-keeping procedures is the most basic tool of accounting—the **accounting equation:**

Assets = Liabilities + Owners' Equity

After each financial transaction (e.g., payments to suppliers, sales to customers, wages to employees), the accounting equation must be in balance. If it isn't, then an accounting error has occurred. To better understand the importance of this equation, we must understand the terms *assets*, *liabilities*, and *owners' equity*.

Assets and Liabilities   An **asset** is any economic resource that is expected to benefit a firm or an individual who owns it. Assets include land, buildings, equipment, inventories, and payments due the company (accounts receivable). Google, the Internet search and information provider, for example, held assets amounting to $57.851 billion at year-end 2010.[12]

A **liability** is a debt that a firm owes to an outside party. The total of Google's liabilities—all the debt owed to others—was $11.610 billion at the end of 2010.

Alex Segre/Alamy

The inventory at this auto dealership is among the company's assets: The cars constitute an economic resource because the firm will benefit financially as it sells them.

Certified Fraud Examiner (CFE) professional designation administered by the Association of Certified Fraud Examiners in recognition of qualifications for a specialty area within forensic accounting

Sarbanes-Oxley Act of 2002 (Sarbox or Sox) enactment of federal regulations to restore public trust in accounting practices by imposing new requirements on financial activities in publicly traded corporations

Accounting Equation Assets = Liabilities + Owners' Equity; used by accountants to balance data for the firm's financial transactions at various points in the year

Asset any economic resource expected to benefit a firm or an individual who owns it

Liability debt owed by a firm to an outside organization or individual

Owners' Equity You may have heard of the *equity* that a homeowner has in a house—that is, the amount of money that could be made (or lost) by selling the house and paying off the mortgage. Similarly, **owners' equity** is the amount of money that owners would receive if they sold all of a company's assets and paid all of its liabilities. Google's financial reports for 2010 declared shareholders' equity of $46.241 billion. For the Google example, we see that the accounting equation is in balance, as it should be.

$$\text{Assets} = \text{Liabilities} + \text{Owners' Equity}$$
$$\$57.851 = \$11.610 + \$46.241 \text{ billion}$$

We can rewrite the equation to highlight how owners' equity relates to assets and liabilities.

$$\text{Assets} - \text{Liabilities} = \text{Owners' Equity}$$

Another term for this is *net worth*: the difference between what a firm owns (assets) minus what it owes (liabilities) is its net worth, or owners' equity. If a company's assets exceed its liabilities, owners' equity is *positive*. At Google, owners' equity is $46.241 billion (= $57.851 – $11.610). If the company goes out of business, the owners will receive some cash (a gain) after selling assets and paying off liabilities. If liabilities outweigh assets, owners' equity is *negative*; assets are insufficient to pay off all debts, and the firm is bankrupt. If the company goes out of business, the owners will get no cash, and some creditors won't be paid.

Owners' equity is meaningful for both investors and lenders. Before lending money to owners, for example, lenders want to know the amount of owners' equity in a business. A larger owners' equity indicates greater security for lenders. Owners' equity consists of two sources of capital:

1 The amount that the owners originally invested

2 Profits (also owned by the owners) earned by and reinvested in the company

When a company operates profitably, its assets increase faster than its liabilities. Owners' equity, therefore, will increase if profits are retained in the business instead of paid out as dividends to stockholders. Owners' equity also increases if owners invest more of their own money to increase assets. However, owners' equity can shrink if the company operates at a loss or if owners withdraw assets.

Financial Statements

3 Describe the three basic financial statements and show how they reflect the activity and financial condition of a business.

As noted previously, accountants summarize the results of a firm's transactions and issue reports to help managers make informed decisions. Among the most important reports are **financial statements,** which fall into three broad categories: *balance sheets, income statements,* and *statements of cash flows.* Together, these reports indicate the firm's financial health and what affected it. In this section, we discuss these three financial statements as well as the function of the budget as an internal financial statement.

Balance Sheets

Balance sheets supply detailed information about the accounting equation items: *assets, liabilities,* and *owners' equity.* Because they also show a firm's financial condition at one point in time, they are sometimes called *statements of financial position.* Figure 14.1 is a simplified presentation of the balance sheet for Google, Inc.

Assets From an accounting standpoint, most companies have three types of assets: *current, fixed,* and *intangible.*

Google, Inc.
Summary of Balance Sheet (condensed)
as of December 31, 2010
(in millions)

Assets		**Liabilities and Shareholders' Equity**	
Current assets:		Current liabilities:	
Cash	$13,630	Accounts payable	$6,137
Marketable securities	21,345	Other	3,859
Other	6,587	**Total current liabilities**	**$9,996**
Total current assets	**$41,562**		
		Long-term liabilities:	
Fixed assets:		All long-term debts	$0
Property and equipment, net	$7,759	Other	1,614
Other	1,230	**Total long-term liabilities**	**$1,614**
Total fixed assets	**$8,989**		
		Total liabilities	**$11,610**
Intangible assets:			
Intangible assets	$1,044	Shareholders' equity:	
Goodwill	6,256	Paid-in capital	$18,373
Total intangible assets	**$7,300**	Retained earnings	27,868
		Total shareholders' equity	**$46,241**
Total assets	**$57,851**		
		Total liabilities and shareholders' equity	**$57,851**

Google's balance sheet for year ended December 31, 2010. The balance sheet shows clearly that the firm's total assets are equal to its total liabilities and owners' equity.

Figure 14.1 Google's Balance Sheet
Source: Modified from "Google Inc. (GOOG)," *Yahoo! Finance,* accessed March 3, 2011 at http://finance.yahoo.com/q/bs?s=GOOG+Balance+Sheet&annual

Current Assets **Current assets** include cash and assets that can be converted into cash within a year. The act of converting something into cash is called *liquidating*. Assets are normally listed in order of **liquidity**—the ease of converting them into cash. Debts, for example, are usually paid in cash. A company that needs but cannot generate cash—a company that's not "liquid"—may be forced to sell assets at reduced prices or even to go out of business.

By definition, cash is completely liquid. *Marketable securities* purchased as short-term investments are slightly less liquid but can be sold quickly. These include stocks or bonds of other companies, government securities, and money market certificates. Many companies hold other nonliquid assets such as *merchandise inventory*—the cost of merchandise that's been acquired for sale to customers and is still on hand. Google has no merchandise inventory because it sells services rather than physical goods.

Fixed Assets **Fixed assets** (such as land, buildings, and equipment) have long-term use or value, but as buildings and equipment wear out or become obsolete, their value decreases. Accountants use **depreciation** to spread the cost of an asset over the years of its useful life. To reflect decreasing value, accountants calculate an asset's useful life in years, divide its worth by that many years, and subtract the resulting amount each year. Every year, therefore, the remaining value (or net value) decreases on the books. In Figure 14.1, Google shows fixed assets of $8.99 (rounded) billion after depreciation.

Intangible Assets Although their worth is hard to set, **intangible assets** have monetary value in the form of expected benefits, which may include fees paid by others

Owners' Equity amount of money that owners would receive if they sold all of a firm's assets and paid all of its liabilities

Financial Statement any of several types of reports summarizing a company's financial status to stakeholders and to aid in managerial decision making

Balance Sheet financial statement that supplies detailed information about a firm's assets, liabilities, and owners' equity

Current Asset asset that can or will be converted into cash within a year

Liquidity ease with which an asset can be converted into cash

Fixed Asset asset with long-term use or value, such as land, buildings, and equipment

Depreciation accounting method for distributing the cost of an asset over its useful life

Intangible Asset nonphysical asset, such as a patent or trademark, that has economic value in the form of expected benefit for obtaining rights or privileges—including patents, trademarks, copyrights, and franchises—to your products. **Goodwill** is the amount paid for an existing business beyond the value of its other assets. A purchased firm, for example, may have a particularly good reputation or location. Google declares both intangible assets and goodwill in its balance sheet.

Liabilities   Like assets, liabilities are often separated into different categories. **Current liabilities** are debts that must be paid within one year. These include **accounts payable (payables)**—unpaid bills to suppliers for materials as well as wages and taxes that must be paid in the coming year. Google has current liabilities of $10.00 (rounded) billion. **Long-term liabilities** are debts that are not due for at least a year. These normally represent borrowed funds on which the company must pay interest. The long-term liabilities of Google are $1.61 (rounded) billion.

Owners' Equity   The final section of the balance sheet in Figure 14.1 shows owners' equity (shareholders' equity) broken down into *paid-in capital* and *retained earnings*. When Google was first formed, it sold a small amount of common stock that provided its first paid-in capital. **Paid-in capital** is money invested by owners. Google's paid-in capital had grown to $18.37 billion by year-end 2010, and includes proceeds from Google's initial public offering of stock in 2004 that created additional funds that were needed for expansion.

  Retained earnings are net profits kept by a firm rather than paid out as dividend payments to stockholders. They accumulate when profits, which can be distributed to shareholders, are kept instead for the company's use. At the close of 2010, Google had retained earnings of $27.87 billion. The total of stockholders' equity—paid-in capital plus retained earnings—had grown to $46.24 billion.

  The balance sheet for any company, then, is a barometer for its financial condition at one point in time. By comparing the current balance sheet with those of previous years, creditors and owners can better interpret the firm's financial progress and future prospects in terms of changes in its assets, liabilities, and owners' equity.

Income Statements

The **income statement** is sometimes called a **profit-and-loss statement** because its description of revenues and expenses results in a figure showing the firm's annual profit or loss. In other words,

$$\text{Profit (or Loss)} = \text{Revenues} - \text{Expenses}$$

  Popularly known as the *bottom line*, profit or loss is probably the most important figure in any business enterprise. Figure 14.2 shows the 2010 income statement for Google, whose bottom line was $8.50 (rounded) billion. The income statement is divided into four major categories: *revenues*, *cost of revenues*, *operating expenses*, and *net income*. Unlike a balance sheet, which shows the financial condition at a specific *point in time*, an income statement shows the financial results that occurred during a *period of time*, such as a month, quarter, or year.

Revenues   When a law firm receives $250 for preparing a will or a supermarket collects $65 from a grocery shopper, both are receiving **revenues**—the funds that flow into a business from the sale of goods or services. In 2010, Google reported revenues of $29.32 (rounded) billion from the sale of advertising and web-search services to Google Network members, such as AOL.

Cost of Revenues (Cost of Goods Sold)   In the Google income statement, the **cost of revenues** section shows the costs of obtaining the revenues from other companies during the year. These are fees Google must pay its network members—revenue sharing from advertising income—and also include expenses arising from the operation of Google's data centers, including labor, energy, and costs of processing customer transactions. The cost of revenues for Google in 2010 was $10.42 (rounded) billion.

Google, Inc.
Summary of Income Statement (condensed)
as of December 31, 2010
(in millions)

Revenues (gross sales)		**$29,321**
Cost of revenues	10,417	
Gross profit		**$18,904**
Operating expenses:		
Research Development	3,762	
Selling, Administrative and General	4,761	
Total operating expenses		**$8,523**
Operating income (before taxes)		10,381
Income taxes*		1,876
Net income		**$8,505**

*approximated

Figure 14.2 **Google's Income Statement**
Source: Modified from "Google Inc. (GOOG)," *Yahoo! Finance*, accessed March 3, 2011 at http://finance.yahoo.com/q/is?s=GOOG+Income+Statement&annual

Google's income statement for year ended December 31, 2010. The final entry on the income statement, the bottom line, reports the firm's profit or loss.

While cost of revenues is a relevant income statement category for service providers like Google, goods producers do not use it. Instead, income statements for manufacturing firms such as Procter & Gamble use the corresponding category, **cost of goods sold:** costs of obtaining materials to make products sold during the year.

Gross Profit Managers are often interested in **gross profit,** a preliminary, quick-to-calculate profit figure that considers just two pieces of data—revenues and cost of revenues (the direct costs of getting those revenues)—from the income statement. To calculate gross profit, subtract cost of revenues from revenues obtained by selling the firm's products.

Operating Expenses In addition to costs directly related to generating revenues, every company has general expenses ranging from erasers to the CEO's salary. Like cost of revenues and cost of goods sold, **operating expenses** are resources that must flow out of a company if it is to earn revenues. As shown in Figure 14.2, Google had operating expenses of $8.53 billion (rounded).

Research development expenses result from exploring new services and technologies for providing them to customers. *Selling expenses* result from activities related to selling goods or services, such as sales-force salaries and advertising expenses. *Administrative and general expenses*, such as management salaries and maintenance costs, are related to the general management of the company.

Goodwill amount paid for an existing business above the value of its other assets

Current Liability debt that must be paid within one year

Accounts Payable (Payables) current liability consisting of bills owed to suppliers, plus wages and taxes due within the coming year

Long-Term Liability debt that is not due for at least one year

Paid-In Capital money that is invested in a company by its owners

Retained Earnings earnings retained by a firm for its use rather than paid out as dividends

Income Statement (Profit-and-Loss Statement) financial statement listing a firm's annual revenues and expenses so that a bottom line shows annual profit or loss

Revenues funds that flow into a business from the sale of goods or services

Cost of Revenues costs that a company incurs to obtain revenues from other companies

Cost of Goods Sold costs of obtaining materials for making the products sold by a firm during the year

Gross Profit preliminary, quick-to-calculate profit figure calculated from the firm's revenues minus its cost of revenues (the direct costs of getting the revenues)

Operating Expenses costs, other than the cost of revenues, incurred in producing a good or service

Operating and Net Income   **Operating income** compares the gross profit from operations against operating expenses. This calculation for Google ($18.90 billion – $8.52 billion) reveals an operating income, or income before taxes, of $10.38 billion. Subtracting income taxes from operating income ($10.38 billion – $1.88 billion) reveals **net income (net profit or net earnings).** Google's net income for the year was $8.50 billion (rounded).

The step-by-step information in an income statement shows how a company obtained its net income for the period, making it easier for shareholders and other stakeholders to evaluate the firm's financial health.

Statements of Cash Flows

Some companies prepare only balance sheets and income statements. However, the SEC requires all firms whose stock is publicly traded to issue a third report, the **statement of cash flows,** which describes yearly cash receipts and cash payments. Since it provides the most detail about how the company generates and uses cash, some investors and creditors consider it one of the most important statements of all. It shows the effects on cash of three aspects of a business: *operating activities*, *investing activities*, and *financing activities*. Google's 2010 statement (simplified) of cash flows is reproduced in Figure 14.3.

- Cash Flows from Operations. This first section of the statement concerns main operating activities: cash transactions involved in buying and selling goods and services. For the Google example, it reveals how much of the year's cash balance results from the firm's main line of business—sales of advertising and web-search services. Operating activities at Google contributed net cash inflows amounting to $11.08 (rounded) billion in 2010.

- Cash Flows from Investing. The second section reports net cash used in or provided by investing. It includes cash receipts and payments from buying and selling stocks, bonds, property, equipment, and other productive assets. These sources of cash are not the company's main line of business. Purchases of property, equipment, and investments made by Google consumed $10.68 billion of net cash. A cash outflow is shown in parentheses.

- Cash Flows from Financing. The third section reports net cash from all financing activities. It includes cash inflows from borrowing or issuing stock, as well as outflows for payment of dividends and repayment of borrowed money. Google's financing activities provided a net cash inflow of $3.05 billion.

Figure 14.3 **Google's Statement of Cash Flows**
Source: Modified from "Google Inc. (GOOG)," *Yahoo! Finance,* accessed March 3, 2011 at http://finance.yahoo.com/q/cf?s=GOOG+Cash+Flow&annual

Google, Inc.
Summary of Statement of Cash Flows (condensed)
as of December 31, 2010
Increase (Decrease) in Cash
(in millions)

Net cash provided by operating activities		**$11,081.**
Cash from investments:		
Purchases of property, equipment, and investments	(11,974.)	
Cash inflows from investment activities	1,294.	
Net cash used in investing activities		**(10,680.)**
Cash flows from financing activities:		
Purchase of stock	(801.)	
Borrowings	3,463.	
Other	388.	
Net cash provided by financing activities		**3,050.**
Net increase in cash		3,451.
Cash at beginning of year		10,179.
Cash at end of year		**$13,630.**

Google's statement of cash flows for year ended December 31, 2010. The final entry shows year-end cash position resulting from operating activities, investing activities, and financing activities.

The overall change in cash from these three sources is $3.45 (rounded) billion for the year. The amount is added to the beginning cash (year-end cash from the 2009 balance sheet) to arrive at 2010's ending cash position of $13.63 billion. When creditors and stockholders know how a firm obtained and used funds during the course of a year, it's easier for them to interpret year-to-year changes in the balance sheet and income statement.

The Budget: An Internal Financial Statement

For planning, controlling, and decision making, the most important internal financial statement is the **budget**—a detailed report on estimated receipts and expenditures for a future period of time. Although that period is usually one year, some companies also prepare three- or five-year budgets, especially when considering major capital expenditures. The budget differs from the other statements we have discussed in that budgets are not shared outside the company; hence the "internal financial statement" title.

Although the accounting staff coordinates the budget process, it needs input from many areas regarding proposed activities and required resources. Figure 14.4 is a sales budget for a hypothetical wholesaler, Perfect Posters. In preparing the budget, accounting must obtain from the sales group projections for units to be sold and expected expenses for the coming year. Then, accounting draws up the final budget and, throughout the year, compares the budget to actual expenditures and revenues. Discrepancies signal potential problems and spur action to improve financial performance.

Reporting Standards and Practices

4 Explain the key standards and principles for reporting financial statements.

Accountants follow standard reporting practices and principles when they prepare external reports. The common language dictated by standard practices and spelled out in GAAP is designed to give external users confidence in the accuracy

---

Perfect Posters, Inc.
555 RIVERVIEW, CHICAGO, IL 60606

Perfect Posters, Inc.
Sales Budget
First Quarter, 2012

	January	February	March	Quarter
Budgeted sales (units)	7,500	6,000	6,500	20,000
Budgeted selling price per unit	$3.50	$3.50	$3.50	$3.50
Budgeted sales revenue	**$26,250**	**$21,000**	**$22,750**	**$70,000**
Expected cash receipts:				
From December sales	$26,210			$26,210
From January sales	17,500	$8,750		26,250
From February sales		14,000	$7,000	21,000
From March sales			15,200	15,200
Total cash receipts:	**$43,710**	**$22,750**	**$22,200**	**$88,660**

Figure 14.4 Perfect Posters' Sales Budget

Operating Income gross profit minus operating expenses

Net Income (Net Profit, Net Earnings) gross profit minus operating expenses and income taxes

Statement of Cash Flows financial statement describing a firm's yearly cash receipts and cash payments

Budget detailed statement of estimated receipts and expenditures for a future period of time

and meaning of financial information. The GAAP principles cover a range of issues, such as when to recognize revenues from operations and how to make full public disclosure of financial information. Without such standards, users of financial statements wouldn't be able to compare information from different companies, and would misunderstand—or be led to misconstrue—a company's true financial status. Forensic accountants such as PricewaterhouseCoopers's Al Vondra watch for deviations from GAAP as indicators of possible fraudulent practices.

Revenue Recognition and Activity Timing   The reporting of revenue inflows, and the timing of other transactions, must abide by accounting principles that govern financial statements. **Revenue recognition,** for example, is the formal recording and reporting of revenues at the appropriate time. Although a firm earns revenues continuously as it makes sales, earnings are not reported until the *earnings cycle* is completed. This cycle is complete under two conditions:

1 The sale is complete and the product delivered.

2 The sale price has been collected or is collectible (accounts receivable).

The end of the earnings cycle determines the timing for revenue recognition in a firm's financial statements. Suppose a toy company in January signs a sales contract to supply $1,000 of toys to a retail store, with delivery scheduled in February. Although the sale is completed in January, the $1,000 revenue should not then be recognized because the toys have not been delivered and the sale price is not yet collectible, so the earnings cycle is incomplete. Revenues are recorded in the accounting period—February—in which the product is delivered and collectible (or collected). This practice ensures that the statement gives a fair comparison of what was gained (revenues) in return for the resources that were given up (cost of materials, labor, and other production and delivery expenses) for the transaction.

Full Disclosure   To help users better understand the numbers in a firm's financial statements, GAAP requires that financial statements also include management's interpretations and explanations of those numbers. This is known as the **full disclosure** principle. Because they know about events inside the company, managers prepare additional information to explain certain events or transactions or to disclose the circumstances behind certain results. For example, earlier annual reports and financial statements filed by Borders, the well-known bookseller, had discussed the competitive and economic risks facing the company before it eventually filed for bankruptcy in 2011. The disclosures noted that consumer spending trends were shifting to Internet retailers and eBooks, and away from in-store purchasing, thus posing risks for Borders' cash flows and overall financial condition. Management's discussion noted there could be no assurance that Borders would muster adequate financial resources to remain competitive and, indeed, it soon happened. Upon filing for bankruptcy, Borders' liabilities of $1.29 billion had surpassed its assets of $1.28 billion.[13]

5 Describe how computing financial ratios can help users get more information from financial statements to determine the financial strengths of a business.

Analyzing Financial Statements

Financial statements present a lot of information, but how can it be used? How, for example, can statements help investors decide what stock to buy or help lenders decide whether to extend credit? Answers to such questions for various stakeholders—employees, managers, unions, suppliers, the government, customers—can be answered as follows: Statements provide data, which can, in turn, reveal trends and be applied to create various *ratios* (comparative numbers). We can then use these trends and ratios to evaluate a firm's financial health, its progress, and its prospects for the future.

MANAGING IN TURBULENT TIMES

The "Fairness" Dilemma: What's an Asset's Real Value?

Think of a personal possession, such as a car. What is its monetary worth, or value? Is it the amount you paid, or what you could get by selling it today, or what you would expect if you sell two years from now? Businesses face similar questions when valuing assets on the balance sheet. Consider the Boston home buyer who paid $475,000 in 2006 when a bank generously valued the property at more than $525,000, allowing the new homeowner to borrow the full amount of the purchase price. The bank's asset (the mortgage loan) was valued at $475,000 and the borrower's property was valued at $525,000. Today, the borrower has vacated the house, unable to make payments. The bank holds the repossessed the property; it is unsellable at a $360,000 asking price. In the event of future economic recovery, the bank expects that the property will be worth at least $500,000. So, what should be the asset value on the balance sheet—$475,000 or $360,000 or $500,000? Many other firms in addition to banks are grappling with such questions in the plunging real estate market.[14]

The core problem is market shutdown: In a recession, there is no functioning market that sets a "fair market price" for many assets. With no buyers, once-valuable properties and financial investments have become "toxic assets": They are unsellable, often having no current market value. Difficulty worsens when market shutdown runs headlong into an accounting rule known as "mark-to-market," resulting in potential business closures.[15]

Mark-to-market—or "fair value accounting"—requires that assets be priced on balance sheets at current market value. That forces a major write-down for toxic assets at companies facing inactive markets for housing, cars, and financial securities, and it forces accounting losses that may cause "bleeding" companies to fold. Advocates for relaxing mark-to-market argue that presently distressed assets will become more valuable later, as the economy recovers, so currently depressed values are not at all "fair" indicators of their worth. Instead, they say, mark-to-market exaggerates the scale of their losses in an economic downturn.[16]

ericsphotography/iStockphoto

Relief for some troubled firms came in early 2009, with unusual action by the U.S. Financial Accounting Standards Board (FASB), an independent organization that sets accounting guidelines. FASB relaxed mark-to-market accounting for financial institutions. Banks now have more flexibility for valuing toxic assets, using estimates from their internal computer models instead of reporting assets at currently distressed market prices. Opponents to the change, however, warn that relaxed rules could let banks hide the true, low value of assets and deceive investors at a time when trust in financial reporting is most needed.[17]

MyBizLab

Ratios are normally grouped into three major classifications:

1 **Solvency ratios** for estimating short-term and long-term risk

2 **Profitability ratios** for measuring potential earnings

3 **Activity ratios** for evaluating management's use of assets

Depending on the decisions to be made, a user may apply none, some, or all of these ratios.

Revenue Recognition formal recording and reporting of revenues at the appropriate time

Full Disclosure guideline that financial statements should not include just numbers but should also furnish management's interpretations and explanations of those numbers

Solvency Ratio financial ratio, either short- or long-term, for estimating the borrower's ability to repay debt

Profitability Ratio financial ratio for measuring a firm's potential earnings

Activity Ratio financial ratio for evaluating management's efficiency in using a firm's assets

Solvency Ratios: Borrower's Ability to Repay Debt

What are the chances that a borrower will be able to repay a loan and the interest due? This question is first and foremost in the minds of bank lending officers, managers of pension funds and other investors, suppliers, and the borrowing company's own financial managers. Solvency ratios provide measures of a firm's ability to meet its debt obligations.

The Current Ratio and Short-Term Solvency   **Short-term solvency ratios** measure a company's liquidity and its ability to pay immediate debts. The most commonly used of these is the **current ratio,** or "banker's ratio." This measures a firm's ability to generate cash to meet current obligations through the normal, orderly process of selling inventories and collecting revenues from customers. It is calculated by dividing current assets by current liabilities. The higher a firm's current ratio, the lower the risk to investors.

As a rule, a current ratio is satisfactory at 2:1 or higher—that is, if current assets more than double current liabilities. A smaller ratio may indicate that a firm will have trouble paying its bills.

How does Google measure up? Look again at the balance sheet in Figure 14.1. Judging from current assets and current liabilities at the end of 2010, we see that

$$\frac{\text{Current assets}}{\text{Current liabilities}} = \frac{\$41.56 \text{ billion}}{\$10.00 \text{ billion}} = 4.2$$

The industry average for companies that provide business services is 1.4. Google's current ratio of 4.2 indicates the firm is a good short-run credit risk.

Long-Term Solvency   Stakeholders are also concerned about long-term solvency. Has the company been overextended by borrowing so much that it will be unable to repay debts in future years? A firm that can't meet its long-term debt obligations is in danger of collapse or takeover—a risk that makes creditors and investors quite cautious. To evaluate a company's risk of running into this problem, creditors turn to the balance sheet to see the extent to which a firm is financed through borrowed money. Long-term solvency is calculated by dividing **debt**—total liabilities—by owners' equity. The lower a firm's debt, the lower the risk to investors and creditors. Companies with more debt may find themselves owing so much that they lack the income needed to meet interest payments or to repay borrowed money.

Leverage   Sometimes, high debt can be not only acceptable, but also desirable. Borrowing funds gives a firm **leverage**—the ability to make otherwise unaffordable investments. In *leveraged buyouts*, firms have willingly taken on sometimes huge debts to buy out other companies. If owning the purchased company generates profits above the cost of borrowing the purchase price, leveraging often makes sense. Unfortunately, many buyouts have caused problems because profits fell short of expected levels or because rising interest rates increased payments on the buyer's debt.

Profitability Ratios: Earnings Power for Owners

It's important to know whether a company is solvent in both the long and the short term, but risk alone is not an adequate basis for investment decisions. Investors also want some indication of the returns they can expect. Evidence of earnings power is available from profitability ratios, such as *earnings per share*.

Earnings per Share   Defined as net income divided by the number of shares of common stock outstanding, **earnings per share** determines the size of the dividend that a firm can pay shareholders. As an indicator of a company's wealth potential, investors use this ratio to decide whether to buy or sell the firm's stock. As the ratio goes up, stock value increases because investors know that the firm can better afford to pay dividends. Naturally, stock loses market value if financial statements report a decline in earnings per share. For Google, we can use the net income total from the

ENTREPRENEURSHIP AND NEW VENTURES

How Will Twitter Turn Tweets into Treasure?

Widely accepted accounting measurements provide useful information about established firms but are a bit foggier with start-ups. Consider the continuing questions from the investment community about Twitter's ambiguous financial status. With several firms interested in buying Twitter, how can they know its market value, variously estimated to have risen from an early $300 million up to $4.5 billion in 2011, without solid financial data? The real numbers are confidential in closely held Twitter. As to its profitability, Twitter reports, "we spend more money than we make." Since Twitter was launched in 2006, its total losses have not been reported publicly. When (and how) will losses blossom into profitability? As stated by cofounder and former CEO Evan Williams, "We will make money, and I can't say exactly how because... we can't predict how the businesses we're in will work." And until they know *how*, they don't know *when* profits will occur.[18]

Twitter's balance sheet is another source of ambiguity. The accounting equation requires a fixed relationship among three items: Assets = Liabilities + Owners' Equity. Twitter insiders have a clear accounting of its outstanding liabilities. Paid-in capital (a part of shareholders' equity) is known, too: It includes the cofounders' personal investments plus a series of venture capital infusions, bringing the suspected total to over $800 million.

Questions also arise for valuing assets. For example, Twitter acquired the assets of *Values of n* to get needed technology and intellectual property into its operations. Exactly how Twitter will use them is unknown, so how should they be valued? Twitter's greatest asset is a massive loyal customer base with a phenomenal growth rate—190 million visitors per month and 65 million Tweets daily—and its enormous advertising potential. Celebrities, media, politicians, and organizations such as Papa Johns, American Red Cross, Warner Bros Pictures, and Toyota USA are using Twitter for sales and marketing promotions. Should this untapped advertising potential be recognized as an intangible asset? At what value? While the company's market, customer base, and products are rapidly emerging, how should its many assets—tangible and intangible—be valued? On what basis can those valuations be justified? Clearly, these issues at Twitter are less well settled than at well-established firms.[19]

MyBizLab

Pixellover RM 1/Alamy

income statement in Figure 14.2, together with the number of outstanding shares of stock, to calculate earnings per share as follows:

$$\frac{\text{Net income}}{\substack{\text{Number of} \\ \text{common shares} \\ \text{outstanding}}} = \frac{\$8{,}505.0 \text{ million}}{\substack{321.5 \text{ million} \\ \text{shares of stock}}} = \frac{\$26.45}{\text{per share}}$$

This means that Google had net earnings of $26.45 (rounded) for each share of stock during 2010. In contrast, Time Warner's recent earnings were $2.25 per share, while Microsoft earned $2.34.

Short-Term Solvency Ratio financial ratio for measuring a company's ability to pay immediate debts

Current Ratio financial ratio for measuring a company's ability to pay current debts out of current assets

Debt company's total liabilities

Leverage ability to finance an investment through borrowed funds

Earnings Per Share profitability ratio measuring the net profit that the company earns for each share of outstanding stock

Activity Ratios: How Efficiently Is the Firm Using Its Resources?

The efficiency with which a firm uses resources is linked to profitability. As a potential investor, you want to know which company gets more mileage from its resources. Information obtained from financial statements can be used for *activity ratios* to measure this efficiency. For example, two firms use the same amount of resources or assets to perform a particular activity. If Firm A generates greater profits or sales, it has used its resources more efficiently and so enjoys a better activity ratio. It may apply to any important activity, such as advertising, sales, or inventory management. Consider the activity of using the firm's resources to increase sales. As an example, suppose from its income statements we find that Google increases its annual sales revenues and does it without increasing it operating costs. Its sales activity has become more efficient. Investors like to see these year-to-year increases in efficiencies because it means the company is getting "more bang for the buck"—revenues are increasing faster than costs.

6 | Discuss the role of ethics in accounting.

Bringing Ethics into the Accounting Equation

The purpose of ethics in accounting is to maintain public confidence in business institutions, financial markets, and the products and services of the accounting profession. Without ethics, all of accounting's tools and methods would be meaningless because their usefulness depends, ultimately, on veracity in their application.

Why Accounting Ethics?

Amidst a flurry of unscrupulous activity, ethics remains an area where one person who is willing to "do the right thing" can make a difference—and people do, every day. The role of ethics in the ground-breaking scandal from a decade ago remains a classic example: Refusing to turn a blind eye to unethical accounting around her at Enron, Lynn Brewer tried to alert people inside about misstatements of the company's assets. When that failed, she, along with colleagues Sherron Watkins and Margaret Ceconi, talked with the U.S. Committee on Energy and Commerce to voice concerns about Enron's condition. To Brewer, maintaining personal and professional integrity was an overriding concern, and she acted accordingly.

AICPA's Code of Professional Conduct   The **code of professional conduct** for public accountants in the United States is maintained and enforced by the AICPA. The institute identifies six ethics-related areas—listed in Table 14.3—with which accountants must comply to maintain certification. Comprehensive details for compliance in each area are spelled out in the AICPA Code of Professional Conduct. The IMA maintains a similar code to provide ethical guidelines for the management accounting profession.

In reading the AICPA's Code, you can see that it forbids misrepresentation and fraud in financial statements. Deception certainly violates the call for exercising moral judgments (in "Responsibilities"), is contrary to the public interest (by deceiving investors) and does not honor the public trust (in "The Public Interest"). Misleading statements destroy the public's confidence in the accounting profession and in business in general. While the Code prohibits such abuses, its success depends, ultimately, on its acceptance and use by the professionals it governs.

Violations of Accounting Ethics and GAAP   Unethical and illegal accounting violations have dominated the popular press in recent years. Some of the more

TABLE 14.3   Highlights from the Code of Ethics for CPAs

By voluntarily accepting Certified Public Accountant membership, the accountant also accepts self-enforced obligations, listed below, beyond written regulations and laws.

Responsibilities as a Professional	The CPA should exercise their duties with a high level of morality and in a manner that is sensitive to bringing credit to their profession.
Serving the Public Interest	The CPA should demonstrate commitment to the profession by respecting and maintaining the public trust and serving the public honorably.
Maintaining Integrity	The CPA should perform all professional activities with highest regards for integrity, including sincerity and honesty, so as to promote the public's confidence in the profession.
Being Objective and Independent	The CPA should avoid conflicts of interest, and the appearance of conflicts of interest, in performing their professional responsibilities. They should be independent from clients when certifying to the public that the client's statements are true and genuine.
Maintaining Technical and Ethical Standards	The CPA should exercise "due care," through professional improvement, abiding by ethical standards, updating personal competence through continuing accounting education, and improving the quality of services.
Professional Conduct in Providing Services	The CPA in public practice should abide by the meaning and intent of the Code of Professional Conduct when deciding on the kinds of services and the range of actions to be supplied for clients.

Source: Based on "Code of Professional Conduct," *AICPA*, at http://infotech.aicpa.org/Resources/Privacy/Federal+State+and+Other+Professional+Regulations/AICPA+Code+of+Professional+Conduct/.

notorious cases, listed in Table 14.4, violated the public's trust, ruined retirement plans for thousands of employees, and caused shutdowns and lost jobs. As you read each case, you should be able to see how its violation relates to the presentation of balance sheets and income statements in this chapter. In each case, adversity would have been prevented if employees had followed the code of professional conduct. In each case, nearly all of the code's six ethics-related areas were violated. And in every case, "professionals" willingly participated in unethical behavior. Such was the impetus for Sarbox.

TABLE 14.4   Examples of Unethical and Illegal Accounting Actions[20]

Corporation	Accounting Violation
AOL Time Warner	America Online (AOL) inflated ad revenues to keep stock prices high before and after merging with Time Warner.
Cendant	Inflated income in financial statements by $500 million through fraud and errors.
HCA, Columbia/HCA	Defrauded Medicare, Medicaid, and TRICARE through false cost claims and unlawful billings (must pay $1.7 billion in civil penalties, damages, criminal fines, and penalties).
Tyco	CEO Dennis Kozlowski illegally used company funds to buy expensive art for personal possession (he received an 8- to 25-year prison sentence).
Waste Management	Overstated income in financial statements (false and misleading reports) by improperly calculating depreciation and salvage value for equipment.
WorldCom	Hid $3.8 billion in expenses to show an inflated (false) profit instead of loss in an annual income statement.

Code of Professional Conduct code of ethics for CPAs as maintained and enforced by the AICPA

7 Describe the purpose of the International Accounting Standards Board and explain why it exists.

Internationalizing Accounting

Accounting in its earliest forms is known to have existed more than 7,000 years ago in Mesopotamia and Egypt for recording trade transactions and keeping track of resources. With the passage of time each country or region's accounting practices were refined to meet its needs in commerce while also accommodating local cultural traditions and developments in its laws. While unique practices served each region well, they later posed problems as international business became prominent. By the late 20th century it was apparent that the upsurge in multinational organizations and the global economy demanded more uniformity among accounting practices. The development of "universal" procedures would allow governments and investors in, say, China, Brazil, and Italy to read, interpret, and compare financial statements from all those countries, whereas such comparisons even today are difficult if not sometimes impossible.

International Accounting Standards Board

Established in 2001 and housed at London, England, the **International Accounting Standards Board (IASB)** is an independent, nonprofit organization responsible for developing a set of global accounting standards, and for gaining the support and cooperation of the world's various accounting organizations to implement those standards.

IASB's 15 board members from various countries are full-time accounting experts with technical and international business experience.[21] Because the Board cannot command sovereign nations to accept its recommended standards, its commitment to gaining cooperation around the world is a continuing task. Yet, international acceptance is essential for success. Accordingly, the Board's task is a long-term process that requires working with various countries to design proposed standards. As an example, for any IASB proposal to be accepted in the U.S., it must first be approved by the U.S.-based Financial Accounting Standards Board (FASB) and by the U.S. Securities and Exchange Commission. However, IASB's efforts extend beyond the U.S., to all nations. The expected timeline reaches beyond 2015 for convergence of the many local GAAP's into one global set of practices.

Why One Set of Global Practices?

Although more than 100 countries have adopted IASB's accounting practices, nearly 40 others, including China, Canada, and the U.S., continue to use their national GAAPs.[22] U.S.-based global companies such as Google, Caterpillar, and Microsoft may prepare different financial reports using local accounting practices for each country in which they conduct business. They also report the company's overall performance in a set of consolidated statements that combines the financial results of all its global affiliates, using U.S.-GAAP. Using different accounting standards, however, can result in vastly different pictures of a firm's financial health. Income statements, balance sheets, and statements of cash flows using local GAAPs versus IASB practices, for example, may contain conflicting information with inconsistencies leading to confusion and misunderstandings among investors and other constituents. To emphasize this point, Sir David Tweedie, Chairman of the IASB notes that a company using IASB standards can report balance sheet figures that are twice the size of those using U.S. GAAP accounting standards.[23] Which of the reports tells how well the company is doing? Such inconsistencies in reporting are unacceptable in a global economy and, accordingly, protection against them is a goal of IASB.

Example Areas Targeted for Aligning U.S. GAAP and IASB   Among the many differences between the practices of U.S. GAAP and IASB—some reports identify more than 400 such discrepancies—the following examples illustrate some discrepancies and proposals for convergence toward universal standards in financial reporting.

In valuing assets (reported on the balance sheet), U.S. GAAP allows an asset to be written down if for some reason its value decreases. However, the value cannot later be rewritten up, even if it its actual value has increased. IASB standards, in contrast, do allow such write-ups reflecting increased market value, so the reported value of a company's assets can be quite different, depending upon the chosen accounting system.[24]

In revenue recognition—when revenues from customers should be recognized (reported), and in what amounts—on the income statement, the U.S. GAAP and IASB procedures differ. A current joint proposal, if approved, would remove existing inconsistencies and provide a single standard that recognizes revenue at the time the goods and services are transferred to the customer, and in the amounts that are expected to be received (or are received) from the customer.[25]

In de-valuing of financial assets—such as writing down bad loans in the financial crisis—both U.S. GAAP and IASB currently use the same procedure: After a loss occurs (but not until after the fact) the loan's value can be written down in the firm's financial statements, reflecting its lower value. Both groups, however, believe an "expected loss model" that recognizes (and reports) likely loan losses *ahead of time* will provide more timely information for investors and financial planners. A joint proposal for such a procedure has been presented.[26]

In fair value disclosure the FASB and IASB jointly propose new standards for improving the comparability of fair value disclosures in financial statements. Unlike dissimilar disclosure practices among many local GAAPs, both groups want the reported "fair value" for an asset, a liability, and an item in shareholders' equity to have the same meaning under both FASB and IASB procedures. The disclosure should identify the techniques and inputs used to measure fair value so that users can more clearly assess and compare financial statements.[27]

Timetable for Implementation   The U.S. Securities and Exchange Commission has targeted 2015 as the earliest date that U.S. companies will be required to use IASB procedures for financial reporting. First, however, IASB must demonstrate that its standards are developed adequately for use in the U.S. financial reporting system. This would include assuring that investors have developed an understanding of and education in using IASB standards. Accounting education, too, must be updated to prepare U.S. accounting students for IASB, as well as updating practitioners in CPA firms. AICPA has announced plans to test for knowledge of international standards in CPA examinations by 2012. Finally, the SEC must make a decision to phase in IASB all at once or, instead, to sequence its adoption beginning with a limited number of companies before final phase-in.[28]

International Accounting Standards Board (IASB) organization responsible for developing a set of global accounting standards and for gaining implementation of those standards

Johnny Lye/Shutterstock

Continued from page 357

Fraud-Finding and Fraud-Prevention: The Stakes Are Getting Higher

Fraudulent insurance claims are on the upswing: A private investigator films an injury victim throwing the neck brace into the back seat of his car after leaving the doctor's office, a homeowner inflates the cost of articles stolen in an alleged burglary, and victims of car wrecks from years past suddenly submit injury claims. Employees, too, are a source of fraud: The U.S. Commerce Department estimates that one-third of business shutdowns are due to employee theft. Inventory stolen from the firm's warehouse is resold; the company's strategic inside information is stolen and sold to a competitor; and employees receive reimbursement for falsely inflated business expenses. [29]

The broad scope of fraud—its costs, who commits it and how, and how it is detected—is revealed in *Global Fraud Studies* conducted by the Association of Certified Fraud Examiners (ACFE).[30] Fraud typically costs organizations five percent of their annual revenues, but small businesses are especially vulnerable because they usually have fewer internal controls for protecting their resources. Employees in the United States commit more cases of fraud than do managers, while top-level executives and owners are least involved. However, it comes as no surprise that financial losses by higher-level perpetrators is typically ten times that of other employees. The most common kind of fraud is asset theft—stealing cash, falsifying business expenses, forging checks, and stealing noncash assets. The Chief Financial Officer of a Florida tree farm, for example, falsified checks and misused company credit cards to embezzle $10 million, earning a 96-month prison sentence and a $14 million fine.[31] The least-common organizational fraud and the costliest by far, is financial statement manipulation. In 2011, for example, the officer of an investment company was convicted of lying to investors using quarterly statements reporting inflated earned interest on bank accounts. The result was a 36-month prison sentence and an order to pay bilked investors some $183 million in restitution.

How do they get caught? Most commonly, detection starts from tips by employees. While internal audits are somewhat effective, external audits are less effective than commonly believed, and less than detection by accident! The CFE study concludes any organization's number-one safeguard is employee education in recognizing, reporting, and preventing fraud.

QUESTIONS FOR DISCUSSION

1 What factors do you think are most important in choosing among various methods to protect against fraud in your firm?

2 Suppose you are hoping for a career as a certified fraud examiner. How do recent trends in fraud provide new opportunities for such a career?

3 An external auditor, such as a CPA firm's accountant, may suspect some irregularities in a client firm's accounting practices. In what ways might a certified fraud examiner be of assistance?

4 Consider the anti-fraud training for a company's employees. Which four (or more) topics should be included in that training?

5 What ethical issues, if any, are involved in a decision to investigate a suspected case of fraud in a firm's accounting activities?

SUMMARY OF LEARNING OBJECTIVES   MyBizLab

1. **Explain the role of accountants and distinguish between the kinds of work done by public accountants, private accountants, management accountants, and forensic accountants. (p. 358–363)**
The role of accountants is to maintain a comprehensive system for collecting, analyzing, and communicating financial information for use by external constituents and within firms for planning, controlling, and decision making. It measures business performance and translates the results into information for management decisions. *Certified public accountants (CPAs)* are licensed professionals who provide auditing, tax, and management advisory services for other firms and individuals. Only CPAs can audit a firm's financial statements, and CPAs are always independent of the firms they audit. Many businesses hire their own salaried employees—*private accountants*—to perform internal accounting activities, such as internal auditing, taxation, cost analysis, and budgeting. Among private accountants, *certified management accountants* have passed the profession's experience and examination requirements for proficiency to provide internal accounting services that support managers in various activities (such as marketing, production, and engineering). *Forensic accountants* use accounting for legal purposes by providing investigative and litigation support in crimes against companies, crimes by companies, and civil cases.

2. **Explain how the accounting equation is used. (pp. 363–364)**
Accountants use the following equation to balance the data pertaining to financial transactions:

$$\text{Assets} - \text{Liabilities} = \text{Owners' Equity}$$

After each financial transaction (e.g., payments to suppliers, sales to customers, wages to employees), the accounting equation must be in balance. If it isn't, then an accounting error has occurred. The equation also provides an indication of the firm's financial health. If assets exceed liabilities, owners' equity is positive; if the firm goes out of business, owners will receive some cash (a gain) after selling assets and paying off liabilities. If liabilities outweigh assets, owners' equity is negative; assets aren't enough to pay off debts. If the company goes under, owners will get no cash and some creditors won't be paid, thus losing their remaining investments in the company.

3. **Describe the three basic financial statements and show how they reflect the activity and financial condition of a business. (pp. 364–369)**
Accounting summarizes the results of a firm's transactions and issues reports—including *financial statements*—to help managers and other stakeholders make informed decisions. (1) The *balance sheet* (sometimes called the *statement of financial position*) supplies detailed information about the accounting equation items—assets, liabilities, and owners' equity—that together are a barometer of the firm's financial condition at a point in time. By comparing the current balance sheet with those of previous years, creditors and owners can better interpret the firm's financial progress and future prospects. (2) The *income statement* (sometimes called a *profit-and-loss statement*) describes revenues and expenses to show a firm's annual profit or loss during a period of time, such as a year. (3) A publicly traded firm must issue a *statement of cash flows*, which describes its yearly cash receipts (inflows) and payments (outflows). It shows the effects on cash during the year from three kinds of business activities: (a) cash flows from operations, (b) cash flows from investing, and (c) cash flows from financing. The statement of cash flows then reports the overall change in the company's cash position at the end of the accounting period.

4. **Explain the key standards and principles for reporting financial statements. (pp. 369–370)**
Accountants follow standard reporting practices and principles when they prepare financial statements. Otherwise, users wouldn't be able to compare information from different companies, and they might misunderstand—or be led to misconstrue—a company's true financial status. The following are two of the most important standard reporting practices and principles: (1) *Revenue recognition* is the formal recording and reporting of revenues in financial statements. All firms earn revenues continuously as they make sales, but earnings are not reported until the earnings cycle is completed. This cycle is complete under two conditions: (a) The sale is complete and the product delivered; (b) the sale price has been collected or is collectible. This practice assures interested parties that the statement gives a fair comparison of what was gained for the resources that were given up. (2) *Full disclosure* recognizes that a firm's managers have inside knowledge—beyond just the numbers reported in its financial statements—that can explain certain events, transactions, or otherwise disclose the circumstances behind certain results. Full disclosure means that financial statements include management interpretations and explanations to help external users understand the financial information contained in statements.

5. **Describe how computing financial ratios can help users get more information from financial statements to determine the financial strengths of a business. (pp. 370–374)**
Financial statements contain data that can be used in *ratios* (comparative numbers) to analyze the financial health of a company in terms of solvency, profitability, and efficiency in performing activities. Ratios can help creditors, investors, and managers assess a firm's current status and check its progress by comparing current with past statements. *Solvency ratios* use balance sheet data to measure the firm's ability to meet (repay) its debts. The *current ratio* measures the ability to meet current (short-term) liabilities out of current assets. *Long-term solvency ratios* compare the firm's total liabilities (including long-term debt) against the owners' equity. High indebtedness (a high ratio) can be risky because it requires payment of interest and repayment of borrowed funds that may not be available. *Profitability ratios*, such as earnings per share, measure current and potential earnings. *Activity ratios* reflect management's use of assets by measuring the efficiency with which a firm uses its resources for a particular activity, such as sales, advertising, or inventory management. Sales efficiency, for

example, can be measured from income statement data for annual sales revenues as compared with sales expenses. Sales efficiency has increased if the year-to-year growth in sales revenues is larger than the growth in sales expenses.

6. **Discuss the role of ethics in accounting. (pp. 374–375)**
The purpose of ethics in accounting is to maintain public confidence in business institutions, financial markets, and the products and services of the accounting profession. Without ethics, all of accounting's tools and methods would be meaningless because their usefulness depends, ultimately, on truthfulness in their application. Accordingly, professional accounting associations enforce codes of professional conduct that include ethics-related areas, such as the accountant's responsibilities, the public interest, integrity, and due care. The associations include ethics as an area of study to meet requirements for certification. The codes prohibit, among other areas, misrepresentation and fraud in financial statements. While the accounting profession relies generally on self-compliance to professional codes, accounting associations maintain ethical conduct committees to receive allegations, hold hearings, reach settlements, and impose penalties for misconduct. The flare-up of unethical and illegal corporate accounting violations

was the impetus for the Sarbanes-Oxley Act of 2002, thus placing even greater emphasis and public awareness on the importance of ethics in accounting.

7. **Describe the purpose of the International Accounting Standards Board and explain why it exists. (pp. 376–377)**
The International Accounting Standards Board (IASB) is an independent, nonprofit organization established for the purpose of developing a set of global accounting standards, and for gaining the support and cooperation of the world's various accounting organizations to implement those standards. It exists because the upsurge in multinational organizations and the global economy demands more uniformity among accounting practices, so that accounting reports become more understandable across nations and regions. Although more than 100 countries have adopted IASB's accounting practices, nearly 40 others continue to use their national accounting standards that are often not comparable and can result in vastly different pictures of a firm's financial health. The development of "universal" procedures would allow governments and investors everywhere to read, interpret, and compare financial statements from every country, whereas such comparisons even today are difficult if not sometimes impossible.

KEY TERMS   MyBizLab

accounting (p. 358)
accounting equation (p. 363)
accounting information system (AIS) (p. 358)
accounts payable (payables) (p. 366)
activity ratio (p. 371)
asset (p. 363)
audit (p. 359)
balance sheet (p. 364)
bookkeeping (p. 358)
budget (p. 369)
Certified Fraud Examiner (CFE) (p. 362)
certified management accountant (CMA) (p. 361)
certified public accountant (CPA) (p. 359)
code of professional conduct (p. 374)
controller (p. 358)
core competencies for accounting (p. 360)
cost of goods sold (p. 367)
cost of revenues (p. 366)
current asset (p. 365)

current liability (p. 366)
current ratio (p. 372)
debt (p. 372)
depreciation (p. 365)
earnings per share (p. 372)
financial accounting (p. 358)
financial statement (p. 364)
fixed asset (p. 365)
forensic accounting (p. 361)
full disclosure (p. 370)
generally accepted accounting principles (GAAP) (p. 359)
goodwill (p. 366)
gross profit (p. 367)
income statement (profit-and-loss statement) (p. 366)
intangible asset (p. 365)
International Accounting Standards Board (IASB) (p. 376)
leverage (p. 372)
liability (p. 363)
liquidity (p. 365)
long-term liability (p. 366)

management accountant (p. 361)
management advisory services (p. 360)
managerial (management) accounting (p. 359)
net income (net profit, net earnings) (p. 368)
operating expenses (p. 367)
operating income (p. 368)
owners' equity (p. 364)
paid-in capital (p. 366)
private accountant (p. 361)
profitability ratio (p. 371)
retained earnings (p. 366)
revenue recognition (p. 370)
revenues (p. 366)
Sarbanes-Oxley Act of 2002 (SARBOX or SOX) (p. 362)
short-term solvency ratio (p. 372)
solvency ratio (p. 371)
statement of cash flows (p. 368)
tax services (p. 360)

QUESTIONS AND EXERCISES

QUESTIONS FOR REVIEW

1. Who are the users of accounting information, and for what purposes do they use it?
2. Identify the three types of services performed by CPAs.
3. Explain the ways in which financial accounting differs from managerial (management) accounting.
4. Discuss the activities and services performed by forensic accountants.
5. What are the three basic financial statements, and what major information does each contain?
6. Explain how financial ratios allow managers to gain additional information from financial statements.

QUESTIONS FOR ANALYSIS

7. If you were planning to invest in a company, which of the three types of financial statements would you most want to see? Why?
8. Suppose that you, as the manager of a company, are making changes to fully comply with provisions of the Sarbanes-Oxley Act. Your company traditionally has relied on CPA firms for auditing, tax services, and management services. What major changes will your company need to make?

9. Consider possible reasons why it is taking so long for IASB's international accounting standards to become fully adopted for use in the United States. Using the Internet as your source for information, identify five or more barriers that have deterred implementation of the standards, and explain how (or why) each has (or is) causing implementation delays.

APPLICATION EXERCISES

10. Interview an accountant at a local firm. How does the firm use budgets? How does budgeting help managers plan business activities? How does budgeting help them control activities? Give examples.
11. Interview the manager of a local retailer, wholesale business, or manufacturing firm about the role of ethics in that company's accounting practices. Is ethics in accounting an important issue to the manager? If the firm has its own private accountants, what measures are taken for ensuring ethical practices internally? What steps, if any, does the company take to maintain ethical relationships in its dealings with CPA firms?

BUILDING YOUR BUSINESS SKILLS

Putting the Buzz in Billing

Goal
To encourage you to think about the advantages and disadvantages of using an online system for handling accounts receivable and accounts payable electronically.

Method

Step 1
As the CFO of a Midwestern utility company, you are analyzing the feasibility of switching to a totally electronic bill-paying system. You decide to discuss the ramifications of the choice with three associates (choose three classmates to take on these roles). Your discussion requires that you research existing electronic payment systems. Specifically, using online and library research, you must find out as much as you can about the electronic bill-paying systems developed by Visa, Intuit, IBM, and the Checkfree Corporation.

Step 2
After you have researched this information, brainstorm the advantages and disadvantages of switching to an electronic system.

FOLLOW-UP QUESTIONS

1. What cost savings are inherent in the electronic system for both your company and its customers? In your answer, consider such costs as handling, postage, and paper.
2. What consequences would your decision to adopt an electronic system have on others with whom you do business, including manufacturers of electronic processing equipment, the U.S. Postal Service, and banks?
3. Switching to an electronic system would mean a large capital expense for new computers and software. How could analyzing the company's income statement help you justify this expense?
4. How are consumers likely to respond to paying bills electronically? Are you likely to get a different response from individuals than you get from business customers?

EXERCISING YOUR ETHICS: INDIVIDUAL EXERCISE

Give and Take with Accounting Clients

The Situation

CPAs rely on access to private information from clients for preparing financial documents. As professionals, accountants also charge fees for their services. Occasionally, however, the obligations of both parties become blurred when disputes arise, causing strained client-CPA relationships.

The Dilemma

Aaron Ault delivered original expense and income records so that his CPA, Katrina Belinski, could prepare financial statements for Ault's small business firm. Three months later, Katrina delivered the completed financial statements together with a fee for services to Ault. Aaron was surprised at what he regarded as excessive fees in the accountant's invoice and refused to make payment. Katrina, in turn, refused Ault's request for return of his original documents until such time as Ault paid for services rendered.

Unable to retrieve his documents, Ault filed a complaint with the Professional Ethics Executive Committee of the AICPA. The charge was violation of Rule 501—Acts Discreditable. Upon hearing the case, a settlement agreement was reached between the AICPA and the accountant. Its stipulations included the following: (1) a two-year suspension of the accountant from membership in the AICPA, and (2) the accountant must complete the AICPA course entitled Professional Ethics, with a passing grade of 90 or above.

QUESTIONS TO ADDRESS

1 What are the ethical issues in this situation?
2 What are the basic arguments for and against Aaron Ault's position in this situation? For and against Katrina Belinski's position?
3 What do you think of the AICPA's ruling in this situation? What would you do if you were placed in the role of ethics representative for the AICPA?

EXERCISING YOUR ETHICS: TEAM EXERCISE

Confidentially Yours

The Situation

Accountants are often entrusted with private, sensitive information that should be used confidentially. In this exercise, you're encouraged to think about ethical considerations that might arise when an accountant's career choices come up against a professional obligation to maintain confidentiality.

The Dilemma

Assume that you're the head accountant in Turbatron, a large electronics firm that makes components for other manufacturing firms. Your responsibilities include preparing Turbatron's financial statements that are then audited for financial reporting to shareholders. In addition, you regularly prepare confidential budgets for internal use by managers responsible for planning departmental activities, including future investments in new assets. You've also worked with auditors and CPA consultants who assess financial problems and suggest solutions.

Now let's suppose that you're approached by another company, Electroblast, one of the electronics industry's most successful firms, and offered a higher-level position. If you accept, your new job will include developing Electroblast's financial plans and serving on the strategic planning committee. Thus, you'd be involved not only in developing strategy but also in evaluating the competition, perhaps even using your knowledge of Turbatron's competitive strengths and weaknesses. Your contractual commitments with Turbatron do not bar you from employment with other electronics firms.

Team Activity

Assemble a group of four to five students and assign each group member to one of the following roles:
- Head accountant (leaving Turbatron)
- General manager of Turbatron
- Shareholder of Turbatron
- Customer of Turbatron
- General manager of Electroblast (if your team has five members)

ACTION STEPS

1 Before hearing any of your group's comments on this situation, and from the perspective of your assigned role, are any ethical issues confronting the head accountant in this situation? If so, write them down.
2 Return to your group and reveal ethical issues identified by each member. Were the issues the same among all roles or did differences in roles result in different issues?
3 Among the ethical issues that were identified, decide as a group which one is most important for the head accountant. Which is most important for Turbatron?
4 What does your group finally recommend be done to resolve the most important ethical issue(s)?
5 What steps do you think Turbatron might take in advance of such a situation to avoid any difficulties it now faces?

VIDEO EXERCISE   MyBizLab

POPS DINER

Learning Objectives

The purpose of this video is to help you:

1 Understand the role of accounting and distinguish between financial and managerial accounting.
2 Describe the equation underlying the balance sheet and explain each of the components.
3 Explain the purpose of the income statement and the equation it represents.

Synopsis

POPS Diner is a relatively new business with iconic roots. Built on the legendary Route 66 as it passes through Oklahoma, POPS is a retail location selling over 600 kinds of soda. However, POPS is so much more. The ultra-modern building was designed by a nationally acclaimed architect and includes a 66 foot high soda bottle made of steel and LED lights. The site includes a gas station, restaurant, shake shop, gift shop, and convenience store, each embodying a 1950s design. While POPS is certainly unique, just like other businesses, the owners and managers rely upon their accounting system to provide information for making decisions within the business and to communicate results to interested parties outside POPS.

DISCUSSION QUESTIONS

1 Who are the potential users of POPS accounting information?
2 What is financial accounting? What types of reports are parts of the financial accounting function?
3 What is managerial accounting and how does it differ from financial accounting? How will managers at POPS use this information?
4 What is the basic equation underlying the balance sheet? Describe the major components of the balance sheet for POPS Diner.
5 What does the income statement reveal to users? Explain the major sections of the income statement for POPS Diner.

Online Exploration

POPS Diner's website (http://route66.com) is as unique at its location and marketing strategy. Click on the "About POPS" link and take a look at a few of the videos to get a better sense of POPS and its iconic brand. As a privately owned company, POPS doesn't have to disclose its financial statements to the general public. After gaining a better understanding about POPS, describe how managers at POPS might use ratio analysis to evaluate their operations.

END NOTES

[1] Adam Piore, "Fraud Scene Investigator," *Portfolio*, (March 10, 2008), at http://www.portfolio.com/careers/job-of-the-week/2008/03/10/Forensic-Accountant-Al-Vondra; Kartik Goyal and Subramanian Sharma, "India Orders Fraud Office Probe Into Satyam Computer Accounts, *Bloomberg.com*, January 13, 2009, at http://www.bloomberg.com/apps/news?pid=20601091&refer=india&sid=ayhBmRJs7nh0.

[2] Adam Smith, "The Reasons Fraud Spikes in a Recession," *Time*, May 20, 2009, at http://www.time.com/time/business/article/0,8599,1899798,00.html; "Recession-Proof Career: Forensic Accounting and IT Auditing Financial Fraud Increases in Economic Recessions," *UAB Media Relations*, November 6, 2008, at http://main.uab.edu/Sites/MediaRelations/articles/54133/; Will Kenyon, "Five Tips for Combating Fraud in the Recession," *Finance Week*, March 23, 2009, at http://www.financeweek.co.uk/risk/five-tips-combating-fraud-recession; "2010 Report to the Nations on Occupational Fraud and Abuse," *Association of Certified Fraud Examiners* (ACFE, Austin, TX, 2010), accessed at http://www.acfe.com/rttn/rttn-2010.pdf.

[3] See Marshall B. Romney and Paul John Steinbart, *Accounting Information Systems*, 11th ed. (Upper Saddle River, NJ: Prentice Hall, 2009), Chapter 1.

[4] See Anthony A. Atkinson, Robert S. Kaplan, Ella Mae Matsumura, and S. Mark Young, *Management Accounting*, 5th ed. (Upper Saddle River, NJ: Prentice Hall, 2007), Chapter 1.

[5] See Walter T. Harrison and Charles T. Horngren, *Financial Accounting and Financial Tips*, 7th ed. (Upper Saddle River, NJ: Prentice Hall, 2007), Chapter 1.

[6] "Public Accounting Tips," *LifeTips.com*, accessed 9/13/2010 at http://accountingjobs.lifetips.com/cat/64430/public-accounting/index.html; "Business Glossary," *AllBusiness.com*, accessed 3/20/2011 at http://www.allbusiness.com/glossaries/review/4954577-1.html.

[7] See Alvin A. Arens, Randal J. Elder, and Mark S. Beasley, *Auditing and Assurance Services: An Integrated Approach*, 13th ed. (Upper Saddle River, NJ: Prentice Hall, 2010), Chapter 1.

[8] See Meg Pollard, Sherry T. Mills, and Walter T. Harrison, *Financial and Managerial Accounting* Ch. 1–14 (Upper Saddle River, NJ: Prentice Hall, 2008), Chapter 1.

[9] Myra A. Thomas, "It's Not About Balance—It's About Reality," *Jobs in the Money* (November 30, 2007), at http://www.jobsinthemoney.com/news.php?articleID=513.

[10] D. Larry Crumbley, Lester E. Heitger, and G. Stevenson Smith, *Forensic and Investigative Accounting*, 4th ed. (Chicago: CCH Incorporated, 2009), Chapter 1.

[11] "Executive Summary of the Sarbanes-Oxley Act of 2002 P.L. 107–204," Conference of State Bank Supervisors, at http://www.csbs.org/legislative/leg-updates/Documents/ExecSummary-SarbanesOxley-2002.pdf; "Sarbanes-Oxley Executive Summary," *Securities Law Update* (Orrick, Herrington & Sutcliffe LLP), August 2002, at http://www.orrick.com/fileupload/144.pdf.

[12] "Google Inc. (GOOG)," *Yahoo! Finance,* accessed March 3, 2011 at http://finance.yahoo.com/q/bs?s=GOOG+Balance+Sheet&annual.

[13] "Borders Files for Bankruptcy, to Close 200 Stores," *Reuters,* February 16, 2011 at http://www.reuters.com/article/2011/02/17/us-borders-idUSTRE71F2P220110217.

[14] Iain MacWhirter, "Mortgage Madness Will End in Inflation, Inflation, Inflation OPINION," *The Sunday Herald,* September 16, 2007, at http://findarticles.com/p/articles/mi_qn4156/is_20070916/ai_n20503579/.

[15] Louis R. Woodhill, "One Way to Deal With Toxic Assets," *Real Clear Markets,* January 23, 2009, at http://www.realclearmarkets.com/articles/2009/01/one_way_to_deal_with_toxic_ass.html; Patrick F. Gannon, "Demystifying Mark-To-Market," *Forbes.com,* April 21, 2009, at http://www.forbes.com/2009/04/21/mark-to-market-personal-finance-guru-insights-accounting-standards.html.

[16] Steven L. Henning, "Controlling the Real-World Risks of Mark-to-Market Valuation," *WebCPA,* June 1, 2009, at http://www.webcpa.com/ato_issues/2009_9/-50466-1.html?pg=3; John Berlau, "The Mark-to-Market Relief Rally," *OpenMarket.org,* April 2, 2009, at http://www.openmarket.org/2009/04/02/the-mark-to-market-relief-rally/.

[17] "Instant View: U.S. Eases Mark-to-Market Accounting, April 2, 2009, *Reuters,* at http://www.reuters.com/article/2009/04/02/us-financial-accounting-instantview-idUKTRE5314PX20090402; John Berlau, "The Mark-to-Market Relief Rally," *OpenMarket.org,* April 2, 2009, at http://www.openmarket.org/2009/04/02/the-mark-to-market-relief-rally/; Elizabeth Williamson and Kara Scannell, "Momentum Gathers to Ease Mark-to-Market Accounting Rule," *WSJ.com,* October 2, 2008, at http://online.wsj.com/article/SB122290736164696507.html.

[18] Rafe Needleman, "Twitter CEO: The Revenue's Coming Soon, But I Won't Tell You How," *CNet.com,* December 2, 2008 at http://news.cnet.com/8301-17939_109-10112037-2.html; Chris Snyder, "Twitter Could 'Go for Years' without Earning a Dime, Investor Says," *Epicenter: The Business of Tech,* February 13, 2009, at http://www.wired.com/epicenter/2009/02/twitter-still-l/; "JPMorgan Twitter Deal Is Said to Value Startup at $4.5 Billion," *MoneyNews.com,* March 1, 2011, at http://www.moneynews.com/FinanceNews/JPMorgan-Twitter-Deal-Value/2011/03/01/id/387853.

[19] Erick Schonfeld, "Costolo: Twitter Now Has 190 Million Users Tweeting 65 Million Times a Day," *TechCrunch,* June 8, 2010 at http://techcrunch.com/2010/06/08/twitter-190-million-users/; Kate Kaye, "Tracking 'Promoted Trends': Twitter Draws Diverse Advertisers," *ClickZ,* March 2, 2011, at http://www.clickz.com/clickz/news/2030238/tracking-promoted-trends-twitter-draws-diverse-advertisers; "What Is Twitter Worth? Twitter Is Valued at Over $4 Billion Dollars," *Wealthvest,* January 26, 2011, at http://www.wealthvest.com/blog/tag/twitter-stock-symbol/.

[20] "The Corporate Scandal Sheet," Citizen Works (August 2004), at http://www.citizenworks.org/enron/corp-scandal.php; "Largest Health Care Fraud Case in U.S. History Settled," Department of Justice (June 26, 2003), at http://www.usdoj.gov/opa/pr/2003/June/03_civ_386.htm; "Waste Management, Inc. Founder and Three Other Former Top Officers Settle SEC Fraud Action for $30.8 Million," U.S. Securities and Exchange Commission, Litigation Release No. 19351 (August 29, 2005), at http://www.sec.gov/litigation/litreleases/lr19351.htm; "Kozlowski Is Found Guilty," TheStreet.com (June 17, 2005), at http://www.thestreet.com/story/10228619/1/kozlowski-is-found-guilty.html; "SEC Charges Time Warner with Fraud...," U.S. Securities and Exchange Commission, Release 2005–38 (March 21, 2005), at http://www.sec.gov/news/press/2005-38.htm.

[21] "IASB and FASB Propose a New Joint Standard for Revenue Recognition," *Financial Accounting Standards Board,* June 24, 2010 at http://www.fasb.org/cs/ContentServer?c=FASBContent_C&pagename=FASB%2FFASBContent_C%2FNewsPage&cid=1176156953088.

[22] "IFRS Overview," *NYSSCPA.ORG,* accessed March10, 2011 at http://www.nysscpa.org/ifrs/overview.htm.

[23] "IASB and FASB Propose to Align Balance Sheet Netting Requirements Differences in IFRS and US GAAP Offsetting Requirements to be Eliminated," *FASB: Financial Accounting Standards Board,*" (news release) January 28, 2011, at http://www.fasb.org/cs/ContentServer?c=FASBContent_C&pagename=FASB/FASBContent_C/NewsPage&cid=1176158186333.

[24] John Briginshaw, "What Will the International Financial Reporting Standards (IFRS) mean to Businesses and Investors?" *Graziadio Business Review,* 2008, Volume 11 Issue 4, at http://gbr.pepperdine.edu/2010/08/what-will-the-international-financial-reporting-standards-ifrs-mean-to-businesses-and-investors/.

[25] "IASB and FASB Propose a New Joint Standard for Revenue Recognition," *Financial Accounting Standards Board,* June 24, 2010 at http://www.fasb.org/cs/ContentServer?c=FASBContent_C&pagename=FASB%2FFASBContent_C%2FNewsPage&cid=1176156953088.

[26] "IASB and FASB Propose Common Solution for Impairment Accounting," *FASB: Financial Accounting Standards Board,*" (news release) January 31, 2011, at http://www.fasb.org/cs/ContentServer?c=FASBContent_C&pagename=FASB/FASBContent_C/NewsPage&cid=1176158192211.

[27] "FASB, IASB Propose Changes in Fair Value Standards," *Insurance Networking News,* June 29, 2010, at http://www.insurancenetworking.com/news/insurance_fair_value_standards_accounting_IASB_FASB_GAAP_IFRS-25136-1.html; "Measurement Uncertainty Analysis Disclosure for Fair Value Measurements," *International Accounting Standards Board,* June 2010, at http://www.iasb.org/NR/rdonlyres/07855A41-D0A9-4197-ADF9-15A1088E466A/0/EDMeasurementUncertaintyAnalysis0610.pdf.

[28] Alexandra Defelice and Matthew G. Lamoreaux, "No IFRS Requirement Until 2015 or Later Under New SEC Timeline," *Journal of Accountancy,* February 24, 2010, at http://www.journalofaccountancy.com/Web/20102656.htm; Remi Forgeas, "IFRS Deadline Is Fast Approaching in the U.S.," *CPA2Biz,* December 20, 2010, at http://www.cpa2biz.com/Content/media/PRODUCER_CONTENT/Newsletters/Articles_2010/CPA/Dec/IFRSDeadline.jsp; "IFRS Roadmap Milestones," *IFRS USA,* accessed March 10, 2011 at http://ifrsusa.wordpress.com/ifrs-roadmap-milestones/.

[29] Katy Stech, "Fighting Fraud: Link Between Bogus Insurance Claims, Recession is Murky," *The Post and Courier*, August 9, 2010, at http://www.postandcourier.com/news/2010/aug/09/fighting-fraud/; Randy Southerland, "Recession Pressures May Boost Employee Fraud," *Atlanta Business Chronicle*, August 19, 2010, at http://www.bizjournals.com/atlanta/stories/2010/08/23/focus9.html; "Fraud to Thrive Beyond the Economic Downturn," *Lloyd's*, January 18, 2010, at http://www.lloyds.com/News-and-Insight/News-and-Features/Business-Risk/Business-2010/Fraud_to_thrive_beyond_the_economic_downturn;

[30] "2010 Report to the Nations on Occupational Fraud and Abuse: 2010 Global Fraud Study," *Association of Certified Fraud Examiners* (ACFE, Austin, TX, 2010), accessed at http://www.acfe.com/rttn/rttn-2010.pdf.

[31] "Examples of Corporate Fraud Investigations—Fiscal Year 2010," IRS.gov, at http://www.irs.gov/compliance/enforcement/article/0,,id=213768,00.html; "Examples of Corporate Fraud Investigations—Fiscal Year 2011," IRS.gov, at http://www.irs.gov/compliance/enforcement/article/0,,id=228084,00.html.

15 Money and Banking

A Tale of Two Worlds in Banking

Once upon a time, in an economic climate far, far away, banking was a steady, quiet, money-making industry regarded by some as, well, rather mundane or even boring. Nothing is further removed from the turbulent and controversial world of banking today.

Banking's external environments—especially economic, global, and political-legal—are significantly demanding and challenging, starting with the largest national banking systems, and continuing on down to the smallest community banks. Following the global economic meltdown of 2008, the U.S. Federal Reserve Bank and European Central Bank, for example, have taken ambitious steps to staunch the damage at thousands of banks in their jurisdictions. Individual banks, both large and small, are redefining the products they offer, changing sources of revenue to compete and survive, and otherwise addressing obligations to the communities they serve.

Governments are relying on banks as instruments of national policy for economic stability, using diverse responses for different conditions. We see, for example, while central banks in China and India are raising key interest rates, those in the euro zone and the U.S. are holding rates at near-historic lows, because remedies for stagnant economies differ from cures for those that are booming. Countries with severe downturns, high unemployment, and increasing national debt—the U.S., Portugal, Greece, Ireland, and Spain among

> *After reading this chapter, you should be able to:*
>
> 1 Define *money* and identify the different forms that it takes in the nation's money supply.
> 2 Describe the different kinds of financial institutions that compose the U.S. financial system and explain the services they offer.
> 3 Explain how financial institutions create money and describe the means by which they are regulated.
> 4 Discuss the functions of the Federal Reserve System and describe the tools that it uses to control the money supply.
> 5 Identify three important ways in which the money and banking system is changing.
> 6 Discuss some of the institutions and activities in international banking and finance.

others—use low interest rates and financial bail-outs to stimulate borrowing and create jobs. Meanwhile, banks in China and India are increasing lending rates to make borrowing more expensive for businesses and consumers. The goal is to slow down rapid economic expansion and reduce fears of runaway inflation. At the same time, Japan's economy—broken by a terrible earthquake and tsunami—needs lower interest rates for easier borrowing to rebuild the devastated economy.[1]

Countries with massive debt face double-trouble for recovery: The first is difficulty borrowing outside money for economic recovery, although some have received emergency financing from the International Monetary Fund. Second, when national debt increases, the value of its currency falls on foreign exchange markets, its money then buys less than before, so each of its citizens suffers lower real wealth.[2]

Our story continues on page 406.

Our story continues on page 406.

Jeffrey Blackler/Alamy

WHAT'S IN IT FOR ME?

Dealing in matters of money is vastly more complicated than counting the cash and coins in your pocket, especially when technology and globalization come into play. At its core are questions about where money comes from, how national economies depend on it, and the public's trust in its value. This chapter will give you a solid understanding of the different forms of money and how its supply is created and controlled by different kinds of financial institutions and government regulations.

MyBizLab Where you see MyBizLab in this chapter, go to **www.mybizlab.com** for additional activities on the topic being discussed.

What Is Money?

When someone asks you how much money you have, do you count the dollar bills and coins in your pockets? Do you include your checking and savings accounts? What about stocks and bonds? Do you count your car? Taken together, the value of all these combined is your personal wealth. Not all of it, however, is "money." This section considers more precisely what *money* is and does.

The Characteristics of Money

Modern money generally takes the form of stamped metal or printed paper issued by governments. Theoretically, however, just about anything *portable*, *divisible*, *durable*, and *stable* can serve as **money**. To appreciate these qualities, imagine using something that lacks them—for example, a 1,000-pound cow used as a unit of exchange in ancient agrarian economies.

- **Portability.** Try lugging 1,000 pounds of cow from shop to shop. In contrast, modern currency is light and easy to handle.

- **Divisibility.** How would you divide your cow if you wanted to buy a hat, a book, and a radio from three different stores? Is a pound of head worth as much as a pound of leg? Modern currency is easily divisible into smaller parts with fixed values—for example, a dollar for ten dimes.

- **Durability.** Your cow will lose value every day (and eventually die). Modern currency, however, neither dies nor spoils, and if it wears out, it can be replaced. It is also hard to counterfeit—certainly harder than cattle breeding.

- **Stability.** If cows were in short supply, you might be able to make quite a deal for yourself. In the middle of an abundant cow year, however, the market would be flooded with cows, so their value would fall. The value of our paper money also fluctuates, but it is considerably more stable and predictable.

The Functions of Money

Imagine a successful cow rancher who needs a new fence. In a *barter economy*—one in which goods are exchanged directly for one another—he or she would have to find someone who is willing to exchange a fence for a cow (or parts of it). If no fence maker wants a cow, the rancher must find someone else—for example, a wagon maker—who does want a cow. Then, the rancher must hope that the fence maker will

© Thinkstock Images/Getty Images

Cattle are not portable, divisible, durable, or stable, making them an unsuitable medium of exchange in the modern monetized economy.

trade for a new wagon. In a money economy, the rancher would sell his or her cow, receive money, and exchange the money for such goods as a new fence.

Money serves three functions:

1 **It is a medium of exchange.** Like the rancher "trading" money for a new fence, money is used to buy and sell things. Without money, we would be bogged down in a system of barter.

2 **It is a store of value.** Pity the rancher whose cow gets sick on Monday and who wants to buy some clothes on the following Saturday, by which time the cow may have died and lost its value. In the form of currency, however, money can be used for future purchases and "stores" value.

3 **It is a measure of worth.** Money lets us measure the relative values of goods and services. It acts as a measure of worth because all products can be valued and accounted for in terms of money. For example, the concepts of $1,000 worth of clothes or $500 in labor costs have universal meaning.

Ton Koene/Picture Contact BV/Alamy

Instead of using a modern monetary system, traders like Muhammed Essa in Quetta, Pakistan, transfer funds through handshakes and code words. The ancient system is called *hawala*, which means "trust" in Arabic. The worldwide *hawala* system, though illegal in most countries, moves billions of dollars past regulators annually and is alleged to be the system of choice for terrorists because it leaves no paper trail. [3]

M-1: The Spendable Money Supply

For money to serve its basic functions, both buyers and sellers must agree on its value, which depends in part on its *supply*—how much money is in circulation. When the money supply is high, the value of money drops. When it is low, that value increases.

Unfortunately, there is no single agreed-upon measure of the supply of money. The oldest and most basic measure, **M-1,** counts only the most liquid, or spendable, forms of money—cash, checks, and checking accounts.

- Paper money and metal coins are **currency (cash)** issued by the government and widely used for small exchanges. Law requires creditors to accept it in payment of debts.

- A **check** is essentially an order instructing a bank to pay a given sum to a payee. Checks are usually, but not always, accepted because they are valuable only to specified payees and can be exchanged for cash.

- **Checking accounts,** or **demand deposits,** are money because their funds may be withdrawn at any time on demand.

These are all noninterest-bearing or low–interest-bearing forms of money. As of January 2011, M-1 in the United States totaled $1.85 trillion. [4]

Money object that is portable, divisible, durable, and stable, and that serves as a medium of exchange, a store of value, and a measure of worth

M-1 measure of the money supply that includes only the most liquid (spendable) forms of money

Currency (Cash) government-issued paper money and metal coins

Check demand deposit order instructing a bank to pay a given sum to a specified payee

Checking Account (Demand Deposit) bank account funds, owned by the depositor, that may be withdrawn at any time by check or cash

M-2: M-1 Plus the Convertible Money Supply

M-2, a second measure of the money supply, is often used for economic planning by businesses and government agencies. **M-2** includes everything in M-1 plus other forms of money that are not quite as liquid—short-term investments that are easily converted to spendable forms—including *time deposits, money market mutual funds,* and *savings accounts.* Totaling $8.84 trillion in January 2011, M-2 accounts for most of the nation's money supply.[5] It measures the store of monetary value available for financial transactions by individuals and small businesses. As this overall level increases, more money is available for consumer purchases and business investments. When the supply is tightened, less money is available; financial transactions, spending, and business activity slow down.

Unlike demand deposits, **time deposits,** such as certificates of deposit (CDs), have a fixed term, are intended to be held to maturity, cannot be transferred by check, and pay higher interest rates than checking accounts. Time deposits in M-2 include only accounts of less than $100,000 that can be redeemed on demand, with penalties for early withdrawal.

With **money market mutual funds,** investment companies buy a collection of short-term, low-risk financial securities. Ownership of and profits (or losses) from the sale of these securities are shared among the fund's investors.

Figure 15.1 shows how M-1 and M-2 have grown since 1979. For many years, M-1 was the traditional measure of liquid money. Because it was closely related to gross domestic product, it served as a reliable predictor of the nation's real money supply. This situation changed in the early 1980s, with the introduction of new types of investments and the easier transfer of money among investment funds to gain higher interest returns. As a result, M-2 today is regarded as a more reliable measure than M-1.

Credit Cards and Debit Cards: Plastic Money?

The use of credit and debit cards has become so widespread that many people refer to them as "plastic money." Credit cards, however, are not money and, accordingly, are not included in M-1 or M-2 when measuring the nation's money supply. Why? Because spending with a credit card creates a debt, but does not move money until later when the debt is paid by cash or check. Debit card transactions, in contrast, transfer money immediately from the consumer's bank account, so they affect the money supply the same way as spending with a check or cash, and are included in M-1.[6]

While consumers enjoy the convenience of credit cards, they also are finding that irresponsible use of the cards can be hazardous to your financial health. A discussion on managing the use of credit cards is presented in Appendix III: Managing Your Personal Finances.

2 *Describe the different kinds of financial institutions that compose the U.S. financial system and explain the services they offer.*

The U.S. Financial System

Many forms of money depend on the existence of financial institutions that provide money-related services to both individuals and businesses. Just how important are these financial institutions, how do they work, and what are some of the services that they offer? The sections that follow explain their role as creators of money and discuss the regulation of the U.S. banking system.

Financial Institutions

The main function of financial institutions is to ease the flow of money from users with surpluses to those with deficits by attracting funds into checking and savings accounts. Incoming funds will be loaned to individuals and businesses and perhaps invested in government securities. U.S. consumers have access to more than 90,000 U.S. branches and offices of *commercial banks, savings institutions, credit unions,* and various *nondeposit institutions.*

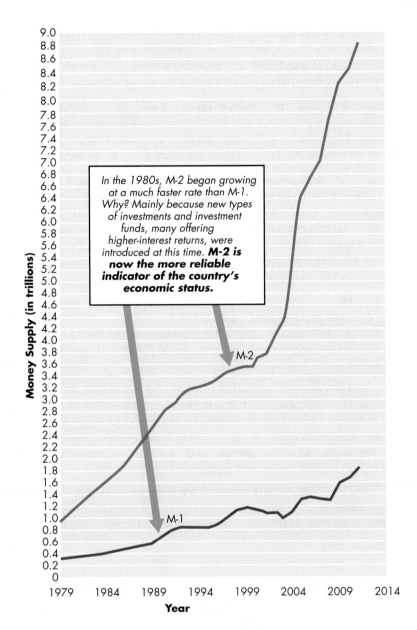

Figure 15.1 **Money Supply Growth**
Source: "Money stock measures," Federal Reserve, at **http//www.federalreserve.gov/releases/h6/**, accessed 4/16/2011.

In the 1980s, M-2 began growing at a much faster rate than M-1. Why? Mainly because new types of investments and investment funds, many offering higher-interest returns, were introduced at this time. **M-2 is now the more reliable indicator of the country's economic status.**

Commercial Banks Federally insured **commercial banks** accept deposits, make loans, earn profits, and pay interest and dividends. Some 6,400 commercial banks range from the very largest institutions in New York, such as Citigroup, Bank of America, and JPMorgan Chase, to tiny banks dotting the rural landscape. Bank liabilities—holdings owed to others—include checking accounts and savings accounts. U.S. banks hold assets totaling more than $12 trillion, consisting of a wide variety of loans to individuals, businesses, and governments.[7]

Savings Institutions Savings institutions include mutual savings banks and savings and loan associations. They are also called *thrift institutions* because they were established decades ago to promote the idea of savings among the general population.

M-2 measure of the money supply that includes all the components of M-1 plus the forms of money that can be easily converted into spendable forms

Time Deposit bank funds that have a fixed term of time to maturity and cannot be withdrawn earlier or transferred by check

Money Market Mutual Fund fund of short-term, low-risk financial securities purchased with the pooled assets of investor-owners

Commercial Bank company that accepts deposits that it uses to make loans, earn profits, pay interest to depositors, and pay dividends to owners

Savings and Loan Associations   Like commercial banks, **savings and loan associations (S&Ls)** accept deposits, make loans, and are owned by investors. Most S&Ls were created to encourage savings habits and provide financing for homes; they did not offer check services. Today they have ventured into a variety of other loans and services.

Mutual Savings Banks   In a **mutual savings bank,** all depositors are considered owners of the bank. All profits are divided proportionately among depositors, who receive dividends. More than 700 U.S. mutual savings banks attract most of their funds in the form of savings deposits, and funds are loaned out in the form of mortgages.

Credit Unions   A **credit union** is a nonprofit, cooperative financial institution owned and run by its members. Its purpose is to promote *thrift*—careful management of one's money or resources—and to provide members with a safe place to save and borrow at reasonable rates. Members pool their funds to make loans to one another. Each credit union decides whom it will serve, such as a group of employees, people in a particular community, or members of an association. Many universities, for example, have credit unions, as does the U.S. Navy, among the nation's nearly 8,000 credit unions.

Nondeposit Institutions   A variety of other organizations take in money, provide interest or other services, and make loans. Unlike commercial banks, these *nondeposit institutions* use inflowing funds for purposes other than earning interest for depositors. Four of the most important are *pension funds, insurance companies, finance companies,* and *securities investment dealers.*

1 A **pension fund** is a pool of funds that is managed to provide retirement income for its members. *Public pension funds* in the U.S. include Social Security and the nearly $3 trillion in retirement programs for state and local government employees. *Private pension funds*, operated by employers, unions, and other private groups, cover about 43 million people and have total assets of $13 trillion, down from $15 trillion before the recent recession.[8]

2 **Insurance companies** accumulate money from premiums charged for coverage. They invest these funds in stocks, real estate, and other assets. Earnings pay for insured losses, such as death benefits, automobile damage, and healthcare expenses.

The Prime Rate Every bank receives a major portion of its income from interest paid on loans by borrowers. As long as terms and conditions are clearly revealed to borrowers, banks may set their own interest rates, within limits set by each state. Traditionally, banks only offered the lowest rate, or **prime rate**, to their most creditworthy commercial customers. Most commercial loans are set at markups over prime, like prime + 1, which means 1 percent over the prime rate. To remain competitive with lower-interest foreign banks, U.S. banks offer some commercial loans at rates below prime. Figure 15.2 shows the changes in the prime rate since 2000. Lower rates in 2008–2011 encouraged banks to continue lending in the economic downturn.

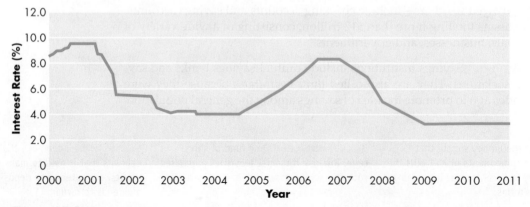

Figure 15.2 **The Prime Rate**
Source: http://www.federalreserve.gov/releases/h15/data/annual/h15_prime_na.txt.

3 **Finance companies** specialize in making loans to businesses and consumers. HFC Beneficial, for example, offers mortgage refinancing and personal loans. Commercial finance companies lend to businesses needing capital or long-term funds. Consumer finance companies devote most of their resources to providing small noncommercial loans to individuals.

4 **Securities investment dealers (brokers)**, such as Merrill Lynch and A. G. Edwards Inc., buy and sell stocks and bonds for client investors. They also invest in securities—they buy stocks and bonds for their own accounts in hopes of reselling them later at a profit. These companies hold large sums of money for transfer between buyers and sellers. (We discuss the activities of brokers and investment banking more fully in Chapter 16.)

The Growth of Financial Services

The finance business today is highly competitive. No longer is it enough for commercial banks to accept deposits and make loans. Most, for example, also offer bank-issued credit and debit cards, safe-deposit boxes, ATMs, electronic money transfer, and foreign currency exchange. In addition, many offer pension, trust, international, and brokerage services and financial advice.

Pension and Trust Services   **Individual retirement accounts (IRAs)** are tax-deferred pension funds that wage earners and their spouses can set up to supplement other retirement funds. Advantages and drawbacks to various kinds of IRAs—*traditional, Roth, and education*—are discussed in Appendix III.

Many commercial banks offer **trust services**—the management of funds left in the bank's trust. In return for a fee, the trust department will perform such tasks as making your monthly bill payments and managing your investment portfolio. Trust departments also manage the estates of deceased persons.

International Services   Suppose a U.S. company wants to buy a product from a Chinese supplier. For a fee, it can use one or more of three services offered by its bank:

1 Currency Exchange: It can exchange U.S. dollars for Chinese yuan to pay the supplier.

2 Letters of Credit: It can pay its bank to issue a **letter of credit**—a promise by the bank to pay the Chinese firm a certain amount if specified conditions are met.

3 Banker's Acceptances: It can pay its bank to draw up a **banker's acceptance**, which promises that the bank will pay some specified amount at a future date.

A banker's acceptance requires payment by a particular date. Letters of credit are payable only after certain conditions are met. The Chinese supplier, for example, may not be paid until shipping documents prove that the merchandise has been shipped from China.

Savings and Loan Association (S&L) financial institution accepting deposits and making loans primarily for home mortgages

Mutual Savings Bank financial institution whose depositors are owners sharing in its profits

Credit Union nonprofit, cooperative financial institution owned and run by its members, usually employees of a particular organization

Pension Fund nondeposit pool of funds managed to provide retirement income for its members

Insurance Company nondeposit institution that invests funds collected as premiums charged for insurance coverage

Prime Rate interest rate available to a bank's most creditworthy customers

Finance Company nondeposit institution that specializes in making loans to businesses and consumers

Securities Investment Dealer (Broker) financial institution that buys and sells stocks and bonds both for investors and for its own accounts

Individual Retirement Account (IRA) tax-deferred pension fund that wage earners set up to supplement retirement funds

Trust Services management by a bank of an estate, investments, or other assets on behalf of an individual

Letter of Credit bank promise, issued for a buyer, to pay a designated firm a certain amount of money if specified conditions are met

Banker's Acceptance bank promise, issued for a buyer, to pay a designated firm a specified amount at a future date

MANAGING IN TURBULENT TIMES

Getting Serious with Credit Standards

While banks try to avoid drowning in bad loans, borrowers and lenders alike are questioning how the banks got into the current financial mess. Many observers blame subprime mortgage lending. Unlike prime mortgages, subprime loans are made to high-risk borrowers—those with bad credit histories, excessive debt, inadequate income, or other indicators that they will not repay the lender. In return for riskier loans, borrowers pay higher interest rates. As the housing market tumbled, delinquencies skyrocketed on millions of subprime loans. Whereas about 6 percent of mortgage loans were uncollectable from 2000 to 2005, thereafter delinquencies increased, nearing 30 percent by 2008, and on into 2010. Lenders extended too much credit to weak borrowers.[9]

Reports indicate that the subprime crisis can be traced to overly relaxed credit standards. One study found that many loan applications listed fraudulent information. Some borrowers, taking advantage of lax lending practices to live beyond their means, lied about their income and assets in order to secure loans. Other misinformation can be attributed to mortgage brokers eager to get otherwise unqualified borrowers approved for loans. Some lenders went so far as to have a relative pose as a borrower's fake employer and falsify W-2 forms to gain approval. These problems were compounded further by those within the banking and finance system who knew that rampant fraud was occurring but looked the other way, as long as profits kept rolling in.[10]

Now stuck with uncollectable loans, unsellable foreclosed properties, and big financial losses, the industry is tightening

DNY59/iStockphoto.com

credit standards and lending practices. Federal bank examiners, for example, are insisting that loan officers use greater caution and judgment to identify credit-worthy borrowers and avoid weak loans. Lenders are switching to independent real estate appraisers who have no direct contact with loan officers, to get accurate rather than inflated property appraisals. Along with requiring bigger down payments, lenders are requiring higher minimum credit scores. Lenders are also reducing limits on credit card balances. With a dire lesson learned, it appears that tighter standards are here for the foreseeable future.[11]

MyBizLab

Financial Advice and Brokerage Services   Many banks, both large and small, help their customers manage their money. Depending on the customer's situation, the bank, in its role as financial advisor, may recommend different investment opportunities. The recommended mix might include CDs, mutual funds, stocks, and bonds. Many banks also serve as securities intermediaries, using their own stockbrokers to buy and sell securities and their own facilities to hold them.

Electronic Funds Transfer   **Electronic funds transfer (EFT)** provides for payments and collections by transferring financial information electronically. Consumers using debit cards instead of writing personal checks enjoy EFT's convenience and speed at the checkout. In addition, EFT systems provide automatic payroll deposit, ATM transactions, bill payment, and automatic funds transfer. Such systems can help a businessperson close an important business deal by transferring money from San Francisco to Miami within a few seconds. The U.S. Treasury reports that it costs $1.03 to issue a check payment, but only $0.105 to issue an EFT payment. The U.S. Social Security system expects savings of over $1 billion during the next decade by phasing out paper check payments by 2013, and instead using paperless payments for federal benefits.[12]

Automated Teller Machines   **Automated teller machines (ATMs)** allow customers to withdraw money, make deposits, transfer funds between accounts, and access information on their accounts. About 420,000 machines are located in U.S. bank buildings and other locations.[13] Increasingly, ATMs have become multilingual global fixtures. As Figure 15.3 shows, among the world's more than 2 million ATMs, most are located outside the United States, and many U.S. banks offer international ATM services. China is expected to become the world's largest ATM market by 2015.

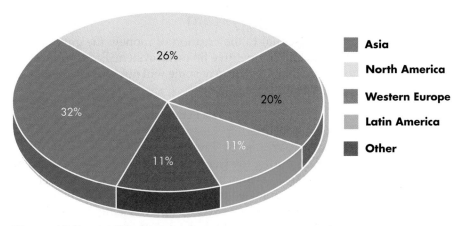

Figure 15.3 Global Dispersion of ATMs

Financial Institutions Create Money and Are Regulated

3 Explain how financial institutions create money and describe the means by which they are regulated.

Financial institutions provide a special service to the economy: They create money. They don't print bills and mint coins, but by taking in deposits and making loans, they expand the money supply.

As Figure 15.4 shows, the money supply expands because banks are allowed to loan out most (although not all) of the money they take in from deposits. If you deposit $100 in your bank and banks are allowed to loan out 90 percent of all their deposits, then your bank will hold $10 in reserve and loan $90 of your money to borrowers. (You still have $100 on deposit.) Meanwhile, a borrower—or the people paid by the borrower—will deposit the $90 loan money in a bank (or banks). The bank will then have another $81 (90 percent of $90) available for new loans. The banks, therefore, have turned your original $100 into $271 ($100 + $90 + $81). The chain continues, with borrowings from one bank becoming deposits in the next.

Deposit	Money Held in Reserve by Bank	Money to Lend	Total Supply
$100.00	$10.00	$90.00	**$190.00**
90.00	9.00	81.00	**271.00**
81.00	8.10	72.90	**343.90**
72.90	7.29	65.61	**409.51**
65.61	6.56	59.05	**468.56**

Figure 15.4 How Banks Create Money

Electronic Funds Transfer (EFT) communication of fund-transfer information over wire, cable, or microwave

Automated Teller Machine (ATM) electronic machine that allows bank customers to conduct account-related activities 24 hours a day, 7 days a week

Regulation of the Banking System

Because commercial banks are essential to the creation of money, the government regulates them to ensure a sound and competitive financial system. Federal and state agencies regulate banks to ensure that the failure of some will not cause the public to lose faith in the banking system itself.

Federal Deposit Insurance Corporation   The **Federal Deposit Insurance Corporation (FDIC)** supervises banks and insures deposits in banks and thrift institutions. The FDIC is a government agency, created by President Franklin D. Roosevelt to restore public confidence in banks during the Depression era. More than 99 percent of the nation's commercial banks and savings institutions pay fees for membership in the FDIC. In return, the FDIC guarantees the safety of all accounts—checking, savings, and certificates of deposit (CDs)—of every account owner up to the current maximum of $250,000. If a bank collapses, the FDIC promises to pay each depositor for losses up to $250,000 per account. A person with more money can establish accounts in more than one bank to protect sums in excess of $250,000. (A handful of the nation's 6,400 commercial banks are insured by states rather than by the FDIC.) To ensure against multiple bank failures, the FDIC maintains the right to examine the activities and accounts of all member banks.

Devout Muslims can't pay or receive interest—a fact that tends to complicate banking operations. Because money has to work in order to earn a return, institutions like the Shamil Bank in Bahrain invest deposits directly in such ventures as real estate and pay back profit shares rather than interest.

The Role of the FDIC in Bank Failures What happens with banks that fail, such as the nearly 300 U.S. banks that failed in slow-down years 2009–2010? The FDIC becomes responsible for disposing of failed banks. One option is to sell them to other banks that are then responsible for the liabilities of the failed banks. Alternatively, the FDIC can seize the assets of the failed banks and undertake two activities: (1) Pay insurance to depositors and (2) dispose of the banks' assets and settle their debts, all at the lowest cost to the FDIC's insurance deposit fund. The resulting net gain (or loss) is put into (or paid from) the insurance deposit fund. As the recession of 2007–2009 deepened, this fund had dwindled to $13 billion in 2009, down from $45 billion in 2008, before recovering to $18 billion in 2010. With more bank closures expected, the FDIC was raising assessments against member banks to restore the fund's reserves.[14]

4 Discuss the functions of the Federal Reserve System and describe the tools that it uses to control the money supply.

The Federal Reserve System

Perched atop the U.S. financial system and regulating many aspects of its operation is the **Federal Reserve System (the Fed),** the nation's central bank, established by Congress in 1913. This section describes the structure of the Fed, its functions, and the tools it uses to control the nation's money supply.

The Structure of the Fed

The Fed consists of a board of governors, a group of reserve banks, and member banks. As originally established by the Federal Reserve Act of 1913, the system consisted of 12 relatively autonomous banks and a seven-member committee whose powers were limited to coordinating the activities of those banks. By the 1930s, however, both the structure and function of the Fed had changed dramatically.

The Board of Governors   The Fed's board of governors consists of seven members appointed by the U.S. President for overlapping terms of 14 years. The chair of the board serves on major economic advisory committees and works actively with the administration to formulate economic policy. The board plays a large role in controlling the money supply. It alone determines the reserve requirements, within statutory limits, for depository institutions. It also works with other members of the Fed to set discount rates and handle the Fed's sale and purchase of government securities.

Reserve Banks   The Fed consists of 12 districts, as shown in Figure 15.5. Each Federal Reserve Bank holds reserve deposits from and sets the discount rate for commercial banks in its geographic region. Reserve Banks also play a major role in the nation's check-clearing process.

Open Market Committee   The Federal Open Market Committee is responsible for formulating the Fed's monetary policies to promote economic stability and growth by managing the nation's money supply. Its members include the Board of Governors, the president of the Federal Reserve Bank of New York, and the presidents of four other Reserve Banks, who serve on a rotating basis.

Member Banks   All nationally chartered commercial banks and some state-chartered banks are members of the Fed. The accounts of all member bank depositors are automatically covered by the FDIC.

Other Depository Institutions   Although many state-chartered banks, credit unions, and S&Ls do not belong to the Fed, they are subject to its regulations, pay deposit insurance premiums, and are covered by the FDIC or the National Credit Union Administration (NCUA).

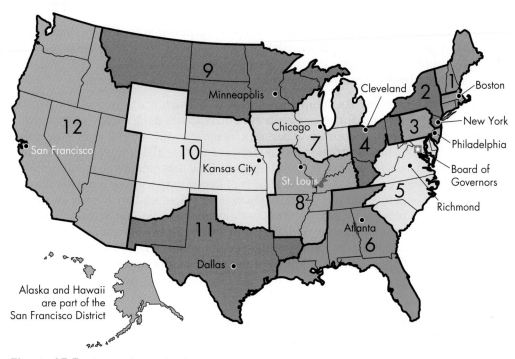

Figure 15.5 **The Twelve Federal Reserve Districts**
Source: http://www.federalreserve.gov/otherfrb.htm

Federal Deposit Insurance Corporation (FDIC) federal agency that guarantees the safety of deposits up to $250,000 in the financial institutions that it insures

Federal Reserve System (The Fed) central bank of the United States, which acts as the government's bank, serves member commercial banks, and controls the nation's money supply

The Functions of the Fed

In addition to chartering national banks, the Fed serves as the federal government's bank and the "bankers' bank," regulating a number of banking activities. Most importantly, it controls the money supply.

The Government's Bank   The Fed produces the nation's paper currency and decides how many bills to produce and destroy. It also lends money to the government by buying bonds issued by the Treasury Department to help finance the national deficit.

The Bankers' Bank   Individual banks that need money can borrow from the Fed and pay interest on the loans. In addition, the Fed provides storage for commercial banks, which are required to keep funds on reserve at a Federal Reserve Bank.

Creatas/jupiterimages

Check Clearing The Fed also clears checks for commercial banks to ensure that cash is deducted from the check writer's bank account and deposited into the check receiver's account. With electronic payments, however, the number of paper checks processed is falling, with 9.5 billion cleared by the Fed in 2008, down from a peak of 60 billion in 2000. Consumers prefer the convenience of debit and credit cards and electronic transactions such as direct deposits and online payments. Even with paper checks, however, the clearing is faster because banks now send the Fed some 60 million electronic images daily to be processed (instead of shipping the checks). As a result, the Fed now has just one full-service check-processing site, instead of the 45 locations needed as recently as 2003.[15]

Controlling the Money Supply   The Fed is responsible for the conduct of U.S. **monetary policy**—the management of the nation's economic growth by managing the money supply and interest rates. By controlling these two factors, the Fed influences the ability and willingness of banks throughout the country to loan money.

Inflation Management As defined in Chapter 1, *inflation* is a period of widespread price increases throughout an economic system. It occurs if the money supply grows too large. Demand for goods and services increases, and the prices of everything rise. To reduce China's inflationary conditions in 2010–2011, for example, banking officials decreased the money supply, hoping to slow that nation's economic growth. In contrast, *deflation* occurs when the supply of goods outpaces the supply of money, so demand for goods and services falls. Decreasing prices lead businesses to cut output, and unemployment rises. The Fed, with its goal of economic stability, uses the money supply to avoid extreme inflation or deflation. Because commercial banks are the main creators of money, much of the Fed's management of the money supply takes the form of regulating the supply of money through commercial banks.

The Tools of the Fed

According to the Fed's original charter, its primary duties were to supervise banking and to manage the nation's currency. The duties of the Fed have evolved to include an emphasis on the broad economic goals as discussed in Chapter 1, especially growth and stability. The Fed's role in controlling the nation's money supply stems from its role in setting policies to help reach these goals. To control the money supply, the Fed uses *reserve requirements*, *interest rate controls*, and *open-market operations*.

Reserve Requirements   The **reserve requirement** is the percentage of its deposits that a bank must hold, in cash or on deposit, with a Federal Reserve Bank. High requirements mean that banks have less money to lend and the money supply is reduced. Conversely, low requirements permit the supply to expand. Because the Fed sets requirements for all depository institutions, it can adjust them to make changes to the overall supply of money in the economy.

Interest Rate Controls   As the bankers' bank, the Fed loans money to banks. The interest rate on these loans is known as the **discount rate.** If the Fed wants to reduce the money supply, it increases the discount rate, making it more expensive for banks to borrow money and less attractive for them to loan it. Conversely, low rates encourage borrowing and lending and expand the money supply.

More familiar to consumers, the **federal funds rate** (or **key rate**) reflects the rate at which commercial banks lend reserves to each other, usually overnight. While the Fed can't actually control this rate, which is determined by the supply and demand of bank reserves, it can control the supply of those reserves to create the desired rate. By instructing its bond traders to buy fewer government bonds, the supply of reserves was decreased, resulting in a series of key rate increases—from a then-historic low of 1 percent in 2004 up to 5.25 percent in 2006—to slow a booming U.S. economy. The Fed then reversed its policy as the economy lost momentum, cutting the target rate gradually down to a then-record low, 0.25 percent in 2008 to boost the economy during the recession, and then to 0.00–0.25 percent to encourage the 2011 recovery.[16]

Open-Market Operations   **Open-market operations** refer to the Fed's sale and purchase of securities (usually U.S. Treasury notes and short-term bonds) in the open market, as directed by the Fed's Open-Market Committee. Open-market operations are particularly effective because they act quickly and predictably on the money supply. The Fed buys securities from a commercial dealer, whose bank account is credited for the transaction, thus giving that bank more money to lend, so this transaction expands the money supply.

The opposite happens when the Fed sells securities. Selling treasury securities to investors allows the U.S. government to raise money and contract the money supply. These securities may include Treasury bills (T-bills), T-notes, and T-bonds with maturity dates ranging from short-term (a few weeks) to long-term (up to 30 years). Treasury securities are highly liquid because they are actively traded on national securities markets, and traditionally have been considered a risk-free investment because they are backed by the U.S. government.

Fed Uses Massive Bond Purchases to Stem Recession   In 2009, the Fed launched its most aggressive buying of long-term Treasury bonds in history—$300 billion—to fight the recession. The purchases were intended to push up market prices for Treasuries and thereby drive down interest rates. As long-term Treasury rates fell, other interest rates soon followed, including rates for home mortgages, business loans, and consumer loans. Overall lower interest rates were expected to encourage more widespread borrowing and lending to get the economy moving. However, continuing weakness led to the Fed's 2010–2011 ground-breaking move in launching a further $600 billion purchase of Treasury debt. While some claim the move is essential for economic recovery, critics fear it may stimulate destructive spiraling inflation[17]

The Changing Money and Banking System

5 Identify three important ways in which the money and banking system is changing.

The U.S. money and banking systems continue to change today. Government emergency intervention aims to stabilize a troubled financial system. Enforcement of anti-terrorism regulations deters criminal misuse of the financial system. And with

Monetary Policy management of the nation's economic growth by managing the money supply and interest rates

Reserve Requirement percentage of its deposits that a bank must hold in cash or on deposit with the Fed

Discount Rate interest rate at which member banks can borrow money from the Fed

Federal Funds Rate (Key Rate) interest rate at which commercial banks lend reserves to each other, usually overnight

Open-Market Operations the Fed's sale and purchase of securities in the open market

the expansion of banking services, electronic technologies affect how you obtain money and how much interest you pay for it.

Government Intervention for Stabilizing the U.S. Financial System

The financial world was shaken with the 2008 collapse of Lehman Brothers, the leading U.S. investment bank. Lehman's bankruptcy was soon followed by the threat of another giant's demise, as Bear Stearns teetered and then was bought by JPMorgan Chase. But JPMorgan Chase's purchase of Bear Stearns became possible only when the Federal Reserve stepped forward with $26 billion to guarantee potential losses on Bear Stearns's assets. With a goal of stabilizing the fractured financial system, the government continues its unprecedented infusion of funding for U.S. financial institutions.

Government Emergency Investment   By mid-2009, the Fed's investments reached nearly $300 billion, mostly in lending programs to commercial banks. Banks used the loans to get rid of bad mortgages and other hard-to-sell assets, thereby gaining cash for lending to bank customers. Another source of funds, the Troubled Asset Relief Program (TARP), a temporary program under the U.S. Treasury, was included in the government's bailout efforts. TARP support included $15 billion to auto-financing companies at risk of failure and $235 billion in direct investments to some 600 banks to encourage lending. Other government sources provided over $130 billion to rescue Freddie Mac and Fannie Mae, two government-sponsored enterprises on the verge of financial failure. Freddie Mac and Fannie Mae (also known as FM2) buy home mortgages from the original lenders—for example, from banks—and hold them or resell them. In 2008, FM2 held 80 percent of U.S. home mortgages, many of which turned bad in the collapsed housing market, and many more that continue to default today. As a result, critics are questioning whether the government should be involved in the mortgage loan business.[18]

Assurances of Repayment   In return for its investments, the government imposes various kinds of assurances. The Fed's loans to banks, for example, are secured by the banks' assets. That is, the Fed holds some of the banks' assets, such as commercial loans, residential mortgages, and asset-backed securities as collateral until the banks repay the Fed. In return for TARP funds, the U.S. Treasury holds preferred stock (dividend-paying ownership shares) of the banks. The Treasury also holds *warrants*—which give the right to buy shares of the banks' stock in the future at a preset price. In addition to creating the government's precedent-setting part ownership, TARP also imposes stricter executive compensation requirements. In the bailout of Freddie Mac and Fannie Mae, both firms were taken over by the Federal Housing Finance Agency (FHFA) because the failure of either would severely damage global financial markets along with the U.S. economy. FHFA took full control over the two firms' assets and operations.[19]

Anti-Crime and Anti-Terrorism Regulations

Enforcement of anti-terrorism regulations deters criminal misuse of the financial system. Under provisions of the *Bank Secrecy Act (BSA)*, the U.S. Department of the Treasury imposed a $24 million fine on the New York branch of a Jordan-based Arab Bank for failing to implement required monitoring and record-keeping methods to deter funding of crimes. The enforcement of BSA regulations includes tracking and reporting on suspicious transactions, such as a sudden increase in wire transfers or cash transactions exceeding $10,000, to cut off funding of criminal and terrorist activities.[20]

Banks are subject to prosecution when they fail to maintain systems for identifying and reporting suspicious activities that indicate possible drug transactions and money laundering. In violation of the BSA, a Miami, Florida, bank agreed to pay a $55 million penalty to the U.S. government following charges that it did not operate an effective anti-money laundering program. A Puerto Rico bank was assessed a $21 million penalty for not filing suspicious activity reports when repeated cash deposits were made into one account, often in paper bags in small denominations, totaling $20 million. A California bank was cited for not maintaining an effective anti-money laundering program when proceeds from cocaine sales were transferred from Mexico for deposit into accounts at the bank.[21]

The *USA PATRIOT Act*, passed in 2001 and designed to reduce terrorism risks, requires banks to better know the customer's true identity by obtaining and verifying their name, address, date of birth, and Social Security (or tax identification) number. They must also implement a *customer identification program (CIP)* to verify identities, keep records of customer activities, and compare identities of new customers with government terrorist lists. Enforcement resides with examiners from the Department of the Treasury.

The Impact of Electronic Technologies

Banks are among the most enthusiastic adopters of technology to improve efficiency and customer service. In addition to EFT systems and mobile devices, banks offer access via telephone, TV, and Internet banking, which allow customers to make around-the-clock transactions. Each business day, trillions of dollars exist in and among banks and other financial institutions in purely electronic form. Each day, the Fed's Fedwire funds transfer system—the world's largest electronic payments system—processes about $4 trillion in transactions for some 8,900 financial institutions.

Automated Clearing House (ACH) Network   ACH is an electronic funds transfer system that provides interbank clearing of electronic payments for the nation's financial institutions. The ACH network allows businesses, government, and consumers to choose an electronic-over-paper alternative for payments (instead of written checks); the system is green, safe, and efficient.

ACH payments include:

- Internet-initiated debit and credit payments by businesses and consumers

- B2B electronic payments

- Direct deposit of payroll, Social Security benefits, and tax refunds

- Federal, state, and local tax payments

- E-checks

- Direct payment of consumer bills: mortgages, loans, utility bills, and insurance premiums

- E-commerce payments

In 2009, the ACH system processed some 19 billion payments that were initiated or received by customers at 15,000 U.S. businesses and financial institutions. Those payments totaled more than $30 trillion. With the federal government's use of ACH, each direct deposit that replaces a check saves $0.925. With more than 1 billion direct deposits for 2009, the federal savings was more than $1 trillion.

The ACH system is governed by NACHA—The Electronic Payments Association—which administers and enforces the association's strict *NACHA Operating Rules* for sound risk management practices. Although NACHA was formed within the American Bankers Association, it later became an independent not-for-profit association that launched the Accredited ACH Professional program and established the system's operating rules.[22]

Check 21: Making the Paper Check Go Away   The *Check Clearing for the 21st Century Act (Check 21)*, which became federal law in 2004, allows a receiving bank to make an electronic image of a paper check and electronically send the image to the paying bank for instant payment instead of waiting days for the paper check to wind its way back to the sender. More banks are adopting check image processing (Check 21) and benefitting from its speed and cost efficiency: less paper handling, reduced reliance on physical transportation, faster collection times, and elimination of expensive float. Today, almost 99 percent of the items processed by the Fed are images instead of in paper form. The days of writing a check, mailing it, and having several days to put money in the account to cover it are numbered, due to faster check clearing.[23]

ENTREPRENEURSHIP AND NEW VENTURES

Cultivating a Social Side for Community Banking

While the U.S. banking system struggles in a distressed economy, smaller community banks are confronted with vigorous challenges from larger banks that stretch across state lines, competing for local consumers and commercial customers. State-chartered Fidelity Bank, serving Central Massachusetts, is an example. With headquarters in Leominster (population 41,000) and full-service facilities in five nearby towns, Fidelity's primary competitive advantage is its commitment to long-term community relationships developed since being established in 1888.

Unlike many smaller banks across the nation, Fidelity experienced a relatively successful year, remaining financially sound through the challenging 2009 economic environment. Consumer and business deposit accounts increased, a record number of first mortgage loans were issued, many borrowers refinanced their homes at lower interest rates to reduce monthly payments, and the bank's commercial lending operation gained recognition by the Small Business Administration for offering new business loan products, with faster and more effective approval processes. By streamlining its services, customers can use mobile banking—"like carrying a branch bank in your pocket"—for "anywhere/anytime" access to their accounts, and text-messaging provides quick information on account balances.[24]

Fidelity's newest initiative, launched in 2011, is a social media program for strengthening customer and community relationships. It aims for broader exposure of the bank's brand through a visible and widespread presence in the social media. The focal resource is a publicly accessible blog, available at Fidelity's website, designed to encourage communications among customers, bank employees, and the local communities-at-large. Its content is then broadcast outward in digital space via connectivity with social media including Twitter, YouTube, LinkedIn, and Facebook. Aided by social media specialists—Digital Brand Expressions—Fidelity's upgraded media reach involves increasing the bank's listings in major search engines, expanding key-word links from other websites,

and utilizing podcasts for competitive advantage. The program enables monitoring of how Fidelity is being talked about in the social media, frequencies of messages, and then taking steps to guide employees toward more effective communicating with constituents. Measurements of frequencies for social network mentions and types of message content can then be compared to changes in product acceptance—savings, loans, investments, and insurance—among consumers and business customers. The results will enable the bank to determine the success of its social media program in terms of profitability and customer satisfaction.[25]

MyBizLab

Paul Rapson/Alamy

Blink Credit Card   "Blink" technology uses a computer chip that sends radio-frequency signals in place of the magnetic strips that have been embedded in credit cards for the past 30 years. The "contactless" payment system lets consumers wave the card in front of a merchant's terminal, at a gas pump or in a department store, without waiting to swipe and sign. Radio-frequency identification, while new to credit cards, is familiar on toll roads with electronic passes that allow drivers to avoid waiting in line to pay.

Debit Cards   Unlike credit cards, **debit cards** do not increase the funds at an individual's disposal but allow users only to transfer money between accounts to make retail purchases. Debit cards are used more than credit cards as payment for U.S. consumer transactions. However, the risk of financial loss is greater for debit cards.

Federal law limits the credit card user's liability to $50 for stolen or fraudulent use. Protection against debit card losses can be higher—ranging up to $500—depending on how quickly the lost card is reported. [26]

Many stores use **point-of-sale (POS) terminals** to communicate relevant purchase information with a customer's bank. A customer inserts a card, and the bank automatically transfers funds from the customer's account to the store's account.

Smart Cards   A **smart card** has an embedded computer chip that can be programmed with "electronic money." Also known as *electronic purses* or *stored-value cards*, smart cards have existed for more than a decade. They are most popular in gas-pump payments, followed by prepaid phone service, ATMs, self-operated checkouts, vending machines, and automated banking services.[27]

International Banking and Finance

6 Discuss some of the institutions and activities in international banking and finance.

Electronic technologies permit nearly instantaneous financial transactions around the globe. These business exchanges—the prices asked and paid—are affected by *values of the currencies* among the various nations involved in the transactions. Once agreements are reached, the *international payments process* that moves money between buyers and sellers on different continents is not subject to any worldwide policy system beyond loosely structured agreements among countries.

Currency Values and Exchange Rates

Euros, pesos, dollars, and yen—money comes in all sizes and stripes. With today's global activities, travelers, shoppers, investors, and businesses often rely on banks to convert their dollars into other currencies. When it comes to choosing one currency over others, the best choice changes from day to day. Why? Because every currency's value changes, reflecting global supply and demand—what traders are willing to pay—for one currency relative to others. One index for the value of the U.S. dollar, for example, is the average of its foreign exchange values against the currencies of a large group of major U.S. trading partners. The resulting **exchange rate**—the value of one currency compared to the value of another—reveals how much of one currency must be exchanged for another. At any one time, then, some currencies are "strong"—selling at a higher price and worth more—while others are "weak." Rates of exchange among currencies are published daily in financial media around the world, and at online foreign currency exchange (forex) markets.[28]

Citizens of the Republic of Belarus, along with visitors from other countries, rely on information about current exchange rates between the Belarusian ruble (Br) and currencies of other countries. The BelarusBank is a local provider of currency exchange services.

Tatyana Zenkovich/Photoshot

Debit Card plastic card that allows an individual to transfer money between accounts

Point-of-Sale (POS) Terminal electronic device that transfers funds from the customer's bank account to pay for retail purchases

Smart Card credit-card-sized plastic card with an embedded computer chip that can be programmed with electronic money

Exchange Rate the value of one currency compared to the value of another

Strong Currency or Weak: Which Is Better?   Most people would prefer a "strong" currency, right? Well, not so fast. It depends on how it will be used. Using money for international activities, such as taking a vacation, for example, is one of those "good news–bad news" situations.

Consider the euro, at times up as much as 83 percent against the U.S. dollar since 2002. As a citizen in one of the 23 euro-area countries—for example, France—you chose wisely in delaying that U.S. vacation until 2011. Each euro in 2011 paid for about $1.45 of the trip, but it would have covered only $0.87 in 2002. That's the good news: The stronger euro means more purchasing power against the weaker dollar. It's bad news, though, for French innkeepers because Americans go elsewhere to avoid expensive European travel—it takes $1.45 for €1 of vacation cost, up from $0.83 nine years earlier. Simply put, that $0.83 cup of coffee at a French sidewalk café in 2002 now costs you $1.45. In this example of the U.S. dollar to euro, your purchasing power has declined as the dollar has weakened against the euro.

The stronger euro has proven to be a stumbling block for Europe's economy, especially for industries that export to non-euro countries with weaker currencies. Prices (in U.S. dollars) had to be increased, for example, on German-made Mercedes and BMW auto exports to the United States to cover the higher euro-based manufacturing costs, causing weaker U.S. demand and sales. While the weaker dollar has hurt many European firms that export products to the U.S., others have gained by increasing their U.S. investments. When DaimlerChrysler, for example, produces Mercedes M-class autos in Alabama, it pays in weaker dollars for manufacturing them, exports cars to Europe, and sells in euros for windfall profits. On balance, however, many euro-based firms have faced sagging sales, with slower revenue growth due to a strong euro.

Bank Policies Influence Currency Values   In managing the money supply and interest rates, the Fed strongly influences the dollar's strength against other currencies. The European Central Bank (ECB) has the same role in the euro zone. The raising of interest rates tends to increase an economic system's currency value, whereas lowering the rate has the opposite effect. Europe's economic recovery is slower than desired when the euro is strong because euro-zone companies are less competitive against global counterparts. Even so, the European Central Bank (ECB) refuses to weaken the euro by cutting interest rates. With lower rates, the supply of euros would increase, and the price of euros would fall—stimulating Europe's economy. But, the ECB fears, it would also stimulate too much inflation.

In contrast, the U.S. Federal Reserve continues with low interest rate policies to stimulate the ailing economy, and in doing so contributes to weakening the dollar. The weaker dollar makes U.S. goods cheaper and more attractive on the world's markets, thus increasing U.S. export sales. At the same time, the weaker dollar makes foreign imports more expensive, so U.S. consumers can afford fewer imported products, many of which are available only from foreign manufacturers. Some must-have commodities, too, such as petroleum, are priced worldwide in U.S. dollars, so as the dollar's value falls, the price of oil increases because it takes more of those weaker U.S. dollars to buy each barrel.[29] We see, then, some of the ways that banking and banking policies significantly influence currency values.

The International Payments Process

Financial settlements between buyers and sellers in different countries are simplified through services provided by banks. For example, payments from U.S. buyers start at a local bank that converts them from dollars into the seller's currency—for example, into euros to be sent to a seller in Greece. At the same time, payments and currency conversions from separate transactions also are flowing between Greek businesses and U.S. sellers in the other direction.

If trade between the two countries is in balance—if money inflows and outflows are equal for both countries—then *money does not actually have to flow between the two countries.* If inflows and outflows are not in balance at the U.S. bank (or at the Greek bank), then a flow of money—either to Greece or to the United States—is made to cover the difference.

International Bank Structure

There is no worldwide banking system comparable, in terms of policy making and regulatory power, to the system of any industrialized nation. Worldwide banking stability relies on a loose structure of agreements among individual countries or groups of countries.

Two United Nations agencies, the World Bank and the International Monetary Fund, help to finance international trade. Unlike true banks, the **World Bank** (technically, the International Bank for Reconstruction and Development) provides only a very limited scope of services. For instance, it funds national improvements by making loans to build roads, schools, power plants, and hospitals. The resulting improvements eventually enable borrowing countries to increase productive capacity and international trade.

Another U.N. agency, the **International Monetary Fund (IMF),** is a group of some 150 nations that have combined resources for the following purposes:

- To promote the stability of exchange rates

- To provide temporary, short-term loans to member countries

- To encourage members to cooperate on international monetary issues

- To encourage development of a system for international payments

The IMF makes loans to nations suffering from temporary negative trade balances. By making it possible for these countries to continue buying products from other countries, the IMF facilitates international trade. However, some nations have declined IMF funds rather than accept the economic changes that the IMF demands. For example, some developing countries reject the IMF's requirement that they cut back social programs and spending in order to bring inflation under control.

World Bank UN agency that provides a limited scope of financial services, such as funding improvements in underdeveloped countries

International Monetary Fund (IMF) UN agency consisting of about 150 nations that have combined resources to promote stable exchange rates, provide temporary short-term loans, and serve other purposes

Jeffrey Blackler/Alamy

Continued from page 387

Shakeups Bring a Wakeup Call to Banking

The failure of Crescent Bank and Trust in Jasper, Georgia, will cost the FDIC more than $240 million and that's just one example among the 157 U.S. bank failures in 2010, after another 140 closures in 2009, the highest since 1992.[30] The nation's remaining 6,400 lenders, too, are shaken by the housing market collapse. As uncollectable loans increase, banks are left with unsellable foreclosed properties, and housing values are continuing to fall.

Along with industry giants, hundreds of smaller U.S. banks face additional losses of billions on commercial loans for office buildings, shopping malls, and apartment projects. Revenues lost from uncollectable loans are unavailable to lend, and banks are trying to shore up cash by selling off assets, cutting costs, or hoarding funds rather than making loans. As cash dwindles, financial losses foreshadow more bank closures.

To regain profits, larger banks are charging for formerly "free" services. Bank of America, for example, charges additional monthly fees for an account if you want to get paper statements or want to bank with a teller. "Free checking" is dwindling away as banks begin charging a fee for each check. Smaller banks, in contrast, hope to keep those traditionally free services as a strategy for attracting customers for survival.[31]

Adding fuel to the revenue fire is the Federal Reserve Board's proposal to limit debit-card fees that banks and credit card companies charge merchants when customers pay with debit cards. Stores pay usage fees between 1 and 2 percent of each sale, totaling some $16 billion from 38 billion debit card transactions annually. The Fed proposal would limit the fee to 12 cents per transaction, thus reducing bank/card company revenues down to just $5 billion. The issue for banks then becomes one of finding new revenue sources to make up for such large losses.[32]

Taking lessons from the continuing financial crisis, regulators are proposing broader rules to provide future global stability in banking. Regulators from more than 20 nations have proposed the "Basel (Switzerland) III Requirements" to be adopted by 2019. They call for banks to keep larger cushions of cash on hand to guard against future losses, with tighter rules on loans to businesses and consumers.[33]

QUESTIONS FOR DISCUSSION

1 Under what economic conditions might you expect the Fed to raise interest rates? To lower them? Explain.

2 With continuing high unemployment, increasing numbers of home buyers are unable to meet home mortgage payments, forcing banks to either foreclose on these properties, or find other ways to handle non-payments on loans. What action would you propose instead of foreclosure? Identify the consequences you would expect from that action.

3 Suppose you are a businessperson planning to build a new facility in either the United States or the euro zone. How might your choice of where and when to build be influenced by monetary policies of the European Central Bank and the Fed?

4 Why do economically stressed countries with massive debt have difficulty borrowing outside money needed for economic recovery? Explain.

5 If banks are required to keep larger cushions of cash on hand rather than loaning out that money (as proposed in the Basel III Requirements), in what ways will the U.S. economy be affected?

SUMMARY OF LEARNING OBJECTIVES   MyBizLab

1. **Define _money_ and identify the different forms that it takes in the nation's money supply. (pp. 388–390)**
Any item that's _portable, divisible, durable,_ and _stable_ satisfies the basic characteristics of money. Money also serves as a _medium of exchange_, a _store of value_, and a _measure of worth_. The nation's money supply is usually measured in two ways. _M-1_, the spendable money supply, includes the most liquid (or spendable) forms of money: currency (cash), checks, and checking accounts (demand deposits). _M-2_ includes M-1 plus other forms of money that are not quite as liquid but are converted easily to spendable forms: time deposits, money market funds, and savings accounts.

2. **Describe the different kinds of financial institutions that compose the U.S. financial system and explain the services they offer. (pp. 390–395)**
Commercial banks offer checking accounts and accept deposits that they use to make loans and earn profits for shareholders. They also offer (1) pension and trust services, (2) international services, (3) financial advice and brokerage services, (4) ATMs, and (5) other forms of electronic banking. _Savings and loan associations_ are owned by shareholders. S&Ls accept deposits and make loans, and offer many of the same services as commercial banks. In _mutual savings banks_, all depositors are owners of the bank, and all profits are divided among them. _Credit unions_ are nonprofit cooperative financial institutions, owned and run by their members who pool their funds to make loans to one another at reasonable rates. Other organizations called _nondeposit institutions_—pension funds, insurance companies, finance companies, and securities investment dealers—take in money, provide interest or other services, and make loans.

3. **Explain how financial institutions create money and describe the means by which they are regulated. (pp. 395–396)**
The money supply expands because banks can loan out most of the money they take in from deposits. The loans create additional deposits as follows: Out of a deposit of $100, the bank may hold $10 in reserve and loan 90 percent—$90—to borrowers. There will still be the original $100 on deposit, and borrowers (of the $90) will also deposit the $90 loans in their banks. Now, the borrowers' banks have $81 of new deposits available for new loans (90 percent of $90). Banks, therefore, have turned the original $100 deposit into $271 ($100 + $90 + $81) of deposits.
    The government regulates commercial banks to ensure a sound financial system. The _Federal Deposit Insurance Corporation (FDIC)_ insures deposits and guarantees the safety of all deposits up to $250,000. To ensure against failures, the FDIC examines the activities and accounts of all member banks and thrift institutions.

4. **Discuss the functions of the Federal Reserve System and describe the tools that it uses to control the money supply. (pp. 396–399)**
The _Federal Reserve System (the Fed)_ is the nation's central bank. As the government's bank, the Fed produces currency and lends money to the government. As the bankers' bank, it lends money to member banks, stores reserve funds for banks, and clears checks for them. The Fed's Open Market Committee is responsible for formulating the monetary policies to promote economic stability and growth by managing the nation's money supply. Among its tools for controlling the money supply, the Fed specifies _reserve requirements_, it sets the _discount rate_ at which it lends money to banks, and it conducts _open-market operations_ to buy and sell securities.

5. **Identify three important ways in which the money and banking system is changing. (p. 399–403)**
(1) The Federal Reserve took unprecedented investment actions to stabilize the U.S. financial system following the collapse of major banks in 2008. Commercial banks received massive loans to cover bad mortgages and other toxic assets, and to encourage lending to stimulate the sagging economy. (2) Anti-crime and anti-terrorism regulations have been enacted to detect and abate use of the financial system for illegal purposes. The Bank Secrecy Act requires financial institutions to deter funding of crimes by tracking and reporting suspicious transactions. The USA PATRIOT Act requires banks to implement a customer identification program to verify identities and compare them with government lists of terrorists. (3) In addition to EFT systems and mobile devices, banks offer access through telephone, TV, and Internet banking. _Electronic check clearing_ speeds up the check-clearing process, and the "blink" credit card speeds up consumer checkout by replacing magnetic strip cards with contactless cards. _Debit cards_ allow the transfer of money from the cardholder's account directly to others' accounts.

6. **Discuss some of the institutions and activities in international banking and finance. (pp. 403–405)**
Changes in currency values and exchange rates reflect global supply and demand for various currencies. Policies by central banks on money supplies and interest rates influence the values of currencies on the foreign currency exchange markets. Country-to-country transactions rely on an international payments process that moves money between buyers and sellers in different nations. If trade between two countries is in balance—if money inflows and outflows are equal for both countries—money does not have to flow between the two countries. If inflows and outflows are not in balance, then a flow of money between them is made to cover the difference.

Because there is no worldwide banking system, global banking stability relies on agreements among countries. Two United Nations agencies help to finance international trade: (1) The *World Bank* funds loans for national improvements so borrowers can increase productive capacity and international trade. (2) The *International Monetary Fund* makes loans to nations suffering from temporary negative trade balances and to provide economic and monetary stability for the borrowing country.

KEY TERMS   MyBizLab

automated teller machine (ATM) (p. 394)
banker's acceptance (p. 393)
check (p. 389)
checking account (demand deposit) (p. 389)
commercial bank (p. 391)
credit union (p. 392)
currency (cash) (p. 389)
debit card (p. 402)
discount rate (p. 399)
electronic funds transfer (EFT) (p. 394)
exchange rate (p. 403)
Federal Deposit Insurance Corporation (FDIC) (p. 396)

federal funds rate (key rate) (p. 399)
Federal Reserve System (the Fed) (p. 396)
finance company (p. 393)
individual retirement account (IRA) (p. 393)
insurance company (p. 392)
International Monetary Fund (IMF) (p. 405)
letter of credit (p. 393)
M-1 (p. 389)
M-2 (p. 390)
monetary policy (p. 398)
money (p. 388)
money market mutual fund (p. 390)

mutual savings bank (p. 392)
open-market operations (p. 399)
pension fund (p. 392)
point-of-sale (POS) terminal (p. 403)
prime rate (p. 392)
reserve requirement (p. 398)
savings and loan association (S&L) (p. 392)
securities investment dealer (broker) (p. 393)
smart card (p. 403)
time deposit (p. 390)
trust services (p. 393)
World Bank (p. 405)

QUESTIONS AND EXERCISES

QUESTIONS FOR REVIEW

1. Explain the four characteristics of money.
2. What are the components of M-1 and M-2?
3. Explain the roles of commercial banks, savings and loan associations, credit unions, and nondeposit institutions in the U.S. financial system.
4. Describe the structure of the Federal Reserve System.
5. Show how the Fed uses the discount rate to manage inflation in the U.S. economy.

QUESTIONS FOR ANALYSIS

6. Do you think credit cards should be counted in the money supply? Why or why not? Support your argument by using the definition of *money*.
7. Should commercial banks be regulated, or should market forces be allowed to determine the kinds of loans and the interest rates for loans and savings deposits? Why?
8. Customers who deposit their money in online-only checking and savings accounts can often get higher interest rates than

at brick-and-mortar banks. Why do you think that online banks can offer these rates? What might be some drawbacks to online-only banking?

APPLICATION EXERCISES

9. Consider historical currency exchange rates for the U.S. dollar versus China's yuan and Japan's yen. If you had bought those currencies with dollars five years ago, what would be their dollar values today?
10. Start with a $1,000 deposit and assume a reserve requirement of 15 percent. Now trace the amount of money created by the banking system after five lending cycles.
11. Interview the manager of a local commercial bank. Identify the ways in which the bank has implemented requirements of the Bank Secrecy Act and the USA PATRIOT Act. What costs has the bank incurred to implement the federal requirements?

BUILDING YOUR BUSINESS SKILLS

Four Economists in a Room

Goal
To encourage you to understand the economic factors considered by the Fed in determining current interest rates.

Background Information
One of the Fed's most important tools in setting monetary policy is the adjustment of the interest rates it charges member banks to borrow money. To determine interest rate policy, the Fed analyzes current economic conditions from its 12 districts. Its findings are published eight times a year in a report commonly known as the "Beige Book."

Method
Step 1
Working with three other students, access the Fed's website at www.federalreserve.gov/. Look for the heading "A-Z Index," and then in the index click on the subheading "Beige Book." When you reach that page, read the summary of the current report.

Step 2
Working with group members, study each of the major summary sections:
- Consumer spending
- Manufacturing
- Construction and real estate
- Banking and finance
- Nonfinancial services
- Labor market, wages, and pricing
- Agriculture and natural resources

Working with team members, discuss ways in which you think key information contained in the summary might affect the Fed's decision to raise, lower, or maintain interest rates.

Step 3
Using an online search engine, find articles published in *Barron's*, the highly respected financial publication. Look for articles published immediately following the appearance of the most recent "Beige Book." Search for articles analyzing the report. Discuss with group members what the articles say about current economic conditions and interest rates.

Step 4
Based on your research and analysis, what factors do you think the Fed will take into account to control inflation? Working with group members, explain your answer in writing.

Step 5
Working with group members, research what the Fed chairperson says about interest rates. Do the chairperson's reasons for raising, lowering, or maintaining rates agree with your group's analysis?

FOLLOW-UP QUESTIONS
1. What are the most important factors in the Fed's interest rate decision?
2. Consider the old joke about economists that goes like this: When there are four economists in a room analyzing current economic conditions, there are at least eight different opinions. Based on your research and analysis, why do you think economists have such varying opinions?

EXERCISING YOUR ETHICS: INDIVIDUAL EXERCISE

Telling the Ethical from the Strictly Legal

The Situation
When upgrading services for convenience to customers, commercial banks are concerned about setting prices that cover all costs so that, ultimately, they make a profit. This exercise challenges you to evaluate one banking service—ATM transactions—to determine if any ethical issues also should be considered in a bank's pricing decisions.

The Dilemma
A regional commercial bank in the western United States has more than 300 ATMs serving the nearly 400,000 checking and savings accounts of its customers. Customers are not charged a fee for their 30 million ATM transactions each year, as long as they use their bank's ATMs. For issuing cash to noncustomers, however, the bank charges a $3 ATM fee. The bank's officers are reexamining their policies on ATM surcharges because of public protests against other banks with similar surcharges in Santa Monica, New York City, and Chicago. Iowa has gone even further, becoming the

first state to pass legislation that bans national banks from charging ATM fees for noncustomers. To date, the courts have ruled that the access fees are legal, but some organizations—such as the U.S. Public Interest Research Group (PIRG)—continue to fight publicly against them.

In considering its current policies, our western bank's vice president for community relations is concerned about more than mere legalities. She wants to ensure that her company is "being a good citizen and doing the right thing." Any decision on ATM fees will ultimately affect the bank's customers, its image in the community and industry, and its profitability for its owners.

QUESTIONS TO ADDRESS
1 From the standpoint of a commercial bank, can you find any economic justification for ATM access fees?
2 Based on the scenario described for our bank, do you find any ethical issues in this situation? Or do you find the main issues legal and economic rather than ethical?
3 As an officer for this bank, how would you handle this situation?

EXERCISING YOUR ETHICS: TEAM EXERCISE

Banker's Predicament: National Security Versus Customer Privacy

The Situation

With recent increases in crime and terrorism, many citizens are hearing about information activities by organizations that previously were considered intrusive. Under provisions of the Bank Secrecy Act and the USA PATRIOT Act, for example, financial institutions now scour transactions of customers more intensely than before. Does increased monitoring of transactions information raise any ethical problems for customers, owners, or employees?

The Dilemma

Bill Decker got irritated when his application to open a checking account at Forthright National Bank was delayed by lengthy identification-verifying procedures at the bank. Months later he was offended to learn that the bank was tracking deposit and checking activities in his account. As he vented his anger to Gloria Liu, the employee that reviews customers' transactions, she tried to explain the bank's obligations to do their part in detecting suspicious activities and preventing terrorism. Surprised by these comments, Bill insisted on finding out just how much Gloria knows about his personal financial situation. "Do you know who I have transactions with through your bank? Are you tracking them, too? With whom are you sharing this information? Does it affect my credit rating?" As the conversation heated up, Gloria decided that her boss, Carolyn Kleen, should be called, especially when Bill indicated that assistance from a civil liberties group might be appropriate for addressing his privacy concerns.

Team Activity

Assemble a group of four students and assign each group member to one of the following roles:

- Bill Decker (bank customer)
- Gloria Liu (bank employee)
- Carolyn Kleen (vice president, financial security)
- Karl Marcks (bank stockholder, investor)

ACTION STEPS

1 Before hearing any of your group's comments on this situation, and from the perspective of your assigned role, do you think there are any ethical issues with Forthright National Bank's security-screening program? If so, write them down.

2 Before hearing any of your group's comments, and from the perspective of your assigned role, what do you think are the main problems with the bank's security-screening program? Write them down.

3 Return to your group and share the ethical issues and problems identified by each member. Were the issues and problems the same among all roles, or did difference in roles result in different issues and problems?

4 Among the ethical issues identified, decide as a group which one is most important for the bank to resolve. Likewise, for potential problems, which is the most important one for the bank?

5 What does your group recommend be done to resolve the most important ethical issue? How should the most important problem be resolved?

VIDEO EXERCISE   MyBizLab

BANCFIRST

Learning Objectives

The purpose of this video is to help you:

1 Relate the characteristics of money to the U.S. currency system.

2 Explain the functions of money and the role that financial institutions play in this process.

3 Describe the role of the Fed in regulating the money supply.

Synopsis

BancFirst is an Oklahoma-based bank with over 75 branches and many more ATM locations. While there were many causes of the recent financial crisis, banking institutions were at the center. Banks like BancFirst take deposits from individuals and businesses and make loans with this money. Before making loans, lending officers evaluate the credit-worthiness of applicants and try to make loans to those who are likely to repay their loans in full and on time. In spite of their best efforts, some loans will not repaid and banks will have to write these off, removing them from their books and financial statements. Normally, banks expect that less than one percent of their loans will be uncollectible. However,

during the recent financial crisis, the default rate soared. As a result, banks became overly cautious and made very few loans. With few loans, the money supply became tighter, prompting the Fed to take action.

DISCUSSION QUESTIONS

1 What is money? Relate the four characteristics of money to the U.S. currency system.

2 Money plays an important role in our economy. What are the functions of money?

3 How do financial institutions like BancFirst create money? How would tighter credit standards affect this process?

4 What is the Federal Reserve? What are the major functions of the Fed?

5 Explain the tools that the Federal Reserve uses to control the money supply.

Online Exploration

Deposits at BancFirst (www.bancfirst.com) are insured by the FDIC, an independent agency of the U.S. government. Follow the link from BancFirst's website to the FDIC (www.fdic.gov). What does the FDIC insure and what are the limitations of this insurance? What implications does this have for depositors?

END NOTES

1 "Why Did the ECB Raise Interest rates?" http://www
.ibtimes.com/articles/131734/20110407/why-ecb-raise-
interest-rates.htm; "Central Bank Raises Interest Rates
Again," http://www.bendbulletin.com/article/20110406/
NEWS0107/104060346/; "China Raises key Interest Rates
By Quarter Percentage…," http://www.startribune.com/
business/119239139.html; "India Raises Interest Rates for
Eighth Time…," http://www.bloomberg.com/news/2011-
03-17/india-raises-interest-rates-for-eighth-time-in-a-
year-to-reduce-inflation.html; "Patricia Kowsmann and
Charles Forelle, "Portugal Pleads for Rescue," *The Wall
Street Journal*," April 7, 2011, Page A1; "EU/IMF Bailout
for Ireland….," *International Business Times*, http://hken.
ibtimes.com/articles/84575/20101122/ireland-bailout.htm;
Michael Winfrey, "Past EU/IMF Bailouts Show Risks, Pluses
for Greece," *Reuters*, May 4, 2010, http://www.reuters.
com/article/2010/05/04/us-greece-bailouts-analysis-idUS-
TRE6434XY20100504.

2 Steve Schifferes, "'$10 Trillion' Credit Crunch Cost," *BBC News*,
July 31, 2009, http://news.bbc.co.uk/2/hi/8177814.stm;
Kimberly Amadeo, "Value of the U.S. Dollar," January 10,
2011, at http://useconomy.about.com/od/tradepolicy/p/
Dollar_Value.htm.

3 See David B. Caruso, "Official: Money Network Linked to NYC
Terror Suspect," Associated Press, May 14, 2010, accessed at
http://www.aolnews.com/2010/05/14/u/.

4 "Money Stock Measures," Federal Reserve, at http://www
.federalreserve.gov/releases/h6/, accessed April 16, 2011.

5 Ibid.

6 *Federal Reserve Bank of San Francisco*, Accessed April 18, 2011, at
http://www.frbsf.org/education/activities/drecon/2005/0509
.html.

7 *Board of Governors of the Federal reserve System*, April 15, 2011,
at http://www.federalreserve.gov/releases/h8/current/default
.htm .

8 Watson Wyatt, "2010 Global Pension Assets Study," *Towers
Watson*, accessed April 16, 2011 at http://www
.towerswatson.com/assets/pdf/966/GPAS2010.pdf;
Joshua Brockman, "Stocks Weigh Down U.S. Pension
Funds," *NPR*, July 15, 2009, at http://www.npr.org/tem-
plates/story/story.php?storyId=100818937; William
Selway, "U.S. Government Pensions Gain 5.5% as Stock
Market Rises," *Bloomberg*, March 31, 2011, at http://www
.bloomberg.com/news/2011-03-31/u-s-government-
pensions-gain-5-5-as-stock-market-rises-1-.html;
"Private Pension Plan Bulletin," *U.S. Department of Labor
Employee Benefits Security Administration*, December
2010, at http://www.dol.gov/ebsa/pdf/2008pensionplan
bulletin.pdf.

9 Shane M. Sherland, "The Past, Present, and Future of Subprime
Mortgages," *Finance and Economics Discussion Series,
Divisions of Research and Statistics and Monetary Affairs:
Federal Reserve Board* (Washington, DC; November
2008); Michael Gerrity, "MBA Reports Mortgage Loan
Delinquencies, Foreclosure Starts Decrease in Q2,"
World Property Channel, August 26, 2010, at http://www

.worldpropertychannel.com/us-markets/residential-real-
estate-1/real-estate-news-mortgage-bankers-association-
national-delinquency-survey-delinquency-rate-for-mort-
gage-loans-foreclosure-actions-bank-foreclosures-loan-
default-rates-3077.php.

10 Richard Bitner, "Confessions of a Subprime Lender,"
Newsweek (March 12, 2008), at http://www.newsweek.
com/id/121512/page/1; Tyler Cowen, "So We Thought.
But Then Again…" *New York Times* (January 13, 2008),
at http://www.nytimes.com/2008/01/13/business/13view.
html?_r=2&scp=1&sq=Tyler+Cowen&oref=login&oref
=slogin; Robert H. Frank, "Don't Blame All Borrowers,"
Washington Post (April 27, 2008), at http://www
.washingtonpost.com/wp-dyn/content/article/2008/04/25/
AR2008042502783.html.

11 Bert Ely, "Don't Push Banks to Make Bad Loans," *The Wall
Street Journal*, February 2, 2009, page A17; Jeannine
Aversa, "Banks Aren't Budging on Tight Lending
Standards," *HuffingtonPost.com*, February 2, 2009, at
http://www.huffingtonpost.com/2009/02/02/banks-
arent-budging-on-ti_n_163325.html; Jeremy M. Simon,
"Lending Standards Keep Tightening, Fed Says,"
CreditCards.com, May 4, 2009, at http://www.creditcards.
com/credit-card-news/2009-q1-senior-loan-officers-sur-
vey-lending-standards-tighten-1276.php; Danny King,
"Banks Tighten Mortgage Standards for FHA-Insured
Loans," *DailyFinance*, November 17, 2010, at http://www.
dailyfinance.com/story/credit/banks-tighten-mortgage-
standards-for-fha-insured-loans-fico-score/19722792/;
Rex Nutting, "Most Banks Tighten Credit Standards
Further, Fed Says," *Market Watch*, May 4, 2009, at http://
www.marketwatch.com/story/most-banks-tighten-
credit-standards-further.

12 "Electronic Funds Transfer," Accessed April 20, 2011, at
http://fms.treas.gov/eft/index.html; "Government to Phase
Out Checks in March 2013," *Columbia Daily Tribune*,
December 21, 2011 at http://www.columbiatribune.com/
news/2010/dec/21/government-to-phase-out-checks-in-
march-2013/.

13 "China to Become World's Largest ATM Market by 2015,"
SmartCards Trends, September 30, 2010, at http://
www.smartcardstrends.com/det_atc.php?idu=12793&ma
in=ea272859892ed0adacb020e361fae6e0; Frederick Lowe,
"China Expected to Become the World's Top ATM Market,"
ATM Marketplace, September 30, 2010, at http://www
.atmmarketplace.com/article_print/176973/China-expected-
to-become-the-world-s-top-ATM-market; "Global ATM
Market to Pass 2.5 Million by 2013," *the-infoshop.com* (press
release), September 10, 2008, at http://www.the-infoshop
.com/press/rbr71603_en.shtml.

14 Brian W. Smith and Melissa R. Hall, "Troubled Banks and
Failed Banks: Opportunities for Investment," *Pratt's
Journal of Bankruptcy Law*, accessed April 20, 2010 at
http://www.lw.com/upload/pubContent/_pdf/pub2296_1.
pdf; Ralph F. MacDonald III, Christopher M. Kelly, Brett
P. Barragate, Kevyn D. Orr, and James C. Olson, "United

States: Bank Failures in 2008 and a Look Ahead to 2009," *Jones Day*, January 28, 2009, at http://www.mondaq.com/article.asp?articleid=72796; "2008-2011 bank Failures in the United States," *Wikipedia*, at http://www.wikipedia.org/wiki/2008_United_States_bank_failures, accessed April 20 2011; Rob Williams, "How Secure Is the FDIC Deposit Insurance Fund?" *Charles Schwab*, September 16, 2009, at http://www.schwab.com/public/schwab/research_strategies/market_insight/investing_strategies/other_choices/how_secure_is_the_fdic_deposit_insurance_fund.html.

15 Katy Jacob, Daniel Littman, Richard D. Porter, and Wade Rousse, "Two Cheers for the Monetary Control Act," *Chicago Fed Letter (June 2010, Number 275): The Federal Reserve Bank of Chicago*, at http://www.chicagofed.org/digital_assets/publications/chicago_fed_letter/2010/cfljune2010_275.pdf; Paul W. Bauer and Geoffrey R. Gerdes, "The Check Is Dead! Long Live the Check! A Check 21 Update," *Federal Reserve Bank of Cleveland*, September 21, 2009, at http://www.clevelandfed.org/research/commentary/2009/0609.cfm; Jim Savage, "Federal Reserve Banks Complete Check Processing Infrastructure Changes," *Board of Governors of the Federal Reserve System*, March 2, 2010, at http://www.federalreserve.gov/newsevents/press/other/20100302a.htm.

16 "Intended Federal Funds Rate, Change and Level," *Board of Governors of the Federal Reserve System*, at http://www.federalreserve.gov/monetarypolicy/openmarket.htm, accessed April 21, 2011.

17 Jon Hilsenrath and Liz Rappaport, "Fed Inches Toward Plan to Purchase U.S. Bonds," *The Wall Street Journal*, January 29, 2009, page A4; Neil Irwin, "Fed to Pump $1.2 Trillion into Markets," *The Washington Post*, March 19, 2009, at http://www.washingtonpost.com/wp-dyn/content/article/2009/03/18/AR2009031802283.html; Rita Nazareth, "Most U.S. Stocks Rise on Durable Goods, Pare Gains on Fed," *Bloomberg.com*, June 24, 2009, at http://www.bloomberg.com/apps/news?pid-20670001&sid=a_dIjb; Jon Hilsenrath, "Fed to Keep Lid on Bond Buys," *The Wall Street Journal*, June 12, 2009, at http://www.online.wsj.com/article/SB124477575898508951.html; Jon Hilsenrath, "Fed Treads Into a Once-Taboo Realm," *The Wall Street Journal*," November 5, 2010, page A6.

18 David Goldman, "CNNMoney.com's Bailout Tracker," *CNNMoney.com*, accessed April 21, 2011, at http://money.cnn.com/news/storysupplement/economy/bailouttracker/.

19 Michael R. Crittenden, "Regulators See Risk in U.S. Bank Stakes, *The Wall Street Journal*, April 24, 2009, at http://online.wsj.com/article/SB124051525463449225.html; Rebecca Christie, "Treasury May Keep U.S. Bank Stakes After Buyback (Update 3)," *Bloomberg.com*, April 17, 2009, at http://www.bloomberg.com/apps/news?pid=newsarchive&sid=a9F3N8vvrHgY; David Goldman, "CNNMoney.com's Bailout Tracker," *CNNMoney.com*, April 21, 2011, at http://money.cnn.com/news/storysupplement/economy/bailouttracker/; Mark Jickling, Fannie Mae and Freddie Mac in Conservatorship," *CRS Report for* Congress, September

15, 2008, at http://fpc.state.gov/documents/organization/110097.pdf.

20 "U.S. Authorities Fine Arab Bank," *Al Bawaba* (August 18, 2005), 1; Paul R. Osborne, "BSA/AML Compliance Provides Opportunity to Improve Security and Enhance Customer Experience," *ABA Bank Compliance*, July/August 2005, 4.

21 Jason Webb, "American Express Bank Forfeits $55 Million for Bank Secrecy Act Violations," *Associated Content*, August 7, 2007, at http://www.associatedcontent.com/article/339208/american_express_bank_forfeits_55_million.html?cat=17; "Banco Popular de Puerto Rico Enters into Deferred Prosecution Agreement with U.S. Department of Justice," *U.S. Department of Justice*, January 16, 2006, at http://www.usdoj.gov/opa/pr/2003/January/03_crm_024.htm; Union Bank of California Enters into Deferred Prosecution Agreement and Forfeits $21.6 Million to Resolve Bank Secrecy Act Violations," *U.S. Department of Justice*, September 17, 2007, at http://www.usdoj.gov/opa/pr/2007/September/07_crm_726.html.

22 "Supporting the Nation's Payment System," *The Federal Reserve Bank of Philadelphia*, April 22, 2011, at http://www.philadelphiafed.org/about-the-fed/who-we-are/payment-system.cfm; "Intro to the ACH Network," *NACHA: The Electronic Payments Association*, accessed April 22, 2011, at http://nacha.org/c/intro2ach.cfm; "NACHA Reports 18.76 Billion ACH Payments in 2009," *NSF Check Processing*, April 7, 2010, at http://www.nsfcheckprocessing.com/achnetwork.htm.

23 Katy Jacob, Daniel Littman, Richard D. Porter, and Wade Rousse, "Two Cheers for the Monetary Control Act," *Chicago Fed Letter (June 2010, Number 275): The Federal Reserve Bank of Chicago*, at http://www.chicagofed.org/digital_assets/publications/chicago_fed_letter/2010/cfljune2010_275.pdf; Paul W. Bauer and Geoffrey R. Gerdes, "The Check Is Dead! Long Live the Check! A Check 21 Update," *Federal Reserve Bank of Cleveland*, September 21, 2009, at http://www.clevelandfed.org/research/commentary/2009/0609.cfm; Jim Savage, "Federal Reserve Banks Complete Check Processing Infrastructure Changes," *Board of Governors of the Federal Reserve System*, March 2, 2010, at http://www.federalreserve.gov/newsevents/press/other/20100302a.htm.

24 "The New Normal: Annual Report 2009," *Fidelity Bank*, accessed April 13, 2011 at http://www.fidelitybankonline.com/home/fiFiles/static/documents/AnnualReport2009.pdf; "Fidelity Bank launches Innovative Social Media Program," *Citi biz list*, February 15, 2011, at http://boston.citybizlist.com/7/2011/2/15/Fidelity-Bank-Launches-Innovative-Social-Media-Program-.aspx.

25 "Digital Brand Expressions," accessed April 12, 2011 at http://www.digitalbrandexpressions.com.

26 Martin Kaste, "Consumers Opt For Debit Over Credit Cards," NPR, June 28, 2009, at http://www.npr.org/templates/story/story.php?storyId=105974724.

27 "About Smart Cards: Introduction: Primer," *Smart Card Alliance*, accessed April 22, 2011, at http://www.smartcardalliance.org/pages/smart-cards-intro-primer.

28 "Summary Measures of the Foreign Exchange Value of the Dollar," *Federal Reserve Statistical Release H:10*, accessed April 23, 2011 at http://www.federalreserve.gov/releases/H10/Summary/.

29 Kimberly Amadeo, "Value of the U.S. Dollar," *About.com*, accessed April 23, 2011, at http://useconomy.about.com/od/tradepolicy/p/Dollar_Value.htm.

30 "Bank Failures in Brief: 2010," *FDIC*, accessed April 4, 2011 at http://www.fdic.gov/bank/historical/bank/2010/index.html; Associated Press, "U.S. Bank Failures Surpass 100," *Columbia Daily Tribune*, July 26, 2010, Page 5B.

31 Associated Press, "Shrinking Profits Kill Bank Freebie," *Columbia Daily Tribune*, October 20, 2010, Page 5B.

32 Associated Press, "Bankers, Merchants Feud Over Fees," *Columbia Daily Tribune*, March 14, 2011, Page 7B.

33 David Enrich and Damian Paletta, "Global Bank Pact Advances," *The Wall Street Journal*, June 4, 2010, page A1, A14; Associated Press, "Bankers Outline New Global Rules," *Columbia Daily Tribune*, September 13, 2010, page 6B.

16 Managing Finances

Investing in Green

Traders are accustomed to using financial markets for investing in just about everything, ranging from pig bellies to movie production, in hopes of gaining a profit. New financial markets for commodities known as carbon credits, however, are driven, not just by profit motive, but by a sense of social responsibility. The economic incentives of emissions trading (ET) bring together both environmental polluters and green investors in an effort to both turn a profit and save the planet. In 2009, the U.S. Congress proposed a version of ET called Cap and Trade.

Here's how ET works: Regulators in various countries are setting limits on the amounts of industrial pollutants that can be released. A leading example, the European Union's Emissions Trading Scheme (ETS), was started by the European Commission in 2005 to meet carbon reductions in accordance with the Kyoto Protocol on Climate Change. The ETS annually sets a cap for the total amount of carbon dioxide (CO_2) emissions allowed for each EU member state and company. The state totals and the EU total cannot exceed the caps.

Companies are issued a permit containing a number of "credits" (or "allowances") representing the right to emit a certain amount of CO_2. Any company producing below its CO_2 cap can sell its surplus allowances to other, more pollution-prone companies that need more credits to keep operating. That's where trading comes into play—it's like a stock

After reading this chapter, you should be able to:

1 **Explain the concept of the time value of money and the principle of compound growth.**
2 **Identify the investment opportunities offered by mutual funds and exchange-traded funds.**
3 **Describe the role of securities markets and identify the major stock exchanges and stock markets.**
4 **Describe the risk–return relationship and discuss the use of diversification and asset allocation for investments.**
5 **Describe the various ways that firms raise capital and identify the pros and cons of each method.**
6 **Identify the reasons a company might make an initial public offering of its stock and explain how stock value is determined.**
7 **Explain how securities markets are regulated.**

exchange that quickly matches up buyers and sellers of emissions credits.

With emissions trading, environmentally oriented companies (so-called green companies) sell unneeded emissions allowances and gain a financial return on past investments for reducing pollution. Such companies view environmental cleanup not as an expense, but as a responsible investment. Other companies, finding it cheaper to avoid such investments, are facing higher costs as they bid for others' unused carbon credits. The trading scheme is adding a new financial incentive for cleaner industries that reduce carbon emissions and other greenhouse gases.[1]

Our opening story continues on page 436.
Our opening story continues on page 436.

WHAT'S IN IT FOR ME?

Emissions trading is just one of countless activities drawing investors of every kind to the world's financial markets. Businesses from all over the world, representing every industry, converge there each day, seeking funds that can be used to finance their endeavors and pay off their debts. Individual investors gather as well, in person or—more often—online, looking to make their money "work" for them. This chapter will help you understand the various ways this is possible, whether your goals are short- or long-term, whether you are motivated by the desire for profit or security, or simply because you enjoy the challenges inherent in the successful raising and investing of capital.

MyBizLab Where you see MyBizLab in this chapter, go to **www.mybizlab.com** for additional activities on the topic being discussed.

© Corbis

1 Explain the concept of the time value of money and the principle of compound growth.

Maximizing Capital Growth

Wise investments are the key to growing your money, especially if you are seeking to build capital to start your own business or simply as a cushion for a sound financial future. In searching for investment opportunities, a number of concepts come into play for evaluating alternative investments and sorting out the good from the bad.

The Time Value of Money and Compound Growth

The **time value of money**, perhaps the single most important concept in business finance, recognizes the basic fact that, while it's invested, money grows by earning interest or yielding some other form of return. Time value stems from the principle of **compound growth**—the cumulative growth from interest paid to the investor over given time periods. With each additional time period, interest payments accumulate and earn more interest, thus multiplying the earning capacity of the investment.

The Rule of 72

How long does it take to double an investment? A handy rule of thumb is called the "Rule of 72." You can find the number of years needed to double your money by dividing the annual interest rate (in percent) into 72. If, for example, you reinvest annually at 8 percent, you'll double your money in about 9 years:

$$\frac{72}{8} = 9 \text{ years to double the money}$$

The Rule of 72 can also calculate how much interest you must get if you want to double your money in a given number of years: Simply divide 72 by the desired number of years. If you want to double your money in 10 years, you need to get 7.2 percent:

$$\frac{72}{10} = 7.2 \text{ percent interest needed to double the money}$$

The lesson for the investor is clear: seek *higher* interest rates because money will double more frequently.

Making Better Use of Your Time Value   What if you invested $10,000 at seven percent interest for one year? You would earn $700 on your $10,000 investment. If you reinvested the principal amount plus the interest you earned during the first year, and reinvested interest annually for another four years, you'd end up with $14,025. Now, if you were planning for retirement and reinvested that money at the same interest rate for another 25 years, you could retire with $76,122—almost eight times the amount you started with!

Figure 16.1 illustrates how the returns from an initial investment of $10,000 accumulate substantially over longer periods of time. Notice that the gains for the last 10 years are much greater than for the first 10 years, illustrating the power of compound growth. Each year, the interest rate is applied to a larger sum. Notice also the larger gains from higher interest rates. Even a seemingly small increase in interest rates, from 7% to 8%, results in much larger accumulations.

As you can see from Figure 16.1, the best way to take advantage of the time value of money is to obtain a high rate of return on your investment. However, various kinds of investments offer opportunities for fulfilling different financial objectives, such as aggressive growth, financial safety, and others.

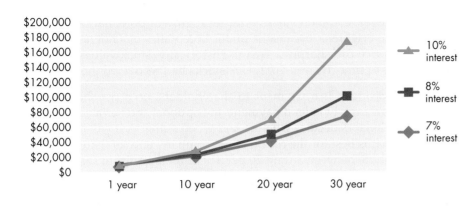

Figure 16.1 **Amount to Which an Initial $10,000 Investment Grows**

Common Stock Investments

History has shown that one way to achieve a high rate of return, compared with many other ways, is to invest in the stock market. A **stock** is a portion of the ownership of a corporation. The company's total ownership is divided into small parts, called *shares*, that can be bought and sold to determine how much of the company (how many shares of stock) is owned by each shareholder. This widespread ownership has become possible because of the availability of different types of stocks and because markets have been established that enable individuals to conveniently buy and sell them.

While several types of stock exist, common stock is the most prominent. A share of **common stock** is the most basic form of ownership in a company. Individuals and other companies purchase a firm's common stock in the hope that it will increase in value and provide dividend income; in addition, each common share has a vote on major issues that are brought before the shareholders.

Stock values are usually expressed in two different ways: as market value and book value.

1 A stock's real value is its **market value**—the current price of a share in the stock market. Market value reflects the amount that buyers are willing to pay for a share of the company's stock.

2 The **book value** for a share of common stock is determined as the firm's owners' equity (from the balance sheet) divided by the number of common shares owned by all shareholders. Book value is used as a comparison indicator because the market value for successful companies is usually greater than its book value. Thus, when market price falls to near book value, some profit-seeking investors buy the stock on the principle that it is underpriced and will increase in the future.

Investment Traits of Common Stock   Common stocks are among the riskiest of all investments. Uncertainties about the stock market itself can quickly change a given stock's value. Furthermore, when companies have unprofitable years, or when economic conditions go sour, they often cannot pay dividends and potential investors become wary of future stock values, so share price drops. U.S. stocks, for example, lost over half their value in the recession years 2008 and early 2009. On the upside, however, common stocks offer high growth potential; when a company's performance brightens, because of public acceptance of a hot new product, for example, share price can sharply increase. Historically, stock values generally rise with the passage of time. By mid-2011, U.S. stocks had recovered their lost values.

Dividends   A **dividend** is a payment to shareholders, on a per-share basis, from the company's earnings. Dividend payments are optional and variable—the corporation's board of directors decides whether and when a dividend will be paid, as well as the amount that is best for the future of the company and its shareholders. Many companies distribute between 30 and 70 percent of their profits to shareholders. The so-called **blue-chip stocks**—those issued by the strongest, well-established, financially sound and respected firms, such as Coca-Cola and ExxonMobil—have historically provided investors steady income through consistent dividend payouts. However, some firms, especially fast-growing companies, do not pay dividends; instead, they use cash earnings for expanding the company so that future earnings can grow even faster. What's more, any company can have a bad year and decide to reduce or omit dividend payments to stockholders.

2 Identify the investment opportunities offered by mutual funds and exchange-traded funds.

Investing to Fulfill Financial Objectives

As an alternative to buying stock, mutual funds and exchange-traded funds are popular because they offer attractive investment opportunities for various financial objectives and often do not require large sums of money for entry. In addition, the simple and easy transaction process makes them accessible to the public.

Mutual funds are created by companies such as T. Rowe Price and Vanguard that pool cash investments from individuals and organizations to purchase bundles of stocks, bonds, and other securities. The bundles are expected to appreciate in market value and otherwise produce income for the mutual fund and its investors. Thus, investors, as part owners, expect to receive financial gains as the fund's assets become increasingly valuable. If you invest $1,000 in a mutual fund with assets worth $100,000, you own 1 percent of that fund. Investors in **no-load funds** are not charged sales commissions when they buy into or sell out of funds. Investors in **load funds** generally pay commissions of 2 percent to 8 percent.

Reasons for Investing

It's relatively easy to open a mutual fund account online or by phone. There are numerous funds that meet any chosen financial objective. The funds vary in their investment goals: Different funds are designed to appeal to the different motives and goals of investors. Three of the most common objectives are financial stability, conservative growth, and aggressive growth.

- **Stability and Safety** Funds stressing safety seek only modest growth with little fluctuation in principal value regardless of economic conditions. They include *money market mutual funds* and other funds that preserve the fund holders' capital and reliably pay current income. Typical assets of these funds include lower-risk U.S. corporate bonds, U.S. government bonds, and other similarly safe short-term securities that provide stable income from interest and dividends.

- **Conservative Capital Growth** Mutual funds that stress preservation of capital and current income, but also seek some capital appreciation, are called *balanced funds*. Typically, these funds hold a mixture of long-term municipal bonds, corporate bonds, and common stocks with good dividend-paying records for steady income. The common stocks offer potential for market appreciation (higher market value), though there is always the risk of price declines if the general stock market falls.

- **Aggressive Growth** *Aggressive growth funds* seek maximum long-term capital growth. They sacrifice current income and safety by investing in stocks of new (and even troubled) companies, firms developing new products and technologies, and other higher-risk securities. They are designed for investors who can accept the risk of loss inherent in common stock investing with severe price fluctuations, but also the potential for superior returns over time.

Most Mutual Funds Don't Match the Market

Many, but not all, mutual funds are managed by "experts" who select the fund's stocks and other securities that provide the fund's income. Unfortunately, some estimates indicate that up to 80 percent of these managed funds do not perform as well as the average return of the overall stock market, due to costly management expenses and underperforming stocks.[2] This underperformance disadvantage has resulted in the emergence of passively managed mutual funds such as index funds, which nearly match the performance of a particular market. As an example, the widely watched S&P 500 market index, which is discussed later, consists of 500 specific common stocks. Any mutual fund company can establish its own index fund by purchasing shares of those same 500 companies, thus matching the market performance of the S&P 500. The selection of which stocks to purchase in an index fund is relatively automatic—it holds many of the same stocks as the market it tracks—and requires little human input, thus reducing management expenses.

Exchange-Traded Funds

As with an index mutual fund, an **exchange-traded fund (ETF)** is a bundle of stocks (or bonds) that are in an index that tracks the overall movement of a market; unlike a mutual fund, however, an ETF can be traded like a stock. Each share of an ETF rises and falls as market prices change continuously for the market being tracked.

Advantages of ETFs

ETFs offer three areas of advantage over mutual funds: They can be traded throughout the day like a stock, they have low operating expenses, and they do not require high initial investments. Because they are traded on stock exchanges (hence, "exchange traded"), ETFs can be bought and sold—priced continuously—any time throughout the day. This *intraday trading* means you can time your transaction during the day to buy or sell when (or if) the market reaches a desired price. Mutual fund shares, in contrast, are priced once daily, at the end of the day. Thus, when you buy or sell during the day, you don't find out the share price until after the day has ended.

Whereas many mutual funds pass the costs of expensive active management onto shareholders, an ETF is bound by a rule that specifies what stocks will be purchased and when; once the rule is established, little or no active human decisions are involved. The *lower annual operating expenses* mean that, for the buy-and-hold investor, annual fees for ETFs are as low as 0.09 percent of assets; annual fees for mutual funds average 1.4 percent.[3]

Finally, unlike mutual funds, ETFs require no minimum investment, meaning they offer *ease of entry* for investors getting started without much money.[4] On the other hand, because ETFs must be bought and sold through a broker, they require

---

Dividend payment to shareholders, on a per-share basis, out of the company's earnings

Blue-Chip Stock common stock issued by a well-established and respected company with a sound financial history and a stable pattern of dividend payouts

Mutual Fund company that pools cash investments from individuals and organizations to purchase a portfolio of stocks, bonds, and other securities

No-load Fund mutual fund in which investors pay no commissions when they buy in or sell out

Load Fund mutual fund in which investors are charged sales commissions when they buy in or sell out

Exchange-Traded Fund (ETF) bundle of stocks or bonds that are in an index that tracks the overall movement of a market but, unlike a mutual fund, can be traded like a stock

payment of a brokerage commission (transaction fees). Traders who buy and sell frequently can end up paying more in transactions fees, even surpassing a mutual fund's high management expenses.[5]

3 Describe the role of securities markets and identify the major stock exchanges and stock markets.

The Business of Trading Securities

Stocks, bonds, and mutual funds are known as **securities** because they represent *secured*, or financially valuable claims on the part of investors. The markets in which stocks and bonds are sold are called **securities markets.** By facilitating the buying and selling of securities, the securities markets provide the capital that companies rely on for survival. Mutual funds, on the other hand, are not bought and sold on securities markets, but are managed by financial professionals in the investment companies that create, buy, and sell the funds.

Primary and Secondary Securities Markets

In **primary securities markets,** new stocks and bonds are bought and sold by firms and governments. Sometimes, new securities are sold to single buyers or small groups of buyers. These so-called *private placements* are desirable because they allow issuers to keep their plans confidential.

Most new stocks and some bonds are sold on the wider public market. To bring a new security to market, the issuing firm must get approval from the U.S. **Securities and Exchange Commission (SEC)**—the government agency that regulates U.S. securities markets. The firm also relied, traditionally, on the services of an **investment bank**—a financial institution that specialized in issuing and reselling new securities. All that changed, however, in the financial collapse of 2008, when the bankruptcy of Lehman Brothers became the largest bankruptcy in U.S. history, Bear Stearns was purchased by JPMorgan Chase, and the two remaining large U.S. investment banks—Morgan Stanley and Goldman Sachs—were allowed to become bank holding companies (much like a commercial bank).[6] Although the companies' structures have changed, they still provide three important investment banking services:

1 They advise companies on the timing and financial terms of new issues.

2 They *underwrite*—that is, they buy and assume liability for—new securities, thus providing the issuing firms with 100 percent of the money (less commission). The inability to resell the securities is a risk that the banks must bear.

3 They create distribution networks for moving new securities through groups of other banks and brokers into the hands of individual investors.

New securities, however, represent only a small portion of traded securities. *Existing* stocks and bonds are sold in the much larger **secondary securities market,** which is handled by such familiar bodies as the New York Stock Exchange and, more recently, by online trading with electronic communication networks.

Stock Exchanges

Most of the buying and selling of stocks, historically, has been handled by organized stock exchanges. A **stock exchange** is an organization of individuals coordinated to provide an institutional auction setting in which stocks can be bought and sold.

Founded in 1792 and located at the corner of Wall and Broad Streets in New York City, the New York Stock Exchange sees billions of shares change hands each day.

Peter Foley/EPA/Newscom

The Trading Floor   Each exchange regulates the places and times at which trading may occur. The most important difference between traditional exchanges and the electronic market is the geographic location of the trading activity. Brokers at an exchange trade face-to-face on the *trading floor* (also referred to as an *outcry market*). The electronic market, on the other hand, conducts trades electronically among thousands of dealers in remote locations around the world.

Trading floors today are equipped with vast arrays of electronic communications equipment for displaying buy and sell orders or confirming completed trades. A variety of news services furnish up-to-the-minute information about world events and business developments. Any change in these factors, then, may be swiftly reflected in share prices.

The Major Stock Exchanges   Among the stock exchanges that operate on trading floors in the United States, the New York Stock Exchange is the largest. Today it faces stiff competition from both the electronic market in the United States—NASDAQ—and large foreign exchanges, such as those in London and Tokyo.

The New York Stock Exchange   For many people, "the stock market" means the *New York Stock Exchange (NYSE)*. Founded in 1792, the NYSE is the model for exchanges worldwide. The merger with Euronext in 2007 formed NYSE Euronext, bringing together marketplaces across Europe and the United States. Only firms meeting certain minimum requirements—earning power, total value of outstanding stock, and number of shareholders—are eligible for listing on the NYSE.[7]

Today's NYSE is a *hybrid market* that utilizes both floor and electronic trading. When a client places an order through a brokerage house or online, it is transmitted to a broker on the NYSE floor. Floor brokers who want to trade that stock meet together to agree on a trading price based on supply and demand, and the order is executed. Alternatively, buyers can use the NYSE's Direct+ service to automatically execute trades electronically.

Global Stock Exchanges   As recently as 1980, the U.S. market accounted for more than half the value of the world market in traded stocks. Market activities, however, have shifted as the value of shares listed on foreign exchanges continues to grow. Table 16.1 identifies several stock exchanges, among hundreds of exchanges around the world, and

TABLE 16.1   Selected Global Stock Exchanges and Markets[9]

Country/Region	Stock Exchange	Total Value of Trades, Year Ended 31 December 2010 (billions of U.S. dollars)
Australia	Australian Securities Exchange	1,602
Brazil	Sao Paulo Stock Exchange	868
Canada	Toronto Stock Exchange	1,368
China	Shanghai Stock Exchange	4,496
Hong Kong	Hong Kong Stock Exchange	1,496
Japan	Tokyo Stock Exchange	3,787
United Kingdom	London Stock Exchange	2,741
United States/Europe	NYSE/Euronext	19,813

Securities stocks, bonds, and mutual funds representing secured, or asset-based, claims by investors against issuers

Securities Markets markets in which stocks and bonds are sold

Primary Securities Market market in which new stocks and bonds are bought and sold by firms and governments

Securities and Exchange Commission (SEC) government agency that regulates U.S. securities markets

Investment Bank financial institution that specializes in issuing and reselling new securities

Secondary Securities Market market in which existing (not new) stocks and bonds are sold to the public

Stock Exchange an organization of individuals to provide an institutional auction setting in which stocks can be bought and sold

the annual dollar volume of shares traded at each exchange. While new exchanges are emerging in Vietnam, Laos, and Rwanda, earlier startups are flourishing in cities from Shanghai to Warsaw, and others are merging or partnering in different regions. NYSE Euronext, for example, gained a valuable presence in the Middle East by joining with Qatar Exchange, which enables Qatar to become a stronger international exchange.[8]

The NASDAQ Market The **National Association of Securities Dealers Automated Quotation (NASDAQ) system**, the world's oldest electronic stock market, was established in 1971. Whereas buy and sell orders to the NYSE are gathered on the trading floor, NASDAQ orders are gathered and executed on a computer network connecting 350,000 terminals worldwide. Currently, NASDAQ is working with officials in an increasing number of countries in replacing the trading floors of traditional exchanges with electronic networks like NASDAQ's.

The stocks of some 3,000 companies, both emerging and well known, are traded by NASDAQ. Examples include Marvell, Apple, Microsoft, and Staples. Although the volume of shares traded surpasses that of the New York Stock Exchange, the total market value of NASDAQ's U.S. stocks is less than that of the NYSE.

International Consolidation and Cross-Border Ownership   A wave of technological advances, along with regulatory and competitive factors, is propelling the consolidation of stock exchanges and the changeover from physical to electronic trading floors across international borders. Electronic communication networks have opened the door to around-the-clock and around-the-globe trading. Every major European stock exchange had gone electronic by the close of the twentieth century, and the United States is catching up. Stock exchanges that don't have enough savvy with electronic technologies to stay competitive are merging or partnering with those having more advanced trading systems. The intensified competition among stock exchanges is resulting in speedier transactions and lower transaction fees for investors.[10]

Non-Exchange Trading: Electronic Communication Networks

The SEC in 1998 authorized the creation of **electronic communication networks (ECNs)**—electronic trading systems that bring buyers and sellers together outside traditional stock exchanges by automatically matching buy and sell orders at specified prices. ECNs have gained rapid popularity because the trading procedures are fast and efficient, often lowering transaction costs per share to mere pennies. They also allow after-hours trading (after traditional markets have closed for the day) and protect traders' anonymity.[11]

ECNs must register with the SEC as broker-dealers. The ECN then provides service to subscribers, that is, other broker-dealers and institutional investors. Subscribers can view all orders at any time on the system's website to see information on what trades have taken place and at what times.[12] Individual investors must open an account with a subscriber (a broker-dealer) before they can send buy or sell orders to the ECN system.

Individual Investor Trading

While half of all U.S. citizens have some form of ownership in stocks, bonds, or mutual funds, more than half of the adults have holdings worth $5,000 or more.[13] Many of these investors are novices who seek the advice of experienced professionals, or brokers. Investors who are well informed and experienced, however, often prefer to invest independently without outside guidance.

Stock Brokers   Some of the people on the trading floor are employed by the stock exchange. Others are trading stocks for themselves. Many, however, are **stock brokers** who earn commissions by executing buy and sell orders for outside customers. Although they match buyers with sellers, brokers do not own the securities. They earn commissions from the individuals and organizations for whom they place orders.

Discount Brokers As with many other products, brokerage assistance can be purchased at either discount or at full-service prices. Discount brokers, such as E*TRADE and Scottrade, offer well-informed individual investors who know what they want to buy or sell a fast, low-cost way to participate in the market. Sales personnel receive fees or salaries, not commissions. Unlike many full-service brokers, many discount brokers do not offer in-depth investment advice or person-to-person sales consultations. They do, however, offer automated online services, such as stock research, industry analysis, and screening for specific types of stocks.

Full-Service Brokers Despite the growth in online investing, full-service brokers remain an important resource, both for new, uninformed investors and for experienced investors who don't have time to keep up with all the latest developments. Full-service firms such as Merrill Lynch offer clients consulting advice in personal financial planning, estate planning, and tax strategies, along with a wider range of investment products. In addition to delivering and interpreting information, financial advisors can point clients toward investments that might otherwise be lost in an avalanche of online financial data.

Online Investing The popularity of online trading stems from convenient access to the Internet, fast, no-nonsense transactions, and the opportunity for self-directed investors to manage their own investments while paying low fees for trading.

Online investors buy into and sell out of the stocks of thousands of companies daily. Consequently, keeping track of who owns what at any given time has become a monumental burden. Relief has come from **book-entry ownership**. Historically, shares of stock have been issued as physical paper certificates; now they are simply recorded in the companies' books, thereby eliminating the costs of storing, exchanging, and replacing certificates.

Tracking the Market Using Stock Indexes

For decades investors have used stock indexes to measure market performance and to predict future movements of stock markets. Although not indicative of the status of individual securities, **market indexes** provide useful summaries of overall price trends, both in specific industries and in the stock market as a whole. Market indexes, for example, reveal bull and bear market trends. **Bull markets** are periods of rising stock prices, generally lasting 12 months or longer; investors are motivated to buy, confident they will realize capital gains. Periods of falling stock prices, usually 20 percent off peak prices, are called **bear markets**; investors are motivated to sell, anticipating further falling prices.

As Figure 16.2 shows, the past three decades have been characterized primarily by bull markets, including the longest in history, from 1981 to the beginning of 2000. In contrast, the period 2000 to 2003 was characterized by a bear market. The period 2007–2009 was the second-worst bear market of all time, exceeded only by that of 1929–1932.[14] The data that characterize such periods are drawn from four leading market indexes: the Dow Jones, Standard & Poor's, NASDAQ Composite, and the Russell 2000 (not shown in Figure 16.2).

National Association Of Securities Dealers Automated Quotation (NASDAQ) System world's oldest electronic stock market consisting of dealers who buy and sell securities over a network of electronic communications

Electronic Communication Network (ECN) electronic trading system that brings buyers and sellers together outside traditional stock exchanges

Stock Broker individual or organization that receives and executes buy and sell orders on behalf of outside customers in return for commissions

Book-Entry Ownership procedure that holds investors' shares in book-entry form, rather than issuing a physical paper certificate of ownership

Market Index statistical indicator designed to measure the performance of a large group of stocks or track the price changes of a stock market

Bull Market period of rising stock prices, lasting 12 months or longer, featuring investor confidence for future gains and motivation to buy

Bear Market period of falling stock prices marked by negative investor sentiments with motivation to sell ahead of anticipated losses

Figure 16.2 Bull and Bear Markets
Source: Dow Jones Industrial Average," MSN.com, at http://moneycentral.msn.com/investor/charts/chartdl.aspx?PT=7&compsyms=&D4=1&DD=1&D5=0&DCS=2&MA0=0&MA1=0&CP=1&C5=1& Yahoo! Finance, at http://finance.yahoo.com.

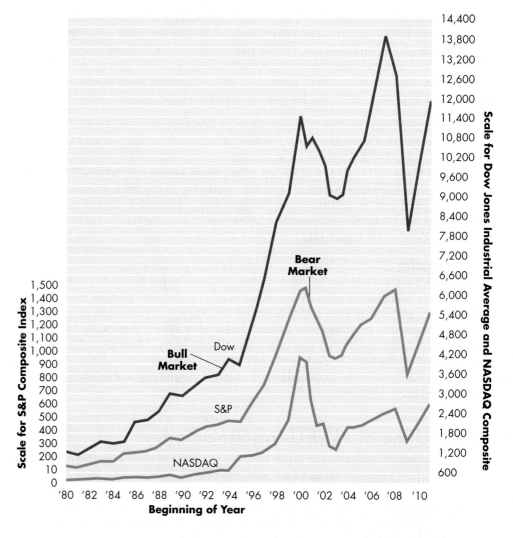

The Dow   The **Dow Jones Industrial Average (DJIA)** is the oldest and most widely cited U.S. market index. It measures the performance of the industrial sector of the U.S. stock markets by focusing on just 30 blue-chip, large-cap companies as reflectors of the economic health of the many similar U.S. firms. The Dow is an average of the stock prices for these 30 large firms, and traders and investors use it as a traditional barometer of the market's overall movement. Because it includes only 30 of the thousands of companies on the market, the Dow is only an approximation of the overall market's price movements.

Over the decades, the Dow has been revised and updated to reflect the changing composition of U.S. companies and industries. Recent modifications occurred in 2008–2009, when three companies were added—Kraft Foods, insurance giant Travelers Companies, and technology titan Cisco Systems—replacing insurance company American International Group, banker Citigroup, and auto icon General Motors. Replacing the three outgoing firms, all facing substantial financial and restructuring upheavals, the new additions better represent today's food- and technology-based economy and the prominence of the financials industry.[15]

The S&P 500   Because it considers very few firms, the Dow is a limited gauge of the overall U.S. stock market. The **S&P 500**—the Standard and Poor's Composite Index—is a broader report, considered by many to be the best single indicator of the U.S. equities market. It consists of 500 large-cap stocks, including companies from various sectors—such as information technology, energy, industrials, financials, health care, consumer staples, and telecommunications—for a balanced representation of the overall large-cap equities market.

ENTREPRENEURSHIP AND NEW VENTURES

An Entrepreneurship of Evil

Bernard Madoff's scheme was not a new idea; it dates back to 1899, when a New Yorker, William Miller, cheated investors out of $1 million. Miller's method was popularized by Boston businessman Charles Ponzi, who, in 1919 to 1920, swindled millions of dollars from unsuspecting investors; he expected to net a 50 percent profit in 90 days. Madoff's contribution to Ponzi-scheme history is the enormity of its size and duration: It reached more than $50 billion, perhaps up to $65 billion, and lasted at least 10 years. So convincing was his sales pitch that the $100,000 minimum investment was paid willingly by a star-studded list, including the Wilpon family (owner of the New York Jets), actor Kevin Bacon, Baseball Hall of Famer Sandy Koufax, and Steven Spielberg, along with a host of banks, universities, churches, and charities.

Ponzi victims over the decades fit a certain pattern: Many are unsophisticated investors, do not rely on a professional representative, believe that unusually high returns are realistic, and place unfounded faith in personal relationships and tips that lure them into making bad decisions. That's how Ponzi connivers operate—by offering abnormally large returns, deflecting prying questions and doubts with personal reassurances and high dividends, and bolstering the scheme's allure by paying high returns to early investors by using new money raised from new clients. As word of high payoffs spreads, more new investors are attracted; otherwise, the scheme falls apart, and the investments disappear. Without an ever-growing pool of new clients, the payoff money runs dry.

Madoff's scheme collapsed when nervous investors, worried about the economic downturn in 2008, asked to withdraw their money. As new money ran dry, the fraud was soon exposed; a federal judge, calling the scheme especially evil, ordered that Bernard Madoff Investment Securities LLC be liquidated, and sentenced Madoff to a 150-year prison term. Meanwhile, victims have filed more than 15,000 claims against the fraud. Investor claims may be eligible for up to $500,000 each from the Securities Investment Protection Corporation (SIPC), a private fund authorized by Congress

Steven Hirsch/Splash News/Newscom

to protect securities investors. Some of the massive losses, but certainly not all, may be recovered from the liquidated company's assets. Meanwhile, the end question from Madoff's evil remains unanswered: What percentage of losses will be recovered?[16]

MyBizLab

The NASDAQ Composite   Because it considers more stocks, some Wall Street observers regard the **NASDAQ Composite Index** as one of the most useful of all market indexes. Unlike the Dow and the S&P 500, all NASDAQ-listed companies, not just a selected few, are included in the index for a total of approximately 3,000 firms, mostly in the U.S. but in other countries as well. However, it includes a high proportion of technology companies, including small-company stocks, and a smaller representation of other sectors—financial, consumer products, and industrials.

Dow Jones Industrial Average (DJIA) oldest and most widely cited market index based on the prices of 30 blue-chip, large-cap industrial firms on the NYSE

S&P 500 market index of U.S. equities based on the performance of 500 large-cap stocks representing various sectors of the overall equities market

Nasdaq Composite Index market index that includes all NASDAQ-listed companies, both domestic and foreign, with a high proportion of technology companies and small-cap stocks

The Russell 2000   Investors in the U.S. small-cap market are interested in the **Russell 2000 Index**—a specialty index that measures the performance of the smallest U.S. companies based on market capitalization. As the most quoted index focusing on the small-cap portion of the U.S. economy, its stocks represent a range of sectors such as financials, consumer discretionary, health care, technology, materials, and utilities.

Index-Matching ETFs   Countless other specialty indexes exist for specific industries, countries, and economic sectors to meet investors' diverse needs. Additionally, many exchange-traded funds are available to investors for duplicating (or nearly duplicating) the market performance of popular stock-market indexes. For example, one ETF, Standard & Poor's Depository Receipts (SPDRS, known as *Spiders*), owns a portfolio of stocks that matches the composition of the S&P 500 index. Similarly the Fidelity® NASDAQ Composite Index® Tracking Stock holds a portfolio of equities for tracking the NASDAQ Composite Index.

4   Describe the risk–return relationship and discuss the use of diversification and asset allocation for investments.

The Risk–Return Relationship

Individual investors have different motivations and personal preferences for safety versus risk. That is why, for example, some individuals and firms invest in stocks while others invest only in bonds. While all investors anticipate receiving future cash flows, some cash flows are more certain than others. Investors generally expect to receive higher returns for higher uncertainty. They do not generally expect large returns for secure, stable investments like government-insured bonds. Each type of investment, then, has a **risk–return (risk–reward) relationship:** Whereas safer investments tend to offer lower returns, riskier investments tend to offer higher returns (rewards).

Figure 16.3 shows the general risk–return relationship for various financial instruments, along with the types of investors they attract. Thus, conservative investors, who have a low tolerance for risk, will opt for no-risk U.S. Treasury Bills, or even intermediate-term high-grade corporate bonds that rate low in terms of risk on future

Figure 16.3 *Potential Financial Returns Rise with Riskier Investments.*
Carl Beidelman, *The Handbook of International Investing* (Chicago, 1987), p. 133. © The McGraw-Hill Companies, Inc.

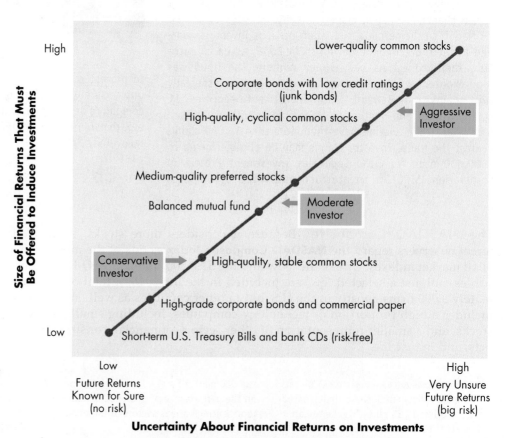

Uncertainty About Financial Returns on Investments

returns, but also low on the size of expected returns. The reverse is true of aggressive investors who prefer the higher risks and potential returns from long-term junk bonds and common stocks.[17]

Investment Dividends (or Interest), Appreciation, and Total Return

In evaluating potential investments, investors look at returns from dividends (or from interest), returns from price appreciation, and total return.

Dividends   The returns from stock dividends are commonly referred to as the **current dividend yield** (or, in the case of interest from a loan, the **interest dividend yield**), and are figured by dividing the yearly dollar amount of dividend income by the investment's current market value. In 2011, for example, each share of AT&T stock was receiving annual dividends payments of $1.72. If, on a particular day, the share price was $31.80, the current yield would be 5.41% ($1.72/$31.80 × 100). This dividend can then be compared against current yields from other investments. Larger dividend yields, of course, are preferred to smaller returns.

Fantasy Stock Markets Enthusiasts of baseball, football, and hockey aren't the only fans energized by fantasy games. Fantasy stock markets are all the rage for learning how securities markets work, for trying your hand at various investment strategies, and earning a fantasy fortune (or going broke!). Internet-based games, including free ones such as *Wall Street Survivor* and *How the Market Works*, provide an investment experience that is educational, challenging, and entertaining. Starting with an initial sum in virtual cash with which to manage their own fantasy portfolio of real companies, participants must live with real market results. It's a learn-by-doing experience—using web-based symbol lookups to enter stock-ticker symbols, searching various information sources for research on companies of interest, making buy-and-sell decisions, and then discovering the financial results as real market prices change for the portfolio holdings. Many students and business practitioners are finding these "games" to be a valuable resource for learning the "how to" of online investing.

Price Appreciation   Another source of returns depends on whether the investment is increasing or decreasing in dollar value. **Price appreciation** is an increase in the dollar value of an investment. Suppose, for example, you purchased a share of AT&T stock for $31.80, then sold it one year later for $33.40. The price appreciation is $1.60 ($33.40 – 31.80). This profit, realized from the increased market value of an investment, is known as a **capital gain.**

Total Return   The sum of an investment's current dividend (interest) yield and capital gain is referred to as its total return. Total return cannot be accurately evaluated until it's compared to the investment that was required to get that return. Total return as a percentage of investment is calculated as follows:

$$\text{Total return (\%)} = (\text{Current dividend payment} + \text{Capital gain})/$$
$$\text{Original investment} \times 100.$$

Russell 2000 Index specialty index that uses 2,000 stocks to measure the performance of the smallest U.S. companies

Risk–Return (Risk–Reward) Relationship principle that safer investments tend to offer lower returns whereas riskier investments tend to offer higher returns (rewards)

Current/Interest Dividend Yield yearly dollar amount of income divided by the investment's current market value, expressed as a percentage

Price Appreciation increase in the dollar value of an investment at two points in time (the amount by which the price of a security increases)

Capital Gain profit realized from the increased value of an investment

To complete our AT&T example, the total return as a percentage of our one-year investment would be 10.44% [($1.72 + $1.60)/$31.80 × 100]. Note that larger total returns are preferred to smaller ones.

Managing Risk with Diversification and Asset Allocation

Investors seldom take an extreme approach—total risk or total risk avoidance—in selecting their investments. Extreme positions attract extreme results; instead, most investors select a mixed portfolio of investments—some riskier and some more conservative—that, collectively, provides the overall level of risk and financial returns that feels comfortable. After determining the desired *risk-return* balance, they then achieve it in two ways: through *diversification* and *asset allocation*.

Diversification   **Diversification** means buying several different kinds of investments rather than just one. For example, diversification as applied to common stocks means that you invest in stocks of several different companies. The risk of loss is reduced by spreading the total investment across different stocks because although any one stock may tumble, the chances are less that all of them will fall at the same time. More diversification is gained when assets are spread across a variety of investment alternatives—stocks, bonds, mutual funds, precious metals, real estate, and so on. Among the tragedies in recent years are sufferings of the lifelong employees who did not have diversified investments and, instead, had all their retirement funds invested in their firm's stock. This was an extremely risky position, as they sorrowfully learned. When their firm's stock took a free fall due to a market collapse or scandals, their retirement funds disappeared.

Asset Allocation   **Asset allocation** is the proportion—the relative amounts—of funds invested in (or allocated to) each of the investment alternatives. You may decide for example, to allocate 50 percent of your funds to common stocks, 25 percent to a money market mutual fund, and 25 percent to a U.S. Treasury bond mutual fund. Ten years later, with more concern for financial safety, you may decide on a less risky asset allocation of 20 percent, 40 percent, and 40 percent in the same investment categories, respectively. In this example, the portfolio has been changed from moderate-risk to lower-risk investments for the purpose of preserving the investor's accumulated capital. The asset allocation was changed accordingly.

Performance Differences for Different Portfolios   Once an investment objective with acceptable risk level is chosen, the tools of diversification and asset allocation are put to use in the investor's portfolio. A **portfolio** is the combined holdings of all the financial investments—stocks, bonds, mutual funds, real estate—of any company or individual.

Just like investors, investment funds have different investment objectives—ranging from aggressive growth/high risk to stable income/low volatility—and their holdings are diversified accordingly among hundreds of company stocks, corporate bonds, or government bonds that provide the desired orientation. The money in a diversified portfolio is allocated in different proportions among a variety of funds; if all goes according to plan, most of these funds will meet their desired investment objectives and the overall portfolio will increase in value.

Financing the Business Firm

5 Describe the various ways that firms raise capital and identify the pros and cons of each method.

If you invest wisely, you may earn enough money to start your own firm—but that's only the first step in the complicated process of financing a business. Every company needs cash to function. Although a business owner's savings may be enough to get a firm up and running, businesses depend on sales revenues to survive. When current sales revenues are insufficient to pay for expenses, firms tap into various other sources of funds, typically starting with the owners' savings—as discussed in Chapter 14, owners contribute funds, or paid-in capital, from their own pockets. If a firm needs more money, they can turn to borrowing from banks, soliciting cash from private outside investors, or selling bonds to the public.

Secured Loans for Equipment

Money to purchase new equipment often comes in the form of loans from commercial banks. In a **secured loan (asset-backed loan)** the borrower guarantees repayment of the loan by pledging the asset as **collateral** to the lender. That is, if the borrower defaults, or fails to repay the loan, the bank can take possession of his or her assets and sell them to recover the outstanding debt. However, as we learned in the 2007–2009 recession, assets from loans defaulted by businesses and home buyers may have little or no value.

Principal and Interest Rates   The amount of money that is loaned and must be repaid is called the **loan principal.** However, borrowers also pay the lender an additional fee, called **interest,** for the use of the borrowed funds. The amount of interest owed depends on an **annual percentage rate (APR)** that is agreed on between the lender and borrower. The interest amount is found by multiplying the APR by the loan principal.

Working Capital and Unsecured Loans from Banks

Firms need more than just fixed assets for daily operations; they need current, liquid assets available to meet short-term operating expenses such as employee wages and marketing expenses. The firm's ability to meet these expenses is measured by its working capital:

$$\text{Working capital} = \text{Current assets} - \text{Current liabilities}$$

Positive working capital means the firm's current assets are large enough to pay off current liabilities (see Chapter 14). Negative working capital means the firm's current liabilities are greater than current assets, so it may need to borrow money from a commercial bank. With an **unsecured loan,** the borrower does not have to put up collateral. In many cases, however, the bank requires the borrower to maintain a *compensating balance*—the borrower must keep a portion of the loan amount on deposit with the bank in a non–interest-bearing account.

Firms with bad credit scores typically cannot get unsecured loans. Because access to such loans requires a good credit history, many firms establish a relationship with a commercial bank and, over time, build a good credit record by repaying loan principal and interest on time.

In extreme conditions, however, even a good credit history may not be enough. During the deepening recession, the cash shortages at most banks prevented loans of nearly any kind to business customers, thereby slowing down the economy even more. Even after vast injections of cash from TARP and other government sources, banks lagged far behind in supplying loans to meet working-capital needs of cash-strapped business borrowers.

Angel Investors and Venture Capital

Once a business has been successfully launched it needs additional capital for growth. Outside individuals who provide such capital are called **angel investors.** In

---

Diversification purchase of several different kinds of investments rather than just one

Asset Allocation relative amount of funds invested in (or allocated to) each of several investment alternatives

Portfolio combined holdings of all the financial investments of any company or individual

Secured Loan (Asset-Backed Loan) loan to finance an asset, backed by the borrower pledging the asset as collateral to the lender

Collateral asset pledged for the fulfillment of repaying a loan

Loan Principal amount of money that is loaned and must be repaid

Interest fee paid to a lender for the use of borrowed funds; like a rental fee

Annual Percentage Rate (APR) one-year rate that is charged for borrowing, expressed as a percentage of the borrowed principal

Unsecured Loan loan for which collateral is not required

Angel Investors outside investors who provide new capital for firms in return for a share of equity ownership

return for their investment, angel investors typically expect a sizable piece of ownership in the company (up to 50 percent of its equity). They may also want a formal say in how the company is run. If the firm is bought by a larger company or if it sells its stock in a public offering, the angel may receive additional payments.

Angel investors help many firms grow rapidly by providing what is known as **venture capital**—private funds from wealthy individuals or companies (see Chapter 3) that seek investment opportunities in new growth companies. In most cases, the growth firm turns to venture capital sources because they have not yet built enough credit history to get a loan from commercial banks or other lending institutions.

Sale of Corporate Bonds

Corporations can raise capital by issuing bonds. A **corporate bond** is a formal pledge (an IOU) obligating the issuer to pay interest periodically and repay the principal at maturity (a preset future date) to the lender. The federal government also issues bonds to finance projects and meet obligations, as do state and local governments (called *municipal bonds*).

Characteristics of Corporate Bonds

The bondholder (the lender) has no claim to ownership of the company and does not receive dividends. However, interest payments and repayment of principal are financial obligations; payments to bondholders have priority over dividend payments to stockholders in cases of financial distress.

Each new bond issue has specific terms and conditions spelled out in a **bond indenture**—a legal document identifying the borrower's obligations and the financial returns to lenders. One of the most important details is the **maturity date** (or **due date**), when the firm must repay the bond's **face value** (also called **par value,** or the amount purchased) to the lender.

Corporate bonds have been traditionally issued to fund outstanding debts and major projects for various lengths of time. Short-term bonds mature in less than five years after they are issued. Bonds with 5- to 10-year lives are considered intermediate term, while anything over 10 years is considered long term. Longer-term corporate bonds are somewhat riskier than shorter-term bonds because they are exposed to greater unforeseen economic conditions that may lead to default.

Default and Bondholders' Claim

A bond is said to be in **default** if the borrower fails to make payment when due to lenders. Bondholders may then file a **bondholders' claim**—a request for court enforcement of the bond's terms of payment. When a financially distressed company cannot pay bondholders, it may seek relief by filing for **bankruptcy**—the court-granted permission not to pay some or all debts. After a restructured General Motors emerged from bankruptcy in 2009, the holders of GM's $24 billion in bonds continue to wonder how much payment, if any, they will recover from the financially strapped company.

Risk Ratings

To aid investors in making purchase decisions, several services measure the default risk of bonds. Table 16.2, for example, shows the rating systems of two well-known services, Moody's and Standard & Poor's. The highest (safest) grades are AAA and Aaa, and the lowest are C and D, representing very speculative and highly risky bonds. Low-grade bonds are usually called *junk bonds*. Negative ratings do not necessarily keep issues from being successful. Rather, they raise the interest rates that issuers must offer to attract lenders.

Flawed Ratings Misread Recession Risks

The financial meltdown of 2008 has raised questions about whether any good purpose is being served by credit-rating

TABLE 16.2 Bond Rating Systems				
Rating System	**High Grades**	**Medium Grades (Investment Grades)**	**Speculative**	**Poor Grades**
Moody's	Aaa, Aa	A, Baa	Ba, B	Caa to C
Standard & Poor's	AAA, AA	A, BBB	BB, B	CCC to D

MANAGING IN TURBULENT TIMES

Staying Afloat in a Sea of Falling Home Values

While questions remain on causes of the U.S. credit crisis, consensus has emerged that two financial giants—Fannie Mae and Freddie Mac—contributed significantly to the downfall. Senator John McCain said the companies were the "catalyst—the match that started this forest fire." Representative Henry Waxman, citing irresponsible investments and ignoring credit risks, noted that the companies' "own risk managers warned time after time of the dangers of investing in the subprime market." Unlike prime mortgages, subprime loans are made to high-risk borrowers.[20]

In 2008, to support the housing market, the U.S. government took over these two companies, which had losses totaling over $100 billion and which owned or guaranteed nearly $6 trillion in outstanding home mortgage debt. The top executives at both companies were fired, and day-to-day operations were placed under control of the Federal Housing Finance Agency. The government also committed up to $200 billion in bailout funds to each firm, if needed, to avoid further meltdown.[21]

Freddie Mac and Fannie Mae, also known as FM2, are federally backed, publicly traded companies chartered by Congress. They were created decades ago to keep the housing market flowing by making home mortgage money more available. FM2 buy mortgage loans from loan-making financial institutions, such as banks, then bundle them together into securities that are insured by FM2 and sold to investors. Before 1992, FM2 applied stricter credit standards, refusing to buy and resell subprime mortgages; banks that made subprime loans had to accept the

Fannie Mae

risks by holding them. When lenders failed to repay, the failed loans became the bank's loss. Since 1992, with FM2's acceptance of subprime mortgages, lending risks have been transferred from banks to FM2 on a massive scale. By selling their subprime loans to FM2, banks receive new cash to lend without being saddled with the risky subprimes. As housing values continue to fall and loan defaults grow, the mortgage-backed securities issued by FM2 are under increasing risk of default, and the U.S. government faces prospects of repaying an ocean of money—perhaps more than $1 trillion—to insured securities investors.[22]

MyBizLab

agencies. Among other investors, California Public Employees Retirement Fund (Calpers), the nation's largest public pension fund, has filed a suit against the three top agencies—Moody's, Standard & Poor's, and Fitch—charging losses caused by "wildly inaccurate and unreasonably high" credit ratings. Calpers officials relied on ratings for investments that turned sour—many failing altogether. Skepticism of agencies' ratings has soared following the collapse of highly rated giants such as Lehman Brothers, Goldman Sachs, and Citigroup, along with high ratings on billions of dollars of mortgage-backed securities that eventually became toxic. Recent lawsuits, including those by the states of Ohio and Connecticut, accuse credit rating agencies of reckless assessments that misled investors.[18]

Highly Rated Securities Turn Toxic **Mortgage-backed securities (MBS)** became a trillion-dollar investment industry during the pre-2007 housing market boom years. Financial institutions bundled home mortgages into packages and resold

---

Venture Capital private funds from wealthy individuals seeking investment opportunities in new growth companies

Corporate Bond formal pledge obligating the issuer (the company) to pay interest periodically and repay the principal at maturity

Bond Indenture legal document containing complete details of a bond issue

Maturity Date (Due Date) future date when repayment of a bond is due from the bond issuer (borrower)

Face Value (Par Value) amount of money that the bond buyer (lender) lent the issuer and that the lender will receive upon repayment

Default failure of a borrower to make payment when due to a lender

Bondholders' Claim request for court enforcement of a bond's terms of payment

Bankruptcy court-granted permission for a company to not pay some or all debts

Mortgage-Backed Security (MBS) mortgages pooled together to form a debt obligation—a bond—that entitles the holder (investor) to cash that flows in from the bundled mortgages

them as securities to eager investors who trusted in the securities' risk ratings given by Moody's, Standard & Poor's, and Fitch. Each MBS is a group of mortgages bundled together to form a debt obligation—a bond—that entitles the holder (investor) to the cash that flows in from the mortgages. Unknown to investors, some $3 trillion of MBSs contained subprime mortgages—high-risk loans to applicants with bad credit, low income, and low down payments—most of whom had received very high ratings (AAA) by credit-rating agencies. With flawed risk assessments, investors were left with little or nothing when the housing and financial markets collapsed.[19]

6 Identify the reasons a company might make an initial public offering of its stock and explain how stock value is determined.

Becoming a Public Corporation

Initial public offerings (IPOs)—the first sale of a company's stock to the general public—are a major source of funds that fuel continued growth for many firms, as well as introduce numerous considerations inherent in running a public company.

Going Public Means Selling Off Part of the Company

Private owners lose some control of the company when shares are sold to the public. Common shareholders usually have voting rights in corporate governance, so they elect the board of directors and vote on major issues put forth at the company's annual shareholders' meeting. Anyone owning a large proportion of the company's shares gains a powerful position in determining who runs the corporation and how.

At an extreme, a **corporate raider**—an investor conducting a type of hostile (unwanted) takeover—buys shares on the open market, attempting to seize control of the company and its assets. The raider then sells off those assets at a profit, resulting in the company's disappearance.

A company is ripe for raiding when its stock price falls so shares can be cheaply bought, although its assets still have high value.

Stock Valuation

There are many factors that affect a stock's value, which in turn affect the value of the business. In addition, different investors measure value differently, and their measurements may change according to circumstance. Because of the uncertainties involved in stock prices, investment professionals believe day-to-day prices to be a generally poor indicator of any stock's real value. Instead, a long-run perspective considers the company's financial health, past history of results and future forecasts, its record for managerial performance, and overall prospects for competing successfully in the coming years. Accordingly, any stock's value today looks beyond the current price and is based on expectations of the financial returns it will provide to shareholders during the long run.

Why Shares Are Different Prices   In April 2011 the price of Google Inc. was about $590 per share on the New York Stock Exchange, while GE shares traded at about $20, and Delta Airlines shares were priced at about $10. Berkshire Hathaway shares traded for $125,000.[23]

In early 2011 Google shares were trading at $586 per share.

Why such differences? One reason is supply and demand for each company's shares; another is because some corporations want the shares to sell within a particular price range, say between $20 and $80, believing it will attract a larger pool of investors. If the price gets too high, many investors can't afford to buy shares. A company can restore shares to the desired lower range by a **stock split**—a stock dividend paid in additional shares to shareholders. Here's how it works. Suppose company X has 100,000 common shares outstanding that are trading at $100 per share, but the company wants it priced in the $20 to $80 range. X can declare a 2-for-1 stock split, meaning the company gives shareholders one additional share for each share they own. Now X has 200,000 shares outstanding but its financial performance has not changed, so the stock price immediately falls to $50 per share. Every shareholder's investment value, however, is unchanged: they previously owned one share at $100, and now they own two shares at $50 each.

Comparing Prices of Different Stocks Consider a trading day in early May, 2011 when PepsiCo's share price was $69.31, while Coca-Cola was $28.89 per share. Does the price difference mean that PepsiCo is a better company than Coca-Cola, because its shares are more expensive? Or does it mean that Coke shares are a better value because they can be bought at a lower price than PepsiCo's? In fact, neither of these two reasons is correct. Share prices alone do not provide enough information to determine which is the better investment. Table 16.3 can help us make a better comparison with further information.

First, earnings per share (EPS) are greater for PepsiCo. Even though you pay more to own a PepsiCo share, earnings per dollar of investment are less than for Coke ($3.74 earnings/$69.31 investment = $0.054; versus $1.80 earnings/$28.89 investment = $0.062): PepsiCo's earnings were more than 5 cents for each dollar of its share price, whereas Coca-Cola earned more than 6 cents. Coca-Cola generated more earnings power for each dollar of shareholder investment.

Now consider annual dividends paid to shareholders. The dividend yield from Coca-Cola was 1.84%. That is, the dividend payment amounted to a 1.84% return on the shareholder's $28.89 investment, or $0.53 ($28.89 × 1.84%). PepsiCo's dividend payment was about $2.04 ($69.31 × 2.95%), representing a somewhat larger return (yield) on shareholder investment than Coca-Cola.

Based on this limited information, it's not clear which of the two companies is the better investment. A more complete evaluation would compare historical performance consistency over a period of several years, along with indicators of each firm's prospects for the future.

Market Capitalization

A widely used measure of corporate size and value is known as **market capitalization (market cap)**—the total dollar value of all the company's outstanding shares, calculated as the current stock price multiplied by the number of shares outstanding. As indicated in Table 16.4, the investment industry categorizes firms according to size of capitalization.

Investors typically regard larger market caps as less risky, and firms with small market caps (small-cap firms) as being particularly risky investments.

TABLE 16.3   Financial Comparison: Coca-Cola and PepsiCo[24]

	Coca-Cola	PepsiCo
Recent price	$28.89	$69.31
EPS	$1.80	$3.74
Dividend yield	1.84%	2.95%

TABLE 16.4   Corporation Sizes Based on Capitalization

Capitalization Category	Range of Capitalization
Micro-Cap	below $250 million
Small-Cap	$250–$2 billion
Mid-Cap	$2 billion–$10 billion
Large-Cap	over $10 billion

Initial Public Offering (IPO) first sale of a company's stock to the general public

Corporate Raider investor conducting a type of hostile corporate takeover against the wishes of the company

Stock Split stock dividend paid in additional shares to shareholders, thus increasing the number of outstanding shares

Market Capitalization (Market Cap) total dollar value of all the company's outstanding shares

In mid-2011 China's CNOOC Ltd. share price was $17.98, and there were 44.67 billion common shares outstanding. Its market cap was over $800 billion, making the oil-and-gas producer the largest company in the world.

Frederic J. Brown/AFP/Getty Images/Newscom

Choosing Equity Versus Debt Capital

Firms can meet their capital needs through two sources: debt financing (from outside the firm) or equity financing (putting the owners' capital to work).

Pros and Cons for Debt Financing   Long-term borrowing from sources outside the company—**debt financing**—via loans or the sale of corporate bonds is a major component in most U.S. firms' financial planning.

Long-Term Loans   Long-term loans are attractive for several reasons:

- Because the number of parties involved is limited, loans can often be arranged very quickly.
- The firm need not make public disclosure of its business plans or the purpose for which it is acquiring the loan. (In contrast, the issuance of corporate bonds requires such disclosure.)

Long-term loans also have some disadvantages. Borrowers, for example, may have trouble finding lenders to supply large sums. Long-term borrowers may also face restrictions as conditions of the loan. For example, they may have to pledge long-term assets as collateral or agree to take on no more debt until the loan is paid.

Corporate Bonds   Bonds are attractive when firms need large amounts for long periods of time. The issuing company gains access to large numbers of lenders through nationwide bond markets. On the other hand, bonds entail high administrative and selling costs. They may also require stiff interest payments, especially if the issuing company has a poor credit rating. Bonds also impose binding obligations on the firm, in many cases for up to 30 years, to pay bondholders a stipulated sum of annual or semiannual interest, even in times of financial distress. If the company fails to make a bond payment, it goes into default.

Pros and Cons for Equity Financing   Although debt financing often has strong appeal, **equity financing**—looking inside the company for long-term funding—is sometimes preferable. Equity financing includes either issuing common stock or retaining the firm's earnings.

The Expense of Common Stock   The use of equity financing by means of common stock can be expensive because paying dividends is more expensive than paying bond interest. Interest paid to bondholders is a business expense and therefore a tax deduction for the firm. Payments of cash dividends to shareholders are not tax deductible.

Retained Earnings as a Source of Capital   As presented in Chapter 14, *retained earnings* are net profits retained for the firm's use rather than paid out in dividends to stockholders. If a company uses retained earnings as capital, it will not have to borrow money and pay interest. If a firm has a history of reaping profits by reinvesting retained earnings, it may be very attractive to some investors. Retained earnings, however, mean smaller dividends for shareholders. This practice may decrease the demand for—and the price of—the company's stock.

7 Explain how securities markets are regulated.

Regulating Securities Markets

The U.S. government, along with various state agencies, plays a key role in monitoring and regulating the securities industry.

The Securities and Exchange Commission

The U.S. Securities and Exchange Commission (SEC) is the regulation and enforcement agency that oversees the markets' activities, including the ways securities are issued. The SEC was created in 1934 to prevent the kinds of abuses that led to the stock market crash of 1929. The SEC regulates the public offering of new securities by requiring that all companies file prospectuses before proposed offerings commence. To protect investors from fraudulent issues, a **prospectus** contains pertinent information about both the offered security and the issuing company. False statements are subject to criminal penalties.

The SEC also enforces laws against **insider trading**—the use of special knowledge about a firm for profit or gain. It is illegal, for example, for an employee of a firm to tell others about an anticipated event that may affect the value of that firm's stock, such as an acquisition or a merger, before news of that event is made public. Those in possession of such insider knowledge would have an unfair advantage over other investors.

Regulations Against Insider Trading

In March 2011 the U.S. Attorney began criminal trial in New York against Raj Rajaratnam, founder of Galleon Group, on charges that the billionaire fund manager profited from illegal stock tips with a network of financial insiders. Reports indicate the accused gained profits of up to $60 million by using illicit information—confidential company information not available to the public—revealing that stock prices of various companies would be increasing or falling. In conjunction with his arrest in 2009, charges were leveled against 26 others in the case—executives and securities traders—nineteen of whom pleaded guilty. In May

Steven Hirsch/Splash News/Newscom

54-year old Raj Rajaratnam was sentenced to 11 years in federal prison after being convicted for insider trading.

2011, Rajaratnam was convicted on 14 charges and faces possible maximum prison sentences totaling up to 205 years. In addition to the criminal trial, he faces additional civil charges brought by the Securities and Exchange Commission. As a U.S. Attorney stated some years earlier, "Insider trading is a crime. Corporate executives are prohibited from enriching themselves while the public remains in the dark about the true financial condition of their companies."[25]

The SEC offers a reward to any person who provides information leading to a civil penalty for illegal insider trading. The courts can render such a penalty of up to three times the illegal profit that was gained, and the reward can, at most, be 10 percent of that penalty.

Along with the SEC's enforcement efforts, the stock exchanges and securities firms have adopted self-regulation by participating with the Financial Industry Regulatory Authority (FINRA) in detecting and stopping insider action, and violations of other industry regulations. Established in 2003, FINRA's mission is to protect U.S. investors by overseeing the nation's brokerage firms and securities representatives. The major U.S. stock markets are under contract that allows FINRA to regulate those markets by writing rules, examining securities firms, enforcing the rules, and enforcing federal securities laws as well.

Debt Financing long-term borrowing from sources outside a company

Equity Financing using the owners' funds from inside the company as the source for long-term funding

Prospectus registration statement filed with the SEC, containing information for prospective investors about a security to be offered and the issuing company

Insider Trading illegal practice of using special knowledge about a firm for profit or gain

© Corbis

Continued from page 415

U.S. Cap and Trade Experiment Is Put on Hold

Amidst an unfavorable political climate, industry objections, and a suspicious EU experience, 2010 legislation to cap U.S. carbon emissions came to an abrupt halt in the Senate. It would have increased costs to businesses and consumers at a time of economic sluggishness, high unemployment, and burgeoning national debt. It would have included a market for trading U.S. emissions allowances. If the legislation had become law, the Chicago Climate Exchange (CCX), with voluntary trading launched in 2003, provided a ready-made market for the new emissions credits; 450 major organizations were CCX members, committed to meeting annual CO2 reduction targets. Members had received allowances based on measured emissions levels. Thereafter, by exceeding scheduled targets, surplus reductions became unused allowances that could be sold, or banked for later use. Firms failing to meet targets had to purchase allowances on the CCX market.[26]

Would the U.S. system avoid problems experienced in the EU system? Some say no, because emissions—unlike gold, cattle, and corn—cannot be measured accurately. Some EU companies are believed to be reporting false measurements; by initially exaggerating the firm's emissions, they receive an inflated number of allowances and gain bonus profits by selling the excess allowances. They can also inflate reported emissions reductions and sell the extra allowances for profit.[27] Critics also cite the unpredictability of allowance prices on the trading markets—costs for emitting a ton of carbon dioxide vary from below [euro]10 to more than [euro]30. Analysts insist that, until they trade near [euro]100, prices won't encourage serious investments for reducing CO2 emissions.[28]

While the EU experience remains controversial and the U.S. cap-and-trade program has stalled, others are going forward. China, for example, is planning to curb inflated greenhouse gas emissions from its expanding manufacturing industries. Striving for a 45 percent reduction of carbon discharges by 2020, climate officials are getting advice from EU leaders for developing China's centralized emissions trading program.[29]

QUESTIONS FOR DISCUSSION

1 If the proposed 2010 legislation had become law, do you believe it would have been desirable for the U.S. cap-and-trade market to become part of a global (multinational) emissions-trading market? Explain why, or why not.

2 Should future U.S. emissions-trading markets be regulated? If yes, in what ways and by what regulatory agency? If no, identify possible risks that may result.

3 Suppose you are CEO of a firm whose activities are known to release CO2 emissions. What factors would you consider in evaluating your possible opposition to mandatory emissions reductions? What factors would you consider in evaluating your support of mandatory cap-and-trade?

4 Suppose you are a potential investor in several companies in various industries. In what ways would your investment decisions be influenced by enactment of mandatory cap-and-trade legislation?

5 Consider a voluntary emissions reduction program that includes allowances trading, such as the Chicago Climate Exchange system, as an alternative to mandatory cap-and-trade. Can a voluntary program succeed in the United States? Explain why, or why not.

SUMMARY OF LEARNING OBJECTIVES   MyBizLab

1. **Explain the concept of the time value of money and the principle of compound growth. (pp. 416–418)**
The time value of money, perhaps the single most important concept in business finance, recognizes the basic fact that, while it's invested, money grows by earning interest or yielding some other form of return. Time value stems from the principle of compound growth—the accumulative growth from interest paid to the investor over given time periods. With each additional time period, interest payments accumulate and earn more interest, thus multiplying the earning capacity of the investment.

2. **Identify the investment opportunities offered by mutual funds and exchange-traded funds. (pp. 418–420)**
As an alternative to buying stock, mutual funds and exchange-traded funds are popular because they offer attractive investment opportunities for various financial objectives and often do not require large sums of money for entry. In addition, the simple and easy transaction process makes them accessible to the public. It's relatively easy to open a mutual fund account online or by phone. There are numerous funds that meet any chosen financial objective. Three of the most common objectives are financial stability, conservative growth, and aggressive growth. ETFs offer three areas of advantage over mutual funds: They can be traded throughout the day like a stock, they have low operating expenses, and they do not require high initial investments. Because they are traded on stock exchanges (hence, "exchange traded"), ETFs can be bought and sold—priced continuously—any time throughout the day. Mutual fund shares, in contrast, are priced once daily, at the end of the day.

3. **Describe the role of securities markets and identify the major stock exchanges and stock markets. (pp. 420–426)**
The markets in which stocks and bonds are sold are called securities markets. By facilitating the buying and selling of securities, the securities markets provide the capital that companies rely on for survival. In primary securities markets, new stocks and bonds are bought and sold by firms and governments. *Existing* stocks and bonds are sold in the much larger secondary securities market, which is handled by such familiar bodies as the New York Stock Exchange, the NASDAQ market in the United States, various foreign exchanges such as the London Stock Exchange and the Tokyo Exchange, and by online trading with other stock exchanges around the globe.

4. **Describe the risk–return relationship and discuss the use of diversification and asset allocation for investments. (pp. 426–428)**
The risk–return relationship is the principle that investors expect to receive higher returns for riskier investments and lower returns for safer investments. Diversification and asset allocation are tools for helping investors achieve the desired risk–return balance for an investment portfolio. *Diversification* means buying several different kinds of investments to reduce the risk of loss if the value of any one security should fall. *Asset allocation* is the proportion of overall money invested in each of various investment alternatives so that the overall risks for the portfolio are low, moderate, or high, depending on the investor's objectives and preferences.

5. **Describe the various ways that firms raise capital and identify the pros and cons of each method. (pp. 428–432)**
Firms often begin with the owner's personal savings. As more money is needed it is obtained from banks, cash from private investors, by issuing bonds, or selling stock. Long-term borrowing through loans or the issuing of bonds is attractive because they can be arranged quickly and do not require public disclosure of the borrower's business plans. However, lenders may place restrictions as conditions of the loan. Payments to bondholders have priority over dividend payments to stockholders. If the borrower fails to make a bond or loan payment, even in times of financial distress, the bond goes into default. Equity financing—issuing common stock or retaining the firm's earnings—can be expensive if dividends are paid because dividend payments are not a tax deduction for the firm, whereas interest paid on loans and bonds is a tax-deductible business expense. Going public by issuing common stock gives up part ownership to shareholders, resulting in less control over company issues by the company's founders. Angel investors, too, expect a sizable share of ownership and a formal say in how the company is run.

6. **Identify the reasons a company might make an initial public offering of its stock and explain how stock value is determined. (p. 432–434)**
The initial public offering (IPO)—the first sale of a company's stock to the general public—is a major source of funds for fueling the growth of many firms. IPOs reach far more potential investors, thereby providing access to a larger pool of funds than is available from the owner's personal funds and other private sources. A stock's real value is its market value—the current price of a share in the stock market. Market value reflects the amount that buyers are willing to pay for a share of the company's stock at any given time. However, the valuing of any stock today looks beyond the current price and is based on expectations of the financial returns it will provide to shareholders during the long run. A long-run perspective considers the company's financial health, past history of results and future forecasts, its record for managerial performance, and overall prospects for competing successfully in the coming years.

7. Explain how securities markets are regulated.
    (pp. 434–435)
    The U.S. Securities and Exchange Commission (SEC) is the regulation agency that oversees the markets' activities. The SEC regulates the public offering of new securities by requiring companies to file prospectuses before proposed offerings commence. The prospectus contains information about the offered security and the

issuing company. False statements are subject to criminal penalties. The SEC also enforces laws against insider trading—the use of special knowledge about a firm for profit or gain. Along with the SEC's enforcement, the stock exchanges and securities firms have adopted self-regulation by participating with the Financial Industry Regulatory Authority (FINRA) in detecting and stopping violations of industry regulations.

KEY TERMS   MyBizLab

angel investors (p. 429)
annual percentage rate (APR) (p. 429)
asset allocation (p. 428)
bankruptcy (p. 430)
bear market (p. 423)
blue-chip stock (p. 418)
bond indenture (p. 430)
bondholders' claim (p. 430)
book value (p. 417)
book-entry ownership (p. 423)
bull market (p. 423)
capital gain (p. 427)
collateral (p. 429)
common stock (p. 417)
compound growth (p. 416)
corporate bond (p. 430)
corporate raider (p. 432)
current/interest dividend yield (p. 427)
debt financing (p. 434)
default (p. 430)
diversification (p. 428)
dividend (p. 418)
Dow Jones Industrial Average (DJIA) (p. 424)

electronic communication network (ECN) (p. 422)
equity financing (p. 434)
exchange-traded fund (ETF) (p. 419)
face value (par value) (p. 430)
initial public offering (IPO) (p. 432)
insider trading (p. 435)
interest (p. 429)
investment bank (p. 420)
load fund (p. 418)
loan principal (p. 429)
market capitalization (market cap) (p. 433)
market index (p. 423)
market value (p. 417)
maturity date (due date) (p. 430)
mortgage-backed security (MBS) (p. 431)
mutual fund (p. 418)
NASDAQ Composite Index (p. 425)
National Association of Securities Dealers Automated Quotation (NASDAQ) system (p. 422)

no-load fund (p. 418)
portfolio (p. 428)
price appreciation (p. 427)
primary securities market (p. 420)
prospectus (p. 435)
risk–return (risk–reward) relationship (p. 426)
Russell 2000 Index (p. 426)
S&P 500 (p. 424)
secondary securities market (p. 420)
secured loan (asset-backed loan) (p. 429)
securities (p. 420)
Securities and Exchange Commission (SEC) (p. 420)
securities markets (p. 420)
stock (p. 417)
stock broker (p. 422)
stock exchange (p. 420)
stock split (p. 433)
time value of money (p. 416)
unsecured loan (p. 429)
venture capital (p. 430)

QUESTIONS AND EXERCISES

QUESTIONS FOR REVIEW
1. Explain the concept of the *time value of money*.
2. What do mutual funds and exchange-traded funds offer, and how do they work?
3. Identify the various characteristics of corporate bonds.
4. How does the market value of a stock differ from the book value of a stock?
5. How do firms meet their needs through debt financing and equity financing?

QUESTIONS FOR ANALYSIS

6. After researching several stocks online, you notice that they have continually fluctuated in price. What might be the reason for this? Is a higher-priced stock a better investment than a lower-priced stock? What factors would you consider in purchasing stocks?

7. Which type of fund do you think you would invest in, a mutual fund or an exchange-traded fund? What is the difference, and why would you favor one over the other?

8. Suppose that you are a business owner and you need new equipment and immediate funds to meet short-term operating expenses. From what sources could you gain the capital you need, and what are some of the characteristics of these sources?

APPLICATION EXERCISES

9. Go to http://www.sec.gov to research how a new security is approved by the Securities and Exchange Commission. What is the process involved and how long would it take? Next, contact a financial institution such as Merrill Lynch and request information about their procedures for issuing or reselling new securities. Share this information with your classmates.

10. If you are not currently involved in investing, imagine that you are analyzing potential investments to build your portfolio. Create a mock portfolio with the investments you would obtain. How would you apply diversification and asset allocation to ensure that your risk–return balance is at a point at which you are comfortable?

BUILDING YOUR BUSINESS SKILLS

Market Ups and Downs

Goal
To encourage you to understand the forces that affect fluctuations in stock prices.

Background Information
Investing in stocks requires an understanding of the various factors that affect stock prices. These factors may be intrinsic to the company itself or part of the external environment.

- Internal factors relate to the company itself, such as an announcement of poor or favorable earnings, earnings that are more or less than expected, major layoffs, labor problems, new products, management issues, and mergers.
- External factors relate to world or national events, such as wars, recessions, weather conditions that affect sales, the Fed's adjustment of interest rates, and employment figures that are higher or lower than expected.

By analyzing these factors, you will often learn a lot about why a stock did well or why it did poorly. Being aware of these influences will help you anticipate future stock movements.

Method

Step 1
Working alone, choose a common stock that has experienced considerable price fluctuations in the past few years. Here are several examples (but there are many others): IBM, JPMorgan Chase, AT&T, Amazon.com, United Health Care, and Apple. Find the symbol for the stock (for example, JPMorgan Chase is JPM) and the exchange on which it is traded (JPM is traded on the NYSE).

Step 2
Use online searches to find a source that provides a historical picture of daily stock closings. Find your stock, and study its trading pattern.

Step 3
Find four or five days over a period of several months or even a year when there have been major price fluctuations in the stock. Then research what happened on that day that might have contributed to the fluctuation.

Step 4
Write a short analysis that links changes in stock price to internal and external factors. As you analyze the data, be aware that it is sometimes difficult to know why a stock price fluctuates.

Step 5
Get together with three other students who studied different stocks. As a group, discuss your findings, looking for fluctuation patterns.

FOLLOW-UP QUESTIONS

1. Do you see any similarities in the movement of the various stocks during the same period? For example, did the stocks move up or down at about the same time? If so, do you think the stocks were affected by the same factors? Explain your thinking.

2. Based on your analysis, did internal or external factors have the greater impact on stock price? Which factors had the more long-lasting effect? Which factors had the shorter effect?

3. Why do you think it is so hard to predict changes in stock price on a day-to-day basis?

EXERCISING YOUR ETHICS: INDIVIDUAL EXERCISE

Are You Endowed with Good Judgment?

The Situation

Every organization faces decisions about whether to make conservative or risky investments. Let's assume that you have been asked to evaluate the advantages and drawbacks of conservative versus risky investments, including all relevant ethical considerations, by Youth Dreams Charities (YDC), a local organization that assists low-income families in gaining access to educational opportunities. YDC is a not-for-profit firm that employs a full-time professional manager to run daily operations. Overall, governance and policy making reside with a board of directors—10 part-time, community-minded volunteers who are entrusted with carrying out YDC's mission.

For the current year, 23 students receive tuition totaling $92,000 paid by YDC. Tuition comes from annual fund-raising activities (a white-tie dance and a seafood carnival) and from financial returns from YDC's $2.1 million endowment. The endowment has been amassed from charitable donations during the past 12 years, and this year it has yielded some $84,000 for tuitions. The board's goal is to increase the endowment to $4 million in five years to provide $200,000 in tuition annually.

The Dilemma

Based on the finance committee's suggestions, the board is considering a change in YDC's investment policies. The current, rather conservative, approach invests the endowment in low-risk instruments that have consistently yielded a 5-percent annual return. This practice has allowed the endowment to grow modestly (at about 1 percent per year). The remaining investment proceeds (4 percent) flow out for tuition. The proposed plan would invest one-half of the endowment in conservative instruments and the other half in blue-chip stocks. Finance committee members believe that—with market growth—the endowment has a good chance of reaching the $4 million goal within five years. While some board members like the prospects of faster growth, others think the proposal is too risky. What happens if, instead of increasing, the stock market collapses and the endowment shrinks? What will happen to YDC's programs then?

QUESTIONS TO ADDRESS

1. Why might a conservative versus risky choice be different at a not-for-profit organization than at a for-profit organization?
2. What are the main ethical issues in this situation?
3. What action should the board take?

EXERCISING YOUR ETHICS: TEAM EXERCISE

Serving Two Masters: Torn Between Company and Client

The Situation

Employees in financial services firms are sometimes confronted by conflicting allegiances between the company and its clients. In managing customers' stock portfolios, for example, the best timing for buy and sell decisions for clients' financial positions may not be the most profitable for the financial manager's firm. Investment managers, as a result, must choose a "right" course of action for reconciling possible conflicting interests.

The Dilemma

George Michaels is a customer portfolio manager employed by Premier Power Investments Company, one of the top 10 financial services firms on the West Coast. His 35 clients—individual investors—have portfolios with market values ranging from $400,000 to $4 million in stocks, bonds, and mutual funds. Clients generally rely on George's recommendations to buy, sell, or hold each security based on his knowledge of their investment goals and risk tolerance, along with his experience in keeping up with market trends and holding down transaction costs. Premier Power Investments Company earns sales commissions ranging from 2 percent to 4 percent of market value for each buy and sell transaction.

On Monday morning, George's boss, Vicky Greene, informs George that due to Premier Power Investments Company's sagging revenues, it is to everyone's benefit to increase the number of transactions in customers' portfolios. She suggests that he find some different and attractive securities to replace existing securities for his customers. As George thinks about possible ways for accelerating his buy and sell recommendations, he has qualms about the motivation behind Vicky's comments. He is unsure what to do.

Team Activity

Assemble a group of four to five students and assign each group member to one of the following roles:

- George Michaels (employee)
- Vicky Greene (employer)
- Portfolio owner (customer)
- Owner (one of many outside shareholders of Premier Power Investments Company)
- SEC representative (use this role only if your group has at least five members)

ACTION STEPS

1 Before hearing any of your group's comments on this situation, and from the perspective of your assigned role, do you think there are any ethical issues with this situation? If so, write them down.

2 Return to your group and reveal any ethical issues that were identified by each member. Be especially aware to see if the different roles resulted in different kinds of ethical issues. Why might role differences result in dissimilar priorities on ethical issues?

3 For the various ethical issues that were identified, decide as a group which one is the most important for Premier Power Investments to resolve. Which issue is second in importance?

4 From an ethical standpoint, what does your group finally recommend be done to resolve the most important ethical issue? To resolve the second most important ethical issue?

VIDEO EXERCISE   MyBizLab

Capital Advisors

Learning Objectives

The purpose of this video is to help you:

1 Explain how companies use debt and equity to finance their operations.

2 Describe the advantages and disadvantages of debt and equity financing.

3 Understand how individuals make investment decisions over their lifetime.

Synopsis

While many businesses will remain small, many entrepreneurs wish to expand their operations, yet lack the money to do so. Companies may fund their expansion through issuing securities (stocks and bonds) or finding venture capital. While issuing securities provides the money needed for a company to grow, it also provides an investment opportunity for individuals and businesses. Investing in securities can allow an investor to build wealth through the accumulation of income or appreciation in value. Those who wish to purchase stock may consider income, blue chip, growth, cyclical, or defensive stocks, depending on their investment objectives. A more balanced portfolio may be achieved through additional investment in secured or unsecured corporate bonds. While some investors prefer to select individual securities for their portfolios, many others rely on mutual funds. Mutual funds are professionally managed portfolios of securities. They provide diversification of risk and greater liquidity than investment in individual stocks or bonds. However, investors in mutual funds will pay a portion of their earnings for management expenses. By carefully considering their investment options, individuals may invest in securities and build wealth for the future.

DISCUSSION QUESTIONS

1 What are the two general options for companies that wish to raise money for expansion?

2 What are the advantages and disadvantages of bonds as a way of raising capital?

3 What are the advantages and disadvantages of stocks as a way of raising capital?

4 What questions should an investor ask before investing in securities?

5 How do investment decisions change over a client's lifetime?

Online Exploration

The website of the Securities and Exchange Commission describes a threefold mission: protecting investors; maintaining fair, orderly, and efficient markets; and facilitating capital formation. As people depend on the securities markets to save for retirement, pay for college, and allow for the purchase of a home, protecting investors is central to the commission's activities. The SEC's investor website (www.investor.gov) provides a wealth of information for those who are considering investing in the market, including suggestions for investing across the life cycle, financial calculators, and worksheets. From the "Introduction to the Markets" link, click on the option "Roadmap to Saving and Investing". The first step in creating a financial plan is establishing goals. Identify at least three tools for setting financial goals.

END NOTES

1 John Carey, "House Passes Carbon Cap-and-Trade Bill," *Bloomberg Businessweek*, June 26, 2009, at http://www.businessweek.com/blogs/money_politics/archives/2009/06/house_passes_ca.html.

2 "Advantages and Disadvantages of Mutual Funds," *The Motley Fool*, at http://www.fool.com, accessed February 11, 2008; "Who Pays for Cap and Trade?" *The Wall Street Journal*, March 9, 2009, at http://online.wsj.com/article/SB123655590609066021.html.

3 "Why Exchange-Traded Funds?" *Yahoo*! Finance Exchange-Traded Funds Center, at http://finance.yahoo.com/etf/education/02, on January 16 2008.

[4] Andrew Bary, "Embracing ETFs," *Barron's*, November 15, 2010, pages 29–34.

[5] Ibid.

[6] "U.S. Investment Banking Era Ends," *UPI.com*, September 22, 2008, at http://www.upi.com/Business_News/2008/09/22/US-Investment-banking-era-ends/UPI-96221222086983/.

[7] New York Stock Exchange, July 22, 2009, at http://www.nyse.com.

[8] "The State of Qatar Launches 'Qatar Exchange' as it Signs Today Formal Terms of Strategic Partnership with NYSE Euronext," *NYSE News Release*, June 19, 2009, at http://www.nyse.com/press/1245406656784.html.

[9] "List of Stock Exchanges," Based on http://en.wikipedia.org/wiki/List_of_stock_exchanges.

[10] "Chronology—Recent Consolidation Moves by Exchanges," *Reuters*, February 13, 2008, at http://www.reuters.com/article/idUSB27064320070223; Randy Grossman, "The Inevitable Stock Exchange Consolidation," *Advanced Trading*, June 16, 2006, at http://www.advancedtrading.com/showArticle.jhtml?articleID=196900426

[11] "Electronic Communication Networks (ECNs)," *U.S. Securities and Exchange Commission*, at http://www.sec.gov/answers/ecn.htm, accessed July 3, 2008; "Electronic Communication Network," *InvestorWords.com*, at http://www.investorwords.com/1679/Electronic_Communication_Network.html, accessed July 3, 2008.

[12] "Electronic Communication Networks (ECNs)," *U.S. Securities and Exchange Commission*, at http://www.sec.gov/answers/ecn.htm, accessed July 3, 2008; "Island ECN—How Island Works," at http://ecommerce.hostip.info/pages/636/Island-Ecn-HOW-ISLAND-WORKS.html, accessed January 16, 2008.

[13] "Just 25% Recognize That Most Americans Are Investors," *Rasmussen Reports*, February 11, 2011, at http://www.rasmussenreports.com/public_content/business/general_business/february_2011/just_25_recognize_that_most_americans_are_investors.

[14] Steven E. Norwitz (editor), "A Bear Market of Historic Proportions," *T. Rowe Price Report*, Spring 2009, page 1.

[15] "Dow Jones to Change Composition of the Dow Jones Industrial Average," *Dow Jones (Press Release)*, June 1, 2009, at http://www.djindexes.com/mdsidx/html/pressrelease/press-release-archive.html#20090601.

[16] Alex Altman, "A Brief History of: Ponzi Schemes," *Time*, January 8, 2009, at http://www.time.com/time/magazine/article/0,9171,1870510,00.html; "How Much Did Madoff Scheme Cost?" *CNNMoney.com*, January 5, 2009, at http://money.cnn.com/2009/01/02/news/companies/madoff/index.htm; "The Man Who Figured Out Madoff's Scheme," *CBS News*, June 14, 2009, at http://www.cbsnews.com/stories/2009/02/27/60minutes/main4833667.shtml; Associated Press, "Investors Named in Madoff List," *Columbia Daily Tribune*, February 5, 2009, page 7B; Diana B. Henriques, "Claims Over 15,400 in Fraud by Madoff," *The New York Times*, July 9, 2009, at http://www.nytimes.com/2009/07/10/business/10madoff.html?ref=nyregion.

[17] Carl Beidelman, *The Handbook of International Investing* (Chicago, 1987), p. 133.

[18] Ajay Kumar, "Can We Trust Moody's, Fitch, Standard & Poor?" *CommodityOnline*, at http://www.commodityonline.com/printnews.php?news_id=15888, accessed July 22, 2009; David Evans and Caroline Salas, "Flawed Credit Ratings Reap Profits as Regulators Fail (Update 1)," *Bloomberg.com*, April 29, 2009, at http://www.bloomberg.com/apps/news?pid=20670001&sid=au4oIx.judz4; Leslie Wayne, "Calpers Sues over Ratings of Securities," *The New York Times*, July 15, 2009, at http://www.nytimes.com/2009/07/15/business/15calpers.html; David Segal, "Ohio Sues Rating Firms for Losses in Funds," *The New York Times*, November 20, 2009, at http://www.nytimes.com/2009/11/21/business/21ratings.html; Lynn Hume, "Connecticut AG Sues All Three Rating Agencies, The Bond Buyer, July 31, 2008, at http://www.bondbuyer.com/issues/117_145/-292250-1.html.

[19] "Mortgage-Backed Securities," *U.S. Securities and Exchange Commission*, June 25, 2007, at http://www.sec.gov/answers/mortgagesecurities.htm; "Mortgage-Backed Security," *riskglossary.com*, at http://www.riskglossary.com/link/mortgage_backed_security.htm, accessed July 24, 2009.

[20] David Goldman, "Fannie, Freddie Ignored Warning Signs," *CNNMoney.com*, December 9, 2008, at http://money.cnn.com/2008/12/09/news/economy/fannie_freddie_hearing/index.htm?postversion=2008120910.

[21] Glenn Somerville, "U.S. Seizes Fannie, Freddie, Aims to Calm Markets," Reuters, September 7, 2008, at http://www.reuters.com/article/newsOne/idUSN0527106320080907.

[22] Tara Kaprowy, "Root Causes of Financial Crisis Complicated," *The Sentinel Echo*, September 30, 2008, at http://www.sentinel-echo.com/local/local_story_274154552.html; Neil Irwin, "Fed to Pump $1.2 Trillion into Markets," *The Washington Post*, March 19, 2009, at http://www.washingtonpost.com/wp-dyn/content/article/2009/03/18/AR2009031802283.html; David Goldman, "Fannie, Freddie Ignored Warning Signs," *CNNMoney.com*, December 9, 2008, at http://money.cnn.com/2008/12/09/news/economy/fannie_freddie_hearing/index.htm?postversion=2008120910; Joe Reeser, "The Real Cause of the Current Financial Crisis," OpEdNews.com, September 27, 2008, at http://www.opednews.com/articles/The-Real-Cause-of-the-Curr-by-Joe-Reeser-080926-83.html.

[23] New York Stock Exchange at http://www.nyse.com/.

[24] *CNN Money.com*, May 6, 2011 at http://investing.money.msn.com/investments/company-report?symbol=US%3aPEP; *CNN Money.com*, May 6, 2011 at http://investing.money.msn.com/investments/company-report?symbol=CCE.

[25] Reuters, "Rajaratnam Insider Trading Trial Begins," March 9, 2011, Huffington Post, at http://www.huffingtonpost.com/2011/03/09/rajaratnam-trial_n_833326.html; U.S. Department of Justice, "Joseph P. Nacchio Indicted by Federal Grand Jury: Former Chief Executive Officer of Qwest Communications Charged with Insider Trading, Selling Over $100 Million Stock," (December 20, 2005), at http://lawprofessors.typepad.com/whitecollarcrime_blog/files/nacchio_indictment.pdf.

[26] Marianne Lavelle, "A U.S. Cap-and-Trade Experiment To End," *National Geographic News*, November 3, 2010,

at http://news.nationalgeographic.com/news/news/energy/2010/11/101103-chicago-climate-exchange-cap-and-trade-election/; "US Senate Drops Bill to Cap Carbon Emissions," *GuardianNews*, July 23, 2010, at http://www.guardian.co.uk/environment/2010/jul/23/us-senate-climate-change-bill; Gerard Wynn and Pete Harrison, "U.S. Cap and Trade Plans Risk European Mistakes," *Reuters*, May 15, 2009, at http://www.reuters.com/article/2009/05/15/us-carbon-usa-analysis-idUSTRE54E4EZ20090515; Nathanial Gronewold, "Chicago Climate Exchange Closes Nation's First Cap-And-Trade System but Keeps Eye to the Future," *The New York Times*, January 3, 2011, at http://www.nytimes

.com/cwire/2011/01/03/03climatewire-chicago-climate-exchange-closes-but-keeps-ey-78598.html.

[27] Nathaniel Gronewold, "3. Markets: Europe's Carbon Emissions Trading—Growing Pains or Wholesale Theft?" *E&E Publishing LLC*, January 31, 2011, at http://www.eenews.net/public/climatewire/2011/01/31/3.

[28] Martin Livermore, "Cap and Trade Doesn't Work," *The Wall Street Journal*, June 25, 2009, at http://online.wsj.com/article/SB124587942001349765.html.

[29] "EU Advises China on Cap and Trade," *Carbon Positive*, November 8, 2010, at http://www.carbonpositive.net/viewarticle.aspx?articleID=2170.

Risk Management

In this appendix, we describe other types of risks that businesses face, and analyze some of the ways in which they typically manage them.

Coping with Risk

Businesses constantly face two basic types of **risk**—uncertainty about future events. **Speculative risks**, such as financial investments, involve the possibility of gain or loss. **Pure risks** involve only the possibility of loss or no loss. Designing and distributing a new product, for example, is a speculative risk—the product may fail, or it may succeed and earn high profits. In contrast, the chance of a warehouse fire is a pure risk.

For a company to survive and prosper, it must manage both types of risk in a cost-effective manner. We can define the process of **risk management** as conserving the firm's earning power and assets by reducing the threat of losses due to uncontrollable events. In every company, each manager must be alert for risks to the firm and their impact on profits.

The risk-management process usually involves five steps:

Step 1: Identify Risks and Potential Losses   Managers analyze a firm's risks to identify potential losses.

Step 2: Measure the Frequency and Severity of Losses and Their Impact   To measure the frequency and severity of losses, managers must consider both history and current activities. How often can the firm expect the loss to occur? What is the likely size of the loss in dollars?

Step 3: Evaluate Alternatives and Choose the Techniques That Will Best Handle the Losses Having identified and measured potential losses, managers are in a better position to decide how to handle them. They generally have four choices:

- A firm opts for **risk avoidance** by declining to enter or by ceasing to participate in a risky activity.
- When avoidance is not practical or desirable, firms can practice **risk control**—the use of loss-prevention techniques to minimize the frequency or severity of losses.
- When losses cannot be avoided or controlled, firms must cope with the consequences. When such losses are manageable and predictable, the firm may decide to cover them out of company funds. The firm is said to assume or retain the financial consequences of the loss; hence, the practice is known as **risk retention**.

- When the potential for large risks cannot be avoided or controlled, managers often opt for **risk transfer** to another firm—namely, an insurance company—to protect itself.

Step 4: Implement the Risk-Management Program The means of implementing risk-management decisions depend on both the technique chosen and the activity being managed.

- Risk avoidance for certain activities can be implemented by purchasing those activities from outside providers.
- Risk control might be implemented by training employees and designing new work methods and equipment for on-the-job safety.
- For situations in which risk retention is preferred, reserve funds can be set aside from revenues.
- When risk transfer is needed, implementation means selecting an insurance company and buying the appropriate policies.

Step 5: Monitor Results   New types of risks emerge with changes in customers, facilities, employees, and products. Insurance regulations change, and new types of insurance become available. Consequently, managers must continuously monitor a company's risks, reevaluate the methods used for handling them, and revise them as necessary.

Insurance as Risk Management

To deal with some risks, both businesses and individuals may choose to purchase insurance. Insurance is purchased by paying **insurance premiums**—payments to an insurance company to buy a policy and keep it active. In return, the insurance company issues an **insurance policy**—a formal agreement to pay the policyholder a specified amount in the event of certain losses. In some cases, the insured party must also pay a **deductible**, an agreed-upon amount of the loss that the insured must absorb prior to reimbursement. Buyers find insurance appealing because they are protected against large, potentially devastating losses in return for a relatively small sum of money.

With insurance, individuals and businesses share risks by contributing to a fund from which those who suffer losses are paid. Insurance companies are willing to accept these risks because they make profits by taking in more premiums than they pay out to cover policyholders' losses. Although many policyholders are paying for protection against the same type of loss, by no means will all of them suffer such a loss.

Insurable versus Uninsurable Risks Like every business, insurance companies must avoid certain risks. Insurers divide potential sources of loss into *insurable risks* and *uninsurable risks*. They issue policies only for insurable risks. Although there are some exceptions, an insurable risk must meet the following four criteria:

1 *Predictability*: The insurer must be able to use statistical tools to forecast the likelihood of a loss. This forecast also helps insurers determine premiums charged to policyholders.

2 *Casualty*: A loss must result from an *accident*, not from an intentional act by the policyholder. To avoid paying in cases of fraud, insurers may refuse to cover losses when they cannot determine whether policyholders' actions contributed to them.

3 *Unconnectedness*: Potential losses must be random and must occur independently of other losses. No insurer can afford to write insurance when a large percentage of those who are exposed to a particular kind of loss are likely to suffer such a loss. By carefully choosing the risks that it will insure, an insurance company can reduce its chances of a large loss or insolvency.

4 *Verifiability*: Insured losses must be verifiable as to cause, time, place, and amount.

Special Forms of Insurance for Business Businesses have special insurable concerns—*liability, property, business interruption, key person insurance,* and *business continuation agreements.*

Liability Insurance Liability means responsibility for damages in case of accidental or deliberate harm to individuals or property. **Liability insurance** covers losses resulting from damage to people or property when the insured party is judged liable.

A business is liable for any injury to an employee when the injury arises from activities related to the occupation. When workers are permanently or temporarily disabled by job-related accidents or disease, employers are required by law to provide **workers' compensation coverage** for medical expenses, loss of wages, and rehabilitation services.

Property Insurance A firm purchases **property insurance** to cover injuries to itself resulting from physical damage to or loss of real estate or personal property. Property losses may result from fire, lightning, wind, hail, explosion, theft, vandalism, or other destructive forces.

Business Interruption Insurance In some cases, loss to property is minimal in comparison to loss of income. If a firm is forced to close down for an extended time, it will not be able to generate income. During this time, however, certain expenses—such as taxes, insurance premiums, and salaries for key personnel—may continue. To cover such losses, a firm may buy **business interruption insurance**.

Key Person Insurance Many businesses choose to protect themselves against loss of the talents and skills of key employees, as well as the recruitment costs to find a replacement and training expenses once a replacement is hired. **Key person insurance** is designed to offset both lost income and additional expenses.

Business Continuation Agreements Who takes control of a business when a partner or associate dies? Surviving partners are often faced with the possibility of having to accept an inexperienced heir as a management partner. This contingency can be handled in **business continuation agreements**, whereby owners make plans to buy the ownership interest of a deceased associate from his or her heirs. The value of the ownership interest is determined when the agreement is made. Special policies can also provide survivors with the funds needed to make the purchase.

Risk uncertainty about future events

Speculative Risk risk involving the possibility of gain or loss

Pure Risk risk involving only the possibility of loss or no loss

Risk Management process of conserving the firm's earning power and assets by reducing the threat of losses due to uncontrollable events

Risk Avoidance practice of avoiding risk by declining or ceasing to participate in an activity

Risk Control practice of minimizing the frequency or severity of losses from risky activities

Risk Retention practice of covering a firm's losses with its own funds

Risk Transfer practice of transferring a firm's risk to another firm

Insurance Premium fee paid to an insurance company by a policyholder for insurance coverage

Insurance Policy formal agreement to pay the policyholder a specified amount in the event of certain losses

Deductible amount of the loss that the insured must absorb prior to reimbursement

Liability Insurance insurance covering losses resulting from damage to people or property when the insured party is judged liable

Workers' Compensation Coverage coverage provided by a firm to employees for medical expenses, loss of wages, and rehabilitation costs resulting from job-related injuries or disease

Property Insurance insurance covering losses resulting from physical damage to or loss of the insured's real estate or personal property

Business Interruption Insurance insurance covering income lost during times when a company is unable to conduct business

Key Person Insurance special form of business insurance designed to offset expenses entailed by the loss of key employees

Business Continuation Agreement special form of business insurance whereby owners arrange to buy the interests of deceased associates from their heirs

The Legal Context of Business

In this appendix, we describe the basic tenets of U.S. law and show how these principles work through the court system. We'll also survey a few major areas of business-related law.

The U.S. Legal and Judicial Systems

Laws are the codified rules of behavior enforced by a society. In the United States, laws fall into three broad categories according to their origins: *common*, *statutory*, and *regulatory*.

Types of Law

Law in the United States originated primarily with English common law. U.S. law includes the U.S. Constitution, state constitutions, federal and state statutes, municipal ordinances, administrative agency rules and regulations, executive orders, and court decisions.

Common Law Court decisions follow *precedents*, or the decisions of earlier cases. Following precedent lends stability to the law by basing judicial decisions on cases anchored in similar facts. This principle is the keystone of **common law**—the body of decisions handed down by courts ruling on individual cases.

Statutory Law Laws created by constitutions or by federal, state, or local legislative acts constitute **statutory law**. Under the U.S. Constitution, federal statutes take precedence over state and local statutes.

Regulatory Law Statutory law and common law have long histories. Relatively new is **regulatory (or administrative) law**—law made by the authority of administrative agencies.

Although Congress retains control over the scope of agency action, regulations have the force of statutory law once passed. Government regulatory agencies act as a secondary judicial system, determining whether regulations have been violated and then imposing penalties. Much agency activity consists of setting standards for safety or quality and monitoring the compliance of businesses.

Congress has created many new agencies in response to pressure to address social issues. In some cases, agencies were established in response to public concern about corporate behavior. The activities of these agencies have sometimes forced U.S. firms to consider the public interest almost as routinely as they consider their own financial performance.

Keeping an Eye on Business Today a host of agencies regulate U.S. business practices, including:

- Equal Employment Opportunity Commission (EEOC)
- Environmental Protection Agency (EPA)
- Food and Drug Administration (FDA)
- Federal Trade Commission (FTC)
- Occupational Safety and Health Administration (OSHA)

Trends in Deregulation and Regulation Although government regulation has benefited U.S. business in many ways, it is not without its drawbacks. Businesspeople complain—with some justification—that government regulations require too much costly paperwork. Many people in both business and government support broader **deregulation**—the elimination of rules that restrict business activity. Deregulation, they argue, is a primary incentive to innovation; deregulated industries are forced to innovate in order to survive in fiercely competitive industries. Those firms that are already conditioned to compete by being more creative will outperform firms that have been protected by regulatory climates in their home countries.

However, it appears likely that there will be a trend back toward more regulation in the United States, at least for the near future. For one thing, the Democratic party tends to support a larger role for government. Given that the Democrats control both the White House and Congress, more regulation is likely. In addition, many critics blame the financial crisis and economic recession of 2008–2010 on the uncontrolled actions of major U.S. banks and have been calling for more regulation to help prevent a future recurrence of the same mistakes.

The U.S. Judicial System

Much of the responsibility for law enforcement falls to the courts. Litigation is a significant part of contemporary life, and we have given our courts a voice in a wide range of issues, some touching personal concerns, some ruling on matters of public policy that affect all our lives.

The Court System There are three levels in the U.S. judicial system—*federal*, *state*, and *local*. Federal courts hear cases on questions of constitutional law, disputes relating to maritime laws, and violations of federal statutes. They also rule on regulatory actions and on such issues as bankruptcy, postal law, and copyright or patent violation. Both the federal and most state systems embody a three-tiered system of *trial*, *appellate*, and *supreme courts*.

Trial Courts At the lowest level of the federal court system are the **trial courts**, the general courts that hear cases not specifically assigned to another court. Every state has at least one federal trial court, called a *district court*.

Trial courts also include special courts and administrative agencies. Special courts hear specific types of cases, such as cases involving tax evasion, fraud, international disputes, or claims against the U.S. government. Within their areas of jurisdiction, administrative agencies also make judgments much like those of courts.

Courts in each state deal with the same issues as their federal counterparts. However, they may rule only in areas governed by state law. For example, a state special court would hear a case involving state income tax laws. Local courts in each state system also hear cases on municipal ordinances, local traffic violations, and similar issues.

Appellate Courts A losing party may disagree with a trial court ruling. If that party can show grounds for review, the case may go before a federal or state **appellate court**. These courts consider questions of law, such as possible errors of legal interpretation made by lower courts. They do not examine questions of fact.

Supreme Courts Cases still not resolved at the appellate level can be appealed to the appropriate state supreme courts or to the U.S. Supreme Court. If it believes that an appeal is warranted or that the outcome will set an important precedent, the U.S. Supreme Court also hears cases appealed from state supreme courts.

Business Law

Most legal issues confronted by businesses fall into one of six basic areas: *contract*, *tort*, *property*, *agency*, *commercial*, or *bankruptcy law*. These areas cover a wide range of business activity.

Contract Law

A **contract** is any agreement between two or more parties that is enforceable in court. As such, it must meet six conditions. If all these conditions are met, one party can seek legal recourse from another if the other party breaches, or violates, the terms of the agreement.

1 *Agreement.* Agreement is the serious, definite, and communicated offer and acceptance of the same terms.

2 *Consent.* A contract is not enforceable if any of the parties has been affected by an honest mistake, fraud, or pressure.

3 *Capacity.* To give real consent, both parties must demonstrate legal **capacity** (competence). A person under legal age (usually 18 or 21) cannot enter into a binding contract.

4 *Consideration.* An agreement is binding only if it exchanges **considerations**—items of value. Note that items of value do not necessarily entail money. Contracts need not be rational, nor must they provide the best possible bargain for both sides. They need only include legally sufficient consideration. The terms are met if both parties receive what the contract details.

5 *Legality.* A contract must be for a lawful purpose and must comply with federal, state, and local laws and regulations.

6 *Proper form.* A contract may be written, oral, or implied from conduct. It must be written, however, if it involves the sale of land or goods worth more than $500. It must be written if the agreement requires more than a year to fulfill. All changes to written contracts must also be in writing.

Breach of Contract Contract law offers a variety of remedies designed to protect the reasonable expectations of the parties and, in some cases, to compensate them for actions taken to enforce the agreement. As the injured party to a breached contract, any of the following actions might occur:

- You might cancel the contract and refuse to live up to your part of the bargain.
- You might sue for damages up to the amount that you lost as a result of the breach.
- If money cannot repay the damage you suffered, you might demand specific performance, or require the other party to fulfill the original contract.

Tort Law

Tort law applies to most business relationships *not governed by contracts*. A **tort** is a *civil*—that is, noncriminal—injury to people, property, or reputation for which compensation must be paid. Trespass, fraud, defamation, invasion of privacy, and even assault can be torts, as can interference with contractual relations and wrongful use of trade secrets. There are three classifications of torts: *intentional*, *negligence*, and *product liability*.

Laws codified rules of behavior enforced by a society

Common Law body of decisions handed down by courts ruling on individual cases

Statutory Law law created by constitution(s) or by federal, state, or local legislative acts

Regulatory (Administrative) Law law made by the authority of administrative agencies

Deregulation elimination of rules that restrict business activity

Trial Court general court that hears cases not specifically assigned to another court

Appellate Court court that reviews case records of trials whose findings have been appealed

Contract agreement between two or more parties enforceable in court

Capacity competence required of individuals entering into a binding contract

Consideration item of value exchanged between parties to create a valid contract

Tort civil injury to people, property, or reputation for which compensation must be paid

Intentional Torts **Intentional torts** result from the deliberate actions of another person or organization. To remedy torts, courts will usually impose **compensatory damages**—payments intended to redress an injury actually suffered. They may also impose **punitive damages**—fines that exceed actual losses suffered by plaintiffs and are intended to punish defendants.

Negligence Torts Most suits involve charges of **negligence**—conduct that falls below legal standards for protecting others against unreasonable risk.

Product Liability Torts In cases of **product liability**, a company may be held responsible for injuries caused by its products.

Strict Product Liability Since the early 1960s, businesses have faced a number of legal actions based on the relatively new principle of **strict product liability**—the principle that liability can result not from a producer's negligence but from a defect in the product itself. An injured party need only show the following:

1 The product was defective.

2 The defect was the cause of injury.

3 The defect caused the product to be unreasonably dangerous.

Because plaintiffs need not demonstrate negligence or fault, these suits have a good chance of success.

Property Law

Property is anything of value to which a person or business has sole right of ownership. Legally speaking, the right of ownership is itself property.

Within this broad general definition, we can divide property into four categories:

1 **Tangible real property** is land and anything attached to it.

2 **Tangible personal property** is any movable item that can be owned, bought, sold, or leased.

3 **Intangible personal property** cannot be seen but exists by virtue of written documentation.

4 **Intellectual property** is created through a person's creative activities.

Protection of Intellectual Rights The U.S. Constitution grants protection to intellectual property by means of copyrights, trademarks, and patents. Copyrights and patents apply to the tangible expressions of an idea, not to the ideas themselves.

Copyrights **Copyrights** give creators exclusive ownership rights to their intellectual property. Copyrights extend to creators for their entire lives and to their estates for 70 years thereafter.

Trademarks Because the development of products is expensive, companies must prevent other firms from using their brand names. Often, they must act to keep competitors from seducing consumers with similar or substitute products. A producer can apply to the U.S. government for a **trademark**—the exclusive legal right to use a brand name.

Trademarks are granted for 20 years and may be renewed indefinitely if a firm continues to protect its brand name. If a firm allows the brand name to lapse into common usage, it may lose protection. Common usage takes effect when a company fails to use the ® symbol to indicate that its brand name is a registered trademark. It also takes effect if a company seeks no action against those who fail to acknowledge its trademark.

Patents **Patents** provide legal monopolies for the use and licensing of manufactured items, manufacturing processes, substances, and designs for objects. A patentable invention must be *novel*, *useful*, and *nonobvious*. Patents are valid for 20 years, with the term running from the date on which the application was *filed*, not the date on which the patent itself was *issued*.

Restrictions on Property Rights Property rights are not always absolute. For example, rights may be compromised under the following circumstances:

• Utility companies typically have rights called *easements*, such as the right to run wire over private property or to lay cable or pipe under it.

• Under the principle of **eminent domain**, the government may, upon paying owners fair prices, claim private land to expand roads or erect public buildings.

Agency Law

The transfer of property often involves agents. An **agent** is a person who acts for and in the name of another party, called the **principal**. Courts have ruled that both a firm's employees and its outside contractors may be regarded as its agents.

Authority of Agents Agents have the authority to bind principals to agreements. They receive that authority, however, from the principals themselves; they cannot create their own authority. An agent's authority to bind a principal can be **express**, **implied**, or **apparent**.

Responsibilities of Principals Principals have several responsibilities to their agents. They owe agents reasonable compensation, must reimburse them for related business expenses, and should inform them of risks associated with their business activities. Principals are liable for actions performed by agents *within the scope of their employment*. If agents make untrue claims about products or services, the principal is liable for making amends. Employers are similarly responsible for the actions of employees. Firms are often liable in tort suits because the courts treat employees as agents. Businesses are also increasingly being held accountable for *criminal* acts by employees. Court findings have argued that firms are expected to be aware of workers' negative propensities, to check their employees' backgrounds, and to train and supervise employees properly.

Commercial Law

Managers must be well acquainted with the most general laws affecting commerce. Specifically, they need to be familiar with the provisions of the **Uniform Commercial Code (UCC)**, which describes the rights of buyers and sellers in transactions. One key area of coverage by the UCC, contracts, was discussed earlier. Another key area is warranties.

A **warranty** is a seller's promise to stand by its products or services if a problem occurs after the sale. Warranties may be express or implied. The seller specifically states the terms of an **express warranty**, while an **implied warranty** is dictated by law. Implied warranties embody the principle that a product should (1) fulfill the promises made by advertisements and (2) serve the purpose for which it was manufactured and sold. It is important to note, however, that warranties, unlike most contracts, are easily limited, waived, or disclaimed. Consequently, they are the source of tort action more often, as dissatisfied customers seek redress from producers.

Bankruptcy Law

Both organizations and individuals can seek debt relief by filing for bankruptcy—the court-granted permission not to pay some or all incurred debts. Many individuals and businesses file for bankruptcy each year, and their numbers continue to increase. Three main factors account for the increase in bankruptcy filings:

1 The increased availability of credit

2 The "fresh-start" provisions in current bankruptcy laws

3 The growing acceptance of bankruptcy as a financial tactic

In some cases, creditors force an individual or firm into **involuntary bankruptcy** and press the courts to award them payment of at least part of what they are owed. Far more often, however, a person or business chooses to file for court protection against creditors. In general, individuals and firms whose debts exceed total assets by at least $1,000 may file for **voluntary bankruptcy**.

Business Bankruptcy   One of three plans resolves a business bankruptcy:

1 Under a *liquidation plan*, the business ceases to exist. Its assets are sold and the proceeds are used to pay creditors.

2 Under a *repayment plan*, the bankrupt company simply works out a new payment schedule to meet its obligations. The time frame is usually extended, and payments are collected and distributed by a court-appointed trustee.

3 *Reorganization* is the most complex form of business bankruptcy. The company must explain the sources of its financial difficulties and propose a new plan for remaining in business. Reorganization may include a new slate of managers and a new financial strategy. A judge may also reduce the firm's debts to ensure its survival.

Legislation passed since 1994 restricts how long a company can protect itself in bankruptcy while continuing to do business. Critics have charged that many firms

---

Intentional Tort tort resulting from the deliberate actions of a party

Compensatory Damages monetary payments intended to redress injury actually suffered because of a tort

Punitive Damages fines imposed over and above any actual losses suffered by a plaintiff

Negligence conduct that falls below legal standards for protecting others against unreasonable risk

Product Liability tort in which a company is responsible for injuries caused by its products

Strict Product Liability principle that liability can result not from a producer's negligence but from a defect in the product itself

Property anything of value to which a person or business has sole right of ownership

Tangible Real Property land and anything attached to it

Tangible Personal Property any movable item that can be owned, bought, sold, or leased

Intangible Personal Property property that cannot be seen but that exists by virtue of written documentation

Intellectual Property property created through a person's creative activities

Copyright exclusive ownership right belonging to the creator of a book, article, design, illustration, photo, film, or musical work

Trademark exclusive legal right to use a brand name or symbol

Patent exclusive legal right to use and license a manufactured item or substance, manufacturing process, or object design

Eminent Domain principle that the government may claim private land for public use by buying it at a fair price

Agent individual or organization acting for and in the name of another party

Principal individual or organization authorizing an agent to act on its behalf

Express Authority agent's authority, derived from written agreement, to bind a principal to a certain course of action

Implied Authority agent's authority, derived from business custom, to bind a principal to a certain course of action

Apparent Authority agent's authority, based on the principal's compliance, to bind a principal to a certain course of action

Uniform Commercial Code (UCC) body of standardized laws governing the rights of buyers and sellers in transactions

Warranty seller's promise to stand by its products or services if a problem occurs after the sale

Express Warranty warranty whose terms are specifically stated by the seller

Implied Warranty warranty, dictated by law, based on the principle that products should fulfill advertised promises and serve the purposes for which they are manufactured and sold

Involuntary Bankruptcy bankruptcy proceedings initiated by the creditors of an indebted individual or organization

Voluntary Bankruptcy bankruptcy proceedings initiated by an indebted individual or organization

International Law general set of cooperative agreements and guidelines established by countries to govern the actions of individuals, businesses, and nations

have succeeded in operating for many months under bankruptcy protection. During that time, they were able to cut costs and prices, not only competing with an unfair advantage, but also dragging down overall industry profits. The new laws place time limits on various steps in the filing process. The intended effect is to speed the process and prevent assets from being lost to legal fees.

MyBizLab

Gain hands-on experience through an interactive, real-world scenario. This chapter's simulation entitled Business Law is located at www.mybizlab.com.

The International Framework of Business Law

Laws vary from country to country, and many businesses today have international markets, suppliers, and competitors. Managers need a basic understanding of the international framework of business law that affects the ways in which they can do business. Issues, such as pollution across borders, are matters of **international law**—the very general set of cooperative agreements and guidelines established by countries to govern the actions of individuals, businesses, and nations themselves.

International law has several sources. One source is custom and tradition. Among countries that have been trading with one another for centuries, many customs and traditions governing exchanges have gradually evolved into practice. Although some trading practices still follow ancient unwritten agreements, there has been a clear trend in more recent times to approach international trade within a more formal legal framework. Key features of that framework include a variety of formal trade agreements.

Another important source of international law is the formal trade treaties that nations negotiate with one another. Governing entities such as the WTO and the EU, for instance, also provide legal frameworks within which participating nations agree to abide.

Managing Your Personal Finances

Dealing with personal finances is a lifelong job involving a crucial choice between two options:

1 Committing to the rational management of your personal finances by controlling them, helping them grow, and therefore enjoying greater personal satisfaction and financial stability.

2 Letting the financial chips fall where they may and hoping for the best (which seldom happens) and therefore inviting frustration, disappointment, and financial distress.

Personal finance management requires consideration of cash management, financial planning and control, investment alternatives, and risk. Let's start by looking at one key factor in success: the personal financial plan. We'll then discuss the steps in the planning process and show how you can make better decisions to manage your personal finances.

Building Your Financial Plan

Financial planning is the process of looking at your current financial condition, identifying your goals, and anticipating steps toward meeting those goals. Because your goals and finances will change as you get older, your plan should always allow for revision. Figure AIII.1 summarizes a step-by-step approach to personal financial planning.

Assessing Your Current Financial Condition

The first step in developing a personal financial plan is assessing your current financial position. Your **personal net worth** is the value of all your assets minus all your

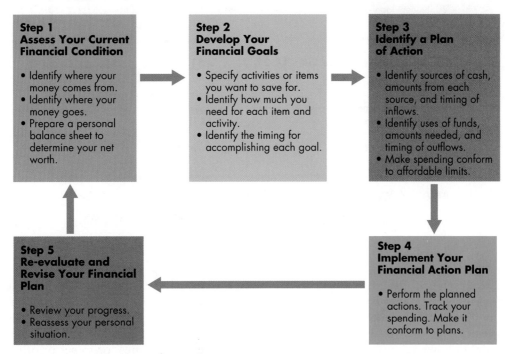

Step 1
Assess Your Current Financial Condition

- Identify where your money comes from.
- Identify where your money goes.
- Prepare a personal balance sheet to determine your net worth.

Step 2
Develop Your Financial Goals

- Specify activities or items you want to save for.
- Identify how much you need for each item and activity.
- Identify the timing for accomplishing each goal.

Step 3
Identify a Plan of Action

- Identify sources of cash, amounts from each source, and timing of inflows.
- Identify uses of funds, amounts needed, and timing of outflows.
- Make spending conform to affordable limits.

Step 4
Implement Your Financial Action Plan

- Perform the planned actions. Track your spending. Make it conform to plans.

Step 5
Re-evaluate and Revise Your Financial Plan

- Review your progress.
- Reassess your personal situation.

Figure AIII.1 Developing a Personal Financial Plan

Financial Planning process of looking at one's current financial condition, identifying one's goals, and anticipating requirements for meeting those goals

Personal Net Worth value of one's total assets minus one's total liabilities (debts)

Assets: What You Own		Example Numbers	Your Numbers
LIQUID ASSETS:			
1. Cash	$	300	_____
2. Savings	+	3,700	_____
3. Checking	+	1,200	_____
INVESTMENTS:			
4. IRAs	+	12,400	_____
5. Securities	+	500	_____
6. Retirement Plan	+	—	_____
7. Real Estate (other than primary residence)	+	—	_____
HOUSEHOLD:			
8. Cars (market value)	+	18,000	_____
9. House (market value)	+	—	_____
10. Furniture	+	3,400	_____
11. Personal Property	+	6,600	_____
12. Other assets		—	_____
13. Total Assets (add lines 1-12)		**= $46,100**	_____
Liabilities (Dept): What You Owe			
CURRENT LIABILITIES:			
14. Credit-card balance	$	1,300	_____
15. Unpaid bills due	+	1,800	_____
16. Alimony and child support	+	—	_____
LONG-TERM LIABILITIES:			
17. Home mortgage	+	—	_____
18. Home equity loan	+	—	_____
19. Car loan	+	4,100	_____
20. Student loan	+	3,600	_____
21. Other liabilities	+	2,400	_____
22. Total Liabilities (add lines 14-21)		**= $13,200**	_____
Net Worth			
23. Total Assets (line 13)		$46,100	_____
24. Less: Total Debt (line 22)	–	13,200	_____
25. Results: Net Worth		**= $32,900**	_____

Figure AIII.2 Worksheet for Calculating Net Worth

liabilities (debts) *at the present time.* The worksheet in Figure AIII.2 provides some sample calculations for developing your own personal "balance sheet." Because assets and liabilities change over time, updating your balance sheet not only allows you to monitor changes, but also provides more accurate information for realistic budgeting and planning.

Develop Your Financial Goals

Step 2 involves setting three different types of future goals: *immediate* (within one year), *intermediate* (within

five years), and *long-term* (more than five years). The worksheet in Figure AIII.3 will help you establish these goals. By thinking about your finances in three different time frames, you'll be better able to set measurable goals and completion times, or to set priorities for rationing your resources if, at some point, you're not able to pursue all your goals.

Because step 3 (identifying a plan of action) and step 4 (implementing your plan) will affect your assets and liabilities, your balance sheet will change over time. As a result, step 5 (reevaluating and revising your plan) needs periodic updating.

Name the Goal	Financial Requirement (amount) for This Goal	Time Frame for Accomplishing Goal	Importance (1= highest, 5 = lowest)
Immediate Goals:			
Live in a better apartment	_____	_____	_____
Establish an emergency cash fund	_____	_____	_____
Pay off credit-card debt	_____	_____	_____
Other	_____	_____	_____
Intermediate Goals:			
Obtain adequate life, disability, liability, property insurance	_____	_____	_____
Save for wedding	_____	_____	_____
Save to buy new car	_____	_____	_____
Establish regular savings program (5% of gross income)	_____	_____	_____
Save for college for self	_____	_____	_____
Pay off major outstanding debt	_____	_____	_____
Make major purchase	_____	_____	_____
Save for home remodeling	_____	_____	_____
Save for down payment on a home	_____	_____	_____
Other	_____	_____	_____
Long-Term Goals:			
Pay off home mortgage	_____	_____	_____
Save for college for children	_____	_____	_____
Save for vacation home	_____	_____	_____
Increase personal net worth to $___ in ___ years.	_____	_____	_____
Achieve retirement nest egg of $___ in ___ years.	_____	_____	_____
Accumulate fund for travel in retirement	_____	_____	_____
Save for long-term care needs	_____	_____	_____
Other	_____	_____	_____

Figure AIII.3 Worksheet for Setting Financial Goals

Making Better Use of the Time Value of Money

As discussed in Chapter 16, the value of time with any investment stems from the principle of compound growth—the compounding of interest received over several time periods. With each additional time period, interest receipts accumulate and earn even more interest, thus, multiplying the earning capacity of the investment. Whenever you make everyday purchases, you're giving up interest that you could have earned with the same money if you'd invested it instead. From a finan-cial standpoint, "idle" or uninvested money, which could be put to work earning more money, is a wasted resource.

Planning for the Golden Years

The sooner you start saving, the greater your financial power will be—you will have taken advantage of the time value of money for a longer period of time. Consider coworkers Ellen and Barbara, who are both planning to retire in 25 years, as can be seen in Figure AIII.4.

Over that period, each can expect a 10 percent annual return on investment (the U.S. stock market averaged more than 10 percent for the 75 years before the 2008-2010 recession). Their savings strategies, however, are different: Barbara begins saving immediately, while Ellen

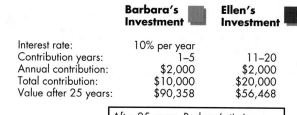

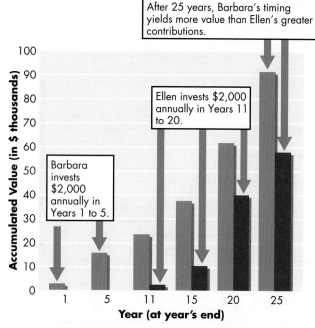

Figure AIII.4 Compounding Money over Time

plans to start later but invest larger sums. Barbara will invest $2,000 annually for each of the next 5 years (years 1 through 5), for a total investment of $10,000. Ellen, meanwhile, wants to live a little larger by spending rather than saving for the next 10 years. Then, for years 11 through 20, she'll start saving $2,000 annually, for a total investment of $20,000. They will both allow annual returns to accumulate until they retire in year 25. Ellen expects to have a larger retirement fund than Barbara because she has contributed twice as much, but she is in for a surprise. Barbara's retirement wealth will be much larger—$90,364 versus Ellen's $56,468—even though she invested only half as much. Barbara's advantage lies in the length of her savings program. Her money is invested longer—over a period of 21 to 25 years—with interest compounding over that range of time. Ellen's earnings are compounded over a shorter period—6 to 15 years. Granted, Ellen may have had more fun in years 1 to 10, but Barbara's retirement prospects look brighter.

Time Value as a Financial-Planning Tool

A good financial plan takes into account future needs, the sources of funds for meeting those needs, and the time needed to develop those funds. When you begin your financial plan, you can use various time-based tables to take into account the time value of money. Figure AIII.5 shows how much a $1.00 investment will grow over different lengths of time and at different interest rates.

A timetable like this can determine the factor at which your money will multiply over a given period of time and at a given interest rate. It can also help you determine how long and at what interest rate you will need to invest to meet your financial goals. For example, if you wanted to double your money in less than 10 years, you would have to find an interest rate of return of at least 8%. The catch is that to obtain a high interest rate, you will have to make riskier investments, such as buying stocks. Because higher interest rates carry greater risks, it is unwise to "put all your eggs in one basket." A sound financial plan will include more conservative investments, such as a bank savings account, to mitigate the risks of more speculative investments.

Conserving Money by Controlling It

A major pitfall in any financial plan is the temptation to spend too much, especially when credit is so easy to get. Because many credit-card issuers target college students and recent graduates with tempting offers appealing to the desire for financial independence, it is important that you arm yourself with a solid understanding of the financial costs entailed by credit cards. The same lessons apply equally to other loans—home mortgages, cars, and student financial aid.

n	1%	2%	4%	6%	8%	10%
1	1.010	1.020	1.040	1.060	1.080	1.100
2	1.020	1.040	1.082	1.124	1.166	1.210
3	1.030	1.061	1.125	1.191	1.260	1.331
4	1.041	1.082	1.170	1.262	1.360	1.464
5	1.051	1.104	1.217	1.338	1.469	1.611
6	1.062	1.126	1.265	1.419	1.587	1.772
7	1.072	1.149	1.316	1.504	1.714	1.949
8	1.083	1.172	1.369	1.594	1.851	2.144
9	1.094	1.195	1.423	1.689	1.999	2.358
10	1.105	1.219	1.480	1.791	2.159	2.594
15	1.161	1.346	1.801	2.397	3.172	4.177
20	1.220	1.486	2.191	3.207	4.661	6.727
25	1.282	1.641	2.666	4.292	6.848	10.834
30	1.348	1.811	3.243	5.743	10.062	17.449

Note: n = Number of time periods   % = Various interest rates

Figure AIII.5 Timetable for Growing $1.00

| Balance = $5,000 | MPD 3% | | MPD 5% | | MPD 10% | |
APR	Months	Costs	Months	Costs	Months	Costs
6%	144	$5,965.56	92	$5,544.58	50	$5,260.74
9%	158	$6,607.24	96	$5,864.56	51	$5,401.63
12%	175	$7,407.50	102	$6,224.26	53	$5,550.32
18%	226	$9,798.89	115	$7,096.70	55	$5,873.86
21%	266	$11,704.63	123	$7,632.92	57	$6,050.28

Note: MPD = Minimum Payment Due   APR = Annual Percentage Rate

Figure AIII.6   Paying Off Credit-Card Debt

Credit Cards: Keys to Satisfaction or Financial Handcuffs?

Although some credit cards don't charge annual fees, all of them charge interest on unpaid (outstanding) balances. Figure AIII.6 reprints part of a page from Bankrate.com's credit-card calculator at www.bankrate.com/brm/calc/MinPayment.asp. Using the table as a guide, suppose you owe $5,000 for credit-card purchases, and your card company requires a minimum monthly payment (minimum payment due [MPD]) of 5 percent of the unpaid balance. The interest rate is 18 percent APR (annual percentage rate) on the outstanding balance.

If you pay only the monthly minimum, it will take you 115 months—over 9 1/2 years—to pay off your credit-card debt. During this time you will pay $2,096.70 in interest, almost half again the principal balance! Repayment takes so long because you are making only the MPD, which decreases with each monthly payment.

Save Your Money: Lower Interest Rates and Faster Payments

Figure AIII.6 confirms two principles for saving money that you can apply when borrowing from any source, not just credit cards: Look for lower interest rates and make faster repayments.

Seeking Lower Interest Rates   Look again at Figure AIII.6 and compare the cost of borrowing $5,000 at 18 percent with the cost of borrowing it at 9 percent. If you assume the same 5 percent minimum monthly payment, a 9 percent APR will save you $1232.14 in interest during the repayment period—a nearly 59 percent savings.

Making Faster Payments   Because money has a time value, lenders charge borrowers according to the length of time for which they borrow it. In general, longer lending periods increase the cost, while shorter periods are cheaper. Using Figure AIII.6, compare the costs of the 5 percent MPD with the faster 10 percent MPD. The faster schedule cuts the repayment period from 115 to 55 months and, at 18 percent APR, reduces interest costs by $1,222.84.

Combining both faster repayment and the lower interest rate cuts your total interest cost to $450.30—a savings of $1,695.07 over the amount you'd pay if you made slower repayments at the higher rate.

Declining Asset Value: A Borrower's Regret

Financially speaking, nothing's more disappointing than buying an expensive item and then discovering that it's not worth what you paid. For example, if you buy a $5,000 used car with a credit card at 18 percent APR and make only the MPD, as in the example above, you'll end up spending a total of $7,407.50 over 9 1/2 years. By that time, however, the car you bought will be worth less than $1,000. Some of this loss in asset value can be avoided through realistic planning and spending—by knowing and staying within your financial means.

Financial Commitments of Home Ownership

Deciding whether to rent or buy a home involves a variety of considerations, including life stage, family needs, career, financial situation, and preferred lifestyle. If you decide to buy, you have to ask yourself what you can afford, and that requires asking yourself questions about your personal financial condition and your capacity for borrowing. Figure AIII.7 summarizes the key considerations in deciding whether to rent or buy.

How Much House Can You Afford?

Buying a home is the biggest investment in most people's lives. Unfortunately, many make the mistake of buying a house that they can't afford, resulting in unnecessary stress and even devastating financial loss. This happened on a massive scale in the housing downfall that began in 2007 and continues today. The seeds for destruction

Renting	Buying
• No down payment to get started	• Must make payments for mortgage, property taxes, and insurance
• Flexibility to leave	• Equity builds up over time
• No obligation for upkeep or improvements	• More privacy
• No groundskeeping	• Value of property may increase
• Easy cash-flow planning (a single monthly payment)	• Lower income taxes: mortgage-interest and property tax payments reduce taxable income
• May provide access to recreation and social facilities	• Financial gains from selling house can be exempt from taxes
• Rental conditions may be changed by owner	• Greater control over use of property and improvements
• Timing for repairs controlled by owner	• The home can become a source of cash by refinancing with another mortgage loan or a home-equity loan

Figure AIII.7 To Buy or Not to Buy

sprouted during the years 2000–2007 when millions of optimistic home buyers borrowed beyond their means by getting larger loans than they could afford. With the rising demand for home ownership, housing prices became inflated and borrowers responded by seeking unrealistically larger loans. They expected market prices would continue to rise indefinitely, thereby providing a profitable investment. Borrowers were aided by lenders using loose credit standards, unlike the time-proven standards presented below, leading to unrealistic repayment requirements. By 2007 the housing market was oversold and the U.S. economy entered a severe recession. With rising unemployment, borrowers were unable to meet monthly payments, especially when interest rates (and thus payments) on loans increased; housing vacancies increased and property values plummeted. Borrowers lost their homes and the equity they had built up in them. Economists predict that the collapsing housing market will continue into 2014.

In addition to loan payments, the typical demands of ownership—time and other resources for maintaining and improving a home—tend to cut into the money left over for recreation, eating out, taking vacations, and so on. You can reduce the financial pressure by calculating in advance a realistic price range—one that not only lets

you buy a house but also lets you live a reasonably pleasant life once you're in it.

Most people need a loan to buy a house, apartment, or condominium. A **mortgage loan** is secured by the property—the home—being purchased. Because the size of a loan depends on the cost of the property, both borrowers and lenders want to know whether the buyer can afford the house he or she wants. To determine how much you can afford, one time-tested (though somewhat conservative) rule recommends keeping the price below 2 1/2 times your annual income. If your income is $48,000, look for a house priced below $120,000.

Any such calculation, however, will give you just a rough estimate of what you can afford. You should also consider how much money you have for a down payment and how much you can borrow. Lending institutions want to determine a buyer's borrowing capacity—the borrower's ability to meet the *recurring costs* of buying and owning.

PITI Every month, the homeowner must pay **prin**cipal (pay back some of the borrowed money), along with **interest, taxes,** and homeowner's **insurance**—PITI, for short. As Figure AIII.8 shows, the size of principal and interest payments depends on (1) the mortgage

Interest Rate (%)	Length of Loan				
	3 Years	5 Years	10 Years	20 Years	30 Years
5.0	$299.71	$188.71	$106.07	$66.00	$53.68
6.0	304.22	193.33	111.02	71.64	59.96
6.5	306.49	195.66	113.55	74.56	63.21
7.0	308.77	198.01	116.11	77.53	66.53
8.0	313.36	202.76	121.33	83.65	73.38
9.0	318.00	207.58	126.68	89.98	80.47
10.0	322.67	212.47	132.16	96.51	87.76
11.0	327.39	217.42	137.76	103.22	95.24
12.0	332.14	222.44	143.48	110.11	102.86

Figure AIII.8 Monthly Payments on a $10,000 Loan

ASSUMPTIONS:

30-year mortgage
Closing costs (fees for property, survey, credit report, title search,
    title insurance, attorney, interest advance, loan origination) = $5,000
Funds available for closing costs and down payment = $25,000
Interest rate on mortgage = $6\frac{1}{2}\%$ per year
Estimated real estate taxes = $200 per month
Estimated homeowner's insurance = $20 month

Example Numbers   Your Numbers

1. Monthly income, gross (before taxes or deductions)........$4,000   _____
2. Apply PITI ratio (0.28 x amount on line 1) to determine
     borrower's payment capacity:
     0.28 x $4,000 = ...$1,120   _____
3. Determine mortgage payment (principal and interest)
     by subtracting taxes and insurance from
     PITI (line 2)..–$ 220   _____
4. **Result: Maximum mortgage payment
     (principal and interest)................................ $900**   _____

5. Using Table Figure AIII.11, find the monthly mortgage payment
     on a $10,000 loan at $6\frac{1}{2}\%$ interest for
     30 years.. $63.21   _____
6. Since each $10,000 loan requires a $63.21 monthly payment,
     how many $10,000 loans can the borrower afford
     with the $900 payment capacity? The answer is
     determined as follows:
         $900.00/$63.21 =
         14.2382 loans of $10,000 each   _____

7. **Result: Maximum allowable mortgage loan** [calculated
     as follows:
         14.2382 loans (from line 6 above)
         x $10,000 per loan] = ...**$142,382**   _____

8. **Result: Maximum house price borrower can afford
     using PITI** (amount of house that can be bought with
     available funds):

         From loan...........................$142,382   _____
         From down payment...........$ 25,000   _____
         Less closing cost................–$ 5,000   _____
                             ....**$162,382**   _____

amount, (2) the length of the mortgage loan, and (3) the interest rate.

In evaluating loan applications, lenders use PITI calculations to estimate the buyer's ability to meet monthly payments. To determine how much someone is likely to lend you, calculate 28 percent of your gross monthly income (that is, before taxes and other deductions). If your PITI costs don't exceed that figure, your loan application probably will receive favorable consideration. With a monthly gross income of $4,000, for example, your PITI costs shouldn't exceed $1,120 (28 percent of $4,000).

Additional calculations show a house price of $162,382 is the most this borrower can afford. Figure AIII.9 gives a sample calculation, and you should be able to make step-by-step computations by plugging your own numbers into the worksheet.

Other Debt In evaluating financial capacity, lenders also look at any additional outstanding debt, such as loans and credit-card bills. They will generally accept indebtedness (including PITI) up to 36 percent of gross income. Because PITI itself can be up to 28 percent, you

Mortgage Loan loan secured by property
(the home) being purchased

might be allowed as little as 8 percent in other long-term debt. With your $4,000 monthly gross income, your total debt should be less than $1,440 ($1,120 for PITI and $320 for other debt). If your total debt exceeds $1,440, you may have to settle for a smaller loan than the one you calculated with the PITI method. Web sites such as http://mortgages.interest.com provide mortgage calculators for testing interest rates, lengths of loans, and other personal financial information.

Cashing Out from Tax Avoidance (Legally)

Personal expenditures always require cash outflows; some also reduce your tax bill and save you some cash. Individual retirement accounts (IRAs) and some education savings accounts have this effect. (Before you commit any money to these instruments or activities, check with an expert on tax regulations; they change from time to time.)

The IRA Tax Break

With a **traditional individual retirement account (IRA)**, you can make an annual tax-deductible savings deposit of up to $5,000, depending on your income level. IRAs are long-term investments, intended to provide income after age 59 1/2. For distant future savings, an IRA boasts immediate cash advantages over a typical savings account because it reduces your current taxable income by the amount of your contribution.

Here's how it works: You're a qualified employee with a federal income tax rate of 20 percent in year 2009. If you contribute $4,000 to an IRA, you avoid $800 in income taxes (0.20 × $4,000 = $800). Your untaxed contributions and their accumulated earnings will be taxed later when you withdraw money from your IRA. The tax break is based on the assumption that, after you retire, you're likely to have less total income and will have to pay less tax on the money withdrawn as income from your IRA.

IRA Risks If you underestimate your future cash requirements and have to withdraw money before you reach 59 1/2, you'll probably get hit with a 10 percent penalty. You can, however, make penalty-free withdrawals under certain circumstances: buying a first home, paying college expenses, and paying large medical bills.

The unpredictability of future income tax rates also poses a financial risk. If tax rates increase substantially, future IRA withdrawals may be taxed at higher rates, which may offset your original tax savings.

Roth IRA versus Traditional IRA The **Roth IRA** is the reverse of the traditional IRA in that contributions are not tax deductible, withdrawals on initial contribution are not penalized, and withdrawals on accumulated earnings after the age of 59 1/2 are not taxed.

Figure AIII.10 shows the significant advantage of this last feature. Accumulated earnings typically far outweigh the initial contribution, so although you pay an extra $1,285 in front-end taxes, you get $40,732 in additional cash at retirement—and even more if income-tax rates have increased.

IRAs and Education Depending on your income level, you can contribute up to $2,000 annually to a Coverdell Education Savings Account (also known as an *Education IRA*) for each child under age 18. As with the Roth IRA, your initial contribution is not tax deductible, your earnings are tax-free, and you pay no tax on withdrawals to pay for qualified education expenses. However, the Education IRA requires that you use the money by the time your child reaches age 30. Funds that you withdraw but don't use for stipulated education expense are subject to taxation plus a 10 percent penalty.

Assumptions: Initial contribution and earnings average 10 percent growth annually. Initial contribution and earnings remain invested for 40 years. Income tax rate is 30 percent.	Traditional IRA	Roth IRA
Initial cash contribution to IRA	$3,000	$3,000
Income tax paid initially: $4,285 income x 30% tax rate = $1,285 tax	0	1,285
Total initial cash outlay	**$3,000**	**$4,285**
Accumulated earnings (40 years)	$132,774	$132,774
Initial contribution	+ 3,000	+ 3,000
Total available for distribution after 40 years	= $135,774	= $135,774
Income tax at time of distribution	− $40,732	0
After-tax distribution (cash)	**= $95,042**	**= $135,774**

Figure AIII.10 Cash Flows: Roth IRA versus Traditional IRA

Protecting Your Net Worth

With careful attention, thoughtful saving and spending, and skillful financial planning (and a little luck), you can build up your net worth over time. Every financial plan should also consider steps for preserving it. One approach involves the risk–return relationship discussed in Chapter 16. Do you prefer to protect your current assets, or are you willing to risk them in return for greater growth? At various life stages and levels of wealth, you should adjust your asset portfolio to conform to your risk and return preferences: conservative, moderate, or aggressive.

Why Buy Life Insurance?   You can think of life insurance as a tool for financial preservation. As explained in Appendix I, a life insurance policy is a promise to pay beneficiaries after the death of the insured party who paid the insurance company premiums during his or her lifetime.

MyBizLab

Gain hands-on experience through an interactive, real-world scenario. This chapter's simulation entitled Personal Finance is located at **www.mybizlab.com**.

What Does Life Insurance Do?   Upon the death of the policyholder, life insurance replaces income on which someone else is dependent. The amount of insurance you need depends on how many other people rely on your income. For example, while insurance makes sense for a married parent who is a family's sole source of income, a single college student with no financial dependents needs little or no insurance.

How Much Should I Buy?   The more insurance you buy, the more it's going to cost you. To estimate the amount of coverage you need, begin by adding up all your annual expenses—rent, food, clothing, transportation, schooling, debts to be paid—that you pay for the dependents who'd survive you. Then multiply the total by the number of years that you want the insurance to cover them. Typically, this sum will amount to several times—even 10 to 20 times—your current annual income.

Why Consider Term Insurance?   *Term insurance* pays a predetermined benefit when death occurs during the stipulated policy term. If the insured outlives the term, the policy loses its value and simply ceases. Term-life premiums are significantly lower than premiums for whole-life insurance.

Unlike term life, *whole-life insurance*—also known as *cash-value insurance*—remains in force as long as premiums are paid. In addition to paying a death benefit, whole life accumulates cash value over time—a form of savings. Paid-in money can be withdrawn; however, whole-life savings earn less interest than most alternative forms of investment.

How Much Does It Cost?   The cost of insurance depends on how much you buy, your life expectancy, and other statistical risk factors. To get the best match between your policy and your personal situation, you should evaluate the terms and conditions of a variety of policies. You can get convenient comparisons on Web sites such as www.intelliquote.com.

Traditional Individual Retirement Account (IRA) provision allowing individual tax-deferred retirement savings

Roth Ira provision allowing individual retirement savings with tax-free accumulated earnings

Glindex

Note: The bracketed page numbers refer to the glossary terms in the text.

A

ABB Asea Brown Boveri, 91

Absenteeism when an employee does not show up for work, [197]

Absolute Advantage the ability to produce something more efficiently than any other country can, [97]

Accommodative Stance approach to social responsibility by which a company, if specifically asked to do so, exceeds legal minimums in its commitments to groups and individuals in its social environment, [49]

Accountability obligation employees have to their manager for the successful completion of an assigned task, 41, [149]

Accounting comprehensive system for collecting, analyzing, and communicating financial information, [359]
    ethics in, 374–375

Accounting Equation Assets = Liabilities + Owners' Equity; used by accountants to balance data for the firm's financial transactions at various points in the year, [363]

Accounting Information System (AIS) organized procedure for identifying, measuring, recording, and retaining financial information for use in accounting statements and management reports, [359]

Accounts Payable (Payables) current liability consisting of bills owed to suppliers, plus wages and taxes due within the coming year, [367]

Acid rain, 43

Acquisition the purchase of one company by another, [79]

Activity Ratio financial ratio for evaluating management's efficiency in using a firm's assets, [371]

Adam Hat Company, 210

Adidas, 234

ADT Ltd., 32

Advanced Development Programs (ADP), 157

Advertising Media variety of communication devices for carrying a seller's message to potential customers, [317]

Advertising promotional tool consisting of paid, nonpersonal communication used by an identified sponsor to inform an audience about a product, [317]
    ethics in, 45
    on Facebook, 80

AES Corporation, 209

Affirmative Action Plan written statement of how the organization intends to actively recruit, hire, and develop members of relevant protected classes, [253]

African Americans, 34, 230

Agent individual or organization acting for and in the name of another party, [449]
    distribution by, 306

Aggregate Output the total quantity of goods and services produced by an economic system during a given period, [17]

Agreeableness, 199

AIDS, 253

AIG, 230

Airbus, 233–234, 275

Airlines industry, 164–166. *See also specific airlines*

Air pollution, 42–43

Amazon.com, 41, 68, 71
    brand awareness for, 287

Amelio, William, 140

American Airlines, 43, 141

American Eagle Outfitters (AEO), 276

American Express, 40, 118, 122

American Federation of Labor and Congress of Industrial Organizations (AFL-CIO), 258

American Marketing Association, 270

American Society for Quality, 175

Americans with Disabilities Act, 248, 252

Anderson, Brad, 128

Angel Investors outside investors who provide new capital for firms in return for a share of equity ownership, [429]

Anheuser-Busch, 42, 252

Annual Percentage Rate (APR) one-year rate that is charged for borrowing, expressed as a percentage of the borrowed principal, [429]

Anti-Virus Software product that protects systems by searching incoming e-mails and data files for "signatures" of known viruses and virus-like characteristics, [347]

Apparent Authority agent's authority, based on the principal's compliance, to bind a principal to a certain course of action, [449]

Appellate Court court that reviews case records of trials whose findings have been appealed, [447]

Apple, 16, 68, 116, 231, 254, 289, 320
    globalization and, 89

Apps, 333–334, 338

Arbitration method of resolving a labor dispute in which both parties agree to submit to the judgment of a neutral party, [261]

Archer Farms, 272

Arthur Andersen, 40

Ash, Mary Kay, 226

Asian Americans, 69, 230

Assembly Line a same-steps layout in which a product moves step by step through a plant on conveyor belts or other equipment until it is completed, [175]

Asset Allocation relative amount of funds invested in (or allocated to) each of several investment alternatives, [429]

Asset any economic resource expected to benefit a firm or an individual who owns it, [363]

Associated Press, 114

Association of Certified Fraud Examiners (ACFE), 356, 378

Association of Southeast Asian Nations (ASEAN) organization for economic, political, social, and cultural cooperation among Southeast Asian nations, [93]

AT&T, 254

Attitudes a person's beliefs and feelings about specific ideas, situations, or people, [201]

Audit systematic examination of a company's accounting system to determine whether its financial reports reliably represent its operations, [359]

Authority power to make the decisions necessary to complete a task, [149]

Auto Clearing House (ACH), 401

Automated Teller Machine (ATM) electronic machine that allows bank customers to conduct account-related activities 24 hours a day, 7 days a week, [395]

Avatar, 288

Avon, 305

Aylett, Matthew, 342

B

Bailouts, 182

Bakery, 98

C

Cabot Cheese, 74

Cafeteria Benefits Plan benefit plan that sets limits on benefits per employee, each of whom may choose from a variety of alternative benefits, [253]

Calvin Klein, 45

Canada, 93, 97, 114

CAN-SPAM Act of 2003, 348

Canyon River Blues, 289

Capacity amount of a product that a company can produce under normal conditions, [173]

Capacity competence required of individuals entering into a binding contract, [447]

Capital funds needed to create and operate a business enterprise, [7]
    small business failure and, 70

Capital Gain profit realized from the increased value of an investment, [427]

Capitalism system that sanctions the private ownership of the factors of production and encourages entrepreneurship by offering profits as an incentive, 4, [11]

Capital Item expensive, long-lasting, infrequently purchased industrial product, such as a building, or industrial service, such as a long-term agreement for data warehousing services, [283]

Carbon offsets, 44

Caring, 36, 37

Cartel association of producers whose purpose is to control supply and prices, [105]

Casualty, of insurable risk, 445

Catalog Showroom bargain retailer in which customers place orders for catalog items to be picked up at on-premises warehouses, [309]

Caterpillar, 184–185

Centralized Organization organization in which most decision-making authority is held by upper-level management, [147]

CereProc, 342

Certified Development Company, 68

Certified Fraud Examiner (CFE) professional designation administered by the Association of Certified Fraud Examiners in recognition of qualifications for a specialty area within forensic accounting, [363]

Certified Management Accountant (CMA) professional designation awarded by the Institute of Management Accountants in recognition of management accounting qualifications, [361]

Certified Public Accountant (CPA) accountant licensed by the state and offering services to the public, [359]

Chain of Command reporting relationships within a company, [141]

Chambers, John, 69

Change management, 131

Charismatic Leadership type of influence based on the leader's personal charisma, [227]

Charities, 33

Check Clearing for the 21st Century Act, 401

Check demand deposit order instructing a bank to pay a given sum to a specified payee, [389]

Checking Account (Demand Deposit) bank account funds, owned by the depositor, that may be withdrawn at any time by check or cash, [389]

Cheer, 15

Chen, Andrew, 80

Chenault, Kenneth, 122

Chettero, Nicole, 89

Chevrolet, 117

Chicago Climate Exchange (CCX), 436

Chief Executive Officer (CEO) top manager who is responsible for the overall performance of a corporation, [79], 118
    leadership by, 228

Chief Financial Officer (CFO), 118

Chief information officer (CIO), 119

Child labor, 86–89

Children's Online Privacy Protection Act, 44

China, 3, 89, 91, 93, 99, 103, 104, 186, 350
    Lenovo in, 138–140

Chiquita, 105

Chocolate, 86–89

Chrysler, 11, 102, 182

CircuitCity, 4, 22, 102, 128

Cisco, 69, 288

Citigroup, 40, 254, 431

Clark Equipment, 148–149

Classical Theory of Motivation theory holding that workers are motivated solely by money, [203]

Clayton Act, 16

Clean Harbors, 71

Clean Water Act, 30

Client-Server Network common business network in which clients make requests for information or resources and servers provide the services, [337]

Clorox, 286, 288

Closely Held (or Private) Corporation corporation whose stock is held by only a few people and is not available for sale to the general public, [77]

Coaching, 229

Coalition an informal alliance of individuals or groups formed to achieve a common goal, [235]

Coast Distribution System, 281

Coblin, James M., 244

Coca-Cola, 15, 80, 100, 287, 289

Code of Professional Conduct code of ethics for CPAs as maintained and enforced by the AICPA, [375]

Collateral asset pledged for the fulfillment of repaying a loan, [429]

Collective Bargaining process by which labor and management negotiate conditions of employment for union-represented workers, [259]

Collectivism, 229–230

Collusion illegal agreement between two or more companies to commit a wrongful act, [45]

Commercial Bank company that accepts deposits that it uses to make loans, earn profits, pay interest to depositors, and pay dividends to owners, [391]

Committee and Team Authority authority granted to committees or teams involved in a firm's daily operations, [149]

Common Law body of decisions handed down by courts ruling on individual cases, [447]

Common Stock most basic form of ownership, including voting rights on major issues, in a company, [417]

Communism political system in which the government owns and operates all factors of production, [11]

Comparative Advantage the ability to produce some products more efficiently than others, [97]

Compensation System total package of rewards that organizations provide to individuals in return for their labor, [249]

Competition vying among businesses for the same resources or customers, [15]
    degrees, 14

Competitive advantage, 97

Competitive environment, 274–275

Competitive Product Analysis process by which a company analyzes a competitor's products to identify desirable improvements, [183]

Compound Growth compounding of interest over time-with each additional time period, interest returns accumulate, [417]

Computer-Aided Design (CAD) IS with software that helps knowledge workers design products by simulating them and displaying them in three-dimensional graphics, [343]

Computer-Aided Manufacturing (CAM) IS that uses computers to design and control equipment in a manufacturing process, [343]

Computer Network group of two or more computers linked together by some form of cabling or by wireless technology to share data or resources, such as a printer, [337]

Conceptual Skills abilities to think in the abstract, diagnose and analyze different situations, and *see* beyond the present situation, [121]

Condé Nast, 80

Conflict of interest, 34

Conscientiousness, 199

Consideration item of value exchanged between parties to create a valid contract, [447]

Consistency dimension of quality that refers to sameness of product quality from unit to unit, [175]

Construction, in small business, 63

Consumer Behavior study of the decision process by which people buy and consume products, [279]

Consumer Bill of Rights, 44, 45

Consumer choice, 4

Consumer Goods physical products purchased by consumers for personal use, [271], 283

Consumerism form of social activism dedicated to protecting the rights of consumers in their dealings with businesses, [45]

Consumer Price Index (CPI) a measure of the prices of typical products purchased by consumers living in urban areas, [23]

The Container Store, 40

Contemporary Landscape Services, 140

Continental, 78

Contingency Planning identifying aspects of a business or its environment that might entail changes in strategy, [131]

Contingent Worker employee hired on something other than a full-time basis to supplement an organization's permanent workforce, [257]

Continuity, with corporations, 75

Contract agreement between two or more parties enforceable in court, [447]

Controller person who manages all of a firm's accounting activities (chief accounting officer), [359]

Controlling management process of monitoring an organization's performance to ensure that it is meeting its goals, [117]

Convenience Good/Convenience Service inexpensive good or service purchased and consumed rapidly and regularly, [283]

Convenience Store retail store offering easy accessibility, extended hours, and fast service, [309]

Cool Whip, 15

Cooperative form of ownership in which a group of sole proprietorships and/or partnerships agree to work together for common benefits, [75]

Coors, 289

Co-pay, 260

Copyright exclusive ownership right belonging to the creator of a book, article, design, illustration, photo, film, or musical work, [449]

Core Competencies For Accounting the combination of skills, technology, and knowledge that will be necessary for the future CPA, [361]

Corporate Blogs comments and opinions published on the web by or for an organization to promote its activities, [289]

Corporate Bond formal pledge obligating the issuer (the company) to pay interest periodically and repay the principal at maturity, [431]

Corporate Culture the shared experiences, stories, beliefs, and norms that characterize an organization, [131]

Corporate Governance roles of shareholders, directors, and other managers in corporate decision making and accountability, [77]

Corporate Raider investor conducting a type of hostile corporate takeover against the wishes of the company, [433]

Corporate Strategy strategy for determining the firm's overall attitude toward growth and the way it will manage its businesses or product lines, [125]

Corporation business that is legally considered an entity separate from its owners and is liable for its own debts; owners' liability extends to the limits of their investments, [75]

advantages, 75
disadvantages, 75–76
foundations of, 49
management of, 77–78
types of, 76–77

Cost of Goods Sold costs of obtaining materials for making the products sold by a firm during the year, [367]

Cost-Of-Living Adjustment (COLA) labor contract clause tying future raises to changes in consumer purchasing power, [261]

Cost of Revenues costs that a company incurs to obtain revenues from other companies, [367]

Cost-Oriented Pricing pricing that considers the firm's desire to make a profit and its need to cover production costs, [301]

Counterproductive Behaviors behaviors that detract from organizational performance, [197]

Coupon sales-promotion technique in which a certificate is issued entitling the buyer to a reduced price, [319]

Courtyard by Marriott, 175

CPA Vision Project, 360

Craftsman, 289

Creative Selling personal-selling task in which salespeople try to persuade buyers to purchase products by providing information about their benefits, [319]

Credit cards, 126, 402, 455

Creditor nation, 21

Credit standards, 394

Credit Suisse First Boston, 40

Credit Union nonprofit, cooperative financial institution owned and run by its members, usually employees of a particular organization, [393], 397

Crisis Management organization's methods for dealing with emergencies, [131]

Cruise lines, 129–130

Culture, leadership and, 229–230

Currency (Cash) government-issued paper money and metal coins, [389]

Current Asset asset that can or will be converted into cash within a year, [365]

Current/Interest Dividend Yield yearly dollar amount of income divided by the investment's current market value, expressed as a percentage, [427]

Current Liability debt that must be paid within one year, [367]

Current Ratio financial ratio for measuring a company's ability to pay current debts out of current assets, [373]

Customer Departmentalization dividing an organization to offer products and meet needs for identifiable customer groups, [145]

Customer Relationship Management (CRM) organized methods that a firm uses to build better information connections with clients, so that stronger company-client relationships are developed, [273]

Customers
in operations process, 169
quality control and, 184
social responsibility for, 43–45
as stakeholders, 39

Customer service improvement, 176

Custom-Products Layout physical arrangement of production activities that groups equipment and people according to function, [175]

Cybermall collection of virtual storefronts (business websites) representing a variety of products and product lines on the Internet, [311]

Cyclical unemployment, 22

D

Daewoo, 91

Daimler, 41

DaimlerChrysler, 258

d'Amore, Massimo F., 145

Data Mining the application of electronic technologies for searching, sifting, and reorganizing pools of data to uncover useful information, [341]

Data raw facts and figures that, by themselves, may not have much meaning, [339]

Data Warehousing the collection, storage, and retrieval of data in electronic files, 272, [341]

Davis, James, 198

The Day After Tomorrow, 42

Debit Card plastic card that allows an individual to transfer money between accounts, [403]

Debt company's total liabilities, [373]

Debt Financing long-term borrowing from sources outside a company, [435]

Debtor nation, 20–21

Decentralized Organization organization in which a great deal of decision- making authority is delegated to levels of management at points below the top, [147]

Decision Making choosing one alternative from among several options, [231]
    behavioral aspects of, 234–235
    hierarchy for, 145–150
    rational, 232–235

Decision-Making Skills skills in defining problems and selecting the best courses of action, [121]

Decision Support System (DSS) interactive system that creates virtual business models for a particular kind of decision and tests them with different data to *see* how they respond, [345]

Deductible amount of the loss that the insured must absorb prior to reimbursement, [445]

Deepwater Horizon (oil rig), 30, 52

Default failure of a borrower to make payment when due to a lender, [431]

Defensive Stance approach to social responsibility by which a company meets only minimum legal requirements in its commitments to groups and individuals in its social environment, [49]

Deflation, 22, 398

Delegation process through which a manager allocates work to subordinates, [149]

Dell, Michael, 61, 120, 186

Dell Computer, 11, 39, 61, 67
    supply chain management at, 186

Demand and Supply Schedule assessment of the relationships among different levels of demand and supply at different price levels, [13]

Demand Curve graph showing how many units of a product will be demanded (bought) at different prices, [13]

Demand the willingness and ability of buyers to purchase a good or service, [13]

Demographic Variables characteristics of populations that may be considered in developing a segmentation strategy, [279]

Denial of service (DoS), 344

Departmentalization process of grouping jobs into logical units, [143]

Department Store large product-line retailer characterized by organization into specialized departments, [307]

Dependability, 170

Depreciation accounting method for distributing the cost of an asset over its useful life, [365]

Depression a prolonged and deep recession, [23]

Deregulation elimination of rules that restrict business activity, [447]

Detailed Schedule schedule showing daily work assignments with start and stop times for assigned jobs, [177]

Dickerson, Ron, 262

Diesel jeans, 15

Digital video recorders (DVRs), 288

Direct Channel distribution channel in which a product travels from producer to consumer without intermediaries, [305]

Direct distribution, 305

Direct (or Interactive) Marketing one-on-one nonpersonal selling by nonstore retailers and B2B sellers using direct contact with prospective customers, especially via the Internet, [319]

Direct-Response Retailing form of nonstore retailing in which firms directly interact with customers to inform them of products and to receive sales orders, [309]

Direct Selling form of nonstore retailing typified by door-to-door sales, [309]

DIRECTTV, 254

Discount brokers, 422

Discount House bargain retailer that generates large sales volume by offering goods at substantial price reductions, [307]

Discount price reduction offered as an incentive to purchase, [305]

Discount Rate interest rate at which member banks can borrow money from the Fed, [399]

Discrimination, 34

Disney, 131, 289

Disney, Roy, 142

Disney, Walt, 116, 142

Disney Magic, 129–130

Distribution Channel network of interdependent companies through which a product passes from producer to end user, [305]

Distribution Mix combination of distribution channels by which a firm gets its products to end users, [305]

Diversification purchase of several different kinds of investments rather than just one, [429]

Divestiture strategy whereby a firm sells one or more of its business units, [79]

Dividend payment to shareholders, on a per-share basis, out of the company's earnings, [419]

Divisional Structure organizational structure in which corporate divisions operate as autonomous businesses under the larger corporate umbrella, [151]

Division department that resembles a separate business in that it produces and markets its own products, [151]

Dole, 105

Domestic Business Environment the environment in which a firm conducts its operations and derives its revenues, [7]

Double Click, 114

Double Taxation situation in which taxes may be payable both by a corporation on its profits and by shareholders on dividend incomes, [77]

Dower's Paradise Laundry, 174

Dow Jones Industrial Average (DJIA) oldest and most widely cited market index based on the prices of 30 blue-chip, large-cap industrial firms on the NYSE, [425]

Dr. Pepper, 285

Duke Energy, 130

Dumping practice of selling a product abroad for less than the cost of production, [105]

Duncan, David, 40

Dunkin' Donuts, 269

Functional Strategy strategy by which managers in specific areas decide how best to achieve corporate goals through productivity, [127]

Functional Structure organization structure in which authority is determined by the relationships between group functions and activities, [151]

G

Gainsharing Plan incentive plan that rewards groups for productivity improvements, [251]

Galleon Group, 435

Gamesa Corporation, 272

GameStop, 42

Gantt Chart production schedule that breaks down large projects into steps to be performed and specifies the time required to perform each step, [179]

Gasoline, 2–4, 24

Gates, Bill, 236

Geek Squad, 128

GEICO, 305

Gender, leadership and, 229

General Agreement on Tariffs and Trade (GATT) international trade agreement to encourage the multilateral reduction or elimination of trade barriers, [93]

General Electric (GE), 124, 154, 166, 210

Generally Accepted Accounting Principles (GAAP) accounting guidelines that govern the content and form of financial reports, 47, [359], 376–377

General Motors, 11, 22, 42, 74, 91, 182, 258, 277

General (or Active) Partner partner who actively manages a firm and who has unlimited liability for its debts, [75]

General Partnership business with two or more owners who share in both the operation of the firm and the financial responsibility for its debts, [73]

Geo-Demographic Variables combination of geographic and demographic traits used in developing a segmentation strategy, [279]

Geographic Departmentalization dividing an organization according to the areas of the country or the world served by a business, [145]

Geographic Variables geographic units that may be considered in developing a segmentation strategy, [279]

Germany, 105, 272

Ghosn, Carlos, 221

Global Business Environment the international forces that affect a business, 6, [7]

Globalization process by which the world economy is becoming a single interdependent system, 63, [89]
    barriers to, 103–105
    entrepreneurship and, 98–99
    management with, 99–103, 121–122
    ups and downs of, 102

Goal objective that a business hopes and plans to achieve, [123]

Goetzmann, Gordon, 39

Goldberg, Whoopi, 308

Goldman Sachs, 431

Goods Operations (Goods Production) activities producing tangible products, such as radios, newspapers, buses, and textbooks, [167]

Goodwill amount paid for an existing business above the value of its other assets, [367]

Goodyear, 252

Google, 68, 71, 112–114, 332
    brand awareness for, 287

Gordon, Gil, 212

Grapevine informal communication network that runs through an organization, [157]

Greenhouse emissions, 42

Green marketing, 44, 274, 414–415

Greenpeace, 52

Grocery Dash, 173

Gross, Bill, 222

Gross Domestic Product (GDP) total value of all goods and services produced within a given period by a national economy through domestic factors of production, [17]

Gross National Product (GNP) total value of all goods and services produced by a national economy within a given period regardless of where the factors of production are located, [19]

Gross Profit preliminary, quick-to-calculate profit figure calculated from the firm's revenues minus its cost of revenues (the direct costs of getting the revenues), [367]

Group manager, 118

Groupware, 339

Grubman, Jack, 40

Grupo Gigante, 105

Gucci, 278

H

H1N1, 130

Hacker cybercriminal who gains unauthorized access to a computer or network, either to steal information, money, or property or to tamper with data, [345]

Halliburton, 246, 251

Hardware physical components of a computer network, such as keyboards, monitors, system units, and printers, [339]

Hastings, Reed, 71, 248

Hawthorne Effect tendency for productivity to increase when workers believe they are receiving special attention from management, [203]

Hayward, Tony, 30

Health care, 11

H-E-B Grocery Company, 314

Henderson, Jill, 201–202

Hershey Foods, 332

Herzberg, Frederick, 204

Hewlett-Packard, 37–38, 115–116, 131, 141, 288
    formal structure at, 156

Hierarchy of Human Needs Model theory of motivation describing five levels of human needs and arguing that basic needs must be fulfilled before people work to satisfy higher-level needs, [205]

High-Contact System level of customer contact in which the customer is part of the system during service delivery, [171]

Hispanics, 69, 230

Hitler, Adolf, 223

HIV, 253

Hoffman, Reid, 291

Home country, 7

Home Depot, 89

Home ownership, 455–458

Hostile Work Environment form of sexual harassment deriving from off-color jokes, lewd comments, and so forth, [255]

The HP Way, 37–38

H&R Block, 286

Human Relations Skills skills in understanding and getting along with people, [121]

Human Resource Management (HRM) set of organizational activities directed at attracting, developing, and maintaining an effective workforce, [245]

Human resource manager, 119

Hurricane Katrina, 32, 45, 254

Hurricane Rita, 45

Hygiene factors, 204–205

Hypertargeting, 80

Hypertext Transfer Protocol (HTTP) communications protocol used for the World Wide Web, in which related pieces of information on separate web pages are connected using hyperlinks, [335]

Hyundai, 91, 288

I

IBM, 48, 69, 74, 100
   Lenovo and, 138–140

IBP, 48

Identity Theft unauthorized use of personal information (such as Social Security number and address) to get loans, credit cards, or other monetary benefits by impersonating the victim, [345]

IKEA, 288

ImClone, 47

Implied Authority agent's authority, derived from business custom, to bind a principal to a certain course of action, [449]

Implied Warranty warranty, dictated by law, based on the principle that products should fulfill advertised promises and serve the purposes for which they are manufactured and sold, [449]

Importer firm that buys products in foreign markets and then imports them for resale in its home country, [101]

Import product made or grown abroad but sold domestically, [89]

Incentive Program special compensation program designed to motivate high performance, [251]

Income Statement (Profit-and-Loss Statement) financial statement listing a firm's annual revenues and expenses so that a bottom line shows annual profit or loss, [367]

Independent Agent foreign individual or organization that agrees to represent an exporter's interests, [101]

India, 103, 186

Individual Differences personal attributes that vary from one person to another, [199]

Individualism, 230

Individual Retirement Account (IRA) tax deferred pension fund that wage earners set up to supplement retirement funds, [393]

Industrial Goods physical products purchased by companies to produce other products, [271]

Industrial Market organizational market consisting of firms that buy goods that are either converted into products or used during production, [281]

Inflation occurs when widespread price increases occur throughout an economic system, [21], 398

Informal groups, 156

Informal Organization network, unrelated to the firm's formal authority structure, of everyday social interactions among company employees, [155]

Information manager, 119

Information meaningful, useful interpretation of data, [339]

Information Resources data and other information used by businesses, [9]

Information Systems Managers managers who operate the systems used for gathering, organizing, and distributing information, [341]

Information System (IS) system that uses IT resources to convert data into information and to collect, process, and transmit that information for use in decision making, [339]

Information Technology (IT) various appliances and devices for creating, storing, exchanging, and using information in diverse modes, including visual images, voice, multimedia, and business data, [331]
   ethics in, 348–349

Initial Public Offering (IPO) first sale of a company's stock to the general public, 79, [433]

Innovation, by small business, 61

Insider Trading illegal practice of using special knowledge about a firm for profit or gain, [47], [435], 435

Institute of Management Accountants (IMA), 361

Institutional Investor large investor, such as a mutual fund or a pension fund, that purchases large blocks of corporate stock, [79]

Institutional Market organizational market consisting of such nongovernmental buyers of goods and services as hospitals, churches, museums, and charitable organizations, [281]

Insurance, in small business, 63

Insurance Company nondeposit institution that invests funds collected as premiums charged for insurance coverage, [393]

Insurance Policy formal agreement to pay the policyholder a specified amount in the event of certain losses, [445]

Insurance Premium fee paid to an insurance company by a policyholder for insurance coverage, [445]

Intangibility, 168–169

Intangible Asset nonphysical asset, such as a patent or trademark, that has economic value in the form of expected benefit, [365]

Intangible Personal Property property that cannot be seen but that exists by virtue of written documentation, [449]

Integrated Marketing Strategy strategy that blends together the Four Ps of marketing to ensure their compatibility with one another and with the company's non-marketing, [277]

Intel, 68

Intellectual Property something produced by the intellect or mind that has commercial value, [345], [449]

Intentional Tort tort resulting from the deliberate actions of a party, [449]

Interactive retailing nonstore retailing that uses a website to provide real-time sales and customer service, [311]

Interbrand, 287

Interest fee paid to a lender for the use of borrowed funds; like a rental fee, [429]

Intermediary individual or firm that helps to distribute a product, [305]

Intermediate Goal goal set for a period of one to five years into the future, [125]

Internal environment, 5

Internal Recruiting considering present employees as candidates for openings, [247]

Internal Revenue Service (IRS), 73, 77

International Accounting Standards Board (IASB) organization responsible for developing a set of global accounting standards and for gaining implementation of those standards, [377]

International communities, as stakeholders, 41

International Competition competitive marketing of domestic products against foreign products, [275]

International Firm firm that conducts a significant portion of its business in foreign countries, [101]

International Law general set of cooperative agreements and guidelines established by countries to govern the actions of individuals, businesses, and nations, [449]

International Monetary Fund (IMF) UN agency consisting of about 150 nations that have combined resources to promote stable exchange rates, provide temporary short-term loans, and serve other purposes, [405]

International Organizational Structures approaches to organizational structure developed in response to the need to manufacture, purchase, and sell in global markets, [153]

Internet gigantic system of interconnected computer networks linked together by voice, electronic, and wireless technologies, 68, 334–337, [335]
   bartering on, 340
   small business and, 65

Internet service providers (ISPs), 348

Liability Insurance insurance covering losses resulting from damage to people or property when the insured party is judged liable, [445]

Licensed Brand brand-name product for whose name the seller has purchased the right from an organization or individual, [289]

Licensing Arrangement arrangement in which firms choose foreign individuals or organizations to manufacture or market their products in another country, [103]

Life insurance, 459

Limited Liability Corporation (LLC) hybrid of a publicly held corporation and a partnership in which owners are taxed as partners but enjoy the benefits of limited liability, [77]

Limited Liability legal principle holding investors liable for a firm's debts only to the limits of their personal investments in it, [75]

Limited Partner partner who does not share in a firm's management and is liable for its debts only to the limits of said partner's investment, [75]

Limited Partnership type of partnership consisting of limited partners and a general (or managing) partner, [75]

Line Authority organizational structure in which authority flows in a direct chain of command from the top of the company to the bottom, [149]

Line Department department directly linked to the production and sales of a specific product, [149]

Linens-N-Things, 4, 128

LinkedIn, 291

Liquidity ease with which an asset can be converted into cash, [365]

Little League, 41

Liu Chuanzhi, 138–139

Livermore, Ann, 115–116

L.L. Bean, 39

Load Fund mutual fund in which investors are charged sales commissions when they buy in or sell out, [419]

Loan Principal amount of money that is loaned and must be repaid, [429]

Local Area Network (LAN) computers that are linked in a small area, such as all of a firm's computers within a single building, [337]

Local communities, as stakeholders, 41

Local Content Law law requiring that products sold in a particular country be at least partly made there, [105]

Location planning, 174

Lockheed Martin, 157, 331, 336

Lockout management tactic whereby workers are denied access to the employer's workplace, [261]

Lombardi, Vince, 226

Long-Term Goal goal set for an extended time, typically five years or more into the future, [125]

Long-Term Liability debt that is not due for at least one year, [367]

Louis Vuitton, 105, 278

Low-Contact System level of customer contact in which the customer need not be part of the system to receive the service, [171]

Lucky jeans, 15

M

M-1 measure of the money supply that includes only the most liquid (spendable) forms of money, [389]

M-2 measure of the money supply that includes all the components of M-1 plus the forms of money that can be easily converted into spendable forms, [391]

Madoff, Bernard, 34, 46, 425

Mail Order (Catalog Marketing) form of nonstore retailing in which customers place orders for catalog merchandise received through the mail, [309]

Make-to-Order Operations activities for one-of-a-kind or custom-made production, [169]

Make-to-Stock Operations activities for producing standardized products for mass consumption, [169]

Malware, 347

Management Accountant private accountant who provides financial services to support managers in various business activities within a firm, [361]

Management Advisory Services assistance provided by CPA firms in areas such as financial planning, information systems design, and other areas of concern for client firms, [361]

Management by Objectives (MBO) set of procedures involving both managers and subordinates in setting goals and evaluating progress, [209]

Management Information System (MIS) computer system that supports managers by providing information-reports, schedules, plans, and budgets-that can be used for making decisions, [343]

Management process of planning, organizing, leading, and controlling an organization's resources to achieve its goals, [115]
    areas of, 118–119
    basic skills of, 120–122

    corporate culture and, 130–131
    globalization and, 121–122
    levels of, 117–118

Managerial (Management) Accounting field of accounting that serves internal users of a company's financial information, [359]

Managerial Ethics standards of behavior that guide individual managers in their work, [33]

Managers, 117–119

Managing emotions, 200

Manufacturing, in small business, 63

Market Capitalization (Market Cap) total dollar value of all the company's outstanding shares, [433]

Market Economy economy in which individuals control production and allocation decisions through supply and demand, [11]

Market Index statistical indicator designed to measure the performance of a large group of stocks or track the price changes of a stock market, [423]

Marketing Manager manager who plans and implements the marketing activities that result in the transfer of products from producer to consumer, 119, [275]

Marketing Mix combination of product, pricing, promotion, and place (distribution) strategies used to market products, [275]

Marketing organizational function and a set of processes for creating, communicating, and delivering value to customers, and for managing customer relationships in ways that benefit the organization and its stakeholders, [271]

Marketing Plan detailed strategy for focusing marketing efforts on consumers' needs and wants, [275]

Market mechanism for exchange between buyers and sellers of a particular good or service, [11]

Market Price (Equilibrium Price) profit-maximizing price at which the quantity of goods demanded and the quantity of goods supplied are equal, [13]

Market Segmentation process of dividing a market into categories of customer types, or "segments," [277]

Market Share (or Market Penetration) company's percentage of the total industry sales for a specific product type, [301]

Market Value current price of a share of stock in the stock market, [417]

Markup amount added to an item's purchase cost to sell it at a profit, [301]

Martha Stewart Living Omnimedia, 152–153

Patent exclusive legal right to use and license a manufactured item or substance, manufacturing process, or object design, [449]

Patriot Act, 255, 401

Pay-for-Knowledge Plan incentive plan to encourage employees to learn new skills or become proficient at different jobs, [251]

Pay for Performance (VARIABLE Pay) individual incentive that rewards a manager for especially productive output, [251]

PayPal, 58

Peanut Corporation of America, 48

Pearson, 122

Penetration Pricing setting an initially low price to establish a new product in the market, [303]

Pension Fund nondeposit pool of funds managed to provide retirement income for its members, [393]

People, 276

PeopleTradingServices.com, 340

PepsiCo, 15, 122, 145

Per-capita income, 90

Perfect Competition market or industry characterized by numerous small firms producing an identical product, [15]

Performance Appraisal evaluation of an employee's job performance in order to determine the degree to which the employee is performing effectively, [249]

Performance Behaviors the total set of work-related behaviors that the organization expects employees to display, [197]

Performance dimension of quality that refers to how well a product does what it is supposed to do, [175]

Permission marketing, 318

Personal Net Worth value of one's total assets minus one's total liabilities (debts), [451]

Personal Selling promotional tool in which a salesperson communicates one-on-one with potential customers, [317]

Person-Job Fit the extent to which a person's contributions and the organization's inducements match one another, [203]

Pert Chart production schedule specifying the sequence of activities, time requirements, and critical path for performing the steps in a project, [179]

Pharmaceutical industry, 34

Physical Distribution activities needed to move a product efficiently from manufacturer to consumer, [311]

Physical Resources tangible items organizations use in the conduct of their businesses, 7, [9]

Picketing labor action in which workers publicize their grievances at the entrance to an employer's facility, [261]

Pixar Animation Studios, 116

Pizza Hut, 125
franchises of, 102

Place (Distribution) part of the marketing mix concerned with getting products from producers to consumers, [277]

Place utility, 167, 271

Planned Economy economy that relies on a centralized government to control all or most factors of production and to make all or most production and allocation decisions, [9], 104

Planning management process of determining what an organization needs to do and how best to get it done, [115]

Poilâne, Lionel, 98

Point-of-Sale (POS) Display sales-promotion technique in which product displays are located in certain areas to stimulate purchase or to provide information on a product, [319]

Point-of-Sale (POS) Terminal electronic device that transfers funds from the customer's bank account to pay for retail purchases, [403]

Political action committee (PAC), 272

Political-Legal Environment the relationship between business and government, [7]

Pollution, 42–43

Polo, 15

Polygraph tests, 248

Portfolio combined holdings of all the financial investments of any company or individual, [429]

Positioning process of establishing an identifiable product image in the minds of consumers, [315]

Positive Reinforcement reward that follows desired behaviors, [209]

Possession utility, 271

Postini, 114

Predictability, of insurable risk, 445

Premium sales-promotion technique in which offers of free or reduced-price items are used to stimulate purchases, [319]

President, 118

Price Appreciation increase in the dollar value of an investment at two points in time (the amount by which the price of a security increases), [427]

Priceline.com, 304

Price Lining setting a limited number of prices for certain categories of products, [305]

Price points, 304

PriceSCAN, 309

Price Skimming setting an initially high price to cover new product costs and generate a profit, [303]

Pricing Objectives the goals that sellers hope to achieve in pricing products for sale, [301]

Pricing process of determining the best price at which to sell a product, [277], [301]
strategies and tactics for, 303–305

Primary agents of interest, 34

Primary Securities Market market in which new stocks and bonds are bought and sold by firms and governments, [421]

Prime Rate interest rate available to a bank's most creditworthy customers, [393]

Principal, interest, taxes, and insurance (PITI), 456–458

Principal individual or organization authorizing an agent to act on its behalf, [449]

The Principles of Scientific Management (Taylor), 203

Private Accountant salaried accountant hired by a business to carry out its day-to-day financial activities, [361]

Private Brand (Private Label) brand-name product that a wholesaler or retailer has commissioned from a manufacturer, [289]

Private Enterprise economic system that allows individuals to pursue their own interests without undue governmental restriction, [15]

Private Warehouse warehouse owned by and providing storage for a single company, [311]

Privatization process of converting government enterprises into privately owned companies, [11]

Proactive Stance approach to social responsibility by which a company actively seeks opportunities to contribute to the well-being of groups and individuals in its social environment, [49]

Process Departmentalization dividing an organization according to production processes used to create a good or service, [143]

Process flowcharts, 176

Procter & Gamble, 290, 341

Product Departmentalization dividing an organization according to specific products or services being created, [143]

Product Differentiation creation of a product feature or product image that differs enough from existing products to attract customers, [275]

Regulatory (Administrative) Law law made by the authority of administrative agencies, [447]

Relationship Marketing marketing strategy that emphasizes building lasting relationships with customers and suppliers, [271]

Reliant Energy, 130

RE/Max, 66, 114–115

Renault, 221

Replacement Chart list of each management position, who occupies it, how long that person will likely stay in the job, and who is qualified as a replacement, [247]

Research and Development (R&D), 285

Research In Motion (RIM), 337

Reseller Market organizational market consisting of intermediaries that buy and resell finished goods, [281]

Reserve Requirement percentage of its deposits that a bank must hold in cash or on deposit with the Fed, [399]

Responsibility duty to perform an assigned task, [149]

Retail distribution, 306

Retailer intermediary who sells products directly to consumers, [305]
  in small business, 62

Retained Earnings earnings retained by a firm for its use rather than paid out as dividends, [367]

Reuters, 114

Revenue Recognition formal recording and reporting of revenues at the appropriate time, [371]

Revenues funds that flow into a business from the sale of goods or services, [367]

Revised Uniform Limited Partnership Act, 73

Revlon, 290

Riceland, 74

Rights, 36, 37

Risk Avoidance practice of avoiding risk by declining or ceasing to participate in an activity, [445]

Risk Control practice of minimizing the frequency or severity of losses from risky activities, [445]

Risk Management process of conserving the firm's earning power and assets by reducing the threat of losses due to uncontrollable events, [445]

Risk Propensity extent to which a decision maker is willing to gamble when making a decision, [235]
  with entrepreneurs, 65

Risk Retention practice of covering a firm's losses with its own funds, [445]

Risk-Return (Risk-Reward) Relationship principle that safer investments tend to offer lower returns whereas riskier investments tend to offer higher returns (rewards), [427]

Risk Transfer practice of transferring a firm's risk to another firm, [445]

Risk uncertainty about future events, [445]

Rockefeller, John D., 41

Ronald McDonald House, 48–49

Roth IRA provision allowing individual retirement savings with tax-free accumulated earnings, [459]

Router, 347

Royal Dutch Shell, 30

Rubbermaid, 156

Russell 2000 Index specialty index that uses 2,000 stocks to measure the performance of the smallest U.S. companies, [427]

S

Sabotage, 197

Saint Luke's Hospital, 183

Saks, 252

Salary compensation in the form of money paid for discharging the responsibilities of a job, [251]

Sales Agent independent intermediary who generally deals in the related product lines of a few producers and forms long-term relationships to represent those producers and meet the needs of many customers, [307]

Sales Promotion short-term promotional activity designed to encourage consumer buying, industrial sales, or cooperation from distributors, [319]

Salmonella, 48

Salvation Army, 33

Same-Steps Layout physical arrangement of production steps designed to make one type of product in a fixed sequence of activities according to its production requirements, [175]

Samsung, 91, 186

Samuel Adams Lager, 123

Sant, Roger, 209

Sarbanes-Oxley Act of 2002 (Sarbox or Sox) enactment of federal regulations to restore public trust in accounting practices by imposing new requirements on financial activities in publicly traded corporations, 47, [363]

Save-A-Lot, 170

Savings and Loan Association (S&L) financial institution accepting deposits

and making loans primarily for home mortgages, [393]

Scardino, Marjorie, 122

Schuessler, Jack, 319

Schultz, Howard, 8, 64, 124, 222, 268, 292

Scientific management, 203

S Corporation hybrid of a closely held corporation and a partnership, organized and operated like a corporation but treated as a partnership for tax purposes, [77]

Sears, 41

Secondary Securities Market market in which existing (not new) stocks and bonds are sold to the public, [421]

Secured Loan (Asset-Backed Loan) loan to finance an asset, backed by the borrower pledging the asset as collateral to the lender, [429]

Securities and Exchange Commission (SEC) government agency that regulates U.S. securities markets, 40–41, 46, 358, [421], 435

Securities Investment Dealer (Broker) financial institution that buys and sells stocks and bonds both for investors and for its own accounts, [393]

Securities Investment Protection Corporation (SIPC), 425

Securities Markets markets in which stocks and bonds are sold, [421]

Securities stocks, bonds, and mutual funds representing secured, or asset-based, claims by investors against issuers, [421]

Security policy, 346

Self-awareness, 200

Service Corps of Retired Executives (SCORE), 68

Service Operations (Service Production) activities producing intangible and tangible products, such as entertainment, transportation, and education, [167]

Services products having nonphysical features, such as information, expertise, or an activity that can be purchased, [271]
  in small business, 62

Seth Thomas, 281

7-Eleven, 66

Sexual Harassment making unwelcome sexual advances in the workplace, 197, [253]

Shares, 417

Shell Oil, 48, 212
  learning organization at, 155

Sherman Antitrust Act, 16

Shopping Agent (E-Agent) e-intermediary (middleman) in the Internet distribution channel that assists users in

earning interest or some other form of return, [417]

TNT Post Group N.V., 11

Tobacco industry, 48

Tomlin, Lily, 308

Top Manager manager responsible for a firm's overall performance and effectiveness, [119]

Tort civil injury to people, property, or reputation for which compensation must be paid, [447]

Toshiba, 91

Total Quality Management (TQM) sum of all activities involved in getting high- quality goods and services into the marketplace, [181]

Toxic assets, 371

Toxic waste disposal, 43

Toyota, 41, 91, 170, 172

Trade Deficit situation in which a country's imports exceed its exports, creating a negative balance of trade, 20–21, [95]

Trademark exclusive legal right to use a brand name or symbol, [449]

Trade Show sales-promotion technique in which various members of an industry gather to display, demonstrate, and sell products, [319]

Trade Surplus situation in which a country's exports exceed its imports, creating a positive balance of trade, [95]

Trading floor, 421

Traditional Individual Retirement Account (IRA) provision allowing individual tax-deferred retirement savings, [459]

Trait Approach to Leadership focused on identifying the essential traits that distinguished leaders, [223]

Transactional Leadership comparable to management, it involves routine, regimented activities, [227]

TransFair, 88–89

Transformational Leadership the set of abilities that allows a leader to recognize the need for change, to create a vision to guide that change, and to execute the change effectively, [225]

Transportation activities in transporting resources to the producer and finished goods to customers, [181]
  in small business, 63

Treasurer, 118

Treaty, 91

Trial Court general court that hears cases not specifically assigned to another court, [447]

Trojan horses, 345–346

Troubled Asset Relief Program (TARP), 400

Trust Services management by a bank of an estate, investments, or other assets on behalf of an individual, [393]

Tupperware, 305

Turner, Ted, 226

Turnover annual percentage of an organization's workforce that leaves and must be replaced, [197]

Tweedie, David, 376

Twitter, 373

Two-Factor Theory theory of motivation holding that job satisfaction depends on two factors, hygiene and motivation, [205]

Tyco International, 32, 42

U

Unconnectedness, of insurable risk, 445

Unemployment the level of joblessness among people actively seeking work in an economic system, [23]

Unethical Behavior behavior that does not conform to generally accepted social norms concerning beneficial and harmful actions, [33]

Uniform Commercial Code (UCC) body of standardized laws governing the rights of buyers and sellers in transactions, [449]

Union Butterfield, 198

United Airlines, 78, 116

United Auto Workers (UAW), 258

United Technologies (UT), 36

United Way, 33, 41

Unlimited Liability legal principle holding owners responsible for paying off all debts of a business, [73]

Unrelated diversification, 125

Unsecured Loan loan for which collateral is not required, [429]

Unstorability, 169

UPS, 152
  materials management at, 180

Urban Outfitters, 7
  decentralization at, 146

U.S. Express, 312

Us Weekly, 276

Utility ability of a product to satisfy a human want or need, 36, 37, [167], [271]

V

Value-Added Analysis process of evaluating all work activities, materials flows, and paperwork to determine the value that they add for customers, [183], 314

Value Package product marketed as a bundle of value-adding attributes, including reasonable cost, [283]

Value relative comparison of a product's benefits *versus* its costs, [271]

Vanderbilt, Cornelius, 41

Variable Cost cost that changes with the quantity of a product produced and sold, [301]

Venture Capital Company group of small investors who invest money in companies with rapid growth potential, [69]

Venture Capital private funds from wealthy individuals seeking investment opportunities in new growth companies, [431]

Verifiability, of insurable risk, 445

Vestibule Training off-the-job training conducted in a simulated environment, [249]

Vice president, 118

Victoria's Secret, 45, 79

Videoconferencing, 336

Video retailing nonstore retailing to consumers via home television, [311]

Vietnam, 104

Vioxx, 44

Viral Marketing type of buzz marketing that relies on the Internet to spread information like a "virus" from person to person about products and ideas, [289]

Virtual leadership leadership in settings where leaders and followers interact electronically rather than in face-to-face settings, [231]

Virtual organization, 154

Viruses, 345–346

Visual Staff Scheduler Pro (VSS Pro), 178

Vitiene, Erika, 173

Vlasic, 143–144

Volkswagen, 91, 126

Voluntary Bankruptcy bankruptcy proceedings initiated by an indebted individual or organization, [449]

Vondra, Al, 356

Vsat Satellite Communications network of geographically dispersed transmitter-receivers (transceivers) that send signals to and receive signals from a satellite, exchanging voice, video, and data transmissions, [337]

W

Wage Reopener Clause clause allowing wage rates to be renegotiated during the life of a labor contract, [261]